41: *Afro-American Poets Since 1955,* edited by Trudier Harris and Thadious M. Davis (1985)

42: *American Writers for Children Before 1900,* edited by Glenn E. Estes (1985)

43: *American Newspaper Journalists, 1690-1872,* edited by Perry J. Ashley (1986)

44: *American Screenwriters,* Second Series, edited by Randall Clark, Robert E. Morsberger, and Stephen O. Lesser (1986)

45: *American Poets, 1880-1945,* First Series, edited by Peter Quartermain (1986)

46: *American Literary Publishing Houses, 1900-1980: Trade and Paperback,* edited by Peter Dzwonkoski (1986)

47: *American Historians, 1866-1912,* edited by Clyde N. Wilson (1986)

48: *American Poets, 1880-1945,* Second Series, edited by Peter Quartermain (1986)

49: *American Literary Publishing Houses, 1638-1899,* 2 parts, edited by Peter Dzwonkoski (1986)

50: *Afro-American Writers Before the Harlem Renaissance,* edited by Trudier Harris (1986)

51: *Afro-American Writers from the Harlem Renaissance to 1940,* edited by Trudier Harris (1987)

52: *American Writers for Children Since 1960: Fiction,* edited by Glenn E. Estes (1986)

53: *Canadian Writers Since 1960,* First Series, edited by W. H. New (1986)

54: *American Poets, 1880-1945,* Third Series, 2 parts, edited by Peter Quartermain (1987)

55: *Victorian Prose Writers Before 1867,* edited by William B. Thesing (1987)

56: *German Fiction Writers, 1914-1945,* edited by James Hardin (1987)

57: *Victorian Prose Writers After 1867,* edited by William B. Thesing (1987)

58: *Jacobean and Caroline Dramatists,* edited by Fredson Bowers (1987)

59: *American Literary Critics and Scholars, 1800-1850,* edited by John W. Rathbun and Monica M. Grecu (1987)

60: *Canadian Writers Since 1960,* Second Series, edited by W. H. New (1987)

61: *American Writers for Children Since 1960: Poets, Illustrators, and Nonfiction Authors,* edited by Glenn E. Estes (1987)

62: *Elizabethan Dramatists,* edited by Fredson Bowers (1987)

63: *Modern American Critics, 1920-1955,* edited by Gregory S. Jay (1988)

64: *American Literary Critics and Scholars, 1850-1880,* edited by John W. Rathbun and Monica M. Grecu (1988)

65: *French Novelists, 1900-1930,* edited by Catharine Savage Brosman (1988)

66: *German Fiction Writers, 1885-1913,* 2 parts, edited by James Hardin (1988)

67: *Modern American Critics Since 1955,* edited by Gregory S. Jay (1988)

68: *Canadian Writers, 1920-1959,* First Series, edited by W. H. New (1988)

69: *Contemporary German Fiction Writers,* First Series, edited by Wolfgang D. Elfe and James Hardin (1988)

70: *British Mystery Writers, 1860-1919,* edited by Bernard Benstock and Thomas F. Staley (1988)

71: *American Literary Critics and Scholars, 1880-1900,* edited by John W. Rathbun and Monica M. Grecu (1988)

72: *French Novelists, 1930-1960,* edited by Catharine Savage Brosman (1988)

73: *American Magazine Journalists, 1741-1850,* edited by Sam G. Riley (1988)

74: *American Short-Story Writers Before 1880,* edited by Bobby Ellen Kimbel, with the assistance of William E. Grant (1988)

75: *Contemporary German Fiction Writers,* Second Series, edited by Wolfgang D. Elfe and James Hardin (1988)

76: *Afro-American Writers, 1940-1955,* edited by Trudier Harris (1988)

77: *British Mystery Writers, 1920-1939,* edited by Bernard Benstock and Thomas F. Staley (1988)

78: *American Short-Story Writers, 1880-1910,* edited by Bobby Ellen Kimbel, with the assistance of William E. Grant (1988)

79: *American Magazine Journalists, 1850-1900,* edited by Sam G. Riley (1988)

(Continued on back endsheets)

Dictionary of Literary Biography ® • Volume One Hundred Fifteen

Medieval Philosophers

Dictionary of Literary Biography ® • Volume One Hundred Fifteen

Medieval Philosophers

Edited by
Jeremiah Hackett
University of South Carolina

A Bruccoli Clark Layman Book
Gale Research Inc.
Detroit, London

Matthew J. Bruccoli and Richard Layman, *Editorial Directors*
C. E. Frazer Clark, Jr., *Managing Editor*

Printed in the United States of America

Published simultaneously in the United Kingdom
by Gale Research International Limited
(An affiliated company of Gale Research Inc.)

The paper used in this publication meets the minimum requirements of American National Standard for Information Sciences—Permanence Paper for Printed Library Materials, ANSI Z39.48-1984. ™

Library of Congress Catalog Card Number 92-46592
ISBN 0-8103-7592-3

In memory of my Parents,
T. J. Hackett & B. T. Meagher

Contents

Plan of the Series

. . . Almost the most prodigious asset of a country, and perhaps its most precious possession, is its native literary product—when that product is fine and noble and enduring.

Mark Twain*

The advisory board, the editors, and the publisher of the *Dictionary of Literary Biography* are joined in endorsing Mark Twain's declaration. The literature of a nation provides an inexhaustible resource of permanent worth. We intend to make literature and its creators better understood and more accessible to students and the reading public, while satisfying the standards of teachers and scholars.

To meet these requirements, *literary biography* has been construed in terms of the author's achievement. The most important thing about a writer is his writing. Accordingly, the entries in *DLB* are career biographies, tracing the development of the author's canon and the evolution of his reputation.

The purpose of *DLB* is not only to provide reliable information in a convenient format but also to place the figures in the larger perspective of literary history and to offer appraisals of their accomplishments by qualified scholars.

The publication plan for *DLB* resulted from two years of preparation. The project was proposed to Bruccoli Clark by Frederick C. Ruffner, president of the Gale Research Company, in November 1975. After specimen entries were prepared and typeset, an advisory board was formed to refine the entry format and develop the series rationale. In meetings held during 1976, the publisher, series editors, and advisory board approved the scheme for a comprehensive biographical dictionary of persons who contributed to North American literature. Editorial work on the first volume began in January 1977, and it was published in 1978. In order to make *DLB* more than a reference tool and to compile volumes that individually have claim to status as literary history, it was decided to organize volumes by topic, period, or genre. Each of these freestanding volumes provides a biographical-bibliographical guide and overview for a particular area of literature. We are convinced that this organization—as opposed to a single alphabet method—constitutes a valuable innovation in the presentation of reference material. The volume plan necessarily requires many decisions for the placement and treatment of authors who might properly be included in two or three volumes. In some instances a major figure will be included in separate volumes, but with different entries emphasizing the aspect of his career appropriate to each volume. Ernest Hemingway, for example, is represented in *American Writers in Paris, 1920-1939* by an entry focusing on his expatriate apprenticeship; he is also in *American Novelists, 1910-1945* with an entry surveying his entire career. Each volume includes a cumulative index of the subject authors and articles. Comprehensive indexes to the entire series are planned.

With volume ten in 1982 it was decided to enlarge the scope of *DLB*. By the end of 1986 twenty-one volumes treating British literature had been published, and volumes for Commonwealth and Modern European literature were in progress. The series has been further augmented by the *DLB Yearbooks* (since 1981) which update published entries and add new entries to keep the *DLB* current with contemporary activity. There have also been *DLB Documentary Series* volumes which provide biographical and critical source materials for figures whose work is judged to have particular interest for students. One of these companion volumes is entirely devoted to Tennessee Williams.

We define literature as the *intellectual commerce of a nation:* not merely as belles lettres but as that ample and complex process by which ideas are generated, shaped, and transmitted. *DLB* entries are not limited to "creative writers" but extend to other figures who in their time and in their way influenced the mind of a people. Thus the series encompasses historians, journalists, publishers, and screenwriters. By this means

*From an unpublished section of Mark Twain's autobiography, copyright © by the Mark Twain Company

readers of *DLB* may be aided to perceive literature not as cult scripture in the keeping of intellectual high priests but firmly positioned at the center of a nation's life.

DLB includes the major writers appropriate to each volume and those standing in the ranks immediately behind them. Scholarly and critical counsel has been sought in deciding which minor figures to include and how full their entries should be. Wherever possible, useful references are made to figures who do not warrant separate entries.

Each *DLB* volume has a volume editor responsible for planning the volume, selecting the figures for inclusion, and assigning the entries. Volume editors are also responsible for preparing, where appropriate, appendices surveying the major periodicals and literary and intellectual movements for their volumes, as well as lists of further readings. Work on the series as a whole is coordinated at the Bruccoli Clark Layman editorial center in Columbia, South Carolina, where the editorial staff is responsible for accuracy of the published volumes.

One feature that distinguishes *DLB* is the illustration policy—its concern with the iconography of literature. Just as an author is influenced by his surroundings, so is the reader's understanding of the author enhanced by a knowledge of his environment. Therefore *DLB* volumes include not only drawings, paintings, and photographs of authors, often depicting them at various stages in their careers, but also illustrations of their families and places where they lived. Title pages are regularly reproduced in facsimile along with dust jackets for modern authors. The dust jackets are a special feature of *DLB* because they often document better than anything else the way in which an author's work was perceived in its own time. Specimens of the writers' manuscripts are included when feasible.

Samuel Johnson rightly decreed that "The chief glory of every people arises from its authors." The purpose of the *Dictionary of Literary Biography* is to compile literary history in the surest way available to us—by accurate and comprehensive treatment of the lives and work of those who contributed to it.

The *DLB* Advisory Board

Foreword

Medieval philosophy is the collective name given to the philosophies of thinkers who lived between the end of the Roman Empire, circa 400, and the beginning of the modern era, circa 1490. With the fall of the Roman Empire and the consequent breakdown of education in the West, a decisive rupture in Western philosophy was avoided due to the labors of Augustine and Boethius; the philosophy of the Latin West in the Middle Ages was built on the foundations of their works.

Roughly speaking, with the exception of John Scottus Eriugena in the ninth-century Carolingian Renaissance, a five-hundred-year dearth of philosophy existed in the Latin West after the death of Boethius in 524. Anselm of Canterbury in the eleventh century was the first major philosopher in the West after Eriugena.

It was the project of Boethius to unite the philosophy of Plato and Aristotle. While he did not fully achieve this goal, he did hand on a combination of Platonism and Aristotelianism, with some mixture of Stoicism. But in general, until the mid thirteenth century, and especially in the School of Chartres in the twelfth century, Platonism was dominant.

The introduction into the West of Aristotelian writings and Arabic scientific treatises from the Islamic world in the first half of the twelfth century was the moment of decisive change. It would take about 150 years for the process of assimilation to be complete. By 1255 the works of Aristotle were required reading for students at the University of Paris, and the study of Greek scientific works, handed on and improved by Arabic scholars, had become an important part of medieval education.

Jewish philosophy was also a strong influence on thirteenth- and fourteenth-century writers in the Latin West; here, Moses Maimonides is the primary figure.

The field of medieval philosophy has given forth much new fruit since the beginnings of modern historical research in the early nineteenth century on the philosophies of the Middle Ages. Since the advent of neo-scholasticism in the 1880s, scholars have labored to produce reliable texts and studies so that modern teachers and students could base their understanding of medieval philosophy on a firm foundation.

Several dictionaries and encyclopedias dealing, in whole or part, with the Middle Ages have appeared in recent years. One thinks immediately of the *Dictionary of the Middle Ages*, published by Charles Scribner's Sons in 1983. *The Cambridge History of Later Medieval Philosophy* appeared in 1982. New and updated editions of standard histories of medieval philosophy such as those of Frederick C. Copleston and Armand A. Maurer have been published. And a new edition of the textbook used in many North American college and university courses, *Philosophy in the Middle Ages: The Christian, Islamic and Jewish Traditions*, by Arthur Hyman and James J. Walsh, appeared in 1984.

This volume of the *Dictionary of Literary Biography* is not meant to repeat what can be found in the above-mentioned works; it is aimed at filling a gap in the available literature. Much new research has taken place in medieval studies since the early 1980s; thus modern high-school, college, and graduate students need accounts of the biographies, bibliographies, and thought of medieval philosophers which are written by experts and are abreast of the most recent developments in the field. *Medieval Philosophers* is targeted at this student audience. But it will also be of use to scholars in the field, who may come to see old portraits in a new light.

This volume will also provide personal and cultural backgrounds which are not found in some other reference works. While philosophy cannot be reduced to either biography or history, philosophers share in cultures, societies, and religions.

Much new work has been done in recent years on medieval Platonism and Stoicism that has not always seen the light of day in the histories, dictionaries, and encyclopedias of philosophy. Often the large shadow of medieval Aristotelianism has prevented themes which are in fact Platonic and Stoic from appearing in their true light. Furthermore, principles of interpretation which are quite complex and organic are frequently sacrificed in attempts to find modern paradigms in medieval problems. To see medieval philosophical problems in the context of the Middle Ages is enormously difficult, but it has been undertaken by the contributors to this volume.

In this volume important and representative thinkers from the traditions of Western medieval philosophy—Jewish, Christian, and Islamic—from the period 345 to 1490 are included. No one school or method of philosophy is privileged. The contributors also have expertise not just in the history of philosophy but also in the fields of study of the various philosophers presented—metaphysics, logic, semantics, natural science, mathematics, epistemology, psychology, philosophy of law, and philosophy of religion. With the virtual explosion of new knowledge about medieval philosophers, such a cooperative effort will be much more useful for students than a work by a single scholar, whose field of expertise must inevitably be limited. The manner of treatment was left up to each contributor, within the bounds of a literary biography.

The philosophers treated in this volume were involved in education, public life, and ecclesiastical administration. Augustine was more a religious thinker than a philosopher, and yet his religious thinking with its personal intensity contains many nuggets of philosophical wisdom. Boethius, Pseudo-Dionysius, and John Scottus Eriugena handed on fragments of the wisdom of antiquity to the Middle Ages and secured the future of philosophy in the Western world. From Anselm to Nicholas of Cusa—that is, from the end of the eleventh century to the end of the fifteenth century—philosophy grew in the fertile ground of the medieval schools. A space was given for the free play of argument and disputation. The crucial revolution took place in the twelfth century with the transmission of Greek philosophy, Islamic science, and Jewish wisdom into Western Latin centers of learning such as Paris, Oxford, Cambridge, Bologna, Cologne. Figures such as al-Farabi, Avicenna, Averroës, Moses Maimonides, and Solomon ibn Gabirol entered, figuratively, into a dialogue with Robert Grosseteste, William of Auvergne, Roger Bacon, Albert the Great, Thomas Aquinas, Bonaventure, Siger of Brabant, and many other Western thinkers who pondered the wisdom coming from Spain and Sicily. This "dialogue" was not merely a rediscovery by the West of Aristotelianism; it was a recovery and a re-creation of all the strands of Western philosophy, including the Stoic, Platonic, Epicurean, and Skeptic traditions. The two names that stand out in this process are William of Auvergne and Grosseteste at the University of Paris and Oxford University, respectively. William and Grosseteste were men of magnificent vision; they were creators of traditions.

As the thirteenth century came to an end, social and political events impinged severely on the world of philosophy. Earlier utopian sentiment and positive excitement gave way to somber assessments of the human condition. Representatives of the religions of the Book—Judaism, Christianity, and Islam—turned inward, and fruitful communication and dialogue among diverse cultures ceased for many centuries. Nevertheless, despite—or even because of—the Parisian condemnations of Aristotelianism in 1277, renewed interest in philosophy and renewed approaches came about. The traditional view of the trajectory of medieval philosophy as an arc with Thomas Aquinas as the high point and the later Middle Ages as a sad decline is no longer tenable. Later thinkers such as Meister Eckhart, William of Ockham, and Nicholas of Cusa made truly creative contributions to philosophy.

In the fourteenth century one witnesses the first stirrings of the breakup of the medieval model. Thinkers as diverse as Hasdai Crescas, Gersonides, Ockham, Marsilius of Padua, and Eckhart reflect this breakup. In Nicholas of Cusa the medieval world finds its final expression, and the modern world begins to dawn.

The Renaissance, when all of the medieval accomplishment would be seen as so much Gothic barbarism, would glory in its newfound independence. The new humanism would quickly forget that its ideas were forged in the smithy of the medieval university and among those scholars such as Bacon, Albert the Great, the "Mertonians," and others who, working in and outside of the universities, were seeking new learning and new science. The Reformation and Counter-Reformation were also deeply influenced by currents of thought coming out of medieval philosophy.

The present volume will have accomplished its intention if it furthers the knowledge of the Middle Ages and of medieval philosophy among modern students by making available to them updated literary biographies of a selection of medieval philosophers. Unfortunately, demands of space limited the number of philosophers who could be treated. In some cases, such as the

School of Chartres, a representative sample had to be chosen. The school of the Victorines at Paris had to be omitted, mainly because this volume deals with philosophers and not theologians. Individual translators of Arabic and Greek works into Latin also could not be treated. This difficulty has been resolved by having an appendix, where the present state of the scholarship is presented by one who has had experience in the field. There are many worthy philosophers who in time will, one hopes, receive renewed study.

—Jeremiah Hackett

Acknowledgments

This book was produced by Bruccoli Clark Layman, Inc. Karen L. Rood is senior editor for the *Dictionary of Literary Biography* series. Philip B. Dematteis was the in-house editor.

Production coordinator is James W. Hipp. Projects manager is Charles D. Brower. Photography editors are Edward Scott and Timothy C. Lundy. Layout and graphics supervisor is Penney L. Haughton. Copyediting supervisor is Bill Adams. Typesetting supervisor is Kathleen M. Flanagan. Systems manager is George F. Dodge. The production staff includes Rowena Betts, Teresa Chaney, Patricia Coate, Janet Connor, Gail Crouch, Henry Cuningham, Margaret McGinty Cureton, Bonita Dingle, Mary Scott Dye, Denise Edwards, Sarah A. Estes, Robert Fowler, Avril E. Gregory, Ellen McCracken, Kathy Lawler Merlette, John Myrick, Pamela D. Norton, Jean W. Ross, Laurrè Sinckler-Reeder, Thomasina Singleton, Maxine K. Smalls, Jennifer C. J. Turley, and Betsy L. Weinberg.

Walter W. Ross and Dennis Lynch did library research. They were assisted by the following librarians at the Thomas Cooper Library of the University of South Carolina: Jens Holley and the interlibrary-loan staff; reference librarians Gwen Baxter, Daniel Boice, Faye Chadwell, Jo Cottingham, Cathy Eckman, Rhonda Felder, Gary Geer, Jackie Kinder, Laurie Preston, Jean Rhyne, Carol Tobin, Virginia Weathers, and Connie Widney; circulation-department head Thomas Marcil; and acquisitions-searching supervisor David Haggard.

The editor extends his gratitude to his teachers in Dublin and Toronto, especially those who are no longer with us: Ludwig Bieler, Michael Bertram Crowe, P. Osmund Lewry, Conor Martin, and James A. Weisheipl. He also thanks his colleagues in the Department of Philosophy at the University of South Carolina for their encouragement and support during the preparation of this volume.

Dictionary of Literary Biography® • Volume One Hundred Fifteen

Medieval Philosophers

Dictionary of Literary Biography

Peter Abelard

(circa 1079 - 21 April 1142)

Peter King
Ohio State University

PRINCIPAL WORKS: *Introductiones Parvulorum* (The Lesser Glosses on Logic, perhaps written circa 1105);
Logica Ingredientibus (The Greater Glosses on Logic, perhaps written circa 1112-1130);
Sic et non (Yes and No, written circa 1117-1128);
Theologia Summi Boni (On the Divine Unity and Trinity, written circa 1118-1120);
Logica Nostrorum Petitioni Sociorum (Glosses on Porphyry's *Isagoge*, perhaps written circa 1122-1125);
Tractatus de Intellectibus (Treatise on Understandings, written circa 1122-1125);
Theologia Scholarium (also known as *Introductio ad Theologiam* [Introduction to Theology], written circa 1125-1130);
Commentaria in Epistolam Pauli ad Romanos (Commentary on the Letter of Saint Paul to the Romans, written circa 1125-1131);
Dialectica (Dialectic, written circa 1130-1140);
Expositio Symboli Apostolorum (Commentary on the Apostle's Creed, written circa 1132-1134);
Expositio orationis dominicae (Commentary on the Lord's Prayer, written circa 1132-1134);
Expositio Fidei Sancti Athanasii (Commentary on the Athanasian Creed, written circa 1132-1134);
Historia Calamitatum (The Story of My Misfortunes, written circa 1132-1133);
Hymnarius Paraclitensis (Hymns for the Paraclete, written circa 1134);
Problemata Heloïssae cum Petri Abaelardi solutionibus (Problems Submitted by Heloïse with Peter Abelard's Solutions, written circa 1134);
Expositio in Hexämeron (Commentary on the Six Days of Creation, written circa 1134-1136);
Theologia Christiana (Christian Theology, written circa 1134-1138);
Dialogus inter Philosophum, Iudaeum, et Christianorum (Dialogue of a Philosopher with a Jew and a Christian, written circa 1138-1142);
Ethica seu Scito Teipsum (Ethics; or, Know Thyself, written circa 1138-1142);
Apologia contra Bernardum (Defense against Bernard, written circa 1140);
Carmen ad Astrolabium Filium (Poem to His Son Astrolabe, written circa 1140);
Sententiae Secundum Magistrum Petrum (Master Peter's Views, date of composition unknown).

EDITIONS: *Ouvrages inedits d'Abélard*, edited by Victor Cousin (Paris: Imprimerie Royale, 1836);
Petri Abaelardi Opera, 2 volumes, edited by Cousin (Paris: Imprimerie Royale, 1859; reprinted, Hildesheim: Olms, 1970);
Petri Abaelardi opera omnia, edited by J.-P. Migne, volume 178 of *Patrologia latina* (Paris: Garnier, 1885);
Peter Abaelards philosophische Schriften, 4 volumes, edited by Bernhard Geyer, Beiträge zur Geschichte der Philosophie und Theologie des Mittelalters, 21 (Münster: Aschendorff, 1919-1933).

CRITICAL EDITIONS: "Peter Abelard's *Historia calamitatum*," edited by Joseph T. Muckle, *Mediaeval Studies*, 12 (1950): 163-213;

Peter Abelard and Héloïse; miniature from a fourteenth-century French manuscript for The Romance of the Rose, *a poem begun by Guillaume de Lorris and completed by Jean de Meun (Musée Condé, Chantilly, ms. 482/665, fol.60v)*

Pietro Abelardo: Scritti filosofici, edited by Mario Dal Pra (Milan: Fratelli Bocca, 1954);

"Abelard's Rule for Religious Women," edited by T. P. McLaughlin, *Mediaeval Studies*, 18 (1956): 241-292;

Dialectica: First Complete Edition of the Parisian Manuscript, edited by L. M. de Rijk (Assen: Van Gorcum, 1956; revised, 1970);

Abaelardiana inedita, edited by Lorenzo Minio-Paluello (Rome: Edizioni di storia e letteratura, 1958);

Pietro Abelardo: Scritti di logica, edited by Dal Pra (Florence: La nuova Italia, 1958);

Petri Abaelardi opera theologica, 2 volumes, edited by Eligius M. Buytaert (Turnholt: Brepolis, 1969);

Dialogus inter philosophum, Iudaeum, et Christianorum, edited by Rudolf Thomas (Stuttgart-Bad Cannstatt: Fromann, 1970);

Peter Abelard's "Hymnarius Paraclitensis," 2 volumes, edited by Josef Szöverffy (Albany, N.Y. & Brookline, Mass.: Classical Folia Editions, 1975);

Peter Abailard: Sic et Non. A Critical Edition, edited by Blanche Boyer and Richard McKeon (Chicago: University of Chicago Press, 1977).

EDITIONS IN ENGLISH: "The Glosses of Peter Abailard on Porphyry (Introduction)," translated by Richard McKeon, in his *Selections from Medieval Philosophers*, volume 1 (New York: Scribners, 1929), pp. 208-258;

Abelard's Christian Theology, translated by J. Ramsay McCallum (Oxford: Blackwell, 1948);

Peter Abelard's Ethics, translated by David E. Luscombe (Oxford: Oxford University Press, 1971);

Dialogue of a Philosopher with a Christian and a Jew, translated by Pierre J. Payer (Toronto: Pontifical Institute of Mediaeval Studies, 1981);

The Hymns of Abelard in English Verse, translated by Jane Patricia (Lanham, Md.: University Press of America, 1986).

Peter Abelard was the teacher of his generation: preeminent as a philosopher, theologian, poet, and musician, he captured the imagination of almost all with whom he came into contact.

His fame as a teacher was unequaled; students traveled from all over Europe to hear him speak, crowds of ordinary people attended his public lectures wherever he went, and it has been said that he was indirectly responsible for the founding of the University of Paris by creating a permanent "deposit" of students in the city. As a philosopher, he brought the investigation of the "old logic" (*logica vetus*) to its heights; as a theologian, he championed the use of reason and intellect in the investigation of matters of faith, putting the word *theology* into use with the meaning it still has today. In philosophy and theology, Abelard's constant and unremitting use of the tools of logic or "dialectic"—argument, objection, example, counterexample, and the like—helped define the Scholastic method, of which an early example is his *Sic et Non* (Yes and No, circa 1117-1128). As a poet and musician, Abelard was renowned for his verses, both secular and sacred, composed in the vernacular and in Latin. He is responsible for some of the earliest extant pieces of "authored" music. Abelard's natural talents alone were formidable. Combined with his quick tongue, undeniable brilliance, sharp wit, dialectical acumen, encyclopedic memory, and flavored with a large dose of arrogance, the force of his personality impressed itself vividly on all his contemporaries. Even his critics and detractors (whom Abelard always referred to as his "enemies") admitted that he never lost an argument, and only those who avoided debating him could ever gain the upper hand over him. And, apart from his intellectual achievements, his luckless affair with Héloïse made him a tragic figure of romance. Abelard seemed larger than life to his contemporaries, and he is all the more so in retrospect.

Abelard's life, unlike those of most medieval thinkers, is well known. Public events are chronicled in a wide variety of sources, and the details of his inner life are revealed in his autobiographical letter *Historia Calamitatum* (The Story of My Misfortunes, circa 1132-1133) and in his correspondence with Héloïse. Yet, despite the wealth of biographical data, the dates of composition and even the number of Abelard's writings remain largely obscure and a matter of controversy among scholars.

Abelard was born circa 1079 in Le Pallet, a small town about twelve miles southeast of Nantes in the independent duchy of Brittany. His parents, Berengar and Lucia, were of the minor nobility. Abelard was the eldest son (and perhaps the eldest child); he had at least three younger brothers, Dagobert, Porcarius, and Ralph, as well as at least one sister, Denise. Abelard received early training in letters at the wishes of his father, most likely from a tutor, and took to his studies naturally; he eventually renounced his primogeniture and the consequent knighthood to pursue philosophy. Abelard's writings reveal a thorough "humanist" grounding in classical literature: he was familiar with the works of Cicero, Horace, Juvenal, Lucan, Ovid, Seneca, and Virgil, as well as postclassical authors such as Augustine, Boethius, Isidore of Seville, and Macrobius.

Abelard's advanced training in philosophy was acquired, following a customary practice of the time, by traveling to study with various thinkers—which may be how he acquired the sobriquet "the Peripatetic of Le Pallet." He studied with Roscelin of Compiègne at Loches near Vannes and with Ulger at the cathedral school associated with Saint Maurice in Angers (and perhaps with Geoffrey Babio and Vasletus there as well). In the first years of the twelfth century Abelard traveled to Paris to study under William of Champeaux, archdeacon of Paris, at the Cloister School of Nôtre Dame. As a student there, Abelard was considered a "clerk" (*clercius*): teachers and students alike were tonsured and wore clerical habits. Although no formal system of education had yet been established, the Cloister School of Nôtre Dame occupied the most eminent position among all the regular cathedral schools in France.

The training Abelard received was almost exclusively devoted to the elements of the classical trivium: grammar, logic, and rhetoric; of these Abelard preferred logic by far, although there is evidence that he wrote a work on grammar (now lost) and that he planned, and perhaps wrote, a work on rhetoric. The "logic" was Porphyry's *Isagoge* (Introduction); Aristotle's *Categories* and *On Interpretation*; Boethius's *On Division*, *On Topical Differences*, *On the Categorical Syllogism*, and *On the Hypothetical Syllogism*. These works were supplemented with Boethius's commentaries on the works of Porphyry, Aristotle, and Cicero: the *Greater Commentary on the "Isagoge,"* the *Commentary on the "Categories,"* the *Lesser Commentary on the "On Interpretation,"* the *Greater Commentary on the "On Interpretation,"* and the *Commentary on Cicero's "Topics."* These works are primarily directed toward theories and problems in formal and informal logic, philosophy of logic, and philosophy of language. The extent to which such theories presuppose a metaphysical basis is controversial, and Abelard, with his genius for controversy, found them fertile ground for argument and debate.

In the early twelfth century there were no clear-cut educational licensing practices, as there were in the late Middle Ages. Teachers gained students simply by ability and reputation, and one way to get a reputation was to win a debate with someone of established celebrity. Abelard, with his outstanding dialectical skills, began to enter into debates with William of Champeaux and so to make a name for himself. As Abelard's reputation began to rise, William's began to fall. Despite William's interference, with some influential help Abelard set up a school in Melun; he soon moved it to Corbeil so that, he says, "I might prove a greater embarrassment [to William of Champeaux] and offer more frequent challenges to debate." Melun was a royal seat, and Corbeil was at this time declared a royal fief; it is possible that the "men of influence" who helped Abelard against William's attempted interference included King Louis the Fat himself. Abelard says that his own reputation for "dialectical skill" was forged at this time, and hence it seems likely that he was lecturing on logic in his schools. The *Introductiones Parvulorum* (Short Indroductions) may date from this period.

Abelard's driving ambition took its toll. After a short period of time he became ill "due to the heavy burden of studies" and returned to his home for several years. The illness may have been a nervous breakdown. Abelard does not discuss his activities during his stay in Brittany, nor of the length of time he was absent from Paris, but he does say that students continued to inquire after him to study dialectic. Abelard returned to Paris sometime between 1108 and 1113 with his ambition intact and his health restored. William of Champeaux had retired in 1108 to the religious center of Saint Victor in Paris (which became an abbey of canons regular under him) and was giving lectures on rhetoric in the associated monastic school.

Abelard went to hear William's lectures and again entered into debate with him. Abelard describes the content of this debate that firmly established his reputation: the problems of universals. In *On Interpretation* Aristotle describes the "universal" as "what is naturally apt to be predicated of many," a description that applies to general and specific terms. Now predication is at least partly a linguistic affair, since one term is predicated of another, and in Abelard's view the metaphysical issue that underlies the problem of universals is whether predication is *more* than linguistic. Given that Socrates and Plato are human, is there something that is common to, or shared by, Socrates and Plato in virtue of which each is human? William of Champeaux initially maintained that there was something common to Socrates and Plato, and Abelard refuted this position. William then changed his view to hold that there is nothing that is common to Socrates and Plato, but that each has some element that can be called "indifferently" the same. Abelard refuted this position as well, and William's lectures at that point, Abelard says, "devolved into so much carelessness that they could scarcely be admitted to be on dialectic at all." Abelard's arguments against both theories are preserved in the beginning of his *Logica Ingredientibus* (Logical Glosses) which may have been started at this time; some further theological objections are added in the later *Logica Nostrorum Petitioni Sociorum* (Glosses on Porphyry's *Isagoge*). The result of this debate was instant acclaim for Abelard: William's students deserted him to study with Abelard, and William's successor at the Cloister School of Nôtre Dame stepped aside for Abelard to lecture on dialectic. Abelard says that William of Champeaux then maneuvered to have his successor removed from his appointment and appointed one of Abelard's rivals, an unnamed person with a reputation in grammar, in his stead. Abelard returned to Melun to teach, shortly afterward transferring his school to the Mont Sainte-Geneviève immediately outside Paris to "besiege" William's new appointee. Further debates and controversy followed, of an unspecified nature, in which Abelard was again the victor.

At some point before 1113, Abelard's mother was preparing to enter a convent (his father had already entered a monastery), and Abelard returned to Brittany for a visit. When he returned to France after 1113 he found that William of Champeaux had become bishop of Châlons-sur-Marne. Abelard then decided to study theology. The reasons behind his decision are none too clear, especially in light of what he was giving up: a successful and remunerative career teaching dialectic. It may be that the example of his parents had turned his mind toward the contemplation of divine things; it may be that he was impressed by William's advancement, which he believed to have been due to his reputation for piety rather than his intellectual ability; it may be that William's departure left room for a master of theology in Paris. Whatever the explanation, Abelard sought out the most eminent teacher of theology of his day, Anselm of Laon, and became his student.

Anselm was one of the compilers of the Ordinary Glosses on the Bible. He followed the traditional *lectio divina* prescribed by the Benedictine Rule: after reading a passage from the Bible, the reigning master would put forward an interpretation (*sententia*) of the sense of the text, which would be expounded and supported by citing various other passages from the Bible and patristic sources (*glossae*). Abelard soon found Anselm's exposition and support of his interpretations to be based on empty rhetoric rather than logical analysis. His attendance at Anselm's lectures became irregular, and he openly voiced his opinion that no instruction was needed to study theology other than the Bible itself and patristic literature. Soon thereafter, perhaps in response to a challenge to these views, Abelard began to offer competing lectures on Ezekiel that were well received by many of Anselm's students. According to Abelard, two students, Alberic of Reims and Lotulph the Lombard, convinced Anselm that he should put a stop to Abelard's lectures. Anselm did so on the ground that any error Abelard might make would be attributable to Anselm himself. Anselm's authority to issue such a prohibition is unclear, but it had an unforeseen result: "a few days after this," Abelard writes, "I returned to Paris, to the school that had long ago been intended for and offered to me." Abelard became the *magister scholarium* at the Cloister School of Nôtre Dame and was adopted into the chapter as a canon.

On his return to Paris, Abelard completed his commentary on Ezekiel (now lost) and held his position "in peace for several years." Given the brevity of his formal studies in theology, it is reasonable to hold that Abelard began to educate himself in patristic literature during this period: his later writings are filled with references to Origen, Jerome, Augustine, Gregory, and other fathers of the church. It may also be that due to his extensive reading he conceived the project of the *Sic et Non*: a series of 158 questions, each of which is furnished with patristic citations that imply a positive answer (*sic*) to the question and other patristic citations implying a negative answer (*non*). Abelard does not attempt to harmonize these apparently inconsistent remarks, but in his preface he lays down rules for proper hermeneutic investigation: look for ambiguity, check the surrounding context, draw relevant distinctions, and the like.

Up to this point, Abelard's single-minded ambition was directed to intellectual pursuits: reading, teaching, and writing. What little energy was left over he devoted to the political aspects of intellectual life. Consequently, he lived ascetically, and in particular was known for his continence. These was no real reason for him to be celibate: the offices of clerk and canon could be held by the laity, and neither required celibacy. Nor was celibacy universally accepted as a requirement for the clergy itself. Only since the Gregorian Reform, begun in the latter part of the eleventh century, had strictures against married priests been put into effect, and the nature and content of the marriage bond (in particular its sacramental status) were still the subject of lively dispute. Abelard's celibacy seems instead a by-product of his driving ambition to make a name for himself in the world of letters. Once he was granted the position at Paris, this ambition was fulfilled, leaving him with time on his hands; and, after several years as *magister scholarium*, Abelard became romantically involved with Héloïse. The events which transpired have been an inspiration to artists ever since. Abelard relates the story as a cold-blooded seduction; Héloïse suggests a tale of passionate first love.

Héloïse was a young woman (*adolescentula*), most likely between fifteen and seventeen years of age, when Abelard met her. Héloïse's mother was named Hersinde; her father and familial background are unknown, though she herself implies that her social status was inferior to Abelard's. She was raised at least in part at the Convent of Sainte Marie of Argenteuil, near Paris, and had acquired a reputation as that rarity of rarities in the Middle Ages: an educated woman. Abelard twice refers to Héloïse knowing Hebrew and Greek as well as Latin, which would make her exceptional among all medieval intellectuals. Héloïse's uncle (likely her maternal uncle) Fulbert was a canon of Nôtre Dame; Héloïse came to Paris and lived with Fulbert, presumably in the cathedral close—traditionally, in a house on the Quai aux Fleurs. Abelard speaks of Fulbert's love for Héloïse and genuine concern for her further education, which seemed largely impossible in the all-male enclave of the schools.

Illumination on the opening page of a thirteenth-century manuscript for Abelard's Historia Calamitatum. *Abelard and Héloïse are depicted, but Héloïse's face has been scratched out. The manuscript was owned in the fourteenth century by Petrarch (Paris MS., Bibliothèque Nationale lat. 2923, f. 1r).*

Fulbert therefore proposed that Abelard enter the household and oversee Héloïse's studies in exchange for his own domestic needs being taken care of. Abelard assented, and the privacy afforded for studies led rapidly to romantic and sexual involvement. By Abelard's own account, his teaching suffered; his inspiration was directed toward writing love lyrics which became quite popular (none have survived, so it is unknown whether they were written in Latin or the vernacular). After "several months" had passed in this way, rumor of the affair reached Fulbert. Abelard left the household but continued to meet Héloïse clandestinely until Fulbert surprised them while they were engaged in sexual intercourse. The separation was more stringent this time. Héloïse discovered that she was pregnant, and Abelard removed her from Fulbert's house one night during Fulbert's absence; Héloïse, disguised as a nun, was sent to Brittany to live with Abelard's sister. She gave birth to a boy, whom she named Astrolabe (perhaps Peter Astrolabe or Astralabe). Abelard later wrote the *Carmen ad Astrolabium Filium* (Poem to His Son Astrolabe, circa 1140), a series of Catonian distichs full of Polonius-type advice for his son, and Héloïse much later requested Peter the Venerable to help Astrolabe acquire a prebend. His death is recorded in the necrology of the Paraclete, the convent later founded by Abelard; nothing else is known of him.

Since Abelard did not accompany Héloïse, it is likely that he continued to teach during this period. While Héloïse was absent from Paris, Abelard approached Fulbert and proposed to marry Héloïse on the condition that the marriage remain secret. Fulbert assented, and Abelard went to Brittany for the more difficult task of persuading Héloïse. As Abelard recounts the story, Héloïse objected on two main grounds: a secret marriage would in fact not appease Fulbert, and any kind of marriage would be a hindrance to Abelard. Two difficult questions are raised by Abelard's proposal and Héloïse's resistance: why should the marriage be kept secret, and how could marriage be a hindrance to Abelard? It has been suggested that marriage would prove a bar to further advancement within the church hierarchy, and also that the idealized conception of a philosopher included freedom from worldly matters, so that the image of a "married philosopher" was ludicrous.

Another of Héloïse's objections to marriage may better explain her resistance: pure and free love is more valuable than marriage; marriage is at best a mundane form of prostitution and the negation of the spiritual worth found in love. During these same years, up to the time of his condemnation at Toulouse in 1119, the monk Henry of Lausanne was preaching against the sacramentalization of marriage, arguing that consent in itself constitutes genuine marriage. Such a view finds expression in Abelard's *Ethica seu Scito Teipsum* (Ethics; or, Know Thyself, circa 1138-1142), which argues that intention alone determines the moral worth of an action; actions of themselves have neither positive nor negative value. Abelard and Héloïse both subscribed to this view. If, as seems likely, they were acquainted with the preaching of Henry of Lausanne, Héloïse may have believed that marriage was at best an empty legal formality and at worst a confusion of mere property relations with the spiritual bond of love. This hypothesis would explain why she insisted that marriage would have been a humiliation for both herself and Abelard, despite their amorous liaison's already being a matter of common knowledge.

Héloïse eventually capitulated to Abelard's proposal, and, leaving Astrolabe with Abelard's sister, they returned to Paris and were secretly married in the presence of Fulbert and some friends and relatives. To preserve the secrecy of the marriage, Héloïse returned to live with Fulbert while Abelard took up residence elsewhere; they met sporadically and furtively. But Fulbert and his relatives began to spread news of the marriage about. Héloïse publicly swore that there was no truth to the reports, adding to her uncle's embarrassment. Fulbert apparently beat Héloïse severely on several occasions. When Abelard learned of the beatings, he removed Héloïse from Fulbert's house and took her to Argenteuil, where he insisted that she wear a nun's habit. Fulbert and his friends and relatives were convinced that Abelard was going to rid himself of Héloïse by making her take vows. One night they bribed one of Abelard's attendants, entered his lodgings, and castrated him.

Abelard writes movingly of his shame and misery. Several letters of consolation written to him still exist; at least one, from his former teacher Roscelin, is maliciously insulting about his castration. Abelard abandoned his teaching position and entered the Benedictine Abbey of Saint Denis in Paris, an unreformed abbey under the leadership of Abbot Adam with close ties to the French court; in obedience to Abelard's wishes, Héloïse became a nun at Argenteuil.

Abelard quickly found the worldly and fashionable life led by the monks at Saint Denis wanting; publicly and privately he objected to their behavior, becoming, in his own words, "a burden and a nuisance" to all. When students began to clamor for Abelard to resume teaching, an equitable bargain was struck: Abelard journeyed to a priory owned by Saint Denis at Maisoncelle-en-Brie, near Provins, and began to teach and write; students flocked after him, and the abbey must have been glad to get rid of him. Abelard says that at this time he primarily worked on theology, though he also lectured on philosophy. He composed a treatise on the unity and trinity of God, the *Theologia Summi Boni* (On the Divine Unity and Trinity, circa 1118-1120), in which he explores the central mystery of the Trinity with the tools of dialectic: questions are raised, authorities cited, distinctions drawn, objections proposed and resolved. Abelard's main argument proceeds through an analysis of the modes of sameness and diversity, and he concludes that the Persons of the Trinity are the same essentially but differ in definition. Many other points are taken up: the identification of Plato's "world-soul" with the Holy Spirit, the generation of the Word from the Father, the claim that all humans naturally have faith in the Trinity.

The dialectical method of Abelard's *Theologia Summi Boni* must have been taken as a direct challenge to traditional theological studies. Alberic and Lotulph, his former fellow students who by this time presided at the school of Reims, persuaded Ralph, the archbishop of Reims, and Conon, bishop of Praeneste and papal legate in France, to convene and preside over a synod in Soissons to examine the content of Abelard's book. No records are preserved from this synod, which was held in April 1121, and Abelard's own account is naturally self-serving, but a few facts are independently attested. First, Geoffrey of Lèves, bishop of Chartres from 1116 to 1149, apparently worked hard on Abelard's behalf. Second, Abelard was at some point apparently given the impression that he should return to Saint Denis while the council deliberated, but before he had an opportunity to do so he was summoned to appear before the council again, and the papal legate pronounced sentence: Abelard was to cast his book into the fire, make a public confession of his faith, and be detained indefinitely at the Cluniac Abbey of Saint Médard in Soissons. The council's refusal to allow Abelard to speak in his own defense during the proceedings was probably contrary to ecclesiastical law.

Conon was apparently uneasy at the political maneuvering that took place during Abelard's trial, and as public opinion moved to condemn the trial as unjust, Conon denounced the "jealousies" that had sponsored it and returned Abelard to Saint Denis. Abelard did not find a friendly welcome, and after a few uneasy months he inflamed the monks of Saint Denis even further by finding documentary evidence in the works of the Venerable Bede that the Saint Denis who was patron saint of the abbey was not in fact the same as Saint Denis (Dionysius), bishop of Athens, known as "the Areopagite." History has shown that Abelard was correct, but his fellow monks were so upset by his charges that they complained to Abbot Adam, who prepared to send Abelard to the king, patron of the monastery, on charges of disrespect for the crown. Abelard fled secretly at night from Saint Denis, taking refuge with Theobald II, Count of Troyes and Champagne (and of Blois and Chartres by inheritance), who allowed Abelard to live in the Priory of Saint Ayoul in Provins. Abelard wrote to Adam in a conciliatory fashion, arguing that it might yet be possible that the founder of the abbey was Saint Denis the Areopagite. When Adam had some business to conduct with Theobald, Abelard relayed through Theobald a request to lead a monastic life elsewhere. But this request was to no avail, since it would be publicly humiliating for Abelard to join another monastery in preference to Saint Denis; Adam insisted that Abelard return, threatening him with excommunication if he did not.

So matters stood for a few days; then Adam suddenly died. He was succeeded in March 1122 by Suger, who would become famous for initiating the Gothic style of architecture when he rebuilt the monastery between 1137 and 1144. Suger; Burchard, the bishop of Meaux; and Abelard met for a conference in which Abelard reiterated his request to be given leave of Saint Denis. Suger demurred, and Abelard appealed to Stephen of Garland, deacon of Nôtre Dame and royal seneschal, to intercede on his behalf. Stephen brought the matter before the king and his council; they decided that Abelard should be granted leave from Saint Denis under the condition that he not come under the authority of any other abbey.

Abelard settled on a wild and uninhabited section of land presented to him in Troyes on the bank of the river Ardusson, four miles southeast of Nogent-sur-Seine in the diocese of Quincy. The archbishop of Quincy, Hatto of Troyes, gave Abelard permission to erect a reed-and-thatch oratory, which he named the Paraclete (Comforter). Abelard says that poverty drove him to return to teaching, and that students flocked to him in such huge numbers that the oratory was rebuilt in wood and stone and greatly enlarged with housing and other buildings. Abelard had returned to the element that suited him best: reading, lecturing, and writing. His reputation continued to spread and increase.

Perhaps in 1125 or 1126 Abelard received an invitation to become abbot of the Monastery of Saint Gildas de Rhuys, on the bay of Quiberon in the diocese of Vannes in Brittany. Abelard accepted after obtaining permission from Suger. It is not known why Abelard again chose to abandon teaching. He vividly describes his fears while at the Paraclete of becoming the target of some new "persecution" by "new apostles" who had risen up against him; the identity of these "new apostles" is not certain, but it seems likely that he had in mind Norbert of Xanten, founder of the Premonstratensian congregation, and Bernard of Clairvaux, the great reformer. Abelard says that his fears were so great that he considered living in a Muslim country to avoid persecution. This may not have been an empty remark: Abelard's *Dialogus inter Philosophum, Iudaeum, et Christianorum* (Dialogue of a Philosopher with a Christian and a Jew, circa 1138-1142) is a fictional debate among a philosopher who is apparently a Muslim, a Jew, and a Christian about the nature of the supreme good and the connection between virtue and happiness; Abelard shows more than a passing familiarity with both Judaism and Islam. The account of Abelard's student Hilary, however, suggests a more mundane reason for Abelard's decision to leave teaching: due to the disorderly behavior of the large number of students gathered there, Abelard had to dissolve the community that had grown up around the Paraclete. Whatever the reason, Abelard left the Paraclete and became abbot of Saint Gildas.

The choice was not a good one. Abelard found the monks barbarous, uncivilized, and immoral; he did not know the local language; the abbey was being heavily taxed by one of the local lords. Abelard attempted without success to reform the practices he found in Saint Gildas, alienating the monks in the process. He fell into a deep depression at his failure but was roused from it by the plight of Héloïse and the nuns of Argenteuil.

In 1128 Suger claimed that he had uncovered a charter showing that the Convent of Sainte Marie of Argenteuil belonged to the Abbey of Saint Denis. Suger presented the claim to Rome, perhaps alleging improper behavior of the nuns as well, and in 1129 ownership of the convent was transferred to Saint Denis by the joint action of Pope Honorius II and King Louis VI. Suger promptly expelled the nuns without making any provision for them. At the time of the expulsion Héloïse was prioress, a position she may have attained as early as 1123. On hearing of the expulsion Abelard left Saint Gildas and handed over the Paraclete and its lands to Héloïse and the nuns who had remained with her, naming Héloïse as abbess. Initially criticized for not helping the nuns at the Paraclete sufficiently, Abelard later visited so frequently that malicious rumors began to spread about his intentions. At some point Héloïse apparently wrote to Abelard that Bernard of Clairvaux had visited the Paraclete and preached to the nuns, and that he took exception to their use of the Vulgate version of the Lord's Prayer in Matthew. This letter is lost, but a short letter Abelard wrote to Bernard, explaining and justifying the nuns' practice, exists. On 20 January 1131 Abelard was present at a gathering in the Benedictine Abbey of Morigny, near Etampes, where Pope Innocent II consecrated the high altar during his progress through France. There Abelard met Bernard in person for the first time. On 28 November 1131 the pope presented a charter to Héloïse as abbess of the Paraclete, confirming the nuns' possession of the gifts they had already received and of all later gifts in perpetuity. The Paraclete remained in existence until the French Revolution.

It is difficult to sort out subsequent events, but it appears that Abelard traveled back to Saint Gildas, left again to visit the Paraclete, and returned once more to Saint Gildas. By the time he wrote his *Historia Calamitatum*, most likely in 1131-1132, he was at Saint Gildas recovering from a fracture caused by a fall from a horse. He tells a harrowing tale of his existence at Saint Gildas: at least twice attempts were made on his life by poison, once while he was celebrating mass (he must therefore have become a priest by this time), and ambushes were set on the roads. Abelard excommunicated some of the monks, expelled others, and made the remainder retake their oaths of allegiance in the presence of a papal legate sent for that purpose. (The request for a papal legate had been one of the reasons for Abelard's presence at Morigny.) But oaths were not strong enough: Abelard was again threatened, this time with a sword to his throat; he escaped only through the intervention of an unnamed secular lord.

These are the circumstances in which Abelard wrote the *Historia Calamitatum*. It purports to be a letter of consolation to a friend, but this may just be a literary device. Abelard may have written it with an eye to its eventual circulation, in hopes of gaining either support for reformation of Saint Gildas or permission to depart. A copy of the letter came to Héloïse, apparently by chance, and the celebrated correspondence between the two ensued. The first pair of exchanges are notable for Héloïse's intensely personal reflections on and reminiscences of their life together and for cool responses from Abelard, who threatened to break off their correspondence if she continued to write in a personal vein. Héloïse's remaining three letters deal with the direction of the Paraclete, and Abelard's responses indicate that he was serious about overseeing the spiritual welfare of the nuns. He sent thirty-four sermons to be read at the Paraclete, some or all of which may have been composed earlier for the monks of Saint Gildas; a psalterium (now lost); many Latin hymns (of which 133 are extant); and several laments. Héloïse sent forty-two questions of biblical interpretation to which Abelard gave carefully reasoned solutions; and apparently at Héloïse's request he wrote the *Expositio in Hexämeron* (circa 1134-1136), a commentary on the six days of creation. Abelard was in residence at Saint Gildas at least for the early exchanges, and there may be references in the letters to Abelard's visiting the Paraclete during the correspondence.

It is not known when Abelard finally left Saint Gildas, only that he did so with his bishop's permission and the right to retain his rank as abbot. According to John of Salisbury, by 1136 Abelard was again teaching on the Mont Sainte-Geneviève in Paris. A plausible hypothesis is that Abelard left Saint Gildas shortly after his initial exchanges with Héloïse and obtained his teaching position through the intercession of the dean of Sainte-Geneviève, Stephen of Garland, who had helped him to leave Saint Denis earlier. Late in 1137 Abelard had to stop teaching and leave the Mont, possibly because of Stephen's loss of influence after the death of King Louis VI on 1 August. The interruption was only temporary, and Abelard returned to teach at Sainte-Geneviève shortly thereafter.

It is not known what Abelard was lecturing on and writing about, but it is clear that some of his works on theology—maybe the *Theologia Christiana* (Christian Theology, circa 1122-1127) or some of the recensions of the *Theologia Scholarium* (School Theology, circa 1135-1138)—were circulating again. In these works Abelard adopts the tone and style of his earlier *Theologia Summi Boni*: they are exercises in dialectical theology. As before, the style and manner of the work led to conflict with those who had a more conservative approach to matters of faith and dogma. In 1139 William, the abbot of the Cistercian Monastery of Signy in the Ardennes, came into possession of Abelard's theological work and was horrified by it. (It is possible that William read a summary of Abelard's teaching rather than a book by Abelard himself.) William was alarmed at the prospect of Abelard's teaching "new things," all the more so because of Abelard's influence and reputation. William sent a list of thirteen heretical points he ascribed to Abelard, accompanied by his own refutations, to the papal legate and to Bernard of Clairvaux. Bernard apparently met with Abelard twice to persuade him to alter his views and restrain his students. When this approach failed, Bernard asked Henry, the archbishop of Sens, who had ecclesiastical authority over the diocese of Paris, and the bishop of Paris to intervene against Abelard. They did not do so but granted Bernard permission to preach to the students in Paris himself. Bernard's sermon is a sharp attack on Abelard, though his name is not mentioned. Abelard's response was to circulate a slightly altered manuscript of his theological work in which some notice is taken of William's criticisms, but without any substantial changes. Bernard then wrote to the pope and the papal curia, sending along his own treatise against Abelard's views. In these letters he also links Abelard to Arnold of Brescia, a severe critic of ecclesiastical practices who argued in particular against church possession of private property. It is possible that Arnold had been a student of Abelard, or that Abelard was sympathetic to Arnold's critique of church property.

Abelard asked the archbishop of Sens to arrange a meeting on 3 June 1140, at which Abelard and Bernard would have a public disputation regarding the points on which they differed. The king and his court were scheduled to be shown the relics in the cathedral that day in the presence of various bishops and dignitaries: Abelard clearly wanted a distinguished audience for what he confidently expected to be his blazing defeat of Bernard in open debate. Bernard initially refused Abelard's invitation on the grounds that one should not debate matters of faith; but his friends prevailed on him to accept. Abelard wrote to his students to enlist their support at Sens. Bernard, however, had no intention of allowing a disputation to be conducted.

Bernard wrote to the bishops who were planning to attend, arguing for his point of view, and he arranged for several bishops sympathetic to his views to be present. He then traveled to Sens a day early and preached against Abelard to the people already assembled there; next, he convened the ecclesiastical authorities present and, after reading aloud a list of Abelard's supposed heresies, secured assent to an inquisition of Abelard the next day. Abelard arrived to find that no debate was to be held; rather, a kangaroo court was prepared to interrogate him. Bernard read aloud nineteen propositions gathered from Abelard's works and, in accordance with the customary procedure in trials for heresy, called on Abelard to defend them, renounce them, or deny his authorship. This question was usually asked as a mere matter of form prior to the real inquiry, assessment, and verdict of the judges. Abelard, however, refused to play the charade: he declared that he would appeal directly to the pope and walked out of the proceedings.

Since Abelard had not formally admitted authorship, the council was at a loss as to how to proceed. It condemned the nineteen propositions, despite Abelard's not admitting that he had written them, and adjourned. The members of the council sent their reports to the pope; Bernard wrote several letters to the pope and the cardinals and had his followers write several more. (It is likely that Bernard himself drafted the "official" report to the pope from the archbishop of Sens.) Meanwhile, Abelard had begun his journey to Rome. He stopped at the Monastery of Cluny at the invitation of its abbot, Peter the Venerable, and began to compose a full-scale refutation of the charges Bernard had brought against him, the *Apologia contra Bernardum* (Defense against Bernard, circa 1140).

On 16 July 1140 a papal rescript was sent to Bernard and the archbishops of Sens and Reims condemning Abelard as a heretic, excommunicating his followers, ordering the burning of his books, and directing that he be confined to a monastery of Bernard's and the bishops' choosing. The news reached Abelard at Cluny, and there can be no doubt that it was a great shock to him: he would never have imagined that he could be condemned without being heard. According to Peter the Venerable, Abelard immediately submitted to the judgment. With the aid of the abbot of Cîteaux, Peter the Venerable set up a meeting between Abelard and Bernard; Abelard traveled to Clairvaux, where he met peacefully with Bernard. Abelard and Peter then returned to Cluny. Peter wrote to the pope, informing him of these matters and requesting that Abelard be allowed to stay at Cluny. The pope gave his permission and lifted Abelard's sentence without objection.

The tomb of Abelard and Héloïse in the Père Lachaise Cemetery, Paris

According to Peter the Venerable, Abelard's behavior at Cluny was exemplary. His health was poor, and it gradually became worse. He was moved to a daughter house of Cluny at Saint-Marcel, near Chalon-sur-Saône, in the hopes that the more temperate climate would help, but he died on 21 April 1142. Peter the Venerable took his body (illegally) to the Paraclete for burial. On Héloïse's death, on 16 May 1163 or 1164, she was interred with Abelard. Their bodies were moved several times; since the nineteenth century they have been in the Père Lachaise Cemetery in Paris.

Several of Abelard's works cannot be dated precisely. A scholarly consensus is forming that his major works on logic, the *Logica Ingredientibus* and the *Dialectica* (Dialectic, circa 1130-1140), were composed fairly close together in time. The *Logica Nostrorum Petitioni Sociorum* and the *Tractatus de Intellectibus* (Treatise on Understandings) have close textual similarities with one another, and the former work also has affinities with the *Theologia Summi Boni.* The *Logica Nostrorum Petitioni Sociorum* is also thought to be later than the major logical works. The *Dialogus inter Philosophum, Iudaeum, et Christianorum* was composed after the *Theologia Christiana,* to which it makes explicit reference. The *Ethica seu Scito Teipsum* is generally agreed to be a late work.

Abelard's legacy has yet to be explored in detail. His students were active as philosophers, theologians, poets, and politicians; they include three popes and several heads of state. There are few explicit references to Abelard's thinking in the later Middle Ages, but it is clear that he had a seminal influence on twelfth-century philosophy and theology, and he may well have affected fourteenth-century philosophical speculation as well. The story of Abelard and Héloïse has been a subject for artists, poets, and writers ever since the twelfth century.

Letters:

"The Personal Letters between Abelard and Heloise," edited by Joseph T. Muckle, *Mediaeval Studies,* 15 (1953): 47-94;

"The Letter of Heloise on Religious Life and Abelard's First Reply," edited by Muckle, *Mediaeval Studies,* 17 (1955): 240-281;

"Abelard's Rule for Religious Women," edited by T. P. McLaughlin, *Mediaeval Studies,* 18 (1956): 241-292;

The Letters of Abelard and Heloise, translated by Betty Radice (New York: Penguin, 1974).

Biographies:

J. G. Sikes, *Peter Abailard* (Cambridge: Cambridge University Press, 1932);

Etienne Gilson, *Héloïse and Abélard,* translated by L. K. Shook (Chicago: Regnery, 1951);

Gonzague True, *Abelard avec et sans Héloïse* (Paris: Fayard, 1956);

Leif Grane, *Peter Abelard: Philosophy and Christianity in the Middle Ages,* translated by Frederick Crowley and Christine Crowley (London: Allen & Unwin, 1970);

D. W. Robertson, Jr., *Abelard and Heloise* (New York: Dial Press, 1972);

Peter Dronke, *Abelard and Heloise in Medieval Testimonies* (Glasgow: University of Glasgow Press, 1976);

David E. Luscombe, *Peter Abelard* (London: Historical Association, 1979).

References:

Raymond Klibansky, "Peter Abailard and Bernard of Clairvaux," *Mediaeval and Renaissance Studies,* 5 (1961): 1-27;

David E. Luscombe, *The School of Peter Abelard: The Influence of Abelard's Thought in the Early Scholastic Period* (Cambridge: Cambridge University Press, 1969);

James Ramsay McCallum, *Abelard's Christian Theology* (Oxford: Blackwell, 1948);

Mary M. McLaughlin, "Abelard as Autobiographer: The Motives and Meaning of His 'Story of Calamities,'" *Speculum,* 42 (July 1967): 463-488;

A. Victor Murray, *Abelard and St. Bernard: A Study in Twelfth Century "Modernism,"* (Manchester, U.K.: Manchester University Press, 1967; New York: Barnes & Noble, 1967);

Charles de Rémusat, *Abélard: Sa vie, sa philosophie et sa théologie,* 2 volumes (Paris: Didier, 1855);

Lucia Urbani Ulivi, *La psicologia di Abelardo e il "Tractatus de intellectibus"* (Rome: Edizioni di storia e letteratura, 1976).

Manuscripts:

Manuscripts of works by Peter Abelard are in the Bibliothèque Nationale and Bibliothèque de l'Arsenal, Paris; the Biblioteca Ambrosiana, Milan; the Preußischer Kulturbesitz, Berlin; and the Bibliothèque Municipale, Lunel.

Albert the Great
(Albertus Magnus)

(circa 1200 - 15 November 1280)

B. B. Price
York University

PRINCIPAL WORKS: *De Natura Boni* (On the Nature of the Good, written circa 1243-1244);
Principium Biblicum (The Biblical Canon, written 1245);
Super Isaiam (Commentary on Isaiah, written between 1245 and 1250);
De Sacramentis (On the Sacraments, written before 1246);
De Incarnatione (On the Incarnation, written before 1246);
De Resurrectione (On the Resurrection, written before 1246);
De Quatuor Coaequaevis (On the Four Coevals, written before 1246);
De Homine (On Humanity, written before 1246);
De Forma Resultante in Speculo (On the Form Which Appears in a Mirror, written before 1248);
De Bono (On the Good, written between 1246 and 1248);
Super Sententiarum (Commentary on Peter Lombard's *Sentences*, written between 1246 and 1249);
Sermones Parisiensis (Paris Sermons, written before 1248);
Quaestiones Theologiae (Theological Questions, written circa 1247-1248);
Super Dionysium De Caelesti Hierarchia (Commentary on [Pseudo-] Dionysius the Areopagite's *On the Celestial Hierarchy*, written circa 1247);
Super Dionysium De Ecclesiastica Hierarchia (Commentary on [Pseudo-] Dionysius the Areopagite's *On the Ecclesiastical Hierarchy*, written circa 1249);
Super Dionysium De Divinis Nominibus (Commentary on [Pseudo-] Dionysius the Areopagite's *On the Divine Names*, written circa 1250);
Super Dionysium De Mystica Theologia (Commentary on [Pseudo-] Dionysius the Areopagite's *On Mystical Theology*, written circa 1250);
Super Epistulas Dionysii (Commentary on the Letters of [Pseudo-] Dionysius the Areopagite, written circa 1250);
Super Ethica, Commentum et Quaestiones (Commentary and Questions on [Aristotle's] *Ethics*, written between 1250 and 1252);
Physica (Physics, written circa 1251);
De Lineis Indivisibilibus (On Indivisible Lines, written circa 1251-1252);
De Caelo et Mundo (On the Heavens and Earth, written circa 1251);
De Natura Loci (On the Nature of Places, written between 1251 and 1253);
De Causis Proprietatum Elementorum (On the Properties of the Elements, written between 1251 and 1253);
De Generatione et Corruptione (On Generation and Corruption, written between 1251 and 1253);
Meteora (Meteorology, written between 1252 and 1254);
Mineralia (Book of Minerals, written between 1252 and 1262);
Super Porphyrium De V Universalis (Commentary on Porphyry's *On the Five Universals*, written between 1252 and 1271);
De Praedicamentis (On the Predicaments, written between 1252 and 1271);
De Sex Principiis (On the Six Principles, written between 1252 and 1271);
De Divisione (On Division, written between 1252 and 1271);
Peri Herimeneias (On Interpretation, written between 1252 and 1271);
Analytica Priora (Prior Analytics, written between 1252 and 1271);
Analytica Posteriora (Posterior Analytics, written between 1252 and 1271);
Topica (Topics, written between 1252 and 1271);
De Sophisticis Elenchis (On Sophistical Refutations, written between 1252 and 1271);
De Anima (On the Soul, written circa 1254);

Albert the Great as he was depicted by Tommaso da Modena in 1352 (Dominican Seminary, Treviso, Italy)

De Nutrimento et Nutribili (On Nutrition, written between 1254 and 1257);
De Sensu et Sensato (On the Senses, written between 1254 and 1257);
De Memoria et Reminiscentia (On Memory and Remembering, written between 1254 and 1257);
De Intellectu et Intelligibili (On the Intellect and the Intelligible, written between 1254 and 1257);
De Somno et Virgilia (On Sleep and Waking, written between 1254 and 1257);
De Spiritu et Respiratione (On Breath and Breathing, written between 1254 and 1257);
De Motibus Animalium (On the Motions of Animals, written between 1254 and 1257);
De Iuventute et Senectute (On Youth and Old Age, written between 1254 and 1257);
De Morte et Vita (On Death and Life, written between 1254 and 1257);
De Fato (On Fate, written 1256);
Super Iohannem (Commentary on John, written circa 1256; revised, 1270 and 1275);
Super Matthaeum (Commentary on Matthew, written between 1257 and 1264; definitive version written after 1270);
Super Marcum (Commentary on Mark, written between 1257 and 1260);
Sermones (Sermons, written circa 1258);
Epistula de Ungelt (Letter on Taxes, written circa 1258);
Quaestiones super De Animalibus (Questions on Aristotle's *On Animals*, written 1258);
De Vegetabilibus (On Plants, written before 1260);
De Animalibus (On Animals, written between 1258 and 1262);
Ethica (Ethics, written before 1261);
Super Lucam (Commentary on Luke, written circa 1261-1262; revised between 1270 and 1275);
De Natura et Origine Animae (On the Nature and Origin of the Soul, written between 1262 and 1264);
De Principiis Motus Processivi (On the Movement of Animals, written between 1262 and 1264);
Metaphysica (Metaphysics, written circa 1262-1263);
De Unitate Intellectus (On the Unity of the Intellect, written circa 1263);
Summa Theologiae sive De Mirabili Scientia Dei (Summary of Theology; or, On the Wondrous Knowledge of God, written between 1263 and 1274);
Politica (Politics, written between 1264 and 1274);
De Causis et Processu Universitatis a Prima Causa (Book of Causes, written between 1267 and 1271);
De XV Problematibus (On Fifteen Problems, written circa 1270);
De Mysterio Missae (On the Mystery of the Mass, written after 1270);
De Corpore Domini (On the Body of the Lord, written after 1270);
Problemata Determinata (Diverse Problems, written April 1271);

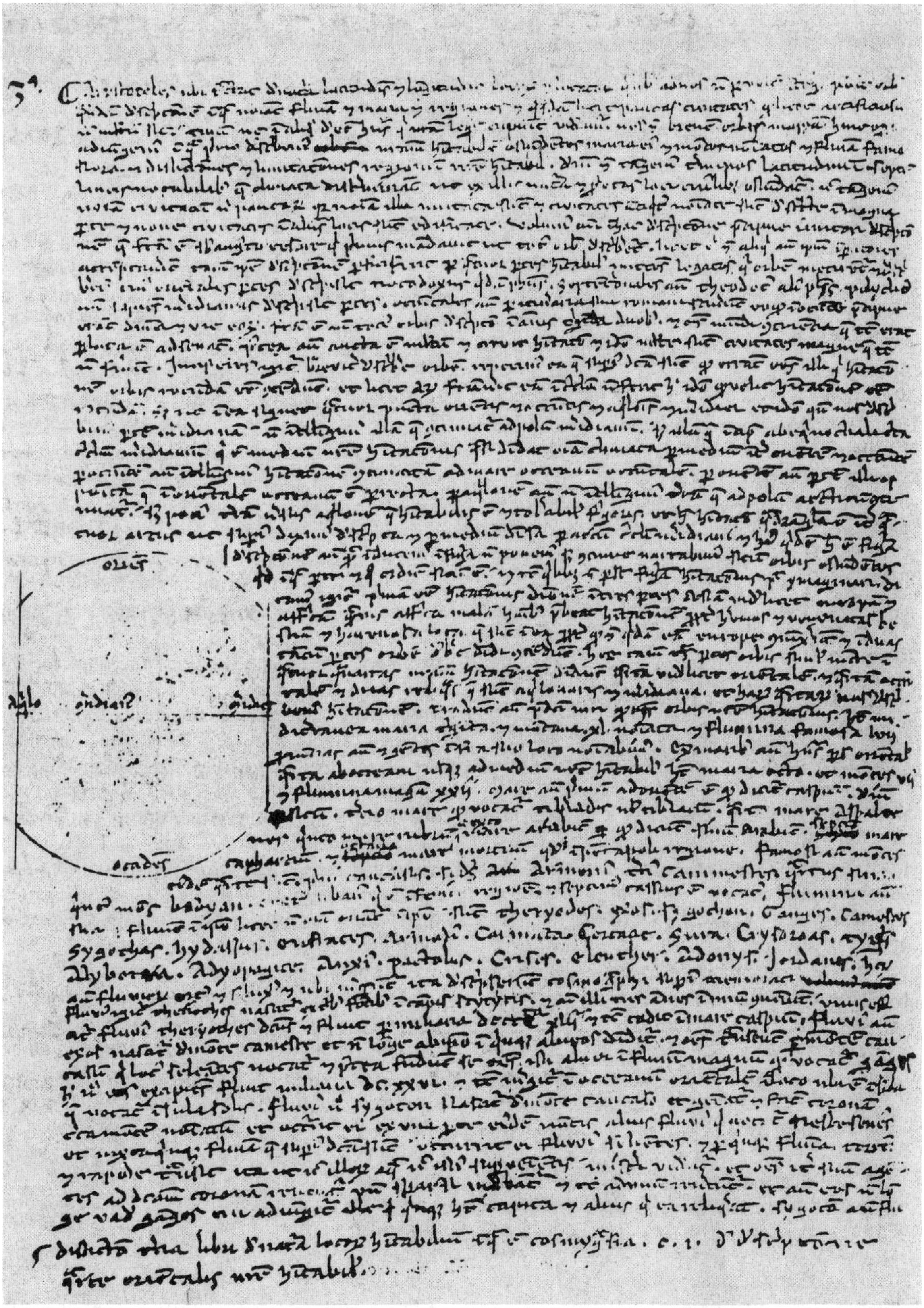

Page from Albert's manuscript for De Natura Loci *(Vienna National Library; Cod. Vindob. 273, fol. 151v)*

Super Iob (Commentary on Job, written 1272 or 1274);

Super Ieremiam (Commentary on Jeremiah, date of composition unknown);

Super Threnos (Commentary on Lamentations, date of composition unknown);

Super Baruch (Commentary on Baruch, date of composition unknown);

Super Ezechielem (Commentary on Ezechiel, date of composition unknown);

Super Danielem (Commentary on Daniel, date of composition unknown);

Super Prophetas Minores (Commentary on the Minor Prophets, date of composition unknown).

EDITIONS: *Opera quæ Hactenus Haberi Potuerunt*, 21 volumes, edited by Peter Jammy (Lyons: Prost & Rigaud, 1651);

Opera Omnia, 38 volumes, edited by Auguste Borgnet (Paris: Vivès, 1890-1899).

CRITICAL EDITION: *Opera Omnia*, 37 volumes published, edited by Bernhard Geyer (Cologne: Monasterii Westfalorum, 1951-).

EDITIONS IN ENGLISH: "*On Plants*, Book VI, Tractate I, chapter 31," edited and translated by Charles Singer, in *Studies in the History and Method of Science*, volume 2, edited by Singer (Oxford: Clarendon Press, 1921), pp. 74-75;

"Albertus Magnus on Comets," edited and translated by Lynn Thorndike, in *Latin Treatises on Comets between 1238 and 1368 A.D.*, edited and translated by Thorndike (Chicago: University of Chicago Press, 1950), pp. 62-76;

Book of Minerals, translated by Dorothy Wyckoff (Oxford: Clarendon Press, 1967);

"Twenty-six Books on Animals" and "Questions 'On Animals,' " extracts translated by Edward Grant, in *A Source Book in Medieval Science*, edited by Grant (Cambridge, Mass.: Harvard University Press, 1974), pp. 654-657, 681-689;

Albert and Thomas: Selected Writings, translated by Simon Tugwell (New York: Paulist Press, 1988).

Albert of Lauingen (also known as Albert of Bollstadt or Albert of Cologne) acquired the title *Magnus* (the Great) from his contemporaries even before his death. By 1280 he had long since entered the company of the major thinkers of the thirteenth century with his writings, his learned counsel, and his role as educator. By one of his most outspokenly critical contemporaries, Roger Bacon, Albert was identified as "the most noted of Christian scholars" and considered an authority on the same level as Aristotle, Avicenna, and Averroës. In 1931 Pope Pius XI, in his canonization address, placed Albert among the most prominent intellectuals ever to have dedicated themselves to Christian thought. In 1941, by decree of Pope Pius XII, Albert was designated the patron saint of natural scientists. The philosopher most responsible for creating the first Christian scientific agenda for the Latin West, Albert was long in receiving "beatific" recognition. With the waning, since the Middle Ages, of the importance of religion in scientific activity, Albert had come to symbolize the role a dedicated religious thinker could play in rendering the beliefs and morals of Christianity significant for science.

Born near Lauingen, in Bavaria, Albert was the son of a German knight who seems to have intended that Albert continue the family's military tradition. At the University of Padua he pursued the study of the medieval liberal arts that was appropriate for a young knight. The passage of Jordan of Saxony, master general of the Dominican order and successor to Saint Dominic, through Padua in the summer of 1223, however, turned Albert from his filial duties. He sought admission into the order despite family opposition and subsequently continued his studies under Dominican directive. Albert spent his novitiate in Germany, where he studied and then taught theology at various priories until the early 1240s. Sent for further study to the Dominican convent of Saint-Jacques at the University of Paris, Albert was graduated master in theology in 1245. The first German to do so, Albert obtained the Dominican teaching chair designated for foreigners; for the rest of his life Paris remained his intellectual home. (A Parisian street near Place Maubert carries his name today.) Albert's encounters in Paris with the "new Aristotle," recently translated from Arabic and Greek, had a permanent effect on his scholarly career; and the wealth of Arabic, Jewish, and pagan learning which was being introduced from Spain, including most recently Averroës' commentaries on Aristotle, was to affect his work at every turn. Among the works of Albert's which survive from this period are *De Natura Boni* (On the Nature of the Good, circa 1243-1244), *De Homine* (On Humanity, before 1246), *De Bono* (On the Good, between 1246 and

1248), and *Super Sententiarum* (between 1246 and 1249), his commentaries on the first three books of the *Libri Quatuor Sententiarum* (Four Books of Sentences, circa 1158) of Peter Lombard.

Perhaps thoughts of an extended teaching appointment in Paris led Albert to begin his exposition of the corpus of Pseudo-Dionysius in the academic year 1247-1248. The Dominican general chapter meeting of June 1248 decreed, however, that one of four new *studia generalia* (general houses of studies) was to be established in Cologne; to Albert this meant a return to his "native" priory. The general chapter sent him to Cologne in August 1248. Establishment of the Cologne *studium generale* was quickly completed; by 1250 a palatial residence next to the Dominican priory had been purchased. Albert presided for six years over the *studium*, where he continued to teach Thomas Aquinas, a novice in the Dominican order who had been permitted to follow the master from Paris. The regimen of work and prayer and the religious importance given to scholarship by Albert deeply appealed to Thomas. With Albert's encouragement Thomas returned to study in Paris in 1252. By that time Albert had begun to be sought out as an arbiter in disputes; archbishops and laypeople alike regularly placed demands on the time he could devote to teaching and writing.

In 1254 Albert became prior provincial of the province of Teutonia, which included modern Germany, Austria, Switzerland, Alsace, Lorraine, Luxembourg, Belgium, Holland, and parts of Poland, Lithuania, Italy, France, and Latvia. The new position entailed a great deal of administrative duty, but Albert was not one to let such demands deter him from scholarship. He made regular visits on foot to all of the more than sixty houses of his province, including those of Milan, Florence, and Paris. His visits provided inspiration to his intellectual work. His travels in the Harz Mountains and along the Rhine and Elbe rivers added firsthand experiences to his earliest interests in meteorology and mineralogy, and the libraries of certain houses afforded him a chance to read books as yet unknown in Cologne.

In 1256 Albert was ordered by Pope Alexander IV to the papal court at Anagni to defend the mendicant Dominican and Franciscan Orders against the secular masters of the University of Paris. Led by William of Saint-Amour, the secular masters were antagonistic to the presence of the mendicants as teaching masters at the university. Albert was instrumental in obtaining the condemnation of an inflammatory work by William and the continued right of mendicants to teach.

In 1257 Albert resigned the post of provincial but was called two and a half years later to become bishop of Regensburg. In 1261 he resigned the episcopal see; thereafter he served only short terms as arbitrator or papal legate, as when preaching the crusade from 1263 to 1264. Albert settled in Cologne at the Dominican priory of Heilige Kreuz in 1269 and lived there until his death at the age of "eighty years or more" on 15 November 1280. Although he may have visited other Dominican houses in Germany during his last years, it is doubtful that he ever again went as far afield as Paris.

Having been requested by his Dominican brethren to explain the works of Aristotle, by 1250 Albert had drawn up a plan for explaining the whole of human learning that bore a systematic connection to the Aristotelian corpus of works on the natural sciences, logic, the moral sciences, and metaphysics. Albert's ambitious undertaking, which amounted to thirty-nine works at its completion, was carried out from 1250 until his return to Cologne in 1269.

His *Physica* (Physics, circa 1251), *De Lineis Indivisibilibus* (On Indivisible Lines, circa 1251-1252), *De Caelo et Mundo* (On the Heavens and Earth, circa 1251), and *De Natura Loci* (On the Nature of Places, between 1251 and 1253) were all written in Cologne, as were most probably his *De Causis Proprietatum Elementorum* (On the Properties of the Elements, between 1251 and 1253), *De Generatione et Corruptione* (On Generation and Corruption, between 1251 and 1253), and *Mineralia* (Book of Minerals, between 1252 and 1262)—certainly while Albert was still teaching, before he was drawn from his priory into extensive travel. Some of the works are definitely direct products of Albert's regent mastership, such as his *Super Ethica, Commentum et Quaestiones* (Commentary and Questions on Aristotle's *Ethics*, between 1250 and 1252), which was delivered as lectures and reported by Thomas Aquinas. *De Anima* (On the Soul, circa 1254) is the first work clearly written after he had been elected prior provincial. Following its rapid composition, both the further empirical information and new texts gathered on provincial visits offered Albert ideas for his *De Motibus Animalium* (On the Motions of Animals, between 1254 and 1257) and *De Natura et Origine Animae* (On the Nature and Origin of the Soul, between 1262 and 1264). Two of his most exciting textual discoveries were made on his sec-

Albert as depicted in a fifteenth-century painting by Justus van Ghent (Palazzo Barbarini, Rome)

ond visit to Italy from August 1261 to February 1263. One was a new translation of Aristotle's *Politics* by William of Moerbeke, on which Albert proceeded—most unusually for him—to write a literal commentary. The other was an authentic work by Aristotle, *On the Progression of Animals.* Having already completed his own *De Motibus Animalium* Albert excitedly compared Aristotle, through an exposition of the newly discovered work, with his "own ingenuity." Between April 1260 and December 1261, while bishop of Regensburg, Albert must have written at least part of *De Animalibus* (On Animals): in book 7 he refers to his observations "in my villa above the Danube," which can only be a reference to the episcopal castle of Donaustauff, just outside of Regensburg on the Danube. Much of books 22 through 26, which are a typical medieval bestiary, also derive from his personal observations.

For the most part, Albert's treatment of the Aristotelian corpus eludes the simple categories of commentary and paraphrase. To provide the assistance for understanding the texts of Aristotle his Dominican brethren had requested of him, Albert chose the manner of the *postilla,* or continuous reading of the source text without making actual mention of it. From the beginning of Albert's project, his commentary on the *Physics,* his approach was to discuss, through explanatory phrases and illustrations, concepts such as motion, change, nature, cause, chance, and fate; and to explain arguments, often with the interpolation of extensive digressions. Whenever possible, Albert would use simultaneously more than one translation of the Aristotelian work, oscillating between their readings. He would include reflections on other authors' comments on the particular text or subject matter under scrutiny. He saw himself as an Aristotelian, but of a critical, realist posture, with a firm Christian faith and alert to what he perceived to be Aristotle's gaps or omissions. He saw parts or all of his *De Causis Propietatum Elementorum, Mineralia, De Nutrimento et Nutribili* (On Nutrition, between 1254 and 1257), *De Intellectu et Intelligibili* (On Intellect and the Intelligible, between 1254 and 1257), *De Spiritu et Respiratione* (On Breath and Breathing, between 1254 and 1257), *De Motibus Animalium, De Morte et Vita* (On Death and Life, between 1254 and 1257), *De Vegetabilibus* (On Plants, before 1260), *De Animalibus,* and an intended *De Astronomia* (On Astronomy) as supplements to what was wanting in the work of Aristotle.

Albert's long digressions are laced with the reflections of many authors: Church Fathers; pagan and Arabic philosophers; Aristotelians, among whom he lists al-Kindi, al-Farabi, and Alexander of Aphrodisias; Platonists or Stoics, including Avicenna, Pseudo-Dionysius, and Augustine; as well as contemporaries such as Aquinas, William of Saint-Amour, Ulrich of Strasbourg, Robert Kilwardby, and Siger of Brabant. Albert adopted the perspective of an elucidator, which has led to an intense discussion of whether the doctrines espoused are to be taken as his own. To confuse matters further, Albert added both frequent disavowals and many references to his own experiences. Albert's language is direct, despite the intricate philosophical vocabulary of the thirteenth-century Scholastics; his accounts of events are brief but evocative. His philosophical intensity is driven by his desire to resolve synthetically the difficulties encountered in other schools of philosophy, notably Epicurean, Platonist, and Averroist.

Albert's philosophical works explaining the Aristotelian corpus fall into four groups: natural scientific, logical, ethical, and metaphysical. They follow the plan of Aristotle's treatises, representing each area of his study from physics, psychology, astronomy and astrology, geography, zoology, botany, meteorology, and mineralogy to the categories and the analysis of logical arguments, to ethical questions and the discussion of first being. In his works on the natural sciences, Albert was not content to make reflections on general principles. For him the value of the principles was in their application to detailed investigations of causes: "it is necessary to get down to the details so that the primary agent in each individual case may be ascertained." Albert was persuaded that experience alone is reliable concerning individual things: "We pass over what the ancients have written on this topic because their statements do not agree with experience." He showed that a cicada goes on singing in its breast after its head has been cut off and that, contrary to the then-current story, ostriches to whom he offered iron did not eat and digest the metal, although they would eat stones and bones broken into bits. "Experience," he contends, is "much more profitable than teaching by [logical] demonstration."

Further, he insisted that "it is not the part of natural science to receive accounts but to enquire into the causes in the matters of nature." According to Albert, natural scientists can achieve causal explanations of any phenomenon by working back analytically from some regularly observed change to the natural agent predetermined to produce such a result. That the end of the analytic road will be celestial phenomena is part of the Aristotelian-Ptolemaic view of a geocentric universe. The ultimate cause of the universe, however, must lie outside the natural realm. Seeking causes in nature was not for Albert contrary to a religious outlook, yet he did acknowledge the need to reconcile the natural causality of the stars, planets, and earthly bodies with the voluntary, free causality of the human will.

Albert's crypt, under the Andreas Cloister of the Dominican Fathers, Cologne

Albert starts from the premise that all natural events are due ultimately to divine will; it is God acting through natural causes who brings about natural phenomena. The intermediate causes between God and human beings, however, have been eliminated; Albert ascribes all actions initiated by human beings to the free will and reason of the soul, which directly—unlike the human body, which is subject to natural causal influence—is affected by God alone. Albert saw it as his task, however, not to undertake an investigation of the divine will itself—that task, he thought, was one for theology, not philosophy—but to discover how natural causes serve as divine instruments. In so doing, Albert found himself coming to a greater awe of the divine will. He became increasingly aware of the degree to which miraculous events, such as the deluge or the eclipse at Christ's crucifixion, could only have been caused by the extraordinary intervention of God; natural causes could not have brought about their occurrence.

Logical, ethical, and metaphysical writings comprise the balance of Albert's exposition of the Aristotelian corpus. Like Aristotle, Albert understood logic to be the study of the methods of proceeding from the known to the unknown. Knowledge of nature can be obtained from experience and observation; knowledge of the "metaphysical"—that which is "above nature"— must be learned from authoritative writings and ultimately from God.

Metaphysics is the search for knowledge of the most general attributes: being, unity, and goodness. Universal being, according to Albert, exists in three ways: "before" individuation (*ante rem*) in the divine intellect; in the individual (*in re*) as the principle of unity in the plurality of things individualized through matter; and "after" individuation (*post rem*) as abstracted by the human mind. God creates all other beings ex nihilo; in themselves they are nothing. They do not have their own power to be but are conserved in existence by God. Each thing imitates God to the degree that it can. God draws from matter the forms that lie dormant within it.

For Albert the ultimate barrier to the extended use of scientific reasoning and to the "natural" comprehension of the First Being is that "the human soul cannot come to know naturally that whose principles it has within itself." The ethical works of Albert reveal the two kinds of "principles" the soul has by virtue of God: innate conscience and infused virtues. The innate conscience provides the individual with the ability to know the principles of good conduct; the divinely infused virtues of faith, hope, and charity, acquired by divine grace, strengthen the relationship between the individual soul and God. Albert maintained, in opposition to the Latin followers of Averroës, the individuality of the human soul both during life on earth and after the death of the individual's body.

All of Albert's writings are thoroughly Christian in spirit. He did not believe in "double truths," one known by faith and the other, contradicting it, knowable through reason; he maintained that all that is really true cannot be contradicted either by faith or by reason. At the same time, Albert affirmed that human beings, while they can come to know much through experience and reason, possess the profound capacity of faith to know certain otherwise inaccessible mysteries. His theological works are devoted both to biblical exegesis and to systematic theology. His most important theological works are six written at the University of Paris on the sacraments, the Incarnation, the Resurrection, the four coevals, humanity, and the good; his late *Summa Theologiae* (Summary of Theology, between 1263 and 1274); his expositions of the Pseudo-Dionysian writings; and his works of biblical exegesis, many of which were completed during his stay in Italy. In his religious works Albert stresses that humanity is an effect of the greatest cause, God. God is both free and omnipresent; he is actualizing a well-ordered plan. Human life is ideally the active discovering of that plan; once it has been perceived, if only in part, human acts of free will can effect the continuing realization of the divine course. Albert's beliefs in this regard parallel those of Augustine and Peter Lombard. Under the influence of Aristotle and Boethius, Albert also concerned himself greatly with the distinctions between theology and other human intellectual endeavors.

Until the process of critically editing all of Albert's works is complete, several assessments remain difficult. The first concerns the authenticity of certain works attributed to Albert. Volume forty of the Cologne edition (1951-) will be devoted to works which, while doubtful, have a long tradition of ascription to him. Among such works are several included in the Borgnet edition (1890-1899): *De laudibus B. Mariae Virginis*, *Mariale*, and *Biblia Mariana*. Others that have circulated widely under Albert's name include *De Secretis Naturae* (On the Secrets of Nature) and *Speculum Astronomiae* (The Mirror of Astronomy). A second question concerns works Albert is said to have written on astronomy and poetics which have not yet been found. A third issue concerns the revisions that Albert's work underwent, either by his own hand or by those of scribes. Some of the difficulty in dating Albert's writings stems from the fact that the extant texts contain many revisions. It has been posited that conflicting assertions in Albert's works, such as that concerning the possibility of melting iron which is asserted in the *Meteora* (Meteorology, between 1252 and 1254) and denied in the *De Mineralia*, could be due to one work having been revised but not the other. A complete study of Albert's thought will only be possible when the editing task is finished.

For his writings as well as his vocational duties, Albert received recognition even during his lifetime. He was the only Scholastic to be called "the Great"; the parallel of his writings with the Aristotelian works must have given a kind of epic perspective to his contribution, leading as well to the titles of *Doctor universalis* and *Doctor expertus* even during his lifetime. Some of his pupils became disciples; next to Aquinas, Albert's best-known student was Ulrich of Strasbourg, who called his master "a man so superior in every science, that he can fittingly be called the wonder and miracle of our time." Siger of Brabant, a contemporary of Thomas in Paris, considered Albert and Thomas "the principal men in philosophy." By the late fifteenth century Albert was so popularly called *magnus in magia* (great in magic) that a canonization process well under way was halted under charges of sorcery. In 1622 Albert was beatified by Gregory XV.

References:

Joseph von Bach, *Des Albertus Magnus Verhältniss zu der Erkenntnislehre der Griechen, Lateiner, Araber und Juden* (Vienna: Braumüller, 1881; reprinted, Frankfurt am Main: Minerva, 1966);

Ingrid Craemer-Ruegenberg, *Albertus Magnus* (Munich: Beck, 1980);

Stanley B. Cunningham, "Albertus Magnus and the Problem of Moral Virtue," *Vivarium*, 7 (November 1969): 81-119;

Alan De Libera, *Albert le Grand et la Philosophie* (Paris: Librairie Philosophique J. Vrin, 1990);

Leonard A. Kennedy, "St. Albert the Great's Doctrine of Divine Illumination," *Modern Schoolman*, 40 (November 1962): 23-37;

Francis J. Kovach and Robert W. Shahan, eds., *Albert the Great: Commemorative Essays* (Norman: University of Oklahoma Press, 1980);

Adolf Layer and Max Springer, *Albert von Lauingen* (Lauingen: Historischen Verein Dillingen an der Donau, 1980);

Gilles Meersseman, *Introductio in Opera omnia B. Alberti Magni* (Bruges: Bayaert, 1931);

Gerbert Meyer and Albert Zimmermann, eds., *Albertus Magnus - Doctor universalis: Festschrift der deutschen Dominikaner zum 700. Todestag Albert des Grossen* (Mainz: Grünewald, 1980);

Karl Schmieder, *Alberts des Grossen Lehre vom naturlichen Gotteswissen* (Freiburg im Breisgau: Herder, 1932);

Thomas M. Schwertner, *St. Albert the Great* (New York & Milwaukee: Bruce, 1932);

Lynn Thorndike, *A History of Magic and Experimental Science*, volume 2 (New York, 1923), pp. 517-592, 692-750;

Richard F. Waskell, "Logic, Language, and Albert the Great," *Journal of the History of Ideas*, 34 (July-September 1973): 445-450;

James A. Weisheipl, ed., *Albertus Magnus and the Sciences: Commemorative Essays* (Toronto: Pontifical Institute of Mediaeval Studies, 1980).

Manuscripts:

A list of the more than two thousand extant manuscripts of Albert the Great's works can be found in Winfrid Tauser, *Die Werke des Albertus Magnus in Ihrer Handschriftlichen Uberlieferung*, Part 1: *Die Echten Werke* (Cologne: Monasterii Westfalorum, 1982).

Anselm of Canterbury

(1033 - 21 April 1109)

Thomas A. Losconcy
Villanova University

PRINCIPAL WORKS: *Monologion* (Soliloquy, written 1076);

Proslogion (An Address of the Mind to God, written 1077-1078);

De Grammatico (On the Word *Grammaticus*, written 1080-1085);

De Veritate (Concerning Truth, written 1080-1085);

De Libertate Arbitrii (On Freedom of Choice, written 1080-1085);

De Casu Diaboli (On the Fall of the Devil, written 1085-1090);

Epistola de Incarnatione Verbi (Letter on the Incarnation of the Word, written 1094);

Cur Deus Homo (Why God Became Human, written circa 1094-1098);

De conceptu Virginalis et de Originali Peccato (On the Virgin Conception and Original Sin, written 1099-1100);

Meditatio Redemptionis Humanae (Meditation on the Redemption of Humanity, written 1099-1100);

De Processione Spiritus Sancti (On the Procession of the Holy Spirit, written 1102);

Epistola de Sacrificio Azimi et Fermentati (Letter on the Sacrifice of Leavened and Unleavened Bread, written 1106-1107);

Epistola de Sacramentis Ecclesiae (Letter on the Sacraments of the Church, written 1106-1107);

De Concordia Praescientiae et Praedestinationis et Gratiae Dei cum Libero Arbitrio (On the Harmony of the Foreknowledge, the Predestination, and the Grace of God with Free Choice, written 1107-1108);

Meditatio ad Concitandum Timorem (Meditation for Arousing Dread, written 1108).

CRITICAL EDITION: *Sancti Anselmi Opera Omnia*, 6 volumes, edited by Franciscus S. Schmitt (volume 1, Seckau: 1938; republished, Edinburgh: Nelson, 1946; volume 2, Rome, 1940; volumes 3-6, Edinburgh: Nelson, 1946-1951; all 6 volumes republished in 2, with new introduction, Stuttgart-Bad Cannstatt: Frommann, 1968).

EDITIONS IN ENGLISH: *The Devotions of Saint Anselm, Archbishop of Canterbury*, edited by Clement C. J. Webb (London: Methuen, 1903);

Proslogium; Monologium; an Appendix, In Behalf of the Fool, by Gaunilon; and Cur Deus Homo, translated by Sidney Norton Deane (Chicago: Open Court, 1903);

The De Grammatico of St. Anselm: The Theory of Paronymy, translated by Desmond P. Henry (Notre Dame, Ind.: University of Notre Dame Press, 1964);

St. Anselm's Proslogion: With, A Reply on Behalf of the Fool by Gaunilo, and the Author's Reply to Gaunilo, translated by Maxwell J. Charlesworth (Oxford: Clarendon Press, 1965);

Theological Treatises, 3 volumes, edited and translated by Jasper Hopkins and Herbert Richardson (Cambridge, Mass.: Harvard Divinity School Library, 1965-1967);

Why God Became Man, and The Virgin Conception and Original Sin, translated by Joseph M. Colleran (Albany, N.Y.: Magi Brooks, 1969);

The Prayers and Meditations of Saint Anselm, translated by Benedicta Ward (Harmondsworth, U.K.: Penguin, 1973);

Anselm of Canterbury, 4 volumes, translated by Hopkins and Richardson (London: SCM Press, 1974-1976; Toronto & New York: Mellen Press, 1974-1976);

A New, Interpretive Translation of St. Anselm's Monologion and Proslogion, translated by Hopkins (Minneapolis: Banning Press, 1986).

Like Augustine, Anselm was a leading churchman and bishop of his day. In his writings he focused on many of the same issues as Augustine: truth, the existence of God, evil, the Fall of humanity and Original Sin, divine foreknowl-

Anselm of Canterbury, as depicted in a fifteenth-century altarpiece by Luca della Robbia (Galleria della Collegiata, Empoli)

edge, freedom of the will, and grace. And, like Augustine, he corresponded with many of his fellow bishops and with secular authorities. Still, Anselm was a Benedictine monk while Augustine was not. Anselm's education was primarily in the writings of Church Fathers and leaders, whereas Augustine's was a classical one. Augustine was bishop of a young and growing church that was actively shaping its doctrines and had to deal with the Roman Empire, while Anselm's church had traditions and established institutional forms and existed in an age in which nations were seeking their respective identities. Finally, Augustine's rhetorical skill and training and Anselm's keen absorption in the power of logic would result in marked differences in their writing styles and approaches to problems.

Anselm was born in Aosta, in Piedmont, in 1033. His family was one of means but was not affluent. His childhood was noteworthy for strong disagreements with his father, Gundulf; when his mother, Ermenberga, died, Anselm left home at the age of twenty-three. He wandered through France, passed some time in the schools of Fleury-sur-Loire and Chartres, and arrived in Normandy in 1059. The Benedictine Abbey of Bec, sixteen miles southwest of Rouen, attracted Anselm's interest because of its renowned prior, Lanfranc, a fellow Italian.

At about this time Anselm's father died, leaving his property to his son. Rather than return home, however, Anselm became a novice at Bec in 1060. When Lanfranc left for a new monastery at Caen in 1063, Anselm replaced him as prior at Bec. On the death of Herluin, the abbot of Bec, in 1078, Anselm became the abbot.

As abbot, Anselm gained social prestige and a wide reputation as a counselor and adviser. He wrote to such personages as Baldwin I, King of Jerusalem; Matilda, Countess of Tuscany; the king of the Scots; the high king of Ireland; and the earl of Orkney. He was summoned to hear the dying confession of William the Conqueror at Rouen in 1087.

In 1078 Anselm had visited Lanfranc, who had been archbishop of Canterbury since 1070. The visit made a favorable impression on the English, and in 1089, at the death of Lanfranc, Anselm was viewed as the logical successor. But William Rufus, the king of England, kept the see vacant for four years so that he could collect its revenues. On 6 March 1093 Anselm was offered the see. He refused, but the English bishops thrust the archiepiscopal staff into Anselm's hand and forcibly brought him to the church, where he was inducted into the office. After William Rufus agreed to meet certain of his terms, Anselm was enthroned on 25 September 1093 and began what was to be a stormy relationship with William Rufus over the powers of church and state.

In 1097 Anselm left Canterbury for Rome without William Rufus's permission. From 1097 to 1100 he endured a kind of self-imposed exile. In 1100 William Rufus was killed in a hunting accident, and the new king, Henry I, invited Anselm to return. But a dispute erupted with Henry over lay investiture of clergy, and Anselm journeyed back to Rome in 1103. He remained in exile until a settlement was reached with Henry in 1107. Anselm died on the Wednesday before Easter, 21 April 1109.

An anecdote is told about an incident a few days before his death: one of the monks gathered around his bed remarked that Anselm would probably die by Easter. Anselm is alleged to have said: "If it is His will I shall gladly obey, but if He should prefer me to stay with you just long enough to solve the question of the origin of the soul which I have been turning over in my mind, I would gratefully accept the chance, for I doubt whether anybody else will solve it when I am gone."

Anselm did not commence writing until nearly ten years after his entry at Bec. It is clear from his work that he had absorbed much from reading the writings of Augustine. In addition, the mature date at which he began his literary output resulted in the rapid appearance of careful and often interconnected works which are clearly placed in an overall program.

In the *De Grammatico* (On the Word *Grammaticus*, 1080-1085) Anselm shows the power of logic and analysis to tease out the meanings of terms and to reach definitions of important notions. The reliance on this approach to philosophizing appears many times in his treatises. In the *De Libertate Arbitrii* (On Freedom of Choice, 1080-1085) he resorts to this methodology to establish the will's condition in different states of its relation to God and grace. Again, in section 4 of his rejoinder to Gaunilo, included in the *Proslogion* (An Address of the Mind to God, 1077-1078), he undertakes a prolonged discussion of the difference between understanding and thinking in one's knowledge of existence. Section 9 of the rejoinder probes the logic of understanding something versus thinking of it. The same technique is also evident in his treatment of the different applications of truth in the *De Veritate* (Concerning Truth, 1080-1085). Some scholars, such as Desmond P. Henry, see logical analysis and distinction as Anselm's forte and perhaps as a forerunner of symbolic and linguistic analysis in the late medieval period. Others, including Marcia L. Colish, think that Anselm's logical and grammatical expertise is subordinate to the larger issues and ideas he treats.

The writings that have attracted the greatest interest are Anselm's *Monologion* (Soliloquy, 1076) and *Proslogion*; the *Pro Insipiente* (Reply on Behalf of the Fool), written by the monk Gaunilo but always copied with the *Proslogion* at Anselm's directive; and Anselm's rejoinder to Gaunilo. Anselm's preface to the *Proslogion* recounts how the series was begun as a result of his fellow monks' desire to have some reassurance that God exists. The *Monologion* provides three arguments: the "highest good" argument, the "supreme nature" argument, and the "highest being" argument. Anselm maintains that there is one Being which, whether viewed as the "highest good," the "supreme nature," or the "highest being," is that on which all other beings depend for their existence.

Anselm endeavored to reduce the arguments of the *Monologion* to a single argument that would be briefer and easier for the monks to read in chapter 2 of the *Proslogion*. This so-called ontological argument has inspired a deluge of reactions, defenses, and interpretations over the centuries that has eclipsed all that has been written about his other works taken together. The tide of reactions was accidentally assisted by Anselm himself when he insisted that Gaunilo's reaction to his argument be included in all copies of the *Proslogion* along with his own rejoinder to Gaunilo. Gaunilo's presentation in *Pro Insipiente* lent itself to easy circulation as a summary of Anselm's argument, which is directed against the fool who "hath said in his heart, There is no God" (Ps. 14:1 and 53:1). As Gaunilo characterizes Anselm's procedure: "Let one doubt or deny that there is a nature such that no greater can be thought. In the foregoing [*Proslogion*] he is told, *first* of all, that its being is proved in this way: when he himself denies or doubts that there is such a nature he already had it in his understand-

Anselm's seal (from the New Catholic Encyclopedia, *1967)*

ing, for every time he hears that nature mentioned he understands what is mentioned. In the *second* place the foregoing proves that what he understands is of necessity not in the understanding alone but among things as well. The latter point is proved in this fashion: that which is also among things is greater than that which is merely in the understanding, but if there be something which is merely in the understanding, anything which is among things as well must be greater still. Accordingly the greater than everything will be less than something and will not be greater than everything. This surely is a contradiction in terms. Accordingly of necessity—the argument runs—that which is greater than everything whose being in the understanding was already proved is not merely in the understanding but is among things as well: for it cannot otherwise be greater than everything." Gaunilo takes Anselm's argument to involve a move from mental existence to extramental existence. Gaunilo argues vehemently against this move, and later Thomas Aquinas and Immanuel Kant rejected the validity of Anselm's argument on the ground that the conclusion contains more than the premises allow.

Gaunilo's objection to Anselm's argument has two parts. First, he argues that there is no way Anselm could obtain from this world an adequate concept of God: "on the one hand I cannot think when I hear nor possess in my intellect that which is greater than all things thinkable (which we say can be no other than God Himself) in terms of a thing specifically or generically known to me; and on the other hand I cannot think that that which is greater than all things thinkable is God Himself of whose nonbeing I can think for this very same reason. For I cannot know the thing itself and I cannot conjecture it from the similitude since, indeed, you yourself hold that the nature is such that there can be no other like it." Moreover, even if one could gain some idea of God, Gaunilo refuses to grant that Anselm's specific formulation, "that whose greater is unthinkable," will permit him to pass from the mental formulation to the extramental reality. To this end, he offers his "Lost Island Argument": one could just as easily claim that the most beautiful possible island must exist somewhere, just because we can conceive it. In his rejoinder to Gaunilo, Anselm denounces Gaunilo's portrayal of his argument as like that of the "Lost Island": "I announce with full confidence: let one discover for me (whether in actual reality or only in his thinking) an existing thing other than that 'whose greater is unthinkable' to which one can validly tailor the pattern of my argumentation; I will discover and bestow upon him that Lost Island never to be lost again." He bolsters this remark with the comment: "First, you often repeat that I say, 'What is greater than all things is in the intellect, and if it is in the intellect it is also among things. For otherwise the greater than all things would not be greater than all things.' Nowhere in all my remarks can anyone find a proof of that sort." Anselm maintains that he never intended to suggest an argument passing from thought to some extramental reality.

In chapter 3 of the *Proslogion* Anselm addresses God: "And, indeed, whatever there is other than you alone can be thought not to be. You alone, then, more truly than all, and therefore, more than all have being. For whatever else there is has being not so truly and for that reason has being less." Anselm wants to focus on the uniqueness of God. The being of all things in the universe which one can observe is less true than God's being. Anselm is arguing from what he understands about the being of the things which he can observe to a conclusion about the being of God. All beings other than God are able not to be; that is, they possess no inherent necessity to exist. But the being of things can provide one with information about a supreme—and supremely unknowable—being. In chapter 16 of the *Proslogion* Anselm writes: "Lord, this is truly that inaccessible light in which You dwell. For truly there is no other thing which penetrates this light so as to see You there. Therefore, I do indeed not see this light: it is much too much for me; and for all that, whatever I see I see through that light. Just as the weak eye (which does see) sees through the light of the sun—the light it cannot look up to in the sun itself. My understanding cannot look at that light."

Anselm points out that there is a crucial distinction to be made between understanding something to exist and thinking about its existence. In the case of understanding a thing to exist one is dealing with the present existence of a thing; the only true judgment in such a case is "It exists." One cannot truthfully think the thing's nonexistence. But when one thinks about the existence of such a thing one comes to realize that its nonexistence is *thinkable* (*cogitari*) even when one understands (*intelligere*) its present existence. It is only a being wholly unlike such beings whose nonexistence is unthinkable.

In the *Proslogion* Anselm is insistent that the intellect can know something of such a being from the things it does experience. In the rejoinder to Gaunilo he sets forth how the intellect can move from the being of things it does know to a knowledge of a being than which no greater can be thought. He refers to this movement as a kind of "conjuring": "You make another point about that 'than which no greater is thinkable': in terms of a thing known to you whether in genus or in species you are unable—so you say—to think it when you hear it or to possess it in your understanding, since you have not known the thing itself nor known one similar to it from which you could conjure it up. Plainly the situation is other than this. For every lesser good is similar to a greater good at least insofar as it is good. Therefore, to every reasonable mind—since from lesser goods we rise to those greater goods from which another greater is thinkable—it is clear that we are able to conjure up [*coniicere*] that than which nothing greater is thinkable. For example, who is not able to think this, even though he may not believe that this is among things, I mean: if there is a good which has a beginning and an end, that good is a better good which may begin to be and yet has no end; and as the second of these is a better good than the first so a third is a better good than the second, a third which has neither end nor beginning even if it everlastingly proceeds through the present from the past into the future. And whether there be among things something of this kind or not, is not that a far better good which has no needs and can in no way be changed or altered? Is this then unthinkable, or is there a greater good than this thinkable? Or is this then not, among the things than which the greater is validly thinkable: to conjure up that than which no greater is thinkable? There is therefore a way in which that 'than which no greater is thinkable' can be conjured up." While things necessarily exist, as regards their present existing, the limitations and conditions of their existence disclose an inherent contingency that points to another way of existing: one in which existence is inherent, by nature, and necessary.

Contrary to what is generally believed about Anselm's "ontological argument," therefore, he does not think that the existence of God is self-evident. It is the analysis of the being of the things of this world that directs the intellect to the existence of a divine being.

Chapter 5 of the *Proslogion* opens: "What (*Quid*) then are you, Lord God, than whom a greater is unthinkable?" This chapter initiates a series of chapters ostensibly designed to answer the question; but the enterprise is judged impossible in chapter 15. Anselm never responds to his question, "What?," in these chapters. Rather than answer what God is he designates God's existence as the "highest," "greatest," and "most unlike" all others. In chapter 14 he reflects: "Have you then, my soul, discovered what you are seeking? You were seeking for God and you discovered him to be a thing, the highest of all things, a thing whose better cannot be thought. And this is life itself, it is light, it is wisdom, it is goodness, it is eternal blessedness and blessed eternity. And this is everywhere and always. How if you have not found your God: how is it that he is this which you did find and how did you understand him to be that with such firm truth and truthful firmness? But if you discovered him: how is it that you have no sense of having discovered him? Lord God, why does my soul have no sense of You if my soul has discovered You? Has my soul not discovered you? Has my soul not discovered that You are light and truth? . . . Or is it the truth and the light that it saw; and for all that has not yet seen You because it saw You only to some extent, but did not see You as You are?"

Chapter 15 states the conclusion to be reached as a consequence of this series of chapters: "Therefore, Lord, You are not only that whose greater is unthinkable; but You are something greater than the thinkable. For something of this sort can indeed be thought to be; if You are not this very thing, something greater than You are is thinkable. But to do this is impossible." Anselm now is aware that the "what" of God remains completely beyond human grasp. On the other hand, he does not relinquish the claim that some being as this is able to be thought by a human being. He is not, however, speaking of knowledge of the being's *nature* but of knowledge of its *existence*.

Anselm's dialogue *De Veritate* is a reworking of Augustine's view of the universe as a manifestation of an "order" *(ordo)* set by God. Augustine treated evil as a disorder—a case of acting or existing in a manner other than that intended in the divine scheme of things. Anselm replaces Augustine's "order" with the notion of the "rightness" *(rectitudo)* of things, actions, and the will—as a matter of whether or not they exist or occur in the "right way" or "wrong way" for them to be. Anselm can discern an "ought" in the very being of things and actions.

Anselm commences his exploration of truth by considering the truth of propositions. He puts forward the traditional claim that a proposition is true "When what it affirms to exist does exist" (*vera propositio significat esse quod est*). But as the teacher and student in the dialogue examine the issue more closely, Anselm points to an inner and outer truth to every proposition. In one sense every proposition is "correct and true because it signifies in accordance with its mere power of signifying." Signifying ability belongs to a proposition always and by nature. When, however, one considers the external truth of a proposition, its truth is determined on the basis of whether it correctly states what is or is not. In this situation the truth of the proposition can change with time. Anselm then proceeds to direct attention to an order of truth itself: the proposition can be judged by a truth in which it occurs, a truth caused by the Supreme Truth, God: "We speak improperly when we speak of 'the truth of this or that thing.' For truth has its own being and is not really *in* or *from* or *on account of* the things in which it is said to be. But when things are in accordance with that truth which is always present when they are as they ought to be, then we say 'the truth of this thing' or 'the truth of that thing.' "

Having established the meaning of the "truth of propositions" and the conditions for anything's participation in truth, Anselm briefly comments upon the various loci of truth in the universe. "Whoever thinks something to exist which does exist thinks as he ought; therefore, his thought is correct." The truth of the will is "that correctness of the will which we call uprightness"; this "uprightness" means that the will actually wills that for which it was made: "Whoever wills what he should is said to do what is right and good: and so he is included among those who do the truth." The "Supreme Truth" transcends any norm of rightness or obligation, since it is the cause of all else and all others are obligated to it. From his analysis of truth Anselm brings away a sense of truth as obligatory and a view of natures as having certain inherent requirements.

In *De Concordia Praescientiae et Praedestinationis et Gratiae Dei cum Libero Arbitrio* (On the Harmony of the Foreknowledge, the Predestination, and the Grace of God with Free Choice, 1107-1108) Anselm treats will and such related issues as freedom, predestination, and evil. He begins by distinguishing three senses of will: as instrument, as affection or inclination of this instrument, and as use of this instrument. In the first sense, will is something possessed internally by human beings. By means of this power or instrument one moves oneself to choose and to act. The willed object is the external factor in the willed action. The goodness or badness of willed actions results from two elements: the kind of will with which one wills and the kind of object willed.

In the second sense of will one is said to be inclined toward willing or desiring something. Anselm divides this inclination of the will into two sorts of affections (*affectiones*): an inherent and ineradicable affection toward one's well-being and a disposition toward justice or uprightness of will for its own sake. The first sort of affection, that inherent in the will, enables Anselm to maintain that the will's freedom of choice is natural and still exists even after the Fall. It is manifest in the common occurrence of a preference for one thing over another. The second sort of affection is the superior one. A will acting from this purity of motive experiences no compulsion and so acts most in keeping with itself. Anselm presents the notion in the following exchange between the student (S) and teacher (T) in the dialogue:

S— When a just man wills what he wought to will, then—insofar as he is to be called just—he keeps uprightness-of-will only for its own sake. By contrast, someone who wills what he ought to will but does so only if compelled to or only if induced by external rewards, does not keep uprightness-of-will for its own sake, but keeps it for the sake of something else—if he should at all be said to keep it.

T— Then, that will is just which keeps its uprightness on account of that uprightness itself.

S— Either that will is just or no will is.

This willing of the just or upright for its own sake empowers the will to seek the right object from the right motivation and to escape the intensity of affection that typifies bodily passion. A kind of natural "freedom of choice" inherent to the will is never lost to it, even after the Fall. Thus, one chooses among objects on the basis of intensity of one's likes or dislikes of them. But when it comes to acting and choosing in a "moral manner," then one must include the second motivation for action, that of the good will that chooses the right object, in the right way, for the right reasons. This sort of will, Anselm thought, is lost through the Fall, and consequently the ability to will for the right moral motives—to will aright—can only be achieved by the will that is brought into alignment through God's grace with its original condition before the Fall; it is then able to will things correctly for what they are and in regard to how they bear on one's ultimate object of the will, God.

Anselm's third sense of will pertains to the actual willing of an object. The object should be in keeping with both of the will's affections, but he places a primacy on the second affection's ability to color the action itself.

Two problems for any position that maintains free will are those of evil and divine foreknowledge. Anselm addresses the problem of evil in several of his treatises, but the longest and most thorough consideration is in the *De Casu Diaboli* (On the Fall of the Devil, 1085-1090). Anselm subscribes to the Augustinian position that evil is essentially a privation of being and hence is intrinsically nothing.

On the issue of divine foreknowledge Anselm again takes an approach reminiscent of that of Augustine. Anselm contends that if God foreknows an action that is to occur without necessity, then God must necessarily know it as such an action. It follows that if one were to sin, then God would foreknow not only that one would sin but also that one would sin without necessity. If one sins without necessity, then one sins freely.

Anselm introduced to the West the idea of proving the existence of God. He engaged the diverse problems of the nature of the human will and began a reintroduction of some of the classical insights into knowledge, will, logic, and human nature to the West. He reacquainted the West with the meaning of "nature" within the context of a Divine order, and affirmed the "rights" of nature within such an order.

Biographies:

Eadmer, *The Life of St. Anselm, Archbishop of Canterbury*, edited and translated by Richard W. Southern (London & New York: Nelson, 1962);

Southern, *Saint Anselm: A Portrait in a Landscape* (Cambridge: Cambridge University Press, 1990).

References:

Marilyn M. Adams, "Hell and the God of Justice," *Religious Studies*, 11 (December 1975): 433-447;

Adams, "Was Anselm a Realist? The *Monologium*," *Franciscan Studies*, 32 (1972): 5-14;

Robert M. Adams, "The Logical Structure of Arguments," *Philosophical Review*, 80 (January 1971): 28-54;

R. E. Allen, "The Ontological Argument," *Philosophical Review*, 70 (January 1961): 56-66;

William P. Alston, "The Ontological Argument revisited," *Philosophical Review*, 69 (October 1960): 452-474;

Leslie Armour, "The Ontological Argument and the Concept of Completeness and Selection," *Review of Metaphysics*, 14 (December 1960): 280-291;

Allan Bäck, "Existential Import in Anselm's Ontological Argument," *Franciscan Studies*, 41 (1981): 97-109;

Hans Ur von Balthasar, "La *Concordantia Libertatis* chez saint Anselme," in his *L'Homme devant Dieu: Mélanges offerts au Père Henri de Lubac*, volume 2 (Paris: Aubier, 1964), pp. 29-45;

Albert G. A. Balz, "Concerning the Ontological Argument," *Review of Metaphysics*, 7 (December 1953): 207-224;

R. L. Barnett, "Anselm and the Fool," *International Journal for Philosophy of Religion*, 6 (Winter 1975): 201-218;

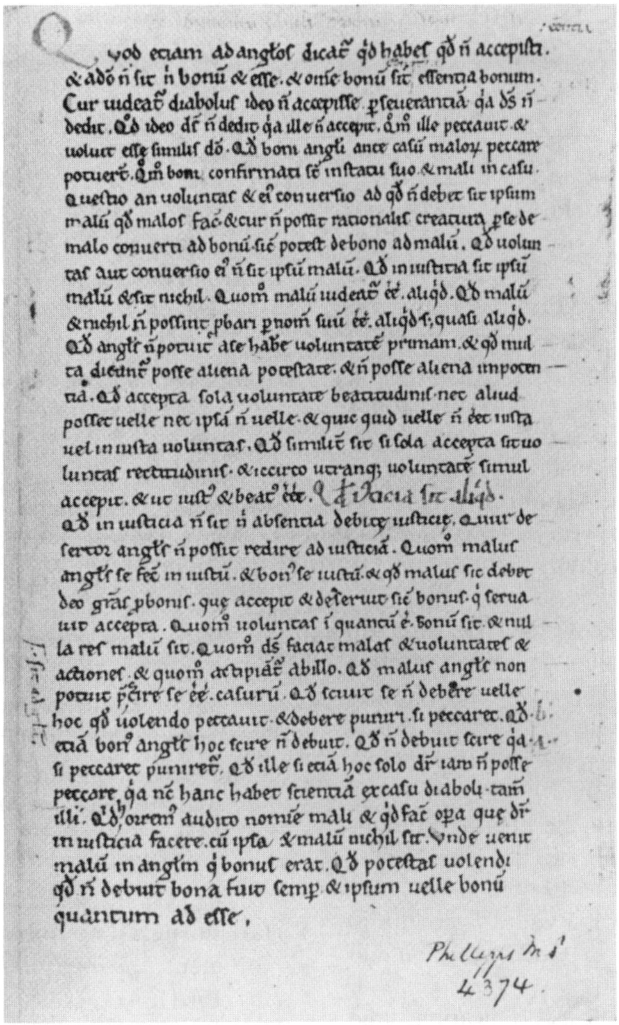

Page from the manuscript for a late-twelfth-century French translation of Anselm's De Casu Diaboli, *written in minuscule script style of the time (from the* New Catholic Encyclopedia, *1967)*

Karl Barth, *Fides quaerens intellectum* (Munich: Kaiser, 1931); translated by Ian W. Robertson as *Anselm: Fides Quaerens Intellectum* (London: SCM Press, 1960);

R. Robert Basham, "The 'Second Version' of Anselm's Ontological Argument," *Canadian Journal of Philosophy*, 6 (1976): 665-683;

William H. Baumer, "Ontological Arguments Still Fail," *Monist*, 50 (January 1966): 130-144;

Ferdinand Bergenthal, "Ist der 'ontologische Gottesbeweis' Anselms von Canterbury ein Trugschluss?," *Philosophisches Jahrbuch*, 59 (1949): 155-168;

Rudolph Berlinger, "Zur Sprachmetaphysik des Anselm von Canterbury: Eine spekulative Explikation," *Analecta Anselmiana*, 5 (1976): 99-112;

Eugene Beurlier, "Les rapports de la raison et de la foi dans la philosophie de saint Anselme," *Revue de philosophie*, 15 (1909): 692-723;

Robert Brecher, *Anselm's Argument* (Aldershot, U.K. & Brookfield, Vt.: Gower, 1985);

Brecher, " 'Greatness' in Anselm's Ontological Argument," *Philosophical Quarterly*, 24 (April 1974): 97-105;

Paul M. van Buren, "Anselm's Formula and the Logic of 'God,' " *Religious Studies*, 9 (September 1973): 279-288;

Richard Campbell, "Anselm's Background Metaphysics," *Scottish Journal of Theology*, 33, no. 4 (1980): 317-343;

Campbell, *From Belief to Understanding: A Study of Anselm's Proslogion Argument on the Existence of God* (Canberra: Australian National University Press, 1976);

Maxwell J. Charlesworth, "St. Anselm's Argument," *Sophia,* 1 (1962): 25-36;

Imelda Choquette, "*Voluntas, Affectio* and *Potestas* in the *Liber De Voluntate* of St. Anselm," *Mediaeval Studies,* 4 (1942): 61-81;

Marcia L. Colish, "Eleventh-Century Grammar in the Thought of St. Anselm," in *Arts liberaux au Moyen Age* (Paris: Vrin, 1969), pp. 785-795;

Michel Corbin, "De L'impossible en Dieu. Lecture du 8e chapitre du dialogue de saint Anselme sur la liberté," *Revue des sciences philosophiques et théologiques,* 66 (October 1982): 523-550;

Corbin, "L'événement de Verité: Lecture du *de Veritate* d'Anselme de Cantorbéry," in his *L'Inouî de Dieu: Six études christologiques* (Paris: Desclée De Brouwer, 1980), pp. 59-107;

Corbin, "Se tenir dans la vérité: Lecture du chapitre 12 du dialogue de saint Anselme sur la Verite," in *Spicilegium Beccense II: Actes du colloque international du CNRS: Etudes anselmiennes IVe Session: Les mutations socioculturelles au tournant des XIe-XIIe siècles,* edited by Raymond Foreville (Paris: Editions du Centre national de la Recherche Scientifique, 1984), pp. 649-666;

William J. Courtenay, "Necessity and Freedom in Anselm's Conception of God," *Analecta Anselmiana,* 4 (1976): 39-64;

Patricia Crawford, "Existence, Predication, and Anselm," *Monist,* 50 (January 1966): 109-124;

R. Crouse, "The Augustinian Background of St. Anselm's Concept of *Justitia,*" *Canadian Journal of Theology,* 4 (1958): 111-119;

Stephen T. Davis, "Anselm and Gaunilo on the 'Lost Island,'" *Southern Journal of Philosophy,* 13 (Winter 1975): 435-448;

Howard L. Dazeley and Wolfgang L. Gombocz, "Interpreting Anselm as Logician," *Synthese,* 40 (January 1979): 71-96;

Philip E. Devine, "'Exists' and St. Anselm's Argument," *Grazer philosophische Studien,* 3 (1977): 59-70;

Devine, "The Religious Significance of the Ontological Argument," *Religious Studies,* 11 (March 1975): 97-116;

Donald F. Duclow, "Structure and Meaning in Anselm's *De Veritate,*" *American Benedictine Review,* 26 (December 1975): 406-417;

Gillian R. Evans, *Anselm and a New Generation* (New York: Oxford University Press, 1980);

Evans, *Anselm and Talking about God* (Oxford: Oxford University Press, 1978);

Evans, "*Inopes verborum sunt Latini*: Technical Language and Technical Terms in the Writings of St. Anselm and Some Commentators of the Mid-twelfth Century," *Archives d'histoire doctrinale et littéraire du Moyen Age,* 53 (1976): 113-134;

Evans, "The 'Secure Technician': Varieties of Paradox in the Writings of St. Anselm," *Vivarium,* 13 (May 1975): 1-21;

Evans, ed., *A Concordance to the Works of St. Anselm,* 4 volumes (Millwood, N.Y.: Kraus, 1984);

B. Geyer, "Zur Deutung von Anselms Cur deus homo," *Theologie und Glaube,* 34 (1942): 203-210;

Etienne Gilson, "Sens et nature de l'argument de saint Anselme," *Archives d'histoire doctrinale et littéraire du moyen âge,* 9 (1934): 5-51;

Paul Gochet, "Le Dieu d'Anselme et les apparences de la raison," *Revue internationale de philosophie,* 26 (1972): 187-198;

Wolfgang L. Gombocz, "Anselm über Sinn und Bedeutung," *Anselm Studies,* 1 (1983): 125-141;

Charles Hartshorne, *Anselm's Discovery* (LaSalle, Ill.: Open Court, 1965);

Hartshorne, "The Logic of the Ontological Argument," *Journal of Philosophy,* 58 (17 August 1961): 471-473;

Hartshorne, "What Did Anselm Discover?," in his *Insights and Oversights of Great Thinkers: An Evaluation of Western Philosophy* (Albany: State University of New York Press, 1983), pp. 93-103;

Desmond P. Henry, *Commentary on De Grammatico: The Historical-Logical Dimensions of a Dialogue of St. Anselm's* (Boston: Reidel, 1974);

Henry, *The De Grammatico of Saint Anselm* (Notre Dame, Ind.: University of Notre Dame Press, 1964);

Henry, *The Logic of Saint Anselm* (Oxford: Clarendon Press, 1967);

Henry, "The *Proslogion* Proofs," *Philosophical Quarterly,* 5 (April 1955): 147-151;

Henry, "Why 'Grammaticus'?," *Archivum Latinitatis Medii Aevi,* 28 (1958): 165-180;

John Hick and Arthur C. McGill, eds., *The Many-faced Argument: Recent Studies of the Ontological Argument for the Existence of God* (New York: Macmillan, 1967);

Jasper Hopkins, "Anselm on Freedom and the Will: A Discussion of G. Stanley Kane's Interpretation of Anselm," *Philosophy Research Archives*, 9 (1983): 471-493;

Hopkins, *A Companion to the Study of St. Anselm* (Minneapolis: University of Minnesota Press, 1972);

Hopkins, *A New Interpretive Translation of St. Anselm's Monologion and Proslogion* (Minneapolis: Banning Press, 1986);

Leroy T. Howe, "One God, One Proof," *Southern Journal of Philosophy*, 6 (Winter 1968): 235-245;

G. Stanley Kane, *Anselm's Doctrine of Freedom and the Will* (New York: Mellen Press, 1981);

Kane, "Elements of Ethical Theory in the Thought of St. Anselm," *Studies in Medieval Culture*, 12 (1978): 61-71;

Klaus Kienzler, *Glauben und Denken bei Anselm von Canterbury* (Vienna: Herder, 1981);

Helmut K. Kohlenberger, ed., *Sola ratione: Anselm-Studien für Pater Dr. h.c. Franciscus Salesius Schmitt OSB zum 75. Geburtstag am 20. Dez. 1969* (Stuttgart-Bad Cannstatt: Frommann-Holzboog, 1970);

Heinz Külling, *Wahrheit als Richtigkeit: Eine Untersuchung zur Schrift* 'De veritate' *von Anselm von Canterbury* (New York: Lang, 1984);

Paul G. Kuntz, "The God We Find: The God of Abraham, the God of Anselm, and the God of Weiss," *Modern Schoolman*, 47 (May 1970): 433-453;

Ernst Lohmeyer, *Die Lehre vom Willen bei Anselm von Canterbury* (Leipzig: Berger, 1914);

Thomas A. Losconcy, "Anselm's Response to Gaunilo's Dilemma—An Insight Into the Notion of 'Being' Operative in the *Proslogion*," *New Scholasticism*, 56 (Spring 1982): 207-216;

Henri de Lubac, " 'Seigneur, je cherche ton visage': Sur le chapitre XIV[e] du Proslogion de saint Anselme," *Archives de philosophie*, 39 (April-June 1976): 201-225; (July-September 1976): 407-426;

Norman Malcolm, "Anselm's Ontological Arguments," *Philosophical Review*, 69 (January 1960): 41-62; reprinted in *The Ontological Argument*, edited by Alvin Plantinga (Garden City, N.Y.: Doubleday, 1965), pp. 136-159;

T. L. Miethe, "The Ontological Argument: A Research Bibliography," *Modern Schoolman*, 54 (January 1977): 148-166;

Anton C. Pegis, "St. Anselm and the Argument of the 'Proslogion,' " *Mediaeval Studies*, 28 (1966): 228-267;

Alvin Plantinga, "Kant's Objection to the Ontological Argument," *Journal of Philosophy*, 63 (13 October 1966): 537-546;

Plantinga, "The Ontological Argument," in his *God, Freedom, and Evil* (Grand Rapids, Mich.: Eerdmans, 1977), pp. 85-112;

Plantinga, "A Valid Ontological Argument?," *Philosophical Review*, 70 (January 1961): 93-101; reprinted in *The Ontological Argument*, edited by Plantinga (Garden City, N.Y.: Doubleday, 1965), pp. 160-171;

Vincenzo Poletti, *Anselmo d'Aosta, filosofo mistico* (Faenza: Lega, 1975);

Robert Pouchet, *La rectitudo chez saint Anselme* (Paris: Etudes Augustiniennes, 1964);

Cyril Charles Richardson, "The Strange Fascination of the Ontological Argument," *Union Seminary Quarterly Review*, 18 (November 1962): 1-21;

Victor W. Roberts, "The Relation of Faith and Reason in St. Anselm of Canterbury," *American Benedictine Review*, 21 (September 1970): 389-406;

R. Roques, "*Derisio, Simplicitas, Insipientia*: Remarques mineurs sur la terminologie de saint Anselme," *L'Homme devant Dieu: Mélanges offerts au père H. de Lubac*, 57 (1963): 47-61;

Roques, "La méthode de Saint Anselme dans le 'Cur Deus homo,' " *Aquinas: Ephemerides thomisticae*, 5 (1962): 3-57;

Gregory Schufreider, *An Introduction to Anselm's Argument* (Philadelphia: Temple University Press, 1978);

Adolf Schurr, "Vie et réflexion selon Saint Anselme," *Archives de philosophie*, 35 (January-March 1972): 111-126;

John R. Sheets, "Justice in the Moral Thought of St. Anselm," *Modern Schoolman*, 25 (January 1948): 132-139;

Robert D. Shofner, *Anselm Revisited* (Leiden: Brill, 1974);

Frederick Sontag, "The Meaning of 'Argument' in Anselm's Ontological 'Proof,' " *Journal of Philosophy*, 64 (10 August 1967): 459-486;

Richard W. Southern, "Anselm at Canterbury," *Anselm Studies*, 1 (1983): 7-22;

Southern, *Saint Anselm and His Biographer: A Study of Monastic Life and Thought, 1059-c.1130* (Cambridge and New York: Cambridge University Press, 1963);

Southern and Franciscus S. Schmitt, *Memorials of St. Anselm* (London: Published for the British Academy by Oxford University Press, 1969);

A. Stolz, "Das *Proslogion* des hl. Anselm," *Revue Bénédictine*, 47 (1935): 331-347;

Stolz, " 'Vere esse' im Proslogion des hl. Anselm," *Scholastik*, 9 (1934): 400-409;

Thomas F. Torrance, "Ethical Implications of Anselm's De veritate," *Theologische Zeitschrift*, 24 (September-October 1968): 309-319;

Sally N. Vaughn, "St. Anselm of Canterbury: The Philosopher-saint as Politician," *Journal of Medieval History*, 1 (October 1975): 279-305;

Paul Vignaux, "Nécessité des raisons dans le Monologion," *Revue des sciences philosophiques et théologiques*, 64 (January 1980): 3-25;

John Visvader, "Anselm's Fool," *Studies in Religion/Sciences Religieuses*, 9 (1980): 441-449;

Jules Vuillemin, *Le Dieu d'Anselme et les apparences de la raison* (Paris: Editions Montaigne, 1971);

Vuillemin, "Id quo nihil maius cogitari potest. Über die innere Möglichkeit eines rationalen Gottesbegriffs," *Archiv für Geschichte der Philosophie*, 53 (1971): 279-299;

Albert W. Wald, "The Fool and the Ontological Status of St. Anselm's Argument," *Heythrop Journal*, 15 (October 1974): 406-422;

Douglas N. Walton, "St. Anselm and the Logical Syntax of Agency," *Franciscan Studies*, 36 (1976): 298-312;

Hans-Joachim Werner, "Anselm von Canterburys Dialogue 'De veritate' und das Problem der Begründung praktischer Sätze," *Salzburger Jahrbuch für Philosophie*, 20 (1975): 119-130;

Henry G. Wolz, "The Empirical Basis of Anselm's Arguments," *Philosophical Review*, 60 (July 1951): 341-361.

Thomas Aquinas

(1224 or 1225 - 7 March 1274)

Edward A. Synan
Pontifical Institute of Mediaeval Studies, Toronto

Thomas Aquinas; detail from The Crucifixion *by Fra Angelico, in the refectory of San Marco, Florence*

PRINCIPAL WORKS: *De Fallaciis ad Quodsam Nobiles Artistas* (Fallacies; for Noblemen Studying Arts, written circa 1244-1245);

De Propositionibus Modalibus (On Modal Propositions, written circa 1244-1245);

Scriptum in IV Libros Sententiarum (Writing on the Four Books of the *Sentences*, written 1252-1257;

De Ente et Essentia (On Being and Essence, written 1253);

De Principiis Naturae (On the Principles of Nature, written 1253);

Contra Impugnantes Dei Cultum et Religionem (Against Those Impugning the Worship of God and Religion, written 1256);

Quaestiones Disputatae de Veritate (Disputed Questions on Truth, written 1256-1259);

Postilla super Isaiam (Exposition of Isaiah, written circa 1256-1259);

Quaestiones Quodlibetales (Quodlibetal Questions, written 1256-1272);

In Librum Boethii de Trinitate Expositio (Exposition of Boethius's *On the Trinity*, written 1257-1258);

In Librum Boethii de Hebdomadibus Expositio (Exposition of Boethius's *De Hebdomadibus*, written 1257-1258);

In Librum Dionysii de Divinis Nominibus (Exposition of [Pseudo-]Dionysius's *The Divine Names*, written 1258-1265);

De Rationibus Fidei contra Saracenos, Graecos et Armenos ad Cantorem Antiochiae (Arguments for the Faith, against Saracens, Greeks, and Armenians, to The Chanter of Antioch, written circa 1259);

Summa de Veritate Catholicae Fidei contra Gentiles (Summary of the Truth of the Catholic Faith against the Gentiles, written 1259-1264);

Contra Errores Graecorum (Against the Errors of the Greeks, written circa 1262);

De Emptione et Venditione (On Buying and Selling on Time, written 1263);

Quaestiones Disputatae de Potentia Dei (Disputed Questions on the Power of God, written 1265);

De Regno: Ad Regem Cypri (On Kingship: To the King of Cyprus, written 1265-1266);

Compendium Theologiae (Compendium of Theology, written 1265-1269);

Summa Theologiae (Summary of Theology, written 1265-1273);

In Libros Posteriorum Analyticorum (Commentary on Aristotle's *Posterior Analytics*, written between 1265 and 1273);

In Libros De Anima (Commentary on Aristotle's *On the Soul*, written between 1265 and 1273);

In Libros De Caelo et Mundo (Commentary on Aristotle's *On the Heaven and Earth*, written between 1265 and 1273);

In X Libros Ethicorum (Commentary on Aristotle's *Nicomachean Ethics* in Ten Books, written between 1265 and 1273);

In Libros De Generatione et Corruptione (Commentary on Aristotle's *On Generation and Corruption*, written between 1265 and 1273);

In Libros Peri Hermeneias (Commentary on Aristotle's *On Interpretation*, written between 1265 and 1273);

In Libros De Memoria et Reminiscentia, et De Sensu et Sensato (Commentaries on Aristotle's *On Memory and Reminiscence* and *On Perception*, written between 1265 and 1273);

In XII Libros Metaphysicorum (Commentary on Aristotle's *Metaphysics* in Twelve Books, written between 1265 and 1273);

In Libros Meteorologicorum (Commentary on Aristotle's *Meteorology*, written between 1265 and 1273);

In VIII Libros Physicorum (Commentary on Aristotle's *Physics* in Eight Books, written between 1265 and 1273);

In Libros Politicorum (Commentary on Aristotle's *Politics*, written between 1265 and 1273);

Quaestiones Disputatae de Malo (Disputed Questions on Evil, written 1267);

Quaestiones Disputatae de Spiritualibus Creaturis (Disputed Questions on Spiritual Creatures, written 1267);

Catena Aurea (The Golden Chain, written circa 1269);

De Regimine Judaeorum (On the Governance of Jews, written circa 1269);

Expositio super Primam et Secundam Decretalem (Exposition on the First and Second Decretal, written circa 1269);

Quaestio Disputatae de Anima (Disputed Question on the Soul, written 1269);

Quaestiones Disputatae de Virtutibus (Disputed Questions on Virtue, written 1269-1272);

Quaestiones Disputatae de Unione Verbi Incarnati (Disputed Questions on the Union of the Incarnate Word, written 1269-1272);

In Job Expositio (Exposition of the Book of Job, written between 1269 and 1272);

In Evangelium Joannis Expositio (Exposition of the Gospel of John, written between 1269 and 1272);

Lectura super Matthaeum: Reportatio (Lecture on the Gospel according to Matthew: Transcription written between 1269 and 1272);

De Unitate Intellectus contra Averroistas (On the Unity of the Intellect against the Averroists, written 1270);

De Substantiis Separatis (On Separate Substances, written 1271);

De Aeternitate Mundi (On the Eternity of the World, written 1271);

In Librum De Causis (Exposition of the Book of Causes, written 1271);

De Perfectione Spiritualis Vitae (On the Perfection of the Spiritual Life, written 1271);

Contra Pestiferam Doctrinam Retrahentium Homines a Religionis Ingressu (Against the Teaching of Those Who Drag Back Those Entering Religion, written 1271);

Expositio in Orationem Dominicam (Commentary on the Lord's Prayer, written 1271);

De Motu Cordis (On the Movement of the Heart, written 1271).

EDITIONS: *Opera omnia*, 25 volumes (Parma: Fiaccadori, 1852-1873; reprinted, New York: Musurgia, 1948-1950);

Opera omnia, 34 volumes (Paris: Vives, 1871-1880).

CRITICAL EDITION: *Opera Omnia*, 52 volumes to date (Rome: Leonine Commission, 1882-).

EDITIONS IN ENGLISH: *Catena Aurea: Commentary on the Four Gospels Collected out of the Works of the Fathers by S. Thomas Aquinas*, 8 volumes, translated by J. D. Dalgairns, M. Pattison, and T. D. Ryder (Oxford: Parker, 1841-1844);

The "Summa Theologica" of St. Thomas Aquinas, Literally Translated by Fathers of the English Dominican Province, 22 volumes (London: Washbourne 1911-1925; New York, Cincinnati & Chicago: Benziger, 1911-1925);

The Summa contra Gentiles of St. Thomas Aquinas, Literally Translated by the English Dominican Fathers from the Latest Leonine edition, 4 volumes (London: Burns, Oates & Washbourne, 1924-1929; New York, Cincinnati & Chicago: Benziger, 1924-1929);

Basic Writings of St. Thomas Aquinas, 2 volumes, edited by Anton C. Pegis (New York: Random House, 1945);

Thomas Aquinas: On Spiritual Creatures, translated by M. C. Fitzpatrick and J. J. Wellmuth (Milwaukee: Marquette University Press, 1949);

St. Thomas Aquinas: On Being and Essence, translated by Armand A. Maurer (Toronto: Pontifical Institute of Mediaeval Studies, 1949; revised, 1968);

De anima, in the Version of William of Moerbeke; and The Commentary of St. Thomas Aquinas, translated by Kenelm Foster and Silvester Humphries (London: Routledge & Kegan Paul, 1951; New Haven: Yale University Press, 1951);

Truth, 3 volumes, translated by Robert J. Mulligan, James V. McGlynn, and Robert W. Schmidt (Chicago: Regnery, 1952-1954);

St. Thomas Aquinas: The Division and Methods of the Sciences, translated by Maurer (Toronto: Pontifical Institute of Mediaeval Studies, 1953);

St. Thomas Aquinas On the Truth of the Catholic Faith: Summa contra Gentiles, Book One: God, translated by Pegis (Garden City, N.Y.: Hanover House, 1955); *Book Two: Creation*, translated by J. F. Anderson (Garden City, N.Y.: Image Books, 1956); *Book Three: Providence*, translated by Vernon J. Bourke (Garden City, N.Y.: Hanover House, 1956); *Book Four: Salvation*, translated by C. J. O'Neil (Garden City, N.Y.: Hanover House, 1957);

Thomas Aquinas: Treatise on Separate Substances, translated by Francis J. Lescoe (West Hartford, Conn.: St. Joseph's College, 1959);

Thomas Aquinas: Commentary on the Metaphysics of Aristotle, 2 volumes, translated by John P. Rowan (Chicago: Regnery, 1961);

Thomas Aquinas: Aristotle on Interpretation. Commentary by St. Thomas and Cajetan, translated by Jean T. Oesterle (Milwaukee: Marquette University Press, 1962);

Thomas Aquinas: Commentary on Aristotle's Physics, translated by Richard J. Blackwell, Richard J. Spath, and W. Edmund Thirlkel (London: Routledge & Kegan Paul, 1963);

St. Thomas Aquinas: Summa theologiae, Latin Text and English, 61 volumes, translated by Dominicans of the English Province, edited by Thomas Gilby (New York: McGraw-Hill, 1964-1980; London: Eyre & Spottiswoode, 1964-1980);

Commentary on Saint Paul's Epistle to the Galatians by St. Thomas Aquinas, translated by F. R. Larcher (Albany, N.Y.: Magi Books, 1966);

Commentary on Saint Paul's Epistle to the Ephesians by St. Thomas Aquinas, translated by M. L. Lamb (Albany, N.Y.: Magi Books, 1966);

Thomas Aquinas: On the Unity of the Intellect against the Averroists, translated by B. H. Zedler (Milwaukee: Marquette University Press, 1968);

Commentary on Saint Paul's First Letter to the Thessalonians and the Letter to the Philippians by St. Thomas Aquinas, translated by Larcher & M. Duffy (Albany, N.Y.: Magi Books, 1969);

Saint Thomas Aquinas: Commentary on the Posterior Analytics of Aristotle, translated by Larcher (Albany, N.Y.: Magi Books, 1970);

Thomas Aquinas: Faith, Reason and Theology, translated by Maurer (Toronto: Pontifical Institute of Mediaeval Studies, 1987).

Thomas Aquinas is rivaled in reputation as the paramount Christian intellectual only by Augustine. Venerated within the Catholic church as a saint and as a normative theologian, Aquinas is esteemed in secular circles as a figure of enduring philosophical and cultural significance as well as the archetypal voice of medieval Christianity. Hardly a single modern collection of philosophical arguments for the reality of God, for instance, omits the "five ways" formulated by Aquinas in his *Summa Theologiae* (Summary of Theology, 1265-1273).

The enormous mass of manuscript works by Aquinas provided, early in the history of printing, for the production of complete, or nearly complete, printed editions of his almost one hundred certainly authentic works, many of them multivolume studies. In modern times this process has reached its apex in the "critical edition" commissioned by Pope Leo XIII and named from this circumstance the Leonine Edition; this work continues to be carried on by the Leonine Commission, teams of scholars in various countries. Later volumes of this edition are notable not only for the most reliable text that can be achieved by scientific method but also for the high quality of the introductions to the various volumes and for the systematic identification of the sources used by Aquinas. A fifty-volume set of concordances and indices produced by R. Busa with the collaboration of IBM, the *Index Thomisticus* (1974-1980), has transformed Thomistic research by listing in alphabetical order every word of every work, set out in boldface type in the sentence in which it occurs with a full reference to the best available edition of the work. While the Leonine Edition and the Busa index are in Latin, the most significant works of Aquinas are available in most international modern languages: Italian, Spanish, French, German, English, Dutch, and the rest.

Biographical and bibliographical data on Aquinas derive principally from documents associated with his canonization by the Roman Catholic church. This step entailed a legal investigation of his life and virtues, testimony under oath by knowledgeable witnesses, and finally, a judgment by the Roman See. There were two legal processes, one at Naples in 1319 and one in 1321 at Fossanova, where he had died. His canonization was proclaimed with exceptional solemnity by Pope John XXII in 1323. Members of the Order of Preachers, to which Aquinas had belonged, had begun shortly after his death to promote the canonization of their eminent colleague. To that end the Dominican historians Thomas of Cantimpré, Tolomeo di Lucca, and Gerard de Frachet included anecdotal material on Aquinas in their general chronicles of the time. Three other Dominicans—William Tocco, Peter Calo, and Bernard Gui—produced formal biographies; the Latin texts of these three "saint's lives" and the canonization documents are available in a sound, if not "critical," edition as *Fontes vitae Sancti Thomae Aquinatis*, edited by Dominicus M. Prümmer and Marie Hyacinthe Laurent (1912-1937). As for Aquinas's works, several near-contemporary catalogues, including the Catalogue of Stams and the Catalogue of Prague, provide guidance to modern bibliographers.

This external documentation of the life and works of Aquinas often can be rendered more precise through an exacting analysis of data internal to his writings. The use or nonuse of a given translation into Latin of a work by Aristotle, for instance, may qualify the statement of a chronicler that a work was produced by Aquinas during the reign of a particular pope. Because Aquinas was not mechanically consistent in his use of such materials, however, this approach demands extreme caution.

Aquinas was born between 1222 and 1227, most probably in 1224 or 1225, at Roccasecca, a family castle near Naples in a fertile district known as the "Terra di lavoro" or the "Roman Campagna." This district formed a part of the mainland territory of the Kingdom of Sicily and was under the rule of the Holy Roman Emperor Frederick II. The family name stems from the ancient Roman city of Aquino, the residence and perhaps the birthplace of the Roman satirist Juvenal. The title "Count" of Aquino became extinct with the death of the last count, Lano IV, in 1137; Landulf, the father of Thomas, was a *miles* (knight; that is, a member of the military caste); there are many indications of this military ambience in the writings of Thomas Aquinas. By a first wife, whose name is not known, Landulf was the father of three sons: Filippo, Adenolfo, and Giacomo. The last was a cleric whose name occurs in the record of a lawsuit brought against an election in which he had been involved; the election was canceled as a violation of church law. After the death of his first wife Landulf married Theodora, a noblewoman from Theate in the environs of Naples. No evidence supports the claim of older historians that Theodora was "sister to the queens of Sicily and Aragon." Theodora bore Landulf a large second family. There were at least four daughters: Marotta, who became abbess of Santa Maria di Capua; Maria, who married Guglielmo of San Severino; Theodora, wife of Count Roger of San Severino; and one who was killed by lightning as an infant. The Adelasia who married Roger of Aquila, Count of Traetto and Fondi, is perhaps a fifth daughter. There were four sons: Aimo (Aimone, Haymo) went to the Holy Land as a crusader with Frederick II in 1229, was captured and held for ransom by a Christian warlord on Cyprus, and was released at the instance of Pope Gregory IX. Reginald (Rinaldo) served in the imperial forces and was a troubadour as well as a knight. A series of poems in the courtly love tradition by a Rinaldo d'Aquino may be his, and a Rinaldo d'Aquino was given favorable mention by Dante for expertise in the vernacular. Reginald's life ended in disaster; accused of complicity in an assassination plot against Frederick II in 1246, he was tortured and executed. Thomas counted Reginald a "martyr" who had died in the cause of church and faith at the hands of the repeatedly excommunicated Frederick. Nothing is known of another son, Landulf, except that he died within the lifetime of Thomas, who was convinced that his brother was "in purgatory." Thomas was the youngest son of his father's second marriage and thus, according to feudal conventions, was suitable for service to the church. When he was about five years old his parents entrusted him to the Benedictine monks of the nearby Abbey of Monte Cassino, probably as an oblate, that is, a child "offered" to the monastery for training with the expectation that on reaching a suitable age he might freely undertake monastic vows. Local gossip had it that the family hoped that one day Thomas might become abbot of the rich and famous monastery. Thomas remained with the monks until 1239, and it was there that he received his earliest formal education.

Nothing is known in any direct way as to what that education was, but it was surely at Monte Cassino that Aquinas was first instructed in Latin, the tongue in which all of his certainly authentic works survive. His Latin is correct and fluent, but it is the living Latin of his century, neither Augustan "golden age" prose nor the quantitative poetry of the humanist scholars of the Renaissance. Latin was the normal medium for the liturgical life of the church and for academic, scientific, and diplomatic communication until the mid seventeenth century. While it was less radical than the populist slide of Latin into the "romance" vernaculars, there was a continuing transformation of Latin by cosmopolitan medieval Europeans. New conceptions demanded new terms: theology, philosophy, law, technology, and trade generated new words as the need arose. The new terms were matched by shifts in orthography and in syntactical usage. Diphthongs became single vowels; it was easier to write *quod* (that) with a subjunctive verb than to honor the accusative and infinitive construction. Among medieval logicians, to be sure, there are turns of speech that repel even the least punctilious Latinists. John Duns Scotus wrote a Latin to match his abstruse thought, and his major opponent a few years later, William of Ockham, was hardly superior. Both had the justification of intricate material; modern logicians, with their symbols as substitutes for words, had a first life among the logicians of the thirteenth and fourteenth centuries. No more than the medievals can modern logicians express their insights in Ciceronian periods.

Thomistic Latin is the technical language of the schools. Flexible, precise, often abstract, it is admirably fitted to express speculation in the Aristotelian and Neoplatonic traditions. With his almost exact contemporary, Bonaventure (also an Italian), Aquinas wrote a Latin more elegant than that of Duns Scotus and Ockham. Aquinas was also capable of smooth and elegant latinity when writing "prologues" for Scholastic treatises or composing liturgical texts.

Aquinas's primary education clearly included the *ars dictaminis* (art of dictating letters). It must further have included instruction in arithmetic and possibly in geometry. It is improbable that he received instruction in the remaining two liberal arts, dialectic and astronomy.

In the minds of the monks and in that of Aquinas himself the most important instruction at Monte Cassino was a thorough formation in religious belief and practice. Over and over Aquinas was to defend the right of the mendicant orders (the Franciscans and Dominicans) to receive young boys as candidates for training in the religious life, more than once drawing a parallel with the training of future knights in the skills and mystique of knighthood. The warmth of address in his last extant writing, a letter to the abbot of Monte Cassino, convinced at least one modern specialist that the letter must be the work of a Benedictine rather than of the Dominican Aquinas. The truth is rather, as the editor of the critical edition of this document remarked, that to the end of his life Aquinas retained profound respect for the abbot of what Saint Benedict, the founder of monasticism in the West, had termed "a school of the Lord's service." For Aquinas, the Abbey of Monte Cassino was indeed the school in which he absorbed the biblical and ecclesial traditions of prayer, self-denial, love of God, and love of neighbor.

In 1239 Frederick II disrupted the monastery of Monte Cassino, and the abbot seems to have advised the parents of its students to send them to the relatively new *studium* (university) at Naples, established in 1224 by the same Frederick to supply his administration with competent officials. In medieval educational practice the foundation of public universities was normally a papal prerogative.

At Naples, Aquinas encountered two influences that were to be of incalculable effect on his life: Aristotelian thought and Dominican spirituality. At Naples he met not only the thought of Aristotle—who was to become "the Philosopher" for medievals—but also the "Peripatetic" tradition of philosophical speculation as it was qualified by Neoplatonic efforts to harmonize Plato and Aristotle as well as by Islamic commentaries. From the beginning the "Aristotelianism" of Aquinas developed under the aegis of the Muslim commentators Avicenna (ibn Sina), al-Farabi, and Averröes (ibn Rushd).

Avicenna set an influential example for Aquinas. Works of his which circulated in Latin translation as *De Anima* (On the Soul) and *Metaphysica* (Metaphysics) are not commentaries on Aristotle's texts, but paraphrases of them; and Avicenna did not hesitate to introduce non-Aristotelian positions. His astronomical views, for instance, had prompted Moses Maimonides in the twelfth century to remark that whereas Aristotle is reliable for what is located beneath the "sphere of the moon," he is no guide on what is above that sphere. A roughly parallel attitude with respect to Aristotle would mark the early work of Aquinas. In his *De Ente et Essentia* (On Being and Essence, 1253) for instance, Aquinas would produce an incontrovertibly "Aristotelian" manual, but like Maimonides and Avicenna before him, he would neither accept the restrictions of a mere commentator nor refrain from the most fundamental doctrinal adjustments. Aristotle made grammatical and logical distinctions between the use of the verb *to be* in its existential and in its merely copulative functions and considered existence as philosophically irrelevant. To say *man*, *one man*, or *existing man* is to engage in merely verbal variations; such must be the case if philosophy deals solely with universal essences and not with the singulars in which essences are given only a transitory reality. In Aristotle's thought the essence of man is eternal and a suitable subject for philosophical investigation, whereas Socrates comes into and out of reality, a suitable subject for history—than which even poetry is "more philosophical." In his eternal cosmos Aristotle counted the singular instantiation of an eternal essence as of no philosophical value beyond providing an object of sensation from which, by the action of intellect, one can abstract the necessary, philosophically significant essence.

In contrast, Aquinas would hold that actually to be is the ultimate ground of reality, of value, and of fulfillment. Thus it seems legitimate to speak of *De Ente et Essentia* as an independent essay in the Peripatetic tradition that has been written as an Avicennian paraphrase rather than a phrase-by-phrase commentary.

This early style would shift in the mature Aquinas to one more redolent of Averröes. Those later, formal expositions of Aristotelian works can be called "Averroistic" in their style, if not in their content. They proceed by the sort of painstaking, phrase-by-phrase exegesis of the Philosopher's text that earned ibn Rushd his honorific title of "the Commentator." Aquinas, despite his sensitivity to the value of literary styles and of philosophical materials, would remain his own master, transforming the materials he adopted from the great Greeks and Muslims. His purpose as a master of theology was consistently a theological one, no matter how austerely he distinguished between what can be known through native rationality and what can be grasped only through faith. In his own view, as he would state it in *In Librum Boethii de Trinitate Expositio* (Exposition of Boethius's *On the Trinity*, 1257-1258), he was "transforming the water of philosophy into the wine of theology," an evocation of the miracle of Cana (John 2:1-11).

At Naples the man who was to become the greatest of Christian Aristotelians was able to study the Philosopher with a freedom not then available at the University of Paris, where lecturing on the texts of Aristotle was forbidden until those texts had been purged of errors (for instance, of arguments to the effect that the world is eternal). By a paradox, Aquinas first learned his Aristotle thanks to an anticlerical, if not an anti-Christian, emperor in that emperor's secular university. Tradition has preserved the names of two masters with whom Aquinas studied at Naples: Peter of Ireland for the philosophy of nature and Master Martin for grammar and dialectic (that is, literature and logic).

For Thomas it was more significant to have met a team of Dominicans at Naples than to have encountered Aristotle. Meeting those friars led this knight's son, whose family had sent him to a long-established and powerful monastery, to choose the vocation of a beggar in the service of the gospel. Like his discovery of Aristotelian thought, his discovery of the Dominicans was an experience Thomas found exciting and liberating. The Dominican order, like that of the Franciscans, had been founded as an orthodox response to grassroots aspirations to evangelical poverty and simplicity. During the twelfth century those aspirations, often on the part of the laity, had frequently slipped into excesses, violence, and heresy. To a dedicated poverty Saint Dominic had added a concern for theologically adequate preaching, for he believed that it was better to persuade heretics by preaching than to destroy them by the legalized violence of crusade and civil prosecution. A new world had been opened to the West by the recovery of Aristotle's science; the Dominican movement opened to Aquinas, on the plane of faith and even of mysticism, horizons of comparable novelty.

Still short of his majority, in 1245 Thomas applied to the Dominicans for admission into their ranks and was accepted. (The correct term for a member of the Dominican and Franciscan orders is *friar*—that is, "brother," derived from the Latin term *frater*. *Monk*, by contrast, designates a member of the older orders, notably that of the Benedictines or of the various religious foundations following the Rule of Saint Benedict, for instance, the Cistercians.) With several other friars, the master general among them, Aquinas began walking northward. He intended to go from Naples to Rome and then to Bologna and ultimately to Paris, where he was to fulfill his novitiate as a preaching friar.

The journey was cut short by a dramatic intervention on the part of the Aquino family. Thomas's father having died in 1243, it was presumably Donna Theodora who authorized an effort to disengage her youngest son from his Dominican vocation. Perhaps she was disappointed that he had not chosen the Benedictine order; perhaps it was simply that the vocation of a begging friar seemed unsuitable for the son of even minor nobility. A more plausible and certainly more respectable motive would be maternal feeling: she may have been moved by a desire to see her son once more before losing him to the religious life. In any case, Aquinas's older brother, the Lord Rinaldo, who had been serving in the emperor's military camp at Acquapendente, swooped down with his retainers on the party of unarmed friars. Aquinas was abducted and taken to successive family strongholds—first Montesangiovanni and then his birthplace, Roccasecca. Tradition indicates that Aquinas underwent at least a year and perhaps two years of what seems to have been a kind of "house arrest" rather than imprisonment in any crueler form. It was during this time (1244-1245) that he seems to have begun his writing career; the period is the most likely one for the production of two short essays on logic, perhaps reflections of his training at Naples with Master Martin: *Fallacies; for Noblemen Studying Arts* and *Modal Propositions*. (The editor of the Leonine Edition has relegated these texts to an appendix owing to their dubious authenticity; but several works ascribed to Aquinas—including the certainly authentic *De Ente et Essentia*—are thought to have their origin in the needs of his fellow students, and as a member of the nobility Aquinas may have had an empathy with the struggles of less endowed members of his class to master the logic of necessity, contingency, possibility, and the rest.)

During this period of confinement, it was alleged by his biographers, a prostitute was smuggled into his room in a fruitless effort to undermine his religious vocation. After he had driven her out, the chroniclers continued, Aquinas experienced a mystical girding by an angel against any future peril to his chastity. Historians have been reserved in crediting these accounts. Still, the times were harsh; if the angel was legendary, the prostitute may not have been fictitious, despite the frequency with which similar tales are told of other saints. In the end his family gave up their efforts to shake his vocation and Aquinas was permitted to proceed to the Dominican novitiate at Paris.

As a young friar Aquinas was assigned in Paris to the Dominican *studium generale* (general house of studies), the convent of Saint-Jacques on the Left Bank. There his Dominican confreres held two chairs of theology within the university structure, one for members of the French Province and one open to members of "external" Dominican provinces. The celebrated Albert of Lauingen—"Albert the Great"—held the external chair. After a year or two Aquinas was assigned to go with Albert to Cologne, where Albert had been charged with founding a new *studium generale* for the order.

Historically sound evidence, laced with what are likely legendary expansions, exists for the years 1248 to 1252, which Aquinas spent at Cologne as Albert's student. A set of notes in Aquinas's own inept handwriting stems from a course given by Albert on the *Nicomachean Ethics* of Aristotle. As Thomas had first met with the doctrine of Aristotle at Naples, so at Cologne he encountered for the first time the works of a Christian writer whose texts then (and for many years to come) circulated under the name of "Dionysius the Areopagite." The author of the collection was identified with the member of the city council of Athens, the Areopagus—so named from its situation on the Hill of Ares (Mars)—who had been one of the few converts gained by Paul's preaching there (Acts 17:34). Modern scholarship sees in the figure of "Dionysius" a Neoplatonic Christian of Monophysite tendencies, probably from Syria, writing at about the year 500; he is now usually referred to as Pseudo-Dionysius. Medieval authors, Aquinas with the rest, gave him next to scriptural authority as an immediate convert of the Apostle. Aquinas may have completed at Cologne the biblical studies necessary for the degree of *biblicus* (bachelor of the Bible); this possibility would account for his work on Jeremiah and Lamentations, the quality of which does not match his mature scriptural exegesis. Some scholars, however, date that part of his training after his return to Paris in 1252. At Cologne Aquinas was ordained a priest.

What are probably legendary embroideries on this historically secure account are tales of his nickname "the dumb ox"—"ox" because he was tall and heavy, "dumb" (*mutus*) because he could not speak German—along with the claim that Albert commented: "The world will be filled with his lowing!" According to another anecdote, his fellow students called him out of his cell one day to "see a flying ox" and ridiculed his simplicity in having answered their call; his somewhat self-righteous response was: "I knew that an ox cannot fly, but not that a religious can lie." Finally, there is the story of the well-meaning fellow student who volunteered to help him with difficult material and then found that Thomas understood it better than did the volunteer tutor.

It is certain that Albert recommended to their superiors in the order that Thomas be assigned "to read"—that is, lecture—on the *Libri Quatuor Sententiarum* (Four Books of Sentences (circa 1157-1158) of Peter Lombard as "bachelor of the *Sentences*" (*sententiarius*) at Paris. Since Aquinas returned to Paris in 1252 and completed his tour as bachelor of the *Sentences* in 1256, he either first completed his work as *biblicus* at Paris (on the hypothesis that he had not done so at Cologne) and then acted as *sententiarius* during the time that remained, or he spent the full four years on the four books of the *Sentences*.

The author of the *Sentences*, Peter Lombard, had been a theologian at Paris and later bishop of the same city a century before Aquinas arrived there. Peter organized a vast collection of short quotations from the works of Christian Fathers and doctors, arranged them with a minimum of explanation, and did so approximately in the order of the articles in the creeds. Such were the "sentences," the views or convictions of Christian authorities of the first rank. Peter's four-volume collection was first adopted as a basis for theological instruction by the Franciscan master Alexander of Hales in 1222; it would remain in that role until the end of the eighteenth century. A younger bachelor would "read" this work to beginners in "cursory" fashion; an older, "formed," bachelor, the *sententiarius*, along with other requirements, made good his claim to the degree of master of theology by presenting the *Sentences* in "magistral" fashion: he would raise problems, give arguments for and against his own position, and finally "determine" or "solve" the problems. He was not permitted to use the notes of another. Aquinas fulfilled the requirements under Master Elias Brunet, who held the external chair of theology at Saint-Jacques.

The period from 1252 to 1257 was tumultuous for the mendicants in the University of Paris. "Secular masters"—theologians from among the diocesan clergy—impugned the right claimed by the mendicants to teach and to administer sacraments. Led by William of Saint-Amour, the secular masters succeeded for a time in their antimendicant campaign with Pope Innocent IV and managed to delay the acceptance of Aquinas (and of the Franciscan Bonaventure) into the ranks of the regent masters of theology. The next pope, Alexander IV, who took office in 1254, was sympathetic to the mendicants, and pressure from him finally effected the reception of Aquinas and Bonaventure by the "consortium of masters" in August 1257. Aquinas and Bonaventure had by then fulfilled all academic regulations and had in fact been teaching as masters—Aquinas since September 1256. Aquinas wrote in defense of the mendicants *Contra Impugnantes Dei Cultum et Religionem* (Against Those Impugning the Worship of God and Religion, 1256), a title in which the term *religion* must be read as "the religious life" of mendicants. From his reception Aquinas held the external chair of the Dominicans in succession to Brunet, his own master, and would do so until 1259.

Three well-known terms which designate the three functions of a master of theology—*to preach, to read*, and *to dispute*—have precise technical meanings. It was a master's role "to preach" in the sense of addressing a university audience on its intellectual level in matters of faith and morals. This kind of preaching is not to be confused with popular preaching, which the biographers report was notably well done by Aquinas because he spoke in terms the people could understand—in the vernacular and eschewing the technicalities of the lecture hall. Thus he met the standard of the order in that he excelled both as a popular preacher and as a theologian who could address his peers successfully. Second, the master was obligated "to read" in the sense of presenting texts and conveying their meaning. In an age of manuscript books a student's contact with most written material would be by hearing rather than by reading it himself. The student would make his own notes on the basic text and on the master's elucidations; he could not hope to own every text for which he would be responsible, owing to the enormous cost of works written on parchment by professional scribes. The performance of the master, therefore, was what would now be called a lecture. This responsibility of the master is visible in many of the works of Aquinas: a section of text by Aristotle or Boethius, skillfully "divided," is followed by a *lectio* organized in an Averroistic sequence of short phrases, explained one by one. Furthermore, despite the prominence of the *Sentences*, the fundamental duty of the master was the daily *lectio* on sacred Scripture (the "master of theology" was often dubbed "master of the sacred page," that is, of the Bible). The master "lectured" to his own students only; this restriction did not obtain with respect to the third magisterial duty, "to dispute" in an organized debate. Here the issue was normally set by the master in the form of a question that could be answered affirmatively or negatively; his own bachelors argued for and against the issue. On the second day the master would determine the problem, taking into account the arguments of the bachelors on the day before. Twice a year, however, a master might announced himself ready to debate a question *de quodlibet* (on anything you like). Quodlibetal questions were held during Advent and Lent. Aquinas has left so many quodlibetal questions that his academic self-confidence is beyond cavil.

A master's teaching naturally led to publication. At Paris a master could register a work with the guild of stationers by submitting it in the form in which he wished it to circulate. The stationers would then rent out *peciae* (pieces), folded parchment leaves of standard size on which a portion of a registered work was written. A stationer's list would indicate to a prospective borrower the number of *peciae* necessary for an entire work and the rent required for each one. The borrower could then take the *pecia* for copying by a professional scribe; when he returned it to the stationer he could rent the next *pecia* in sequence until he had procured the complete work. Many extant manuscripts of works by Aquinas carry in the margins indications of where one *pecia* ends and another begins. This sequence is often visible to modern experts even when marginal *pecia* markings are lacking: They observe minute variations in the ink, the pen, even in the size of the letter forms between one *pecia* and the next.

During his first Parisian regency Aquinas registered a range of works that set the general lines of his lifetime production. In those years he wrote up the definitive version of the work he had done as *sententiarius* under the title *Scriptum in IV Libros Sententiarum* (Writing on the Four Books of the *Sentences*). To this systematic theology he added the *Quaestiones Disputatae de Veritate* (Disputed Questions on Truth), dated by the Leonine editor A. Dondaine between spring 1256 and early summer 1259. In exegetical studies it is generally held that this period was marked by his *Postilla super Isaiam* (Exposition of Isaiah). According to Aquinas, theological argument can proceed only from the "literal" sense of a biblical passage, not from one of the "mystical" or "spiritual" senses. By "literal sense" Aquinas meant every level of meaning of which the inspired human author was aware; this sense could, therefore, include parables, figures of speech, literary forms employed for rhetorical purposes, and so on; it is not restricted to a superficial or mechanical interpretation of the words. With the *Scriptum in IV Libros Sententiarum* and the *Quaestiones Disputatae de Veritate* Aquinas began a long effort of Scholastic, scientific theologizing; with the *Exposition of Isaiah* he made a beginning of serious exegetical theology. Yet another type of theological work was inaugurated by his two expositions of heavily Neoplatonic treatises by Boethius: a work on the Trinity and that known to the Middle Ages as *Hebdomads* ("sevens"). These relatively short Boethian treatises were subjected to close and philosophically acute analyses. The first was completed certainly before 1260-1261, when Annibald de Annibaldis, a *sententiarius* working under the direction of Aquinas as regent master, cited the trinitarian opuscule in his own work on the *Sentences*; the second is believed on internal criteria to belong to the same period. Philosophy also presided over his celebrated essay *De Ente et Essentia* as well as *De Principiis Naturae* (On the Principles of Nature, 1253). Yet another aspect of his lifetime literary activity is represented by the polemical *Contra Impugnantes Dei Cultum et Religionem*. In the first Parisian regency also Aquinas began the *Summa de Veritate Catholicae Fidei contra Gentiles* (Summary of the Truth of the Catholic Faith against the Gentiles, 1259-1264). This survey of Christian theology was probably composed in response to requests from Dominican missionaries in Spain, much of which remained under Muslim domination in intellectual as well as in military-political matters. (Tradition ascribes such a request to Saint Raymond of Peñafort.) The term *gentiles* in the title designates any who hold faiths other than the Catholic, whether Jews, Muslims, or Christian heretics. Muslims were perceived as experts in philosophy rather

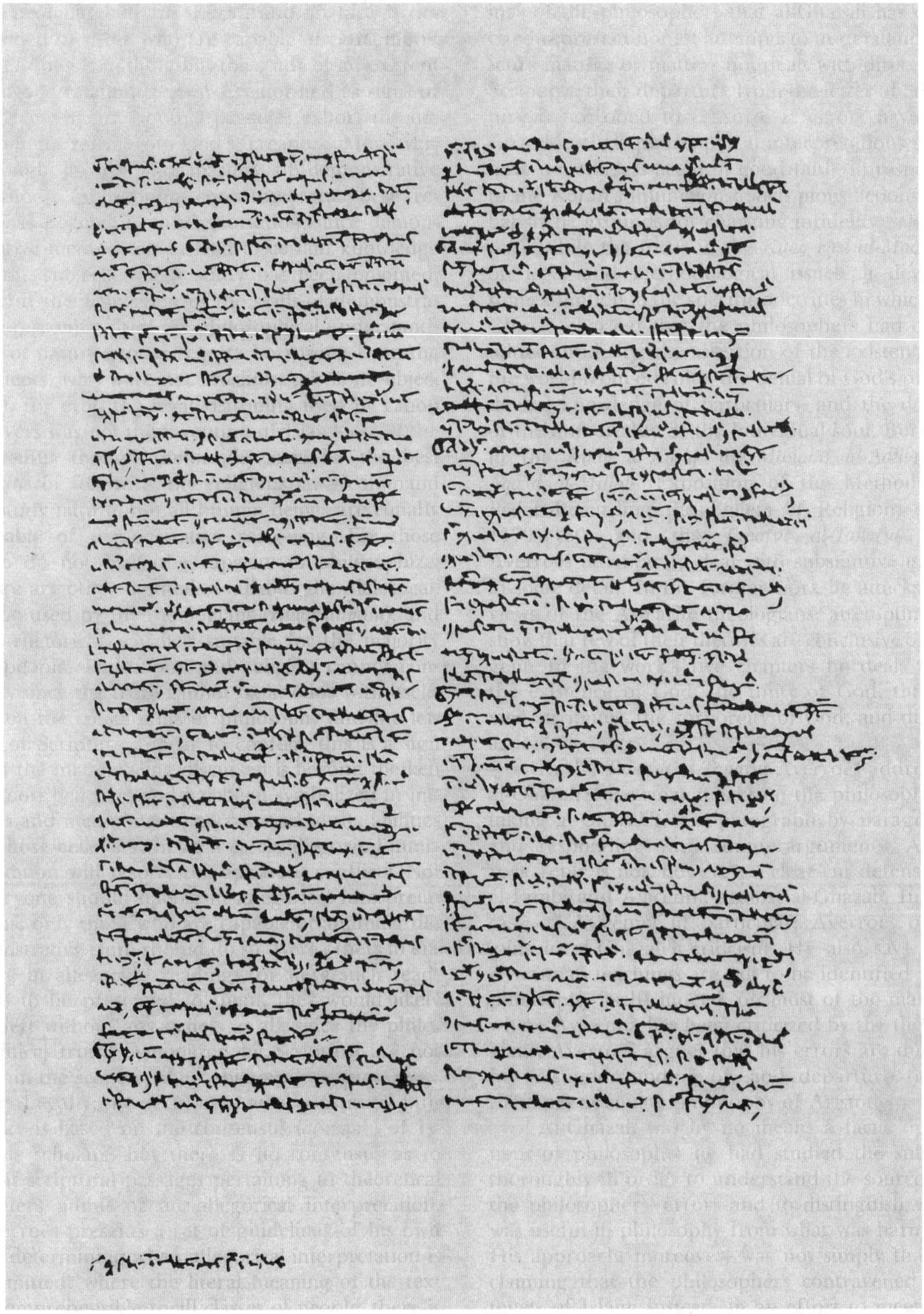

Page from book 2 of the Summa contra Gentiles, *in Aquinas's handwriting (Ambrosian Library, Milan)*

than in a biblically grounded, revealed text.

This side of Aquinas's bibliography accounts for a paradoxical interpretation of his place in the tradition. His heavily "philosophical" texts and his expertise in handling philosophical materials have blurred the ultimately theological preoccupation which made him, in his own eyes and in those of his contemporaries, not a philosopher but a theologian. Today he is often seen as the preferred "philosopher" rather than as one of the preferred theologians of the Catholic church. This situation would surely have been a matter of consternation to him: as a master in theology he looked on purely human disciplines, *artes*, as the "vassals" of sacred doctrine. His prestige in philosophical circles is matched by a loss of standing in modern theological circles; his thirteenth-century exegesis preceded crucial advances in linguistics, philology, archaeology, and literary criticism which began in the seventeenth century and still continue. Aquinas lacked knowledge of any oriental language; thus his biblical exegesis was his best reading of the Latin Vulgate and is so temporally determined as to be of primarily historical interest today. While his insistence (with all first-rank theologians of his own time) on the absolute priority of the "literal" sense of Scripture undoubtedly contributed to keeping biblical scholars of the next generation from dissipating their energies on often fanciful, if devotionally precious, "spiritual" interpretations, his exegetical work remains irredeemably "medieval."

On the other hand, a most enduring aspect of his theological work has been a brilliant development of philosophical insights applied to theological materials. His metaphysical insistence on the priority of the act of being in the structure of created things and his conviction of the omnipresent "analogy of being" are visible in the work of his first Parisian regency. G. K. Chesterton was right to have ended his brief, brilliant *St. Thomas Aquinas: The Dumb Ox* (1933) with the wry reflection that from "so small a book about so big a man" something must be left out and the hope that readers would understand why he had "left out the only important thing": the master of paradox had spoken with incisive intuition of the philosophy, but not of the theology, and still less of the mysticism of Saint Thomas.

In addition to his normal duties as regent master at Saint-Jacques, Aquinas was charged to serve on a commission of five masters (one of whom was his former master Albert) to make recommendations for the organization of studies in Dominican houses. One recommendation was that each house *lector*, a certified resident theologian, have an assistant, and that the *lector*'s classes be compulsory for all members of the house, even for the prior. With his own appointments as *lector*, at Orvieto in 1261 and at Rome in 1268, Aquinas would have an opportunity to put into practice the educational policies he had helped formulate at Paris.

The first Italian period in Aquinas's teaching career was spent in Dominican houses of study rather than in universities. Beginning in 1259 he gave systematic courses in theology to the *fratres communes*, the "common run of friars" who were in training for the characteristic Dominican apostolate of preaching and of spiritual, moral guidance, particularly through the confessional. Although not destined for university theology, the *fratres communes* often had distinguished careers in the church. Aquinas can be seen as a conscious reformer of Dominican education. His intention seems to have been to move the center of gravity from what he judged an excessively pragmatic training of confessors and preachers to a pastoral formation embedded in speculative as well as practical theology.

Assigned to the convent of San Domenico at Naples, the scene of his own enlistment in the Order of Preachers, Aquinas seems to have continued to prepare the last three of the four books of his *Summa de Veritate Catholicae Fidei contra Gentiles* for publication; the project extended to about 1264. The date is suggested by borrowings from its text in an opuscule directed by Aquinas to a "Chanter of Antioch" in which he provided materials for the defense of Christian doctrine against opponents who flourished in the Near East: Jews, Muslims, and Byzantine Christians. The Chanter had asked for "moral and philosophical arguments . . . ones Saracens accept." Like the summary against the gentiles, the *De Rationibus Fidei contra Saracenos, Graecos et Armenos ad Cantorem Antiochiae* (Arguments for the Faith, against Saracens, Greeks, and Armenians, to The Chanter of Antioch, circa 1259) contributed to the perception of Aquinas as a philosopher rather than as a theologian.

At Naples Aquinas was given the services of the distinguished Reginald of Piperno as *socius* (companion) and assistant; their association would continue until Aquinas's death. This talented and erudite Dominican was to act not only as secretary in the production of the formidable Thomistic corpus but also as the saint's confessor.

His reminiscences would be cited in the Naples canonization process.

In 1260 Aquinas was named a "preacher general" for the Naples convent, an appointment that entailed his attendance at the annual provincial "chapters" (conferences) which set policy for the Roman province of the order. In 1261 he was transferred from Naples to the Dominican convent (not to the papal court) in the papal city of Orvieto as *lector* of that house. A momentous circumstance of this transfer is that Pope Urban IV came into residence there in 1262. Until his death this pope was to make repeated demands on the learning of Aquinas, and such requests resulted in some of Aquinas's most significant works. One of these is an evaluation of *A Book on Trinitarian Faith,* a collection of Greek theological texts—not all of them authentic—which were circulating in southern Italy, where Byzantine influence was strong. Modern scholarship has established that this collection was probably composed in the years 1254 to 1256 and then translated into Latin by Nicholas of Durazzo, who became bishop of Cotrone in 1254. Aquinas seems to have had access to at least a part of this work when composing his *Contra Impugnantes Dei Cultum et Religionem.* The evaluation of this collection by Aquinas has been preserved under an infelicitous title: *Contra Errores Graecorum* (Against the Errors of the Greeks, circa 1262). Although it presents the positions of Latin Christianity on several controversial issues—the papal primacy, the insertion of the term *filioque* (and from the Son) into the Nicene Creed to designate the "procession" of the Holy Spirit from the Son as well as from the Father, the use of unleavened bread for the Eucharist, and purgatory—the work was perceived as sufficiently irenic for a later pope, Gregory X, to direct that Aquinas bring it to the Second Council of Lyons, a general council of the church convoked in the interest of reunion between Greek and Latin Christians. (The death of Aquinas was to occur at an early stage of his journey toward Lyons.) As is often the case in a Thomistic work, the prologue gives an "above-the-fray" context to what follows. He points out that doubts can arise from ancient writers who had done their work before the appearance of various heresies had made the orthodox more cautious in expression. A parallel source of doubts on ancient authors arises from the fact that "many things which sound right in Greek do not sound right in Latin." A most notable instance of his conciliatory stance in this work is the recommendation that the Boethian tradition of "word-by-word" translation of technical texts be replaced by an effort to reexpress the intention of the author. Aquinas wrote that the Greek term *hypostasis,* intended by Greek theologians to convey the notion named by their Latin counterparts' *persona* (person), is the literal equivalent of the Latin term *substantia* (substance). The result was that where a Greek author spoke of "three *hypostases*" to mean what a Latin would express as "three Persons," a Latin would be scandalized by what would seem to be an affirmation of three divine substances, in short, tritheism—three gods rather than one God subsistent in three Persons.

A Thomistic work on the four Gospel accounts traditionally named *Catena Aurea* (The Golden Chain, circa 1269) is an erudite weaving together of patristic texts in a continuous gloss on the Gospel. The *Catena Aurea* has been as esteemed outside the Roman Catholic communion as within; it was included in the nineteenth-century Anglican "Library of the Fathers," edited by E. B. Pusey, John Keble, and John Henry Newman, moving spirits of the Oxford Movement. This work, too, was encouraged by Pope Urban IV, who had asked Aquinas to compose the Corpus Christi liturgy. It was during Urban's pontificate that Aquinas wrote his *In Job Expositio* (Exposition of the Book of Job, written between 1269 and 1272), a deliberate departure from the heavily "mystical" interpretation of Job by Pope Gregory I (the Great) in the late sixth century.

Dignitaries other than popes profited from the theological and general competence of Aquinas. A woman who has been identified as either the countess of Flanders or the duchess of Brabant asked for his views on her responsibilities to the Jews under her jurisdiction, particularly on the issue of "usury," the taking of interest on loans—a practice forbidden by church canons. He responded with a substantial essay on the legal and moral aspects of her role, *De Regimine Judaeorum* (On the Governance of Jews, circa 1269). Since nothing suggests that the unnamed king of Cyprus to whom *De Regno* (On Kingship, 1265-1266) is dedicated had asked for the treatise, nor that it was a spontaneous gesture by Aquinas, it may be that a superior's command underlies this unfinished analysis of a king's role. Like the countess or the duchess, a James of Viterbo asked for a moral analysis of issues in the ethics of business and received in reply the brief *De Emptione et Venditione* (On Buying and Selling on Time, 1263), in which Aquinas asserts that modifications of the "just price" in view of delay in payment or delivery constitute usury and thus are immoral.

The most momentous assignment of this period spent in the Roman province came from Aquinas's own Order of Preachers: a commission to establish a house of studies for young Dominicans at Santa Sabina in Rome was addressed to him from the annual provincial chapter held at Anagni in 1265. As preacher general of the Naples convent he may be assumed to have attended this chapter and thus may have had some influence in setting the terms of his commission.

Aquinas spent three productive years at Santa Sabina. To that stay are dated his *Quaestiones Disputatae de Potentia Dei* (Disputed Questions on the Power of God, 1265), perhaps also his *Quaestiones Disputatae de Malo* (Disputed Questions on Evil, 1267), and the seventh through eleventh *Quaestiones Quodlibetales*. He produced a notable insertion on the divine attributes for his long-circulating early work on the *Sentences*, and there is compelling evidence that he began a fresh course on the *Sentences*. A Dominican who had been his student at Santa Sabina, Tolomeo of Lucca, testified for the canonization inquiry that he had seen at the Dominican house at Lucca a copy of a work on the *Sentences* composed by Aquinas at Rome "as a master," but, he reported, it later disappeared. (A considerable portion, perhaps all that Aquinas completed, of this commentary seems to have been recovered: notes comprising about ninety articles have been found on the guard folios and in the margins of a manuscript at Lincoln College, Oxford, of the first book of the *Scriptum in IV Libros Sententiarum* Aquinas had published after his lectures as *sententiarius* in Paris. Leonard E. Boyle argues that the long series of notes is based on a student's *reportatio* of the Roman fresh start on the *Sentences* by Aquinas.)

All of these works pale by comparison to the *Summa Theologiae*, which was begun during the Roman teaching period—perhaps, one might speculate, because Aquinas, hoping to do better than he had done as a *sententiarius*, had begun a new version of his understanding of the *Sentences*, abandoned it, and started his definitive presentation of theology as a whole. Here, too, investigation by Boyle throws new light on some old conundrums that surround the *Summa Theologiae*. A first puzzle is that the *Summa Theologiae* does not fit into medieval university programs in theology: those conservative institutions were to continue to structure their degree work in theology on the *Sentences* until at least the sixteenth century. Second, statistics on manuscript distribution of the work establish that the various "Parts" circulated independently and in unequal measure, the "Second Part of the Second Part" leading the field as the most copied section. Third, this most widely copied portion falls into the genre of handbooks for confessors and directors of souls, a genre that was to flourish long after the death of Aquinas. A final puzzle has been the meaning of the compressed and enigmatic "prologues" that introduce the various "Parts," the most puzzling of all being the prologue to the "First Part." There Aquinas speaks of the teacher's role in dealing not only with "advanced" students but also with "beginners and novices"; university students of theology were graduates in arts and so could hardly appear as academic infants to be fed with "milk, not with solid food" (1 Cor. 3:1) suitable for adults.

All these difficulties fade away when it is recognized that the students to whom this work was directed were "the common run of friars" at Santa Sabina and that Aquinas had been given a free hand to organize their teaching in whatever way seemed to him most effective. Hence the relative economy of arguments for the affirmative and the negative in each article. In the celebrated "five ways" to demonstrate rationally the reality of God, for instance, he counted two arguments for atheism with their refutations sufficient, and there are seldom more than three or four such exchanges in any article. "Doublets" in his *Quaestiones Disputatae*, on the other hand, normally exhibit long chains of arguments and counterarguments. As the prologue to the First Part of the *Summa Theologiae* puts it, the "multiplication of useless questions, articles, and arguments" contribute to "distaste and confusion in the minds of students." The prologue also adverts to unfortunate results that stem in part from "necessary points" being transmitted in haphazard fashion "according to what the exposition of books requires or . . . opportunities provided by debates. . . ."; one thinks of Peter Lombard's ordering of theology according to the articles of the creed and of "disputed questions—above all, of those "on anything you like."

Aquinas met these difficulties by what Marie Dominique Chenu has identified as an organizational plan redolent of Christian Neoplatonism. The "many" of created things has proceeded from a One, no longer the One of Plato and Plotinus but the One Lord of Deuteronomy 6:4, the triune God of the New Covenant and the Church. The human multitude returns to the One by the exercise of virtuous freedom; Jesus and his Church constitute the "Christian" conditions of that return. The highly speculative First Part of the *Summa Theologiae* deals with God, creation, and the nature of the human being in our concrete, fallen state. The Second Part is an introduction to moral living that sets out the goal of humanity, the nature of moral choice, the passions and their moral implications, sinfulness in general, the analogical sweep of "law," and the grace of God; the First Part of the Second Part provides a speculative ground for the praxis of the Second Part of the Second Part. The work concludes with a Third Part, unfinished at the death of Aquinas, in which the theme of Incarnation of the eternal Word in Jesus leads into a treatise on the Church and sacraments. Of the "seven sacraments" established by twelfth-century theologians, baptism, confirmation, Eucharist, and penance are treated, the last incompletely; marriage, holy orders, and the final anointing of the dying, as well as "the Last Things"—death, judgment, heaven, and hell—are lacking. These issues are dealt with in a "supplement" compiled by fourteenth-century editors who collected texts by Aquinas on the themes he had not reached in the *Summa Theologiae* and put them together in the style of that work.

Aquinas's summary of all Christian belief, directed to a nonuniversity audience, ranks among the classics of the Christian tradition. Its order; lucidity; respect for sources, whether biblical, ecclesial, philosophical, or simply the dicta of classical authors in their fields; and especially the cogency of argument have merited the esteem of all generations since. The theology is that of 1265 to 1273; but, like all classics, the *Summa Theologiae* transcends its time.

One of the most attractive of the expositions by Aquinas is of the *De Divinis Nominibus* (The Divine Names, circa 500) of Pseudo-Dionysius, whose works he had first encountered when studying under Albert the Great at Cologne. This exposition must have been written before May 1268: in that month William of Moerbeke completed his Latin version of the *Elements of Theology* by the pagan Neoplatonist Proclus; the silence of the exposition of the *De Divinis Nominibus* on this work would be inexplicable had it been available to Aquinas at the time of writing. The same date functions as one before which the Thomistic exposition of the *Liber de Causis* (Book of Causes)—until then ascribed to Aristotle by the learned world—could not have been written. With the appearance of the *Elements of Theology* in Latin translation Aquinas saw immediately that the *Liber de Causis* was nothing more than Proclus's work in abridged form. This feat of internal criticism of the *Liber de Causis* has earned Aquinas high praise as a predecessor of the Renaissance usually thought to have begun with Petrarch in the following century, in particular, of the achievement of Giovanni de Matociis in distinguishing the two Plinys.

Modern scholarship reinforces the traditional ascription to Aquinas of the liturgy for the Eucharist. Between 1261 and 1264 Pope Urban IV commissioned Aquinas to compose the liturgy for what was then a new feast. The task included the selection of appropriate biblical texts as well as the composition of hymns. (In addition to these Latin hymns, a vernacular sonnet on honor is ascribed to Aquinas by a single manuscript.)

In 1265 Pope Clement IV succeeded Urban IV. Clement is said to have offered Aquinas the archbishopric of Naples, and Aquinas is said to have declined. William of Tocco, with a fine medieval disregard for chronology, recounts Clement's readiness to grant Aquinas "dignities and income" just before mentioning a papal offer of funds in support of Aquinas's family as his brothers fled from the vengeance of Frederick II; this second, accepted, benefaction must have been an act of Innocent IV, since it was during that pontificate—in 1250—that Frederick died.

It is unclear whether Clement intervened in the transfer of Thomas from Santa Sabina to the papal city of Viterbo in 1267. This assignment has given rise to the inference that Aquinas may have been a house theologian for the pope, a predecessor of the later (and still current) appointment of a distinguished Dominican theologian as "Master of the Sacred Palace." In any event, his *Quaestiones Disputatae de Spiritualibus Creaturis* (Disputed Questions on Spiritual Creatures, 1267) can be assigned to his time at Viterbo. A notable intervention of this period was made by Aquinas at the instance of his Dominican master general, John of Vercelli: the Dominican theologian, Peter of Tarentaise, had been denounced for alleged theological shortcomings, and John asked Aquinas to evaluate 108 articles abstracted from Peter's works. Despite some incidental reservations on details, Aquinas judged the attack to be a cal-

Fourteenth-century fresco in the Spanish Chapel of the Cloister of Santa Maria Novella, Florence, traditionally called The Triumph of Saint Thomas Aquinas. *Aquinas is seated on a throne at the center, surrounded by figures representing the virtues, the sciences, the liberal arts, biblical characters, and heretics.*

umny, and Peter's future career as archbishop, then cardinal, and briefly (from January to June 1276) as pope under the name Innocent V vindicated that judgment.

In 1267 Aquinas attended a general chapter of his order at Bologna. In 1268 or 1269 he was reappointed to the external chair of theology at Saint-Jacques in Paris; by then he had completed his *Quaestio Disputate de Anima* (Disputed Question on the Soul, 1269). The transfer to Paris was motivated by renewed attacks on the mendicants by secular masters, but also by the rise of a philosophical naturalism in the faculty of arts, often called "Latin Averroism" or "radical Aristotelianism."

During this second Parisian period Aquinas extended his series of disputed questions with *Quaestiones Disputatae de Virtutibus* (Disputed Questions on Virtue, 1269-1272), *Quaestiones Disputatae de Unione Verbi Incarnati* (Disputed Questions on the Union of the Incarnate Word, 1269-1272), and *Quaestiones Quodlibetales* 1-6 and 12. In exegetical studies during those years Aquinas wrote on the Gospel according to John and, less successfully, on Matthew, along with reports on certain epistles of Paul. He also produced an imposing number of Aristotelian expositions, along with extended and penetrating expositions of other philosophical texts. The explanation of pagan philosophical texts was in no sense a duty for masters of theology; Aquinas's apprenticeship under Albert, who had struggled to make Aristotle "intelligible to the Latins," here had a most fruitful consequence. Aquinas was convinced, as Augustine had been, that although faith remains the ultimate criterion of truth, genuine philosophical insights cannot be in conflict with what Christianity teaches. Aquinas felt free to subsume philosophy within his theological resources; the "water" of philosophy thus became the "wine" of theology. Aquinas's Aristotelian expositions written in Paris include those on the logical treatises *On Interpretation* and *Posterior Analytics*, as well as on *On the Soul, On Perception, On Memory and Reminiscence*, the *Physics*, and the *Nicomachean Ethics*.

Two essays of the second Parisian period bear witness to his involvement in the defense of the mendicants: *De Perfectione Spiritualis Vitae* (On the Perfection of the Spiritual Life, 1271) and *Contra Pestiferam Doctrinam Retrahentium Homines a Religionis Ingressu* (Against the Teaching of Those Who Drag Back Those Entering Religion, 1271). These tracts had in view William of Saint-Amour and Gerard of Abbeville, whereas *De Unitate Intellectus contra Averroistas* (On the Unity of the Intellect against the Averroists, 1270) and *De Aeternitate Mundi* (On the Eternity of the World, 1271) were directed against the excessive naturalism that was perceived as flourishing in the faculty of arts at Paris. *De Unitate Intellectus* was a refutation of the "Averroistic" claim that the Philosopher had demonstrated a single "active intellect" for the whole human race and *De Aeternitate Mundi* a refutation of the parallel claim that Aristotle had demonstrated the eternity of the world. On the alleged eternity of the world it may be noted that the Jewish sage Moses Maimonides in his *Moreh Nevukhim* (Guide of the Perplexed, 1190) had defended the position Aquinas was to adopt: that Aristotle had not demonstrated the point but had given only rhetorical, probable arguments. Still, Aquinas was in the uncomfortable position of opposing, on the one hand, the Averroistic masters of arts and, on the other hand, traditionalist theologians who claimed to be able to demonstrate that the world is not eternal. Aquinas responded with passion against the notion that a conclusion opposed to an article of faith might be validly deduced from premises formulated with philosophical truth.

In Lent 1272 the University of Paris went on strike, but, perhaps because he was primarily associated with Saint-Jacques, Aquinas seems to have continued to teach. He seems also to have continued work on the *Summa Theologiae*.

In 1272 a general chapter of his order gave Aquinas the assignment of establishing a theological *studium* for the Roman province; the chapter left to his discretion the location, the personnel, and even the number of students to be admitted. The Dominican convent in Naples in which he established the *studium* was not only located in proximity to the university that Aquinas had attended in his youth but was supported by the pro-Dominican Charles I of Anjou, the king of Sicily. There is secure evidence that the king assigned Aquinas a stipend of one ounce of gold each month, apparently the standard rate for university teaching at the time. Charles evidently considered the Dominican theological *studium* an adjunct of the royal university.

At Naples Aquinas wrote an exposition of Aristotle's *On Generation and Corruption* and finished his work on the Philosopher's *On Heaven and Earth* and *Meteorology*, begun in Paris. The Naples manuscripts of his exposition of Aristotle's *Metaphysics* guarantee that it is to this period that this formidable work belongs. It was at Naples, too, that Aquinas wrote commentaries on Psalms 1-51.

In addition to his academic exertions Aquinas was involved, as executor of the will of Count Roger of Aquila, in what seem to have been intricate legal and economic affairs. The count died in the summer of 1272, and Aquinas's role lends some weight to the view that his widow, Adelasia, was a sister of Thomas. The episode bears witness to an expertise on fiscal matters that goes beyond the usual theological pronouncements by Aquinas on usury and just-price theory. Furthermore, there is sound evidence that an October application to the king by Aquinas for a royal license in connection with certain irregularities in the dead count's affairs led to considerable esteem for Aquinas, for it was later in the same month that Charles made the allocation of a monthly ounce of gold.

Biographers have understandably seen in this laborious period at Naples the pressure of excessive work such as must have caused a physical, if not a mental, breakdown. On 6 December 1273, while celebrating mass in the chapel of Saint Nicholas at Naples, Aquinas suffered "an astounding change." Experts on mysticism recognize in descriptions of this event signs compatible with a mystical experience, whereas modern medical practitioners see the symptoms of a cerebral accident. Aquinas's final illness came upon him some weeks later at the castle of Maenza on the Campagna road to Rome as he was traveling to Lyons to take part in the church council. According to his secretary-companion Reginald of Piperno, he forthwith "hung up his writing instruments." The *Summa Theologiae* had been brought to Part 3, Question 90, Article 4. To Reginald's protest that he must go on to complete the work Aquinas answered: "Reginald, I cannot . . . in comparison with what I have seen in prayer all that I have written seems to me as if it were straw." During the nine weeks of life that remained to Aquinas this literary abnegation was twice suspended, and on both occasions for the benefit of others. First, there was the letter to the abbot of Monte Cassino, where Aquinas had received his primary education. A passage in Saint Gregory the Great's *Books of Morals on Job*, where the pope had commented on Job 22:16 by introducing the confrontation between the Prophet Isaiah and King Hezekiah (Isa. 38:1-8), had bewildered the monks, and the abbot had requested that Aquinas give the monks a lecture on the reconciliation of God's unfailing knowledge of the future with genuine human freedom.

In the letter he made a creative use of Aristotle and Boethius in combination. From the *On Interpretation* of the Philosopher he took materials to settle an issue that could not have arisen in Aristotle's universe; from Boethius's *De Consolatione Philosophiae* (The Consolation of Philosophy, 524) he took a striking image: the mountain-peak observer of the rising sun and a walking human being. Aristotle had noted that "what is [the case] must needs be [the case] when it is [the case]." Thus there is a necessity embedded within contingent facts; yet for the Philosopher, on the eve of a naval battle, the statement that it will or will not occur can be neither "actually true" nor "actually false." God, wrote Aquinas, sees everything from an atemporal, eternal perspective—the Boethian "total and simultaneous possession of life without end, and perfect"; for him our "past" and our "future" are "present." As the mountainside observer did not warp the necessity of the sun's rising, nor the contingency and voluntariness of a human's walking, so God's unfailing knowledge of our future—his present—does not impinge on the contingency or the voluntary character of that future. All of this Aquinas expressed with elegance and force in a letter that honors the medieval conventions of the *ars dictandi* (art of dictating letters) but is grounded in the Ciceronian conception of an effective oration. Although he was a dying man, Aquinas retained full control of his extraordinary speculative capacities at least to the point of writing this last extant work.

Finally, on his deathbed in the Cistercian monastery of Fossanova Aquinas dictated an exposition of the Canticle of Canticles—Solomon's Song of Songs—as a guest-gift; no copy of this work is known to be extant. Aquinas died on 7 March 1274.

Bibliographies:

Pierre Mandonnet and Jean Destrez, *Bibliographie thomiste* (Le Saulchoir, Belguim: Revue des sciences philosophiques et théologiques, 1921); revised edition, edited by Marie Dominique Chenu (Paris: Vrin, 1960);

Vernon J. Bourke, "Thomistic Bibliography, 1920-1940," *Modern Schoolman*, supplement to volume 21 (1945).

Biographies:

Dominicus M. Prümmer and Marie Hyacinthe Laurent, eds., *Fontes vitae Sancti Thomae Aquinatis*, 6 volumes (Toulouse: Privat & Revue thomiste, 1912-1937);

Jacques Maritain, *The Angelic Doctor: The Life and Thought of St. Thomas Aquinas* (London: Sheed & Ward, 1931);

G. K. Chesterton, *St. Thomas Aquinas: The Dumb Ox* (London: Hodder & Stoughton, 1933);

Maritain, *St. Thomas Aquinas, Angel of the Schools*, translated by James F. Scanlon (London: Sheed & Ward, 1946);

Angelus Walz, *Saint Thomas Aquinas: A Biographical Study*, translated by Sebastian Bullough (Westminster, U.K.: Newman Press, 1951);

Frederick C. Copleston, *Aquinas* (Harmondsworth, U.K.: Penguin, 1955);

Kenelm Foster, *The Life of Saint Thomas: Biographical Documents* (London & Baltimore: Helicon Press, 1959);

Marie Dominique Chenu, *St Thomas d'Aquin et la théologie* (Paris: Editions du Seuil, 1959);

Vernon J. Bourke, *Aquinas's Search for Wisdom* (Milwaukee: Bruce, 1965);

James A. Weisheipl, *Friar Thomas D'Aquino* (Garden City, N.Y.: Doubleday, 1974).

References:

James F. Anderson, *The Bond of Being: An Essay on Analogy and Existence* (St. Louis: Herder, 1949);

Anderson, *The Cause of Being: The Philosophy of Creation in St. Thomas* (St. Louis: Herder, 1952);

Anderson, *An Introduction to the Metaphysics of St. Thomas Aquinas* (Chicago: Regnery, 1953);

Dennis Bonnette, *Aquinas's Proofs for God's Existence* (The Hague: Nijhoff, 1972);

Leonard E. Boyle, "Alia lectura fratris Thome," *Mediaeval Studies*, 45 (1983): 418-429;

Boyle, *The Setting of the* Summa theologiae *of Saint Thomas* (Toronto: Pontifical Institute of Mediaeval Studies, 1982);

David Burrell, *Aquinas: God and Action* (Notre Dame, Ind.: University of Notre Dame Press, 1979);

R. Busa, *Index Thomisticus*, 50 volumes (Stuttgart: Frommann-Holzboag, 1974-1980);

Leonard Callahan, *A Theory of Esthetic According to St. Thomas Aquinas* (Washington, D.C.: Catholic University of America, 1927);

Marie Dominique Chenu, *Towards Understanding Saint Thomas*, translated by Albert M. Landry and Dominic Hughes (Chicago: Regnery, 1964);

Roy J. Deferrari, Sister M. Inviolata Barry, and Ignatius McGuiness, *A Lexicon of St. Thomas Aquinas Based on the Summa Theologica and Selected Passages of His Other Works*, 5 volumes (Washington, D.C.: Catholic University of America Press, 1948-1953);

James C. Doig, *Aquinas on Metaphysics* (The Hague: Nijhoff, 1972);

A. Dondaine, *Secrétaires de Saint Thomas* (Rome: Editori di S. Tommaso, S. Sabina, 1956);

H.-F. Dondaine, "Alia lectura fratris Thome, (Super 1 Sent.)?" *Mediaeval Studies*, 42 (1980): 308-336;

Cornelio Fabro, *Esegesi Tomistica* (Rome: Libreria editrice della Pontifica Università lateranensa, 1969);

Fabro, *La nozione metafisica di partecipazione secondo S. Tommaso* (Turin: Società editrice internazionale, 1950);

Fabro, *Partecipazione e causalità secondo S. Tommaso d'Aquino* (Turin: Società editrice internazionale, 1960);

Louis-Bertrand Geiger, *La Participation dans la philosophie de saint Thomas d'Aquin* (Paris: Vrin, 1942);

Thomas Gilby, *The Political Thought of Thomas Aquinas* (Chicago: University of Chicago Press, 1958);

Etienne H. Gilson, *The Christian Philosophy of St. Thomas Aquinas: With a Catalogue of St. Thomas's Works by I. T. Eschmann*, translated by L. K. Shook (New York: Random House, 1956);

Martin Grabmann, *Die Werke des hl. Thomas von Aquin*, third edition (Münster: Aschendorff 1949);

P.-M. Gy, "L'office du Corpus Christi et S. Thomas d'Aquin: Etat d'une recherche," *Revue des sciences philosophiques et théologiques*, 64 (1980): 491-507;

Robert J. Henle, *Saint Thomas and Platonism: A Study of the Plato and Platonici Texts in the Writings of Saint Thomas* (The Hague: Nijhoff, 1956);

Harry V. Jaffa, *Thomism and Aristotelianism: A Study of the Commentary by Thomas Aquinas on the Nicomachean Ethics* (Chicago: University of Chicago Press, 1952);

Anthony Kenny, *Aquinas: A Collection of Critical Essays* (Garden City, N.Y.: Doubleday, 1969);

Kenny, *The Five Ways* (London: Routledge & Kegan Paul, 1969);

George P. Klubertanz, *St. Thomas Aquinas on Analogy: A Textual Analysis and Systematic Synthesis* (Chicago: Loyola University Press, 1960);

Wolfgang Kluxen, *Philosophische Ethik bei Thomas von Aquin* (Mainz: Matthias-Grünewald, 1964);

Dom C. Lambot, "La bulle d'Urbain IV à Eve de Saint-Martin sur l'institution de la Fête-Dieu," *Scriptorium*, 2 (1948): 69-77; reprinted, *Revue Bénédictine*, 79 (1969): 261-270;

Jacques Maritain, *Art and Scholasticism* (New York: Scribners, 1930);

Ralph McInerny, *St. Thomas Aquinas* (Boston: Twayne, 1978);

McInerny, *Thomism in the Age of Renewal* (Garden City, N.Y.: Doubleday, 1966);

Hans Meyer, *The Philosophy of St. Thomas Aquinas*, translated by Frederic Eckhoff (St. Louis & London: Herder, 1944);

John Naus, *The Nature of the Practical Intellect According to St. Thomas Aquinas* (Rome: Libreria editrice dell'Università Gregoriana, 1959);

Joseph Owens, *St. Thomas and the Future of Metaphysics* (Milwaukee: Marquette University Press, 1957);

Owens, *St. Thomas Aquinas on the Existence of God* (Albany: State University of New York Press, 1980);

Josef Pieper, *Guide to Thomas Aquinas*, translated by Richard and Clara Winston (New York: Pantheon, 1962);

Pieper, *The Silence of St. Thomas: Three Essays*, translated by John Murray and Daniel O'Connor (New York: Pantheon, 1957; London: Faber & Faber, 1957);

Karl Rahner, *Geist in Welt: Zur Metaphysik der endliche Erkenntnis bei Thomas von Aquin* (Innsbruck: Raunch, 1939);

Santiago María Ramírez, *De Auctoritate Doctrinali Sancti Thomae Aquinatis* (Salamanca: Apud Sanctum Stephanum, 1952);

Herman Reith, *The Metaphysics of St. Thomas Aquinas* (Milwaukee: Bruce, 1958);

J. K. Ryan, "St. Thomas and English Protestant Thinkers," *New Scholasticism*, 22, no. 1 (1948): 1-33; 22, no. 2 (1948): 126-208;

Ludwig Schütz, *Thomas-Lexikon* (New York: Ungar, 1957);

Edward A. Synan, "Aquinas and His Age," in *Calgary Papers* (Toronto: Pontifical Institute of Mediaeval Studies, 1978), pp. 1-25;

Synan, "St. Thomas Aquinas and the Profession of Arms," *Mediaeval Studies*, 50 (1988): 404-437;

Synan, *Thomas Aquinas: Propositions and Parables* (Toronto: Pontifical Institute of Mediaeval Studies, 1979);

Johannes Ude, *Die Autorität des HL. Thomas von Aquin als Kirchenlehrer* (Salzburg: Pustet, 1932);

Michael Wittman, *Die Ethik des hl. Thomas von Aquin* (Munich: Heuber, 1933);

R. J. Zawilla, "The 'Historiae Corporis Christi' Attributed to Thomas Aquinas: A Theological Study of Their Biblical Sources," Ph.D. dissertation, University of Toronto, 1985.

Manuscripts:

Work by independent scholars on the manuscripts of Aquinas seems now to be impracticable in view of the enormous number of manuscripts and the accelerating productivity of the Leonine Commission, the scholars charged with critical editions of all the works by Aquinas. Their work is complicated by a double manuscript tradition of certain works, a "university" and a "conventual" tradition.

Augustine (Aurelius Augustinus)

(13 November 354 - 28 August 430)

Frederick Van Fleteren
LaSalle University

PRINCIPAL WORKS: *Contra Academicos* (Against the Academics, written 386);
De Beata Vita (The Happy Life, written 386);
De Ordine (On Order, written 386);
De Magistro (On the Teacher, written 387);
De Libero Arbitrio (On Free Choice, written 388-395);
De Vera Religione (On True Religion, written 390);
Enarrationes in Psalmos (Commentaries on the Psalms, written 392-420);
De Doctrina Christiana (On Christian Teaching, written 396-426);
Confessiones (Confessions, written 397-401);
De Trinitate (On the Trinity, written 399-418);
De Genesi ad Litteram (A Literal Commentary on Genesis, written 400-415);
De Civitate Dei (The City of God, written 412-425);
Tractatus in Iohannis Evangelium (Treatise on the Gospel of St. John, written 413-418);
Retractationes (Retractations, written 427).

EDITIONS: *De Arte Praedicandi* [*De Doctrina Christiana*] (Strasbourg, 1465);
Confessiones, edited by Jean Matelin (Strasbourg: Matelin, 1465-1470?);
De Civitate Dei (Subiaco: Sweynheim & Pannartz, 1467);
De Trinitate, edited by Henry of Rimini (Strasbourg, 1474);
De Vera Religione, edited by Martinus Flach (Strasbourg, 1489);
Explanatio Psalmorun, edited by Johann Amerbach (Basel: Amerbach, 1489);
De Libero Arbitrio (Parma, 1491);
Sermones, edited by Amerbach (Basel: Amerbach, 1497);
De Magistro, edited by J. Badius (Paris: Badius, 1502);
Retractiones, edited by A. Dodon (Basel: Amerbach, 1505-1506);
De Genesi ad Litteram, edited by Amerbach (Basel: Amerbach, 1506);
Contra Academicos, edited by Amerbach (Basel: Amerbach, 1506);
De Beata Vita, edited by Amerbach (Basel: Amerbach, 1506);
De Ordine, edited by Amerbach (Basel: Amerbach, 1506);
De Libero Arbitrio, edited by Amerbach (Basel: Amerbach, 1506);
Patrologia Latina, volumes 32-46, edited by J.-P. Migne (Paris: D'Enfer, 1841-1842); revised by Palémon Glorieux as *Pour revaloriser Migne*, volumes 32-44 (Lille: Facultés catholiques, 1952);
Miscellanea Agostiniana, 2 volumes, edited by Germain Morin (Rome: Tipografia Poliglotta Vaticana, 1930-1931);
Stromata, edited by Walter Green (Utrecht & Antwerp: Spectrum, 1955).

CRITICAL EDITIONS: *Corpus Scriptorum Ecclesiasticorum Latinorum*, volumes 28, 33, 40,

Augustine as depicted in a detail of a fourteenth-century tempera painting by Simone Martini (Fitzwilliam Museum, Cambridge)

63, 74, 77, 80, 85, edited by Joseph Zycha, Emanuel Hoffman, Pium Knoell, Walter Green, Guenther Weigel, and Michael Zelzra (Prague, Vienna & Leipzig: Tempsky-Tempsky-Freytag/Hölder-Pchler-Tempsky, 1896-1963);

S. Aureli Augustini Confessionum Libri Tredecim, edited by Knoell and Martinus Skutella (Leipzig: Teubner, 1934);

Corpus Christianorum, volumes 27, 29, 32, 36, 38-41, 47-48, 50, 57, edited by Green, L. Verheijen, K.-D. Daur, R. Willems, D. Eligius Dekkers, Johannes Fraipont, Cyril Lambot, Bernard Dombart, Alphonse Kalb, Joseph Martin, W. J. Mountain, and Almut Mutzenbacher (Turnhout: Brepols, 1954-1984).

EDITIONS IN ENGLISH: *A Worke, Of the Predestination of Saints, Wrytten by the Famous Doctor S. Augustine . . . and Translated by Nycolas Lesse . . . Item, Another Worke of the Sayde Augustyne Entytuled Of the Vertue of Perseueraunce to Thend, Translated by the Sayd Nycolas Lesse* (London: Imprinted by the wydowe of Ihon Herforde for Gwalter Lynnem, 1550);

Two Bokes of the Noble Doctor and B. S. Augustine, Thone Entiteled Of the Predestiuacion of Saintes, Thother Of Perseueraunce unto Thende, translated by John Scory (Emden: Egidius van der Erve, 1556?);

Of the Citie of God, with the Learned Comments of Io. Lod. Vives, translated by John Healey (London: G. Eld, 1610; revised edition, London: G. Eld & M. Flesher, 1620);

The Confessions of the Incomparable Doctour S. Augustine, translated by Tobie Matthew (Saint Omer, France, 1620); revised by Roger Hudleston (London: Burns, Oates & Washbourne, 1923);

Saint Augustine's Confessions, Translated, and with Some Marginall Notes Illustrated wherein Diuers Antiquities Are Explayned and the Marginall Notes of a Former Popish Translator [Tobie Matthew] *Answered*, translated by William Watts (London: Printed by Iohn Norton for John Parker, 1631; Boston, 1843; London: Heinemann, 1912; New York: Macmillan, 1912);

Saint Austins Care for the Dead or His Bouke Intitled De Cura pro Mortuis, Translated for the Use of Those Who Ether Have Not His Volumes or Have Not Knowledge in the Latine Tungue (Paris?, 1636);

The Kernell or Extract of the Historicall Part of S. Augustin's Confessions, Together with All the Most Affectuous Passages Thereof Taken out of That Whole Booke and Seuered from Such Parts as Are Obscure (Paris, 1638);

The Judgment of the Learned and Pious St. Augustine, Concerning Penal Laws against Conventicles and for Unity in Religion, Deliver'd in His 48th Epistle to Vincentius (London: Printed for James Collins, 1670);

S. Augustine's Confessions, with the Continuation of His Life to the End Thereof Extracted out of Possidius and the Fathers Own Unquestioned Works, Translated into English, translated by Abraham Woodhead (London: Printed in the year, 1679);

St. Augustine's Confessions; or, Praises of God in Ten Books, Newly Translated into English from the Original Latin (Dublin: P. Wogan, 1807);

"Augustine, On the Art of Preaching," translated by Oliver A. Taylor, *Biblical Repository*, 3 (July 1833): 569-612;

The Confessions, translated by E. B. Pusey (Oxford: Parker, 1838; New York: Dutton, 1907);

Sermons on Selected Lessons of the New Testament, 2 volumes, translated by Richard Gell MacMullen (Oxford: Parker, 1844-1845);

Seventeen Short Treatises, translated by C. L. Cornish and H. Browne (Oxford: Parker, 1847);

Expositions on the Book of Psalms by St. Augustine, 6 volumes, translated by John E. Tweed and others, edited by Pusey and Charles Marriott (Oxford: Parker, 1847-1857);

Homilies on the Gospel according to St. John and on His First Epistle, 2 volumes, translated by Browne (Oxford: Parker, 1848-1849);

The Works of Aurelius Augustine: A New Translation, 15 volumes, edited by Marcus Dods (Edinburgh: Clark, 1872-1876);

Confessions of S. Augustine: Ten Books, a New Translation, translated by William Henry Hutchings (London: Rivingtons, 1878);

On Faith and the Creed: Dogmatic Teaching of the Church of the Fourth and Fifth Centuries, Being a Translation of the Several Treatises Contained in the Compilation Entitled De Fide et Symbolo, translated by Charles A. Heurtley (Oxford & London: Parker, 1886);

A Select Library of the Nicene and Post-Nicene Fathers of the Christian Church, volumes 1-8, edited by Philip Schaff and others (volumes 1-4, Buffalo, N.Y., 1886-1887; volumes 5-8, New York: Christian Literature Co., 1887-1888);

Three Anti-Pelagian Treatises of S. Augustine, Viz., De Spiritu et Littera, De Natura et Gratia, and De Gestis Pelagii, translated with analyses by Francis Henry Woods and John Octavius Johnston (London: Nutt, 1887);

The Confessions of St. Augustine, edited by Alexander Smellie (London: Melrose, 1897);

The Confessions of St. Augustine, translated, with notes and introduction, by Charles Bigg (London: Methuen, 1898);

Thirteen Homilies of St. Augustine on St. John XIV, In Joh. Ev. Tractatus LXVII-LXXIX, translated by Hugh Fraser Stewart (Cambridge: Cambridge University Press, 1900; revised, 1902);

The Soliloquies of St. Augustine, translated, with notes and introduction, by Rose Elizabeth Cleveland (Boston: Little, Brown, 1910);

Treatise of Saint Aurelius Augustine . . . On the Catechizing of the Uninstructed, translated by E. Phillips Barker (London: Methuen, 1912);

How to Help the Dead: A Translation of St. Augustine's De Cura Gerenda pro Mortius [sic], A. D. 411, translated by Mary H. Allies (London: Burns & Oates, 1914);

The Philosophy of Teaching: A Study in the Symbolism of Language. A Translation of St. Augustine's De Magistro, translated by Francis E. Tourscher (Philadelphia: Reilly, 1924);

Readings from St. Augustine on the Psalms, translated by Joseph Rickaby (London: Burns, Oates & Washbourne, 1925);

St. Augustine: On the Spirit and the Letter, translated by W. J. Sparrow Simpson (London: Society for the Propagation of Christian Knowledge, 1925; New York & Toronto: Macmillan, 1925);

De Catechizandis Rvdibvs, Liber Vnvs, translated, with an introduction and commentary, by Joseph Patrick Christopher (Washington, D.C.: Catholic University of America Press, 1926);

De Doctrina Christiana, Liber Qvartvs: A Commentary, with a Revised Text, Introduction, and Translation, translated by Sister Thérèse Sullivan (Washington, D.C.: Catholic University of America Press, 1930);

De Quantitate Animae, the Measure of the Soul: Latin Text with English Translation and Notes, translated by Tourscher (Philadelphia: Reilly, 1933; London: Herder, 1933);

The Teaching of St. Augustine on Prayer and the Contemplative Life: A Translation of Various Passages from the Saint's Sermons and Other Writings, translated by Hugh Pope (London: Burns, Oates & Washbourne, 1935);

An Augustine Synthesis, edited by Erich Przywara (London: Sheed & Ward, 1936);

De Beata Vita, Happiness: A Study, Latin Text with English Translation and Notes, translated by Tourscher (Philadelphia: Reilly, 1937);

De Libero Arbitrio (Libri Tres), The Free Choice of the Will (Three Books): Latin Text with English Translation and Notes, translated by Tourscher (Philadelphia: Reilly, 1937);

Concerning the Teacher (De Magistro) and On the Immortality of the Soul (De Immortalitate Animae) by St. Aurelius Augustine, translated by

George G. Leckie (London & New York: Appleton-Century, 1938);

The Happy Life of Aurelius Augustine, translated by Ludwig Schopp (Saint Louis & London: Herder, 1939);

St. Augustine: On Music, Books I-VI, translated by R. Catesby Taliaferro (Annapolis, Md.: St. Johns Bookstore, 1939);

Divine Providence and the Problem of Evil: A Translation of St. Augustine's De Ordine, with Annotations, translated by Robert P. Russell (New York: Cosmopolitan Science and Art Service Co., 1942);

The Rule of Our Holy Father St. Augustine, Bishop of Hippo, translated by Tourscher, revised by Russell (Villanova, Pa.: Province of St. Thomas of Villanova, 1942);

Answer to Skeptics: A Translation of St. Augustine's Contra Academicos, translated by Denis J. Kavanagh (New York: Cosmopolitan Science and Art Service Co., 1943);

The Confessions of St. Augustine, translated by Francis Joseph Sheed (New York: Sheed & Ward, 1943; London: Sheed & Ward, 1944);

De Beata Vita, translated by Ruth Allison Brown (Washington, D.C.: Catholic University of America Press, 1944);

The City of God, 2 volumes, translated by Healey, revised by R. V. G. Tasker (London: Dent, 1945; New York: Dutton, 1945);

De Libero Arbitrio Voluntatis: St. Augustine on Free Will, translated by Carroll M. Sparrow (Charlottesville: University of Virginia Press, 1947);

Faith, Hope and Charity, translated and annotated by Louis A. Arand (Westminster, Md.: Newman Bookshop, 1947);

Like as the Hart, by St. Augustine: Being His Enerratio super Psalmum XLI *Translated by an Unknown Sixteenth-Century Writer*, edited by G. Desmond Schlegel (Oxford: Blackfriars, 1947);

The Lord's Sermon on the Mount, translated by John J. Jepson (Westminster, Md.: Newman Press, 1948);

Basic Writings of St. Augustine, 2 volumes, edited by Whitney J. Oates (New York: Random House, 1948);

The Greatness of the Soul; The Teacher, translated and annotated by Joseph M. Colleran (Westminster, Md.: Newman Press, 1950);

Introduction to St. Augustine: The City of God, Being Selections from De Civitate Dei, Including Most of the XIXth Book, with Text, Translation, and Running Commentary, translated by Reginald H. Barrow (London: Faber & Faber, 1950);

The City of God, 3 volumes, translated by Gerald G. Walsh, Grace Monahan, and Demetrius B. Zema (Washington, D.C.: Catholic University of America Press, 1950-1954);

Against the Academics, translated by John J. O'Meara (Westminster, Md.: Newman Press, 1950 [i.e., 1951]);

Commentary on the Lord's Sermon on the Mount, with Seventeen Related Sermons, translated by Kavanagh (Washington, D.C.: Catholic University of America Press, 1951);

De Utilitate Ieiunii: A Text with a Translation, Introduction, and Commentary, translated by S. Dominic Ruegg (Washington, D.C.: Catholic University of America Press, 1951);

Confessions, in Thirteen Books: A New English Translation from the Original Latin, edited by J. M. Lelen (New York: Catholic Book Publishing Co., 1952);

Sermons for Christmas and Epiphany, translated and annotated by Thomas C. Lawler (Westminster, Md.: Newman Press, 1952);

Treatises on Various Subjects, edited by Roy J. Deferrari, translated by Mary S. Muldowney and others (New York: Fathers of the Church, 1952);

The Confessions of St. Augustine, Book VIII, edited and translated by C. S. C. Williams (Oxford: Blackwell, 1953);

Confessions, translated by Vernon J. Bourke (New York: Fathers of the Church, 1953);

Earlier Writings, translated by John H. S. Burleigh (Philadelphia: Westminster Press, 1953);

Enchiridion; or, Manual to Laurentius Concerning Faith, Hope, and Charity, Translated from the Benedictine Text, with an Introduction and Notes, translated by Ernest Evans (London: Society for the Propagation of Christian Knowledge, 1953);

On True Religion, translated by Burleigh (Philadelphia & London: Westminster Press, 1953);

De Natura Boni of St. Augustine: A Translation with an Introduction and Commentary, translated by A. Anthony Moon (Washington, D.C.: Catholic University of America Press, 1955);

Later Works, translated by John Burnaby (Philadelphia: Westminster Press, 1955);

The Problem of Free Choice, translated and annotated by Mark Pontifex (Westminster, Md.: Newman Press, 1955);

Confessions and Enchiridion, translated and edited by Albert C. Outler (Philadelphia: Westminster Press, 1955);

Sancti Aurelii Augustini, De Excidio Urbis Romae Sermo: A Critical Text and Translation, edited and translated by Marie Vianney O'Reilly (Washington, D.C.: Catholic University of America Press, 1955);

Treatises on Marriage and Other Subjects, translated by Charles T. Wilcox, edited by Deferrari (New York: Fathers of the Church, 1955);

The De Dono Perseverantiae of St. Augustine, translated by Mary A. Lesousky (Washington, D.C.: Catholic University of America Press, 1956);

The De Haeresibus of St. Augustine, translated, with an introduction and commentary, by Liguori G. Müller (Washington, D.C.: Catholic University of America Press, 1956);

The Rule of St. Augustine, Commentary by Blessed Alphonsus Orozco, translated by Thomas A. Hand (Westminster, Md.: Newman Press, 1956);

Against Julian, translated by Matthew A. Schumacher (New York: Fathers of the Church, 1957);

Against the Academicians: Contra Academicos, translated by Mary Patricia Garvey (Milwaukee: Marquette University Press, 1957);

The City of God against the Pagans, 7 volumes, translated by George E. McCracken, William M. Green, David S. Wiesen, Philip Levine, and William Chase Greene (Cambridge, Mass.: Harvard University Press, 1957-1960; London: Heinemann, 1957-1960);

On Christian Doctrine, translated by D. W. Robertson, Jr. (New York: Liberal Arts Press, 1958);

Nine Sermons of Saint Augustine on the Psalms, translated by Edmund Hill (New York: Kennedy, 1959);

Of True Religion, translated by Burleigh (Chicago: Regnery, 1959);

Selected Easter Sermons, translated by Philip T. Weller (Saint Louis: Herder, 1959);

Sermons on the Liturgical Seasons, translated by Muldowney (New York: Fathers of the Church, 1959);

The Confessions of St. Augustine, translated by John K. Ryan (Garden City, N.Y.: Doubleday, 1960);

St. Augustine on the Psalms, 2 volumes, translated and annotated by Scholastica Hebgin and Felicitas Corrigan (Westminster, Md.: Newman Press, 1960);

John Shines through Augustine: Selections from the Sermons of Augustine on the Gospel according to Saint John, translated by A. P. Carleton (London: United Society for Christian Literature, 1960; New York: Association Press, 1961);

Confessions, translated by R. S. Pine-Coffin (Baltimore: Penguin, 1961);

The Political Writings of St. Augustine, edited by Henry Paolucci (Chicago: Regnery, 1962);

Selected Writings, edited by Roger Hazelton (Cleveland: Meridian, 1962);

City of God, abridged and translated by J. W. C. Wand (London: Oxford University Press, 1963);

Confessions: A New Translation, translated by Rex Warner (New York: New American Library, 1963);

The Trinity, translated by Stephen McKenna (Washington, D.C.: Catholic University of America Press, 1963);

The Essential Augustine, edited by Bourke (New York: New American Library, 1964);

Introduction to the Philosophy of St. Augustine: Selected Readings and Commentaries, edited by John A. Mourant (University Park: Pennsylvania State University Press, 1964);

On Free Choice of the Will, translated by Anna S. Benjamin and L. H. Hackstaff (Indianapolis: Bobbs-Merrill, 1964);

The Catholic and Manichaean Ways of Life: De Moribus Ecclesiae Catholicae et de Moribus Manichaeorum, translated by Donald A. Gallagher and Idella J. Gallagher (Washington, D.C.: Catholic University of America Press, 1966);

Selected Sermons, translated and edited by Quincy Howe, Jr. (New York: Holt, Rinehart & Winston, 1966);

The Free Choice of the Will, translated by Russell (Washington, D.C.: Catholic University of America Press, 1968);

The Retractions, translated by Mary Inez Bogan (Washington, D.C.: Catholic University of America Press, 1968).

Augustine is one of the major thinkers in the history of Western thought. Born during the decline of the Roman Empire, he provided a bridge between the thought of ancient Greece, interpreted in the light of the Judeo-Christian Scriptures, and the Middle Ages. His authority reigned supreme during the latter period and has remained unparalleled throughout the history of Christianity. But even were he not a transitional figure with a foot in both the ancient and modern worlds, the nature and scope of his writings would have assured him a high place in the history of the West.

Augustine was born on 13 November 354 in Tagaste in Numidia Cirtensis, North Africa (now Souk-Ahras, Algeria), of a Roman father, Patricius, and a local tribeswoman, Monica. In his *Confessiones* (Confessions, 397-401) Augustine contrasts the hot-blooded, semicultured character of his father with the common sense and saintliness of his mother. Although such a contrast must be seen against the background of Augustine's thesis in the *Confessiones*—the wretchedness (*miseria*) of man and the mercy (*misericordia*) of God, and Augustine's view of Monica as the agent of God's grace in his life—there is no more reason to doubt the veracity of this characterization than to doubt anything else in the *Confessiones*. It is certain that Monica exerted a powerful influence over the career and conversion of her son.

Within the confines of his father's tenuous means and the decadence of the late Roman Empire, Augustine received a good education first at Tagaste, then at nearby Madauros, and finally—after a year of idleness caused by his father's poverty—at Carthage. He studied grammar and rhetoric, the master of which was the Roman orator, statesman, and philosopher Cicero. At the age of nineteen Augustine read Cicero's now-lost *Hortensius*, an introduction to the philosophic life in the manner of Aristotle that inspired in Augustine the desire for wisdom. Augustine's search for wisdom led him into Manichaeanism.

The Manichaeans were a Gnostic sect, widespread in the Middle East and northern Africa in the fourth century. Basing a dualistic doctrine of good and evil on a special revelation supposedly given to their founder, Manes, the Manichaeans promised the young Augustine an understanding of the universe that did not require an appeal to faith. Further, they offered him a deterministic explanation of the existence of evil that left human beings free of personal responsibility. Though Augustine never became one of the elect, he used the influential positions of many Manichaeans within the Roman Empire to advance his career well into his late twenties. Gradually, however, he became disenchanted with Manichaeanism because it did not provide the understanding it had promised but rather demanded belief in an absurd system. Abandoning Manichaeanism after finding that one of its leading spokesmen, Faustus, could not answer his questions, the young African entered a period of provisional skepticism. Augustine had familiarized himself with various philosophies, but regret for his rash adherence to Manichaeanism made him hesitant to commit to any other doctrine; following Cicero, he believed truth to be an ideal, unattainable by man.

Throughout this period, Augustine advanced in his chosen profession of rhetoric. He taught the subject in his hometown of Tagaste, then in Carthage, Rome, and Milan; in Milan he attained the post of state rhetor for public occasions. During this time he lived with a woman from Numidia whom he loved and who bore him a son, Adeodatus (the name means "Gift of God"). But advancement in his career demanded a wife with money. When Monica chose a young woman not yet of legal age for him to marry, his former mistress left for Africa, vowing never to love another man; Adeodatus remained with Augustine. Until he could marry his mother's choice, Augustine lived with another woman. Though Augustine later chastised himself for these relationships, such ties were not unusual in ancient Roman society, where it was impossible to marry outside of one's social class. Further, as a catechumen, a Christian was not necessarily expected to give up cohabitation.

Augustine became an ardent admirer of the sermons of Ambrose, the bishop of Milan, who used the Neoplatonic writings of Plotinus and Porphyry in his preaching. As part of an informal circle of Christian Neoplatonists, Ambrose imparted to Augustine two teachings which remained with him for the rest of his life: the spirituality of the human soul, in which its *imago Dei* consists, and the "spiritual exegesis" of the Scriptures.

Thus prepared, Augustine read some treatises by Plotinus and Porphyry. In book 7 of the *Confessiones* he describes the effect of these writings on him as an intellectual conversion. Many of the doctrines Augustine espoused throughout his life originated from this early reading of the Neoplatonists: the relationship between the Father and the Son, taken from the Neoplatonic relationship between the One and the Intellect; the doctrine of creation; the theory of illumination; the spirituality of the human soul; a metaphysics of being and nonbeing; the transcendentality of goodness; and a theory of divine providence and the harmony of the universe. The principal doc-

Fresco including the earliest known depiction of Augustine, executed circa 600 (Lateran, Rome)

trine Augustine derived from these books, however, was their teaching on the destiny of humanity. Even in his later years Augustine held the Neoplatonists to be the closest of all philosophers to the Christians because both agreed that possession of the summum bonum caused humans to be happy. The young Augustine thought that such happiness was attainable in this life; later, through his closer reading of the Epistles of Paul, he realized it to be attainable only in the next. The essential difference between Augustine and the Neoplatonists was on the Incarnation. Christ becoming human while remaining God was central to Christianity but impossible for the Neoplatonists. In Neoplatonism any concourse with the material world would involve a diminution of God's being. As a result, the Neoplatonic universe was peopled with *daemons*, partially spiritual and partially material beings that mediated between God and man. Following Paul, Augustine places Christ's mediation in the fact that he is both God and human.

The chief immediate effect that the reading of the Neoplatonist books had on Augustine, he believed, was the ascent of his soul to God. On at least one occasion during this period Augustine achieved what he considered a vision of the divine. Such an ascent demanded moral and intellectual purification (*katharsis*) in the manner of the Neoplatonists; unlike the Neoplatonic ascent, it also demanded faith and grace. The ascensional motif remained with Augustine throughout his works, and his belief in the importance of the *exercitatio animae* (training of the mind) to understand the truths of faith stems from this period.

Augustine's account of the ascent of his soul raises the question of whether he should be considered a mystic. If mysticism is defined in the broadest sense as a belief that one has experienced direct intellectual contact with the divine, then Augustine had mystical experiences.

Augustine saw similarities between the Neoplatonic and Christian conceptions of the godhead. He identified the Father with the Plotinian One and the Son with the Plotinian *Nous* (Intellect). In Neoplatonic thought, the *Nous* contained the Platonic Forms. For Augustine, Christ is present to every person, and the Forms are present to humans through Christ. Such is the Augustinian interpretation of John 1:9, which says that Christ "is the true light which enlightens every man coming into the world" (*lumen uerum, quod inluminat omnem hominem uenientem in hunc mundum*). Knowledge of the Forms constitutes, for Augustine, a "memory of the present." This is Augustine's theory of illumination. Augustine incorporates Plato's Forms into the divine mind and indicates that humans have some mediate vision of them in this life.

In book 8 of the *Confessiones* Augustine tells of his conversion to Christianity in 386. In the garden of his house in Milan, Augustine, hearing children singing "*tolle, lege; tolle, lege*" (take up and read, take up and read), read the Epistle to the Romans 13:13—"Not in rioting and drunkenness, not in promiscuity and licentiousness, not in quarreling and jealousy, but put on the Lord Jesus Christ and take no care for the flesh in its desires"—and was immediately converted. Some scholars have held that Augustine was actually converted to Neoplatonism in 386 and only later, in 391, to Christianity. Most scholars, however, do not question the reality of Augustine's conversion to Christianity, insofar as he understood it, in 386. Augustine says in the *Confessiones* that he read the Neoplatonist works through the prism of the New Testament, not vice versa. It was Christian teaching that formed for him the criteria for the acceptance or rejection of Neoplatonic thought.

Augustine saw Christianity and Neoplatonism for the most part as compatible; when he did find them in conflict, he chose decisively for Christianity. He tried to incorporate what he learned of Greek metaphysics into his worldview; nevertheless, it is certain that Augustine did more to stem the tide of Platonism in the West than he did to promote it.

More than anything else, Augustine saw his conversion as the triumph of humility over pride. People cannot save themselves; they are saved by the grace of God. For the remainder of his life Augustine saw the story of humanity in terms of pride and humility: "Every other sin is concerned with the commission of evil deeds; but pride lurks even in good works, seeking to destroy them. And what good is there in giving all one's goods to the poor, even in becoming poor oneself, if the miserable soul is more given to pride in despising riches than it had been in possessing them." Humility is the specifically Christian virtue and the one virtue necessary for salvation.

The result of Augustine's conversion was the decision, in the autumn of 386, to lead a celibate life in a kind of philosophic-monastic community at the villa of Cassiciacum. Together with his mother, his son, and some students, friends, and other relatives, Augustine discussed questions concerning the ultimate human destiny, its attainability, the unacceptability of skepticism, divine providence, and the use of the liberal arts to attain the vision of God. After his baptism by Ambrose in Milan in April 387 and Monica's death shortly afterward in Ostia, near Rome, Augustine returned to Africa in 388 to begin a life of philosophical monasticism in his hometown of Tagaste. During this time he began to discuss the question of the freedom of the will. Humanity, he says, is placed in a midway position in creation between God and things eternal, on the one hand, and material things, on the other. By the use of the will, humans should turn toward the eternal and immutable and away from the material and changeable. In this emphasis on the will Augustine distinguishes himself from Platonism. Later, in his dispute with Pelagius and his followers, Augustine would modify his views on the ability of the will to choose the good.

Augustine mentions in his *Retractationes* (Retractations, 427) that a central part of his thinking during this period was a project on the liberal arts. The purpose of the project was to purify the mind so that it could attain the vision of God. Augustine later realized that he had asked too much of the liberal arts. Nevertheless, in the *De Doctrina Christiana* (On Christian Teaching, 396-426), Augustine puts forth a program of the study of the liberal arts for the Christian. Christianity is a religion of the book, and Augustine wanted to place the secular learning of his time at the disposal of interpreters of the Scriptures. He took the passage in Exodus in which the Jews were told to take gold out of Egypt to indicate that Christianity was to use the gold of secular science for its own purposes. Truth, wherever it was found, was ultimately God's. The influence of Augustine's notions of the liberal arts and the unity of truth is evident in the Christian commitment to the liberal arts in the Middle Ages.

Influenced by the Platonic tradition, Augustine held that it was not possible for one person to place ideas into the mind of another; one had only words at one's disposal, and they could not produce this result. The teacher can merely serve as the occasion whereby the student confronts the truth which resides within him. Words can serve as an admonition but cannot deliver the truth. The dictum *foris monet, intus docet* (he admonishes externally, he teaches internally) summarizes Augustine's views on this subject. Christ, the interior master, enlightens everyone. This doctrine influenced Martin Luther.

In 391, while visiting the port city of Hippo in North Africa in an effort to found a monastic community there, Augustine was invited to succeed the aging bishop Valerius. Somewhat against his will, he was immediately ordained. He was consecrated cobishop in 395 and became bishop of the diocese of Hippo on Valerius's death in 396. From the day of his ordination, Augustine's primary work was sacerdotal and episcopal; his prodigious literary output was actually his secondary occupation. Whenever a problem arose in the African church, it was Augustine to whom that church turned. He was its literary and theological representative to churches in Europe and Asia, the defender of orthodoxy within the church, and the defender of Christendom against the pagans. The growing significance of Augustine gave Hippo an ecclesiastical importance out of proportion to its size. Augustine always considered the episcopacy to be a burden rather than an honor.

Augustine's extant writings include 93 works in 232 books; more than 300 letters, many of which are works in themselves; and more than 500 sermons. Serving as the basis for most of medieval thought, his writings have remained among the most influential in the history of the West. They may be divided into three periods: the anti-Manichaean period, from 386 to 400; the anti-Donatist period, from 400 to 412; and the anti-Pelagian period, from 412 to 430.

Several of Augustine's major themes were developed as responses to Manichaean positions. Manichaean rationalism promised the young Augustine complete understanding without appeal to faith; he left Manichaeanism precisely because it could not deliver on this promise. Eventually he developed a position of mitigated rationalism, in which both faith and reason have a place. Reason's task is to give rational explanations, insofar as this is possible, for what we believe; to use reason for other purposes is mere idle curiosity. Faith has a temporal priority since we need to believe before we can attempt to understand; reason can give a deeper appreciation of what we believe. Augustine's celebrated dictum on faith and reason occurs in *Sermo* (Sermon) *XLIII*: "Every man wishes to understand; there is no one who does not so wish. Not all men wish to believe. A man says to me: I would understand so that I might believe; I respond: Believe that you might understand." Augustine did not share the optimism of his disciple of six centuries later, Anselm, on the ability of reason to comprehend the truths of faith. Augustine's position has much more in common with that of Thomas Aquinas than is commonly recognized.

Manichaeanism had also attracted the young Augustine with its deterministic explanation of evil: the universe was composed of two opposed principles of good and evil. The cosmic struggle was carried out in each individual in such a way that the principle of evil, rather than the person, was responsible for immorality.

In response to Manichaean dualism, Augustine posited the free choice of the human will as the cause of evil. Influenced by Ambrose and Neoplatonism, Augustine sees humanity in a median position between higher and lower goods. All things are good; it is the human use of them

Saint Augustine in His Study, *painted in 1480 by Sandro Botticelli (Church of All Saints, Florence)*

which can be evil. Moral evil consists in choosing lower goods in preference to higher goods; moral goodness lies in choosing higher goods in preference to lower goods or in using lower goods to attain higher ones. The highest being—God—is being in its fullest sense; all other beings are composed of being and nonbeing. Complete evil would be absolute nonbeing; thus it cannot exist. The centrality of the will in the thought of Augustine overturns the intellectualism of the Greek world. Human happiness lies not only in the possession of truth by the intellect but also in possession of the good by the will. Love becomes the center of human existence, and one's place in the universe is determined by what one loves. This is the meaning of the phrase in the *Confessiones: "Amor meus, pondus meus"* (My love is my weight). Later, in *De Civitate Dei* (The City of God, 412-426), Augustine divides people into two societies according to their respective loves.

In the *Confessiones* Augustine says that his inability to conceive spirit constituted the single greatest impediment to his conversion. This inability Augustine attributed to the materialism of the Manichaeans. Through the preaching of Ambrose and the works of the Neoplatonists, Augustine began to understand spiritual existence. Spirit has no need of a place in which to exist. God exists in neither time nor space; the human soul exists in time but not in space. A spiritual being exists where it acts; its being is not parceled out.

The Manichaeans had pointed out several apparent contradictions in the Bible, particularly in the first chapters of Genesis. Likewise, the variation in moral precepts from one book to another did not go unnoticed. Augustine believed in the literal meaning of the scriptural text, but he included figurative and allegorical interpretations as part of the literal meaning. When literal exegesis, understood in this broad sense, fails, Augustine turns to "spiritual exegesis." Augustine derived the notion of spiritual exegesis from Ambrose, who, using the Pauline text "The letter killeth, but the spirit giveth life" (2 Cor. 3:6) as his inspiration, found meaning in the Scriptures above and beyond the literal sense. The purpose of reading and meditating on the Scriptures was to raise one above the material to the spiritual; this idea owes something to Platonism. Using this kind of exegesis, Augustine avoided the materialistic explanations of the Manichaeans. He carried the method far beyond its use by those who had gone before him. Modern scholarship finds some Augustinian exegesis rather bizarre; nevertheless, his explanations almost always remain well within the mainstream of Christian thinking.

The Manichaeans held that procreation of children was immoral, that it was the bringing of human beings into an evil world. Augustine says that the purposes of marriage are the procreation and rearing of children and the mutual care and support of the spouses for one another. He does not speak of primary and secondary purposes of marriage, as later theologians would. Rather, he distinguishes between the *bonum prolis* (good of the offspring), the *bonum fidis* (good of the faith), and the *bonum sacramenti* (good of the sacrament) in marriage. The first good deals with the procreation and rearing of children; the second is the honor and trust by which the spouses give power over their bodies to each other for the sexual act; the third is the indissolubility of marriage. Although the mutual love of the spouses was a purpose of marriage, Augustine did not see sexual intercourse as promoting this end; nor did he see the sexual act as a sign of the love between married people. In this respect he differs significantly from modern theory.

Augustine's views on marriage and sex can be seen as an advance over those of many of his predecessors. Gregory of Nyssa and John Chrysostom, for example, held that the differentiation of the sexes was a result of the Fall of humanity. Prior to the Fall, the human race would have been propagated by a spiritual union between unsexed human beings. Early in his career, Augustine toyed with adopting this view; his considered opinion, however, is quite different and more biblical. Following Genesis, Augustine saw that sexual differentiation existed at the creation; the human race, from its very inception, would have to have been procreated by sexual intercourse. The sole difference between the prelapsarian and postlapsarian situations is that in the former case lust (*libido*), which is the result of the Fall (*poena peccati*), would not have been involved. Augustine's views on marriage and sex were thought out in a culture in which love was not a primary reason for marriage and in which promiscuity was rampant. Judged against his own background, Augustine presents a quite balanced view on marriage and sex.

For some time prior to the life of Augustine, the Africans had been searching for the "pure" and "unsullied" church which was to be the spotless bride of Christ; for the better part of two centuries the Donatists had thought of themselves as the true church. Some bishops, clergy, and lay people had handed over (*tradere*) the Scriptures to local authorities to be burned. In the view of the Donatists, these *traditores* had "sold out" the church to the secular powers, and the sacraments administered by these clergy were invalid. This doctrine had created a schism within the African church. Augustine held that the efficacy of the sacraments did not depend on the holiness of the minister; sacraments administered by disloyal clergy were true sacraments. For Augustine, the church was always the church of sinners; it was holy in its founder and in prospect, but sinful in its actual members here below. The triumph of Augustine over Donatism was the triumph of the average Christian over the elitist.

The Donatist controversy was important in another regard. Unity within the church was advantageous to the secular authorities; as a result, the Roman powers attempted to unite the church by political means. Eventually the Donatists were designated as heretics and therefore enemies of the state. They were to be disbanded and their properties given to the Catholics. Originally, Augustine opposed the use of secular force for ecclesiastical purposes, believing that it led to insincere conversions. Gradually, however, he came to embrace the use of secular authority for ecclesiastical purposes. In the first place, the Circumcelliones, a fanatical and vicious arm of the Donatists, had caused much physical harm to the Catholics. Augustine thought that these brigands could only be controlled by the secular authority. Second, he came to see that many of the conversions were indeed sincere and that the African church, so long disunited, had begun to become one as a result of this policy. Because of his acceptance of the use of secular power for ecclesiastical purposes, Augustine is viewed by some as the forerunner of the Inquisition eleven hundred years later. Such a comparison minimizes the differences between fifth-century Africa and sixteenth-century Europe, especially with regard to the importance of the church in secular matters.

The better part of the last two decades of Augustine's life was spent confronting the Welsh monk Pelagius (whose real name was Morgan) and his followers. As Christianity became the religion of the empire, conversion became expedient; insincere conversions were frequent. As a reaction to these insincere conversions, Pelagius and his followers taught that people were able to do good merely if they so willed. Virtue was within the grasp of everyone, unaided by grace. Pelagius even used Augustine's *De Libero Arbitrio* (On Free Choice, 388-395) to support his position that humans can do good without the grace of God.

Augustine saw the teachings of Pelagius as endangering the Pauline doctrine of salvation through grace. Salvation is a freely given gift of God, unable to be merited by humans. People can only do good—can only begin to do good—by the grace of God. During this controversy, Augustine developed a sophisticated doctrine of Original Sin. In various parts of the Old and New Testaments, especially the Epistles of Paul, a person is represented as being in a state of alienation from God prior to any act he or she commits. Augustine asserted that humanity was estranged from God in the first sin of Adam. The *peccatum originale* was passed on from Adam to the human race through the act of intercourse; Original Sin demanded the biological unity of the human race. The result of Original Sin was the concupiscence of the flesh (*concupiscentia carnis*), by which all people are prone to evil prior to any personal act which they might commit.

It is not without justification that Augustine has been named the "Doctor of Grace." He sees three distinct ages for humanity: before the law (*ante legem*), under the law (*sub lege*), and under grace (*sub gratia*). While people of every age were saved through the grace of God, in the last period humanity receives salvation solely through grace. The word *gratia* (grace) derives from *gratis* (freely given). No demand can be placed on the grace of God; otherwise, it would not be grace. Grace is mentioned in Augustine's earlier works, and he goes to great lengths in the *Retractationes* to show the essential harmony between his earlier and later works in this regard, but the doctrine of grace was largely developed during the Pelagian controversy. Paul's comment in the Epistle to the Romans that "God will have mercy on whom He will have mercy" was decisive in Augustine's thinking.

The doctrine of the necessity of grace for salvation led Augustine almost inexorably to extreme views on predestination. Humanity is a *massa damnata* (damned mass) of clay. God makes some vessels to display his mercy, others to display his justice. Passages where Paul apparently speaks of the universality of the offer of salvation are explained by Augustine only with the greatest difficulty. Augustine's views are distinctly different from the later views of John Calvin: Augustine nowhere speaks of predestination to sin, nor does he think that material success in this life is a sign of God's favor in the next. God's salvific plan remained mysterious to Augustine.

Late in his life, Augustine reviewed the entire corpus of his writings in the *Retractationes*, correcting them especially in the light of the Pelagian controversy. There he says that the best way to read his writings is in chronological order; modern scholarship has followed him in this matter. Three of his writings stand out above the rest as works of universal genius: the *Confessiones*, the *De Trinitate* (On the Trinity, 399-418), and the *De Civitate Dei*.

Alone among the works of antiquity, the *Confessiones* gives precise details of the author's life. Nevertheless, it is much more than an autobiography. Written around 400, the *Confessiones* uses the author's life to illustrate a universal theory of humanity. Augustine sees all people as falling from and returning to God; all humans are prodigals, in need of faith to be saved by grace. The denouement of the *Confessiones* comes in book 8 with his conversion to Christianity. Throughout the work Augustine's conviction remains: "Late have I loved thee, O Beauty ever ancient ever new, late have I loved thee" (*Sero to amaui, pulchritudo tam antiqua tam noua, sero te amaui*). The *Confessiones*, however, does much more than propound a thesis. So delicate is Augustine's use of the introspective method that he anticipates, and even goes far beyond, modern analyses of grief, bereavement, friendship, childhood, and teaching.

The *Confessiones* can be read as a literary masterpiece, as a work of profound psychological insight, as a philosophical treatise, and as a work of theological genius. Always the rhetor, Augustine intertwines classical turns of phrase with biblical expressions and Neoplatonic thought with scriptural insights to form a unique synthesis. The work consists of a confession of past sins and God's mercies (books 1 through 9), a confession of Augustine's present state of mind (book 10), and a confession of faith (books 11 through 13). Whether Augustine unifies these strands into one work or whether this complex notion of confession was present in Augustine's intentions from its inception is a question that has vexed the best scholars, both ancient and modern. Surely the *Confessiones* has endured for almost sixteen hundred years because it has captured the human search and struggle for happiness and rest. "You have made us for yourself, O Lord, and our heart is restless until it rests in You" (*Fecisti nos, Domine, ad te et irrequietum est cor nostrum donec requiescat in te*).

Begun about the same time as the *Confessiones* and concluded some twenty years later, the *De Trinitate* contains Augustine's final speculations on the nature of human knowledge of God in this life. From his reading of Plotinus and Porphyry, the young Augustine believed that humanity could attain the final vision of God in this life. His more perceptive reading of the Epistles of Paul in 394-395 caused him to abandon this project. Yet the possibility of human knowledge of God in this life still intrigued him. His final answer to this question, like a good student of Paul, was: Yes, we can know God in this life, but *per speculum et in aenigmate* (through a mirror darkly).

The *De Trinitate* is divided into two parts. The first seven books treat the unity of God through the Scriptures; his exegesis of Exodus 3:14, "*Ego sum qui sum*" (I am That I am), anticipates to some extent the distinction between essence and existence in Thomas Aquinas and is an excellent example of Augustine understanding Greek philosophy through the eyes of the Scriptures. In the final eight books Augustine searched for images of the triune God in creation. In no way is he interested in proving the existence of God; rather, accepting the existence of God on faith, Augustine searches for traces (*vestigia*) of the triune God in this world in order to gain some understanding of the divine nature. From the very beginning, Augustine's thought had been ascensional and triadic, and the *De Trinitate* owes much to these earlier speculations. Augustine rises in a hierarchy of triads from the exterior person to the interior person to the divine. Augustine's insistence on the procession of the Spirit from both the Father and the Son had as an incidental by-product the later Trinitarian controversies between the Eastern and Western churches. It is sometimes alleged that the influence of the *De Trinitate* has led Christian theology to attempt knowledge of God through philosophical means rather than the Scriptures, to place the doctrine of the Trinity logically prior to the doctrine of the Incarnation, and to deemphasize the role of the Incarnation. But from the time of his conversion Augustine saw the essential difference between Platonism and Christianity lying in the possibility of mediation through the Incarnation. The *De Trinitate* is the most pointed example of the Augustinian thesis that there is no distinction between philosophy and theology and that it is the task of philosophy to explain, insofar as possible, the truths accepted by faith.

The *De Civitate Dei* was the most influential Augustinian work throughout the Middle Ages. Written over a period of thirteen years, 412 to 425, the work exemplifies Augustine's lifelong tendency to digress while still tying all strands of his thought together. The occasion of the work was the sack of Rome by the barbarians in 410. The pagans accused the Christians of undermining the empire and blamed the decline of Rome on the adoption of pacifist Christian principles. Marcellinus, the Roman counsel in Carthage and a Christian, asked Augustine to respond to this criticism. Augustine answers that internal decay, not external attack, caused Rome's demise, and that far from causing Rome's collapse, Christianity could have saved the empire. The ancient pagan traditions had procured goods neither of this world nor the next.

Yet the *De Civitate Dei* goes far beyond the mere occasion of the work. Augustine's intention is nothing less than a philosophical-theological interpretation of all of human history: what he theorized concerning his own life in the *Confessiones* he applies to mankind in the *De Civitate Dei.* The moving force behind human history is the free decisions of human beings under the providence and grace of God. History is linear, not cyclical as in the view of many Greeks, including Plato: it started with Creation by God and will end in the Second Coming of Christ. The acceptance of the resurrection of the body places an entirely different perspective on Augustine's view of the world. Unlike the ascetical views expressed in the more Pythagorean sections of Plato's works, and the ascetical and eschatological views of Plotinus and Porphyry, the human body is not something to be fled; it is something to be saved.

In books 1 through 5 Augustine shows that the worship of pagan gods was ineffective for obtaining goods of this world; in books 6 through 10 he shows that such worship could not attain goods of the next life. During the course of this explanation Augustine gives reasons for his opinion that Platonism is the closest of all philosophies to Christianity. Books 11 through 14 deal with the origins, books 15 through 18 with the progress, and books 19 through 22 with the destiny of the City of Man and the City of God. People are divided into two groups, according to the things they love. The City of God is composed of those who love God to the point of having contempt of things in this world; the citizens of the City of Man love things in this world to the point of contempt for God: "Two loves make two cities, namely the love of self up to the contempt of God makes the earthly city; the love of God up to the contempt for self makes the heavenly city. The one glories in itself; the other in the Lord. The one seeks honor from men; for the other, with conscience as its witness, God is its greatest glory. The one raises its head in its own glory; the other says to its God: You are my glory, raising my head. In the one the desire to dominate rules over its leaders or those nations which it subjugates; in the other, the rulers by giving good counsel and the subjects by obeying serve each other in love. The one loves its own strength in its own powers; the other says to its God: *I love you, O Lord, my strength.*" These two cities remain intertwined until the end of time, when they will be separated. It is in the *De Civitate Dei* that Augustine expresses the social doctrine most associated with his name: that people are social by nature but government arises from human sinfulness. The *De Civitate Dei* served as the basis for church-state relations during the Middle Ages.

Augustine's tomb, sculpted in 1362 by Benino da Campione, in the basilica of the church of Saint Peter in Pavia, Italy. Augustine's body was removed from the church of Saint Stephen in Hippo in 710 by Saint Fulgence and sent to Sardinia, where Pope Gregory II ransomed it from the Saracens; he then brought it to Pavia.

In 430 the Vandals laid siege to Hippo. During the siege, on 28 August 430, Augustine died while reciting the penitential Psalms.

Though Augustine has influenced every age since his own, in a sense it was a different Augustine who was important at different times. In the speculations on faith and reason and the ability of the human mind to comprehend the Godhead, it was the Augustine of the *De Trinitate.* In the High Middle Ages, when the relations between church and state were being worked out, it was the Augustine of the *De Civitate Dei* that was influential. During the Reformation and post-Reformation, the works of the Pelagian period on grace as well as the teaching of Christ as the interior master became paramount. During the Renaissance, when the liberal arts again gained ascendancy, it was the Augustine of the *De Doctrina Christiana* who was revered. Today it is the Augustine of the *Confessiones* who reigns. So rich and so diverse was Augustine's writing that, no matter the age or the topic, Augustine's thought has been present. Practically every strain of Christian thought, and many secular ones also, have sought to enlist his aid or have had to counter his opinions. In a real sense, he has defined the mainstream of Western Christian thought.

Letters:

Epistulae, edited by Johann Amerbach (Basel: Amerbach, 1493);

Letters of Saint Augustine, translated by Mary H. Allies (London: Burns & Oates, 1890);

Epistulae, edited by Alois Goldbacher, volumes 34, 44, 57, and 58 of *Corpus Scriptorum Ecclesiasticorum Latinorum* (Prague, Vienna & Leipzig: Tempsky-Tempsky-Freytag, 1895, 1904, n.d., n.d.);

St. Augustine: Select Letters with an English Translation, translated by James Houston Baxter (London: Heinemann, 1930; New York: Putnam's, 1930);

St. Augustine: Letters, 5 volumes, translated by Wilfrid Parsons (New York: Fathers of the Church, 1951-1956);

Epistulae, edited by Johannes Divjak, volume 87 of *Corpus Scriptorum Ecclesiasticorum Latinorum* (Vienna: Hölder-Pichler-Tempsky, 1981).

Biographies:

Gerald Bonner, *St. Augustine of Hippo: Life and Controversies* (London: SCM Press, 1963);

Peter Brown, *Augustine of Hippo: A Biography* (London: Faber & Faber, 1967).

References:

Prosper Alfaric, *L'évolution intellectuelle de saint Augustin: I. Du manicheisme au néoplatonisme* (Paris: Nourry, 1918);

Arthur Hilary Armstrong, *St. Augustine and Christian Platonism* (Villanova, Pa.: Villanova University Press, 1967);

Gustave Bardy, *Saint Augustin, l'homme et l'oeuvre* (Paris: Desclée de Brouwer, 1940);

W. Beierwaltes, *Regio Beatitudinis: Augustine's Concept of Happiness* (Villanova, Pa.: Villanova University Press, 1981);

Gerald Bonner, *Augustine and Modern Research on Pelagianism* (Villanova, Pa.: Villanova University Press, 1970);

Bonner, *God's Decree and Man's Destiny: Studies in the Thought of Augustine of Hippo* (London: Variorum Reprints, 1987);

Vernon J. Bourke, *Augustine's Quest for Wisdom: Life and Philosophy of the Bishop of Hippo* (Milwaukee: Bruce, 1945);

Bourke, *Augustine's View of Reality* (Villanova, Pa.: Villanova University Press, 1964);

Bourke, *Joy in Augustine's Ethics* (Villanova, Pa.: Villanova University Press, 1979);

Charles Boyer, *Christianisme et néo-platonisme dans la formation de saint Augustin* (Rome: Officium libri catholici, 1953);

John Burnaby, *Amor Dei: A Study of the Religion of St. Augustine* (London: Hodder & Stoughton, 1947);

Mary T. Clark, *Augustine, Philosopher of Freedom: A Study in Comparative Philosophy* (New York: Desclée de Brouwer, 1958);

Pierre Courcelle, *Les Confessions de saint Augustin dans la tradition littéraire: Antécédents et postérité* (Paris: Etudes Augustinienne, 1963);

Courcelle, *Recherches sur les Confessions de saint Augustin* (Paris: De Boccard, 1968);

Olivier Du Roy, *L'intelligence de la foi en la Trinité selon saint Augustin: Genese de sa theologie trinitaire jusqu'en 391* (Paris: Etudes Augustiniennes, 1966);

Leo C. Ferrari, *The Conversions of Saint Augustine* (Villanova, Pa.: Villanova University Press, 1984);

Ernest Fortin, *Political Idealism and Christianity in the Thought of St. Augustine* (Villanova, Pa.: Villanova University Press, 1972);

Etienne H. Gilson, *The Christian Philosophy of St. Augustine*, translated by L. E. M. Lynch (New York: Random House, 1960);

H. Hagendahl, *Augustine and the Latin Classics* (Göteborg: Elanders Boktryckeri Aktieboland, 1955);

Ephraem Hendrikx, *Augustins Verhältnis zur Mystik: Eine patristische Untersuchung* (Würzburg: Rita-Verlag, 1936);

Paul Henry, *La vision d'Ostie: Sa place dans la vie et l'oeuvre de St. Augustine* (Paris: Vrin, 1938);

Ragnar Holte, *Béatitude et Sagesse: Saint Augustin et le problem de la fin de l'homme dans la philosophie ancienne* (Paris: Etudes Augustiniennes, 1962);

A.-M. La Bonnardière, *Recherches sur la chronologie augustinienne* (Paris: Etudes Augustiniennes, 1965);

Emilien Lamirande, *Church, State and Toleration: An Intriguing Change of Mind in Augustine* (Villanova, Pa.: Villanova University Press, 1975);

Jean Marie Le Blond, *Les Conversions de Saint Augustin* (Paris: Editions Montaigne, 1950);

O. Lechner, *Idee und Zeit in der Metaphysik Augustins* (Munich: Pustet, 1964);

A. Mandouze, *Saint Augustin: L'Aventure de la raison et de la grâce* (Paris: Etudes Augustiniennes, 1968);

Henri-Irénée Marrou, *St. Augustine and His Influence through the Ages*, translated by Patrick Hepburne-Scott (New York: Harper, 1957; London: Longmans, Green, 1957);

Marrou, *The Resurrection and Saint Augustine's Theology of Human Values* (Villanova, Pa.: Villanova University Press, 1966);

Marrou, *Saint Augustin et la fin de la culture antique* (Paris: De Boccard, 1949);

Robert O'Connell, *Imagination and Metaphysics in St. Augustine* (Milwaukee: Marquette University Press, 1986);

O'Connell, *The Origin of the Soul in St. Augustine's Later Works* (New York: Fordham University Press, 1987);

O'Connell, *St. Augustine's Confessions: The Odyssey of Soul* (Cambridge, Mass.: Belknap Press, 1969);

O'Connell, *St. Augustine's Early Theory of Man, A.D. 386-391* (Cambridge, Mass.: Belknap Press, 1968);

O'Connell, *Saint Augustine's Platonism* (Villanova, Pa.: Villanova University Press, 1984);

Gerald J. P. O'Daly, *Augustine's Philosophy of Mind* (London: Duckworth, 1987);

John Joseph O'Meara, *The Charter of Christendom: The Significance of the City of God* (New York: Macmillan, 1961);

O'Meara, *The Creation of Man in the De Genesi ad Litteram* (Villanova, Pa.: Villanova University Press, 1980);

O'Meara, *Philosophy from Oracles in Augustine* (Paris: Etudes Augustiniennes, 1959);

O'Meara, *Philosophy from Oracles in Eusebius's Praeparatio Evangelica and Augustine's Dialogues at Cassiciacum* (Paris: Etudes Augustiniennes, 1969);

O'Meara, *The Young Augustine: The Growth of Augustine's Mind up to His Conversion* (London: Longmans, Green, 1954);

Eugène Portalié, *A Guide to the Thought of St. Augustine*, translated by Ralph J. Bastian (Chicago: Regnery, 1908);

Michael Schmaus, *Die psychologische Trinitätslehre des heiligen Augustinus* (Münster: Aschendorff, 1927);

Eugène Teselle, *Augustine the Theologian* (London: Burns & Oates, 1970);

Teselle, *Augustine's Strategy as an Apologist* (Villanova, Pa.: Villanova University Press, 1974); & Oates, 1970);

Maurice Testard, *Saint Augustin et Cicéron* (Paris: Etudes Augustiniennes, 1958);

Frederick van der Meer, *Augustine the Bishop*, translated by B. Battershaw and G. Lamb (New York: Sheed & Ward, 1961);

Frederick Van Fleteren and J. Schnaubelt, *Augustine: The Second Founder of the Faith* (New York: Lang, 1990);

Melchior Verheijen, *Eloquentia Pedisequa, observations sur la style des "Confessions" de saint Augustin* (Nijmegen: Dekker & van de Vegt, 1949);

Verheijen, *La règle de saint Augustin* (Paris: Etudes Augustiniennes, 1967);

Verheijen, *St. Augustine's Monasticism in the Light of Acts. 4:32-35* (Villanova, Pa.: Villanova University Press, 1979);

Emilie Zum Brunn, *Le dilemme de l'être et du néant chez Saint Augustin: Des premièrs dialogues aux "Confessions"* (Paris: Etudes Augustiniennes, 1969);

Adolar Zumkeller, *Augustine's Ideal of the Religious Life* (New York: Fordham University Press, 1986).

Averroës
(Abu al-Walid Muhammad ibn Ahmad ibn Muhammad ibn Rushd)

(1126 - December 1198)

Deborah L. Black
Pontifical Institute of Mediaeval Studies, Toronto

PRINCIPAL WORKS: *Al-Mukhtasar al-Saghir fi al-Mantiq* (Epitome of the *Organon*, written circa 1159?);

Jami' Kitab al-Sama' al-Tabi'i (Epitome of Aristotle's *Physics*, written circa 1159?);

Jami' Kitab al-Sama' wa-al-'alam (Epitome of Aristotle's *On the Heavens*, written circa 1159?);

Jami' Kitab al-Athar al-'Ulwiyyah (Epitome of Aristotle's *Meteorology*, written circa 1159?);

Jami' Kitab al-Kawn wa-al-Fasad (Epitome of Aristotle's *On Generation and Corruption*, written circa 1159?);

Jami' Kitab al-Nafs (Epitome of Aristotle's *On the Soul*, written circa 1159?, twice revised);

Jami' Kitab Ma Ba'd al-Tabi'ah (Epitome of Aristotle's *Metaphysics*, written circa 1159?);

Kitab al-Kulliyat fi al-Tibb (Generalities of Medicine, written circa 1162-1169);

Bidayah al-Mujtahid (The Beginning for One Striving for Independent Interpretation, written circa 1167-1168, completed 1188);

Talkhis Kitab al-Maqulat (Middle Commentary on Aristotle's *Categories*, written circa 1168 or earlier);

Talkhis Kitab al-'Ibarah (Middle Commentary on Aristotle's *On Interpretation*, written circa 1168 or earlier);

Talkhis Kitab al-Qiyas (Middle Commentary on Aristotle's *Prior Analytics*, written circa 1168 or earlier);

Talkhis Kitab al-Jadal (Middle Commentary on Aristotle's *Topics*, written April 1168);

Jami' Kitab al-Hiss wa-al-Mahsus (Epitome of Aristotle's *Parva Naturalia*, written January 1170);

Talkhis Kitab al-Sama' al-Tabi'i (Middle Commentary on Aristotle's *Physics*, written March 1170);

Talkhis Kitab al-Sama' wa-al-'Alam (Middle Commentary on Aristotle's *On the Heavens*, written March 1170);

Statue of Averroës by Venancio Vallmitjana, at the University of Barcelona

Jami' li-Kitab al-Hayawan (Epitome of Aristotle's *On the Parts of Animals* and *On the Generation of Animals*, November 1170);

Talkhis Kitab al-Burhan (Middle Commentary on Aristotle's *Posterior Analytics*, written 1170);

Talkhis Kitab al-Athar al-'Ulwiyya (Middle Commentary on Aristotle's *Meteorology*, written circa 1170-1172?);
Talkhis Kitab al-Nafs (Middle Commentary on Aristotle's *On the Soul*, written circa 1170-1180?);
Talkhis Kitab al-Kawn wa-al-Fasad (Middle Commentary on Aristotle's *On Generation and Corruption*, written 1172);
Talkhis Kitab Ma Ba'd al-Tabi'ah (Middle Commentary on Aristotle's *Metaphysics*, written 1174);
Talkhis Kitab al-Khatabah (Middle Commentary on Aristotle's *Rhetoric*, written February 1175; revised July 1175);
Talkhis Kitab al-Shi'r (Middle Commentary on Aristotle's *Poetics*, written circa 1175);
Talkhis Kitab al-Madkhal (Middle Commentary on Porphyry's *Isagoge*, written circa 1175?);
Talkhis Kitab al-Akhlaq (Middle Commentary on Aristotle's *Nicomachean Ethics*, written 1177);
Maqalah fi Jawhar al-Falak [Latin title: *De Substantia Orbis*] (On the Substance of the Celestial Sphere, written 1178);
Kitab Fasl al-Maqal (Decisive Treatise, written circa 1179);
Kitab al-Kashf 'an Manahij al-Adillah fi Aqa'id al-Millah (Exposition of the Methods of Proof Regarding the Beliefs of Religion, written circa 1179-1180);
Tahafut al-Tahafut (The Incoherence of the *Incoherence* [of Al-Ghazali], written circa 1180);
Sharh al-Burhan li-Aristu (Long Commentary on Aristotle's *Posterior Analytics*, written circa 1180);
Tafsir Kitab al-Sama' al-Tabi'i (Long Commentary on Aristotle's *Physics*, written circa 1186);
Tafsir Kitab al-Sama' wa-al-'Alam (Long Commentary on Aristotle's *On the Heavens*, written circa 1188);
Tafsir Kitab al-Nafs (Long Commentary on Aristotle's *On the Soul*, written circa 1190);
Tafsir Ma Ba'd al-Tabi'ah (Long Commentary on Aristotle's *Metaphysics*, written circa 1190);
Talkhis Kitab al-Siyasah Aflatun (Middle Commentary on Plato's *Republic*, written circa 1195?);

EDITIONS: *Tahafut al-Tahafut*, edited by Maurice Bouyges (Beirut: Imprimerie Catholique, 1930);
Tafsir Ma Ba'd al-Tabi'ah, 4 volumes, edited by Bouyges (Beirut: Imprimerie Catholique, 1938-1952);
Rasa'il Ibn Rushd, anonymous edition (Hyderabad: Matba'at Da'irat al-Ma'arif al-'Uthmaniyya, 1947 [edition of various *Short Commentaries* on physics]);
Talkhis Kitab al-Nafs, edited by Fu'ad Al-Ahwani (Cairo: Maktabat al-Nahdah al-Misriyah, 1950 [an edition of the *Epitome of "On the Soul,"* erroneously titled]);
Averrois Cordubensis Commentarium Magnum in Aristotelis De Anima Libros, edited by F. S. Crawford (Cambridge, Mass.: Mediaeval Academy of America, 1953);
Averroes' Tahafut al-Tahafut (The Incoherence of the Incoherence), 2 volumes, translated by Simon Van Den Bergh (London: Luzac, 1954);
Commentarium medium et Epitome in Aristotelis De Generatione and Corruptione libros (Hebrew), edited by Samuel Kurland (Cambridge, Mass.: Mediaeval Academy of America, 1958);
Talkhis Kitab Ma Ba'd al-Tabi'ah, edited by Uthman Amine (Cairo: Mustafa al-Babi al-Halabi, 1958 [an edition of the *Epitome of the "Metaphysics,"* erroneously titled]);
Kitab Fasl al-Maqal, edited by George F. Hourani (Leiden, Netherlands: Brill, 1959);
Talkhis Kitab al-Khatabah, edited by A. R. Badawi (Cairo: Maktabah al-Nahdah al-Misriyah, 1960);
Talkhis Kitab al-Hiss wa-al-Mahsus, edited by Harry Blumberg (Cambridge, Mass.: Mediaeval Academy of America, 1972 [an edition of the *Epitome of the "Parva Naturalia,"* erroneously titled]);
Talkhis Kitab al-Jadal, edited by M. M. Kassem, C. E. Butterworth, and A. A. Haridi (Cairo: General Egyptian Book Organization, 1979);
Talkhis Kitab al-Maqulat, edited by Kassem, Butterworth, and Haridi (Cairo: General Egyptian Book Organization, 1980);
Talkhis Kitab al-'Ibarah, edited by Kassem, Butterworth, and Haridi (Cairo: General Egyptian Book Organization, 1981);
Talkhis Kitab al-Burhan, edited by Kassem, Butterworth, and Haridi (Cairo: General Egyptian Book Organization, 1982);
Talkhis Mantiq Aristu, 3 volumes, edited by Jirar Jihami (Beirut: Al-Maktabah al-Sharqiyya, 1982 [an edition of the *Middle Commentaries* on Aristotle's logic]);
Epitome in Physicorum libros, edited by J. Puig (Madrid: Instituto Hispano-Arabe de Cultura, 1983);

Sharh al-Burhan li-Aristu wa-Talkhis al-Burhan, edited by Badawi (Kuwait: Al-Majlis al-Watani li-al-Thaqafah wa-al-Funun, 1984);

Talkhis Kitab al-Shi'r, edited by Butterworth and Haridi (Cairo: General Egyptian Book Organization, 1986).

EDITIONS IN ENGLISH: *Philosophy and Theology of Averroes*, translated by Jamil-Ur-Rehman (Baroda, India: Widgery, 1921);

Averroes on Aristotle's "On Generation and Corruption," translated by Samuel Kurland (Cambridge, Mass.: Mediaeval Academy of America, 1958);

Averroes; Epitome of "Parva Naturalia," translated by Harry Blumberg (Cambridge, Mass.: Mediaeval Academy of America, 1961);

Averroes on the Harmony of Religion and Philosophy, translated by George F. Hourani (London: Luzac, 1961);

Averroes' Middle Commentary on Porphyry's "Isagoge" and on Aristotle's "Categoriae," translated by H. A. Davidson (Cambridge, Mass.: Mediaeval Academy of America, 1969);

Averroes on Plato's "Republic," translated by Ralph Lerner (Ithaca, N.Y. & London: Cornell University Press, 1974);

Averroes' Three Short Commentaries on Aristotle's "Topics," "Rhetoric," and "Poetics," edited and translated by Charles E. Butterworth (Albany: State University of New York Press, 1977);

The Epistle on the Possibility of Conjunction with the Active Intellect by Ibn Rushd with the Commentary of Moses Narboni, edited (in Hebrew) and translated by Kalman P. Bland (New York: Jewish Theological Seminary of America, 1982);

Averroes' Middle Commentaries on Aristotle's "Categories" and "On Interpretation," translated by Butterworth (Princeton: Princeton University Press, 1983);

Averroes' Middle Commentary on Aristotle's "Poetics," translated by Butterworth (Princeton: Princeton University Press, 1986);

Averroes' De Substantia Orbis, edited (in Hebrew) and translated by Arthur Hyman (Cambridge, Mass.: Mediaeval Academy of America, 1986);

Ibn Rushd's Metaphysics: A Translation with Introduction of Ibn Rushd's Commentary on Aristotle's Metaphysics, Book Lam, translated by Charles Genequand (Leiden, Netherlands: Brill, 1986);

Averroes' Questions in Physics, translated by Helen Tunik Goldstein (Dordrecht, Boston & London: Kluwer Academic, 1991).

Ibn Rushd, known to the Latin West as Averroës, was the most important of the philosophers who lived and wrote in Islamic Spain during the twelfth century and was virtually the last of the great Muslim Aristotelians. His writings and reputation extend not only to philosophy but include medicine and the Islamic religious sciences of law (*figh*) and dialectical theology (*kalam*). Averroës' reputation is linked largely to his commentaries on and explanations of Aristotle's writings, in virtue of which he was known as "The Commentator" in the Christian West. In his own milieu, also, Averroës extended his defense of Aristotelianism in incisive treatises replying to theological and legal challenges to philosophy, in particular those of al-Ghazali.

Averroës' unique combination of philosophical and religious learning made him well qualified to undertake the defense of Aristotelian philosophy by meeting his opponents on their own terms. Born in Cordova in 1126 to a family of distinguished jurisprudents—his grandfather was chief justice of Cordova—Averroës was ensured the best education in law, theology, philosophy, and medicine. He also had a vast knowledge of Arabic literature, a knowledge that he attempts to exploit in his commentary on Aristotle's *Poetics*.

Apart from the details of his early legal education, not much information is available about Averroës' early career or the order of composition of his early extant writings. Some of his works can be dated from information in the manuscript colophons of his texts, but the vast majority of dates can be established only tentatively by extrapolation from the available information. The basic chronology of Averroës' writings was established by Manuel Alonso in 1947 and has been emended by later scholars. In 1986 Miguel Cruz Hernandez produced an updated chronology incorporating the findings of recent scholarship.

According to Alonso, Averroës wrote several of his short treatises and commentaries as early as the 1150s; other scholars suggest that they were written in the 1160s. Averroës says in his commentary on Aristotle's *On the Heavens* that he was in Marrakech in 1153 making astronomical observations; he also may have been helping in the setting up of schools. It was at Marrakech in 1168-1169 that an event took place that would

Averroës (left) conversing with the third-century philosopher Porphyry, on whose Isagoge *Averroës wrote a commentary. The drawing appears in a fourteenth-century herbal,* De Herbis et Plantis, *by Manfredus (Bibliothèque Nationale, Paris, Ms. lat. 6823, fol. 2V)*

prove the focal point of Averroës' philosophical career.

The event was Averroës' introduction to the caliph Abu Ya'qub Yusuf by his fellow Andalusian philosopher Ibn Tufayl. The caliph praised Averroës' reputation and questioned him about his family and his lineage. Soon, however, the caliph began to ask about Averroës' views on the eternity of the world. Well aware that the debate over eternity and creation was a point of intense controversy between theologians and philosophers, Averroës prudently professed ignorance of such lofty philosophical issues. The caliph sensed Averroës' unease and attempted to allay his fears by engaging Ibn Tufayl in a discussion of the questions. Once Averroës realized that the caliph was sympathetic to the study of philosophy, he began to participate in the discussion and offer his own position. As a result, the caliph rewarded Averroës with money, a robe of honor, a steed, and appointment as a judge in Seville.

A further consequence of the meeting occurred when the caliph complained to Ibn Tufayl of the obscurity of the Arabic versions of Aristotle's writings and asked him to compose a series of commentaries and explanations. Ibn Tufayl declined the offer and suggested that Averroës be charged with the task. Averroës accepted the invitation and thus began his career as "The Commentator." Averroës' commentaries on Aristotle are of three types, each of which seems to mark a distinct period in the chronology of his works. There is the short commentary or paraphrase (*jami'* or *mukhtasar*), the middle commentary (*talkhis*), and the great or long commentary (*tafsir* or *sharh*). The purpose and degree of dependence on the original text varies considerably in the three genres. On a few Aristotelian texts Averroës wrote commentaries of all three types; on many others only short and middle commentaries were composed. Some of the commentaries do not survive in Arabic but are extant in Hebrew and Latin translations. Alonso argues that Averroës' shorter commentaries or paraphrases were composed in the 1150s, before the meeting with the caliph; if Alonso's dating is correct, the caliph's commission would be the occasion for Averroës' composition of his middle and great commentaries. Among Averroës' earliest known writings is a set of short commentaries on the *Organon*, as the logical works of Aristotle are called. This series of commentaries includes discussions of Porphyry's *Isagoge* (Introduction), often used as a school text introducing Aristotle's *Categories*, as well as the *Rhetoric* and *Poetics* of Aristotle, which were grouped with the logical treatises in late Greek and medieval taxonomies. The entire corpus of these short logical writings has survived in Arabic, written in Hebrew characters.

One of the principal characteristics of the genre of the short commentary is relative freedom with the text being commented on; the text serves as an occasion for the commentator to present his own views on the philosophical issues discussed, emphasizing the themes that he considers primary and his view of the importance of the topic for philosophy as a whole. Averroës in his short commentaries does not disagree with or depart from Aristotle—Averroës considered it one of his principal tasks to restore Islamic Aristotelianism to its pure form and to ensure that the Stagirite's true views were correctly represented, without contamination from other influences. The liberties taken with the text in the short commentary allow Averroës to present what he believes to be the most essential aspects of various Aristotelian works, instead of concentrating heavily on particular points and detailed arguments.

In his *Al-Mukhtasar al-Saghir fi al-Mantiq* (Epitome of the *Organon*, circa 1159?) Averroës considers the *Organon* as a single, unified treatment of logic; he does not feel bound to treat its individual books as autonomous treatises. Hence, he rearranges his material rather freely. For example, equivocation, a topic discussed in Aristotle's *Categories*, is considered by Averroës in his epitome of Porphyry's *Isagoge*; material from the *Topics* that Averroës felt was useful in the construction of syllogisms intervenes, for pedagogical reasons, between the discussions of the *Prior* and the *Posterior Analytics*; and the discussion of the *Sophistical Refutations* follows that of the *Posterior Analytics* rather than that of the *Topics*. Averroës also prefers titles evocative of the content and purpose of the various logical arts rather than titles echoing the Arabic names for the Aristotelian treatises and includes some elements of non-Aristotelian logic that had worked their way into the Arabic logical tradition.

Averroës' approach to logic in the texts is heavily influenced by al-Farabi's short treatises on the *Organon*, and, like al-Farabi, Averroës expresses considerable optimism about the state of logical sophistication that had been reached in Greek and Islamic philosophy. According to Averroës, logic in his time was a perfected art, and some parts of it, once useful for supporting theories whose certainty was in question, had become superfluous. In his preface Averroës expresses a similar optimism about most of the arts, especially medicine, declaring them already completed "in this our time."

As was customary in Arabic logical writings, Averroës focuses his consideration of logic on what he believes are the two pillars of human knowledge, conception (*tasawwur*; Latin *formatio*) and assent (*tasdiq*; Latin *verificatio*). Conception refers to the formation of concepts, that is, to "the understanding of a thing through what constitutes its substance." Assent, however, involves some act of judgment about the thing conceived, "the understanding of the thing by which some disposition is predicated of it." Conception is achieved by means of definitions and assent by means of the syllogism. Averroës introduces a further fourfold division of logical concerns, distinguishing arts which prepare one for either of these two acts of the intellect by making known the species and varieties of each, and arts which actually produce an act of conception or assent in the mind.

Averroës considered the *Rhetoric* and *Poetics* to be closely linked to the *Topics* in purpose and subject matter, but he classifies these works among the nonnecessary arts, that is, arts which the perfection of logic has rendered superfluous. In his actual treatment of rhetoric and poetics, however, Averroës' comments are somewhat modified. Rhetoric and poetics may not be useful for attaining demonstrative proof, but they contribute to the production of assent in people who are not capable of the rigors of demonstration. Rhetoric and poetics, like dialectic (the subject of the *Topics*), produce assent that is less than demonstratively certain. Dialectic produces supposition or opinion that is near to certainty and usually contains an element of falsehood. It is useful primarily for training in argumentation. Rhetoric produces persuasion, which is defined as a "probable supposition" that is assented to despite awareness that the opinion may be false. Its purpose is to produce assent on a popular level, particularly regarding ethical matters. Poetics aims at evoking an image of something through rhythmic, imitative discourse. While this assent is not an intellectual one and hence is "external to the primary human perfection," it is "highly useful" because it can move the multitude toward a desirable goal or away from an undesirable one. Thus, Averroës sees these three logical arts primarily as political tools, useful for persuading and moving popular audiences but extraneous to the main goals of logic, which he associates with the demonstrative science taught in Aristotle's *Posterior Analytics*.

Averroës also wrote, early in his career, epitomes on all of Aristotle's physical treatises, as well as an epitome of the *Metaphysics*. In these treatises Averroës begins to take issue with his predecessors al-Farabi and Avicenna, charging them with misconstruing Aristotelian philosophy. (Averroës is said to have written a series of polemical treatises against these two philosophers, but they have not survived.) In physics, for example, he challenges Avicenna's interpretation of the notion of corporeal form, a modification of Aristotle's teaching on the nature of prime matter. Corporeal form was posited to account for the elemental qualities common to all material beings; these qualities could not be accounted for through prime matter itself, which was for Aristotle simply the potential for substantial change in all material things. Both Avicenna and Averroës linked corporeal form to the tridimensionality of material beings. But whereas Avicenna held corporeal form to be other than three-dimensionality itself, Averroës identified corporeal form with the body's three-dimensional extension. Moreover, whereas Avicenna had held that metaphysics has the task of proving the existence of matter as a first principle of physics, Averroës claims that the existence of matter is self-evident and requires no proof from a higher science.

Averroës' *Jami' Kitab al-Nafs* (Epitome of Aristotle's *On the Soul*, circa 1159?), along with the roughly contemporary *Epistle on the Possibility of Conjunction*, is the first work in a series of texts which shows Averroës struggling to discover the correct interpretation of Aristotle's teachings on the nature of the human intellect. The epitome of *On the Soul* subscribes to the view, partly inspired by Alexander of Aphrodisias but attributed by Averroës to Ibn Bajja, that the material or potential intellect is a corruptible disposition of the particular images or forms of sensible objects retained in the imaginative faculty. Later Averroës added a note repudiating this teaching; but he justified leaving the text as it was, since it had already been widely read in its original form. Later still, Averroës removed the appended note and inserted a passage that brings the early work in line with his mature views, as expressed in his *Tafsir Kitab al-Nafs* (Long Commentary on Aristotle's *On the Soul*, circa 1190). This revised view is that the material intellect is an eternal substance, for which the imaginative forms are only a subject of truth and source of the content of thought.

Averroës also later revokes some of the views he expresses in his epitome of the *Metaphysics*; for this reason some have considered it to be a spurious work. Still, some elements of Averroës' metaphysical views do remain constant, in particular his critique of Avicenna's claim that metaphysics, rather than physics, demonstrates the existence of God. In the epitome, however, Averroës apparently accepts the Neoplatonic emanative cosmology adhered to by Avicenna and al-Farabi. According to this theory, the universe is a series of emanations, or processions, from God: God thinks his own essence, thereby emanating a single effect, the first Intellect. In this way God's unity is preserved in accordance with the maxim, "From the One only one can proceed." Then the first Intellect contemplates itself and God, producing the souls and spheres of the heavens, as well as further intellects; the tenth intellect, the Agent Intellect, is the immediate cause of the sublunar world. This theory was rejected by Averroës later in his *Tahafut al-Tahafut* (The Incoherence of the *Incoherence*, circa 1180) and in his *Tafsir Ma Ba'd al-Tabi'ah* (Long Commentary on Aristotle's *Metaphysics*, circa 1190), works in which emanation appears to be taken as no more than a metaphor—and an inappropriate one at that.

Averroës' final epitome, devoted to Aristotle's short physical treatises (*Parva Naturalia*), is recorded in manuscript colophons as having been completed in Seville in January 1170. The epitome is Averroës' only commentary on these important treatises, which supplement Aristotle's basic teachings in *On the Soul*. Averroës' epitome comprises discussions of what he says were the only books of the *Parva Naturalia* available in Spain at the time: *On Sense and Sensible Objects*; *On Memory and Recollection*, *On Sleeping and Waking*, and *On Dreams* (all three treated as a single book); and *On Length and Shortness of Life*. Averroës begins with a brief statement of the relationship of these treatises to Aristotle's *On the Soul* and his zoological treatises, identifying their particular concern as that of investigating the faculties of animals insofar as they are besouled: those faculties that belong to the body by virtue of the soul, such as perception and locomotion, and those that belong to the soul by virtue of the body, such as sleep, youth, age, death, life, and disease. The first two books treat the nature of perception and outline Averroës' doctrine of the internal senses. The latter are a set of psychological faculties, posited by medieval philosophers since Avicenna, in an attempt to specify and sharpen Aristotle's account of the imagination. Like his predecessors, Averroës localizes each internal sense in a specific organ or ventricle of the brain. In addition, he outlines a hierarchical scale of abstraction among the internal senses, developing a doctrine espoused by Avicenna. According to Averroës, the internal senses can be ordered according to the degree of abstraction and immateriality by which each of them grasps its proper object; progressing through this scale can be likened to peeling the various rinds or layers from a fruit. The lowest stage of abstraction occurs in the sense object as it exists outside the soul; in the second stage the form is abstracted somewhat and exists in the common sense of the soul; third, and more abstract still, is its existence in the imagination; fourth is its existence in the discriminative faculty; finally, its existence in the memory constitutes the highest degree of abstraction possible on the level of sensation. Averroës here mentions without criticism Avicenna's notion of an estimative faculty, which Averroës prefers to call the discriminative faculty. For Avicenna, it is the faculty whereby nonsensible intentions inhering in sensible things—such as pleasure and pain, good and evil—are grasped; its function is illustrated by the sheep's instinctive fear of the wolf. Later, in his *Tahafut al-Tahafut*, Averroës rebukes Avicenna rather sharply for positing this faculty, claiming that it is a non-Aristotelian innovation which is unnecessary for explaining animal behavior. Averroës' short commentaries on Aristotle's zoological treatises can be dated precisely to November 1169, when he was serving as a judge in Seville: he makes explicit reference to the date and to the difficulty posed by the fact that his library remained in Cordova.

Shortly before completing the short commentaries, Averroës began to turn to writing middle commentaries on Aristotle's works. The middle commentaries are more closely tied to Aristotle's texts, usually following the arguments paragraph by paragraph. Still, the middle commentary presents considerable scope for its author to engage in reflection on the purpose of the text, on the reasons for Aristotle's procedure, and on the best reading of ambiguous passages. But Averroës considers his exegetical works to be first and foremost faithful interpretations of Aristotle's thought, based on careful study of the original texts and free from contamination by non-Aristotelian sources.

It appears from the dates of the middle commentaries that can be fixed precisely that Averroës must have worked on several of them simultaneously during the late 1160s and early to middle 1170s in Cordova and in Seville. Among the earliest are parts of the commentaries on the *Organon*. Like the short commentaries on the *Organon*, the middle commentaries include the *Rhetoric* and *Poetics*, as well as Porphyry's *Isagoge*. In the middle commentaries, however, Averroës expresses doubts about the usefulness of Porphyry's text, and his introduction to the commentary on the *Categories* indicates that his original intention was to omit the *Isagoge* and begin with the *Categories* itself. At the end of the commentary on the *Isagoge* he says that he does not believe that Porphyry's text is of much use for introducing the art of logic; indeed, he doubts whether it can be considered a logical text at all. He assesses its teaching as less than profound, calling it "self-explanatory." But, he says, he had been requested by some friends in Murcia to comment on the book and cast aside his misgivings out of respect for them.

The middle commentary on the *Poetics* has been ridiculed by many literary critics, particularly those working with only the Latin translation. In this text Averroës attempts to apply Aristotle's discussion of poetry, so closely tied to Greek dramatic forms, to the quite different poetry of the Arabs. Averroës substitutes for Aristotle's citations of Homer and the Greek tragedians verses from al-Mutanabbi, Imru' al-Qays, and several other Arabic poets. Well aware of his limited understanding of Greek poetry, Averroës announces his intention to distill the universally applicable rules in the *Poetics*. His interpretation is sometimes hampered by difficulties in the Arabic version of the *Poetics* and by his ignorance of the nature of comedy and tragedy. Averroës' theory of poetry emphasizes its ethical and imaginative aims and became influential among writers in the Latin West.

Several of the middle commentaries have not survived in their Arabic versions; they are available only in Latin or Hebrew translations. The commentary on the *Nicomachean Ethics*, for example, is precious for its relative rarity. The *Nicomachean Ethics* for some reason receives little attention from Arabic commentators; although both Averroës and Ibn Bajja refer to a long commentary by al-Farabi which is now lost, Averroës'

Averroës as depicted in a detail of a fourteenth-century fresco by Taddeo Gaddi, in the Spanish Chapel of the Cloister of Santa Maria Novella, Florence

middle commentary remains the only widely accessible exegesis of this important Aristotelian text.

Closely connected to the commentary on the *Nicomachean Ethics* is a middle commentary on Plato's *Republic*, which survives in Hebrew translation. Aristotle's *Politics* does not seem to have been translated into Arabic, and its place was taken in Islamic philosophy by the *Republic*. Averroës says that the *Nicomachean Ethics* and the *Republic* complement one another and together form the substance of ethical or political philosophy. E. I. J. Rosenthal, an editor and translator into English of Averroës' commentary on the *Republic*, suggests that this text was probably written in the late 1170s, close in time to the middle commentary on the *Nicomachean Ethics*; Alonso, however, considers it to be one of Averroës' last writings from the 1190s. The influence of Plato on Averroës' political thinking is considerable; however pure an Aristotelian Averroës considered himself, his political philosophy is basically Platonic.

In the late 1170s and early 1180s Averroës turned from commenting to defending the pursuit of philosophy against its detractors among theologians and jurists of Islam. Drawing on his meticulous training in theology and canon law and on his practical experience as a judge, Averroës mounted a three-pronged counterattack on the opponents of philosophy in three polemical works.

The *Kitab Fasl al-Maqal* (Decisive Treatise, circa 1179) attempts to answer the serious legal charges leveled against the philosophers by the theologians. Al-Ghazali, in his *Tahafut al-Falasifah* (The Incoherence of the Philosophers, circa 1091-1095), had charged the philosophers with the offense of infidelity (*al-kufr*) on the basis of teachings which he claimed were inimical to Muslim beliefs. Averroës does not address al-Ghazali's charge directly, since his answer was to hinge in part on the claim that such matters should not be publicly discussed lest they threaten the faith of believers. Instead, Averroës attempts to show that the study of philosophy is not prohibited by the Koran and, in fact, is demanded of those who are capable of pursuing it. Philosophy is nothing but the study of all existent beings in relation to their Creator and as signs of him, and many Koranic passages exhort the believer to reflect on God's creation. Moreover, through its use and mastery of demonstrative methods, philosophy constitutes the best response possible to this exhortation, since demonstrative methods alone lead to certain knowledge of the subjects whose study has been enjoined. And if the acquisition of the skills of demonstrative reasoning or of the philosophical understanding of nature should require borrowing from the ancients, who were not Muslims, this is no objection, for even the legal reasoning used by canon lawyers was not the invention of Islam.

But though philosophy may be the best means of following the religious law's command to study nature, not all human beings are equally capable of demonstrative reasoning. For those who do not have the capacity to philosophize, there are other methods available: the dialectical, to be used by the theologians (*mutakallimun*), and the rhetorical, which is suitable for the majority of people. Philosophy and religion cannot conflict, since the truth cannot be at odds with itself. When the conclusions of philosophy and the letter of Scripture appear to conflict, this is a sign that the matter being discussed is beyond the ken of most believers and has been symbolized in images and metaphors to correspond to the abilities of those believers. In such cases, allegorical interpretation will resolve the apparent conflicts. Not everyone should dabble in allegorical interpretations; only those who are capable of attaining demonstrative truth should do so. Were others to engage in allegorical readings, or were such readings to be presented to them, they would likely be left without any beliefs at all, since the philosophical truths symbolized by Scripture are not within the scope of their abilities.

Legally, the decision of what constitutes infidelity is based on the consensus (*al-ijma'*) of Islamic scholars; but there is no consensus as to what scriptural passages pertaining to theoretical matters admit of an allegorical interpretation. Averroës presents a set of guidelines of his own for determining when allegorical interpretation is permitted: where the literal meaning of the text is comprehensible to all classes of people, there is no warrant for allegorizing; but where the meaning is obscure, the learned are permitted to decide if allegory is intended. Since all the teachings of the philosophers that al-Ghazali has criticized represent honest attempts to understand obscure matters or matters not dealt with directly in Scripture, their departure from the letter of Scripture is not open to censure. If errors have occurred in their philosophical interpretations, they have nonetheless acted in good faith, in response to the Koran's injunctions; such pious actions can hardly be grounds for charging infidelity.

While the focus in the *Kitab Fasl al-Maqal* is on legal and methodological issues, it devotes some attention to the specific doctrines in which al-Ghazali charged that the philosophers had committed infidelity: the assertion of the existence of the world from eternity, the denial of God's providential knowledge of particulars, and the denial of the immortality of the individual soul. But it is in the *Kitab al-Kashf 'an Manahij al-Adillah fi Aqa'id al-Millah* (Exposition of the Methods of Proof Regarding the Beliefs of Religion, circa 1179-1180) and the *Tahafut al-Tahafut* that Averroës attempts to deal with substantive issues in some detail. In the former work he attacks the views of the Ash'arite theologians, attempting to show that few of their theories are conclusive or cogent. In the work's five chapters he deals with the existence of God, the unity of God, the divine attributes, the corporeity of God, and divine action.

In the *Tahafut al-Tahafut* Averroës addresses al-Ghazali's doctrinal attacks on the philosophers, taking al-Ghazali's text paragraph by paragraph and responding with counterarguments. Averroës' reply is not, however, a clear-cut defense of al-Farabi and Avicenna against al-Ghazali. In the case of Avicenna in particular, Averroës often joins in al-Ghazali's criticism. He also says that Avicenna's teachings are not to be identified with philosophy itself; indeed, on most of the matters where Avicenna has been criticized by the theologians, Averroës argues that his errors are due to his misunderstanding of, and departure from, the more adequate philosophy of Aristotle.

Al-Ghazali was by no means a facile opponent of philosophy: he had studied the subject thoroughly in order to understand the sources of the philosophers' errors and to distinguish what was useful in philosophy from what was harmful. His approach, moreover, was not simply that of claiming that the philosophers contravened the tenets of Islam; instead, in an effort to meet the philosophers on their own terms, he argued that the conclusions for which they had claimed certitude were inconsistent, contradictory, or at least open to question. The philosophers, in al-Ghazali's view, had overestimated the competence of human reason and had claimed demonstrative certitude in matters in which no such security was possible.

Al-Ghazali's *Tahafut al-Falasifah* and Averroës' reply are both organized around a list of twenty metaphysical and physical propositions which al-Ghazali claims contravene Islamic law. Of these, seventeen are held merely to be innovations that deviate from the mainstream of belief but have not yet been determined to be heretical. Three, however, are cited as instances of infidelity: the world's preeternity, which implies the denial of voluntary creation out of nothing; the denial of divine providence; and the denial of bodily resurrection.

Of the twenty propositions discussed by al-Ghazali, sixteen are drawn from metaphysics. Many of these attack the philosophers' belief in the eternity of the world; others attack their conception of the nature of God and his relation to the created order. In the area of the physical sciences, which in an Aristotelian system includes psychology, al-Ghazali and the philosophers are at odds over propositions regarding the immortality of the soul, the resurrection of the body, and perhaps most well known, the nature of causality.

In the *Tahafut al-Falasifah* al-Ghazali had mounted an attack on the philosophical conception of causality that parallels the skepticism of the eighteenth-century Scottish philosopher David Hume. Al-Ghazali's motive for launching this critique was the desire to preserve God's absolute power over events in the created order so as to allow for the possibility of miracles. Al-Ghazali based his attack on epistemological criteria, arguing that the existence of necessary causal connections is not self-evident but involves inferences beyond what can be immediately observed. When fire and cotton come into contact with one another, we do not see any causal connection between the contact and the subsequent burning; nor is there any contradiction involved if we imagine the contact occurring without burning taking place. The most our observations can support is concomitancy between the so-called cause and effect, not agency or necessitation. The true agent of the burning is God, and our belief in causal connections is the result of a habitual association whose ultimate source is the divine custom of always creating the customary effect simultaneously with its supposed cause.

Replying to this rather devastating attack, Averroës charges al-Ghazali with sophistry, claiming that to deny causality is to deny the possibility of knowledge and ultimately to make all things into an unintelligible and undifferentiated one. Averroës' reply is clearly Aristotelian: to deny the existence of causes is to deny that things have essences that are manifested in the discharge of causal properties and powers: "Denial of cause implies the denial of knowledge, and denial of knowledge implies that neither proof nor definition exist, and that the essential attributions which compose definitions are void." Averroës also offers some explanation as to why someone would be led to doubt the reality of causal connections if the results of such a denial are so drastic: because some causes are not immediately open to observation and legitimately remain in doubt, people such as al-Ghazali fallaciously extend that doubt universally and question the notion of causality itself.

In 1182 Ibn Tufayl retired as court physician to the caliph, and Averroës was recalled to Marrakech to take his place. In 1184 the caliph died and was succeeded by his son, whose support of Averroës continued for about ten years. During this time Averroës returned to explaining the writings of Aristotle, this time in the great or long commentaries.

The method of these commentaries, few of which survive in the original Arabic, is to cite the text paragraph by paragraph and to explain its arguments in detail. Only those Aristotelian texts most central to the Stagirite's views were subjected to this detailed treatment: *Posterior Analytics*, *Physics*, *On the Heavens*, *On the Soul*, and *Metaphysics*. While in most cases the long commentaries supplement and build on interpretations of Aristotle found in their short and middle counterparts, in some instances Averroës' mature views represent a rethinking of basic Aristotelian positions. In the *Tafsir Ma Ba'd al-Tabi'ah* (Long Commentary on Aristotle's *Metaphysics*, circa 1190) Averroës' abandonment of the theory of emanation and his return to the Aristotelian position that God's link to the universe is one of final causality is most significant. It has been suggested that his efforts to address al-Ghazali's devastating critique of emanationism in the *Tahafut al-Falasifah* caused him to recognize the difficulties in the theory.

In a similar way Averroës' long commentary on Aristotle's *On the Soul* modifies the doctrine of intellect found in the earlier commentaries. In this instance, however, the change of position was due not to the pressures of outside criticism but to a lifelong struggle to sort out the host of interpretations of Aristotle's cryptic remarks in book 3, chapters 4 and 5. In the commentary the views of other commentators, such as Alexander of Aphrodisias, Themistius, and Ibn Bajja, are scrutinized and subjected to criticism; Ibn Bajja's view is closest to that of Averroës himself in his earlier period. In his final position Averroës considers the intellect an eternal substance, common to all human beings, which is particularized by the images that provide it with the content of its thought (its "subject of truth," in Averroës' phrase).

Around 1195 Averroës incurred the displeasure of the caliph and was banished to Lucena, a small town near Cordova, along with other philosophers; their books were censored or burned in a general suppression of the study of philosophy. While there are suggestions that Averroës exasperated the caliph by his excessive familiarity, it is more likely that the caliph's actions were more political than personal and were designed to gain the support of powerful theologians and lawyers. Averroës' exile and disgrace were short-lived, and he was soon able to return to Marrakech. But he died in December 1198 at the age of seventy-two, only a short time after his return.

Averroës' influence on Islam was limited, but in Jewish and Christian circles his impact was tremendous. In the West his work spawned several controversies, and his name was associated with a group of philosophers, the Latin Averroists, who strove to defend the autonomy of philosophical study. Averroës' teaching on the unicity of the intellect in particular became a focal point for controversy between church authority and the arts faculties of the Western universities and prompted Albert the Great and Thomas Aquinas to write treatises denouncing the theories of Averroës and his followers. Still, Averroës' commentaries on Aristotle were consulted as a matter of course by philosophers and theologians seeking a careful and appreciative exegesis of the Stagirite's philosophy. In the nineteenth and early twentieth centuries Averroës was sometimes viewed as an unoriginal thinker who was slavishly devoted to Aristotle yet who often unwittingly misrepresented the latter's thought. With increased study of Averroës' works within their own context, a much richer picture of his thought has arisen. While he remains an important and appreciative guide to Aristotle, Averroës' originality, in particular as manifested in his polemical and political treatises, is widely acknowledged.

Bibliography:

Philip W. Rosemann, "Averroes; A Catalogue of Editions and Scholarly Writings from 1821 Onwards," *Bulletin de philosophic médiévale*, 30 (1988): 153-221.

Biography:

Miguel Cruz Hernandez, *Abu-L-Walid Ibn Rushd (Averroes): Vida, Obra, Pensamiento, Influencia* (Cordoba: Caja de Ahorros, 1986).

References:

Michel Allard, "Le rationalisme d'Averroès d'après une étude sur la création," *Bulletin d'Etudes Orientales*, 14 (1952-1954): 7-59;

Manuel Alonso, *Teología de Averroes: Estudios y Documentos* (Madrid: Consejo Superior de Investigaciones Científicas, Instituto "Miguel Asin," Escuelas de Estudios Arabes de Madrid y Granada, 1947);

R. Arnaldez, "La pensée religieuse d'Averroès I: La doctrine de la Création dans le *Tahāfut*," *Studia Islamica*, 7 (1957): 99-114;

Arnaldez, "La pensée religieuse d'Averroès II: La théorie de Dieu dans le *Tahafut*," *Studia Islamica*, 8 (1957): 15-28;

Iysa A. Bello, *The Medieval Islamic Controversy between Philosophy and Orthodoxy: Ijma' and Ta'wil in the Conflict between Al-Ghazali and Ibn Rushd* (Leiden, Netherlands: Brill, 1989);

Charles E. Butterworth, "Averroës: Politics and Opinion," *American Political Science Review*, 66 (September 1972): 894-901;

Butterworth, "Ethics and Classical Islamic Philosophy: A Study of Averroës' *Commentary on Plato's Republic*," in *Ethics in Islam*, edited by R. G. Hovannisan (Malibu, Cal.: Undena, 1985), pp. 17-45;

Butterworth, "New Light on the Political Philosophy of Averroës," in *Essays on Islamic Philosophy and Science*, edited by George F. Hourani (Albany: State University of New York Press, 1975), pp. 118-127;

Herbert A. Davidson, "Averroes on the Material Intellect," *Viator*, 17 (1986): 91-137;

Davidson, "*Averrois Tractatus de Animae Beatitudine*," in *A Straight Path: Studies in Medieval Philosophy and Culture. Essays in Honor of Arthur Hyman*, edited by Ruth Link-Salinger and others (Washington, D.C.: Catholic University of America Press, 1988), pp. 57-73;

Majid Fakhry, *Islamic Occasionalism and its Critique by Averroës and Aquinas* (London: Allen & Unwin, 1958);

Fakhry, "Philosophy and Scripture in the Theology of Averroës," *Mediaeval Studies*, 30 (1968): 78-89;

Léon Gauthier, *Ibn Rochd (Averroès)* (Paris: Presses Universitaires de France, 1948);

Gauthier, *La théorie d'Ibn Rochd (Averroès sur les rapports de la religion et de la philosophie)* (Paris: Leroux, 1909);

George F. Hourani, "Averroes on Good and Evil," *Studia Islamica*, 16 (1962): 13-40;

Arthur Hyman, "Aristotle's 'First Matter' and Avicenna's and Averroes' 'Corporeal Form,' " in *Harry Austyn Wolfson Jubilee Volume* (Jerusalem: American Academy for Jewish Research, 1965), pp. 385-406;

Hyman, "Aristotle's Theory of the Intellect and its Interpretation by Averroes," in *Studies in Aristotle*, edited by Dominic J. O'Meara, Studies in Philosophy and the History of Philosophy, 9 (Washington, D.C.: Catholic University of America Press, 1981), pp. 161-191;

Alfred Ivry, "Averroes and the West: The First Encounter/Nonencounter," in *A Straight Path: Essays in Honor of Arthur Hyman*, edited by Link-Salinger and others (Washington, D.C.: Catholic University of America Press, 1988), pp. 142-158;

Ivry, "Averroes on Causation," in *Studies in Jewish Religious and Intellectual History*, edited by Raphael Loewe and Siegfried Stern (Alabama: University of Alabama Press, 1979), pp. 143-156;

Ivry, "Averroes on Intellection and Conjunction," *Journal of the American Oriental Society*, 86 (1966): 76-85;

Ivry, "Towards a Unified View of Averroes' Philosophy," *Philosophical Forum*, 4 (Fall 1972): 87-113;

Ivry, "The Will of God and the Practical Intellect of Man in Averroes' Philosophy," *Israel Oriental Studies*, 9 (1979): 377-391;

Jean Jolivet, ed., *Multiple Averroès: Actes du Colloque International organisé à l'occasion du 850e anniversaire de la naissance d'Averroès, Paris 20-23 septembre, 1976* (Paris: Belles-Lettres, 1978);

Barry S. Kogan, *Averroes and the Metaphysics of Causation* (Albany: State University of New York Press, 1985);

Kogan, "Averroes and the Theory of Emanation," *Mediaeval Studies*, 43 (1981): 384-404;

Kogan, "Eternity and Origination: Averroes' Discourse on the Manner of the World's Existence," in *Islamic Theology and Philosophy: Essays in Honor of George F. Hourani*, edited by Michael Marmura (Albany: State University of New York Press, 1984), pp. 203-235;

Kogan, "The Philosophers al-Ghazali and Averroës on Necessary Connection and the Problem of the Miraculous," in *Islamic Philosophy and Mysticism*, edited by Parviz Morewedge (Delmar, N.Y.: Caravan Books, 1981), pp. 113-132;

Oliver Leaman, *Averroes and His Philosophy* (Oxford: Oxford University Press, 1988);

Edward H. Madden, "Averroes and the Case of the Fiery Furnace," in *Islamic Philosophy and Mysticism*, edited by Parviz Morewedge (Delmar, N.Y.: Caravan Books, 1981), pp. 133-150;

Muhsin Mahdi, "Averroës on Divine Law and Human Wisdom," in *Ancients and Moderns*, edited by Joseph Cropsey (New York: Basic Books, 1964);

Mahdi, "Remarks on Averroes' *Decisive Treatise*," in *Islamic Theology and Philosophy: Essays in Honor of George F. Hourani*, edited by Michael Marmura (Albany: State University of New York Press, 1984), pp. 188-202;

Ernst Renan, *Averroès et l'Avveroisme: Essai historique*, third edition (Paris: Calman-Levy, 1866; reprinted, New York: Olms, 1986);

Stephen C. Tornay, "Averroes' Doctrine of the Mind," *Philosophical Review*, 52 (March 1943): 270-282;

Dominique Uvvoy, *Ibn Rushd (Averroes)*, translated by Olivia Stewart (London & New York: Routledge, 1991);

Harry Austrin Wolfson, "The Plurality of Immovable Movers in Aristotle and Averroes," *Harvard Studies in Classical Philology*, 63 (1958): 233-253;

Wolfson, "The Twice-Revealed Averroes," *Speculum*, 36 (1961): 373-393;

Beatrice Zedler, "Averroes and Immortality," *New Scholasticism*, 28 (October 1954): 436-453;

Zedler, "Averroes on the Possible Intellect," *Proceedings of the American Catholic Philosophical Association*, 25 (1951): 164-178.

Avicenna
(Abu 'Ali al-Husayn ibn 'Abd-Allah ibn Sina)

(980 - 1037)

Michael E. Marmura
University of Toronto

PRINCIPAL WORKS: *Al Qanun fi al-Tibb* (Canon of Medicine, written between 1012 and 1022);

Al-Shifa' (Healing, written between 1020 and 1027);

Al-Najat (Salvation, written circa 1027);

Daneshnama-yi 'Ala'i (The Book of Science Dedicated to 'Ala' al-Dawla, written circa 1027);

Kitab Al-Isharat wa al-Tanbihat (The Book of Remarks and Directives, written between 1030 and 1034);

Fi Ithbat al-Nubuwwat (On the Proof of Prophecies, date of composition unknown);

Al-Falsafa al-Mashriqiyya (The Eastern Philosophy, date of composition unknown);

Sirat al-Shaykh al-Ra'is (The Life of the Leading Master, date of composition unknown).

EDITIONS: *Al-Qanun fi al-Tibb* (Rome: Medici Press, 1593);

Al-Qanun fi al-Tibb (Cairo: Bulaq, 1877);

Al-Najat, edited by M. S. Kurdi (Cairo: Matba'at al-Sa'ada, 1938);

Risale-ye-Mantiq, edited by Muhammad Mo'in and S. M. Mishkat (Tehran: Anjumani athar-i milli, 1952);

Tabi'iyyat, edited by Mishkat (Tehran: Anjumani athar-i milli, 1952);

Ilahiyyat, edited by Mo'in (Tehran: Anjumani athar-i milli, 1952);

Al-Shifa; al-Mantiq; al-Taba'iyyat; al-Riyadiyyat; Ilahiyyat, 23 volumes, edited by I. Madkour and others (Cairo: Al-Hay'a al-Misriyya al-'Amma li al-Kitab, 1953-1982);

Kitab Al-Isharat wa al-Tanbihat, with the commentary of Nasir al-Din al-Tusi, 3 volumes, edited by S. Dunya (Cairo: Dar al-Ma'arif, 1958);

Kitab Al-Isharat wa al-Tanbihat, with the summary (*Lubab*) of Fakhr al-Din al-Razi, edited by M. Shehaby (Tehran: Publications of the University of Tehran, 1960);

Pakistani stamp commemorating Avicenna

Al-Qanun fi al-Tibb (Baghdad: Matba at al-Muthanna, 1970);

Al-Najat, edited by M. Fakhry (Beirut: Dar al-Afaq al-Jadida, 1985).

CRITICAL EDITIONS: *Kitab Al-Isharat wa al-Tanbihat*, edited by G. Forget (Leiden: Brill, 1892);

Fi Ithbat al-Nubuwwat, edited by Michael E. Marmura (Beirut: Da al-Nahar, 1968);

Al-Najat, edited by M. T. Daneshpazuh (Tehran: Intisharat-i Daneshgah-i Tihran, 1985).

EDITIONS IN ENGLISH: *A Compendium on the Soul by Abû-'Aly al-Husayn ibn 'Abdallah ibn Sînâ*, translated by Edward Abbott Van Dyck (Verona: Paderno, 1906);

Avicennae De congelatione et conglutinatione lapidum, Being Sections of the Kitâb al-Shifâ': The Latin and Arabic Texts with an English Translation of the Latter and with Critical Notes, edited and translated by E. J. Holmyard and D. C. Mandeville (Paris: Geuthner, 1927);

A Treatise on the Canon of Medicine of Avicenna, Incorporating a Translation of the First Book, translated by O. Cameron Gruner (London: Luzac, 1930);

"A Treatise on Love by Ibn Sina," translated by Emil L. Fackenheim, *Medieval Studies*, 7 (1945): 208-228;

Avicenna on Theology, translated by Arthur J. Arberry (London: Murray, 1951);

Avicenna's Psychology: An English Translation of Kitab al-Najat, Book II, Chapter VI with Historico-philosophical Notes and Textual Improvements on the Cairo Edition, translated by Fazlur Rahman (London: Oxford University Press, 1952);

"Avicenna: *Healing: Metaphysics X*," and "Avicenna: *On the Proof of Prophecies and the Interpretation of the Prophets' Symbols and Metaphors*," translated by Michael E. Marmura, in *Medieval Political Philosophy: A Sourcebook*, edited by Ralph Lerner and Muhsin Mahdi (New York: Free Press of Glencoe, 1963), pp. 98-121;

Arabic Phonetics: Ibn Sina's Risalah on the Points of Articulation of the Speech Sounds, translated by Khalil I. Semaan (Lahore: Ashraf, 1963);

Avicenna's Poem on Medicine, translated by Haven C. Krueger (Springfield, Ill.: Thomas, 1963);

The General Principles of Avicenna's Canon of Medicine, edited and translated by Mazhar H. Shah (Karachi: Naveed Clinic, 1966);

"Ibn Sina's 'Essay on the Secret of Destiny,'" translated by George F. Hourani, *Bulletin of the School of Oriental and African Studies*, 29 (1966): 25-48;

Avicenna's Treatise on Logic: Part One of the Danesh-Name Alai, translated by Farhang Zabeeh (The Hague: Nijhoff, 1971);

The Metaphysics of Avicenna (Ibn Sina): A Critical Translation-Commentary and Analysis of the Fundamental Arguments in Avicenna's Metaphysics in the Danish Nama-i 'Ala'i (the Book of Scientific Knowledge), translated by Parviz Morewedge (New York: Columbia University Press, 1973; London: Routledge & Kegan Paul, 1973);

The Propositional Logic of Avicenna: A Translation from al-Shifa': al-Qiyas, translated by Nabil Shehaby (Boston & Dordrecht: Reidel, 1973);

The Life of Ibn Sina, edited and translated by William E. Gohlman (Albany: State University of New York Press, 1974);

"Avicenna's Chapter, 'On the Relative,' in the *Metaphysics* of the *Shifa*," translated by Marmura, in *Essays on Islamic Philosophy and Science*, edited by Hourani (Albany: State University of New York Press, 1975), pp. 83-99;

"Avicenna's Chapter on Universals in the *Isagoge* of his *Shifa*," translated by Marmura, in *Islam: Past Influence and Present Challenge*, edited by Alford T. Welch and Pierre Cachica (Edinburgh: Edinburgh University Press, 1979), pp. 34-56;

"Avicenna on the Division of the Sciences in the *Isagoge* of the *Shifa*," translated by Marmura, *Journal of the History of Arabic Science*, 4 (1980): 1241-1251;

"Avicenna on Causal Priority," translated by Marmura, in *Islamic Philosophy and Mysticism*, edited by Morewedge (Delmar, N.Y.: Caravan Books, 1981), pp. 65-83;

Remarks and Admonitions, translated by S. Inati (Toronto: Pontifical Institute of Mediaeval Studies, 1984);

"Avicenna on Primary Concepts," translated by Marmura, in *Logos Islamikos: Studia Islamica in Honorem Georgii Michaelis Wickens*, edited by Roger M. Savory and Dioisius A. Agius (Toronto: Pontifical Institute of Mediaeval Studies, 1984), pp. 219-239;

"Autobiography," translated by Dimitri Gutas, in *Avicenna and the Aristotelian Tradition*, edited by Gutas (Leiden: Brill, 1988), pp. 23-30.

Abu 'Ali al-Husayn ibn 'Abd-Allah ibn Sina, known in the West as Avicenna, was born in Bukhara, Persia, in 980. His father had come from Balkh to Bukhara to administer some royal estates. Bukhara was the tenth-century capital of the Samanids, a Persian dynasty theoretically acting on behalf of the Abbasid caliphate but actually quite independent of it. The Samanid rulers were noted for their patronage of the sciences and the arts. Avicenna's father was a member of the heterodox Ismaili sect, whose theology and religious philosophies embodied Neoplatonic ideas. As a boy Avicenna listened to his father and brother discuss the Ismaili doctrine of the mind and the soul. "I would listen to what they were saying and understand it," he writes, "but my soul would not accept it." His statement is significant not only because it seems to dissociate him from Ismailism but also because it indicates that he was exposed at an early age to some form of philosophical thought, however elementary.

His formal education, however, began in a traditional Islamic manner with the study of the Koran (which he completed at the age of ten), Arabic belles lettres, and Islamic law; his father also sent him to a greengrocer who taught him arithmetic. The transition toward a formal study of Greek philosophy began when al-Natili, who claimed to be a philosopher, came to Bukhara. Avicenna's father employed al-Natili as a tutor to his precocious son. Al-Natili introduced Avicenna to the rudiments of logic, geometry, and astronomy. The pupil did not have great regard for the abilities of his teacher, who at any rate soon left Bukhara. Throughout his autobiography Avicenna unabashedly extols his own intellectual powers, indicating that he was largely self-taught. But while there is certainly no false modesty in his autobiographical sketch, there are indications in it, supported by his statements elsewhere, that the stress on his self-education and his own intellectual prowess is also intended to illustrate a central point in his epistemology: the role played in the acquisition of knowledge by intuition, that is, the grasping of a syllogistic middle term without instruction.

After the departure of al-Natili, Avicenna devoted some time to the study of medicine, which, he says, "is not among the difficult sciences. . . . Hence, I excelled in it in the shortest of times so that the outstanding physicians began to read medicine under my instruction." He practiced medicine, discovering methods of treatment derived from experience. "Throughout all this," he continues, "I was busy with law, engaging myself in legal disputation, being at the time sixteen years old."

He then returned to logic and philosophy, devoting a year and a half to their intensive study. "During this period," he writes, "I did not sleep one night in its entirety, nor did I preoccupy myself by day with anything else. . . . When puzzled by a problem, being unable to grasp the middle term of a syllogism, I would frequent the mosque, pray and beseech the Creator of All to disclose what is closed and render the difficult easy." He mastered the logical, natural, and mathematical sciences; "divine science"—metaphysics—however, posed a major difficulty for him. "I read [Aristotle's] *Metaphysics*, but did not understand its content and the objective of its author became confused for me so that I repeated its reading forty times and it became memorized for me." With all that, "I neither understood it, nor what is intended by it, despaired of my self, saying, 'there is no way of understanding this book.' " A bookseller persuaded Avicenna to buy a volume that turned out to be *Fi aghrad Kitab al-Huruf* (The Aims of Aristotle's *Metaphysics*, circa 900), by the great medieval Islamic philosopher al-Farabi. The reading of this book, Avicenna says, rendered the objective of the *Metaphysics* clear to him.

An important episode in his education occurred when he was summoned to the Samanid court to join other physicians attending on the ruler, Nuh Ibn Mansur. As court physician Avicenna was given permission to use the well-stocked Samanid library, which gave him access to works in diverse sciences he had not known. He immersed himself in these works, and at the age of eighteen, he says, he completed the study of the various branches of knowledge. Thereafter, he says, he added little to his stock of knowledge, but his understanding of what he had learned deepened.

In 999 Avicenna's father died. After undertaking some administrative duties for the Samanids, whose realm was disintegrating, he left Bukhara and traveled to one princedom after another, serving various rulers. He says nothing about the reasons for these moves. He spent some time at Rayy, which was a center of learning and the abode of 'Abd al-Jabbar, an important representative of the Mu'tazilite, the rationalist school of Islamic theology. Whether or not Avicenna had any personal contact with Mu'tazilite theologians is not known. But his writings embody persistent criticisms of Islamic theology, usually in its Mu'tazilite form. Thus he criticizes both Greek and Islamic atomism, defending Aristotle's views of the potentially infinite divisibility of matter, the doctrine of creation ex nihilo espoused by Islamic theologians, the Mu'tazilite theory that nonexistence is a "something," and their doctrine that the rightness or wrongness of the moral act is intrinsic to it and can be directly apprehended by reason.

Between 1015 and 1022 he was in the city of Hamadan, serving its ruler Shams al-Dawla, as vizier and physician. Internal political turmoil at one point forced him into hiding and resulted in

Illustration in a sixteenth-century manuscript of Mansur's Anatomy *depicting Avicenna lecturing on anatomy (from* The Legacy of Islam, *edited by Sir Thomas Arnold and Alfred Guillaume, 1945)*

a subsequent four-month imprisonment. He left Hamadan disguised as an Islamic mystic, or Sufi, and went to Esfahan; he served its ruler, 'Ala' al-Dawla, and was encouraged to pursue his scientific—including astronomical—and philosophical investigations. In 1030 troops from Ghazna invaded Esfahan and looted his library. He died of colic in 1037 while accompanying his patron on a military expedition against the city of Hamadan, where he was buried.

Despite his duties as physician and administrator, Avicenna's written output was enormous. Some of his works were written in Persian, of which the most important is the *Daneshnama-yi 'Ala'i* (The Book of Science Dedicated to 'Ala' al-Dawla, circa 1027). The main body of his writings, however, is in Arabic. It includes his major medical work, *Al-Qanun fi al-Tibb* (Canon of Medicine, between 1012 and 1022); his philosophical magnum opus, the voluminous *Al-Shifa'* (Healing, between 1020 and 1027); *Al-Najat* (Salvation, circa 1027), largely a condensation of the latter; and *Kitab Al-Isharat wa al-Tanbihat* (The Book of Remarks and Directives, between 1030 and 1034), which sums up his philosophy and gives expression to his mystical thought. In addition to scientific and philosophical works, many in the form of short treatises, he wrote symbolic mystical narratives and Arabic verse. His verse includes a didactic poem on medicine that was influential in both the Islamic world and the medieval Latin West and a moving philosophical ode on the soul.

Avicenna was heir to the tradition of Greek science and philosophy transmitted to the medieval Islamic world mainly by Syriac-speaking Christian scholars. "There is nothing reliable in the books of the ancients," he writes, introducing his *Shifa'*, "but [what] we've included in this book. If something is not found in a place where it is normally found, it would be found in another place where I judge it more fit to be. I have added to this what I have apprehended with my thought and attained through my reflection, particularly in physics, metaphysics and logic." The ingredients of his philosophy derive in large measure from the "books of the ancients," particularly Aristotle, but Avicenna informs them with his own insights and constructs a worldview that is uniquely his. He is noted, on the one hand, for his hard-headed endeavors to solve problems, to analyze, criticize, to draw distinctions, and, in logic, to experiment. On the other hand, he is also noted for his synthetic approach and his attempt to construct a comprehensive philosophical system. Despite human limitations, true knowledge, he held, is in principle attainable. "The purpose of philosophy," he wrote, echoing his predecessor the philosopher al-Kindi, "is to know the true nature of all things to the extent that man is capable of knowing." Avicenna's philosophical system is detailed and is one of the most comprehensive in the history of philosophy.

Avicenna was also indebted to antecedent Islamic thinkers. Thus, for example, although he was highly critical of al-Razi (Rhazes) as a philosopher—particularly of his theory of creation—he was indebted to al-Razi's medical writings. Avicenna held al-Farabi in great esteem; to an extent, Avicenna's emanative metaphysics can be regarded as an expansion on al-Farabi's Neoplatonic metaphysical scheme. The expansion, however, is quite extensive, and Avicenna effects modifications that render the two systems quite distinct. One area in which al-Farabi's influence on Avicenna remains particularly marked is the latter's political philosophy.

Avicenna's philosophy, however abstract it becomes, remains personal. His discussions can be dry and his statements abstruse, but the personal involvement is reflected in a constant quest after truth, a search for answers, an attempt to resolve difficulties, a striving after comprehensiveness. Referring to his *Al-Falsafa al-Mashriqiyya* (The Eastern Philosophy), most of which is lost, he makes a distinction between his "investigatory" approach and the more "natural," spontaneous approach he sometimes adopts. But the motivating spirit behind both approaches strikes one as being the same.

Avicenna's characteristic Aristotelianism is immediately seen in his distinction between physics, mathematics, and metaphysics. With the objects of knowledge of physics and mathematics there is always some "mixture" with matter and motion, but in different ways. In the case of physics the object of knowledge is always mixed with a specific kind of matter—the human being as the object of knowledge in natural science, for example, cannot be separated from the material body of the family animal. With mathematics the object of knowledge is not mixed with a specific kind of matter. In external reality circles and squares must be of some kind of material, but they are not confined to any one kind. As objects of knowledge they undergo abstraction, whereby mathematicians can consider them dissociated from any specific kind of material. The object of metaphysical knowledge is not mixed with matter. In some cases—for example, God and intellect—it is necessarily immaterial. In other cases it can exist with matter but is considered by the metaphysician only abstractly, in dissociation from matter. Thus, unlike the physicist, who is concerned with the cause of a specific material thing, the metaphysician is concerned with causality as such.

A second criterion for the distinction between these three theoretical sciences is their subject matter. They all have as their subject matter "the existent." In physics the existent is considered in terms of motion and change; in mathematics, in terms of quantification. Metaphysics is concerned with the existent simply "inasmuch as it exists" (*al-maw jud bi ma huwa maw jud*) or with "absolute existence" (*al-maw jud al-mutlaq*). It is also concerned with the relation of the existent as such to the ten Aristotelian categories and to the

Iranian stamp with a depiction of Avicenna by Abu'l-Hasan Sádiqí

concomitants that adhere to it. But more basic is its modality: the impossible cannot exist; hence, the existent, according to Avicenna, must either be possible or necessary. To be possible means that a thing's essence, or quiddity, exhibits no internal contradiction that would prevent its existence and nothing that renders its existence necessary. Hence, considered in itself, the possible is that which can exist or not exist. Avicenna held that with the exception of God, in the case of all existents—whether actual or potential, mental or extramental, transient or (as with the existents in the celestial world) eternal—there is a distinction between their essence and their existence, or as he normally puts it, between their quiddity (*al-mahiyya*) and their existence (*al-anniyya*, literally "thatness"). Essence does not include the idea of existence, either external or mental. Existence, in other words, is not a defining characteristic of essence. Moreover, considered in itself, as essence, it excludes not only the idea of existence but also the concomitants of existence: unity and plurality. Illustrating his point, he says that "horseness" as an essence, considered in itself, "is neither one nor many, exists neither externally nor in the soul"; the whole question of existence and its concomitants does not enter into the consideration of "horseness" simply as "horseness."

The essence as such, or as he sometimes terms it, the natural genus, is neither particular nor universal. If, for example, humanity, considered in itself, is particular, then the particular becomes part of its defining characteristic; in that case, in speaking of "humanity," one would necessarily be speaking of only one individual human being. On the other hand, if universality were a defining characteristic of humanity, one could never predicate it of a particular human being. Hence, humanity considered in itself is ontologically "neutral."

Humanity becomes particularized in the external world through the particular circumstances encountered. It becomes universalized in the mind when something is added to it. What is added to it is universality, or, as Avicenna sometimes refers to it, "the logical genus."

It is universality, or logical genus, that renders the essence predicable of many things of a kind. Combined with universality, the essence becomes the universal. The universal, which he also refers to as the mental genus, exists only in the mind. In itself the essence is not a universal, although it is sometimes referred to as such.

This ontological neutrality of the essence as such is used by Avicenna to resolve the metaphysical problem of the one and the many: how can one and the same essence be "found in many" and not *be* many? When the essence is considered in itself, it is totally dissociated from both particularity and universality. It is thus dissociated from the particular circumstances that relate it to one individual and also from the universality that renders it predicable of many. Thus it would be meaningless to speak of humanity as existing in only one individual or in many; humanity as such is neither one nor many. In the definition of humanity "there is nothing except humanity alone."

In making the distinction Avicenna uses language that can lead one to attribute to him the doctrine that existence is "an accident" predicable of essence, and hence that essence is ontologically "prior" to existence. A careful reading of Avicenna shows that this is not his intention. It is true that he speaks in one place of existence as "occurring" to essence; but this is a manner of speaking, meant to emphasize the distinction between essence and existence. The Arabic *'arad* (accident) derives from the verb *'arada* (to occur; in some contexts, to occur accidentally). Hence, the criticism that Averroës levels at Avicenna, that Avicenna regards existence as an accident, is unjust. For Avicenna existence is prior to essence; it forms no part of the essence considered as such and is certainly not an accident that is predicated of it.

The distinction between essence and existence is the basis of Avicenna's causal theory and of his proof for the existence of God. He subscribes to the four Aristotelian causes—material, formal, efficient, and final. His discussions and analyses of the concept of efficient causality, however, are of particular interest because of his endeavor to justify the notion of necessary causal connection. He offers an epistemological justification which influenced medieval Latin thought on the subject; the metaphysical justification, however, involves the essence-existence distinction more directly. This metaphysical justification is less explicitly stated than the epistemological one.

In the epistemological justification Avicenna argues that the experiencing of constantly conjoined events shows only concomitance, not necessary causal connection. (This point was also stressed, for a different reason, by the occasionalist theologians of Islam, who maintained that God alone, through his voluntary action, is the direct cause of all events.) He then argues that in addition to the observation of such regularities there is a "hidden syllogism" to the effect that if these constantly conjoined events were accidental or coincidental, they would not happen always or for the most part. Whether cogent or not, this argument shows Avicenna's awareness of the problem of basing the idea of necessary causal connection on perception alone. The conclusion he draws is that the relationship between cause and effect is a necessary one. It derives from the specific nature of the cause and the specific nature of the effect; the latter is disposed to receive the action of that cause.

The metaphysical justification is embodied in Avicenna's proof of God's existence, which rests on the distinction between essence and existence. An existent is, in itself, either necessary or only possible, for the impossible cannot be an existent. He then proceeds to demonstrate that if it is necessary in itself, it must be one, simple in essence, and uncaused. In other words, it is God. If the existent is, in itself, only possible, then, if it actually exists, its existence must derive from something external to it; its own essence does not yield its existence. If this something is also only possible—hence something that can exist or not exist, act or not act—then another thing must be sought to explain *its* existence; and if this latter is only possible, yet another, and so on. The cause that necessitates the existence of the possible is an essential cause; for Avicenna, the essential cause coexists with its effect. A series of such coexisting causes cannot be infinite, for they would form an actual infinite; but the actual infinite is impossible. An infinite series of accidental or prepa-

كتاب الفاضل جالينوس في فرق الطب للمتعلمين
نقل أبي زيد حنين بن إسحاق المتطبب

Part of a leaf from an eleventh-century Arabic translation of the works of Galen, with notations in Avicenna's handwriting (Bibliothèque Nationale, Paris)

ratory causes that precede each other in time, however, is possible, for the infinite they form is not an actual, coexisting one. But such causes do not bestow existence. If then, the series of essential causes—a series of existents each, in itself, possible but necessitated by another—cannot be infinite, it must terminate in an existent that, in itself, is necessary. This is God.

Avicenna offers several different versions of this proof. What is most characteristic about it is its a priori character: it is not a proof based on our experience of extramental existence, inferring the existence of God from the world we see and touch. The ideas of "the existent," "the thing," and "the necessary" are primary concepts on a par with the self-evident truths of logic, Avicenna says; their presence in the mind does not require experience of the external world. Thus it is through an analysis of the very concept of "the existent" that we prove God's existence.

Moreover, it is through a consideration of the Necessary Existent that we deduce the existence of the world and its order; here, we infer the effect from the cause. In his *Isharat*, after giving a version of his proof of God's existence, Avicenna writes:

> Reflect on how our proof for the existence and oneness of the First and His being free from attributes did not require reflection on anything except His existence itself and how it did not require any consideration of His creation and acting, even though the latter [provides] evidential proof for Him.
>
> This mode, however, is more reliable and noble, that is, where when we consider the state of existence, we find that existence inasmuch as it is existence bears witness to Him, while He thereafter bears witness to all that comes after Him in existence.

The deduction of the existence of the world from God leads to Avicenna's emanative scheme. The scheme has antecedents in al-Farabi's emanative philosophy. From an initial overflow of God, according to al-Farabi, an intelligence emanates. Its contemplation of God and of itself results in the procession of a series of celestial dyads, consisting of bodies and intelligences. Avicenna's emanative scheme, while similar, is triadic. God, the necessary existent, undergoes an eternal act of self-knowledge that results in the emanation from him of an intellect. This intellect, although eternal and immaterial, derives its existence from God. It is thus, in itself, only possible, but it is nec-

Iranian stamp depicting the mausoleum of Avicenna at Hamadan after reconstruction was completed in 1953

essary through another. It eternally contemplates three sorts of existence, each act of contemplation resulting in the necessary emanation from it of an existent. Contemplating God as the necessary existence, it emanates another intellect. Contemplating itself as a necessitated existent, it emanates a soul. Finally, contemplating itself as an existence that, in itself, is only possible results in the necessary emanation from it of a body, the outermost sphere of the heavens. A similar cognitive process is then undergone by the second intelligence, resulting in the necessary emanation from it of another intelligence, another soul, and the sphere of the fixed stars. This cognitive process is repeated by the successive intelligences, resulting in a series of triads, their bodily components consisting of the planetary spheres and those of the sun and the moon. The last celestial intelligence in the series is the active intellect. From the active intellect our world, the world of generation and corruption, emanates. In these triads the intellects are pure minds and, like God, have only universal knowledge. The particulars in the world of generation and corruption are known to them "in a universal way." In other words, they do not know this or that particular individual but only the universal characteristic shared by all individuals of a kind. The celestial souls, on the other hand, move the spheres through their desire of the intelligence in each triad and have a direct influence on the events in the world of generation and corruption. They know these particulars in their particularity and have knowledge of future terrestrial events.

The human soul is an emanation from the active intellect. It is an immaterial substance that is individuated only when it joins the body. This individuality, however, is retained, so that with the death of the body the human soul survives as an individual. The task of the soul in this life is to control and manage the bodily appetites, ideally through the acquisition of theoretical and practical knowledge. For those incapable of philosophy, control of the body is achievable through obedience of the religious law, which is a representation in images and symbols of philosophical truth. Souls that have been untarnished by the body are rewarded in the hereafter by a life of contemplation of the intelligences and of God. Souls that have been tarnished live in torment, longing on the one hand for their bodies and on the other for the now unattainable contemplation of the intelligences and God.

Avicenna offers several demonstrations to prove the immateriality of the soul. A more dramatic way of establishing this immateriality is his example of the man floating in space. He makes it plain that the example is not meant to "prove" the soul's immateriality in the usual sense of "proof." Rather, it is a means of awakening the soul to a direct knowledge of itself and hence of its immateriality, its absolute distinctness from the body—a knowledge the soul always possesses but of which it is often oblivious.

> We must indicate in this place a manner of establishing the existence of the soul we have by way of alerting and reminding, giving an indication that has a strong impact on someone who has the power of noticing the truth himself, without the need of having to educate him, constantly prod him, and divert him from what causes sophistical errors.
>
> We say: The one among us must imagine himself as though he is created all at once and created complete, but that his sight has been veiled from observing external things, and that he is created falling in the air or the void in a manner where he would not encounter air resistance, requiring him to feel, and that his limbs are separated from each other so that they neither meet nor touch. He must then reflect as to whether he will affirm the existence of his self.
>
> He will not doubt his affirming his existence, but with this he will not affirm any limb from among his organs, no internal organ, whether heart or brain, and no external thing. Rather, he would be affirming [the existence of] his self without affirming for it length, breadth and depth. And if in this state he were able to imagine a hand or some other organ, he would not imagine it as part of his self or a condition for its existence.
>
> You know that what is affirmed is other than what is not affirmed and what is acknowledged is other than what is not acknowledged. Hence the self whose existence he has affirmed has a special characteristic of its being his very self, other than his body and organs that have not been affirmed.
>
> Hence the one who affirms has a means to be alerted to the existence of the soul as something other than the body—indeed, other than body—and to his being directly acquainted (*'arif*) with [this existence] and aware of it. If he is oblivious to this, he would require educative prodding.

This act of imagination and contemplation arouses the individual to a direct experiencing of his self. The individual thus attains knowledge that his self is an immaterial entity not merely through syllogistic arguments but directly. Direct self-awareness, Avicenna maintains, is the most basic form of knowledge. Avicenna does not disparage syllogistic knowledge; the quest in science and philosophy is for such knowledge. Moreover, for Avicenna the very structure of the world is rational and syllogistic. But he distinguishes between the direct experiencing of something and the certain knowledge that is attained indirectly through the demonstrative approach.

Avicenna's epistemology is emanative. Theoretical knowledge involves the reception from the active intellect of two types of intelligibles, primary and secondary. The primary consists of primitive concepts, such as that of "the existent," and of self-evident logical truths. These primary intelligibles are received "directly," in the sense that they are received without the need of any preparatory activities of the soul such as perception, imagination, or cogitation. The secondary intelligibles consist of complex concepts and inferences and normally require these preparatory activities for their acquisition.

Intuition, the ability to arrive at a syllogistic term—usually the middle term—without instruction, is the basis of all philosophical and scientific knowledge. Some individuals at some times must have made inferences by apprehending the middle term of an argument without being taught it. This does not mean that all knowledge is attained by the efforts of a single individual; the acquisition of theoretical knowledge is cooperative and accumulative. Thus, "this person would intuit something, that other would learn what this one has intuited and would intuit something else, and so on."

Prophets are an exception to the rule that knowledge is acquired cooperatively. All human beings (provided they are sane and mature) receive the primary intelligibles. Acquisition of the secondary intelligibles, however, is confined to those who have the ability to undergo abstract thinking. The reception of this knowledge requires the preparatory activities of the soul. Sometimes an inference is made intuitively, not only without instruction but with little preparatory activity. The intuitive powers of individuals vary; some take a long time before they intuit a syllogistic term, some take a shorter period. Moreover, some are capable of grasping more than one middle term at a time. Some individuals may be endowed with such powerful intuitive faculties that their souls flare with intuition. They require neither instruction nor the preparatory activities of the soul to intuit instantaneously all or most of the intelligibles in the active intellect. Thus with one single intuitive act, they grasp the entire logical structure of the world as it proceeds from its source. This intellectual vision belongs to prophets, who receive all knowledge directly from the active intellect. This knowledge, acquired by their rational souls, is translated into particular images as it descends into their imaginative faculties. These images are either particular instances of universal truths or symbols of such truths. The language expressing these particular truths and symbols is the language of revelation. Revelation is given in language that is understood by the philosopher and the nonphilosopher alike.

Al-Farabi expressed this notion by saying that religion is the imitation of philosophy: it is a copy of philosophical truth given in the language of the particular, the symbol and metaphor which can be understood by the nonphilosopher. Avicenna, however, also speaks of another type of prophethood, in which the prophet receives the symbols directly from the celestial souls rather than from the celestial intelligences. In either case, for Avicenna as for al-Farabi, the prophet ought to be a philosopher-king. Avicenna's political philosophy is in the tradition of al-Farabi's, which is essentially Platonic.

The prophet's instantaneous vision of the structure of the whole of reality remains an intellectual vision. In the *Isharat*, however, Avicenna indicates that there is a mode of knowing that is beyond this vision, one that is inexpressible by ordinary rational discourse. Avicenna describes the spiritual journey of the *'arif*, "the knower" or "gnostic," in the language of the Islamic mystics, the Sufis. The first stage in the journey is that of will, where a certain quietude of the soul is required. Demonstrative certainty is conducive to bringing about this stage. After completing several more stages the *'arif* plunges into the "sea of arrival," presumably attaining direct experience of the divine. Beyond this stage there are many other stages. But what happens in these stages and beyond cannot be expressed in language.

Although Avicenna left an autobiographical sketch covering a part of his life that was completed (also sketchily) by his pupil, al-Juzjani, little detailed information about his life is available. From his writings and those of his contemporaries, however, one gets certain impressions of his character. He was undoubtedly a man of enormous energy, combining, paradoxically, a strong mystical bent and a definite sensuality. He was "powerful in all his faculties," al-Juzjani writes, "but the copulative faculty among the concupiscible faculties was his strongest and he occupied himself with it a great deal." This activity, al-Juzjani adds, affected his health. One also gets the impression of a man confident of his intellectual and administrative powers. He had enemies as well as friends, students, and devoted followers. One is left, however, with an impression that he was a solitary figure. His poem on the soul, which gives philosophical expression to the concept of man as a stranger in this terrestrial existence, is not without a touch of personal anguish.

References:

Soheil M. Afnan, *Avicenna: His Life and Works* (London: Allen & Unwin, 1959);

Henry Corbin, *Avicenna and the Visionary Recital*, translated by Willard R. Trask (New York: Pantheon Books, 1960);

Louis Gardet, *Le pensée religieuse d'Avicenne (Ibn Sina)* (Paris: Vrin, 1951);

Dmitri Gutas, *Avicenna and the Aristotelian Tradition* (Leiden: Brill, 1988);

M. Mahdi, ed., "Avicenna," in *Encyclopedia Iranica*, volume 3, fascicle 1 (London & Boston: Routledge & Kegan Paul, 1985), pp. 66-110;

Michael E. Marmura, "Avicenna's Chapter on Universals in the *Isagoge* of his *Shifa'*," in *Islam: Past Influence and Present Challenge*, edited by Alford T. Welch and Pierre Cachia (Edinburgh: Edinburgh University Press, 1979), pp. 34-56;

Marmura, "Avicenna's 'Flying Man' in Context," *Monist*, 69 (July 1986): 383-395;

Marmura, "Some Aspects of Avicenna's Theory of God's Knowledge of Pariticulars," *American Journal of Oriental Studies*, 82, no. 3 (1962): 299-312;

Seyyed H. Nasr, *An Introduction to Islamic Cosmological Doctrines* (Cambridge, Mass.: Belknap Press of Harvard University Press, 1964);

G. M. Wickens, ed., *Avicenna: Scientist and Philosopher; A Millenary Symposium* (London: Luzac, 1952).

Roger Bacon

(circa 1214/1220 - 1292)

Jeremiah Hackett
University of South Carolina

PRINCIPAL WORKS: *Quaestiones supra Undecim Prime Philosophiae Aristotelis* (Questions on the Eleventh Book of Aristotle's *First Philosophy* [i.e., *Metaphysics*, Book 12], written circa 1240-1247);

Quaestiones supra Libros Quatuor Physicorum Aristotelis (Questions on the Four Books of Aristotle's *Physics*, written circa 1240-1247);

Quaestiones Altere supra Libros Prime Philosophiae (Alternate Questions on the *First Philosophy*, written circa 1240-1247);

Quaestiones supra Quatuor Libros Prime Philosophiae (Questions on the Four Books of the *First Philosophy*, written circa 1240-1247);

Quaestiones De Plantis (Questions on [Pseudo-Aristotle's] *On Plants*, written circa 1240-1247);

Quaestiones supra Librum De Causis (Questions on *The Book of Causes*, written circa 1240-1247);

Quaestiones Altere supra Libros Octo Physicorum Aristotelis (Alternate Questions on the Eight Books of Aristotle's *Physics*, written circa 1240-1247);

Liber de Sensu et Sensatu (The Book on Sense and What Is Sensed, written circa 1240-1252);

Summa de Sophismatibus et Distinctionibus (Summary of Sophisms and Distinction, written circa 1240-1252);

Summa Grammatica (Summary of Grammar, written circa 1240-1252);

Summulae Dialectices (Summary of Dialectics, written circa 1240-1252);

Metaphysica Fratris Rogeri (The Metaphysics of Brother Roger, written circa 1266);

Opus Maius (Major Work, written circa 1267);

Opus Minus (Minor Work, written circa 1267);

Opus Tertium (Third Work, written circa 1267);

Epistola Fratris Rogeri de Secretis Operibus Artis et Naturae, et de Nullitate Magiae (Letter of Brother Roger on the Secret Works of Art and Nature, and on the Uselessness of Magic, written circa 1267);

Communia Mathematica (Common Topics in Mathematics, written circa 1267);

Secretum Secretorum cum Glossis et Notulis Fratris Rogeri (The Book of the Secret of Secrets with the Glosses and Notes of Brother Roger, written circa 1267);

De Multiplicatione Specierum (On the Multiplication of Species, written circa 1267-1270);

De Speculis Comburentibus (On Burning Mirrors, written circa 1267);

Communia Naturalium (Common Account of Natural Things, written circa 1267-1270);

De Retardatione Senectutis cum Aliis Opusculis de Rebus Medicinalibus (The Prevention of Old Age, with Other Works on Medical Topics, probably written circa 1267-1292);

Compendium Studii Philosophiae (Summary of the Study of Philosophy, written circa 1292);

Compotus Fratris Rogeri (The Compote of Brother Roger, date of composition unknown).

EDITIONS: *Opus Majus ad Clementem Quartum, Pontificem Romanum*, edited by Samuel Jebb (London: Printed by William Bowyer, 1733);

Fr. Rogeri Bacon Opera Quaedam Hactenus Inedita, edited by John Sherren Brewer (London: Longman, Green, Longman & Roberts, 1859; reprinted, Nendeln, Liechtenstein: Kraus, 1965);

The Opus Majus of Roger Bacon, 3 volumes, edited by John Henry Bridges (Oxford: Clarendon

Illumination from a fifteenth-century manuscript for Roger Bacon's De Retardatione Senectutis, *depicting Bacon seated, deep in thought, in the doorway of his convent (Bodleian Library, Oxford University; MS Bodley 211)*

Press, 1897-1900; reprinted, Frankfurt am Main: Minerva, 1964);

"An Unpublished Fragment of a Work by Roger Bacon," edited by F. A. Gasquet, *English Historical Review*, 12 (July 1897): 494-517;

The Greek Grammar of Roger Bacon and a Fragment of His Hebrew Grammar, edited by Edmund Nolan and S. A. Hirsch (Cambridge: Cambridge University Press, 1902);

Un Fragment inédit de l'Opus tertium de R. Bacon precede d'une etude sur ce Fragment, edited by Pierre Duhem (Quaracchi: Saint Bonaventure College Press, 1909);

Fr. Rogeri Bacon Compendium Studii Theologiae, edited by Hastings Rashdall (Aberdeen: Typis academicis, 1911);

Part of the Opus Tertium of Roger Bacon, Including a Fragment Now Printed for the First Time, edited by Andrew George Little, British Society for Franciscan Studies, volume 4 (Aberdeen: Aberdeen University Press, 1912; reprinted, Farnborough, U.K.: Gregg Press, 1966);

"An Unnoticed Treatise of Roger Bacon on Time and Motion," edited by S. Harrison Thomson, *Isis*, 27 (August 1937): 219-224;

"Le Prologue de R. Bacon à son traité De influentiis agentium," edited by F. M. Delorme, *Antonianum*, 18 (1943): 81-90.

CRITICAL EDITIONS: *Opera Hactenus Inedita Fratris Rogeri Baconis*, 12 volumes, edited by Robert Steele, F. M. Delorme, Andrew George Little, and Edward Theodore Withington (Oxford: Clarendon Press, 1905-1940);

Rogeri Baconis Moralis Philosophia, edited by Delorme and Eugenio Massa (Zurich: Thesaurus Mundi, 1953);

"An Unedited Part of Roger Bacon's 'Opus Maius': 'De Signis,'" edited by K. M. Fredborg, Lauge Nielsen, and Jan Pinborg, *Traditio*, 34 (1978): 75-136.

EDITIONS IN ENGLISH: *The Mirror of Alchimy, Composed by the Thrice-Famous and Learned Fryer, Roger Bachon . . . Also a Most Excellent and Learned Discourse of the Admirable Force and Efficacie of Art and Nature, Written by the Same Author: With Certain Other Worthie Treatises of the Like Argument*, translated anonymously (London: Printed by Thomas Creede for Richard Olive, 1597);

Frier Bacon His Discovery of the Miracles of Art, Nature, and Magick, Faithfully Translated out of Dr. Dee's Own Copy by T. M. and Never Before in English (London: Printed for Simon Miller, 1659);

The Cure of Old Age and Preservation of Youth, translated by Richard Browne (London: Printed for Tho. Flesher & Edward Evets, 1683);

Roger Bacon's Letter Concerning the Marvelous Power of Art and of Nature and Concerning the Nullity of Magic, Together with Notes and an Account of Bacon's Life and Work, translated by Tenney L. Davis (Easton, Pa.: Chemical Publishing Co., 1923);

"On the Errors of Physicians," translated by Edward Theodore Withington, in *Essays on the History of Medicine Presented to Karl Sudhoff*, edited by Charles Singer and Henry E. Sigerist (London; Oxford University Press, 1924), pp. 139-157;

The Opus Maius of Roger Bacon, 2 volumes, translated by Roger Belle Burke (Philadelphia: University of Pennsylvania Press, 1928; London: H. Milford, Oxford University Press, 1928);

"The Mirror of Alchemy of Roger Bacon," translated by Davis, *Journal of Chemical Education*, 8 (October 1931): 1945-1953;

"The Errors of the Doctors according to Friar Roger Bacon of the Minor Order," translated by Mary Catherine Welborn, *Isis*, 18 (July 1932): 26-62;

Roger Bacon's Philosophy of Nature: A Critical Edition, with English Translation, Introduction, and Notes, of De multiplicatione specierum *and* De speculis comburentibus, edited and translated by David C. Lindberg (Oxford: Clarendon Press, 1983);

Compendium of the Study of Theology: Edition and Translation with Introduction and Notes, edited and translated by Thomas S. Maloney, Studien und Texte zur Geistesgeschichte des Mittelalters, volume 20 (Leiden: Brill, 1988);

Three Treatments of Universals by Roger Bacon: A Translation with Introduction and Notes, translated by Maloney (Binghamton, N.Y.: Medieval and Renaissance Texts and Studies, 1989).

Information about the life of Roger Bacon is slim; scholars have invented conflicting chronologies and have assumed a great deal about his career. The commonly accepted view is that set out by Theodore Crowley and developed by David C. Lindberg. It takes Bacon's indirect remarks in the *Opus Tertium* (Third Work, circa 1267) as the basis for a firm setting of the whole chronology: "I have laboured much in sciences and languages, and I have up to now devoted forty years [to them] after I first learned the alphabet; and I was always studious. Apart from two of these forty years I was always [engaged] in study [*in studio*], and I have had many expenses just as others commonly have. Nevertheless, provided I had first composed a compendium, I am certain that I could directly teach a solicitous and confident man whatever I knew of those sciences and languages. And it is known that no one worked in so many sciences or languages as I did, nor so much as I did. Indeed, when I was living in the other state of life [as a scholar], people marvelled at the abundance of my work. And still, I was just as involved in studies afterwards as I had been before. But I did not work all that much, since in the pursuit of wisdom this was not required." In the light of this passage, Crowley and Lindberg believe that Bacon was born about 1220. This date of birth would mean that Bacon may have been a student at Oxford from about 1234 to 1241. Andrew George Little, however, argues that *in studio* means "at a university" and that *alphabet* means his early education; he thus places Bacon's birthdate at 1214. For other reasons, Thomas S. Maloney favors Little's view.

In the passage from the *Opus Tertium* Bacon distinguishes two periods in his life. The first is that of the scholar/academic; the second is that spent "in the pursuit of wisdom" as a Franciscan friar. Scholars are unsure about the date of Bacon's inception as master of arts at the University of Paris. Lindberg believes that it was during the 1240s; Maloney puts the date "in or shortly before 1245." But James A. Weisheipl points out that 1237 was a significant date in Bacon's mind, and that Bacon himself attests that he taught in the arts longer than any other master; Weisheipl makes the not improbable assumption that Bacon began teaching at Paris about 1237, and most scholars assume on the basis of obiter dicta by Bacon that he resigned his position about 1247.

Crowley argues that Bacon studied theology under Adam Marsh at Oxford from about 1247 to 1252. He bases his position on three passages from the *Opus Tertium* which give some evidence of personal discourse between Marsh and Bacon. The passages, however, do not prove that Bacon was a theological student under Marsh between

1247 and 1250, when Marsh was regent in theology at Oxford; and there is no other evidence of a return to Oxford by Bacon in 1247.

On the basis of Bacon's own account, it would appear that sometime around 1247 he ceased to preside at the inception of masters in the arts at the University of Paris. For the next ten years, he devoted his private resources to professional work in the arts. From 1256, when he joined the Franciscan Order, until 1266, Bacon remained "studious, " but he no longer worked professionally in the arts. His great reputation as a teacher and researcher was lost, and his Franciscan superiors ordered him to desist from his favorite pursuits. He complained bitterly about this situation. Most of Bacon's ideas were developed out of his reading of the works of Robert Grosseteste. Bacon's originality would seem to lie in two areas: first, he developed some of the ideas in natural philosophy which he found in Grosseteste; second, he set out to make a major synthesis of the natural science, philosophy, and religious teaching of his time. He was above all important in his transmission of Islamic science into the Latin West. His influence in this respect would be felt into the Renaissance.

In much of his early work, Bacon is quite eclectic. He seems to be attempting a fresh synthesis of traditional Latin with Islamic and Jewish philosophical positions.

The most important book in metaphysics which lies behind Bacon's early interpretation of Aristotle is the Neoplatonic *Liber de Causis* (Book of Causes), also known in the thirteenth century under the title *Liber Aristotelis de Expositione Bonitatis Purae* (Book of Aristotle on the Exposition of the Pure Good). This book, whose true origin was identified by Thomas Aquinas as extracts from the *Elements of Theology* of Proclus, is an epitome of pagan Neoplatonism. The work covers many topics, but especially the Neoplatonic doctrine of causality and participation, the nature of the triads, the plentitude of being, the sovereignty of good, the superessentiality of the first cause, the one and the many, and the nature of intelligence.

Next to the *Liber de Causis*, the most important influence on Bacon's ideas about fundamental metaphysical principles such as matter, form, potency and act, and essence and existence is the *Fons Vitae* (Fountain of Life) by the Jewish philosopher Avicebron (Solomon Ibn Gabirol) in the translation of Dominicus Gundissalinus. Also important are the other works of Gundissalinus, such as the *De Processione Mundi* (The Procession of the World).

For Scholastic philosophers of the early thirteenth century, including Bacon, creatures are seen as coming from the creative activity of the first cause, God. Creatures are essentially composite; divine being is marked by simplicity. Although Bacon argues for a composition of being in creatures, he holds that the distinction between essence and existence is a logical and not a metaphysical one; for Bacon, the fundamental distinction in creatures is that between matter and form. He distinguishes between prime matter and natural matter; the latter possesses a form and is involved in actual generation. Matter is a substratum of all forms; it is not an independent substance. The "separated substances" or angels, like humans, are creatures; therefore, they are contingent. That is, they do not possess being in themselves but receive being from the primary cause; they possess matter in the sense of potency, the principle of contingency. But of course, the separated substances have spiritual matter and not corporeal matter.

Bacon's theory of matter and form provides a foundation for his philosophical psychology (theory of the soul). The human embryo evolves through successive stages until the rational soul is infused into it by God. For Bacon, the preceding forms of the soul—the vegetative and the sensitive—coexist in the final form; the lower forms become principles of operation within the higher form. The final form is the perfection of the intermediate forms. Unlike the intermediate forms, which evolve gradually, the final form is introduced immediately. The unity of the substantial form is one of integration and composition; it is not one of simplicity (the doctrine of Aquinas). Interpreting the traditional doctrine (stoic in origin) of the *rationes seminales* (rational seeds), Bacon holds that the whole substantial form is contained in a seed. Thus, matter can be said to have the potency to develop a form; this potency is rather like "desire" or "appetite." The active principle—the agent or cause—comes from outside; but once the active cause operates, the substantial form is educed from matter. Bacon, however, objected to the view, held by some other philosophers and theologians, that there must be a *forma animalitatis* (form of animality) already complete in the soul before the infusion of the rational soul. In that case, the rational soul would be redundant.

Bacon's account of universals in his early works is that the universal term is predicated of many individual things, but the mental concept is not so predicated; thus, the universal is not a concept. Universals in the strict and primary sense, as the foundation of knowledge, are outside the mind in things. There is no direct intuitive knowledge of the individual; science depends on demonstrative reason, and hence on universals. Still, universal being and individual being cannot be separated.

Bacon's logical works from the 1240s and 1250s, such as the *Summa Grammatica* (Summary of Grammar) and *Summulae Dialectices* (Summary of Dialectics), and *Summa de Sophismatibus et Distinctionibus* (Summary of Sophisms and Distinction), place Bacon in the "terminist" tradition of logical and semantic studies, along with William of Sherwood and Robert Kilwardby. Since, in Bacon's view, the imposition of a term involves the imposition of a meaning, great attention must be given to the context of a term. One cannot assume that there is one definite, unchanging meaning corresponding to each term. Thus, the imposition of meaning is not something which happened in the distant past; in every act of communication, there is a new imposition of meaning. There has to be an intention on the part of the speaker and an agreement on the part of the listener. A clear analysis of language to exhibit the various levels of meaning is a prerequisite of doing philosophy. In some aspects, Bacon's theory foreshadows that of William of Ockham. After joining the Franciscan Order, Bacon was domiciled at the Franciscan *studium* (house of studies) in Paris. At the Council of Narbonne in 1260, strict rules were promulgated to control the spread of ideas of Joachim of Fiore among the spiritual Franciscans. The publication of books was restricted; all works had to be submitted to the provincials for examination.

Bacon was entirely frustrated by his situation in the *studium*. Between 1260 and 1264 he made contact with Cardinal Guy Le Gros Foulques. He appears to have given the cardinal the impression that he had major works in philosophy ready for publication, when in fact he was requesting funds to begin a research project. The cardinal was elected pope in early 1265, taking the name Pope Clement IV. Sometime in 1265 or 1266, Bacon contacted Clement through Sir William Bonecor, the ambassador from King Henry III to the pope. In a letter of June 1266 the pope ordered Bacon to send the work in philosophy which he had already requested and also "to reveal to us your remedies for the critical problems to which you have recently called our attention, and this as quickly and as secretly as possible." What emerged from this injunction by Clement IV was a series of writings by Bacon which was completed between 1267 and 1270: the *Opus Maius* (Greater Work), *Opus Minus* (Minor Work), *Opus Tertium*, *De Multiplicatione Specierum* (On the Multiplication of Species), *De Speculis Comburentibus* (On Burning Mirrors), *Communia Naturalium* (Common Account of Natural Things), and *Secretum Secretorum* (The Book of the Secret of Secrets).

Bacon's appeal to the chief authority in medieval Christendom involved going behind the back of the minister general of his order, Bonaventure. Moreover, Bacon had strong views on astrology and alchemy, topics which Bonaventure condemned in the 1260s and early 1270s. Further, Bacon seems to have had a preference for the apocalyptic ideas associated with Joachim of Fiore, thereby allying himself with radical elements in the Franciscan Order. For all of these reasons he would have been open to severe reprimand and even punishment, and he may have been put under house confinement when the authorities in Paris discovered that he had evaded the normal restrictions on writing.

Bacon's literary output between 1266 and 1292 was great; it would appear that most of it was produced in Paris between 1266 and 1277. It was a mixture of polemic and philosophy, in which the main issue was the rise of Latin Averroism in the arts faculty at the University of Paris in the early 1260s. Bacon saw himself as a Christian philosopher in Grosseteste's mold, one who set out to correct and limit the extreme Averroist Aristotelianism of the leading young men in the arts faculty. Bacon also launched an attack on church lawyers and on some theologians. The burden of this attack, which is found in part 1 of the *Opus Maius*, is that the theologians and lawyers were destroying education by condemning Aristotle and science. They ignored the rhetoric and poetics of Aristotle and the new translations of Aristotle's scientific works which had been received from the Islamic world since 1140. Bacon, therefore, saw himself as arguing for a via media between the Scylla of extreme Averroist Aristotelianism and the Charybdis of fideistic theology.

Following the polemic of part 1 of the *Opus Maius*, Bacon opens part 2 with an account of his theory of truth and wisdom, including his schema of a history of philosophy. He begins by telling the reader that "I wish in this second distinction, to point out that there is one perfect wisdom, from whose roots all truth branches out. I say, therefore, that one science is the mistress of the others, namely, theology, to which the remaining sciences are completely necessary, and without which it is not capable of reaching its fulfillment. Theology claims the strength of these sciences for her own law, to whose nod and rule the other sciences subordinate themselves. Or better, there is one perfect wisdom, which is totally contained in Sacred Scripture, and which ought to be unfolded through Canon Law and Philosophy." Wisdom, therefore, is a doctrine, a way of life, and a way of salvation; philosophy is subordinated to Scripture and, by implication, to theology. Philosophy, therefore, is a preamble to faith. The goal of philosophy is a knowledge of things in this world, leading to a knowledge of God. This goal includes the creation of a just and peaceful society on earth as a foretaste of eternal happiness.

This subordination of philosophy to theology shows that Bacon shared the broad vision of a Christian philosophy as one finds it in the works of Bonaventure. The synthesis of religion and Platonic philosophy had existed from the time of the Church Fathers in the early centuries of Christianity; it also existed in Judaism with Philo Judaeus. The main difference in Bacon is that Aristotle replaces Plato as the main authoritative philosopher; just as the Apostle Paul was the authority in Scripture, Aristotle was the authority in philosophy.

Bacon, like Aquinas, had a sense of the history of doctrine. He displays this sense in setting out a "History of Wisdom," a schema of the history of philosophy taken from the account in Augustine's *De Civitate Dei* (The City of God, 412-426), supplemented with that in Abu Mashar's *Introductorium Maius* (Major Introduction) and Josephus's *Antiquities*.

To show that the disclosure of wisdom given to the world was not the sole possession of any one race, Bacon follows Philo in presenting the view that the ancient Hebrews were granted a revelation not only in religious but also in philosophical and scientific matters. There is a universal wisdom which is required for the common happiness of humanity; God revealed this wisdom to the Hebrew prophets. Subsequent philosophers—Indian, Persian, Greek, and Latin—received from the Hebrews the beginnings of philosophy. Unfortunately, a tradition of antiwisdom developed among both the Greeks and the Hebrews. That tradition of antiwisdom is symbolized by the mythical characters of Prometheus and Nimrod. The latter, like Prometheus, stole the divine fire. Worse, he built the Tower of Babel, with the resulting fragmentation of language. Finally, Nimrod boasted that he was the source of wisdom. For Nimrod, there was no such thing as transcendent truth, a truth which is revealed to the human being. In opposition to Nimrod, Bacon identifies Plato, Aristotle, Seneca, Cicero, al-Farabi, and Avicenna as great philosophers because they refer all things to God as an army is referred to its chief. All things must be referred to a primary principle which is objective.

Philosophy is divided into theoretical and practical. Theoretical philosophy is metaphysics, and it refers all things to God as the one primary principle. Practical (that is, moral) philosophy refers all human actions to one final goal. Still, Bacon is adamant that philosophy is not theology. The latter is based on Scripture, the former on the texts of the great philosophers of the past. They also have different methodologies; only in a very attenuated sense do the principles of philosophy enter into the arguments of theology. The principles of philosophy enter more deeply into the principles of the sciences than they do into the principles of theology.

For Bacon, a knowledge of language is the first prerequisite for any entry into philosophy. Bacon laments what he takes to be a decadent state of language studies in the universities of the West. The language of the Latin West has originated from more fundamental languages, namely, Greek and Hebrew. Further, much scientific language is translated from Arabic, and much of the translating is done badly. In the West, according to Bacon, "Boethius alone, the first translator, had full mastery of the languages, and Master Robert Grosseteste, recently Bishop of Lincoln, was the only one who knew the sciences. Certain other translators like Gerard of Cremona, Michael Scot, Alfred the Englishman, Herman the German, whom we saw in Paris, have failed greatly in both languages and sciences, since the same Herman admitted this about himself and others, and their translations make this obvious." Bacon is mostly negative about the translations of the works of Aristotle, especially of the *Poetics* and the *Rhetoric*. The importance of these works is that they are the part of logic which links up with moral philosophy. The

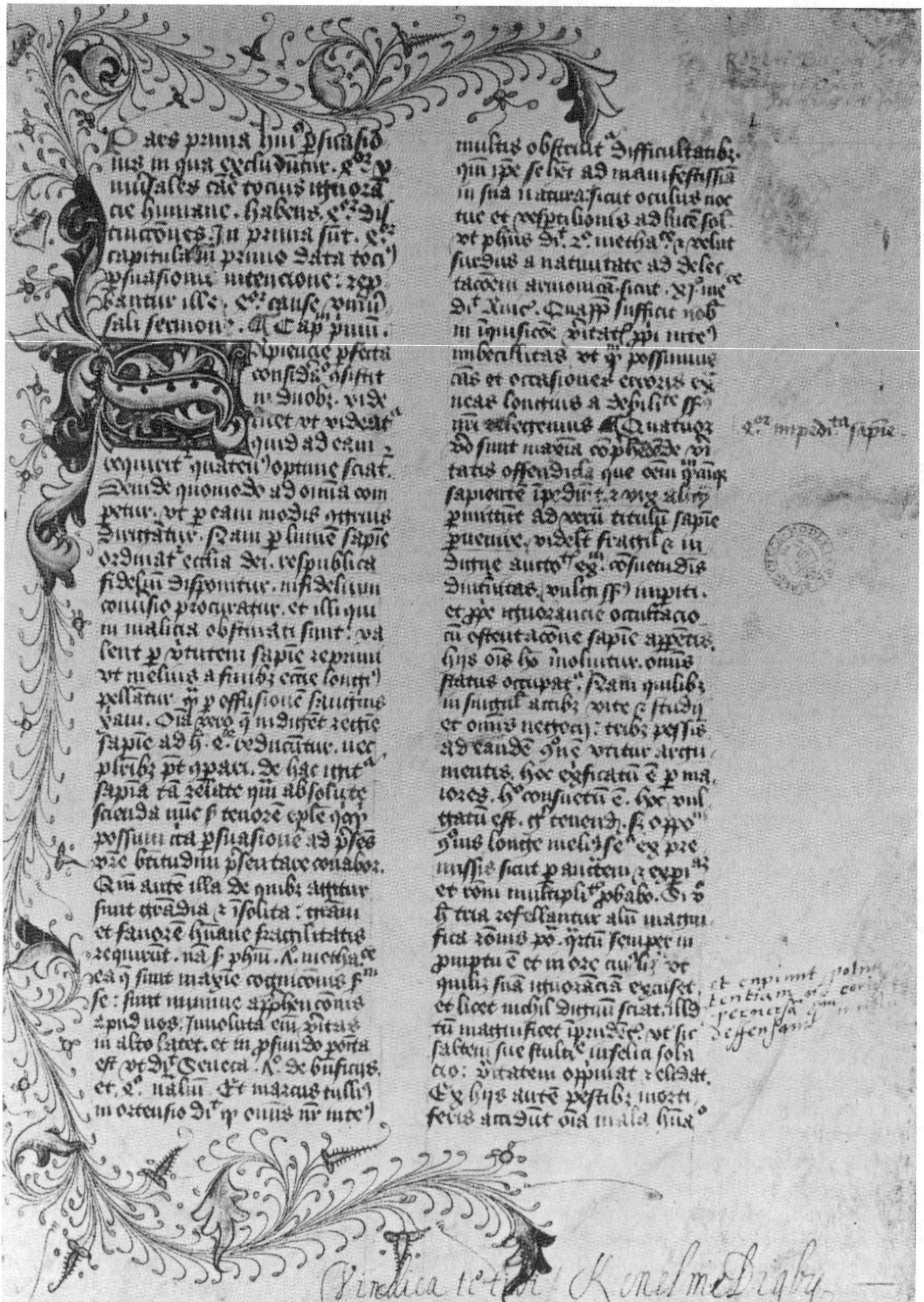

Page from a manuscript, copied circa 1425, for Bacon's Opus Maius *(Bodleian Library, Oxford University; MS. Digby 235)*

most egregious mistake in translation is the terrible state of the Latin Bible; in Bacon's view, the Parisian text is woefully corrupt.

Bacon links up the concern with words to the action of the heavens: the constellations influence human actions. The saints as well as the philosophers, according to Bacon, "performed their wonderful works in their appointed times, so also they formed words, which received great virtue from the Heavenly constellation itself and accordingly they accomplished many things through these words." Therefore, word power, "which is the principal and first work of the rational soul," is influenced by the heavenly powers. The signs of the heavens influence signs in language, and language is a sign system which discloses the structure of the universe.

Discussing the signification of words, Bacon argues that all signification implies the awareness of something. Such awareness does not, however, imply the existence of the object of which one is aware. "It does not follow 'a sign is in act, therefore the thing signified exists,' because nonentities can be signified by words just like entities." Furthermore, a sign is not just that which can appear to a sense faculty: whatever is accessible to the intellect is potentially a sign. This notion of an imperceptible sign is not developed in Bacon's extant works.

Some signs, Bacon says, signify naturally. If something is related to something else, it is a sign by its essence and not by the deliberate intention of an animate agent. Aristotelian science demands knowledge of the cause, whereas knowledge by signs is knowledge from accidents not essential causes. Lactation is an invariable natural sign of an impending birth, but the former does not cause the latter. Lactation is an example of a sign by necessity, as smoke is a natural sign by necessity of fire.

Words, in certain respects, signify as natural signs. Vocal sounds which do not yet have a meaning—nonsense words—are still accompanied by a representation in a speaker's mind; as a result, they are signs of the latter by necessary inference.

Some signs signify not by rational inference but by "configuration and likeness." A sign in this sense is a likeness of what it signifies. An artifact is the visible representation of the model in the mind of the one who made it. An uttered word is analogous to an artifact: uttered words resemble sounds in the mind of a speaker and are signs by configuration of those mental sounds.

Roger Bacon; statue by H. R. Hope-Pinker, Oxford University Museum

Signs which are deliberately given by a soul Bacon divides into signs signifying naturally and signs signifying at pleasure. The natural language of the human reason, acting without deliberation or choice, signifies naturally; groans also function in this natural way. Signs given by a soul signifying at pleasure are imposed signs. Imposition is a free act of the will. Names of things existing outside the mind signify only the things themselves, Bacon says, not the likenesses of those things in the intellect. If one wishes to name the mental representation of the object with the name of the object, one makes a second imposition. But doing so, says Bacon, will lead to equivocation.

The consensus of the scholarship is that Bacon's semiotic theory (theory of signs) was an advance on the received Aristotelian account. It laid the ground for the more advanced theories in the logic of William of Ockham, Thomas Hobbes, and John Stuart Mill.

Part 4 of the *Opus Maius* begins with a rhetorical argument for the value of the study of mathematics. Bacon marshals many authorities, including Pythagoras, Boethius, Ptolemy, Aristotle, and al-Farabi, to give this testimony. Bacon points out that all the other logical categories depend on a knowledge of quantity, and quantity is explained in mathematics. Thus, logic depends on mathematics.

Bacon then offers proofs that every science depends on the application of mathematics: "Wherefore since this knowledge is almost innate, and as it were precedes discovery and learning, or at least is less in need of them than other sciences, it will be first among sciences and will precede others disposing us toward them. Since what is innate or almost so disposes toward what is acquired." Mathematics was the first science acquired by the human race, and among the sciences it is the one which is knowable by the most humans.

Knowledge of nature, God, angels, and the future life is difficult. Bacon says: "when the same things are known both *to us and to nature*, we make much progress in regard to what is known to nature and in regard to all that is there included, and we are able to attain a perfect knowledge of them. But only in mathematics alone, as Averroes says in the first book of the Physics and in the seventh of the Metaphysics and in his commentary on the third book of the Heavens and the World, *are the same things known to us and to nature or simply*. Therefore, we are able to reach directly an intimate knowledge of that science. Since, therefore, we have not this ability in other sciences, clearly mathematics is better known. Therefore, the acquisition of this subject is the beginning of our knowledge." In other words, knowledge in both physics and theology is difficult. In physics one may not always be able to get clear and distinct knowledge due to the opacity of the physical evidence. In theology one is dealing with knowledge due to faith; here, too, one does not have clear and distinct knowledge. Clear and distinct knowledge, where there is an isomorphism between what is known and what is so in fact, is only had in mathematical knowledge: here the concept and the reality coincide.

Finally, only in mathematics, according to Bacon, are we able to arrive at the full truth without error and uncertainty. Therefore, if the other sciences are to have a firm foundation in certainty and truth, they must be founded on a secure knowledge of mathematics. Thus, doubts and uncertainties in the sciences can be cleared away with the help of mathematics: "But mathematics alone, as was shown above, remains fixed and verified for us with the utmost certainty and verification. Therefore by means of this science all other sciences must be known and verified."

In the remainder of *Opus Maius*, part 4, Bacon gives a review of traditional Christian use of mathematics for the computation of the date of Easter, in religious history, and in archaeology. He suggests that mathematics might be used to elucidate religious mysteries. He also argues for the importance of using mathematics in geography. There is some evidence that Christopher Columbus may have known this section.

Parts 5 and 6 are concerned with *perspectiva* (optics) and a *scientia experimentalis* (science of experience), respectively. For Bacon, optics is the key to a universal science. Following Aristotle, he holds that vision alone reveals the differences of things. By means of visual instruments we can view and measure the heavenly bodies and examine impressions generated in the air such as comets and rainbows. Altitude above the horizon can be determined by sighting with instruments such as the astrolabe. It is, of course, possible to learn from books and teachers, but verbal argument must be tested by experience. Bacon describes the "separate science of vision" as "the flower of the whole of philosophy" and says that "through it and not without it can the other sciences be known."

Bacon proceeds to give a full physiology of the eye and the optic nerves, including the sphericity of the eye, the cornea, the albugineus humor, and the uvea. This part of the *Opus Maius* is perhaps the greatest synthesis of theory of vision in the Middle Ages.

The short tract on a science of experience is a development of some ideas Bacon found in Grosseteste's treatise on the rainbow. It should be emphasized that Bacon is not proposing a post-Newtonian notion of an experimental physics; Bacon was a medieval Aristotelian who tried to extend and add to the ideal of a demonstrative science as set out in the *Posterior Analytics* of Aristotle.

Experience for Bacon is twofold; first, there is philosophical-scientific experience by means of observation; second, there is moral-spiritual experience, which is internal. Bacon is in search of a practical science of experience. Just as formal

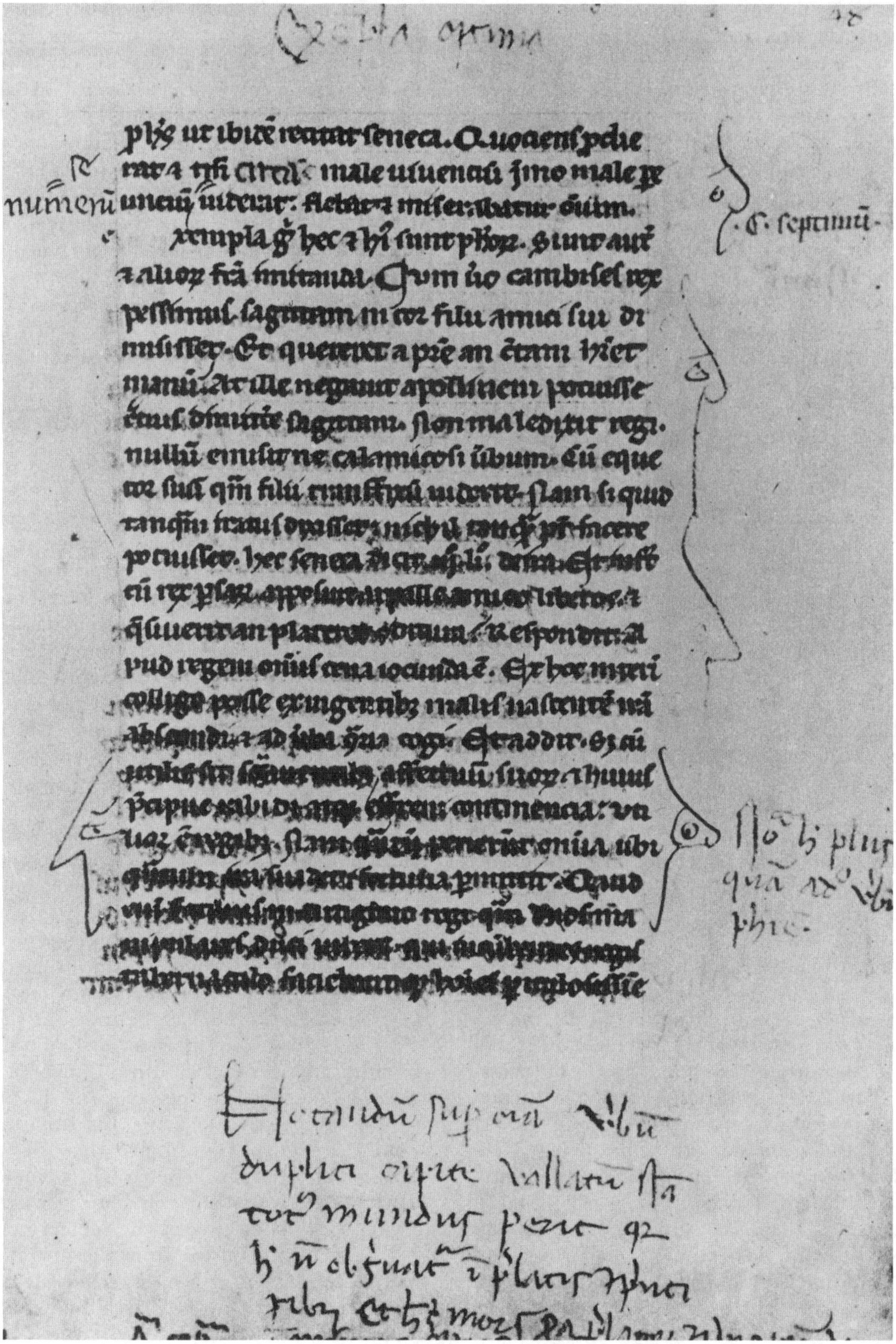

Page from a manuscript for part 7 of the Opus Maius, *with marginal notations and drawings of faces by Bacon. Bacon sent this copy to Pope Clement IV in 1267 (the Vatican, MS. Vat. lat. 429s f. 48r).*

logic provides the rules for argument, this practical science of experience will provide the rules for practical reasoning.

This science has three tasks. The first task is to investigate the conclusions of the other sciences. "For the other sciences know how to discover their principles by experiments, but their conclusions are reached through arguments made from the discovered principles. But if they are to have a particular and complete experience of their conclusions, they must have it with the aid of this science." The second function of the science of experience has to do with the discovery of truth by means of experience alone. Here Bacon is talking about using instruments, such as an astrolabe, or making observations in medicine. The third function, prognostication of the future, aims at the provision of a new social and political order. The four principal divisions of this science are experimental astrology, experimental alchemy, provision of new technology, and application of this technology to the direction of church and state. Experimental science is the directive or political science: it directs the uses of all the other sciences.

The science of experience is the penultimate science; the ultimate science is moral philosophy, treated in part 7 of the *Opus Maius*, titled *Moralis Philosophia*. For Bacon, moral philosophy is the queen of the sciences; it is the goal of the activities of the other sciences. Bacon says that "This science is preeminently active, that is, operative, and deals with our actions in this life and the other." Thus, moral philosophy is concerned with human actions which have to do with good and evil.

Bacon was strongly influenced by Arabic authors, especially al-Farabi, Algazel, Avicenna, and Averroës. The first section of the *Moralis Philosophia*, on metaphysics as a foundation of morality, is taken from Avicenna. It also includes materials from Greek and Latin writers. This section also includes some significant indications of the nature of Bacon's philosophical anthropology (theory of human nature). The second section indicates Bacon's social philosophy, which is taken from Arabic sources. The kernel of the moral philosophy is found in section 3, on virtues and vices. It includes an anthology of passages from Classical authors, especially Seneca, and presents a combination of Aristotelian and Stoic virtue theory. It is evidently aimed at the education of princes. Section 4 includes an attempt to differentiate world religions on the basis of typical features. It treats Judaism, Christianity, Greek and Roman religion, Islam, and Buddhism. Section 5, on persuasion within Christianity, deals with the kind of argument which is needed in religion. Bacon holds that demonstrative reason is to be confined to science; religion requires attention to rhetoric and poetics. The final section is a brief summary concerning forensic rhetoric.

Bacon also wrote many tracts on medicine, especially on the prolongation of old age. And he produced his own edition of the pseudo-Aristotelian *Secretum Secretorum* (*The Book of the Secret of Secrets*, circa 1267), a work which had an enormous impact on medieval political education.

No information is available on Bacon's life from 1278 to 1292. He seems to have been living in Oxford at the Franciscan *studium*. It was in Oxford about 1292 that he produced his *Compendium Studii Theologia* (Compendium of the Study of Theology). This work seems to be a rewrite of the *Opus Maius*. Only parts of it are extant, but it is clear that Bacon lost none of his acerbic temperament in old age. Like the English Renaissance philosopher Hobbes, Bacon ended his days baiting the younger generation at Oxford. He accused the learned theologians of stupidity and maintained that all the errors of contemporary theology and philosophy began around 1250 in Oxford and were still there in 1292. The age of the great Grosseteste had given way, in Bacon's view, to the rule of little minds, such as Richard Rufus of Cornwall: "And I knew well the worst and most foolish [author] of these errors, who was called Richard of Cornwall, a very famous one among the foolish multitude. But to those who knew, he was insane and [had been] reproved at Paris for the errors which he had invented [and] promulgated when lecturing solemnly on the *Sentences* there, after he had lectured on the *Sentences* at Oxford from the year of the Lord 1250. From that [year of] 1250 up till now the multitude has remained in the errors of this master, i.e. for forty years and more, and it is currently gaining strength at Oxford, just where this unlimited madness began." Bonaventure took over much of the teaching on the *Libri Quatuor Sententiarum* (Four Books of Sentences, 1157-1158) of Peter Lombard from Richard of Cornwall; Bacon may have been directing his polemic against both Richard of Cornwall and Bonaventure.

The full extent of Bacon's influence in the history of medieval philosophy has yet to be researched. That it was major is becoming apparent from serious study of fourteenth-century philosophy and has been demonstrated in Katherine H. Tachau's *Vision and Certitude in the Age of Ockham* (1988).

Bibliographies:

Franco Alessio, "Un secolo de studi su Ruggero Bacone (1848-1957)," *Rivista critica de storia della filosofia*, 14 (1959): 81-102;

Mara Huber, "Bibliographie zu Roger Bacon," *Franziskanische Studien*, 65 (1983): 98-102;

Jeremiah Hackett and Thomas S. Maloney, "A Roger Bacon Bibliography (1957-1985)," *New Scholasticism*, 61, no. 2 (1987):184-207.

References:

Efrem Bettoni, "L'Aristotelismo di Ruggero Bacone," *Rivista di filosofia neo-scolastica*, 58 (1966): 541-563;

Davide Bigalli, *I Tartari e l'Apocalisse: Ricerche sull'escatologia in Adamo Marsh e Ruggero Bacone* (Florence: La Nuova Italia, 1971);

H. A. G. Braakhuis, "The Views of William of Sherwood on Some Semantical Topics and Their Relations to Those of Roger Bacon," *Vivarium*, 15 (May 1977): 111-142;

H. L. L. Busard, "Ein mittelalterlicher Euklid-Kommentar, der Roger Bacon zugeschreiben werden Kann," *Archives internationales d'histoire des sciences*, 24 (1974): 199-218;

Roul Carton, *L'Experience mystique de l'illumination interieure chez Roger Bacon* (Paris: Vrin, 1924);

Alastair C. Crombie, *Robert Grosseteste and the Origins of Experimental Science, 1100-1700* (Oxford: Clarendon Press, 1953), pp. 139-162;

Theodore Crowley, *Roger Bacon: The Problem of the Soul in His Philosophical Commentaries* (Louvain: Editions de l'Institute superieur de philosophie, 1950);

Crowley, "Roger Bacon: The Problem of Universals in His Philosophical Commentaries," *Bulletin of the John Rylands Library, Manchester*, 34 (1952): 264-275;

E. Randolph Daniel, "Roger Bacon and the De seminibus scripturarum," *Mediaeval Studies*, 34 (1972): 462-467;

Stewart C. Easton, *Roger Bacon and His Search for a Universal Science: A Reconsideration of the Life and Work of Roger Bacon in the Light of His Own Stated Purposes* (New York: Columbia University Press, 1952);

Sten Ebbesen, "Can Equivocation be Eliminated?," *Studia Mediewistyczne*, 18, no. 2 (1977): 103-124;

Ebbesen, "The Dead Man is Alive," *Synthese*, 40 (January 1979): 43-70;

Ebbesen, "Roger Bacon and the Fools of His Times," *Cahiers de l'Institut du Moyen-Age grec et latin*, volume 3 (Copenhagen: University of Copenhagen Press, 1970), pp. 40-44;

Umberto Eco, and others, "Latratus Canus or The Dog's Barking," in *Frontiers in Semiotics*, edited by John Deeley and others (Bloomington: Indiana University Press, 1966), pp. 63-73;

Malgorzata Frankowska-Terlecka, *Science as Interpreted by Roger Bacon*, translated by Ziemislaw Zienkiwicz (Warsaw: Scientific Publications Foreign Cooperation Center of the Central Institute for Scientific, Technical and Economic Information, 1971);

Frankowska-Terlecka, " 'Scientia' as Conceived by Roger Bacon," *Organon*, 6 (1969): 209-231;

Karin Margarita Fredborg, "Roger Bacon on 'Imposition Vocis ad significandum,' " in *English Logic and Semantics: From the End of the Twelfth Century to the Time of Ockham and Burleigh. Acts of the Fourth European Symposium on Medieval Logic and Semantics, Leiden-Nijmegen, 23-27 April, 1979*, edited by H. A. G. Braakhuis, Artistarium Supplementa, volume 1 (Nijmegen: Ingenium, 1981), pp. 167-191;

Jeremiah Hackett, "The Attitude of Roger Bacon to the *Scientia Experimentalis* of Albertus Magnus," in *Albertus Magnus and the Sciences: Commemorative Essays 1980*, edited by James A. Weisheipl (Toronto: Pontifical Institute of Mediaeval Studies, 1980), pp. 53-72;

Hackett, "Averroes and Roger Bacon on the Harmony of Religion and Philosophy," in *A Straight Path: Studies in Medieval Philosophy and Culture. Essays in Honor of Arthur Hyman*, edited by Ruth Link-Salinger (Washington, D.C.: Catholic University of America Press, 1988), pp. 98-112;

Hackett, "Moral Philosophy and Rhetoric in Roger Bacon," *Philosophy and Rhetoric*, 20, no. 1 (1987): 18-40;

Mara Huber-Legnani, *Roger Bacon: Lehrer der Anschaulichkeit Der franziskanische Gedanke und die Philosophie des Einzelnen*, Freiburgh Hochschul-Sammlung Philosophie, volume 4 (Freiburg: Hochschul, 1984);

Alain de Libera, "Roger Bacon et le probleme de l'appelatio univoca," in *English Logic and Semantics*, edited by Braakhuis, pp. 193-234;

Libera, "Textualité Logique et forme summuliste," in *Archeologie de du signe*, edited by Lucie Brind'Amour and Eugene Vance, Recueils d'études médiévales/Papers in Mediaeval Studies, volume 3 (Toronto: Pontifical Institute of Mediaeval Studies, 1983), pp. 213-234;

David C. Lindberg, "The Genesis of Kepler's Theory of Light: Light Metaphysics from Plotinus to Kepler," *Osiris*, second series 2 (1986): 4-42;

Lindberg, "Lines of Influence in Thirteenth Century Optics: Bacon, Witelo, and Pecham," *Speculum*, 46 (January 1971): 66-83;

Lindberg, *Science in the Middle Ages* (Chicago: University of Chicago Press, 1978);

Lindberg, *Studies in the History of Medieval Optics* (London: Variorum Reprints, 1983);

Lindberg, *Theories of Vision from Al-Kindi to Kepler* (Chicago: University of Chicago Press, 1976);

Andrew George Little, ed., *Roger Bacon: Essays Contributed by Various Writers on the Occasion of the Commemoration of the Seventh Centenary of His Birth* (Oxford: Clarendon Press, 1914; New York: Russell & Russell, 1972);

Thomas S. Maloney, "The Extreme Realism of Roger Bacon," *Review of Metaphysics*, 38 (June 1985): 807-837;

Maloney, "Roger Bacon on the *Significatum* of Words," in *Archeologie du signe*, edited by Brind'Amour and Vance, pp. 187-211;

Maloney, "The Semiotics of Roger Bacon," *Mediaeval Studies*, 45 (1983): 120-154;

Gareth B. Matthews, "A Medieval Theory of Vision," in *Studies in Perception: Interrelations in the History of Philosophy and Science*, edited by Peter K. Machamer and Robert G. Turnbull (Columbus: Ohio State University Press, 1978), pp. 186-199;

A. G. Molland, "Medieval Ideas of Scientific Progress," *Journal of the History of Ideas*, 39 (October-December 1978): 561-577;

Molland, "Roger Baconas Magician," *Traditio*, 30 (1974): 445-460;

Thomas A. Orlando, "Roger Bacon and the *Testimonia gentilium de secta christiana*," *Recherches de theologie ancienne et médiévale*, 43 (1976): 202-218;

Jan Pinborg, "Roger Bacon on Signs: A Newly Recovered Part of the *Opus Maius*," in *Sprache und Erkenntnis im Mittelalter*, volume 29, edited by Jan P. Beckmann and others, Miscellanea Medievalia, volume 13, part 1 (Berlin & New York: De Gruyter, 1981), pp. 403-412;

Georgette Sinkler, "Roger Bacon on the Compound and Divided Senses," in *The Rise of British Logic*, edited by P. Osmund Lewry, Papers in Mediaeval Studies, volume 7 (Toronto: Pontifical Institute of Mediaeval Studies), pp. 145-171;

A. Mark Smith, "Getting the Big Picture in Perspectivist Optics," *Isis*, 72 (1981): 568-589;

Katherine H. Tachau, "The Problem of the *species in medio* at Oxford in the Generation after Ockham," *Mediaeval Studies*, 44 (1985): 394-443;

Tachau, *Vision and Certitude in the Age of Ockham: Optics, Epistemology and the Foundations of Semantics 1250-1350* (Leiden: Brill, 1988);

James A. Weisheipl, "Albertus Magnus and the Oxford Platonists," *Proceedings of the American Catholic Philosophical Association*, 32 (1958): 124-139;

Jan Wrobel, "Le probleme de 'reditio' dans le commentaire a *Liber de causis* de Roger Bacon," *Studia Philosophiae Christianae*, 8, no. 2 (1972): 121-148.

Manuscripts:

The manuscripts of Roger Bacon are in libraries all across Europe. The historian of British Franciscan life Andrew George Little included a list of Bacon manuscripts in the appendix to his *Roger Bacon: Essays Contributed by Various Writers on the Occasion of the Commemoration of the Seventh Centenary of His Birth* (Oxford: Clarendon Press, 1914; New York: Russell & Russell, 1972).

Bernard of Chartres

(circa 1060 - 2 June 1124?)

Paul Edward Dutton
Simon Fraser University

WORKS: *Glosae super Platonem* (Glosses on Plato['s *Timaeus*], written circa 1100-1115);

Poems and aphorisms (written circa 1100-1120); in John of Salisbury, *Metalogicon* (written 1159-1160), sections 1.24, 2.17, 3.2, 3.5; and in John of Salisbury, *Policraticus* (written circa 1160), sections 2.22, 7.13.

EDITIONS: *Ioannis Saresberiensis episcopi Carnotensis Policratici sive de Nugis curialium et vestigiis philosophorum libri VIII*, 2 volumes, edited by Clement C. J. Webb (Oxford: Clarendon Press, 1909);

Metalogicon, edited by Webb (Oxford: Clarendon Press, 1929);

The Glosae super Platonem of Bernard of Chartres, edited by Paul Edward Dutton, Studies and Texts, 107 (Toronto: Pontifical Institute of Mediaeval Studies, 1991).

EDITIONS IN ENGLISH: *Frivolities of Courtiers and Footprints of Philosophers: Being a Translation of the First, Second, and Third Books and Selections from the Seventh and Eighth Books of the* Policraticus *of John of Salisbury*, translated by Joseph B. Pike (Minneapolis: University of Minnesota Press, 1938);

The Metalogicon of John of Salisbury: A Twelfth-Century Defense of the Verbal and Logical Arts of the Trivium (Berkeley & Los Angeles: University of California Press, 1962).

For many years Bernard of Chartres seemed the Socrates of the twelfth century—famous for the profound impression he made upon renowned students such as Gilbert of Poitiers and William of Conches but not known as an author in his own right. Bernard has been considered by some the creator of the intellectual character of the so-called school of Chartres in the twelfth century, especially of its humanist drive to bring poetry, the Latin classics, and Platonic philosophy to bear on the Christian theme of the creation of the universe. The great English humanist John of Salisbury could hardly contain his praise of the master of Chartres, whom he had never met: he called Bernard the most deeply learned man in all of Gaul and the most accomplished Platonist of the twelfth century. Almost the whole of Bernard's considerable reputation as a seminal teacher and Platonic philosopher of the first phase of the twelfth-century renaissance has derived from John of Salisbury's *Metalogicon*. In 1984, however, a set of glosses on Plato's *Timaeus* was attributed to Bernard. With this substantial work, John's testimony, and some documentary evidence from the cartularies of Chartres, a much clearer picture of Bernard of Chartres's influential career as cathedral master and glossator of Plato has begun to emerge.

In the first decade of the twelfth century Bernard was a simple subdeacon of the Cathedral of Chartres. When he had arrived at Chartres is obscure, as are most of the details of his life. He was probably in his forties when he first signed some surviving charters of the cathedral, since his students remembered him from this period as the "old man of Chartres." That he was not a native of Chartres but had moved there from some other region of medieval France may be surmised from Bernard's statement that it was the lot of the scholar to seek out foreign lands. The former assumptions that Bernard was a Breton and that Thierry of Chartres was his brother now seem unlikely.

The subdeacon in Bernard's day was a minor cleric whose function was to assist the priest in the divine service. Bernard's bishop until 1115 was the ecclesiastical reformer Ivo of Chartres, the author or director of several volumes of canon law. Ivo believed that bishops must seek out the best masters of the liberal arts to adorn their cathedral schools. The tradition of interest in the liberal arts at Chartres may be traced to the episcopate of Fulbert in the early eleventh century. (The cathedral in which Bernard served was not the soaring Gothic structure that so enthralls visitors today but a massive Romanesque church, begun by Fulbert, that burned in 1194.)

By 1115 Bernard had been named the master of the cathedral school of Chartres. The late eleventh and early twelfth centuries were the age of the great masters of Europe, such as Manegold of Lautenbach, Anselm of Laon, and William of Champeaux. These men were intellectual magnets, attracting students from all over Europe to their classrooms; their teaching was authoritative, and they were personally admired for their vast learning, moral sobriety, and brilliance. Peter Abelard would directly challenge the unwarranted reliance on authority by the masters he studied under in northern France, but Abelard, too, wished to be a master. It was the rise of the cathedral schools that allowed Europe to move beyond the limited and, perhaps, inhibiting system of monastic schools that had dominated education in the Middle Ages for three hundred years. In Paris the combination of a growing and prosperous city and an established cathedral school was to create the conditions for the birth of a university at the end of the twelfth century. Thus, the cathedral schools of the early twelfth century occupied an important point in the transition of European education from an older institution of learning to the one that still exists. This institutional development was facilitated by that set of circumstances generally subsumed under the title of the twelfth-century renaissance: expanding cities and trade; a growing and more mobile population; and contact with the outside world, most notably with Byzantium and Islam in three crusades. The cathedral schools were also a product of this changing world. The cities that contained them were expanding, and the rise of a class of burghers and merchants made new demands on the cathedral, particularly with regard to the education of its sons. The cathedral school's curriculum was based on the intensive study of a few "worthy" books. Eventually it fell to the university, with its greater gathering of scholars, to incorporate and assimilate the newly translated texts that came north from Spain and Sicily in the later twelfth and thirteenth centuries.

Bernard spent much of his early career teaching town boys the basics of Latin. His students memorized and recited passages from classical authors and were urged to imitate these authors as best they could; if they failed, he might resort to flogging. Master Bernard must have been forced to inflict corporal punishment on very few occasions, since it was claimed that with him as teacher any student could, if he were not persistently dull, learn rudimentary Latin in a year.

Reconstruction by Harry H. Hilberry of the Cathedral of Chartres in Bernard's day. This Romanesque building burned in 1194 and was replaced by the Gothic structure that stands today.

Bernard also drew to Chartres senior students who came seeking instruction in the *lectio philosophorum,* the reading of difficult philosophical texts. In the so-called Six Keys of Learning he set out the discipline these students should strive to acquire in their quest for philosophical enlightenment:

> A humble mind, the zeal to learn, a life
> Of quiet, the silent search, a lack of wealth,
> A foreign land, these are the keys that open,
> When we read, the doors to light our night of ignorance.

Among Bernard's students were the theologian Gilbert of Poitiers, who later came under the cloud of Bernard of Clairvaux's disapproval of inventive thinkers, and William of Conches, the author of the *Philosophia Mundi* (Philosophy of the World, circa 1125-1130), the *Dragmaticon* (circa 1147-1149), and a host of glosses.

With these students, Bernard concentrated on a close and critical reading of philosophical and grammatical texts. The main ones seem to have been the grammar of Priscian, Plato's *Timaeus*, Macrobius's commentary on *The Dream of Scipio*, Porphyry's *Isagoge*, and Boethius's theological and philosophical writings. Bernard's almost boundless respect for these ancient authors is best captured in an aphorism he coined that was borrowed by William of Conches and Isaac Newton. According to John of Salisbury, "Bernard of Chartres used to compare us to dwarfs perched on the shoulders of giants. He pointed out that we see more and farther than our predecessors, not because we have keener vision or greater height, but because we are lifted aloft on their gigantic stature."

The books available in the early twelfth century were essentially those that had been known to the Latin West since Charlemagne's reign three hundred years earlier. Bernard did not live to see that flood of works translated from Greek and Arabic, especially the treatises of Aristotle, that began to flow into Europe after 1135. It was natural, therefore, that he and his fellow masters should concentrate on the intensive explication of the few texts that they had at hand. In this work Bernard proved to be a methodological innovator of some importance, for he perfected a critical methodology for approaching difficult texts: the comprehensive gloss.

In the eleventh century, glosses had been inserted in the margins and between the lines of philosophical texts, but they had been for the most part brief, unsystematic, and concerned with matters of grammar and etymology. Glossators had rarely, thought Bernard and his student William, risen to a real understanding of the text. On the other hand, commentators floated so far above the text in their concentration on its general meaning that they neglected its details and specific meanings. In another aphorism recorded by John of Salisbury, Bernard holds that there are basically three types of intellectual capacities among men: the first flies, the second crawls, and the third walks by the middle way. The one that flies can hold on to nothing solid, for while it learns quickly, it just as quickly forgets. The one that crawls on the ground is stuck there and cannot rise to higher things. The one that walks, however, is firmly grounded in solid things but can climb to higher truths. The comprehensive gloss pioneered by Bernard wedded the best features of the soaring commentary with the chief virtues of the grounded gloss, producing a middle way of steady progress in the critical study of philosophical texts.

The one surviving example of Bernard's technique of glossing employs this method. After introducing the work (the *accessus ad auctorem*), Bernard approaches the text in a regular and systematic fashion. He first considers the larger issues raised by Plato in each section of the *Timaeus*, then descends to a consideration of specific passages, and finally explains any words or phrases that might cause confusion. It is also noteworthy that in this set of glosses Bernard begins to experiment with the question-and-answer method that would figure so large in the universities of the next century. The comprehensive gloss, which became the favored genre of Bernard's students, particularly William, emerged from the needs of Bernard's cathedral classroom: as an active teacher, Bernard had to anticipate the questions that would occur to students faced with puzzling philosophical works.

The chief such work for Bernard was Plato's *Timaeus*, the only Platonic dialogue known in the Latin West for most of the Middle Ages. Early in the fourth century Calcidius had translated a significant portion of the dialogue into Latin and had provided a lengthy commentary. Despite the popularity of the *Timaeus* in later antiquity, especially with Macrobius and Boethius, the work had stirred little interest among early medieval thinkers. Even Eriugena seems not to have been deeply influenced by it, preferring instead his Neoplatonic sources. Late in the eleventh century, however, a new interest in the *Timaeus* began to build, evident in an increase in the number of manuscripts of Calcidius's translation and in the frequency with which these manuscripts received glosses.

Early in the twelfth century Bernard of Chartres composed his *Glosae super Platonem* (Glosses on Plato['s *Timaeus*], circa 1100-1115). This simple set of glosses, probably designed to answer the particular problems of Bernard's students, became the early twelfth century's introduction to Plato's thought. In systematic fashion Bernard glossed the entire translated text. He relied to some extent on Calcidius's commentary but felt free to depart from it on fundamental issues; indeed, one of the accomplishments of Bernard's comprehensive gloss was to free readers of the *Timaeus* from having to consult Calcidius's perplexing and often unsystematic commentary. Bernard tended to remain fairly faithful to what he took to be the meaning of Plato, refusing, for in-

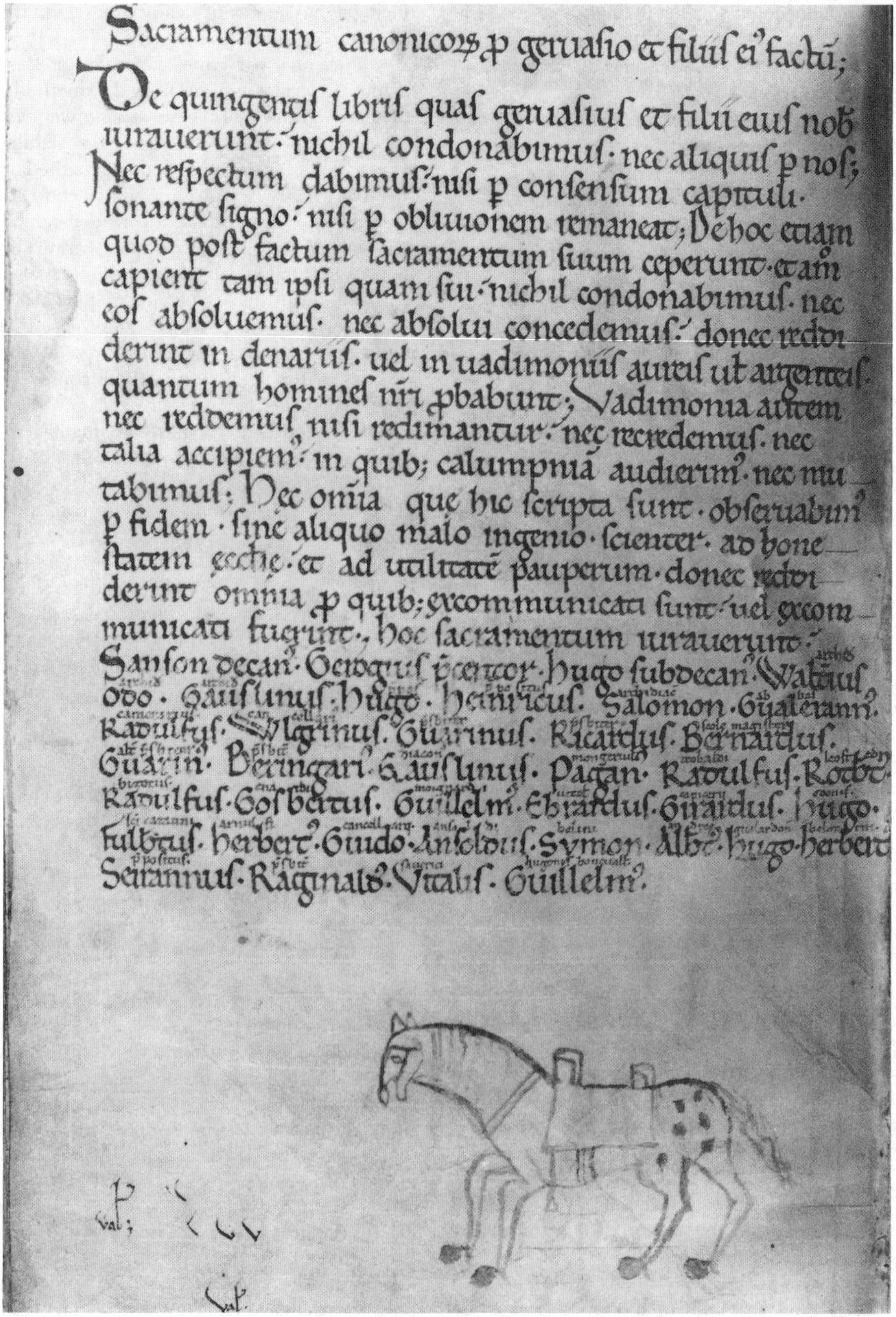

Sacramentum canonicorum pro geruasio et filiis ei' factum;
De quingentis libris quas geruasius et filii eius nob
iurauerunt: nichil condonabimus. nec aliquis pro nos;
Nec respectum dabimus: nisi per consensum capituli.
sonante signo: nisi per obliuionem remaneat; De hoc etiam
quod post factum sacramentum suum ceperunt. et tamen
capient tam ipsi quam sui: nichil condonabimus. nec
eos absoluemus. nec absolui concedemus: donec reddi
derint in denariis. uel in uadimoniis aureis ut argenteis.
quantum homines nostri probabunt; Vadimonia autem
nec reddemus nisi redimantur: nec recredemus. nec
talia accipiemus: in quib; calumpnia audierimus. nec mu
tabimus; Hec omnia que hic scripta sunt. obseruabimus
per fidem. sine aliquo malo ingenio. scienter. ad hone
statem ecclesie. et ad utilitatem pauperum. donec reddi
derint omnia pro quib; excommunicati sunt: uel excom
municati fuerint. Hoc sacramentum iurauerunt:
Sanson decanus. Georgius precentor. Hugo subdecanus. Walterius
Odo. Gauslinus. Hugo. Heinricus. Salomon. Gualerannus.
Radulfus. Vulgrinus. Guarinus. Ricardus. Bernardus.
Guarin. Beringarius. Gauslinus. Pagan. Radulfus. Rotbertus.
Radulfus. Gosbertus. Guillelmus. Ebrardus. Girardus. Hugo.
Fulbertus. Herbertus. Guido. Ansoldus. Symon. Albertus. Hugo. Herbertus.
Serannus. Raginaldus. Vitalis. Guillelmus.

A charter, dating from between 1121 and 1124, in which Bernard is listed among the signatories (Bibliothèque municipiale, Chartres) stance, to Christianize the *Timaeus*. The Bible is virtually absent from Bernard's sources, and he did not associate the world soul with the Holy Spirit, as even Abelard had done. It was probably for his direct approach to the *Timaeus* that John of Salisbury came to think of Bernard as the most accomplished Platonist of his age.

Bernard identified three Platonic principles in the *Timaeus*: God, the Ideas, and *hyle* or primordial matter. Though the Demiourgos of the *Timaeus* is a worker-god, a craftsman who fashioned and ordered already existing but disorderd things, Bernard understandably thought of him as God. God, for him, is the first mover, leading all things from disorder into order because he wished them to be ordered like him. Following Plato, Bernard conceived of God as the best author and best cause of the eternal exemplar of the world.

According to John of Salisbury, Bernard of Chartres was the chief proponent in the twelfth century of the notion that the Platonic Ideas were universals. In the *Glosae super Platonem* the Ideas are defined as the original forms of all things, but they are never mixed in with creatures; they remain in the mind of God, which is inferior to God himself. Thus, the Ideas descend from God but are not identical with him. Instead, they occupy an intermediary position between God and the sensible world. An archetype is a collection of Ideas, and the sensible world is the image of the archetypal or exemplary world. Bernard conceived of the Ideas as universals *ante rem*: they exist but outside of and before created things. The Ideas do not inhere in created things but always stand apart from the corruptible and transitory sensible world. Bernard was, according to John of Salisbury, careful to stress that the Ideas were eternal but not coeternal with God: they existed in the mind of God, which Bernard counted as inferior and subsequent to God himself.

Even though Plato had preferred to think of his third principle as space or, perhaps, a spatial field, not matter, Bernard thought of *hyle* as both space and matter. Without *hyle* it would be impossible for any corporeal thing to exist, but *hyle* remains confused and disordered in itself and can only be obscurely perceived in sensible things. *Hyle*, for instance, cannot be understood through the application of the Aristotelian categories. *Hyle* on its own was passive and inert, and its existence could not explain the creation of things.

The problems facing Bernard were that Plato had never precisely linked his three principles in the *Timaeus* and that Calcidius had downplayed the importance of the Ideas. Thus God, the Ideas, and *hyle* seemed to stand apart from each other, locked in prisons of conceptual rigor and lacking a principle to link their separate activities together into a total system. What could explain, in this system of metaphysically differentiated functions, the appearance of sensible, particular things? How were created things related to *hyle* and to the Ideas created by God?

Bernard arrived at a satisfying solution by creating the concept of native or inhering forms. The problem was, on the one hand, to insure that the Ideas were completely separate from and not mixed in with sensible things and, on the other, to discern a principle of imitation of those exemplars that was in and, therefore, not separable from sensible things. In reading Calcidius's commentary Bernard had encountered the concept of the native species, but Calcidius had employed the phrase simply as a label for visible form. Bernard transformed the concept into the active feature of his metaphysical system. Since the Ideas and *hyle* remain forever distinct from each other, Bernard conceived of the native forms as the mediating images of the Ideas. These native forms, which he likens to a father, enter *hyle*, which takes up the role of the mother, to beget the sensible world. Bernard's native forms, therefore, introduce into the static Platonic cosmos of the *Timaeus* an active or generative force, one that, like the seed of the father in the womb of the mother, sets life in motion.

With the concept of the native forms Bernard also made a significant contribution to the problem of universals. Boethius had framed the issue in terms of the apparently contrary views of Plato and Aristotle: "Plato thinks that genera and species, and the rest, not only are understood as universals, but also are and subsist without bodies; whereas Aristotle thinks that they are understood as incorporeal and universal, but subsist as sensibles." John of Salisbury claimed that Bernard and his followers had labored to reconcile Plato and Aristotle, though he quipped that he found it a vain exercise to attempt to reconcile two dead philosophers who had never agreed while they lived. John underestimated the major thrust of Bernard's metaphysical reconciliation of the differing demands of Platonism and Aristotelianism. The concept of the native forms allowed Bernard to insist on the absolute separateness of the immutable and eternal Ideas and yet to identify the intermediate agent between them and *hyle*. In this way he could reconcile the Platonic intuition of the transcendent Ideas and a practical Aristotelian concern with the observable forms and causes of sensible things. For Bernard, the native forms truly existed as the images of the Ideas but inhered in particular observable things.

In the end, then, Bernard discerned a metaphysical reason for studying the sensible, physical world: the native forms, the images of the pure Ideas of God, were actually present in this world, waiting to be recognized. Bernard thought he had found in the doctrine of the native forms an inherent connection between the imperfect and perfect, between this world and the archetypal world, and between creature and creator. Much of the thought that flowed from the school of Chartres was to share this underlying belief in the knowability of higher things and the meaningfulness of the created world in which human beings live.

By the early 1120s Bernard of Chartres's career was coming to a close. In these years he was named the chancellor of the cathedral, doubtless a great honor and a powerful and remunerative office for the simple subdeacon and master of Chartres. Gilbert of Poitiers wrote his former master a letter at about this time in which he gives thanks that he had enjoyed the benefit of being taught by so great a master. He longed to assist Bernard again in penetrating the truths hidden in the secret folds of philosophy and to drink from the pure and inexhaustible fountain of his master's wisdom. He vowed to attribute whatever good fortune came his way in life, including whatever he himself achieved, to God and his master Bernard.

On 2 June, probably in 1124, Bernard died, bequeathing to his cathedral twenty-four volumes of books. His greatest accomplishment may well have been the tremendous impact he had on a series of students, such as Gilbert of Poitiers and William of Conches, who would play such a large part in shaping the twelfth-century renaissance. The warmth with which they remembered the "old man of Chartres" is evocatively captured in John of Salisbury's *Metalogicon*. Bernard had focused the attention of his students on a group of fundamental ancient books that was to prove a kind of core curriculum for Chartrian thinkers. He had also shown them a critical methodology for analyzing even the most difficult of texts. His general interest in Plato also became theirs, though they were to depart from his basic metaphysical insights. William of Conches's glosses on Plato were to surpass in size and systematic treatment those of his master, but William and other medieval glossators of the *Timaeus* borrowed freely from Bernard's comprehensive gloss. By the end of the twelfth century Bernard of Chartres was largely forgotten; but just as the massive stone crypt of Fulbert supports the magnificent Gothic cathedral of Chartres that rises above it, so Bernard of Chartres's method and interests were the foundation on which the Platonic, classical, and humanist concerns of the school of Chartres were to be erected.

References:

R. R. Bolgar, *The Classical Heritage and Its Beneficiaries from the Carolingian Age to the End of the Renaissance* (Cambridge: Cambridge University Press, 1954; reprinted, New York: Harper & Row, 1964);

M. D. Chenu, *Nature, Man, and Society in the Twelfth Century: Essays on New Theological Perspectives in the Latin West*, edited and translated by Jerome Taylor and Lester K. Little (Chicago: University of Chicago Press, 1968);

A. Clerval, "Bernard de Chartres," *Les lettres chrétiennes*, 4 (1882): 390-397;

Clerval, *Les écoles de Chartres au Moyen Age (du Ve au XVIe siècle)* (Paris: Garnier, 1895; reprinted, Frankfurt am Main: Minerva, 1965);

Paul Edward Dutton, "*Illustre civitatis et populi exemplum*: Plato's *Timaeus* and the Transmission from Calcidius to the End of the Twelfth Century of a Tripartite Scheme of Society," *Mediaeval Studies*, 45 (1983): 79-119;

Dutton, "The Uncovering of the *Glosae super Platonem* of Bernard of Chartres," *Mediaeval Studies*, 46 (1984): 192-221;

Stephen C. Ferruolo, *The Origins of the University: The Schools of Paris and Their Critics, 1100-1215* (Stanford, Cal.: Stanford University Press, 1985);

Eugenio Garin, *Studi sul platonismo medievale* (Florence: Felice le Monnier, 1958);

Stephen Gersh, *Middle Platonism and Neoplatonism: The Latin Tradition*, 2 volumes, Publications in Medieval Studies, The Medieval Institute, University of Notre Dame, 23 (Notre Dame, Ind.: University of Notre Dame, 1986);

Robert Giacone, "Masters, Books and Library at Chartres according to the Cartularies of

Notre Dame and Saint-Père," *Vivarium*, 12 (1974): 30-51;

Margaret Gibson, "The Study of the *Timaeus* in the Eleventh and Twelfth Centuries," *Pensamiento*, 25 (1969): 183-194;

Étienne Gilson, "Le platonisme de Bernard de Chartres," *Revue néo-scholastique de philosophie*, 25 (1923): 5-19;

Tullio Gregory, *Anima mundi: La filosofia di Guglielmo di Conches e la scuola di Chartres*, Pubblicazioni dell'istituto di filosofia dell'universita di Roma, 3 (Florence: Sansoni, 1955);

Gregory, *Platonismo medievale: Studi e ricerche*, Studi storici, 26-27 (Rome: Istituto storico Italiano per il medio evo, 1958);

Nikolaus Häring, "Chartres and Paris Revisited," in *Essays in Honour of Anton Charles Pegis*, edited by J. Reginald O'Donnell (Toronto: Pontifical Institute of Mediaeval Studies, 1974), pp. 268-329;

Charles Homer Haskins, *The Renaissance of the Twelfth Century* (Cambridge, Mass.: Harvard University Press, 1927);

Brian Hendley, "John of Salisbury and the Problem of Universals," *Journal of the History of Philosophy*, 8 (July 1970): 289-302;

Harry H. Hilberry, "The Cathedral at Chartres in 1030," *Speculum*, 34 (October 1959): 561-572;

A History of Twelfth-Century Western Philosophy, edited by Peter Dronke (Cambridge: Cambridge University Press, 1988);

Edouard Jeauneau, "*Lectio philosophorum*": *Recherches sur l'École de Chartres* (Amsterdam: Hakkert, 1973);

Jeauneau, "Nains et géants," in *Entrétiens sur la renaissance du 12ᵉ siècle*, edited by M. de Gandillac and Jeauneau (Paris: Mouton, 1968), pp. 21-52;

Raymond Klibansky, *The Continuity of the Platonic Tradition during the Middle Ages: Outlines of a Corpus Platonicum Medii Aevi* (London: Warburg Institute, 1939; revised and enlarged, 1981);

John Marenbon, *Early Medieval Philosophy (480-1150): An Introduction* (London: Routledge & Kegan Paul, 1983);

G. Paré, A. Brunet, and P. Tremblay, *La renaissance du XIIᵉ siècle: les écoles et l'énseignement*, Publications de l'Institut d'Études Médiévales d'Ottawa, 3 (Paris: Vrin, 1933);

J. Parent, *La doctrine de la création dans l'école de Chartres*, Publications de l'Institut d'Études Médiévales d'Ottawa, 8 (Paris: Vrin, 1938);

Platonismus in der Philosophie des Mittelalters, edited by Werner Beierwaltes, Wege und Forschung, 197 (Darmstadt: Wissenschaftliche Buchgesellschaft, 1969);

Reginald Lane Poole, *Illustrations of the History of Medieval Thought and Learning*, revised edition (New York: Dover, 1960);

Renaissance and Renewal in the Twelfth Century, edited by Robert L. Benson and Giles Constable with Carol D. Lanham (Cambridge, Mass.: Harvard University Press, 1982);

Richard W. Southern, *Medieval Humanism and Other Studies* (New York: Harper, 1970; Oxford: Blackwell, 1984);

Southern, *Platonism, Scholastic Method, and the School of Chartres: The Stenton Lecture of 1978* (Reading, U.K.: University of Reading, 1979);

Winthrop Wetherbee, *Platonism and Poetry in the Twelfth Century: The Literary Influence of the School of Chartres* (Princeton: Princeton University Press, 1972);

Michael Wilks, ed., *The World of John of Salisbury*, Studies in Church History: Subsidia, 3 (Oxford: Blackwell, 1984).

Manuscripts:

Six twelfth-century copies of Bernard of Chartres's *Glosae super Platonem* survive, the earliest being one in the library of Durham Cathedral. All paleographical evidence of Bernard's career—his signature and annotations—was likely lost when the library of the Cathedral of Chartres was destroyed during World War II.

Boethius
(Anicius Manlius Severinus Boethius)

(circa 480 - circa 524)

Ralph McInerny
University of Notre Dame

PRINCIPAL WORKS: *De Institutione Arithmetica* (On Arithmetic, written circa 503);

De Institutione Musica (On Music, written circa 503);

In Isagogen Porphyrii Commenta (First Commentary on Porphyry's *Isagoge*, written 504-505);

De Syllogismo Categorico (On Categorical Syllogisms, written circa 505-506);

In Isagogen Porphyrii Commenta (Second Commentary on Porphyry's *Isagoge*, written circa 507-509);

Liber de Divisione (On Division, written circa 508);

In Categorias Aristotelis (Commentary on Aristotle's *Categories*, written circa 509-510);

Contra Euthycen et Nestorium (Against Eutyches and Nestorius, written circa 512);

Commentarii in Librum Aristotelis Peri Hermeneias (Commentaries on Aristotle's *On Interpretation*, written circa 513-516);

De Syllogismis Hypotheticis (Hypothetical Syllogisms, written after 516);

In Ciceronis Topica (Commentary on Cicero's *Topics*, written circa 518);

De Fide Catholica (On the Catholic Faith, written circa 521);

Quomodo Substantiae in Eo Quod Sint Bonae Sint cum Non Sint Substantialia Bona (Whether Everything That Exists Is Good Just Because It Exists, written circa 521);

De Trinitate (On the Trinity, written circa 521);

Utrum Pater et Filius et Spiritus Sanctus de Divinitate Substantialiter Praedicentur (Whether Father, Son, and Holy Spirit May Be Predicated Substantially of Divinity, written circa 521);

De Consolatione Philosophiae (The Consolation of Philosophy, written circa 524).

EDITIONS: *In Ciceronis Topica Commentarium*, edited by Johann Kaspar Orelli and Johann George Baiter, in *Ciceronis Opera*, volume 5, part 1, edited by Orelli and Baiter (Zurich, 1833);

Boethius plucking the string of a Greek monochord in an illustration from a twelfth-century Canterbury manuscript of one of his works (Ms L1.3.12, fo. 61v; Cambridge University Library)

Opera Omnia, volumes 63-64 of *Patrologia Latina*, edited by J.-P. Migne (Paris: Garnier, 1847);

De Institutione Arithmetica, edited by Gottfried Friedlein (Leipzig: Teubner, 1867);

De Institutione Musica, edited by Friedlein (Leipzig: Teubner, 1867);

De Consolatione Philosophiae, edited by Rudolf Peiper (Leipzig: Teubner, 1871);

Anicii Manlii Severini Boetii Commentarii in Librum Aristotelis Peri Hermeneias, 2 volumes, edited by Karl Meiser (Leipzig, 1877-1880);

Anicii Manlii Severini Boethii in Isagogen Porphyrii Commenta, edited by Georg Schepss and Samuel Brandt, volume 48 of *Corpus Scriptorum Ecclesiasticorum Latinorum* (Leipzig:Tempsky, 1906);

De Syllogismis Hypotheticis, edited by Luca Orbetello (Brescia: Paideia, 1969).

EDITIONS IN ENGLISH: *Boetius, De Consolatione Philosophiae: The Boke of Boecius Called the Comforte of Philosophye or Wysedome, Moche Necessary for All Men to Read and Know*, translated by George Coluile (London: Imprinted by John Cawoode, 1556);

Five Bookes of Philosophicall Comfort, Full of Christian Consolation, Written a 1000 Yeeres Since by Anitius Manlius Torquatus Severinus Boetius: Newly Translated out of Latine, Together with Marginall Notes Explaining the Obscurest Places, translated by "I. T." (London: Printed by I. Windet for Lownes, 1609);

The Consolation of Philosophy, translated by Sir Harry Coningsby (London: Printed by James Flesher for the author, 1664);

Summum Bonum; or, An Explication of the Divine Goodness, in the Words of the Most Renowned Boetius, Translated by a Lover of Truth and Virtue, translated by Edmund Elys (Oxford: Printed by H. Hall for Ric. Davis, 1674);

Of the Consolation of Philosophy, in Five Books, Made English and Illustrated with Notes, translated by Richard, Lord Viscount Preston (London: Printed by J. D. for A. and J. Churchill, 1695);

Ancius Manlius Torquatus Severinus Boetius, His Consolation of Philosophy in Five Books, Translated into English, translated by William Causton (London: Printed for the author, 1730);

Boethius's Consolation of Philosophy, Translated from the Latin with Notes and Illustrations, translated by Philip Ridpath (London: Printed for C. Dilly, 1785);

The Five Books of Anicius Manlius Torquatus Severinus Boethius, On the Consolation of Philosophy, translated by Robert Duncan (Edinburgh: Printed for the translator and sold by William Creech, 1789);

The Consolation of Philosophy of Boethius, Translated into English Prose and Verse, translated by H. R. James (London: Stock, 1897);

The Consolation of Philosophy, translated by W. V. Cooper (London: Dent, 1902);

The Theological Tractates, with an English Translation by H. F. Stewart and E. K. Rand; The Consolation of Philosophy, with the English Translation of "I. T." (1609) Revised by H. F. Stewart (London: Heinemann, 1918; New York: Putnam's, 1918);

The Consolation of Philosophy, translated, with an introduction and notes, by Richard H. Green (Indianapolis & New York: Bobbs-Merrill, 1962); revised edition, edited by S. J. Tester (London: Heinemann, 1973; Cambridge, Mass.: Harvard University Press, 1978);

Boethius's De topicis differentiis, edited and translated by Eleonore Stump (Ithaca, N.Y.: Cornell University Press, 1978);

Boethius's In Ciceronis Topica, translated by Stump (Ithaca, N.Y.: Cornell University Press, 1988);

Fundamentals of Music, translated, with an introduction and notes, by Calvin M. Bower, edited by Claude V. Palisca (New Haven: Yale University Press, 1989).

Looked at from the perspective of his death cell, the career of Boethius does not at first seem much of an argument for the belief that life makes sense. From being the favorite of fortune he has been cast down to the depths. He portrays himself as lamenting his fate until gradually, under the tutelage of Dame Philosophy, the wisdom he had laboriously acquired returned and served him as consolation. His reflections on his unjust treatment became a book which to this day is an all but necessary component of a liberal education.

Boethius was born into a distinguished Roman family around 480, a time when Italy was ruled by barbarian invaders whose legitimacy was grudgingly recognized by the Eastern emperors. His father, Aurelius Manlius Boethius, had served twice under the Visigoth Odoacer as prefect of Rome and once as praetorian prefect; in 487 he became consul.

Orphaned about 488, Boethius was taken into the household of the senator Quintus Aurelius Memmius Symmachus, a cultivated, pious Roman who was well connected both politically and ecclesiastically; Boethius eventually married Symmachus's daughter Rusticiana. In this setting Boethius acquired his love of learning, directed at Greek philosophy, and his Catholic loyalty, ever at the service of orthodoxy. It has been argued that Boethius was educated in Alexandria, and his writings betray close affinities with both Athenian and Alexandrian Neoplatonism. If it is the mark of Neoplatonism to wish to reconcile

Plato and Aristotle, the literary plan Boethius set for himself may be said to bear that mark. He would, he tells his reader, translate into Latin all the works of Aristotle and all the works of Plato and then go on to show their fundamental agreement. It is doubtful that such a task could have been accomplished in a long lifetime, and Boethius was destined to die relatively young. One may lament how little of this great project he managed to complete. On the other hand, one may rejoice that he accomplished as much of it as he did.

Theodoric, an Ostrogoth, deposed Odoacer in 493 and ruled Italy from Ravenna. His reign was in many ways an enlightened one. Members of Roman families continued to hold the traditional posts, he employed them at his court, and he appeared willing to see Arianism as the religion of Goths and Catholicism the religion of Romans. Boethius served the king for many years, beginning around 500. He served a term as consul in 510, as did his two sons in 522; the post was almost entirely a ceremonial one, requiring the outlay of enormous sums of money on the part of the incumbent for the entertainment of the populace. Boethius was named master of the offices by Theodoric in 523, but he soon fell afoul of Theodoric and, abandoned by his fellow senators, was condemned to death for conspiracy. He was executed in Pavia, probably in 524 or 525. As he awaited execution he composed one of the greatest examples of prison literature, *De Consolatione Philosophiae* (The Consolation of Philosophy), a work which vied with the Bible for popularity in the Middle Ages.

De Consolatione Philosophiae is part of an enormous literary output, but this final work is in a class by itself. Boethius's other writings are translations from the Greek, commentaries, original treatises on various liberal arts, and theological treatises.

Boethius has often been accused of plagiarism: some scholars have suggested that his commentaries are near to being translations of Greek commentaries. For example, portions from commentaries of Ammonius (with whom Pierre Courcelle was convinced Boethius studied in Alexandria) are juxtaposed to portions of Boethius's own—and, indeed, to passages from *De Consolatione Philosophiae*, and the close dependence of the latter on the former is pointed out. There are resemblances, some quite close, between such passages, and it is true that Boethius was influenced by the commentaries Alexandrian Neoplatonists wrote on Aristotle; but the charge of plagiarism is overblown. Indeed, one need only remember that Boethius had set himself the task of getting the wisdom of the Greeks into Latin to see how odd it is to look for innovations and fundamental originality in these efforts. Boethius worked quite consciously in a tradition, and the emphasis of his intellectual life is to assimilate that tradition rather than to put a personal stamp on it.

Boethius's writings are the main source for knowledge of the man. His first commentary on Porphyry's *Isagoge* (Introduction, circa 504-505) is cast in the form of a dialogue, and he paints a word picture of his home on Monte Aurelio, the night breeze passing through the house, Boethius sleepless and susceptible to being drawn into the exchange on Porphyry's work. His statement of his great translation project clearly envisages a labor of love rather than an onerous task. And the sadness of *De Consolatione Philosophiae* cannot conceal Boethius's love of learning and of truth. His Christian writings and his allusions to the admired Symmachus provide other hints of the kind of man he was. There is paternal pride in his voice when he notes that his sons served a year as joint consuls. He has been called the last Roman and the first Scholastic; he has also been called a founder of the Middle Ages. It is difficult to overstate his importance as a means whereby some, at least, of pagan philosophy passed into the Christian West and as a Christian whose reflections on his faith influenced the development of medieval philosophy. His gifts ran from logic to poetry, from music to theology, and from rhetoric to arithmetic; he was a statesman who could design and build a water clock.

His translation from Greek into Latin of Porphyry's *Isagoge* and of Aristotle's *Categories* and *On Interpretation*, *Prior Analytics*, *Posterior Analytics*, and *Topics* are extant. Boethius commented on the first two of these works—there are two commentaries on Porphyry as well as on *On Interpretation*, but only one on the *Categories*—but if he commented on the rest, his commentaries have been lost. Boethius also composed original logical works on division, on categorical and hypothetical syllogisms, and on dialectical reasoning to fill in gaps in the field. Besides these logical efforts, Boethius composed two works which fall into what he called the *quadrivium*, the "quadruple way" to wisdom: *De Institutione Arithmetica* (On Arithmetic, circa 503) and *De Institutione Musica* (On Music, circa 503). He may have composed

The earliest known pictorial representation of any of the seven liberal arts—in this case the quadrivium: Music, Arithmetic, Geometry, and Astronomy. This illustration is from a transcription of Boethius's De Institutione Arithmetica *made at Tours, circa 840, for Charles the Bald (Bamberg, Staatsbibliothek, class. 5, fol 9v°, s. ix).*

other mathematical works (there are references to a geometry by him), but they are not extant.

The label Boethius applied to some of these works was to be fateful for medieval education because of the influence of Boethius's contemporary Cassiodorus Senator, founder of a monastery at Vivarium and author of a book which set forth an ideal of conjoining secular and sacred learning. Sacred learning comes, of course, from Scripture; secular learning is organized by Cassiodorus around the notion of the seven liberal arts. The medieval division of the arts into the trivium (grammar, rhetoric, and logic) and the quadrivium (arithmetic, geometry, music, and astronomy) show the influence of Boethius.

There was yet another influence of Boethius on medieval learning. After setting forth accounts of the universals genus, species, difference, property, and accident—knowledge of which is a prerequisite to understanding the *Categories*—Porphyry says that to decide between the Platonic and Aristotelian views on the ontological status of universals would be far too complicated for an introductory work. But Porphyry did formulate the three questions he would not answer, questions which collectively make up what historians call the Problem of Universals. Are genera and species mere figments of the imagination, or do they really exist? If they really exist, are they corporeal or incorporeal? If incorporeal, do they exist with bodies or independent of them?

In both of his commentaries Boethius provides answers to these questions—a quite elaborate answer in his second commentary, where he relies on Alexander of Aphrodisias and gives what he characterizes as an Aristotelian solution. His dwelling on matters Porphyry thought postponable started a tradition that produced luxuriant fruit, one theory of universals succeeding another into the twelfth century.

Boethius's solution to the problem of universals created one of the puzzles associated with him. He gives, he says, an Aristotelian account because he is commenting on an introduction to a work of Aristotle's. Is he suggesting that it is a solution he does not personally accept? Is he an Aristotelian or a Platonist? The question may perhaps be taken to be settled by the remark in *De Consolatione Philosophiae*: "I align myself vigorously with Plato" (*Platoni vehementer assentior*). But in the same work Dame Philosophy speaks approvingly of "my Aristotle."

In his first commentary on Porphyry, Boethius speaks of the three theoretical sciences as concerned with intellectibles, intelligibles, and naturals, a Platonic declension from the eternal and timeless to the changing and temporal. Physical objects are described as fallen versions of intellectibles, contaminated by matter. Chapter 2 of his *De Trinitate* (On the Trinity, circa 521), on the other hand, provides what appears to be a straightforward version of the Aristotelian division of theoretical philosophy as found, for instance, in *Metaphysics* E, 1. Natural philosophy is concerned with things which exist in matter and must be defined with matter; mathematics is concerned with things which exist in matter but are defined without matter; theology is concerned with what both exists and is defined without matter. Since the second text is later and is an original work, not a commentary, it might be taken to express Boethius's own view. But later in the chapter one begins to encounter Platonic Forms, with "earthly man" (*homo terrenus*) apparently being a participation in the Ideal Man. True forms exist apart from matter: "Forms which are in matter and produce a body come from those forms which are outside matter." The Platonic flavor of the passage seems inescapable.

In the tractate *Quomodo Substantiae in Eo Quod Sint Bonae Sint cum Non Sint Substantialia Bona* (Whether Everything That Exists Is Good Just Because It Exists, circa 521) Boethius says that God, the First Good, is essentially good; the question arises as to what is meant when his effects are called good. There seem to be two possibilities: creatures are either good substantially—that is, essentially—or they are good by way of participation. If the first, they are identical with God, which is absurd. But Boethius also denies the second alternative, addressing the question in a geometrical fashion. He sets down a list of axioms, among which is "like attracts like." But the good is that which all things seek. So, to seek the good, things must *be* good. If they were good only by participation, they could be without being good and thus could not pursue the good; but that possibility runs counter to another axiom: that all things seek the good. Thus, the dilemma is encountered that, of the two possible answers, neither is acceptable. Boethius argues that the existent effects of the First Good are good because the First Good is also the First Being. The identity of being and goodness in God trickles down to his effects. Participation, which in the posing of the dilemma was equated with accidental predication—the attribution to something of a quality it can exist with or without—comes to have another meaning in the course of the tractate; Boethius's solution is that the creature participates in goodness in such a way that it cannot exist and fail to be good. The goodness in view here is not of course moral goodness. It may be called ontological goodness or, in medieval terminology, transcendental goodness.

The first axiom set forth at the beginning of the treatise is "What a thing is and for it to be are diverse" (*diversum est esse et id quod est*). Many modern interpreters understand this axiom as a distinction between a nature and the individual that has that nature, for example, between humanity and Socrates. Thomas Aquinas, who commented on this tractate, took Boethius to be saying that for any composite thing, its being the kind of thing it is does not explain why it exists at all. Oddly enough, it is often Thomists—disciples of Thomas—who insist that he got the text wrong. Such Thomists consider this truth—dubbed "the real distinction between essence and existence"—to have been discovered by Thomas; if that were true, he could not, of course, have found it in the text of Boethius. Unfortunately for such Thomists, Thomas is confident that he finds it in Boethius (as well as in many other predecessors). Indeed, given the way it is introduced by Boethius, this truth does not sound like something in need of discovery: Boethius calls his axioms "*communes animae conceptiones*" (the mind's most common understandings)—self-evident truths, assent to which requires only knowledge of what the terms mean. A creature can be good insofar as it exists, without being essentially good. The creature exists because the First Good wills it to be, and, the First Good being the source of its existence, the creature is good just insofar as it exists.

The tractate *De Fide Catholica* (On the Catholic Faith, circa 521) is simply a narrative of the main lines of Christian belief: God one and triune; creation; the fall of man; the covenant with Israel which prepared for the new covenant estab-

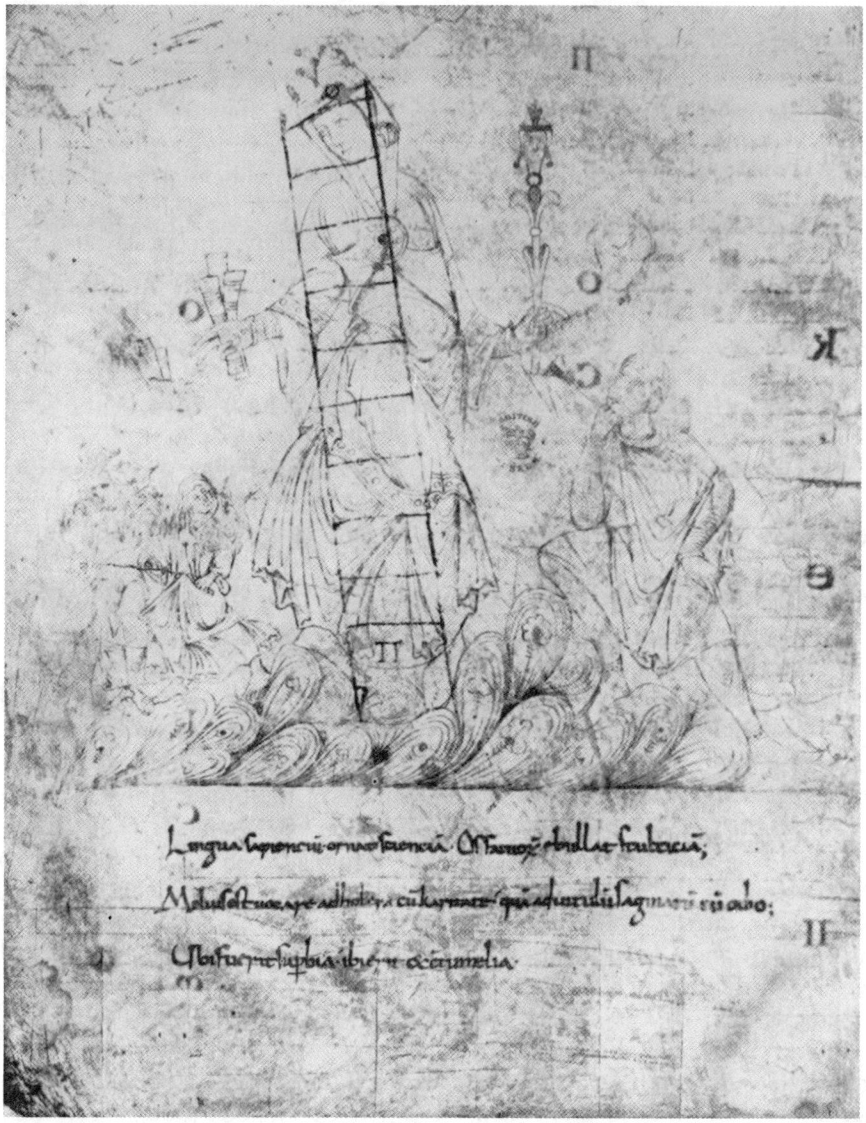

Boethius (right) being visited in his prison cell by Philosophy. This drawing was originally the frontispiece to a transcription of Boethius's De Consolatione Philosophiae, *made prior to 950 (Ms. Harley 2688, f. 22v; British Library).*

lished by Christ, who was both human and divine and whose propitiatory sacrifice reconciles man with God; the sacraments; the preaching of the gospel to the whole world; the end times. "There is therefore now but one expectation of the faithful by which we believe that the end of the world will come, that all corruptible things shall pass away, that men shall rise for the test of the judgment to come, that each shall be rewarded according to his deserts and abide in the lot assigned him perpetually and eternally."

In *Contra Euthycen et Nestorium* (Against Eutyches and Nestorius, circa 512) Boethius established a Latin vocabulary that became part of the patrimony of medieval and later theology, including such terms as *essence, nature, substance, subsistence,* and *existence.* The tractate put before the reader the Greek accounts that Boethius is rendering in Latin and thus served as a linguistic bridge in times when knowledge of Greek was not widespread. If Boethius served as one of the chief conduits whereby Greek philosophy came into the Latin West, he also made important contributions to the mutual understanding of Greek and Latin Christianity.

In this tractate and in *De Trinitate,* both of which are derivative from Augustine, Boethius is intent to show that the Christian belief is not that there are three gods but rather that there are three persons in the one God. *Contra Euthycen et*

Nestorium begins with a vivid mise-en-scène, a meeting of high churchmen and educated laymen at Rome with Boethius and Symmachus in attendance. The opening paragraph of *De Trinitate* provides clues as to Boethius's understanding of the relation between faith and reason; he observes: "We should of course press our inquiry only so far as the insight of man's reason is allowed to climb the height of heavenly knowledge." The tractates assume the truth of the Trinity and Incarnation and seek to bring to bear on them such philosophical knowledge as can diminish their obscurity. The analysis is not meant to establish the truth of the dogma being analyzed; faith is the warrant of the truth of such mysteries. "And I think that the method of our inquiry must be borrowed from what is admittedly the surest source of all truth, namely, the fundamental doctrines of the Catholic faith."

Unlike John Philoponus, a Christian philosopher in Alexandria who formulated lengthy refutations of the claim that the world is eternal, Boethius does not seem to quarrel with the teaching that the world has always been. But this discussion is in *De Consolatione Philosophiae*, and the nature of that work as compared with the tractates makes Boethius a truly enigmatic figure.

Indeed, so striking is the difference between the theological tractates, with their assertion of the Christian faith and careful analysis of its central mysteries and defense of them against heretical interpretations, that *De Consolatione Philosophiae* can leave one wondering whether its author is a pagan philosopher or a Christian thinker. This discrepancy led some scholars to conclude that the tractates could not have been written by Boethius if Boethius was the author of *De Consolatione Philosophiae*, as he indubitably was. This solution to the problem was removed by the discovery of the so-called *Anecdoton Holderi* in which Cassiodorus Senator himself says that Boethius was the author of the tractates as well as of *De Consolatione Philosophiae*. But why would a Christian, unjustly accused and facing execution, not appeal to the innocent victim par excellence for consolation? James Boswell records Samuel Johnson's amazement that Boethius, in such circumstances, showed himself to be a philosopher rather than a Christian.

De Consolatione Philosophiae is made up of five books with alternating prose and verse sections. The thematic question is biblical, reminiscent of the Book of Job: why do the innocent suffer and the wicked prosper? The work opens with Boethius, abject in his death cell, bemoaning his fate and seeking to console himself with poetry. Suddenly an imposing female figure, Dame Philosophy, appears. She is wearing a ladderlike tunic whose rungs represent the liberal arts; embroidered on her garment are the Greek letters *Pi* and *Theta*, symbolizing the two main branches of philosophy, the practical and the theoretical. The dispatch of poetry does not prevent its use in the course of the argument; indeed, the prose sections function as comments on the verse. Plato exiled poetry from his ideal state in the *Republic* and then employed it in the writing of that dialogue; and the plot of the *De Consolatione Philosophiae* recalls the parable of the cave in the *Republic*. Boethius is in a state of forgetfulness; he has lost contact with wisdom; he is so confused as to think that it is fortune which confers happiness on men. A long and arduous dialectic is required to disabuse him of such confusion. Wisdom will be regained when Boethius once more is able to see the goods of fortune from a higher perspective, within a providential order. *De Consolatione Philosophiae* echoes with the arguments of the philosophers, Stoics as well as Platonists and Aristotelians. The emerging question is: What is human happiness? In what does a person's real fulfillment and perfection consist? In riches and pleasure, in honor and fame, in power? Such candidates are weighed and found wanting. They are gifts, things that happen to us, not what we bring about. The focus thus turns to the wellsprings of human agency; but before daring to define true human happiness, one must invoke God's help. God is goodness itself and the human good must be seen in relation to the First Good. Themes from *Quomodo Substantiae in Eo Quod Sint Bonae Sint cum Non Sint Substantialia Bona* recur; there is an account of how Aristotle explained the fortuitous in his *Physics* and *On Interpretation*; there is a contrast of Fate and Providence; there is a discussion of the problem of the compatibility of God's foreknowledge and human free will. The message is clear: a person who turns from the beguiling lures of this world, who devotes himself to virtue and to knowledge, who wins through to clarity on such issues, will have the consolation philosophy can afford in this vale of tears. From this regained perspective, Boethius can accept the injustice that has befallen him and turn his face toward the First Good.

De Consolatione Philosophiae is theological and religious, but the theology and religion are philosophical. Herein lies the enigma for subsequent readers: how could a Christian settle for this? That question will be discussed as long as Boethius is read; no one has ever answered it in a satisfactory way.

Many eminent writers have praised *De Consolatione Philosophiae*. It is difficult to imagine a time when the work will not be read, and read by the general reader. The theological tractates of Boethius must interest anyone concerned with the history of Christian theology, but they can function as bedside reading only for the few. Those whose scholarly concern is the transmission of pagan learning to the Christian West will accord Boethius a primary place in the process. Boethius's book on music was regularly read until the late nineteenth century but perhaps now can claim only historical interest. The accessible Boethius, the Boethius who is read in paperback, on plane and train, in home and on campus, is the author of *De Consolatione Philosophiae*. The poignancy of the narrative is deepened by the knowledge that shortly its author would be put to death. As it happened, Symmachus, his beloved mentor and father-in-law, was executed on the same charge. And Theodoric, their accuser and judge, died shortly thereafter. It is as if the historical events were meant to illustrate the long view advocated by *De Consolatione Philosophiae*.

Biography:

Helen M. Barrett, *Boethius: Some Aspects of His Times and Work* (Cambridge: Cambridge University Press, 1940; New York: Russell & Russell, 1965).

References:

Henry Chadwick, *Boethius: The Consolations of Music, Logic, Theology and Philosophy* (Oxford: Clarendon Press, 1981; New York: Oxford University Press, 1981);

Pierre Courcelle, "The East to the Rescue of Pagan Culture: Boethius," in his *Late Latin Writers and Their Greek Sources*, translated by Harry E. Wedeck (Cambridge, Mass.: Harvard University Press, 1969), pp. 273-330;

C. S. Lewis, *The Discarded Image: An Introduction to Medieval and Renaissance Literature* (Cambridge: Cambridge University Press, 1964), pp. 75-90;

Bruno Maioli, *Teoria dell'essere e dell'esistente e Classificazione delle scienze in M. S. Boezio* (Rome: Bulzoni, 1978);

Ralph McInerny, *Boethius and Aquinas* (Washington, D.C.: Catholic University of America Press, 1990);

Luca Obertello, *Severino Boezio*, 2 volumes (Genoa: Accademia ligure di scienze e lettere, 1974);

Howard R. Patch, *The Tradition of Boethius: A Study of His Importance in Medieval Culture* (New York: Oxford University Press, 1935);

Edward K. Rand, "Boethius, the First of the Scholastics," in his *Founders of the Middle Ages* (Cambridge, Mass.: Harvard University Press, 1928);

Edmund Reiss, *Boethius* (Boston: Twayne, 1982);

David L. Wagner, ed., *The Seven Liberal Arts in the Middle Ages* (Bloomington: Indiana University Press, 1983).

Boethius of Dacia
(Boethius or Boetius of Sweden)

(circa 1240 - ?)

Anthony J. Celano
Stonehill College

PRINCIPAL WORKS: *Opuscula: De Aeternitate Mundi, De Summo Bono, De Somniis* (Opuscula: On the Eternity of the World, On the Supreme Good, On Dreams, written circa 1270-1274);

Modi Significandi sive Quaestiones super Priscianum Minorem (Modes of Signifying; or, Questions on Priscian Minor, written circa 1270-1274);

Quaestiones de Generatione et Corruptione (Questions on Generation and Corruption, written circa 1270-1274);

Quaestiones super Libros Physicorum (Questions on the *Physics*, written circa 1270-1274);

Quaestiones super Librum Topicorum (Questions on the *Topics*, written circa 1270-1274);

Quaestiones super IVm Meteorologicorum (Questions on the Fourth Book of the *Meteorology*, written circa 1270-1274);

Sophismata (Sophisms, written circa 1270-1274).

EDITIONS: "Die *Opuscula, De summo bono sive de vita philosophi* and *De sompniis* des Boetius von Dacien," edited by Martin Grabmann, *Archives d'histoire doctrinale et littéraire du moyen âge*, 6 (1931): 287-317;

Corpus philosophicorum Danicorum Medii Aevi, volumes 1, 2, 4, 6, 8, 9, edited by Géza Sajó, Jan Pinborg, Heinrich Roos, Niels G. Green-Pedersen, Gianfranco Fioravanti, and S. Ebbesen (Copenhagen: Gad, 1969-1979; volume 9 forthcoming).

EDITIONS IN ENGLISH: *Godfrey of Fontaine's Abridgement of Boethius of Dacia's Modi Significandi, sive Quaestiones super Priscianum Minorem*, translated by A. Charlene Senape McDermott (Amsterdam: Benjamins, 1980);

Boethius of Dacia: On the Supreme Good, On the Eternity of the World, On Dreams, translated by John Wippel (Toronto: Pontifical Institute of Mediaeval Studies, 1987);

"Boethius of Dacia: The Sophisma 'Every Man Is of Necessity an Animal,' " translated by Eleonore Stump, in *The Cambridge Translations of Medieval Philosophical Texts*, volume 1 (Cambridge: Cambridge University Press, 1988), pp. 480-510.

Little is known with certainty concerning the life of Boethius of Dacia. Scandinavian in origin, likely Danish, Boethius was identified as a leader of the "radical Averroists" or "heterodox Aristotelians" who taught at the University of Paris in the turbulent early 1270s. Though his birth date is unknown, Boethius certainly was a member of the arts faculty at Paris around 1270. There his impassioned defense of the autonomy of philosophical reason earned the suspicion of more conservative theologians, who included several theses taken from Boethius's writings in the condemnations promulgated by the bishop of Paris Stephen Tempier in 1277. Unlike his contemporary Siger of Brabant, Boethius was never called to face the royal inquisition to defend his philosophical positions. He may have entered the Dominican order some time after 1273, since the so-called Stams Catalogue of Dominican works includes a list of his writings.

If the life of Boethius remains obscure, the picture of his literary activity has become clearer through the historical research of the last half of the twentieth century. Many of Boethius's writings were the products of his magisterial activity at Paris in the years around 1270 and cover a wide range of philosophical topics which were vigorously debated at the university. He commented on the works of Aristotle and considered topics such as supreme human goodness, the eternity of the world, and the nature of the physical and metaphysical sciences. His authentic writings include the logical works *Modi Significandi sive Quaestiones super Priscianum Minorem* (Modes of Signifying; or, Questions on Priscian Minor, circa

1270-1274), *Quaestiones super Librum Topicorum* (Questions on the *Topics*, circa 1270-1274), and *Sophismata* (Sophisms, circa 1270-1274), the works on natural philosophy *Quaestiones de Generatione et Corruptione* (Questions on Generation and Corruption, circa 1270-1274), *Quaestiones super Libros Physicorum* (Questions on the *Physics*, circa 1270-1274), and *Quaestiones super IVm Meteorologicorum* (Questions on the Fourth Book of the *Meteorology*, circa 1270-1274); and *Opuscula: De Aeternitate Mundi, De Summo Bono, De Somniis* (Opuscula: On the Eternity of the World, On the Supreme Good, On Dreams, circa 1270-1274). Boethius certainly composed all of his works before 1277, probably by 1273.

In the logical works Boethius describes the aim and limits of the philosophical science, and his understanding of the boundaries of scientific research affects all his subsequent philosophical conclusions. Scholars such as Géza Sajó, Jan Pinborg, and Paul Wilpert have noted how important the scientific principle "*nullus artifex considerare potest illa quae sunt extra terminos suae scientiae*" (no worker can consider those things which are beyond the limits of his science) is for comprehending the thought of Boethius. This principle guides Boethius in his search for solutions of difficult problems concerning the ability of human reason to unravel the mysteries of the physical universe, the nature of human goodness, and the absolute power of the first cause. It also directs Boethius's understanding of the way in which the philosophy of Aristotle may be applied to questions provoked by religious doctrines.

Science, according to Boethius, must proceed from necessary general principles which permit some conclusion to be deduced concerning the object under study. To gain scientific knowledge the philosopher must formulate principles and conclusions based on the observation of natural phenomena. Boethius adds another condition for the production of scientific knowledge: "all science concerns some being" (*omnis scientia est de aliquo ente*). The philosopher does not merely formulate propositions without regard to observed physical phenomena; he must attempt to reduce individual effects to their true causes. Boethius maintains that logic originated in observations of causal connections between physical events. The first logician, Boethius writes, was not only a dialectician but also a philosopher who correctly identified the relationship between causes and their effects.

Since the logician, as such, does not concern himself with the causal connections within the physical world, logic produces no scientific knowledge; it generates only opinion. Though the conclusion in the argument "Socrates is a man, therefore he is an animal" follows necessarily from the connection between the terms *man* and *animal*, Boethius denies the status of scientific knowledge to the conclusion because its causal connection has not been verified through experience. He maintains the impossibility of formulating true propositions about nonexisting objects, since truth about the world is not derived by supposition alone but through observed causal connections. The statement "Man is an animal" would not be true if no human beings existed, since there would be no way to verify the state of reality which the statement signifies. While Boethius asserts in *Sophismata* that logic can formulate no true proposition about nonexisting objects, he indicates elsewhere that such propositions may be considered true regardless of the object's existence. Whatever Boethius's final thoughts on this problem may have been, he clearly considers logic incapable of producing scientific certainty.

Though logic may not lead to scientific knowledge in the strictest sense, it still may be considered a science within its own limits. Like all sciences, it describes a closed system derived from its own principles. Logical conclusions may be considered necessary insofar as they denote the way in which certain terms are predicated of certain subjects. This formal necessity may or may not describe an actual state of the natural world, but it does permit an informed opinion about the inherence of a predicate within a subject. The method of dialectical argument is therefore useful in moral, mathematical, physical, and metaphysical discourse, since informed opinion is more easily produced than scientific necessity; and concerning beings whose causes are difficult to discover, it is better to have an opinion than to remain wholly ignorant. Logic not only demands that the rules of argument be followed in scientific discourse; it also contributes to a certain type of resolution of difficult problems within these sciences. No philosopher, therefore, should ignore the contributions of logic to more substantive problems.

In his works devoted to natural philosophy, Boethius shows himself to be a careful and diligent expositor of Aristotle's thought. The objects studied in each science determine the aim and limits of the philosopher's quest. The most important element in any discipline is the constant nature of the objects under consideration. In metaphysics, the First Being (God), who is the ultimate cause of all inferior beings, is the primary object of study. All other beings are influenced by the causality of the Supreme Being, whose absolute immutability and perfection elevate metaphysics to the level of the most certain human science.

In the physical world beings undergo constant alteration; the constant element here lies in the relationship between cause and effect. In identifying the natural causes of all change, including generation and corruption, the natural philosopher remains bound by the principles of physical science. These principles assume the existence of matter, the four causes of change (formal, material, efficient, and final) described by Aristotle, and the Aristotelian concepts of act and potency. Regarding the creation of matter, Boethius says: "because the making of matter cannot be natural, no physicist in any book on natural things made mention of it."

Boethius realizes that Aristotle's natural philosophy does not permit the temporal beginning of the universe or the resurrection of the body. He says that no one can offer scientific demonstrations of the possibility of these miraculous events; but because his faith demands belief, Boethius is willing to deny the principles of natural science. Boethius is not advocating a theory of double truth, whereby one conclusion may be philosophically true and its opposite must be true according to faith. Although Boethius has at times been described as an advocate of this doctrine of double truth, he merely allows for the possibility of the causality of the Supreme Being contravening the laws of nature.

In his opusculum *De Aeternitate Mundi* Boethius tries to maintain the integrity of the conclusions of natural philosophers while asserting the absolute verity of the teachings of Christianity. Since faith opposes natural reason on the question of the eternity of the world, Boethius is forced to resort to subtle and carefully formulated arguments to resolve the problem. The philosopher cannot demonstrate either that the world began temporally (*ex novo*) or that it was created from nothing (*ex nihilo*). Change requires a prior moving cause, according to the principles of natural science, so the philosopher assumes motion to be eternal. But the philosopher is also prohibited from demonstrating the creation of the world, since divine volition, on which creation depends, remains hidden from human reason. Although the philosopher denies a temporal beginning to motion, he need not deny the possibility of a higher cause suspending the natural laws and producing an effect which seems impossible. This possibility prevents the philosopher from concluding with certainty that the world is eternal. The Scriptures must be accepted as the final account of the world's origin. In maintaining such a position, Boethius agrees substantially with Thomas Aquinas and opposes the claims of theologians such as Bonaventure, Henry of Ghent, and John Peckham who believed reason sufficient for demonstrating the beginning of the universe.

In another opusculum, *De Summo Bono*, Boethius investigates the highest human good that can be known by reason. He, with Aristotle, concludes that human goodness consists in both moral and intellectual excellence: to achieve supreme goodness one must perform morally good actions as well as come to some understanding of the First Being. There is no greater good "than a cognition of the totality of beings which emanate from the first principle, and therefore a cognition of the first principle itself insofar as such a cognition is possible." Aristotle's description of the desire to know the first cause in Book X of the *Nicomachean Ethics* leads Boethius to align the philosopher's quest for cognition of the First Being with the believer's love of God. Like Thomas Aquinas, Boethius is convinced that the rational moral ideal of intellectual union with the Supreme Being brings man closer to the perfect union between God and man described in the Scriptures.

Boethius's bold use of philosophical language and his unflinching adherence to the principles of philosophy earned him the enmity of the more conservative theologians of the last quarter of the thirteenth century. Propositions concerning the elevated status of philosophers and the denial of reason's ability to demonstrate the creation of the world which were condemned in 1277 were likely taken from his works. But the theologians who were unsympathetic to, and perhaps unaware of, the subtleties of his arguments were unable to face the challenge he brought to their understanding of the relationship between faith and reason. Boethius preferred the confrontation of contradictory positions to the false security of bolstering theological doctrines with faulty philosophical reasoning. He never denied the superiority of faith, since he viewed the relationship between religion and philosophy in the same way he regarded the relationship among the human sciences. A superior science may overrule the conclusions of an inferior one, as the laws of physics supersede merely logical conclusions and as the principles of metaphysics may supplant the deductions of physics. Boethius was too skillful a thinker and too sound a philosopher to accept a theory of double truth. He admitted, however, that human sciences are restricted by their principles and rules, and that faith may provide answers that reason cannot.

References:

T. Bukowski and B. Dumoulin, "L'influence de Thomas d'Aquin sur Boéce de Dacie," *Revue des sciences philosophiques et théologiques*, 57 (1973): 627-631;

Anthony J. Celano, "Boethius of Dacia: On the Highest Good," *Traditio*, 43 (1987): 199-214;

Roland Hissette, *Enquête sur les 219 articles condamnés à Paris le 7 Mars 1277* (Louvain: Publications Universitaires, 1977);

Armand A. Maurer, "Boethius of Dacia and the Double Truth," *Mediaeval Studies*, 17 (1955): 235-239;

Jan Pinborg, "Zur Philosophie des Boethius de Dacia: Ein Überblick," *Studia Mediewistyczne*, 15 (1974): 165-185; reprinted in his *Medieval Semantics: Selected Studies on Medieval Logic and Grammar*, edited by Sten Ebbesen (London: Variorum Reprints, 1984);

Fernand Van Steenberghen, *Thomas Aquinas and Radical Aristotelianism* (Washington, D.C.: Catholic University of America Press, 1980), pp. 95-99;

Paul Wilpert, "Boethius v. Dacien—die Autonomie des Philosophen," *Miscellanea Mediaevalia*, 3 (1964): 135-152.

Bonaventure (Giovanni di Fidanza)

(circa 1217 - 15 July 1274)

Anthony Murphy
Saint Bonaventure University

PRINCIPAL WORKS: *Quaestiones Disputatae de Scientia Christi* (Disputed Questions on Christ's Knowledge, written 1254);

Quaestiones Disputatae de Mysterio Trinitatis (Disputed Questions on the Mystery of the Trinity, written 1254);

Quaestiones Disputatae de Caritate et de Novissimis (Disputed Questions on Charity and the Last Things, written between 1254 and 1257);

De Reductione Artium ad Theologiam (On the Reduction of the Arts to Theology, written circa 1255-1257 or circa 1273);

Breviloquium (Brief Commentary, written 1257);

Itinerarium Mentis in Deum (The Mind's Road to God, written October 1259);

De Triplici Via (The Triple Way, written 1259);

Legenda Major (Long Life of Saint Francis, written 1261);

Collationes de Decem Praeceptis (Collations on the Ten Commandments, written 1267);

Collationes de Septem Donis Spiritus Sancti (Collations on the Seven Gifts of the Holy Spirit, written 1268);

Collationes in Hexaëmeron sive Illuminationes Ecclesiae (Collations on the Six Days of Creation; or, Enlightenment of the Church, written 1273).

EDITIONS: *Doctoris Seraphici S. Bonaventurae Opera Omnia*, 10 volumes (Quaracchi & Firenze: Ad Claras Aquas, 1882-1902);

Collationes in Hexaëmeron et Bonaventuriana quaedem selecta, edited by Ferdinand Delorme (Quaracchi: Ad Claras Aquas, 1934);

Doctoris Seraphici S. Bonaventurae opera theologica selecta, 5 volumes (Quaracchi & Firenze: Ad Claras Aquas, 1934-1965);

Bonaventure, as depicted by Benedetto Bonfigli, 1472 (from Steven Ozment, The Age of Reform, 1250-1550, *1980)*

Obras de San Buenaventura, 6 volumes, edited by León Amoros, Bernardo Aperribay, and Miguel Oromi (Madrid: Biblioteca de Autores Cristianos, 1945-1949).

CRITICAL EDITIONS: *Questions disputées De Caritate, De Novissimis,* edited by Palémon Glorieux (Paris: Editions Franciscaines, 1950);

Sancti Bonaventurae Sermones Dominicales, edited by Jacques Guy Bougerol (Grottaferrata: Collegio S. Bonaventura, Padri Editori di Quaracchi, 1977).

EDITIONS IN ENGLISH: *The Life of the Holie Father S. Francis, Writen by Saint Bonaventure and as It Is Related by the Reverend Father Aloysius Lipomanus, Bishop of Veron, in His Fourth Tome of the Life of Saintes*, translated by Anthony Maria Browne, Viscount Montague (Douay: Printed by Laurence Kellam, 1610);

The Life of the Most Holy Father S. Francis, Written and in One Booke Compiled by That Famous and Learned Man S. Bonaventure, translation attributed to Montague (Douay: Imprinted by Martin Bogard, 1635);

The Life of S. Francis of Assisi: From the "Legenda Santi Francisci" of S. Bonaventure. By the Author of "The Life of S. Teresa," translated by Elizabeth Lockhart, edited by Henry Edward Manning (London: Washbourne, 1868);

"The Soul's Progress in God, Translated from the Latin of Bonaventura ('Itinerarium Mentis in Deum')," translated by Thomas Davidson, *Journal of Speculative Philosophy*, 21 (July 1887): 288-324;

The Life of Saint Francis, translated by E. Gurney Salter (London: Dent, 1904);

The Virtues of a Religious Superior (De Sex alis Seraphim): Instructions by the Seraphic Doctor, St. Bonaventure, translated by Sabinus Mollitor (St. Louis & London: Herder, 1920);

A Franciscan View of the Spiritual and Religious Life: Being Three Treatises from the Writings of Saint Bonaventure, Done into English, translated by Dominic Devas (London: Baker, 1922);

Holiness of Life: Being St. Bonaventure's Treatise De Perfectione Vitae ad Sorores, translated by Laurence Costello (St. Louis & London: Herder, 1923);

The Franciscan Vision: Translation of St. Bonaventure's Itinerarium Mentis in Deum, translated by James Edward O'Mahony (London: Burns & Oates, 1937);

On the Reduction of the Arts to Theology: The First Translation into the American Language of De Reductione Artium et Theologiam, translated by Charles Glenn Wallis (Annapolis: St. John's Press, 1938);

Saint Bonaventure's De Reductione Artium ad Theologiam: A Commentary with an Introduction and Translation, translated by Sister Emma Thérèse Healy (Saint Bonaventure, N.Y.: Saint Bonaventure College, 1939);

Breviloquium, translated by Erwin E. Nemmers (St. Louis & London: Herder, 1946);

"Letter on the Imitation of Christ," translated by M. Brady, *Assisian*, 6 (1946): 160-165;

The Mind's Road to God, translated, with an introduction, by George Boas (New York: Liberal Arts Press, 1953);

"The Rule for Novices," translated by Joseph Mahoney, *Cord*, 4, no. 1 (1954): 10-15; no. 2 (1954): 37-42; no. 3 (1954): 74-77; no. 4 (1954): 118-121;

Saint Bonaventure's Itinerarium Mentis in Deum, with an Introduction, Translation and Commentary, translated by Philotheus Boehner (St. Bonaventure, N.Y.: Franciscan Institute, 1956);

"St. Bonaventure's Conferences on the Gifts of the Holy Spirit," translated by M. Hogan, *Cord*, 7 (1957): 80-156, 217-222, 250-256; 8 (1958): 83-92, 150-159, 175-184;

The Way of Perfection, Based on the Rule for Novices of St. Bonaventura, translated by Anslem Romb, edited by Method C. Billy and Salvator Pantano (Chicago: Franciscan Herald Press, 1958);

"On the Knowability of God," translated by Richard McKeon, in *Selections from Medieval Philosophers*, edited by McKeon, volume 2 (New York: Scribners, 1958), pp. 118-148;

Hymn to the Cross, translated by José de Vinck (Paterson, N.J.: St. Anthony Guild Press, 1960);

The Works of Bonaventure: Cardinal, Seraphic Doctor, and Saint, 5 volumes, translated by de Vinck (Paterson, N.J.: St. Anthony Guild Press, 1960-1970);

"The Life of St. Francis (Legenda Major)" and "The Life of St. Francis (Legenda Minor)," translated by Benen Fahy, in *St. Francis of Assisi: Writings and Early Biographies. English Omnibus of Sources for the Life of St. Francis*, edited by Marion A. Habig (Chicago: Franciscan Herald Press, 1973);

Rooted in Faith: Homilies to a Contemporary World, translated by Marigwen Schumacher (Chicago: Franciscan Herald Press, 1974);

What Manner of Man? Sermons on Christ by St. Bonaventure, translated by Zachary Hayes (Chicago: Franciscan Herald Press, 1974);

Bonaventure, translated by Ewert Cousins (New York: Paulist Press, 1978);

The Disciple and the Master: Sermons of St. Bonaventure on St. Francis, translated by Eric Doyle (Chicago: Franciscan Herald Press, 1983);

St. Bonaventure as a Biblical Commentator: A Translation and Analysis of His "Commentary on Luke," XVIII, 34 - XIX, 42, translated by Thomas Reist (Lanham, Md.: University Press of America, 1985).

The thirteenth century can be characterized as the century of grand intellectual syntheses, and the thought of Saint Bonaventure stands out as a philosophical and theological synthesis equal to that of Thomas Aquinas. One a Franciscan and the other a Dominican, both men were officially recognized as regent masters at the University of Paris on the same day: 12 August 1257. Indeed, the philosophies of Bonaventure and Aquinas have come to represent the two most comprehensive interpretations of the universe as seen by Christians—the synthesis of Aquinas being essentially Aristotelian, while Bonaventure's edifice, attempting to render philosophically intelligible an essentially mystical and religious insight, represents the fullest expression of medieval Augustinianism.

Bonaventure was born in Bagnorea, in Tuscany, Italy, as Giovanni di Fidanza around 1217. His father, also named Giovanni, appears to have been a fairly well-to-do physician; his mother was Maria di Ritello (or Maria Ritella). While a boy, Bonaventure fell seriously ill and was saved from death, he says, only through the miraculous intervention of Saint Francis of Assisi. Although Bonaventure never met the living Francis, he became a follower of Francis for life; it would be no exaggeration to say that Bonaventure's thought was a philosophical and theological embodiment of the spirit and mystical insight of Francis of Assisi.

After receiving his primary education in the Franciscan Monastery of Bagnorea from 1225 to 1235, he entered the faculty of arts at the University of Paris in 1236, becoming bachelor of arts in 1241 and master of arts in 1243. He entered the Franciscan order at Paris in 1243, taking the name Bonaventure. As a Franciscan novice he would have studied theology under Alexander of Hales and John of La Rochelle until their deaths in 1245. In 1248 he became a bachelor in biblical studies and lectured on the Gospel of St. Luke and other scriptural texts.

The next stage of instruction at the university required a lengthy study of and commentary on the *Libri Quatuor Sententiarum* (Four Books of Sentences) of Peter Lombard. Bonaventure's monumental four-volume commentary on the *Sentences*, probably the outstanding example of this genre of medieval literature, was begun in 1250 and completed in 1252. It is his first major attempt at developing a philosophical and theological synthesis. The *Libri Quatuor Sententiarum*, written between 1155 and 1157, had become the official textbook in theology in all Christian universities. The four books of Lombard's work were concerned with the whole range of theological issues: the Trinity and the divine attributes; the creation of the world and of humanity and the Fall; the Incarnation and the virtues; and the sacraments and the Last Things. All these questions were treated by Lombard in a traditional Augustinian manner.

Bonaventure's commentary makes it clear that he, like Augustine, viewed theology as rooted in faith. Theology is faith seeking understanding. Bonaventure had no intention of developing a theology of pure speculation; there is for him an infinite distance between knowing Christ and knowing an axiom of Euclid. The underlying presupposition of Bonaventure's synthesis is that theology is not merely a speculative science but a way of life, existing for no other reason than the formation of saints. The intention is not to know the good in some abstract sense but to become good. This practical understanding of theology points out the gap between Bonaventure's vision and that of Aquinas.

Bonaventure received his licentiate and doctorate from the University of Paris in 1253, meaning that he had the right to teach at the university. It is reasonable to assume that he was a full-time academic at Paris from 1253 until his election as minister general of the Franciscan order on 2 February 1257.

During this period (a time during which Thomas Aquinas was also teaching at Paris), Bonaventure delivered at least three series of disputed questions to the university, a task appropriate to a master. These disputed questions represent his most mature and detailed Scholastic work.

The *Quaestiones Disputatae de Scientia Christi* (Disputed Questions on Christ's Knowledge, 1254) presents the foremost problem of Bonaventurean epistemology; how human beings can have certain knowledge. The answer is found in the Augustinian notion of divine illumination. In Question 2 Bonaventure concludes that God knows the world through the exemplary ideas after which things are patterned; the ideas are regulative principles that constitute the possibilities of both thought and physical reality and render certain knowledge of things possible. In that sense, when human beings know the world with certitude they are in some manner knowing the divine mind itself—or, better yet, the divine mind is knowing the world through them.

One immediate difficulty is that if humans know the world through the mediation of divine ideas, it would seem to follow that they must know as God knows—that is, that they must know things perfectly. Such perfect knowledge may be the case when humans have achieved a state of perfection or blessedness at the end time; but as long as they are beset with all the limitations of the current human condition, as long as they fail to intuit the divine ideas directly but instead always experience them as mixed with the findings of the senses, human knowledge will contain a certain amount of distortion. This mixed mode of perception, a perception of the divine ideas mingled with the report of the senses, Bonaventure refers to as "contuition." Relying on a theme of Saint Paul (1 Cor. 13:12), Bonaventure develops something like an evolutionary theory of knowledge: perfect knowledge, knowledge through the divine ideas, is a regulative ideal postulated at the end of human history yet presently grounding the possibility of certain, yet partially clouded, knowing. Such notions were to receive much greater treatment in the modern era at the hands of such philosophers as G. W. F. Hegel and Charles Sanders Peirce.

Question 1, Article 1 of the *Quaestiones Disputatae de Mysterio Trinitatis* (Disputed Questions on the Mystery of the Trinity, 1254) is "Whether the Existence of God is an Indubitable Truth?" In twenty-nine arguments Bonaventure shows that the existence of God is an analytic truth that cannot be doubted—that no matter where we start our investigation, either with the world or with our own immediate consciousness or with the idea of God, our reason and experience brings us to an immediate awareness of God's existence. Indeed, our idea of God is a priori in the sense that an awareness of God is given along with all other experience. That being the case, the Bonaventurean "proofs" for God's existence are not really proofs at all: it is impossible to prove what is most evident, and nothing, for Bonaventure, could be more evident than God's existence.

In the second article of the same question, "Whether it is a Truth to be Believed that God Is a Trinity?," Bonaventure exhibits an optimism in regard to human reason that far exceeds that of Aquinas. Basing his position on the Anselmian notion of "necessary reasons," Bonaventure holds that it is possible to develop proofs for, or at least render intelligible, the most mysterious truths of the faith, such as the doctrine of the Trinity. The point is not that the human mind unaided by revelation could deduce the existence of the Trinity but rather that once the doctrine is revealed, it is possible for human reason to perceive the doctrine as logically necessary. (Aquinas explicitly rejected the doctrine of necessary reasons.) Bonaventure's notion of the Trinity as a dynamic force is quite different from Aquinas's static view of the Trinity. Some modern commentators, such as Ewert H. Cousins, have suggested that implicit in this dynamic notion of the Trinity is a process metaphysics comparable to that found in the American pragmatist tradition.

After completing the disputed questions Bonaventure wrote the *Breviloquium* (Brief Commentary), a brief, tightly knit summa of theology. Completed in 1257, the last year of Bonaventure's official connection to the University of Paris, this work may be considered his most mature statement in theology during his academic period.

Each chapter of the *Breviloquium* is built on the same model: there are no arguments, no conclusions, no answers to objections, just a rather austere exposition organized for the purposes of personal meditation. The reader is told what to believe and then given an explanation for the belief. The explanatory sections are often prefaced with the expression, "This should be understood as follows." The explanations obey a single law: "The theme of theology is, indeed, God and the first Principle. Rather, being the highest knowledge and the highest teaching, it resolves everything in God as the first and supreme Principle." In Bonaventure's theology all things are from God (emanation), according to God (exemplarity), and for God as an end (consummation). The *Breviloquium* is clearly Augustinian in that theology is seen as a way of rendering the tenets of faith intelligible. Such a procedure is exactly the reverse of the modern approach: the modern mind seeks understanding as a necessary condition for faith. For Bonaventure, the contribution of reason is not so great as to make theology a science in the strict Aristotelian sense; in creating theology, reason must be elevated by an infused gift of faith and understanding.

The key to understanding the Book of Nature, according to Bonaventure, is found in that other great book, the Book of Scripture; Scripture and Nature are embodiments of the same Logos. This connection between the biblical text and nature is stated explicitly in Bonaventure's commentary on the Book of Ecclesiastes (1254-1257): "Every creature is the divine word, because it speaks God." Scripture has four dimensions: breadth, length, height, and depth. The breadth of Scripture consists in the whole extent of the sacred text. Throughout its entire course it contains a rule of knowledge and a form of life. Being the inspired word of the Holy Spirit, Scripture contains all truth necessary for salvation. The length of Scripture presents a supernatural vision of world history from the time of Creation to the ultimate fulfillment. If humans are to understand the course and meaning of creation, they must embrace the whole of it; the vision of the whole is made possible only by Scripture.

The height of Scripture describes the progressive hierarchy of things: the ecclesiastical, the angelical, and the heavenly. Things exist in themselves, but they also exist in our minds when we know them; and finally, they exist as signs or symbols of the Eternal Art, as instances of divine ideas as revealed in the first chapter of the Gospel of John. The depth of Scripture consists in the multiplicity of meanings a word may possess: the literal meaning, the allegorical meaning (an image that is an object of faith), the ethical meaning (definition of what ought to be done), and the anagogic meaning (that which lifts the mind up to the Eternal Good). A study of Scripture in all its four dimensions, especially with respect to its anagogic sense, offers the key to understanding all reality.

The commentary on the Book of Ecclesiastes is a model of literal interpretation. The significance of Ecclesiastes for Bonaventure is that it stresses that humanity is made for knowledge of the eternal—all else is vanity. The influence of Hugh of Saint-Victor appears in the study of vanity under its three aspects of change, curiosity, and frailty. Bonaventure's identification of Original Sin with curiosity in his later works is traceable to this early commentary. Curiosity, for Bonaventure, refers to the attitude of seeing the things of the world as individual substances separated from their eternal source, rather than as signs.

In all of Bonaventure's biblical commentaries the technique is the same: the literal sense is studied first, and sometimes a mystical meaning is introduced. Bonaventure frequently appeals to an ethical meaning to provide the preacher for whom these works are written with an immediate homiletic tool. Because of difficulties that arose during his tenure as minister general of the order, Bonaventure resigned his chair at the university in 1257. His premature removal from the university at age thirty-nine has often been used to justify the claim that Bonaventure's thought never achieved the sophistication of Aquinas's synthesis.

Saint Bonaventure the Seraphic Doctor, *engraving after a painting by Victor (Vittorio) Crivelli*

After 1257 most of Bonaventure's energies were taken up with the troubles and concerns of the Franciscan order during a time of great turmoil over the question of the nature and extent of evangelical poverty. In October 1259, to find some peace of mind, Bonaventure traveled to Mount La Verna, the holiest of all Franciscan shrines and the place where Francis was reputed to have received the stigmata. There, during the feast of Francis, Bonaventure had what he believed to be an insight into the nature of Francis's enlightenment, as well as into the manner of reproducing it. It is these thoughts that are written down in the *Itinerarium Mentis in Deum* (The Mind's Road to God, 1259), a "how-to" manual for mystical experience. Starting with the Augustinian threefold division of the modes of being—the being of the world, the being of the mind, and the being of God—Bonaventure attempts to bring the reader into a direct and immediate experience of God at all levels. Starting with the world, Bonaventure shows that alongside all experiences of nature there is a "contuition" of the divine—all creatures can be perceived, in a truly Franciscan sense, as vestiges of God. Turning to the inner reality of human consciousness, Bonaventure shows in good Augustinian fashion that all internal experience carries with it a "contuition" of the divine insofar as human persons are images of the Trinity. Finally, a meditation on God himself, as both necessary being and the highest good, brings us to a reasoned experience of the Father as source of all being, structure, and intelligibility. The last step is to pass over to the Father as totally unstructured, totally beyond all human understanding. At last we have reached the supreme peace, or mystical union with God, not through discursive knowledge but through a form of intuitive or mystical knowledge that is a knowing through love.

If the years 1253 to 1257 represent the strictly academic phase of Bonaventure's life, 1259 marks the beginning of the mystical phase. He became a mystic without ceasing to be a Scholastic; entering more deeply into the life of Francis, he wrote the *Legenda Major* (Long Life of Saint Francis, 1261). This work, which became the official biography of Francis, attempts to capture the essence of Franciscan spirituality. Bonaventure became responsible for the articulation of the religious insight of Francis of Assisi; it is nearly impossible to speak of the spirituality of Francis without reference to Bonaventure.

Between 1264 and 1274 Bonaventure became progressively more distressed by the growth of Averroistic Aristotelianism. In particular he rejected the teachings of the Latin Averroist, Siger of Brabant, whose influence in university life and thought became ever more pronounced during this time. The three sets of collations, or university sermons—the *Collationes de Decem Praeceptis* (Collations on the Ten Commandments, 1267), the *Collationes de Septem Donis Spiritus Sancti* (Collations on the Seven Gifts of the Holy Spirit, 1268), and the *Collationes in Hexaëmeron sive Illuminationes Ecclesiae* (Collations on the Six Days of Creation; or, Enlightenment of the Church, 1273)—are concerned with refuting the errors of Averroistic Aristotelianism: an overly rationalist approach to ethics that failed to place Christ at the center of the moral life, the doctrine of the eternity of the world, the oneness of the intellect, ethical determinism, the rejection of divine illumination, and the rejection of the Platonic/Augustinian exemplarism that, in Bonaventure's view, was necessary to tie the world to the divine mind.

It is commonplace to situate Bonaventure in the Platonic/Augustinian rather than the Aristotelian tradition, yet the works of Aristotle are cited some 930 times in the Bonaventurean corpus. Indeed, Bonaventure wrote that Aristotle was the "Prince of the Peripatetics," the most excellent of philosophers. There is no doubt that Bonaventure was thoroughly familiar with the works of Aristotle, whom he regarded as the major philosopher of nature. Bonaventure's theory of knowledge, at least at the level of perception, was Aristotelian, recognizing the necessity of sensory perception as the source of universal ideas. However, he rejected the inappropriate use of Aristotelian science in theological matters.

The basic problem was that Aristotle rejected the doctrine of exemplarism. There was no place in Aristotle for the divine mind, or Logos, and so there was no effective way for Aristotle to tie together God and the world. For Aristotle the only causal connection between the unmoved mover and the world was final causality: the world was impelled to the divine by an inherent yearning. God was not tied to the world as universal idea to particular instance; indeed, God could have no knowledge of the world. If that were true, notions of Creation and Providence were nonsense. As Bonaventure grew older he became more and more aware of the implication of Aristotle's rejection of Plato's theory of Ideas: if there were no reality to general ideas apart from their particular instances, the notion of the divine mind and the entire Logos doctrine would become redundant. This implication, Bonaventure believed, would lead to atheism by effectively severing the connection between God and world.

Any radical empiricism that denied the independent existence of general universal ideas or any wholesale rejection of the Augustinian metaphysics of exemplarism was seen by Bonaventure as leading inevitably to the death of belief in God. Like any good Neoplatonist philosopher, Bonaventure saw an underlying unity between the works of Plato and Aristotle: Aristotle was the philosopher of the natural world, Plato the philosopher of the transcendent. The rejection of Platonic general Ideas and the consequent encroachment of Aristotelian concepts into the realm of theology was, for Bonaventure, disastrous. This is the theme of the *Collationes in Hexaëmeron*, begun in 1273. This work, a final synthesis that was never completed because of his premature death, was to develop fully the metaphysics of exemplarism, the centrality of Christ, and the doctrine of illumination as the essential core of any Christian wisdom. By this time Bonaventure's early discomfort with Aristotle had become strident.

In *Collationes in Hexaëmeron* Bonaventure presents a sketch of his entire system: "And this is the whole of our metaphysics: it concerns emanation, exemplarity, and consummation." The Plotinian concept of emanation suggests for Bonaventure that all reality, in differing degrees of perfection, proceeds from God. The material world is nothing other than the material manifestation of the divine Logos, the expression of all of God's creative possibilities. The Bonaventurean notion of exemplarity holds that material reality is an embodiment of the divine idea; thus physical reality has the character of sign or symbol, and the world is more a book to be read than, as Aristotle would have it, a collection of substances. Consummation or enlightened return (*reductio*) concerns the final goal of all created reality: all things have emanated from God and must return to their source. Although this return begins in reason, it is completed in loving mystical union—a union of the soul in darkness granted to saints like Francis before their death. Bonaventure's synthesis is essentially a Trinitarian one, identifying the process of emanation with the power of the Father, the divine mind, or Logos, with the Second Person of the Trinity, and enlightened return with the Holy Spirit.

To many scholars the high point of Bonaventure's work is *De Reductione Artium ad Theologiam* (On the Reduction of the Arts to Theology). The exact date of this work is uncertain; some date it from the magistral period (1255-1257), but others believe that it was written during the same period as the *Collationes in Hexaëmeron*. In any case, this work represents

Bonaventure's most advanced attempt to justify and bring together his entire system. The basic claim is that the meaning of the world lies outside the world. The reference point for all human activity and specifically for all academic activity is reference to the divine reality. Human knowing is but a stage in the quest for wisdom, understood as the contemplative union with God in love. The life of the academic and that of the ascetic are directed to the same end, the experience of God in all the levels of reality. The notion of "reductio" contained in the title of this work is crucial: all rational creative activity, if it is to be meaningful, must "lead back to" an understanding of God as its first principle.

It is at this point that the connection between Bonaventure the scholastic and Bonaventure the mystic follower of Francis becomes clear. The highest good in all human life is the mystical union with God in love; this is the practical purpose of the life of Gospel perfection. This contemplative union with God, this deification, is the practical end of the entire Christian life, whether the Christian be a wandering mendicant or a university scholar. The goal is the same even though the paths may differ. This final goal of contemplative union is developed in chapter 7 of the *Itinerarium Mentis in Deum* and in the two other works given over to a treatment of the mystical life, *De Triplici Via* (The Triple Way, 1259) and the *Legenda Major* (1261). In both of these works the spiritual journey is described as having three distinct phases: the purgative, the illuminative, and the unitive phase. The purgative way consists in the expulsion of sin, the illuminative in the imitation of Christ, and the unitive in contemplative union with God in love. Each way is a stage on the way to blessedness. Purgation leads to peace, illumination to truth, and perfective union to love. Thus, the life of blessedness consists essentially in a life of peace, truth, and love.

In June 1273 Pope Gregory X created Bonaventure cardinal bishop of Albano. Soon afterward, Bonaventure traveled with the pope to prepare for the Second Council of Lyons, which opened on 7 May 1274. On 15 July, in the midst of the council's activity, Bonaventure died suddenly at the age of fifty-seven. His canonization by Pope Sixtus IV took place on 14 April 1482; on 14 March 1588 he was named the sixth doctor of the church (Thomas Aquinas being the fifth) by Sixtus V, with the title "Doctor Seraphicus" (Seraphic Doctor) replacing the earlier "Doctor Devotus" (Devout Doctor).

Although the philosophical works of Bonaventure have been eclipsed by the works of the great Dominican Thomas Aquinas, as well as by later thinkers within his own order such as John Duns Scotus and William of Ockham, the mystical writings of Bonaventure have not been surpassed. Philosophically his work can be seen as the completion of the Augustinian tradition influenced by the lived experience of Francis. In contemporary philosophy, the works of Bonaventure should hold interest for any hermeneutically based attempt to see the world not so much as a collection of separate substances but rather as a system of signs. Some have held that Bonaventure's dynamic notion of the Divinity has echoes in both contemporary process thought and in evolutionary theory. If there is such a connection, it must be traceable to the considerable influence that Bonaventure's thought has had on German philosophy. Some obvious similarities between Bonaventure's philosophy and the thought of the American philosopher Peirce suggest that research into their relation, if any, might prove to be fruitful.

Bibliographies:

Jacques Guy Bougerol, *Bibliographia Bonaventuriana*, volume 5 of his *S. Bonaventura 1274-1974* (Grottaferrata, Italy: Collegio S. Bonaventura, 1974);

Bougerol, ed., *Lexique saint Bonaventure*, 3 volumes (Paris: Editions Franciscaines, 1969).

Biography:

Leonard Lemmens, *Der heilige Bonaventura* (Kempten: Kösel, 1909).

References:

Efrem Bettoni, *Saint Bonaventure*, translated by Angelus Gambatese (Westport, Conn.: Greenwood Press, 1981);

John Borelli, "Matter and Exemplar: Difference-in-Identity in Vijnanabhiksu and Bonaventure," in *Neoplatonism and Indian Thought*, edited by R. Baine Harris (Norfolk, Va.: International Society for Neoplatonic Studies, 1982);

Jacques Guy Bougerol, *Introduction to the Works of St. Bonaventure*, translated by José de Vinck (Paterson, N.J.: St. Anthony Guild Press, 1964);

Bougerol, *S. Bonaventura, 1274-1974*, 5 volumes (Grottaferrata: Collegio S. Bonaventura, 1973-1974);

Ewert H. Cousins, *Bonaventure and the Coincidence of Opposites: The Theology of Bonaventure* (Chicago: Franciscan Herald Press, 1978);

Matthew M. De Benedictis, *The Social Thought of Saint Bonaventure: A Study in Social Philosophy* (Westport, Conn.: Greenwood Press, 1972);

John Dourley, *Paul Tillich and Bonaventure: An Evaluation of Tillich's Claim to Stand in the Augustinian-Franciscan Tradition* (Leiden: Brill, 1975);

Pascal F. Foley, ed., *Proceedings of the Seventh Centenary Celebration of the Death of Saint Bonaventure, St. Bonaventure University, St. Bonaventure, N.Y., July 12-15, 1974* (Saint Bonaventure, N.Y.: Franciscan Institute, 1975);

B. A. Gendreau, "The Quest for Certainty in St. Bonaventure," *Franciscan Studies*, 21 (1961): 104-227;

Etienne Gilson, *The Philosophy of St. Bonaventure*, translated by Dom Illtyd Trethowan and Frank J. Sheed (Paterson, N.J.: St. Anthony Guild Press, 1965);

Zachary Hayes, *The Hidden Center: Spirituality and Speculative Christology in St. Bonaventure* (New York: Paulist Press, 1981);

Louis Mackey, "Redemptive Subversions: The Christian Discourse of St. Bonaventure," in *The Autonomy of Religious Belief: A Critical Inquiry*, edited by Frederick J. Crosson (Notre Dame, Ind.: University of Notre Dame Press, 1981), pp. 38-59;

Mackey, "Singular and Universal: A Franciscan Perspective," *Franciscan Studies*, 17 (1982): pp. 130-164;

Michael P. Malloy, *Civil Authority in Medieval Philosophy: Lombard, Aquinas, and Bonaventure* (Lanham, Md.: University Press of America, 1985);

George F. McLean, ed., *Thomas and Bonaventure; A Septicentenary Commemoration* (Washington, D.C.: American Catholic Philosophical Association, 1974);

Timothy Noone, "A Disputed Question: Whether Whatever Is Known Is Known in the Divine Ideas," in *From Cloister to Classroom*, edited by Ellen Rozanne Elder (Kalamazoo, Mich.: Cistercian Publications, 1986), pp. 154-177;

Steven Ozment, *The Age of Reform, 1250-1550* (New Haven & London: Yale University Press, 1980);

John C. Plott, *A Philosophy of Devotion: A Comparative Study of bhakti and prapatti in Visistadvaita and St. Bonaventura and Gabriel Marcel* (Delhi: Moutilal Banarsidass, 1974);

Alfonso Pompei, ed., *San Bonaventura maestro di vita francescana e di sapienza cristiana*, 3 volumes (Rome: Pontificia facoltà teologica "San Bonaventuro," 1976);

John Francis Quinn, *The Historical Constitution of St. Bonaventure's Philosophy* (Toronto: Pontifical Institute of Mediaeval Studies, 1973);

Joseph Ratzinger, *The Theology of History in St. Bonaventure* (Chicago: Franciscan Herald Press, 1971);

A. Schaefer, "The Position and Function of Man in the Created World According to Saint Bonaventure," *Franciscan Studies*, 20 (1960): 261-316; 21 (1961): 233-382;

Robert W. Shahan and Francis J. Kovach, eds., *Bonaventure and Aquinas: Enduring Philosophers* (Norman: University of Oklahoma Press, 1976);

Emma Spargo, *The Category of the Aesthetic in the Philosophy of St. Bonaventure* (Saint Bonaventure, N.Y.: Franciscan Institute, 1953);

G. H. Tavard, *Transiency and Permanence: The Nature of Theology According to St. Bonaventure* (Saint Bonaventure, N.Y. & Paderborn: Franciscan Institute, 1974);

David Tracy, ed., *Celebrating the Medieval Heritage: A Colloquy on the thought of Aquinas and Bonaventure* (Chicago: University of Chicago, 1978).

Manuscripts:

A manuscript of questions concerning the commentaries on the *Sentences* of Peter Lombard, written circa 1252-1254, is in the town library at Assisi, Italy. A manuscript of disputed questions on the production of things is in the National Library, Florence.

Thomas Bradwardine
(Thomas de Bradwardina)

(circa 1295 - 26 August 1349)

André Goddu
Stonehill College

PRINCIPAL WORKS: *Arithmetica Speculativa* (Speculative Arithmetic, written circa 1325);
Geometria Speculativa (Speculative Geometry, written circa 1325);
Insolubilia (Treatise on Insoluble Sentences, written circa 1325);
Tractatus de Proportionibus Velocitatum in Motibus (Treatise on the Ratios of Velocities in Motions, written 1328);
Tractatus de Continuo (Treatise on the Continuum, written circa 1330);
Tractatus de Futuris Contingentibus (Treatise on Future Contingents, written circa 1340);
Summa de Causa Dei contra Pelagium et de Virtute Causarum ad Suos Mertonenses (Summa to His Fellow Mertonians on the Causality of God against Pelagius and on Causal Power, written 1344);
Sermo coram Edwardo III Epinicius (Victory Sermon in the Presence of Edward III, written 1346).

EDITIONS: *De Proportionibus* (Paris, circa 1481);
Arithmetica speculativa, edited by Pedro Sanchez Ciruelo (Paris: Guy Marchant, 1495);
Geometria speculativa, edited by Sanchez Ciruelo (Paris: Guy Marchant, 1495);
Summa de causa Dei contra Pelagium et de Virtute causarum (Paris, 1495);
Thomae Bradwardini Archiepiscopi olim Cantuarieusis, De causa Dei contra Pelagium et de virtute causarum ad suos Mertonenses libri tres, edited by Henry Savile (London: Ex Officina Nortoniana, Apud I. Billium, 1618; reprinted, Frankfurt am Main: Minerva, 1964);
"Tractatus de continuo," edited by John Murdoch, in his "Geometry and the Continuum in the Fourteenth Century," Ph.D. dissertation, University of Wisconsin, 1957;
"The *Sermo Epinicius* Ascribed to Thomas Bradwardine (1346)," edited by Heiko Oberman and James A. Weisheipl, *Archives d'histoire doctrinale et littéraire du moyen âge,* 25 (1958): 295-329.

EDITIONS IN ENGLISH: *Thomas Bradwardine, His Tractatus de Proportionibus, Its Significance for the Development of Mathematical Physics,* edited and translated by H. Lamar Crosby, Jr. (Madison: University of Wisconsin Press, 1955);
Geometria Speculativa, edited and translated by A. G. Molland, Boethius Texte und Abhandlungen zur Geschichte der exakten Wissenschaften, 18 (Stuttgart: Steiner, 1989).

As European society in the eleventh through the thirteenth centuries increased in population and expanded economically, it became increasingly diversified; more competitive in social, political, and economic contexts; and more specialized and professionalized in areas of administration, law, diplomacy, and teaching. In natural philosophy, the efforts in the twelfth and thirteenth centuries to bring order and even number into understanding the natural world are striking and broadly consistent with the increasing specialization and professionalization of medieval society. In the second half of the thirteenth century in particular, the impulse given to more technical endeavors contributed to the reestablishment of mathematical optics, statics, and kinematics; to the renewal of interest in mathematical astronomy; and to the application of such technical accomplishments to the solution of problems in medicine, particularly the explanation of the effects of compound medicines.

Scholars have also pointed to internal developments in philosophy and theology that inspired ever more subtle, sophisticated, nuanced, and complex solutions to problems among intellectuals, many of whom could no longer be satisfied with the apparently simpler solutions of the past. Many criticized Thomas Aquinas's subtle doctrine

Merton College, Oxford University, where Thomas Bradwardine was a fellow from about 1326 until about 1335

of analogy of proportionality on logical grounds; Thomas's account of qualitative change seemed to close off the very avenues that those interested in a more quantitative approach wanted to adopt. In addition, instruction in the medieval university was structured to encourage criticism and diversity rather than agreement and uniformity. Systems were devised and were apparently desired, but their success seems often more a result of administrative fiat than of intellectual conviction. A "common teaching" may have emerged from the competition of ideas, but even as Western European society began to contract in the fourteenth century, the subtlety of problems and questions about qualities and qualitative phenomena in natural philosophy and theology encouraged the further development of sophisticated linguistic and quantitative techniques.

These developments are exemplified by the so-called Merton School or Merton Calculators of fourteenth-century Oxford University. Describing the achievements of the Merton "Calculators" has been in the twentieth century largely a matter of gradual refinement and ever more precise qualifications of exaggerated and alternating overestimation and underestimation. The appellation "Merton Calculators" is a completely artificial designation, referring principally to four individuals who were students or masters sometime during their careers at Merton College, Oxford, in the fourteenth century. Their real link, however, derives from their common interest in developing techniques for solving a variety of logical dilemmas and mathematical problems applicable to natural philosophy and theology. "Calculator" was the name given apparently by fifteenth-century Italian schoolmen to the chronologically last of these authors, Richard Swineshead, and it has been applied retrospectively to the others. The other principal authors were Thomas Bradwardine, William Heytesbury, and John of Dumbleton.

The sources of these techniques are still a matter of some debate, but they seem to have involved several strands: discussions about the division of the sciences and the relation between mathematics and natural philosophy; debates about the nature of quantity and its relation to substance and quality; the tendency to replace the view of motion as a qualitative accident, a process, with entirely quantitative and relational (or functional) considerations based not on empirical evidence or measurement but on mathematical consistency or coherence and on ontologically reductionist critiques of earlier views; discussion of kinematics and of variations in the intensity of a quality or essence; competing conceptions of medicine as an art and medicine as a science; the emphasis on the empirical, with a corresponding antisystematic and even irrational element in medicine; late-thirteenth-century suggestions that pharmacy ought to be based on more general, rational principles; Averroës' critique of Avicenna's account of combination of accidental forms; the effort to "regulate" and "quantify" intensity and qualitative increase; Arnald of Villanova's synthesis of medical and natural-philosophical discussions of variations in qualitative intensity; and the additive theory of qualitative increase advocated by Richard of Middleton. The proponents of the additive theory of qualitative increase thought of increase in terms of incremental degrees or grades, a notion that was subsequently distinguished from extensive magnitude in order to explain, for example, why the addition of the same degree of heat has different effects in different subjects. These discussions were also influenced by the rediscovery of the Alkindian geometrical relationship between increasing degree and increasing quality. Abu-Yusuf Ya'qub ibn Ishaq al-Kindi, a ninth-century Arabic author at the court of Baghdad, held that the degree of intensity of a quality increases arithmetically as the ratio of one contrary to another contrary increases geometrically. For example, the temperature of a medicine increases arithmetically as the ratio of heat-to-cold increases geometrically; hence, the medicine is hot in the first degree if the ratio of heat-to-cold is two-to-one, it is hot in the second degree if the ratio is four-to-one, in the third degree if the ratio is eight-to-one, and in the fourth degree if the ratio is sixteen-to-one.

The terms that are typically found in Mertonian treatises are *intensity, latitude*, and *extension*. Although these terms did not have the same meanings for all fourteenth-century authors, for the proponents of the additive theory the latitude of a quality was identified with the intensity of a quality at a given point. Hence, latitudes are virtually identical with degrees, and both are regarded as divisible. That is, a degree, according to this view, is not represented by a discrete arithmetical unit but by a continuous geometrical line.

Whether or not all of the earlier medical discussions were known at Oxford is still unclear. Simon Bredon, a fellow of Merton College for at least ten years who is known for his mathematical work, devoted part of a medical book to an exposition of Alkindian pharmacy. Walter of Odington, whose association with Merton is based on the assumption that he is identical with Walter of Evesham, discussed alchemy in Alkindian terms. Others who were Merton fellows and who in one way or other reflect the characteristics associated with Merton College are Thomas Buckingham, Walter Burley, William of Collingham, Walter of Segrave, William of Sutton, and Thomas Wilton. Richard Kilvington (or Kilmington) is often included among the "calculators," as is Roger Swineshead; but, though active at Oxford, they had no known association with Merton College. Although there was no Merton School of Calculators in any strict sense, distinctive characteristics exhibited by Bradwardine, Dumbleton, Heytesbury, and Richard Swineshead justify referring to them as the "Merton Calculators."

Bradwardine was born sometime between 1290 and 1300. The belief that he referred to Chichester as his birthplace is based on a passage in the *Summa de Causa Dei contra Pelagium et de Virtute Causarum* (Summa to His Fellow Mertonians on the Causality of God against Pelagius and on the Causal Power, 1344) as interpreted by Henry of Savile. A closer look at the text, however, raises doubts about this interpretation, leaving it unclear whether Thomas was born while his father was at Chichester. As his name indicates, he was probably born in the village of Bradwardine, and early in his life he was linked with Hartfield and Chichester in southeastern England. The safe conjecture, then, is that he was born and spent his early years in the county of Sussex.

The known records indicate that Thomas was a fellow of Balliol College in 1321, that he matriculated at Merton College, Oxford University, in 1323, and that he was a master of arts in 1326, when he is also first referred to as a fellow of Merton College. He served as proctor of the university in 1325 and again in 1326 or 1327. By 1333 he was a bachelor of theology, and about 1335 he left the university to join the household of Richard de Bury, Bishop of Durham. He served Edward III as royal chaplain in 1338 and 1346, and there are reasons for thinking that Bradwardine performed important diplomatic services in the king's behalf.

By 1348 Bradwardine had received the title of doctor of theology. In 1349 he was consecrated archbishop of Canterbury in Avignon, where, according to some accounts, an unfortunate incident occurred. The pope, Clement VI, was apparently so much under the control of Edward III at the time (within two years of the fall of Calais) that he supposedly remarked that he would have to make a bishop of a jackass if the king of England requested it. While Bradwardine was at the banquet given by the pope, a clown seated on a jackass entered the hall and presented a request to be made archbishop of Canterbury. Appropriate apologies were made by the pope and the cardinals.

On the morning of 23 August 1349, while staying in London, Bradwardine suffered an attack of fever; that evening tumors were observed under his arms. These symptoms, along with the fact that the plague was ravaging London at the time, make it probable that Bradwardine's death on 26 August must be attributed to the plague.

Bradwardine wrote several works of a mathematical and natural-philosophical character, probably between 1321 and 1335. The most impressive of them, and the one that has earned Bradwardine his place in the history of science, is the *Tractatus de Proportionibus Velocitatum in Motibus* (Treatise on the Ratios of Velocities in Motions, 1328). In this treatise Bradwardine introduced a new dynamic law, according to which, in modern terms, a body's velocity will increase arithmetically as the ratio of force to resistance increases geometrically. There are disagreements among experts as to the source of Bradwardine's innovation, but the similarities between Bradwardine's law and Alkindian theory, as well as evidence of the availability of Montpellier medical works in Oxford, lend credibility to the suggestion that Bradwardine knew these works and was influenced by them. The suggestion is also consistent with the otherwise confirmed synthesizing inclinations and interests that Bradwardine possessed. On the other hand, Bradwardine may have arrived at his rules independently, inasmuch as they derive from the generally available medieval theory of proportions and in certain respects differ from the concepts found in the medical rules. In addition, Boethius, Campanus of Novara, and Gerard of Brussels have been singled out as Bradwardine's most important sources in the quadrivial arts.

What is original in Bradwardine's work and approach is the axiomatic basis that he applied to changes in the motions of bodies relative to changes in force and resistance. The immediate sources of such problems were Scholastic interpretations of Aristotle's apparent view about the relation among the speed, force, and resistance of a mobile. Aristotle treated the motions of a body as occurring necessarily in a plenum; the motion, therefore, would be dependent on some relation between the forces moving the body and the forces resisting its motion. It is doubtful that Aristotle intended his remarks to be taken as a law or rule, but in the absence of more clarification it is not difficult to see how his remarks could be so interpreted.

Rather than construct a mathematical analysis for the simplest, abstract, and ideal conditions, the Aristotelian is under the burden of having to derive general laws from concrete cases. The strength of the Aristotelian analysis lies in its adherence to the concreteness of sense experience; its weakness lies in the effort to generalize. Bradwardine's innovation was to analyze the standard accounts of the ratio or proportionality of variations in speed and variations in force and resistance in terms of the mathematics of ratios and proportions. In book 7 of his *Physics* Aristotle proposes as a generalization that twice the velocity of a given motion follows from a doubling of the moving power (force) or from the halving of the resistance of the medium. Whether Aristotle intended this claim to be taken as a dynamic law is doubtful, but whatever the final velocity of a falling body may be, he likely followed common sense in concluding that its final velocity is dependent on the weight (moving power or force) of the body and the resistance of the medium. Bradwardine criticizes the Aristotelian generalization as based on the false assumption that any force, however small, can move any resistance, however large, when, in fact, it is obvious that motion occurs only if the force is greater than the resistance. A true generalization, Bradwardine recognizes, must be valid for every variation of ratio, and it must either rule out the possibility of zero velocity or show that no motion arises only when the ratio of force to resistance is one to one. Bradwardine's solution to this problem is purely mathematical and not based on empirical considerations. He realizes that to double a velocity, the ratio of force to resistance must be squared. For example, if the ratio of force to resistance of a given motion is three to one, then to double the velocity the ratio of force to resistance must be squared, that is, increased to nine to one. Only the ratio squared can double the velocity, only the ratio cubed can triple the velocity, and so forth. Conversely, to halve the velocity the ratio of force to resistance must be reduced to the square root. For example, to halve the velocity of a body with a force-to-resistance ratio of nine to one, the force-to-resistance ratio must be reduced to three to one. Bradwardine's mathematical formula is valid for every variation of velocity, and it rules out the possibility of motion where the resistance is equal to the force, for, according to Bradwardine's law, the velocity of a body with a ratio of force to resistance of one to one is zero. In general form, Bradwardine's conclusion means that velocity increases arithmetically as the ratio of force to resistance increases geometrically.

Although Bradwardine did not produce an adequate dynamics, he did discover proportional relations that fit Aristotelian principles of motion more adequately than the standard generalization did, he was able to state in a general form the medieval mathematics behind his function, and he showed an explicit awareness of fundamental assumptions and of the need to analyze those assumptions.

Because Bradwardine did not teach the members of the Merton "School," his influence on subsequent Mertonians seems to have been largely inspirational. His approach to the problems of physical science inspired others to develop his analysis, to make the resulting analytical techniques part of the teaching of logic, and to apply the techniques to the discussion of fundamental assumptions in natural philosophy and theology. After the fourteenth century, however, the influence of these approaches is found more on the Continent than in England. Bradwardine's reputation as a theologian, however, both in England and on the Continent is attested by his title of *Doctor Profundus* and by Geoffrey Chaucer—perhaps influenced by John Wycliffe—in the "Nun's Priest's Tale":

But what that God forwoot moot nedes be,
After the opynyoun of certeyn clerkis.
Witnesse on hym that any parfit clerk is
That in scole is gret altercacioun
In this matere and gret disputisoun
And hath ben of an hundred thousand men.
But I ne kan nat bulte it to the bren
As kan the holy doctour Augustyn
Or Boece or the Bisshope Bradwardyn:
Wheither that Goddes worthy forewityng
Streyneth me nedely for to doon a thyng
("Nedely" clepe I symple necessitee),
Or ellis if fre choys be graunted me
To do that same thyng or do it noght
Though God forwoot it er that I was wroght,
Or if his wityng streyneth never a del
But by necessitee condicionel—
I wol nat han to do of swich matere.

The belief in an omnipotent and omniscient God has generated many logical and theological puzzles. The mysteries of divine creation and foreknowledge have led some theologians to conclude that God so determines everything that human beings possess no free will, and hence are bound by "symple necessitee." Others have concluded that God's knowledge of the future does not constrain individuals to make the choices that they make, and hence they are bound by a "necessitee condicionel," not simple necessity. The issue is complicated further by the question of whether an individual achieves salvation by works or by the grace of God. In the late fourth and early fifth centuries the monk Pelagius had so stressed the efficacy of works as to imply that individuals *earn* their salvation, thus minimizing God's grace; his views were declared heretical. These problems motivated theologians to formulate sophisticated distinctions intended to preserve a balance between the belief that one's salvation is dependent on the merits of Jesus Christ and the belief that one is responsible for one's response to grace in the performance of salutary actions. In the fourteenth century a view was developed that attributed to individuals a natural capacity to do good but added that whether such naturally good actions were meritorious (led to salvation) depended on God's acceptance of them. Although this thesis is not Pelagian, it was perceived to be so, leading some theologians to adopt the contrary view and to express it in language that suggested that God's grace is so enabling as to determine one's response. The survival of these contrary emphases attests to the difficulty in achieving a proper balance, and a balance between such extremes inevitably appears paradoxical if not contradictory.

Bradwardine's *Summa de Causa Dei contra Pelagium et de Virtute Causarum* is a response to Pelagian views, or to what he perceived to be Pelagian views; hence, it emphasizes the need for God's saving grace and for the merits of Jesus Christ and suggests that human works by themselves are inefficacious for salvation. This interpretation was adopted by Wycliffe, and Bradwardine's treatise is rightly seen as a forerunner of Protestant views that stress one's total worthlessness and dependence upon God for salvation. Of course, if Bradwardine merely intended to correct the overemphasis on the ability to save oneself, he can be read as trying to restore the balance between the need for salvation by Jesus and the obligation to cooperate with God's saving grace. On the other hand, Bradwardine's anti-Pelagian view has its source in an extreme thesis about divine omnipotence that attributed to God the freedom to change the past without contradiction. This strong view of divine omnipotence leads to belief in double predestination, that is, the belief that God elects both the saved and the damned. Although Bradwardine's thesis was controversial and provoked defenses of human freedom, his opinions were not officially censured. On the contrary, his efforts can be counted among those that countered the separation of philosophy from theology. Bradwardine was disturbed by contemporary philosophical discussions of grace and free will; he seems to have been especially disturbed by the tendency of philosophers to emphasize naturalistic explanations of human actions to the detriment of theological and religious points of view. Bradwardine's views exercised a considerable influence, most importantly on Wycliffe, culminating in the later strong doctrines of grace and justification with a corresponding emphasis on penance and biblical faith.

References:

Vern L. Bullough, "Medical Study at Mediaeval Oxford," *Speculum*, 36 (October 1961): 600-612;

Stefano Caroti, ed., *Studies in Medieval Natural Philosophy*, Biblioteca di Nuncius, Studi e Testi, 1 (Florence: Leo S. Olschki, 1989);

Geoffrey Chaucer, "The Nun's Priest's Tale," in *The Canterbury Tales: A Variorum Edition of the Works of Geoffrey Chaucer*, volume 2, edited by Derek Pearsall (Norman: University of Oklahoma Press, 1984), pp. 217-221;

Marshall Clagett, *Giovanni Marliani and Late Medieval Physics* (New York: Columbia University Press, 1941);

Clagett, *Nicole Oresme and the Medieval Geometry of Qualities and Motions* (Madison & London: University of Wisconsin Press, 1968);

Clagett, *The Science of Mechanics in the Middle Ages* (Madison: University of Wisconsin Press, 1959);

William Courtenay, *Schools and Scholars in Fourteenth-Century England* (Princeton: Princeton University Press, 1987);

A. C. Crombie, "Quantification in Medieval Physics," *Isis*, 52 (1961): 143-160;

Alain de Libera, "Bulletin d'histoire de la logique médiévale," *Revue des sciences philosophiques et théologiques*, 71 (1987): 590-634;

Stillman Drake, "Medieval Ratio Theory vs. Compound Medicines in the Origins of Bradwardine's Rule," *Isis*, 64 (March 1973): 67-77;

Pierre Duhem, *Etudes sur Léonard da Vinci*, third series (Paris: Hermann, 1913);

Duhem, *Le Système du monde*, volumes 7-10 (Paris: Hermann, 1956-1959);

A. B. Emden, *A Biographical Register of the University of Oxford* (Oxford: Oxford University Press, 1957), I: 244-246; III: xv-xvi;

Amos Funkenstein, *Theology and the Scientific Imagination from the Middle Ages to the Seventeenth Century* (Princeton: Princeton University Press, 1986);

André Goddu, *The Physics of William of Ockham*, Studien und Texte zur Geistesgeschichte des Mittelalters, 16 (Leiden & Cologne: Brill, 1984);

Edward Grant, *Studies in Medieval Science and Natural Philosophy* (London: Variorum Reprints, 1981);

Grant, ed., *A Source Book in Medieval Science* (Cambridge, Mass.: Harvard University Press, 1974);

Grant and John Murdoch, eds., *Mathematics and Its Application to Science and Natural Philosophy in the Middle Ages* (Cambridge: Cambridge University Press, 1987);

Norman Kretzmann, ed., *Infinity and Continuity in Ancient and Medieval Thought* (Ithaca, N.Y. & London: Cornell University Press, 1982);

Gordon Leff, *Bradwardine and the Pelagians* (Cambridge: Cambridge University Press, 1957);

Christopher Lewis, *The Merton Tradition and Kinematics in Late Sixteenth and Early Seventeenth Century Italy*, Saggi e Testi, 15 (Padua: Editrice Antenore, 1980);

Anneliese Maier, *An der Grenze von Scholastik und Naturwissenschaft*, Studien zur Naturphilosophie der Spätscholastik, 3, second edition, Studi e Testi, 41 (Rome: Storia e Letteratura, 1952);

Maier, *Ausgehendes Mittelalter*, 3 volumes, Studi e Testi, 97, 105, 138 (Rome: Storia e Letteratura, 1964-1977);

Maier, *Metaphysische Hintergründe der spätscholastischen Naturphilosophie*, Studien zur Naturphilosophie der Spätscholastik, 4, Studi e Testi, 52 (Rome: Storia e Letteratura, 1955);

Maier, *Die Vorläufer Galileis im 14. Jahrhundert*, Studien zur Naturphilosophie der Spätscholastik, 1, second enlarged edition, Studi e Testi, 22 (Rome: Storia e Letteratura, 1966);

Maier, *Zwei Grundprobleme der scholastischen Naturphilosophie*, Studien zur Naturphilosophie der Spätscholastik, 2, third expanded edition, Studi e Testi, 37 (Rome: Storia e Letteratura, 1968);

Maier, *Zwischen Philosophie und Mechanik*, Studien zur Naturphilosophie der Spätscholastik, 5, Studi e Testi, 69 (Rome: Storia e Letteratura, 1958);

Alfonso Maierù, *Terminologia logica della tarda scolastico*, Lessico intellettuale europeo, 8 (Rome: Edizioni dell'Ateneo, 1972);

Maierù, ed., *English Logic in Italy in the 14th and 15th Centuries*, History of Logic, 1 (Naples: Bibliopolis, 1982);

Michael McVaugh, "Arnald of Villanova and Bradwardine's Law," *Isis*, 58 (Spring 1967): 56-64;

Jürgen Miethke, "Zur sozialen Situation der Naturphilosophie im späteren Mittelalter," in *Lebenslehren und Weltentwürfe im Übergang vom Mittelalter zur Neuzeit*, edited by Hartmut Boockmann and others, Abhandlungen der Akademie der Wissenschaften in Göttingen, Philologisch-Historische Klasse, third series 179 (Göttingen: Vandenhoeck & Ruprecht, 1989), pp. 249-266;

A. George Molland, "The Geometrical Background to the 'Merton School,' " *British Journal for the History of Science*, 4 (December 1968): 108-125;

John Murdoch, "From Social into Intellectual Factors: An Aspect of the Unitary Character of Late Medieval Learning," in *The Cultural Context of Medieval Learning*, edited by Murdoch and Edith Sylla, Boston Studies in the Philosophy of Science, 26, Synthese Library, volume 76 (Dordrecht & Boston: Reidel, 1975), pp. 271-339;

Murdoch, "Geometry and the Continuum in the Fourteenth Century," Ph.D. dissertation, University of Wisconsin, 1957;

Murdoch, *"Rationes Mathematice": Un aspect du rapport des mathématiques et de la philosophie au moyen âge* (Paris: Palais de la Découverte, 1962);

Murdoch, "Scientia Mediantibus Vocibus: Metalinguistic Analysis in Late Medieval Natural Philosophy," in *Sprache und Erkenntnis im Mittelalter*, 13, no. 1 (1981): 73-106;

Heiko Oberman, *Archbishop Thomas Bradwardine: A Fourteenth Century Augustinian* (Utrecht: Kemink & Zoon, 1957);

F. M. Powicke, *The Medieval Books of Merton College* (Oxford: Oxford University Press, 1931);

Edith D. Sylla, "Medieval Concepts of the Latitudes of Forms: The Oxford Calculators," *Archives d'histoire doctrinale et littéraire du moyen âge*, 40 (1973): 223-283;

Sylla, "Medieval Quantifications of Qualities: The 'Merton School,' " *Archive for History of Exact Sciences*, 8 (1971): 9-39;

Thomas Tanner, *Bibliotheca Britannico-Hibernica* (N.p., 1748; reprinted, Tucson, Ariz.: Audax Press, 1963), p. 237;

Lynn Thorndike, *A History of Magic and Experimental Science*, volume 3 (New York & London: Columbia University Press, 1934), pp. 370-384;

James A. Weisheipl, "Early Fourteenth Century Physics of the Merton 'School' with Special Reference to Dumbleton and Heytesbury," Ph.D. dissertation, Oxford University, 1956;

Weisheipl, "Ockham and Some Mertonians," *Mediaeval Studies*, 30 (1968): 163-213;

Weisheipl, "Repertorium Mertonense," *Mediaeval Studies*, 31 (1969): 174-224.

Manuscripts:

A preliminary checklist of manuscripts of Thomas Bradwardine's authentic and doubtful works has been compiled by James Weisheipl in "Repertorium Mertonense," *Mediaeval Studies*, 31 (1969): 177-183. Most of the manuscripts are located in the libraries and archives of Cambridge, Erfurt, London, Munich, Oxford, Paris, the Vatican, Venice, and Vienna.

Hasdai Crescas

(circa 1340 - 1412?)

Charles H. Manekin
University of Maryland

PRINCIPAL WORKS: *Ketav asher shalah . . . el qehilot Avignon* (Epistle to the Jewish Communities of Avignon, written 19 October 1391);

Sefer Bittul Iqqarei ha-Nozrim (The Book of the Refutation of the Principles of the Christians, written 1397-1398);

Sefer Or Adonai (The Book of the Light of the Lord, written 1405-1410);

Derashat ha-Pesah (Sermon on the Passover, date of composition unknown).

EDITIONS: *Or Adonai* (Ferrara: Abraham Usque, 1555; reprinted, Jerusalem: Makor, 1972);

"Ketav asher shalah . . . el qehilot Avignon," in *Shevet Yehuda*, edited by Meir Wiener (Hannover, 1855), pp. 128-130;

Sefer Or Adonai (Vienna: Adalbert della Torre, 1860);

Sefer Bittul Iqqarei ha-Nozrim, translated into Hebrew by Joseph Shem Tov (Salonica[?], 1860);

Bitul 'ikare ha-Notsrim, Hebrew translation by Shem Tov, edited by Ephraim Deinard (Kearny, N.J., 1904);

"Derashat ha-Pesah," edited by Aviezer Ravitzky, in his *Crescas' Sermon on the Passover and Studies in His Philosophy* (Jerusalem: Israel Academy of Sciences and Humanities, 1988), pp. 128-169;

Sefer Bittul Iqqarei ha-Nozrim, edited by Daniel J. Lasker (Ramat-Gan, Israel: Bar-Ilan University Press & Beer-Sheva University of the Negev Press, 1990).

EDITIONS IN ENGLISH: "Text and Translation of the Twenty-five Propositions of Book I of the Or Adonai," translated by Harry Austryn Wolfson, in his *Crescas' Critique of Aristotle: Problems of Aristotle's Physics in Jewish and Arabic Philosophy* (Cambridge, Mass.: Harvard University Press, 1929), pp. 129-315;

"Epistle to the Jewish Communities of Avignon, October 19, 1391," translated by Franz Kobler, in *Letters of Jews through the Ages*, volume 1, edited by Kobler (London: East and West Library, 1952), pp. 272-275;

"The Book of the Light of the Lord," excerpts translated by Warren Zev Harvey and Seymour Feldman, in *With Perfect Faith: The Foundations of Jewish Belief*, edited by J. David Bleich (New York: Ktav, 1983).

Although Hasdai Crescas was a great leader of Spanish Jewry in the late fourteenth and early fifteenth centuries, he is known today chiefly for his philosophical work *Sefer Or Adonai* (The Book of the Light of the Lord, 1405-1410). In this work Crescas attempted to sound the death knell for the synthesis between Aristotelianism and Judaism achieved by such thinkers as Moses Maimonides and Gersonides. Yet unlike the Jewish opponents of Aristotelianism who attacked the philosophers from orthodox or Cabalistic standpoints, Crescas sought to undermine philosophically the Aristotelian worldview that pervades his predecessors' works. His trenchant critique of Aristotelian physics, especially the notions of time, place, infinity, and motion, shows affinities to the new physics developed at Paris by Nicholas Oresme and prefigured the treatment of these notions during the Renaissance.

It is possible to view Crescas's critique of Jewish Aristotelianism as a natural reaction against an "official" philosophy that had run its course. But the timing of this critique was due to the unusually difficult situation facing Spanish Jewry in the late fourteenth and fifteenth centuries. Persecution of Jews by Christians was widespread during this period; in addition to the normal phenomenon of forced conversion, the Jewish community witnessed a growing number of voluntary conversions out of the faith. Some voluntary converts were Jewish Aristotelians who argued that because ultimate human happiness consists in intellectual perfection, the yoke of the commandments enjoined by the Torah was unnecessary and even harmful for salvation. In attacking Jew-

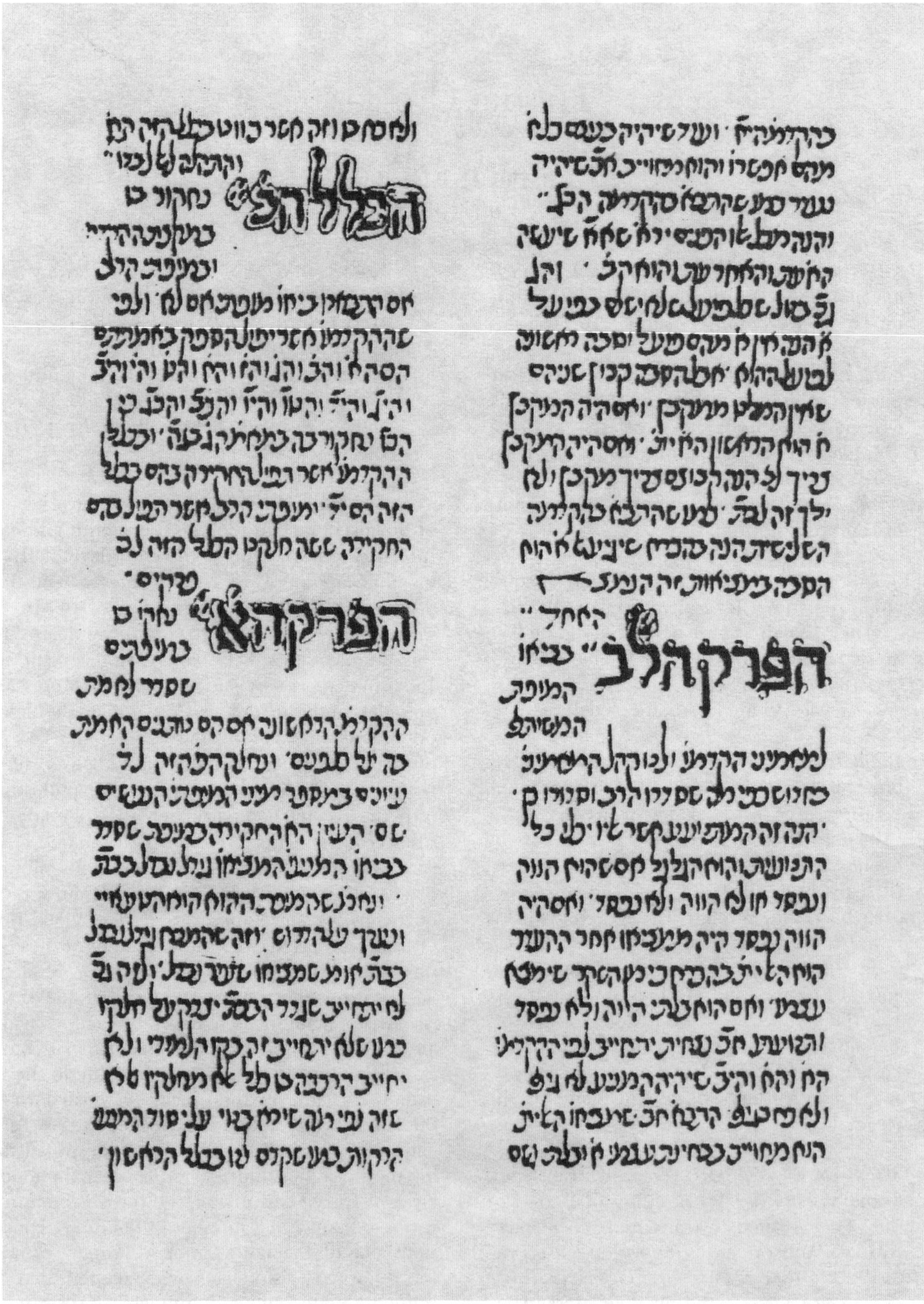

Page from a manuscript for Hasdai Crescas's Sefer Or Adonai *(Spanish Manuscript Adler Collection, Jewish Theological Seminary, New York)*

ish Aristotelianism Crescas was doing more than posing a philosophical alternative—he was fighting for the souls of his fellow Jews.

Although nothing is known of Crescas's family, he was apparently well connected. He was arrested in Barcelona in 1367, together with two rabbis, on the spurious charge of "desecrating the Host"; all three were released. As elsewhere in Christian Europe, the Jews of Aragon came under the direct protection of their king, and it was Crescas's good fortune to be on excellent terms with James I. Awarded the title "member of the royal household," in 1387 he moved to Zaragoza, where he was authorized by the king to enforce bans on recalcitrant Jews and later, in 1390, by the queen to judge cases against Jews who informed on their brethren to the gentile authorities. The latter appointment was intended to act as a check on the power of the local Jewish authorities to prosecute and punish informers, such punishment including flogging and even death.

The turning point of Crescas's life occurred in 1391, when a series of anti-Jewish riots and massacres swept the country. Crescas himself was not in danger, because of his proximity to the court in Zaragoza, but a royal order of protection arrived too late to save the life of his son in Barcelona. His account of the massacres to the Jewish communities in Avignon is a poignant elegy for the martyrs; it is also his earliest extant work. Until his death around 1412 Crescas was engaged in rebuilding the decimated Jewish communities in Aragon and Catalonia. Documents from the last years of the fourteenth century attest to his attempts to resettle Jews and to reframe communal regulations.

The riots of 1391 and the conversionary activity directed toward the Jews provoked a spiritual crisis in Spanish Jewry. Responding to the missionary literature, Crescas wrote a polemic, *Sefer Bittul Iqqarei ha-Nozrim* (The Book of the Refutation of the Principles of the Christians, 1397-1398). The principles he discusses are Original Sin, Redemption, the Trinity, the Incarnation, the Virgin Birth, transubstantiation, baptism, the messiahship of Jesus, the New Testament, and demonology. Like other Jewish philosophical polemicists he argues that these doctrines are self-contradictory and philosophically absurd, although his critique is distinguished from his predecessors' by its comprehensiveness. Crescas occasionally advances arguments whose cogency he will reject in the *Or Adonai*: for example, he argues against the eternal generation of the Son from the Father on the grounds that eternal creation is impossible, a position that he refutes in the later work. Although he may have changed his mind, it is more likely that he preferred to score points in his polemical treatises at the expense of philosophical consistency.

The *Or Adonai* is a philosophical polemic against Jewish Aristotelianism, especially as expounded by Maimonides and Gersonides. It was originally designed as part of a comprehensive two-part work to be called "The Lamp of God," with the second part to be devoted to Jewish law; Crescas undoubtedly hoped that "The Lamp of God" would replace the two great works of Maimonides, the legal code *Mishneh Torah* (Repetition of the Law, 1180) and the philosophical *Moreh Nevukhim* (Guide of the Perplexed, 1190). But he never wrote the second part, and hence his influence on Jewish culture was never nearly as great as that of Maimonides.

The *Or Adonai* is divided into four treatises dealing with, respectively, the "Roots" of the beliefs of the Torah, the "Cornerstones" of the commandments, "True Beliefs" taught by the Torah which are not cornerstones, and "Theories and Opinions" that the mind inclines to accept, although they are not explicitly contained in the Torah. This literary structure was quite innovative; previous works of Jewish philosophy had examined "doctrines and opinions," but never before in a hierarchic structure according to a dogmatic system.

The Roots consist of the existence, unity, and incorporeality of God. To demolish Maimonides' interpretations of these doctrines Crescas attacks the twenty-five Aristotelian principles that Maimonides used to prove them. Crescas realized that when one uses Aristotle to prove the existence of God, the God that is proved is an Aristotelian one. But while his criticism is motivated by considerations of theology, the conception of the universe that emerges foreshadows the post-Aristotelian one. Thus, he advances the conception of an infinite universe consisting of "empty space capable of receiving corporeal extensions" against Aristotle's finite universe that abhors a vacuum. This infinite space contains a plurality of worlds, whereas Aristotle's system rules out more than one. Crescas denies the fundamental Aristotelian distinction between celestial and terrestrial matter and argues instead for one matter whose primary characteristic is tridimensionality. Unlike Aristotle, who views time as contingent on motion, Crescas defines time as "the duration of motion or of rest between two instants." Time understood as duration leads Crescas to conjecture that "the existence of time is only in the soul." Time is divorced from matter, and hence spiritual substances such as the celestial intelligences and God can be said to be in time.

Crescas does not integrate these doctrines into a coherent worldview. Like the eleventh-century Islamic philosopher al-Ghazali, he wants to liberate theology from the straitjacket of Aristotelianism. Thus, whereas medieval Aristotelians preached that an unbridgeable ontological gap lies between God and the world, Crescas speaks of the glory of God pervading the world. Combined with his doctrine of space-as-extension, this position brings him quite close to the radically unorthodox (and un-Aristotelian) position of attributing extension to God—a move made in the seventeenth century by Benedict de Spinoza, who saw in Crescas a forerunner.

Moreover, although God's perfection is incomparable and his essence simple, he possesses "essential attributes" such as eternity, knowledge, and power that are infinite in kind as well as in number. By distinguishing between God's essence and his essential attributes, Crescas is able to claim that the former is unknowable while the latter can be known.

Crescas singles out one attribute for special consideration: joy. God rejoices in the constant overflow of good that he brings into the world. This joy is not the joy of attaining something one lacks, for God lacks nothing. Nor is it the "joy" that, according to the Aristotelians, the Supreme Intellect experiences in contemplating his essence. Rather it is the perfect joy of the giver, who rejoices infinitely in bestowing the good on the recipient; the joy of the lover, who desires the beloved. Crescas does not hesitate to use the term *desire* (*hesheq*) in conjunction with God's love, even though the Aristotelians had argued that desire is an emotion and hence unworthy of an unmoved mover; he says that the term signifies "energetic love" (*ahavah nimrezet*) and cites Scripture to buttress his argument. Through God's love the world exists; while other Jewish thinkers spoke of God's love for humanity, no one emphasized it more than Crescas.

If the Roots are the presuppositions of revelation in general, then the Cornerstones are the presuppositions of the commandments propounded in the Torah. Crescas lists six fundamental doctrines which must be assumed for the system of commandments to be true: God's knowledge of particulars, Providence, God's power, prophecy, human choice, and the purposefulness of the Torah. Although the list looks quite traditional, Crescas's interpretation differs from those of the Aristotelians and the orthodox. Against the Aristotelian Gersonides he affirms God's knowledge of particulars, even of those future events that are determined by human choice. Crescas argues that the entire system of commandments assumes that there is a commander who knows the actions of those he commands and who metes out reward and punishment appropriately. This much is in accord with traditional rabbinic theology. But Crescas goes on to affirm an unorthodox deterministic theory of human action, claiming that human freedom of choice is epistemological and not real: humans only *think* that they choose freely because they are ignorant of the causes determining their choices. But this position is just as much a threat to the system of commandments as the position of Gersonides, for if human choice is predetermined, wherein lies responsibility for human action? Crescas's answer is to link responsibility to the subject's inner acquiescence in the act: one acts freely when one makes the act his own. Although God has determined that the subject will fulfill a commandment, this determination in no way lessens the joy felt by the subject when doing so; this feeling of joy is his reward. Yet Crescas realized that teaching this doctrine might provide an excuse for the wicked, and so he cautioned against disseminating it publicly.

Crescas distinguishes between the Cornerstones that are presupposed by the Torah's system of divine commandments and True Beliefs that are taught by the Torah yet are not fundamental. Although the latter are also dogmas, in that to deny them would be heretical, the system of commandments would not collapse if one of them were omitted. The True Beliefs that are independent of specific commandments are creation ex nihilo, immortality, reward and punishment, bodily resurrection, eternity of the Torah, Mosaic prophecy, the priestly lots, and the messiah; those that relate to specific commandments are the efficacy of prayer and the priestly blessing, the efficacy of repentance, and the power of the Day of Atonement and the other holidays to cause worship of God. Once again Crescas interprets these beliefs in idiosyncratic ways—for example, depicting creation ex nihilo as an eternal emanation from God rather than a temporal production and giving a quasi-rationalistic account of bodily resurrection (the resurrected body, though miraculously created, will possess the same proportion of parts as the original one). His failure to include creation ex nihilo as a fundamental belief directly contradicts the position of Maimonides, who considered it second only to belief in the unity of God.

In the last book of the *Or Adonai* Crescas passes favorable judgment on topics not specifically dealt with in the Torah, such as the perpetual existence of the world in the future, astral influence, the power of amulets, the existence of demons, and the possibility of other worlds. In his treatment of these topics one sees clearly the influence of the thirteenth-century Spanish Cabala, especially that of the Gerona circle. But his use of the Cabala is eclectic and general, with no reference to the elaborate theosophical system of the Zohar or of other classical works of Cabala.

Crescas's systematization of Jewish belief in the *Or Adonai* is not intended to produce a rigid set of dogmas obligatory on every Jew. On the contrary, he argues, against Maimonides, that it is impossible to command belief, for belief is rational and not volitional. For Crescas, knowledge of the beliefs taught by the Torah is important for the proper fulfillment of the actions enjoined on the Jew. Here, too, he differs from the Aristotelians, who saw performance of the commandments as "spiritual exercises" that would free the believer to concentrate on the intellectual contemplation of God. Crescas locates human salvation in the will rather than in the intellect; even a simple child who recites "Amen" to a blessing has a place in the afterlife.

A neglected manuscript of Crescas, *Derashat ha-Pesah* (Sermon on the Passover, composition date unknown), identified and edited by Aviezer Ravitzky in 1988, contains important additional material on Crescas's views on the freedom of the will and determinism, miracles, and the laws concerning the Passover festival. Of particular interest is his doctrine of the inconclusiveness of miracles, which differs entirely from his treatment of miracles in the *Or Adonai.*

Of Crescas's philosophy it has been said that it came too late and too early—too late for the intense Jewish philosophical activity of the thirteenth and fourteenth centuries in southern France and Spain and too early for the new physical theories of the Renaissance. He had no immediate followers, but his reputation guaranteed that his philosophy would not be ignored. Although Jewish philosophers such as Shem Tov ben Joseph ibn Shem Tov (the son of Crescas's translator) and Isaac Abrabanel rejected his arguments, he was well liked by the Renaissance philosopher Giovanni Pico della Mirandola, and he may have influenced Giordano Bruno. Of all subsequent philosophers it was Spinoza who took his theories most to heart.

References:

Phillipp Bloch, *Die Willensfreiheit von Chasdai Kreskas* (Munich: Ackermann, 1879);

Herbert Davidson, "The Principle that a Finite Body Can Contain Only Finite Power," in *Studies in Jewish Religious and Intellectual History: Presented to Alexander Altmann on the Occasion of His Seventieth Birthday*, edited by Siegfried Stein and Raphael Loewe (University: University of Alabama Press, 1979), pp. 75-92;

Seymour Feldman, "The Theory of Eternal Creation in Hasdai Crescas and Some of His Predecessors," *Viator*, 11 (1980): 289-320;

Julius Guttmann, "Das Problem der Willensfreiheit bei Hasdai Crescas und den islamischen Aristotelikern," in *Jewish Studies in Memory of George A. Kohut, 1874-1933* (New York: Alexander Kohut Memorial Foundation, 1935), pp. 325-349;

Warren Z. Harvey, "Kabbalistic Elements in Crescas' *Light of the Lord*," *Jerusalem Studies in Jewish Thought*, 2 (1982-1983): 75-100;

Harvey, "The Term *hitdabbekut* in Crescas' Definition of Time," *Jewish Quarterly Review*, 71 (1980): 44-47;

M. Joel, *Don Chasdai Creskas' Religionsphilosophische Lehren* (Breslau: Schetler, 1886);

Sarah Klein-Braslavy, "Gan-Eden et Gehinnom dans le Systeme de Hasdai Crescas," in *Hommage à Georges Vajda*, edited by Gérard Nahon and Charles Touati (Louvain: Peeters, 1980), pp. 263-279;

Shlomo Pines, *Scholasticism after Thomas Aquinas and the Teachings of Hasdai Crescas and His Predecessors*, Proceedings of the Israel Academy of Sciences and Humanities, volume 1, no. 10 (Jerusalem: Israel Academy of Sciences and Humanities, 1967);

Charles Touati, "Hasday Crescas et ses Paradoxes sur la Liberté," in *Melanges d'Histoire des Religions offerts à Henri-Charles Puech* (Paris: Presses Universitaires de France, 1974), pp. 573-578;

Meyer Waxman, *The Philosophy of Don Hasdai Crescas* (New York: Columbia University Press, 1920);

Harry A. Wolfson, "Crescas on the Problem of Divine Attributes" and "Studies in Crescas," in his *Studies in the History of Philosophy and Religion*, volume 2 (Cambridge, Mass.: Harvard University Press, 1977), pp. 247-333, 458-478.

John Duns Scotus

(circa 1266 - 8 November 1308)

Jerome V. Brown
University of Windsor, Canada

John Duns Scotus, portrait by Justus van Ghent (Palazzo Barberini, Rome)

PRINCIPAL WORKS: *Lectura in Librum Primum Sententiarum* (Lectures on the *Sentences*, Books 1 and 2, written circa 1296?);

Ordinatio (Oxford Commentary on the *Sentences*, written circa 1300?);

Quaestiones super Libros Metaphysicorum Aristotelis (Libros I-IX) (Questions on the *Metaphysics* of Aristotle, Books 1-9, written circa 1300?);

Reportata Parisiensia (Parisian Commentary on the Sentences, written circa 1302-1304?);

Collationes seu Disputationes Subtilissimae (Collations or Most Subtle Disputations, written circa 1302? and circa 1306?);

In Librum Praedicamentorum Quaestiones (Questions on the *Categories*, written after 1304?);

De Interpretatione (Questions on Aristotle's "On Interpretation," written after 1304?);

De Interpretatione (Questions on Books 1 and 2 of Aristotle's "On Interpretation," written after 1304?);

Super Universalia Porphyrii Quaestiones (Questions on the Universals of Porphyry, written after 1304?);

In Libros Elenchorum Quaestiones (Questions on The Sophistic Arguments, written after 1304?);

Quaestiones super Libros Aristotelis De Anima (Questions on Aristotle's *On the Soul*, written after 1304?);

Quaestiones Quodlibetales (Quodlibetal Questions, written circa 1306-1307?);

De Primo Principio (On the First Principle, written circa 1308?);

Theoremata (Theorems, written circa 1308?).

EDITIONS: *Opera Omnia*, 12 volumes, edited by Luke Wadding (London: Durand, 1639; facsimile edition, Hildesheim: Olms, 1968); republished, 26 volumes (Paris: Vivès, 1891-1895; facsimile edition, Westmead, U.K.: Gregg, 1969);

"De Collationibus Ioannis Duns Scoti, Doctoris Subtilis ac Mariani," edited by Carlo Balić, *Bogoslovni Vestnik*, 9 (1939): 185-219.

CRITICAL EDITION: *Opera Omnia*, 18 volumes published, edited by Carlo Balić and others (Vatican City: Typis Polyglotis Vaticanis, 1950-).

EDITIONS IN ENGLISH: *The De Primo Principio of John Duns Scotus: A Revised Text and a Translation*, edited and translated by Evan Roche (Saint Bonaventure, N.Y.: Franciscan Institute, 1949);

"Duns Scotus on the Necessity of Revealed Knowledge: Prologue to the *Ordinatio* of John Duns Scotus," translated by Allan B. Wolter, *Franciscan Studies*, 11 (September-December 1951): 231-272;

Reason and Revelation: A Question from Duns Scotus, translated by Nathaniel Micklem (New York: Nelson, 1953);

"D. Scotus on the Predestination of Christ," translated by Wolter, *Cord*, 5 (December 1955): 366-372;

Duns Scotus: Philosophical Writings. A Selection, edited and translated by Wolter (Edinburgh: Nelson, 1962); republished as *Philosophical Writings: A Selection* (Indianapolis: Hackett, 1987);

John Duns Scotus: A Treatise on God as First Principle, a Revised Latin Text of the De Primo Principio Translated into English along with Two Related Questions from an Early Commentary on the Sentences, edited and translated by Wolter (Chicago: Franciscan Herald Press, 1966);

John Duns Scotus: God and Creatures. The Quodlibetal Questions, translated by Wolter and Felix Alluntis (Princeton & London: Princeton University Press, 1975);

Duns Scotus: Questions on the Metaphysics, Bk. IX, translated by Wolter (Washington, D.C.: Catholic University of America Press, 1981);

John Duns Scotus: Six Questions on Individuation, translated by Wolter (Washington, D.C.: Catholic University of America Press, 1981);

On the Will and Morality, selected and translated by Wolter (Washington, D.C.: Catholic University of America Press, 1986);

John Duns Scotus: Four Questions on Mary, translated by Wolter (Santa Barbara, Cal.: Old Mission, 1988).

John Duns Scotus was called "*Doctor Subtilis*" (the Subtle Doctor), and the title describes the man to the letter. The complexity of his thought and the presence of what can only be termed an absolute glut of distinctions were the bane of friend and foe alike. In 1678 a disciple produced a manual which he felt called upon to announce as *The Theology of Scotus Delivered from Prolixity and Obscurity, and Its Subtlety Vindicated*. It met with limited success, and that, one may surmise, only with those who already counted themselves among Duns Scotus's staunchest supporters. For others, he was forever the original "dunce" ("Duns man"), and no appeal to his learning or wisdom could rescue the name from this ignominious association. When, in the same century in which the disciple's book appeared, a certain lawyer was called "a dunce," he sued and won in spite of the defendant's claim that Duns Scotus was "a great learned man."

But the attraction of a powerful mind dies hard. Gerard Manley Hopkins wrote a sonnet about him, and Thomas Merton came under his spell. The American philosopher Charles Sanders Peirce called him one of the "profoundest metaphysicians that ever lived," and the doctoral dissertation (and first book) of Martin Heidegger was *Die Kategorien- und Bedeutungslehre des Duns Scotus* (Categories and Meaning in Duns Scotus, 1916).

The situation of Heidegger illustrates perfectly the problems presented by the life and works of Duns Scotus. He was working with some logical treatises attributed to Duns Scotus in the first volume of Luke Wadding's edition of Duns Scotus's *Opera Omnia* (Complete Works, 1639), including the *Tractatus de Modis Significandi sive Grammatica Speculativa* (Tractate on the Mode of Signifying, or the Speculative Grammar). He knew enough about Duns Scotus's thought to speculate that this work was probably not by Duns Scotus at all. Some years later, Martin Grabmann picked up the clue and found that Heidegger was right: it was a work of Thomas of Erfurt (circa 1350) that had been included among the works of Duns Scotus.

Practically nothing can be said with certainty about the life of Duns Scotus. What records there are show that he was ordained on 17 March 1291 by Bishop Oliver Sutton at Northampton; that he was at Oxford on 26 July 1300, for his name is on a list of Franciscans given that day to Bishop John Dalderby, requesting permission for them to hear confessions at the friars church in Oxford; and that he commented on the *Libri Quatuor Sententiarum* (Four Books of Sentences, 1157-1158) of Peter Lombard at the University of Paris in the autumn term, 9 October 1302 to April 1303. He was only at Paris a short time before the long-simmering quarrel between Pope Boniface VIII and Philip the Fair over the taxation of church properties broke into the open. Duns Scotus sided with the pope and was exiled; it is not known where he went. He was back in Paris in 1304 but probably did not occupy his chair in the faculty of theology until 1305; within a relatively short time he was teaching in Cologne, where he died on 8 November 1308. He was buried in the Franciscan church near Cologne Cathedral, and his remains are still venerated there. Nothing else is known for certain, not even whether Duns was part of his name or a designation of his place of birth. It is probable, however, that he was from Duns, Scotland, and that his uncle was Elias Duns.

His works were left in a totally unedited state at his death. Not one of them can be dated with any exactness. His earliest disciples acted with more haste than prudence and "completed" works according to their own fancies and designs, using bits and pieces of which some did not even originate from his pen. It cannot be assumed that his commentaries on the logical treatises of Aristotle are early works done while pursuing the master of arts degree preparatory to his study of theology, because the privileges of the mendicant friars included the right to pursue their arts courses in their own houses of study without having to take the master of arts degree in the university. These courses were somewhat less stringent and extensive than the university courses, and therefore they perhaps did not always lead to detailed and lengthy commentaries on Aristotle's works. Often such commentaries did not come until relatively late in a professorial career, after the standard commentary on the *Sentences* of Peter Lombard. Nor is it to be ruled out that these commentaries, in the form of questions on relevant topics, were, as Allan B. Wolter suggests, "discussed privately for the benefit of the Franciscan student philosophers and theologians." The reader must, therefore, be extremely careful about tracing "evolutions" in the thought of Duns Scotus.

Of far greater importance for a proper understanding of the thought of Duns Scotus is an event of singular significance for all late medieval philosophy and theology. In 1277 Pope John XXI, deeply concerned about what was being taught in the faculty of arts at the University of Paris, asked Etienne Tempier, the bishop of Paris, to look into the situation. The concerns were over the teaching of the works of Aristotle, and more particularly of the purely philosophical and hence untheological interpretations put on those works by the Islamic philosopher and greatest commentator on Aristotle, Averroës, and by his predecessor, Avicenna. Tempier could hardly be accused of laxness in his efforts. He assembled a commission of sixteen theologians; it drew up a list of 219 propositions, all of which the bishop condemned on 7 March 1277. On 18 March 1277 Robert Kilwardby, the archbishop of Canterbury, condemned some 30 of the propositions. The affair became known as the Condemnation of 1277, and its central thrust was against the concept of a philosophy independent of theology and on occasion actually opposed to it. There can be no doubt that the condemnation was taken seriously in all quarters: philosophical and theological literature changes after 1277, and the works of Duns Scotus, with their profound subtlety and often hair-splitting exactness, reflect this new attitude. To the old-line Augustinians, Aristotle was an upstart who confused everything. The break with Augustine is at times quite visible in Duns Scotus, but it is effected with such caution that one is bound to wonder at other times whether there has been any real break at all.

The issue of the proper domains of philosophy and theology was a concern of Duns Scotus (albeit an indirect one: he was a metaphysician first and foremost) even in the prologue to the *Ordinatio* (Oxford Commentary on the *Sentences*, circa 1300?). Traditionally, Scholastic philosophers and theologians had seen philosophy, the work of human reason unaided by revelation, as an instrument for the clarification of the truths of the Christian faith; but it often proved a most inadequate and imperfect instrument. The Condemnation of 1277 forced the supporters of philosophical approaches to theological questions to look more carefully at the relationship between

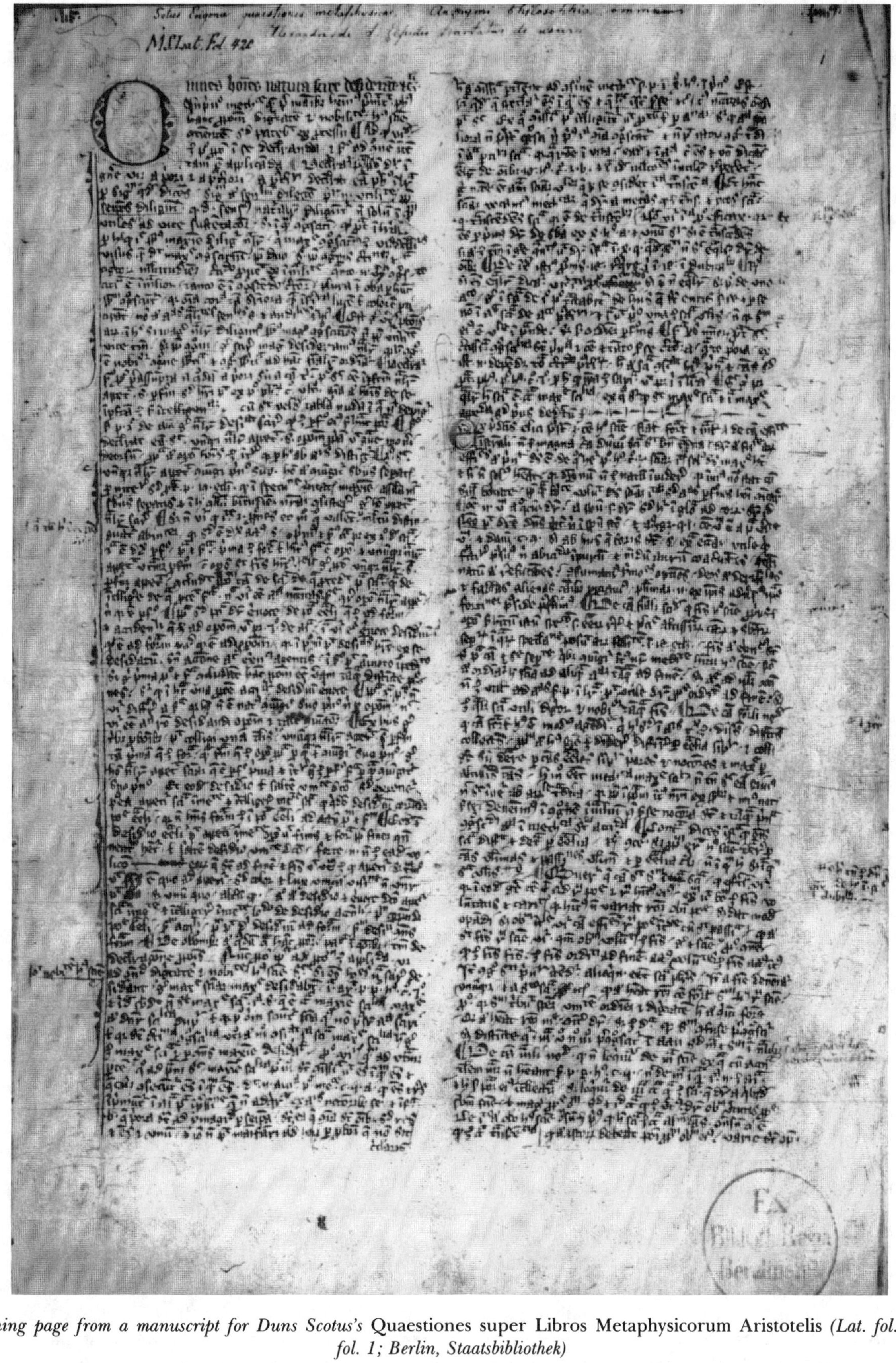

Opening page from a manuscript for Duns Scotus's Quaestiones super Libros Metaphysicorum Aristotelis *(Lat. fol. 420 fol. 1; Berlin, Staatsbibliothek)*

the two disciplines and, consequently, to undertake a closer analysis of the whole idea of deductive science and how it applied to theology. Duns Scotus is perhaps more rigorous than his predecessors in distinguishing between the answers of the philosophers and the theologians to a given question, constantly pointing out the inadequacies of the philosophical answers and explaining what this or that philosopher might have said had he been better at philosophy—not, it should be noted, what he might have said had he had before him the truths of faith.

Duns Scotus's philosophical inclinations, at least, were Aristotelian through and through. He doubted much of the Augustinianism current among the Franciscans before him, and he was the first of them to throw overboard the traditional Augustinian teaching on the need of the human mind for a special divine illumination to know the truth. In this area, as in so many others, he found himself at odds not just with the members of his own order but also with the teachings of Henry of Ghent, secular master of theology at Paris from 1276 to 1292 and perhaps the most influential master in the faculty in the last quarter of the thirteenth century. Henry, who had served on Tempier's commission of theologians, was a supporter of Augustine; whether Duns Scotus studied under him is not known. He was certainly familiar with Henry's works, and it is against those works that his own must be placed and not against the works of Thomas Aquinas, who had died in 1274 and whose work had also been rendered suspect by the Condemnation of 1277.

That Duns Scotus often views Aristotle through the eyeglasses of Avicenna and Averroës made a defensive posture vis-à-vis his philosophical speculations still more imperative. This posture in large measure explains both the incredible complexity of his writings and the difficulties of the reader in trying to come to grips with them. Everything that was philosophical, no matter how remote from the central argument of a question, had to be dealt with at once, together with all possible objections that might be raised; everything was examined from every possible angle. In each of his works, then, one is confronted with a monumental amount of detail designed to dissuade all but the stoutest hearts from finding his meaning. Simplifications of and generalizations about his ideas are virtually impossible: to simplify is to oversimplify; to generalize is to court not merely the exception that proves the rule but so many exceptions that it looks as though there is no rule at all.

The best that can be done is to sketch out some of the central positions that identify "the mind of Duns Scotus." His views on the nature of metaphysics and its place in philosophy owe more to Avicenna than they do to either Aristotle or Averroës. Metaphysics is a demonstrative science, concerned with God and divine things. Certainly there is nothing here to suggest a parting of the ways with either "the Philosopher" (Aristotle) or "the Commentator" (Averroës). But Averroës said that the existence of God is proved in physics, in terms of a first mover, and not in metaphysics. Avicenna, on the other hand, offered a causal proof for the existence of God within metaphysics, and Duns Scotus agreed. There is no reason, he thought, why metaphysics should be subordinated to physics; and in any event, the idea of a "first mover" is itself somewhat suspect. "Whatever is moved is moved by another" is the basis of the proof of the first mover in Aristotle's *Physics*, and Duns Scotus was puzzled by this so-called principle. He did not regard it as self-evident; indeed, he found no shortage of exceptions to it, such as the acts of the human free will and (anticipating the eighteenth-century philosopher David Hume) movements of bodies when other bodies are no longer in contact with them.

God and all other beings were united, in this Avicennian view of metaphysics. This unity is preserved by Duns Scotus in his teachings on the univocity of the concept of being. Being, he says, must be said univocally of all that is; otherwise, being could not be the primary object of the human intellect. In this matter, both the Augustinians and the Aristotelians are in error: God is not the primary object of the human intellect (as the former maintained) but its *highest* object; the essences of material things cannot be the primary object of the human intellect either (as the latter maintained), for then God would be left out of the picture. The powers of the human intellect cannot be restricted in this unjustifiable and inconsistent manner.

Being in its widest extension, therefore, is the proper object of the human intellect. By "being" (*ens*) Duns Scotus seems to have meant anything that could possibly exist—that is, anything the existence of which would not result in contradiction. It is the first of the "transcendentals," since it transcends the Aristotelian categories (substance, quantity, quality, relation,

A depiction of Duns Scotus in a fourteenth-century manuscript (Coll. 215, fol. 1r; Biblioteca dell'accademia dei Concordi, Rovigo, Italy)

place, time, posture, state, action, and passion); for Duns Scotus, anything is a transcendental so long as it can be predicated of reality and cannot be found among the Aristotelian categories ("quantity," then, is not a transcendental; not all being is quantifiable). Being is different from existence, which adds the dimension of extramentality to being. Being is a universal but not a genus to which differences can be added "from the outside." Differences in being arise from within being in the manner of intrinsic modes (*formalitates*). Being, then, is predicated of both God and creatures univocally. But God and creatures are obviously different in their respective being; they must, then, be different intrinsic modes of being. The same is true of what came to be known as the transcendentals in medieval metaphysics: the one, the true, the good, and so forth are intrinsic modes or formalities of being.

Among the transcendentals Duns Scotus includes the "disjunctive transcendentals," such as "caused or uncaused, possible or actual, necessary or contingent." No one of the disjuncts is convertible with being, but each pair of disjuncts is ("All being must be either necessary or contingent," and so on). Finally, there are the transcendentals of absolute perfection: those that can be predicated of being without suggesting any imperfection or limitation. Thus, "being" in itself is such a transcendental, as are "necessary," "actual," "uncaused," and any one of a pair of disjunctive transcendentals that is of greater perfection than the other. The divine attributes are transcendentals of this sort: they can be predicated of some reality—either of God alone (omnipotence, for example), or of God and creatures (knowledge and free will, for example)—and they do not fall under the Aristotelian categories.

Duns Scotus's Aristotelianism was not so all-encompassing as to prevent some Augustinian elements from finding their place in his teachings. For Aristotle, prime matter was pure potentiality. For Duns Scotus, prime matter is perhaps more like Augustine's notion of matter as "nearly nothing." It is something that is capable of taking on further perfections in being. Matter and form are essentially and not just accidentally ordered to each other; an essential unity prevails between matter and the substantial form such that a composite is one by nature. A substantial form cannot also be accidental; in every substantial change, as Aristotle maintains, a substance results, not a substance and an accident. This position illustrates quite well the extreme caution of Duns Scotus when testing the limits of the Condemnation of 1277: an Augustinian view of matter is welded to an Aristotelian view of substance.

Duns Scotus agreed with Avicenna that "horseness [*equinitas*] is only horseness, that of itself it is neither singular nor plural, neither one nor many, etc." Being is indifferent to its further modifications and modalities. Thus, in every being of a particular kind there is a common nature which can only be made singular by having something positive added to it. There is a modality of being which makes the common nature "horseness" into this horse, Citation, or this horse, Black Beauty, or any horse whatever. This positive something is the principle of individuation. It is occasionally referred to as "thisness" (*haecceitas*), but the word appears only infrequently in Duns Scotus's writings.

Individuation is a process rather than a completed state of affairs. Matter is first actualized by the "form of corporeity" (*forma corporeitatis*), and the presence of this form explains the continuing (albeit brief) resemblance between the corpse and the no longer "besouled" living person. The form of corporeity makes matter a physical body. It also prepares the matter to receive a further specification and individuation through the soul. In this way, for example, the common nature of "horseness" is gradually specified to this singular horse (Citation, Black Beauty, Native Dancer), with the common nature remaining after the soul ceases to inform the body of the individual.

Like other medieval philosophers, Duns Scotus recognizes real distinctions between things as well as a distinction of reason in which there are not two things but only two different names (for example, the Morning Star and the Evening Star). There is another distinction, characteristic only of the philosophy of Duns Scotus (though its antecedents are to be found in Avicenna and Henry of Ghent), located between the real distinction and the distinction of reason: it is the "formal distinction in respect of the thing" and is asserted by Duns Scotus to exist *in reality* between two different formalities in the same thing considered as a unified whole. It is rather difficult to say exactly what a "formality" is for Duns Scotus. A formality is supposed to have just enough real being to keep it outside the realm of the being of reason and not so much real being that it can be put into the realm of real extramental and concrete being. Apparently it is something like the Platonic Ideas or Forms.

One area of application of the formal distinction is that of the human soul and its powers or faculties. There is no faculty psychology in Augustine; Duns Scotus is faithful enough to Augustine to want to preserve an integral unity in the human soul, but he is also committed to Aristotle's idea of a plurality of powers in the soul. So he distinguishes the soul and its powers as "formalities" in relation to each other. The will, the intellect, and so on are formalities in relation to the soul, and the soul is a formality in relation to them. The nature of a formality permits Duns Scotus to opt for both the faculty psychology of Aristotle and what he perceives to be a more Augustinian view of the unity of the human being. The effects of the Condemnation of 1277 can be seen here.

The idea of the unified whole is a dominating one in the metaphysics of Duns Scotus. It is behind his ideas on the univocity of the concept of being and on the transcendentals as distinct from being and from each other only in virtue of a formal distinction.

The proof of the existence of God in the *Ordinatio* and in the *De Primo Principio* (On the First Principle, circa 1308?) is Duns Scotus at his most complex. Being that is merely possible cannot account for itself, for then it would have to be actual as well as possible, which is a contradiction. And if there is no cause to account for the actuality of possible being, then there would be possible being prior to actual being, which is absurd. So there will have to be at least one necessary being. Possible being makes no sense without necessarily existing being. The conclusion is that there must be a being necessary in itself which is the cause of the possibility in all other beings, a first being whose very essence is being. If it is not totally actual, then it would be impossible. Self-causality in such a being is viewed by Duns Scotus as absurd. No limits whatsoever can be placed on this first essential cause on which all other beings depend; infinity is identified by Duns Scotus as the most characteristic property of this first being.

This being is necessary in its being, but not necessary in its actions. Here Duns Scotus takes a definite stand against Averroës. God is both completely rational and completely free; there is nothing in the changelessness of the divine nature which mandates a necessary course of behavior for the divine being. The divine essence and the divine will are formally distinct from each other. Thus, the moral law is not determined absolutely by the divine essence, but neither is it the product of capriciousness in the divine will. The divine law is the objective foundation of the moral law and is the product of the divine will operating in accordance with the noncontradictory character of the divine nature. God can change the rules of morality, but he cannot act against his own nature.

The primacy of the will extends also to human psychology. Desire is moved only by what is known, but the impetus toward the object comes from the will. The will is thus the higher faculty: the will moves the intellect to know what it knows. Once again Duns Scotus locates himself within the tradition of Augustine (and, incidentally, puts distance between himself and Aquinas) at the same time as he advances a faculty psychology that is ostensibly more Aristotelian than Augustinian.

Duns Scotus's work is quite capable of generating in his would-be readers a sense of raging despair; it is small wonder that he came to be thought of as "a dunce." But, as with the "dumb ox" Aquinas, whose bellowings were destined to be heard near and far, so too it is with Duns Scotus. He wrote magnificently in defense of Mary, especially of her Immaculate Conception. The Roman Catholic church proclaimed the doctrine on 8 December 1854; the Marian theology of Duns Scotus, as interpreted by his followers, was in large measure responsible.

Bibliographies:

Uriel Smeets, *Lineamenta Bibliographiae Scotisticae* (Rome: Commissio Scotisticae, 1942);

Odulf Schäfer, *Bibliographia de Vita, Operibus et Doctrina Iohannis Duns Scoti, Doctoris Subtilis ac Mariani, Saec. XIX-XX* (Rome: Herder, 1955);

Donald A. Cress, "Toward a Bibliography on Duns Scotus on the Existence of God," *Franciscan Studies*, 35 (1975): 45-65.

References:

Efrem Bettoni, *Duns Scotus: The Basic Principles of His Philosophy*, translated by Bernardine Bonansea (Washington, D.C.: Catholic University of America Press, 1961);

John F. Boler, *Charles Peirce and Scholastic Realism: A Study of Peirce's Relation to John Duns Scotus* (Seattle: University of Washington Press, 1963);

Ioannes Gabriel Boyvim, O.F.M., *Theologia Scoti a prolixitate et subtilitas eius ab obscuritate libera et vindicata* (Paris: Couterot, 1678);

Jerome V. Brown, "Duns Scotus on the Possibility of Knowing Genuine Truth: The Reply to Henry of Ghent in the *Lectura Prima* and in the *Ordinatio*," *Recherches de Théologie Ancienne et Médiévale*, 51 (1984): 136-182;

Brown, "John Duns Scotus on Henry of Ghent's Arguments for Divine Illumination: The Statement of the Case," *Vivarium*, 14 (November 1976): 94-113;

Brown, "John Duns Scotus on Henry of Ghent's Theory of Knowledge," *Modern Schoolman*, 56 (November 1978): 1-29;

Brown, "John Duns Scotus on Mutability and Immutability," in *Studies in Medieval Culture*, edited by John R. Sommerfeldt and Rozanne Elder (Kalamazoo, Mich.: Medieval Institute, 1976), pp. 129-135;

Brown, "The Knowledge Proper to the Separated Soul: Henry of Ghent and John Duns Scotus," *Franziskanische Studien*, 66 (1984): 316-334;

R. Effler, *John Duns Scotus and the Principle "Omne Quod Movetur ab Alio Movetur"* (St. Bonaventure, N.Y.: Franciscan Institute, 1962);

Etienne Gilson, *Jean Duns Scot* (Paris: Vrin, 1952);

Martinus Grabmann, "De Thoma Erfordiensi auctore Grammaticae quae Ioanni Duns Scoto adscribitur speculativae," *Archivum Franciscanum Historicum*, 15 (1922): 273-277;

Martin Heidegger, *Die Kategorien- und Bedeutungslehre des Duns Scotus* (Tübingen: Mohr, 1916);

Allan B. Wolter, *The Transcendentals and Their Function in the Metaphysics of Duns Scotus* (St. Bonaventure, N.Y.: Franciscan Institute, 1946).

Manuscripts:

There are no known manuscripts in the hand of Duns Scotus himself, nor is there any evidence of a manuscript done by a scribe and corrected by him. The principal manuscript of the *Ordinatio* is Assisi, Biblioteca Communalis, codex 137, fol. 1ra-291vb. Also known as "Codex A," it is the base manuscript for the critical edition. For the *Quaestiones super Libros Metaphysicorum Aristotelis* (*Libros I-IX*) the most important manuscript is Berlin, Bibliothek Status, codex latinus fol. 420, fol. 1ra-57va. The critical edition of this work is currently being prepared by the Franciscan Institute at St. Bonaventure University, Saint Bonaventure, New York. The *Quaestiones Quodlibetales* are found in Assisi, Biblioteca Communalis, codex 136, fol. 1ra-57v. The *Lectura in Librum Primum Sententiarum* is in Vatican City, Biblioteca Apostolica, codex palatinus latinus 993, fol. 48ra-98vb, and Padua, Biblioteca Antoniana, codex 178, fol. 1ra-83vb. The *Quaestiones super Libros Aristotelis De Anima* is in Avignon, Bibliothèque Communale, codex 328, fol. 33ra-98ra. For the logical treatises (also being edited by the Franciscan Institute), the principal manuscripts are Berlin, Bibliothek Status, codex 220, fols. 3ra-222r, containing, in order, *Super Universalia Porphyrii Quaestiones*, *In Librum Praedicamentorum Quaestiones*, and *De Interpretatione* (*Quaestiones in I et II Librum Perihermeneias Aristotelis*). The *De Interpretatione*—also known as *In Duos Libros Perihermeneias, Operis Secundi, Quod Apellant, Quaestiones*—is in Vatican City, Biblioteca Apostolica, codex palatinus latinus 870, fol. 47vb-52va. The *In Libros Elenchorum Quaestiones* is in Brussels, Bibliothèque Royale, codex 2908, fol. 101r-119v. Finally, the *De Primo Principio* is in Avignon, Bibliothèque Communale, codex 328, fol. 1ra-32ra, and the *Theoremata* in Newburg Cloister (Klosterneuburg, Germany), Biblioteca Canoniae Sancti Augustini, codex 307, fol. 120va-126v.

Meister Eckhart

(circa 1260 - circa 1328)

Bernard McGinn
University of Chicago

PRINCIPAL WORKS: *Collatio in Libros Sententiarum* (Collation of the Book of Sentences, written circa 1293-1294);

Sermo die Beati Augustini Parisius Habitus (Sermon for the Feast of Saint Augustine Given at Paris, written circa 1293-1294);

Die Rede der Underscheidene (The Counsels on Discernment, written circa 1295-1298);

Tractatus super Oratione Dominica (Treatise on the Lord's Prayer, written before 1300?);

Quaestiones Parisienses, 1-3 (Parisian Questions, written 1302-1303);

Liber Benedictus (The Book "Benedictus," written 1308-1318);

Quaestiones Parisienses, 4-5 (Parisian Questions, written circa 1311-1313);

Opus Tripartitum (Work in Three Parts, written circa 1311-1326): Part One, *Opus Propositionum* (Work of Propositions)—only *Prologi in Opus Tripartitum* (Prologues to the Work in Three Parts) survives; Part Two, *Opus Quaestionum* (Work of Questions—not extant); Part Three, *Opus Expositionum* (Work of Expositions)—includes *Expositio Libri Genesis* (Commentary on the Book of Genesis), *Liber Parabolorum Genesis* (Book of the Parables of Genesis), *Expositio Libri Exodi* (Commentary on the Book of Exodus), *Sermones et Lectiones super Ecclesiastici Cap. XXIV* (Sermons and Lectures on the Twenty-fourth Chapter of Ecclesiasticus), *Expositio Libri Sapientiae* (Commentary on the Book of Wisdom), *Expositio Sancti Evangelii Secundum Iohannem* (Commentary on John), *Sermones* (Latin Sermons);

Von Abgeschiedenheit (On Detachment, written circa 1325?);

Rechtfertigungsschrift (Defense, written 1326);

Granum Sinapis (The Mustard Seed, date and authenticity uncertain);

Sprüche und Legenden (Sayings and Legends, date and authenticity uncertain).

CRITICAL EDITIONS: *Meister Eckhart: Die lateinischen Werke. Herausgegeben im Auftrage der Deutschen Forschungsgemeinschaft*, 6 volumes projected, 5 volumes to date, edited by Joseph Koch (Stuttgart & Berlin: Kohlhammer, 1936-);

Meister Eckhart: Die deutschen Werke. Herausgegeben im Auftrage der Deutschen Forschungsgemeinschaft, 5 volumes projected, 4 volumes to date, edited by Josef Quint (Stuttgart & Berlin: Kohlhammer, 1958-).

EDITIONS IN ENGLISH: *Meister Eckhart's Sermons, First Time Translated into English,* translated by Claud Field (London: Allenson, 1909);

Meister Eckhart, 2 volumes, edited by Franz Pfeiffer, translated by C. de B. Evans (London: Watkins, 1924-1931); republished as *The Works of Meister Eckhart,* 2 volumes (London: Watkins, 1947-1952);

Meister Eckhart: A Modern Translation, translated by Raymond Bernard Blakney (New York & London: Harper, 1941);

Meister Eckhart Speaks: A Collection of the Teachings of the Famous German Mystic, translated by Elizabeth Strakosch (New York: Philosophical Library, 1957);

Meister Eckhart: Selected Treatises and Sermons Translated from Latin and German, with an Introduction and Notes, edited and translated by James M. Clark and John V. Skinner (London: Faber & Faber, 1958);

Master Eckhart: Parisian Questions and Prologues, translated by Armand A. Maurer (Toronto: Pontifical Institute of Mediaeval Studies, 1974);

Meister Eckhart: Sermons and Treatises, 3 volumes, translated by M. O'C. Walshe (volumes 1 & 2, London & Dulverton: Watkins, 1979-1981; volume 3, Dorset: Element Books, 1987);

Breakthrough: Meister Eckhart's Creation Spirituality in New Translation, translated by Matthew Fox and others (Garden City, N.Y.: Doubleday, 1980);

Meister Eckhart: The Essential Sermons, Commentaries, Treatises, and Defense, edited and translated by Edmund Colledge and Bernard McGinn, Classics of Western Spirituality (New York: Paulist Press, 1981);

Meister Eckhart: Teacher and Preacher, edited and translated by McGinn, Frank Tobin, and Elvira Borgstadt, Classics of Western Spirituality (New York: Paulist Press, 1986).

Meister Eckhart is best known as a mystic, a preacher, and a theologian. William of Ockham, who probably learned of him when both men were under investigation at the papal court in Avignon in 1327, thought his views "fantastic, no less heretical than insane." Philosophers in the tradition of Ockham have continued to have doubts about Eckhart; those of other persuasions, such as Nicholas of Cusa in the fifteenth century, G. W. F. Hegel in the nineteenth, and Martin Heidegger in the twentieth, have found in Eckhart's thought a powerful philosophical resource and one of the most important speculative systems in Western thought.

Eckhart himself certainly thought that what he was engaged in teaching and preaching pertained to both philosophy and theology. Throughout his writings the German friar insists not only that revelation and reason cannot disagree (a position held by most Christian theologians) but also that one can use arguments from reason with regard to every truth of the Christian religion (with the possible exception of the manner of Christ's presence in the Eucharist)—a view that, if not unique, is at least unusual. Though Eckhart did admit a diversity of modes of apprehension between the certainty of faith and the probability of reason—in line with Christian Platonic thinkers before him but in an even bolder way—he did not think it necessary to make a distinction in kind between the truths of faith and those of philosophy. Eckhart's major speculative writings, which form the basis for his preaching in both Latin and the vernacular Middle High German, are no less philosophical than they are theological. The purpose of his great *Expositio Sancti Evangelii Secundum Iohannem* (Commentary on John) was, as he put it, "to explain what the Holy Christian faith and the two testaments maintain through the help of the natural arguments of the philosophers." He claimed that all of Scripture teaches natural and moral truths, as well as truths about God.

Late in the third century of the Christian era, the pagan thinker Plotinus reformulated basic philosophical insights inherited from Plato, Aristotle, and the Stoics into a potent new religious and mystical philosophy customarily known as Neoplatonism. Central to Plotinus's philosophy was a dialectical view of the relation between the ultimate ground of all being, which Plotinus referred to as the One, and everything else. Plotinus held the One to be both the immanent depth present within all multiplicity and the transcen-

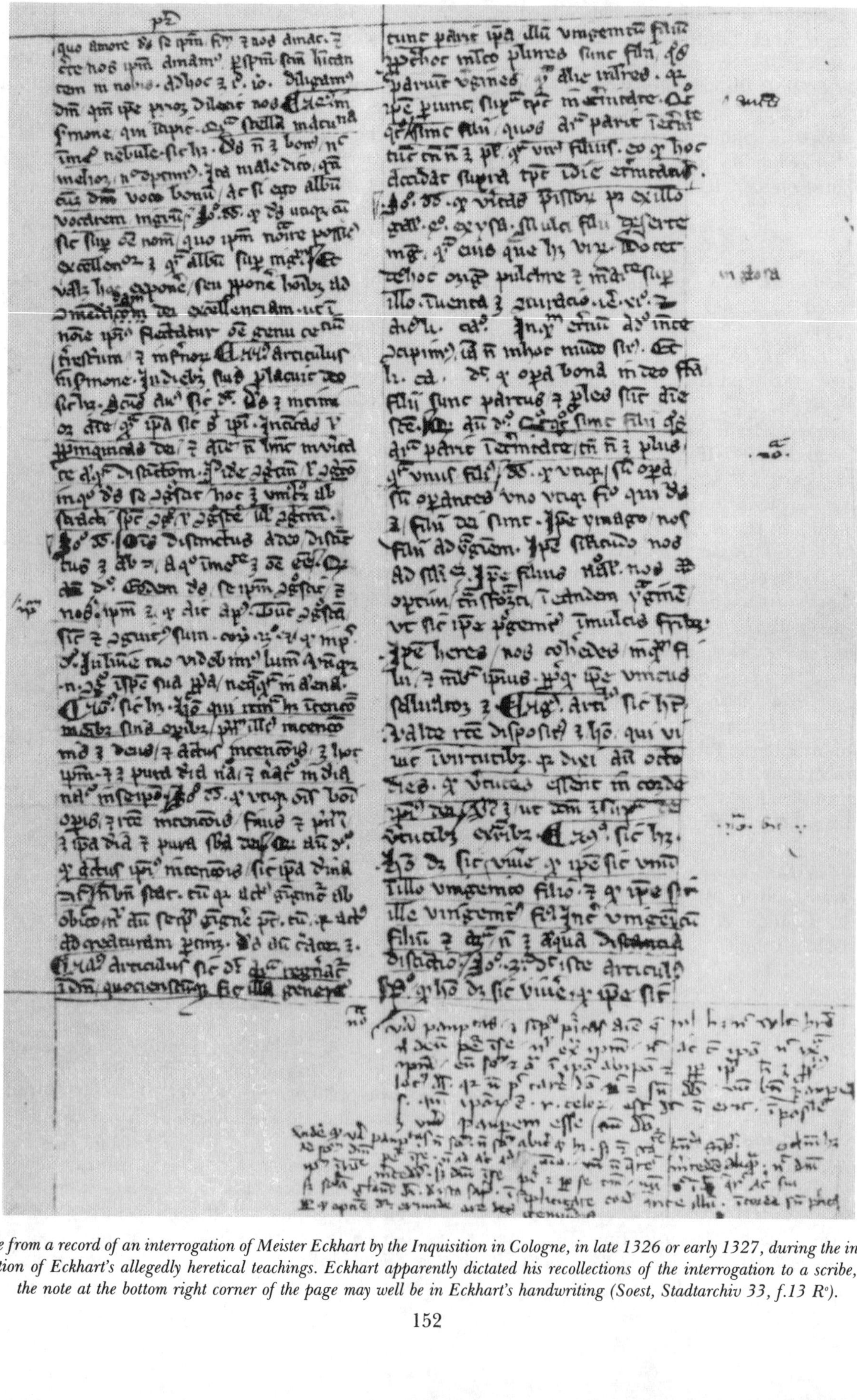

Page from a record of an interrogation of Meister Eckhart by the Inquisition in Cologne, in late 1326 or early 1327, during the investigation of Eckhart's allegedly heretical teachings. Eckhart apparently dictated his recollections of the interrogation to a scribe, but the note at the bottom right corner of the page may well be in Eckhart's handwriting (Soest, Stadtarchiv 33, f.13 R°).

dent source of that multiplicity. Neoplatonic philosophy, developed and modified to accommodate Christian belief in the Trinity, Creation, and the Incarnation, was of central importance in Christian thought during the Middle Ages and beyond. (It was also an important source for much medieval Muslim philosophy and mysticism, and, to a lesser extent, was also found in medieval Judaism.) Eckhart's thought is a particularly powerful form of speculative dialectical Neoplatonism. Though he was certainly an original thinker, his approach to philosophy bears a remarkable affinity to the most speculative, and frequently most "mystical," Neoplatonists—Plotinus and Proclus among the pagans, Ibn al-'Arabi among the Muslims, Pseudo-Dionysius the Areopagite and John Scottus Eriugena among Christians.

Knowledge of Eckhart's life is limited. Born in Hochheim in Thuringia in Germany about 1260 he may have entered the Dominican order as young as fifteen or sixteen, because there is evidence that he was an arts student at the University of Paris during the great debates over the use of Aristotle in the mid 1270s. Eckhart says that he studied with the Dominican scholar Albert the Great; this period would have been during Albert's last years, when he was teaching at the Dominican house of studies in Cologne. Eckhart always considered himself a disciple and defender of Albert's greatest student, Thomas Aquinas, who was dead by the time Eckhart began his studies.

Albert the Great had not only been instrumental in introducing knowledge of Aristotle into the university curriculum but had also emphasized classic Neoplatonic texts, especially the writings of the Pseudo-Dionysius and the *Liber de Causis* (Book of Causes), a Latin translation of an Arabic work derived from the writings of Proclus. Aquinas had taken this effort a step further and had effected a major revision of Christian theology on the basis of a transformed Aristotelianism that included important elements of the Neoplatonic tradition. Thomas's partial condemnation in 1277, and the cloud under which Albert also came, did not halt the intellectual work of the German Dominicans. Contemporaries of Eckhart, such as Dietrich of Freiburg and Berthold of Moosburg, shared many of his philosophical interests. But such speculation remained suspicious to many, especially when Eckhart used some of its most daring forms in his public preaching.

The first secure date in Eckhart's life is 1294, when a document refers to him as a Dominican "lecturer on the *Sentences*" at the University of Paris. This position was the last step before receiving the degree of Master of Theology, the coveted acme of the medieval intellectual world. The brief *Collatio in Libros Sententiarum* (Collation of the Book of Sentences), which many ascribe to him, appears to date from 1293-1294, and the *Sermo die Beati Augustini Parisius Habitus* (Sermon for the Feast of Saint Augustine Given at Paris) and the *Tractatus super Oratione Dominica* (Treatise on the Lord's Prayer) might well come from this period, too. These early works are conventional scholastic pieces; Eckhart was something of a late bloomer.

Eckhart was recalled to Germany in 1294 to serve both as prior of the Dominican house in Erfurt and as vicar of all the Dominican houses in his native Thuringia. After 1298 the Dominican general chapter forbade such dual positions; Eckhart appears to have continued as prior in Erfurt until 1302.

Eckhart's duties as an official in the Dominican order in Germany during these years prompted his first securely datable vernacular work, *Die Rede der Underscheidene* (The Counsels on Discernment, circa 1295-1298). This collection of twenty-three loosely organized chapters of spiritual advice on such conventional themes as obedience, penance, and the reception of the Eucharist, as well as more properly Eckhartian topics such as detachment and the relation of interior and exterior works, is both less and more original than it may at first appear. While it is not as verbally and theologically daring as Eckhart's later vernacular sermons and treatises, many of the main themes of his mature works are expressed here in somewhat more sober fashion. One should also note that a vernacular treatise of this sort, especially one addressed to members of a religious order, was quite a novelty at the time.

Part of Eckhart's fascination, from the literary as well as from the philosophical point of view, is that he is the first major medieval speculative thinker to present his thought in both his mother tongue and in the learned language of the schools. It has been claimed that Eckhart alone was responsible for the creation of a philosophical and theological vocabulary in the German language, but the translation of speculative thought from Latin into the German vernacular was a great cultural achievement to which many writers contributed from the beginning of the second half of the thirteenth century. Despite the role of such figures as Berthold von Regensburg, David of Augsburg, and Mechthild of Magdeburg (all of whom wrote prior to Eckhart), the Dominican friar was undoubtedly the central figure in this remarkable moment in Western culture. Eckhart is the only medieval thinker in whose works one can study the rich interchange between an established speculative vocabulary stretching back more than a thousand years and a rapidly developing vernacular tongue ready to move into new forms of expression. The real Eckhart is neither the Latin Eckhart nor the German Eckhart, but the creative genius forced to relate the two as had no thinker before him.

In 1302 Eckhart was recalled to Paris to serve as regent master in the "extern" (that is, non-French) Dominican chair of theology at the university. It was apparently at this time that "Meister" (Master) Eckhart began to come into his own. The *Quaestiones Parisienses* (Parisian Questions), the first three of which date from this mastership of 1302-1303, already display some of Eckhart's most daring speculative themes. The first question, "Are existence [*esse*] and understanding [*intelligere*] the same in God?," is the most significant. Eckhart begins in good Dominican fashion by citing Aquinas's doctrine of existence as the fundamental attribute of God, only to reverse this position by declaring: "it is not my present opinion that God understands because he exists, but rather that he exists because he understands. God is an intellect and understanding, and his understanding itself is the ground of his existence." Eckhart repeats this claim in other works. For students looking for metaphysical consistency, this argument has provided a problem, because other and presumably later works, both in Latin and in the vernacular, seem to give metaphysical priority to existence or to unity (*unum*) as the fundamental attribute of God. But Eckhart's dialectical thought gives no single transcendental predicate a totally privileged position: all predicates have their uses, but all also have limitations. True love of wisdom (*philosophia*) consists in realizing these limitations in order to begin living the reality they suggest.

The second of the *Quaestiones Parisienses* denies that an angel's understanding is the same as his existence; the third reflects a public disputation between the Franciscan master Gonsalvus of Spain and Eckhart over whether priority was to be given to the will, as the Franciscans held, or the intellect, as the Dominicans contended.

In 1303 Eckhart was again recalled to Germany, this time to take up an even more important administrative and pastoral position as the first provincial of the new Dominican province of Saxony. There he was in charge of forty-seven male houses and an undetermined number of cloisters of nuns. In 1307 he was given the onerous task of serving as the personal vicar of the Dominican master general in reforming the order's houses in Bohemia. During this time Eckhart seems to have become friendly with the Bohemian royal family, especially with Queen Agnes, to whom he dedicated his *Liber Benedictus* (The Book "Benedictus," 1308-1318). His many duties apparently left little time for writing, though it has been suggested that his two Latin sermons on Ecclesiasticus come from this time.

In 1311 the Dominican general chapter held at Naples sent Eckhart to Paris for a second term as regent master, a rare privilege. This two-year period was crucial for the direction of his life and for his subsequent preaching and teaching. It was during this time that he conceived of his massive *Opus Tripartitum* (Work in Three Parts), a project that he says in the prologue he undertook "to satisfy as best he can the wishes of certain zealous brethren who a long time ago persistently urged him and constantly pressed him to put down in writing the topics they were accustomed to hear from him in lectures and other school exercises, in sermons and in daily discussions." In theory, if not in fact (since it was never completed), the *Opus Tripartitum* was one of the most ambitious projects of the age of High Scholasticism.

From its outset the Dominican order had emphasized the best theological education as the necessary preparation for effective preaching. This theological education, as Eckhart conceived it, comprised three levels. The first was to be manifested in the first part of the *Opus Tripartitum*, the *Opus Propositionum* (Work of Propositions), which was designed to lay down the speculative basis for sound teaching and preaching through "a thousand propositions or more, divided into fourteen treatises corresponding to the number of terms of which the propositions are formed." Eckhart provides a list of the fourteen treatises, organized according to opposed terms (such as existence/nothing, one/many, true/false), but only the prologue to the *Opus Propositionum*, treating the first of the "thousand or more" propositions, survives. It is devoted to the proposition "Existence is God" and is a major source of information about Eckhart's metaphysics. This method of argument by analytic investigation of propositions was well known in the Neoplatonic tradition, as evidenced by Boethius's *De Trinitate* (On the Trinity, circa 521) and by the *Liber de Causis*, major sources of Eckhart's thought. In other works Eckhart refers to parts of the *Opus Propositionum* that do not survive; it seems likely that he never finished much of it.

The *Opus Quaestionum* (Work of Questions) which was to follow was apparently to be of more limited scope, dealing with a series of disputed issues following the order of Aquinas's *Summa Theologica*. Nothing of this work survives. The final part of the great project, the *Opus Expositionum* (Work of Expositions), was more directly related to the preparation of friars in the knowledge of Scripture necessary for effective preaching. In this part Eckhart intended to comment on key passages of the Bible and to present model sermons showing how to expound the texts of both testaments. Almost all of what survives of Eckhart's Latin writings belongs to the *Opus Expositionum*. The relative completeness of this part of the *Opus Tripartitum* probably results from his removal from Paris in 1313 to pastoral work in Germany, which would have put the needs of preachers to the fore in his life.

Eckhart's scriptural commentaries are quite different from those of Aquinas and most other exegetes of the time. Instead of giving a continuous explanation of the text, frequently according to an abstract plan, Eckhart interprets selected texts in highly speculative ways as a supplement to the interpretations of the recognized authorities. No Christian writer since Origen had presented so impressive a system of thought through exegesis alone.

Aquinas held that theological argument should be based only on the literal sense of the biblical text. Eckhart, like Origen and Augustine, believed that "Sacred scripture frequently tells a story in such a way that it also contains and suggests mysteries, teaches the nature of things, and directs and orders moral actions." In other words, he was a firm adherent of the superiority of the spiritual sense of the text.

Eckhart's understanding of the spiritual, or "parabolical" sense, as he called it, was deeply influenced by the *Moreh Nevukhim* (Guide of the Perplexed, 1190), by the great Jewish philosopher, legal scholar, and exegete Moses Maimonides. In the prologue to his second commentary on Genesis, the *Liber Parabolorum Genesis* (Book of the Parables of Genesis), Eckhart distinguishes between the "more evident sense," which itself may contain many doctrinal and speculative truths, and "the more hidden sense . . . of the theological, natural and moral truths hidden beneath the form and surface of the literal sense." Eckhart takes the same position as Augustine in insisting that "every true sense is a literal sense," that is, is intended by God.

There are six surviving scriptural commentaries; internal references indicate that there were others that are no longer extant. Of the two interpretations of Genesis, the *Expositio Libri Genesis* (Commentary on the Book of Genesis), like Augustine's *De Genesi ad Litteram* (Literal Commentary on Genesis), concentrates on the speculative truths revealed in the literal sense, while the *Liber Parabolorum Genesis* investigates the mysteries manifested in the parabolical reading. Eckhart also left the *Expositio Libri Exodi* (Commentary on the Book of Exodus) and interpretations of two of the Wisdom books of the Old Testament, *Sermones et Lectiones super Ecclesiastici Cap. XXIV* (Sermons and Lectures on the Twenty-fourth Chapter of Ecclesiasticus) and the important *Expositio Libri Sapientiae* (Commentary on the Book of Wisdom). The longest of the commentaries is that on the Gospel of John, a favorite text for the exposition of the most profound truths about God and the world since the time of the Gnostic exegetes of the second century.

In the prologue to the *Liber Parabolorum Genesis* Eckhart gives a brief sketch of the kinds of truths hidden in the revealed text. Christ, the Truth, is Scripture's "hidden marrow"; the kinds of truths that the Truth reveals in his inspired word include "very many of the properties that belong to God alone, the First Principle"; "the most sacred emanation of the divine Persons with their property of distinction under and in one essence, one act of existence, life and understanding"; and "the production of creatures derived from them as their exemplar." Thus, not only are all the "virtues and principles of the sciences" found in Scripture but also the inner relations of the three Persons of the Trinity "shine out in every natural, ethical and artistic work"—a perfect homology between the natural and supernatural realms.

The Neoplatonists presented their understanding of reality under the metaphor of a process of emanation and return, terms much used by Eckhart both in Latin (*exitus, reditus*) and in the vernacular (*ûzbruch, durchbruch*). The three kinds of truths pertain primarily to the emanation (production or origin) of all things—they answer the fundamental question "Where has the universe come from?" Eckhart's sermons, both the Latin ones preached to a learned audience of clerics and especially the German ones delivered to the laity, were primarily concerned with the process of return—that is, with how the believer uses the knowledge of the divine source of all things to regain its original union with that source. The latter implies and is based on the former; the former is exemplified and realized in the latter. Both sides of Eckhart's work illuminate each other and cannot be fully understood in isolation.

His teaching on the *exitus* is primarily presented in the *Opus Expositionum.* All of Eckhart's teaching and preaching is an exercise in the paradoxical task of speaking of what by definition is unspeakable, the divine mystery. Each individual human person not only expresses the divine ground, as do all other beings, but is also capable of becoming aware of this expression and is therefore in a situation in which speaking about God is always necessary but insufficient. This idea has been proclaimed by thinkers of both East and West, but few have explored it in such challenging ways as did Eckhart. The vernacular works contain not so much the theory of language about God as the actual practice—a series of varying exercises on the possibilities and limitations of speaking about God designed to awaken the hearer to the most vital of all tasks, bringing the divine ground of one's being to conscious awareness as the source of a new way of living. The Middle High German of Eckhart's time lent itself to experiments, both playful and serious, that could not be achieved in the technical Latin of the schools. Eckhart's sermons make more lively reading, but they cannot be fully grasped without the systematic background available only in the Latin works. It is in the school texts that Eckhart presents his important theoretical discussions of the use of language about God.

Like any good Scholastic, Eckhart recognized that clarity and exactitude of presentation depend on a proper understanding of the rules of language and argument. Although he did not comment on Aristotle's logical works or write treatises on logic, as many Schoolmen did, he has several enlightening discussions of two key aspects of logic: predication and analogy. Eckhart tried to present his teaching as traditional, but it is really quite innovative. It should be seen as an example of a Neoplatonic logic based on a different metaphysics from that found in Aristotle's thought. In the prologues to the *Opus Tripartitum* are found references to two kinds of predication, that is, two ways in which predicates are related to subjects in propositions. Two-term propositions (*secundum adiacens*) have the form "X is" (that is, X exists), "X is-one," "X is-true," "X is-good," and the like. Three-termed propositions (*tertium adiacens*) follow the form "X is this thing (or being)," "X is this one-thing," and so on. As he puts it: "When something is called being, one, true good, each of these is a predicate of a proposition, and it lies second to the subject. But when something is called this being, this one, this true, or this good (for example, a man or a stone or the like), then the 'this' and 'this' are the predicate of the proposition, and the general terms just mentioned (for example, 'being') are not predicates, nor do they lie second to the subject, but they connect the predicate with the subject." In two-term propositions the predicates are used "formally and substantively," that is, they are identified with the very substance of the subject, formally considered. For this reason, two-term propositions can be properly used of God alone. On this basis Eckhart establishes four principles central to his metaphysics: "First, God alone is properly being, one, true and good. Second, from him all things are and are one, true and good. Third, all things immediately owe to him the fact that they are one, true and good. Fourth, when I say this being, or this one, or that one . . . , 'this' or 'that' adds absolutely nothing, or makes no addition of entity, unity, truth or goodness to being, one, true, good."

The two kinds of predication express a metaphysical divide between the being of God and that of creatures that is even clearer in Eckhart's treatment of analogy, that is, the way in which terms can be applied both to God and to creatures. Here he borrowed his terminology from Aquinas but used it in quite a different way. Although there are still debates about Thomas's understanding of analogy, the "Angelic Doctor" generally used it to try to build bridges between ordinary predication and the special world of God-language. Eckhart, on the other hand, understood analogy as an expression of the unbridgeable opposition between the divine and the human. In his understanding, if God is truly existence, oneness, and the like, then creatures cannot be said to possess these attributes at all. As the *Sermones et Lectiones super Ecclesiastici Cap.*

XXIV puts it, "Analogates have nothing of the form according to which they are analogically ordered rooted in positive fashion in themselves." This position is the basis of Eckhart's condemned teaching, found in both the Latin and German works, that all creatures are pure nothing. The implication is that if predicates such as existence and oneness are understood in their applications to particular being, then these terms must be denied of God. God, too, is "No-thing." As Eckhart's German Sermon 83 says: "You should love him as he is a non-God, a non-spirit, a non-person, a non-image, but as he is a pure, unmixed, bright 'One,' separated from all duality; and in that One we should eternally sink down, out of something into nothing."

This understanding of analogy suggests a deeper level of language analysis, one which is evident throughout Eckhart's writings. It might be called the "negation of negations" (*negatio negationis, versagen des versagennes*), a phrase that appears in the Latin works and in one vernacular sermon; but the negation of negation is but one expression of an underlying Neoplatonic logic of dialectic, that is, the simultaneous use of mutually opposed terms to suggest the inexpressible divine nature and its relation to the created realm. Dialectical thinking of this sort is not meant to abrogate Aristotelian logic, just as the special qualities of two-term propositions do not exclude a role for three-term ones. Particular beings must always be described in terms of Aristotle's rules, based on the principle of noncontradiction. But God is not a particular being; he is existence, oneness, truth, and goodness themselves. Language used of God and of God's relation to other things demands another kind of logic, the logic of dialectic.

Discussions of dialectic appear several times in the Latin commentaries. The discussion of analogy in the *Sermones et Lectiones super Ecclesiastici Cap. XXIV*, a comment on the text "They that eat me shall yet hunger" (Eccles. 24:29), concludes: "God is inside all things in that he is existence, and thus every being feeds on him. He is also on the outside because he is above all and thus outside all. Therefore, all things feed on him, because he is totally within; they hunger for him, because he is totally without." A passage from the *Expositio Libri Sapientiae* explaining the text "And since it [Wisdom] is one, it can do all things," (Wisd. of Sol. 7:27) goes even deeper in analyzing the nature of the One as the negation of negation. If the "One" is indistinct, that is, not distinguished from anything else, then God is distinguished from his creatures in dialectical fashion—he is the more distinct (or transcendent) the more indistinct (or immanent) he is, and vice versa. A third treatment is found in the *Expositio Libri Exodi* on Exodus 20:4, where Eckhart analyzes the similarity between God and creature to arrive at the conclusion that "nothing is both as dissimilar and similar to anything else as God and the creature. What is as dissimilar and similar to something else as that whose 'dissimilitude' is its very 'similitude,' whose indistinction is its very distinction? God is distinguished from everything created, distinct and finite by his indistinction and his infinity."

Dialectical thought is also at work in Eckhart's most detailed study of the problem of speaking about God. In lengthy remarks on Exodus 15:3 and 20:4 he presents a treatise on the divine names, paying special attention to the methodological issues involved in speaking about God. The treatise was deeply influenced by Eckhart's reading of Maimonides, whose emphasis on the superiority of negative predication in speaking about God had been attacked by Aquinas. Eckhart tried to find a synthesizing position to bring together the theories of philosophers and theologians—pagans, Jews, and Muslims, as well as the Christian teachers.

The Scholastics customarily distinguished a variety of ways to describe how such "transcendental" predicates as *being, good, one*, and the like could be applied both to God and to created things. Such terms might be affirmed of God and creatures in exactly the same way (univocally) or in totally different ways (equivocally)—positions rejected by both Aquinas and Eckhart. More adequate ways of speaking about God traditionally fell under three headings: the way of negation (only negations, such as *nonmaterial, uncaused, infinite*, could be properly applied to God), the way of causality (to apply to God terms taken from created reality is only to affirm that he has caused such reality and not to say anything about the divine nature in itself), and the way of eminence (that predicates derived from experience of created things can be properly affirmed of God but only in some transformed or higher sense). Aquinas's notion of analogy is a good example of the third option. In his treatise, Eckhart at first seems to side with Maimonides in preferring the way of negation: "all things that are positively said of God, even though they are perfections in us, are no longer so in God and are not more perfect than their opposites." But in discussing the predicates *existence* and *unity*, Eckhart constructs his own version of the way of eminence (*via eminentiae*) on familiar dialectical grounds. Speaking of the divine pole of the dialectic, he says, "Therefore, no negation, nothing negative, belongs to God, except for the negation of negation which is what the One signifies when expressed negatively. 'God is one' (Deut. 6:4). The negation of negation is the purest and fullest affirmation—'I am who I am' (Exod. 3:14). It returns upon itself with a full return; it rests upon itself, and through itself it is Existence Itself." Eckhart's dialectic fuses the negative way and the positive moment of the way of eminence into a distinctive theory of God-language.

The German Dominican's dialectical thought shows its originality especially in relation to Christian teaching on the Trinity and on Creation. In both areas Eckhart was bold, controversial—and condemned. Especially noteworthy are the ways in which his dynamic understanding of the Trinity explains both Creation and all forms of operation, and the manner in which the traditional understanding of the Trinity seems to be put at risk by his teaching on the hidden ground of God.

According to Eckhart, "the metaphysician, who considers the entity of things, proves nothing through exterior causes, that is, the efficient and final causes," but rather looks only to the formal cause, the ideal reason or image. Thus, all activity has a single source and a similar structure in the transcendent formality of the inner life of the Trinity. In Latin Sermon 49 Eckhart outlines three stages in the production of existence. The first is an "emanation from the depths in silence, excluding everything that comes from without. It is a form of life, as if you were to imagine something swelling up from itself and in itself and then inwardly boiling without any boiling over . . . The second stage is like the boiling over in the manner of an efficient cause and with a view toward an end by which something produces something else that is from itself, but not out of itself. This production is either out of some other thing (and then it is called 'making') or it is out of nothing." Production out of nothing is Creation.

Inner boiling (*bullitio*) is Eckhart's powerful metaphor for the emanation of the three Persons in the Trinity. Creation and every other kind of making are shadows of the inner-Trinitarian life in which the Father, or Principle, produces the Word, his perfect coessential image, by means of intellectual emanation and coproduces, along with the Word, the Spirit (the Essential Concomitant and Notional Love). The keystone of Eckhart's view of reality is the virtual existence of all things in the Principle, that is, both in the entire Trinity as the efficient cause of the universe and more significantly in the Father as the formal Principle of the perfect Image of the Word that contains the ideas of all things. The richest discussion of how the relation of the Father and the Son shines forth in all reality is found in Eckhart's exposition of John 1:1-5 in the *Expositio Sancti Evangelii Secundum Iohannem*.

The view of creation as a kind of overflow (*ebullitio*) of the process by which the three Persons proceed within the Trinity is at the root of some of Eckhart's views that were subsequently condemned as heretical. Following Avicenna and Aquinas, Eckhart defined Creation as the conferring of existence and the production of all things from nothing, but the heart of his teaching is found in his special reading of the first verse of Genesis. "You must recognize that the 'principle' [*in principio* of Gen. 1:1] in which 'God created heaven and earth' is the Ideal Reason. This is what the first chapter in John says, 'In the principle was the Word.' " Creation in the Principle, as understood by Eckhart, was an eternal creation that stressed the virtual being of all things in the divine source rather than their created particular being.

Eckhart insisted that if God creates, he must do so in the "now" of his eternal present, and that, therefore, Creation must be eternal. Both his Latin and German works contain many passages similar to the three that were drawn from the commentary on Genesis and commentary on John and condemned as heretical after his death. But he also held in the commentary on John that "Exterior creation is subject to time." How can creation be both eternal and temporal? Eckhart's answer was to distinguish between the virtual or intellectual aspects of reality, on the one hand, and the distinct or formally inhering aspects, on the other. "All things are in God as in the First Cause in an intellectual way and in the mind of the Maker. Therefore, they do not have any of their formal existence until they are causally produced and extracted on the outside in order to exist," he says in his commentary on the Book of Wisdom. The virtual existence of all things in God must be eternal; the formally inhering aspect in which things are distinct from God is temporal. In German Sermon 57 Eckhart uses the analogy of a mirror: just as the image of a face in a mirror is always being created by the face as it looks into the mirror and therefore owes its whole being to that exemplar, which is in no way changed by having a reflection, so too created reality is merely a reflection of the being of God. Eckhart's assertion of the eternity of the virtual or ideal aspect of Creation and his insistence on the nothingness of the formal or particular aspect were vigorously attacked by his opponents. They make sense only on the basis of the dialectical view of the relation of God and Creation that his attackers clearly did not share.

Eckhart's trinitarian view of reality has many echoes in the history of Christian thought, notably among the Greek Fathers and in his near contemporary, Bonaventure. Like Bonaventure, Eckhart in some texts stresses the role of the Father as the absolute origin of all things; but in other passages he presents the divine essence or ground as the source or origin of the three Persons in ways that suggest a "God beyond God." In the commentary on John there are two patterns of description of the relation between the essence and the Persons. More frequently, the Father is the One understood as the "Principle without principle" Who produces the Word as Truth and, acting together with the Word, produces the Holy Spirit as Good. A second pattern ascribes Absolute Unity (*unum*) to the divine ground and being, truth, and goodness, respectively, to the Father, Son, and Holy Spirit. Despite this emphasis on the primordiality of the divine ground, Eckhart often speaks of the identity of the Father, Son, and Holy Spirit in traditional fashion. One difficult text from German Sermon 10 insists that the relation between the ground and the Persons should be understood in a dialectical way: "Distinction comes from the Absolute Unity, that is, the distinction in the Trinity. Absolute Unity is the distinction and distinction is the unity. The greater the distinction, the greater the unity, for that is the distinction without distinction."

Eckhart's teaching about the emanation of all things from the hidden depths of God is complemented by what he says about the reverse process, the return of all things to indistinct union with that ground. This doctrine is the primary message of his vernacular works. It is on the basis of this message that Eckhart has been acclaimed as one of the premier mystics in the history of Christianity.

Eckhart's age was one of intense spiritual vitality, in which new forms of religious life and practice were created to meet a hunger for God on the part of people of all walks of life. At the beginning of the thirteenth century the two great mendicant orders, the Dominican and the Franciscan, had been born. The mendicants pioneered a new form of the "apostolic life," that is, the following of Christ and the apostles. Rather than a stable and enclosed monastic piety centered on the celebration of the liturgy, the mendicants believed that the following of Christ meant a life pledged to poverty and preaching for the service of the Christian community. This apostolic way of life soon attracted the intellectual and spiritual elite of the time. In the patriarchal medieval society women could not share in all aspects of the mendicant life, but cloistered houses of Franciscan and Dominican nuns proliferated during the century and became important centers for mystical piety. The spread of Dominican nuns was especially marked in Germany, and there can be no doubt that a good deal of Eckhart's pastoral work and his vernacular preaching were directed to these women.

The desire of women to share in the following of Christ and the apostles, however, was not limited to the mendicant orders. From the end of the twelfth century, beginning in the Lowlands and then spreading to the Rhineland and northern France, women called Beguines lived lives of prayer and service in small communities, generally in an urban environment. They pledged themselves to poverty and celibacy but not under any of the religious rules recognized by church authority; hence, they were viewed with suspicion by many. Nevertheless, these groups produced women with reputations for great sanctity and special, frequently ecstatic, experiences of God. Clare of Assisi and Angela of Foligno among the Franciscans; Beatrice of Nazareth among the Cistercian nuns; Hadewijch of Antwerp, Mechthild of Magdeburg, and Marguerite Porete among the Beguines; and the many German Dominican nuns whose lives and visions were written down in the first half of the fourteenth century testify to the role that women took in the spread of mysticism in the late Middle Ages.

The last centuries of the Middle Ages were also a time of tension within the church and concern over the growth of heresy. Ecclesiastical authorities, including the papacy, often looked on new forms of religious life as dangerous to faith and morals. Inquisitorial proceedings were created during the thirteenth century to ferret out and condemn Waldensians, Albigensians, and other recognized heretics. In the early fourteenth century these proceedings were turned against what were seen as errors of mystical piety, especially as found in the Beguines.

Henry of Friemar, a German Augustinian who taught at Paris from 1307 to 1311, wrote a series of treatises in 1309 against false mystics who claimed to be "perfect and established in a liberty of spirit" and who misunderstood Christian teaching about the birth of the Divine Word in the soul. In Paris on 30 May 1310, probably a few months before Eckhart arrived back in the city for his second regency, Porete was burned at the stake as a relapsed heretic for continuing to disseminate her mystical treatise *Le Mirouer des Simples Ames Anienties* (The Mirror of Simple Souls). At the Council of Vienne in 1311-1312, Pope Clement V issued the bull *Ad Nostrum* condemning eight errors of "the abominable sect of malignant men known as Beghards and faithless women known as Beguines in the kingdom of Germany." Henry of Friemar; Henry of Virneburg, the archbishop of Cologne; and several of Porete's inquisitors were at the council. Eckhart cannot have been ignorant of this flurry of activity, but despite the official reaction against mystical heresy (the so-called heresy of the Free Spirit) he began preaching powerful and powerfully dangerous mystical sermons on his return to Germany in the summer of 1313.

Though some of Eckhart's vernacular sermons probably come from the time of his provincialate, the majority of the authentic pieces seem to date from these last years in Germany (1313 to 1327), when he served in various capacities first in Strasbourg and later in Cologne. Eckhart appears to have functioned as a spiritual guide to the Dominican nuns in the Teutonia province; he also taught at the Dominican house of studies in Cologne, at least in his later years. Like any good member of the Order of Preachers, he would have frequently addressed lay congregations; these congregations would doubtless have included many Beguines, since they customarily worshipped in their parish churches.

Eckhart's sermons present many problems, not only in content but also in transmission. With the exception of the sermon "Von dem edeln Menschen" (Of the Nobleman), there is no evidence that any of the surviving sermons were actually written down by the Meister. They are *reportationes*, texts taken down by others during oral delivery. Unlike most school *reportationes*, they do not appear to have been subsequently checked by the speaker; Eckhart would later complain during his trial: "I am not held to respond to the other articles taken from sermons ascribed to me, since even learned and studious clerics take down what they hear frequently and indiscriminantly in a false and abbreviated way." Nevertheless, even in his defense against the inquisitors Eckhart would admit most of the passages brought against him as authentic. Although the presence of alternate versions of several sermons, and the incompleteness and obscurity of others, render Eckhart's sermons an area filled with pitfalls for the unwary, the labors of generations of scholars, culminating in Josef Quint's superb edition (1958-), provide a solid basis for understanding Eckhart the preacher. It was these vernacular works which assured the Dominican such a profound influence on medieval German culture. While his Latin works survive in only a handful of manuscripts, the German manuscripts number in the hundreds.

Not all of Eckhart's vernacular works were addressed to anonymous audiences. The *Liber Benedictus* (The Book "Benedictus"), a combined work of consolation with an appended sermon, was sent to Queen Agnes of Hungary, probably in 1318. It is the most polished of Eckhart's German writings. The first part, "Daz buoch der götlîchen troestunge" (The Book of Divine Consolation), belongs to a well-known genre of medieval literature, but it does not offer consolation on the basis of philosophical arguments about the nature of providence, as Boethius had in his *De consolatione Philosophiae* (Consolation of Philosophy, circa 524), or even through sharing in the sufferings of Christ, as much late medieval consolation literature did. Rather, Eckhart bases true consolation on detachment, as the way to come to the realization of the identity of ground between God and the soul. Most of the basic elements of his mystical teaching are present in the work in explicit or implicit fashion.

The three parts of "Daz buoch der götlîchen troestunge" repeat the same message; much of Eckhart's vernacular work consists of inventive variations on a few basic themes. He begins by analyzing how the just or good person is identical with divine Justice or Goodness from the formal point of view, a teaching laid out in detail at the beginning of the commentary on John. Such a person "is the begotten son of what is Unbegotten and Begetting, and he shares that one

Coin bearing an effigy of Pope John XXII, who in 1329 condemned twenty-eight propositions attributed to Eckhart (Vatican Library)

same being which Justice has and is." One who can live in this awareness can be troubled by no external thing. In the second and longest part of the work Eckhart supplies thirty topics showing how "he who would in created things love God alone, and who would love created things only in God, he would find true, just and unchanging consolation everywhere." The way to this goal is through detachment (*Abgeschiedenheit*)—"to be naked, poor, empty of all created things lifts the soul up to God." The pure internal activity by which "God brings to birth his Only-Begotten Son" and in which the "flowing out and the springing up of the Holy Spirit" is accomplished takes place in the depths of the truly poor and empty soul. Just as God "loves for love and works for working's sake," such a soul "loves God for the sake of loving God, and performs all his works for the sake of working." This theme of loving and living in complete spontaneity, "without a why" (*sunder warumbe, âne warumbe*), forms one of Eckhart's most characteristic mystical teachings. "Daz buoch der götlîchen troestunge" also makes use of the desert theme, in which the hidden divine One invites the soul out into the wasteland of the union of indistinction, though the work does not develop this theme in the language of "breakthrough" found in some of the sermons.

The sermon "Von dem edeln Menschen" that Eckhart appended to the "Daz buoch der götlîchen troestunge" is an extended treatment of the theme of the ground of the soul, the place where indistinct union with God is always a reality but is not always realized. Eckhart used a variety of metaphors for this hidden reality which lay deeper than all the other powers of the soul. Sometimes he spoke of it as the "ground" (*grunt*); at other times as the "little spark" (*vunkelîn*), "little castle" (*burgelîn*), "uncreated and uncreatable something, or power in the soul" (*ungeschaffen und ungeschepflich kraft in der sêle*), and here as the "nobleman." It was one of the more controversial aspects of his vernacular teaching and was later condemned by the pope.

The sermon analyzes the difference between the inner and the outer man in terms of the distinction between the ground of the soul, "untouched by anything particular," and all the other spiritual and material powers. Only in this inner ground of the soul can indistinct union with God be attained "without a medium" (*âne mittel*). The sermon concludes with one of Eckhart's most striking passages about the encounter between the "nobleman" and the divine lover—" 'I,' says our Lord through the prophet Osee, 'will lead the noble soul out into the desert, and there I will speak to her heart' (Os. 2:14), one with One, one from One, one in One, and in One, one everlastingly. Amen."

Eckhart summarized his usual themes in a well-known passage from German Sermon 53: "When I preach, I am accustomed to speak about detachment, and that a man should be free of himself and of all things; second, that a man should be formed again into that simple good which is God; third, that he should reflect on the great nobility with which God has endowed his soul, so that in this way he may come to wonder at God; fourth, about the purity of the divine nature, for the brightness of the divine nature is beyond words. God is a word, a word unspoken."

Detachment, that is, perfect purity or emptiness, was such an important part of Eckhart's message that he devoted a separate vernacular treatise, *Von Abgeschiedenheit* (On Detachment, circa 1325), to it. This work praises detachment above both humility, the traditional foundation of the virtues, and love, their crown. True detachment, which Eckhart defines as "nothing else than for the spirit to stand as immovable against whatever may chance to it of joy and sorrow, honor, shame and disgrace, as a mountain of lead stands before a little breath of wind," compels God to come down to the soul because the soul is now totally one with God. To be completely empty of all created particular being is to be totally filled with the emptiness of God. "And if the heart is to be willing for that highest place, it must repose in a naked nothingness, and in this there is the greatest potentiality that can be. When the heart that has detachment attains to the highest place, that must be nothingness, for in this is the greatest receptivity."

The fundamental religious practice for Eckhart, the only one that really counted, was the attainment of true detachment from created things. He expressed this freedom from particularity through a series of paradoxical and exaggerated formulas designed to indicate not only the necessity of detachment but also its difficulty. Detachment is an internal attitude; it has no essential relationship to any external activity. This position is the source of Eckhart's indifference to all outward forms or "ways" of piety. He never condemns or attacks them; they are all equally useful, but they are also all equally useless if one allows oneself to become trapped in them. He who seeks God in "ways" will find ways and not God, Eckhart insists. "When people think they are acquiring more of God in inwardness, in devotion, in sweetness and in various approaches than they do by the fireside or in a stable, you are acting just as if you took God and muffled his head up in a cloak and pushed him under a bench." "It is not what we do that makes us holy, but we ought to make holy what we do," as *Die Rede der Underscheidene* expresses it. This emphasis on the interior work was highly suspect to ecclesiastical authorities at a time when some mystics were accused of abandoning both the practices of religion and the Christian virtues to enjoy a hedonistic life of "freedom of the spirit." However true this charge may have been of some, it was certainly not true of Eckhart, whose whole life was devoted to the service of the church. But some of Eckhart's more daring expressions of the implications of detachment, particularly his indifference toward prayer, were later condemned.

This Eckhartian internalism was influenced by the mystical currents of the time, especially as found among women. There can be no doubt that Eckhart was deeply influenced by the women mystics. His use of themes from Porete's *Mirror of Simple Souls*, especially on the destruction of the will (in his German Sermon 52), shows that he did not agree with those who judged her work heretical. Works by Mechthild of Magdeburg (whose *Das fließende Licht der Gottheit* [The Flowing Light of Godhead] Eckhart might have known) and by Porete express the idea of a union of indistinction of the kind later developed by the Meister. Eckhart's stress on interior emptiness or detachment has been seen as a theological transformation of the stress on exterior poverty that was characteristic of the Beguine life. Eckhart's unusual use of feminine imagery in several of his most noted sermons, especially the stress on the soul becoming both a virgin and mother in German Sermon 2 and his inversion of the traditional interpretation of the roles of Mary and Martha in German Sermon 86, may be a reflection of his involvement with audiences of Beguines whose lives were dedicated both to virginity—the detachment by which the soul is free of all things—and to good works in which they give birth every day, "a hundred or a thousand times . . . from that same ground where the Father is bearing his eternal Word." The use of the motif of pregnancy and giving birth is also found in one of the rare passages where Eckhart speaks of his own experience of God. In German Sermon 71, obviously talking about himself, he says: "It seemed to a man as though in a dream—it was a waking dream—that he became pregnant with nothing as a woman does with a child, and in this nothing God was born; he was the fruit of the nothing. God was born in the nothing."

Eckhart's attitude toward the female mysticism of the time, however, also contained elements of critique. This critical stance is most evident in his position on special, or ecstatic, experiences. Most of the major female mystics of the Middle Ages (Porete is an exception) emphasized visionary and ecstatic experiences to such an extent that these experiences seem at times to constitute the core of their mysticism. Though Eckhart admitted the existence of special, direct ecstatic experiences (*raptus* or *excessus*) and referred to the ecstasies of Moses and Paul discussed by Aquinas and traditional authorities, he thought that these experiences were just another "mode" or "way" and did not constitute the inner detachment and awareness of the identity of ground between God and the soul that was the true goal. At times he expresses his criticism quite strongly, placing the visionaries on the same level with those who love God because he has rewarded them with wealth. "Some people want to see God with their own eyes, just as they see a cow; and they want to love God just as they love a cow. You love a cow because of the milk and the cheese and because of your own advantage. This is how all these people act who love God because of external riches or because of internal consolation. They do not love God rightly; rather they love their own advantage," he says in German Sermon 16b.

The truly detached soul finds in its depth that it is identical with the divine ground: "God's ground and the soul's ground are one ground." Eckhart's notion of the union of indistinction between God and the soul was a break with the main tradition in Western Christianity, which had always insisted that union with God did not surpass the level of a loving union of wills. A dialectical union with the ultimate ground, who is always both absolutely transcendent to all things and yet immanent within them, is found in the Neoplatonic tradition and in some contemporary women mystics. Eckhart gave it a full theoretical exposition, perhaps most succinctly in the commentary on the Book of Wisdom: "God is indistinct, and the soul loves to be indistinguished, that is, to be and to become one with God." The vernacular sermons are filled with daring expressions of this doctrine. "God's is-ness (*istikeit*) is my is-ness, neither less nor more," he insisted in Sermon 6, while Sermon 40 says, "Between man and God there is not only no distinction, there is no multiplicity either. There is nothing but one." On the disputed question as to whether this union is achieved through love or knowledge, that is, the power of the will or that of the intellect, Eckhart seems at first to be a standard follower of the Thomistic position which placed the ultimate goal primarily in the intellect. Latin Sermon 29 identifies God with Pure Intellect and avers that "To rise up to intellect, to be attached to it, is to be united to God." But, as usual, things are more complicated than they first appear in Eckhart. Other texts, such as German Sermon 39, go beyond both traditional views—"Some teachers claim that the spirit takes its happiness from love; others claim that it takes it from seeing God. I say, however, that it takes it neither from love nor from knowing nor from seeing." Neither love nor knowledge, as humans understand them at least, can play a part in the final union. German Sermon 83 relates the traditional three supreme powers of the soul—memory, understanding, and will—to the Father, Son, and Holy Spirit, respectively. But just as the divine ground has a dialectical priority to the three Persons, the ground in which humans are absolutely one with God lies beyond these powers. Eckhart's mysticism is not an intellectual one but transcends both intellect and emotion.

Eckhart's assertion of the absolute identity between the divine ground and the human ground has troubled many, both in his own time and later. Accusations of pantheism have been common. His response was to insist that the identity-of-ground formulations were true but that they expressed only one side of the dialectical nature of reality: "the words 'insofar as' [*in quantum*] . . . exclude from the term in question everything that is foreign to it. . . ." In other words, his claim that "the just man insofar as he is just" is identical with Justice [that is, God] is only true when the just man is considered solely from the perspective of justice, not in his total concrete being.

Since we are identical with God in the ground of our being, we must also act as God acts. Among the most shocking of all Eckhart's mystical teachings are his ruminations on this conclusion. The foremost is the birth of the Word in the soul, a theme constantly repeated in the German sermons and also found occasionally in the Latin works. The idea that Christ is born in the hearts of the faithful is an ancient one in Christianity, first found in connection with the sacrament of baptism. The Meister found in this motif a central element for his preaching, one that also forms the basis for his distinctive Christology. Becoming aware of the identity of ground through the process of detachment means recognizing that the dynamic activity in God by means of which the Father gives birth to the Son from all eternity and the Holy Spirit springs up eternally from both is also taking place in the human soul.

German Sermon 6 is a classic presentation of the birth of the Son in the soul. Beginning with a discussion of the relation of the just person and Justice, it proceeds to a detailed investigation of how, since God is always bearing his Son in the now of eternity, and since God's ground and the soul's ground are identical, "He gives me birth, me, his Son, and the same Son." But since the soul's ground is identical with the divine essence, the mystic is also one with the Father giving birth and the Spirit proceeding from the Father. "He [the Father] gives birth not only to me, his Son, but he gives birth to me as himself and himself as me and to me as his being and nature." And "In the innermost source, there I spring out in the Holy Spirit, where there is one life, one being and one work." The repetitions of this theme are manifold throughout the sermons. The implication that Eckhart drew was daring—whatever can be affirmed of the Son in his divine being (and indeed of the Trinity as a whole) can also be affirmed of the just person insofar (*in quantum* again) as the latter is just. This implication is most evident in three of the propositions for which Eckhart was condemned: two passages from German Sermons 5a and 24 claiming that whatever Scripture says of Christ can also be said of every just person and another, from a source that is no longer extant but that is close to a passage in "Daz buoch der gotlîchen troestunge" which says that the just man "performs whatever God performs, and he created the heaven and earth together with God." Finally, in dealing with the Incarnation, Eckhart emphasizes (for example, in German Sermon 46) that Christ assumes human nature as a whole and not an individual human persona. The implication is that because the undifferentiated idea of humanity has always been united to God in the now of eternity, the human person is able to share in the dynamism of the Trinitarian life in an essential way and not merely as a sign, trace, or image of the formal emanation of all things from the divine ground.

The final element in Eckhart's vernacular preaching is the invitation to "break through" (*durchbrechen*) to the hidden depths of the Godhead. At various places in his sermons he explains that sharing in the life of the Trinity is not enough; there is a level beyond even that. A good example occurs in German Sermon 52, where he characterizes true poverty as wanting nothing, knowing nothing, and having nothing. On all three levels the soul needs to go beyond God to reach true poverty and perfect indistinction. "So therefore let us pray to God that we be free of 'God.'" The flowing out of all things by which God becomes God is less noble than the breaking-through, "for in this breaking-through I receive that God and I are one." German Sermon 48 speaks of this breaking-through as a going beyond the Trinity of Persons. The spark in the soul "wants to go into the simple ground, into the quiet desert, into which distinction never gazed, not the Father, nor the Son, nor the Holy Spirit." Here Eckhart's preaching reflects one of the most daring elements of his speculation and brings into question all human conceptions of God.

Eckhart's mysticism of inner awareness of the ground is based on detachment from all created things, but not on flight from the world. Nor did his notion of perfection depend on belonging to any particular order, or following a set way of life. The virginity he counseled was a virginity of intention, being free of all attachment, not a physical virginity. Eckhart's mysticism is "secular" in the sense that it is in the world but not of it. The "living without a why" that constitutes the core of his message about the conduct of the awakened person is pure spontaneous love expressing itself as God does in the dynamic overflow of his being that produces the world. This idea is most forcefully put in Sermon 86 on Mary and Martha, in which Eckhart goes against the whole exegetical tradition in praising Martha, the traditional representative of the active life, above Mary, the type of the contemplative life. For Eckhart, Martha represents someone who "was so grounded in being that her activity did not hinder her."

One other Middle High German text that may well be by Eckhart is a poem written in the form of a liturgical sequence and known as the *Granum Sinapis* (The Mustard Seed, date uncertain). The content of the piece is deeply Eckhartian. Beginning with two strophes on the divine "inner boiling" that produces the Son and Holy Spirit, it describes the "boiling over" of creation in strophe three. Strophes four through eight concern the divine desert and the soul's return to it through perfect detachment. The first strophe provides an indication of the poem's special combination of philosophical and poetical beauty:

In dem begin
hô uber sin
ist ïe daz wort.
ô rîcher hort,
da ïe begin begin gebâr!
ô vader brust,
uz dir mit lust
daz wort ïe vlôz!
doch hat der schôz
daz wort behalden
daz ist wâr.

In the Beginning [that is, Principle]
High above understanding
Is ever the Word.
O rich treasure,
There the Beginning always bore the Beginning.
O Father's breast,
From thy delight
The Word ever flows!
Yet the bosom
Retains the Word,
truly.

Debate as to whether the poem was written by Eckhart has continued in recent literature; today the weight of authority favors its authenticity. The Latin commentary on the poem does not appear to be from Eckhart's pen.

Around 1323 Eckhart appears to have moved to Cologne; several of his sermons give evidence of having been preached in that flourishing center of intellectual and spiritual life. Henry of Virneburg, the archbishop of Cologne, was a noted hunter of heretics, and it was probably at his behest that formal inquisitorial proceedings against Eckhart were begun in 1326. This was a surprising turn of affairs: the Dominicans were the traditional opponents of heresy, and Eckhart was among the most important Dominican friars in Germany. Eckhart's trials in Cologne and then in Avignon were dramatic events in the history of medieval thought and piety.

In such proceedings it was customary for the inquisitors to draw up lists of objectionable articles from the writings of the accused. The evidence that survives concerning Eckhart's trial in Cologne indicates that the inquisitors had compiled four or five lengthy lists of articles from both his Latin and German works. Eckhart's responses to two of these lists survive in a manuscript in Soest that has come to be known as the *Rechtfertigungsschrift* (Defense). On 26 September 1326 Eckhart responded to a list of forty-nine articles and shortly thereafter to one of fifty-nine drawn exclusively from the vernacular sermons.

Eckhart's defense involved both procedural and substantive issues. First, he argued that he could not be a heretic because he had not obstinately taught something he knew was an error: "I can be in error, but I cannot be a heretic, because the first belongs to the intellect, the second to the will." Eckhart said that he was always ready to retract any errors he might have made, and indeed, he admitted that about one-fifth of the propositions were "ill sounding" or sometimes even "erroneous." Rather than retract them, however, in most cases he gave them a benign interpretation, appealing to the good intention he had always had in preaching. Second, Eckhart insisted that the local inquisitorial panel had no jurisdiction over him as a member of an exempt order—"I am not held to respond to you or to anyone except the pope and the University of Paris." In regard to the content of his views, he laid down general principles for interpreting his "uncommon and subtle" declarations and statements and also responded point by point to each of the articles, sometimes at length. A tone of testiness pervades the *Rechtfertigungsschrift*, and Eckhart's explanations are not always convincing.

At the beginning of 1327 Eckhart and his superior, Nicholas of Strasbourg, appealed to Pope John XXII at Avignon, and on 13 February Eckhart preached an emotional defense of his innocence in the Dominican church at Cologne. He then went to Avignon, where Pope John set up a commission of cardinals and theologians to study the lists of articles that had been sent from Cologne. Eckhart was once again called upon to defend himself; one of the two reports the commission sent to the pope survives and contains a summary of his defense. This document (technically a *votum theologicum*) reveals that Eckhart and his questioners were far apart on basic issues of philosophical and theological language. In April 1328 the pope wrote to inform the archbishop of Cologne that the investigation was still going on, although Eckhart was dead. He probably died in the Dominican priory in Avignon.

Finally, on 27 March 1329 Pope John issued the bull *In agro dominico* which officially condemned twenty-eight propositions. The first fifteen are adjudged heretical and include three relating to the eternity of Creation, three concerning the birth of the Son in the soul, one relating to indistinct union, and eight which seemed to conflict with Christian moral teaching or to deny the efficacy of prayer. Articles sixteen through twenty-six were said to be "evil-sounding, and very rash and suspect of heresy, though with many explanations and additions they might take on or possess a Catholic meaning." These articles include two more expressions of the birth of the Son in the soul, several concerning the relation of the interior and exterior work, one denying any distinction in God, another affirming the nothingness of creatures, and a few miscellaneous propositions. Two appended heretical articles, one on the "uncreated something" in the soul, the other denying that God should be called good, are rather puzzling. They are put in a separate category because Eckhart had denied making them; but they are contained in German Sermons 13 and 9, respectively.

The papal bull was issued only for the ecclesiastical province of Cologne, from which the original complaint had come. This limitation may well explain how little it did to stop the proliferation of Eckhartian and pseudo-Eckhartian vernacular sermons and treatises in the late Middle Ages. While Eckhart's Dominican followers, such as Heinrich Suso and Johannes Tauler, continued to respect him and to use his thought, they were conscious of his suspect reputation. Other anonymous scribes and readers appear either to have not cared about the condemnation or to have been ignorant of it. Eckhart's influence and name remained large in German-speaking areas at least until the sixteenth century.

In its preface the papal bull makes special note of the many incorrect statements which Eckhart "put forth especially before the uneducated crowd in his sermons." The public preaching of such complex and speculative thought seems to have been a major factor in getting Eckhart into trouble. In the context of widespread fears about mysticism, especially lay mysticism, on the part of the clergy, and with a pope who was devoted to suppression of all dangerous tendencies, Eckhart's condemnation is not really surprising.

John XXII noted that the Meister had "revoked and deplored" the condemned articles before he died, but the bull included the qualification that he revoked them "insofar as they could generate in the minds of the faithful a heretical opinion, or one erroneous and hostile to the true faith." This qualification is fully in accord with Eckhart's claim in the *Rechtfertigungsschrift* that all that he had written and preached, however difficult and subtle, was intended for the good of the Christian religion.

Eckhart's reputation as a thinker, a teacher, and a preacher was bound to be controversial, whether or not he had been condemned. His considerable fame as a preacher in his own time, his influence in the later Middle Ages, the growing worldwide interest in him since his rediscovery in nineteenth-century Germany, all testify that he is one of those philosophical and theological thinkers who can address a wide audience as much through the speculative power of his thought as through the artistry of his literary presentation.

References:

Karl Albert, *Meister Eckharts These vom Sein: Untersuchungen zur Metaphysik des Opus tripartitum* (Saarbrücken: Universitäts-und Schulbuchverlag, 1976);

Jeanne Ancelet-Hustache, *Master Eckhart and the Rhineland Mystics* (New York: Harper, 1957);

Till Beckmann, *Daten und Anmerkungen zur Biographie Meister Eckharts und zum Verlauf des gegen ihm angestrengten Inquisitionsprozesses* (Frankfurt am Main: Fischer, 1978);

John Caputo, "Fundamental Themes in Meister Eckhart's Mysticism," *Thomist*, 42 (April 1978): 197-225;

Caputo, "The Nothingness of the Intellect in Meister Eckhart's 'Parisian Questions,' " *Thomist*, 39 (January 1975): 85-115;

Edmund Colledge and J. C. Marler, " 'Poverty of the Will': Ruusbroec, Eckhart and *The Mirror of Simple Souls*, in *Jan van Ruusbroec: The Sources, Content and Sequels of His Mysticism*, edited by P. Mommaers and N. de Paepe (Leuven: Leuven University Press, 1984), pp. 14-47;

Ingeborg Degenhardt, *Studien zum Wandel des Eckhartbildes* (Leiden: Brill, 1967);

Donald Duclow, " 'My Suffering Is God': Meister Eckhart's *Book of Divine Consolation*," *Theological Studies*, 44 (December 1983): 570-586;

Heribert Fischer, *Meister Eckhart: Einführung in sein philosophisches Denken* (Munich: Alber, 1974);

Wolfram Malte Fues, *Mystik als Erkenntnis? Kritische Studien zur Meister-Eckhart-Forschung* (Bonn: Bouvier, 1981);

Alois M. Haas, *Nim din selbes war: Studien zur Lehre der Selbsterkenntnis bei Meister Eckhart, Johannes Tauler und Heinrich Seuse* (Freiburg, Switzerland: Universitätsverlag, 1971);

Haas, "Seinsspekulation und Geschöpflichkeit in der Mystik Meister Eckharts," in *Sein und Nichts in der abendländische Mystik*, edited by Walter Strolz (Freiburg, Germany: Herder, 1984), pp. 33-58;

Haas, ed., *Sermo mysticus: Studien zu Theologie und Sprache der deutschen Mystik* (Freiburg, Switzerland: Universitätsverlag, 1979);

Ruedi Imbach, *Deus est Intelligere: Das Verhältnis von Sein und Denken in seiner Bedeutung für das Gottesverständnis bei Thomas von Aquin und in den Pariser Questionen Meister Eckharts* (Freiburg, Switzerland: Universitätsverlag, 1976);

C. F. Kelley, *Meister Eckhart on Divine Knowledge* (New Haven: Yale University Press, 1977);

Karl G. Kertz, "Meister Eckhart's Teaching on the Birth of the Divine Word in the Soul," *Traditio*, 15 (1959): 327-363;

Richard Kieckhefer, "Meister Eckhart's Conception of Union with God," *Harvard Theological Review*, 71 (July-October 1978): 203-225;

Joseph Koch, "Kritische Studien zum Leben Meister Eckharts," *Archivum Fratrum Praedicatorum*, 29 (1959): 1-51; 30 (1960): 1-52;

Koch, "Zur Analogielehre Meister Eckharts," in *Mélanges offerts à Etienne Gilson* (Paris: Vrin, 1959), pp. 327-350;

Alain de Libera, *Le problème de l'être chez Maître Eckhart: Logique et métaphysique de l'analogie* (Geneva: Droz, 1980);

De Libera and Emilie zum Bruun, *Maître Eckhart: Métaphysique de verbe et théologie négative* (Paris: Centre National de la Recherche Scientifique, 1984);

Vladimir Lossky, *Théologie négative et connaissance de Dieu chez Maître Eckhart* (Paris: Vrin, 1960);

Bernard McGinn, "Eckhart's Condemnation Reconsidered," *Thomist*, 44 (July 1980): 390-414;

McGinn, "The God Beyond God: Theology and Mysticism in the Thought of Meister Eckhart," *Journal of Religion*, 61 (January 1981): 1-19;

McGinn, "Meister Eckhart on God as Absolute Unity," in *Neoplatonism and Christian Thought*, edited by Dominic O'Meara (Albany: State University of New York Press, 1982), pp. 128-139;

Dietmar Mieth, *Die Einheit von vita activa und vita contemplativa in den deutschen Predigten und Traktaten Meister Eckharts und bei Johannes Tauler* (Regensburg: Pustet, 1969);

Burkhard Mojsisch, *Meister Eckhart: Analogie, Univozität und Einheit* (Hamburg: Meiner, 1983);

La mystique rhénane: Colloque de Strasbourg 1961 (Paris: Presses Universitaires de France, 1963);

Udo Nix and Raphael Ochslin, eds., *Meister Eckhart der Prediger: Festschrift zum Eckhart-Gedenkjahr* (Freiburg, Germany: Herder, 1960);

Josef Quint, "Einleitung," in *Meister Eckhart: Deutsche Predigten und Traktate* (Munich: Hanser, 1963), pp. 9-50;

Hugo Rahner, "Die Gottesgeburt: Die Lehre der Kirchenväter von der Geburt Christi aus dem Herzen der Kirche und der Gläubigen," *Zeitschrift für katholische Theologie*, 59 (1933): 333-418;

Kurt Ruh, *Meister Eckhart: Theologe; Prediger; Mystiker* (Munich: Beck, 1985);

Ruh, ed., *Altdeutsche und altniederländische Mystik* (Darmstadt: Wissenschaftliche Buchgesellschaft, 1964);

Toni Schaller, "Die Meister-Eckhart Forschung von der Jahrhundertwende bis zur Gegenwart," *Freiburger Zeitschrift für Philosophie und Theologie*, 15 (1968): 262-316, 403-426;

Benno Schmoldt, *Die deutsche Begriffsprache Meister Eckharts* (Heidelberg: Quelle & Meyer, 1954);

Reiner Schürmann, *Meister Eckhart: Mystic and Philosopher* (Bloomington: University of Indiana Press, 1978);

Gabriel Théry, "Contribution a l'histoire du procès d'Eckhart," *La vie spirituelle: Supplement*, 9 (1924): 93-119, 164-183; 12 (1925): 149-187; 13 (1926): 49-95; 14 (1926): 45-65;

Frank Tobin, *Meister Eckhart: Thought and Language* (Philadelphia: University of Pennsylvania Press, 1986);

Shizuteru Ueda, *Die Gottesgeburt in der Seele und der Durchbruch zur Gottheit: Die mystische Anth-*

ropologie Meister Eckharts und ihre Konfrontation mit der Mystik der Zen-Buddhismus (Gütersloh: Mohn, 1965);

Bernard Welte, *Meister Eckhart: Gedanken zu seinen Gedanken* (Freiburg, Germany: Herder, 1979);

Eberhard Winkler, *Exegetische Methoden bei Meister Eckhart* (Tübingen: Mohr, 1965);

Richard Woods, *Eckhart's Way* (Wilmington, Del.: Glazier, 1986).

Manuscripts:

The manuscripts of Eckhart's works reflect the double pattern of the reception of his preaching and teaching—extensive for the vernacular works, especially the sermons, and restricted for the Latin writings. In his edition of 86 Middle High German sermons he considered to be authentic, Josef Quint used 219 manuscripts mostly found in German libraries. Further manuscript discoveries, as well as the possibility of other sermons being genuine, easily expand the number to more than 300 manuscripts. The oldest of these, a fragment (MS 80 18537) in the Germanisches National Museum in Nuremberg, goes back to circa 1300. On the other hand, the manuscript witnesses to the Latin works are few—4 major manuscripts (Erfurt, Trier, Cues, and Berlin) and 10 minor ones. Edmund Colledge and J. C. Marler have suggested that Ms. 33b of the Stadtarchiv in Soest, which contains Eckhart's defense against the inquisitorial proceedings at Cologne, contains marginal expansions in Eckhart's own hand.

John Scottus Eriugena

(circa 810 - circa 877)

Paul Edward Dutton
Simon Fraser University

PRINCIPAL WORKS: *Glossae Diuinae Historiae* (Biblical Glosses, written circa 845-850);

De Diuinae Praedestinatione Liber (Book on Divine Predestination, written circa 850-851);

Carmina (Poems, written circa 850-877);

Annotationes in Marcianum (Annotations on Martianus Capella, written circa 859-860);

Periphyseon (About Nature; also known, incorrectly, as On the Division of Nature, written circa 864-866);

Expositiones in Ierarchiam Coelestem (Explanations of *The Celestial Hierarchy* [of Pseudo-Dionysius], written circa 865-870);

Vox Spiritualis Aquilae . . . (The Voice of the Mystical Eagle . . . [Homily on the Prologue of John], written circa 870-872);

Commentarius in Euangelium Iohannis (Commentary on the Gospel according to John, written circa 875-877).

TRANSLATIONS: *Versio Operum Sancti Dionysii Areopagitae* (Translation of the Works of Saint [Pseudo-]Dionysius the Areopagite, circa 862-864; revised, circa 865-870);

De Imagine (Translation of *On the Image of Man*, by Gregory of Nyssa, circa 862-864);

Ambigua ad Iohannem (Translation of the *Ambigua to John* of Maximus the Confessor, circa 862-864);

Quaestiones ad Thalassium (Translation of the *Questions to Thalassius* of Maximus the Confessor, circa 864-866).

EDITIONS: *Joannis Scoti Erigenæ De Divisione naturæ libri quinque diu desiderati: Accedit appendix ex Ambiguis S(ancti) Maximi Graece et Latine*, edited by Thomas Gale (Oxford: e Theatro Sheldoniano, 1681; reprinted, Frankfurt am Main: Minerva, 1964);

Joannis Scoti Opera quae supersunt omnia, edited by H. J. Floss, in *Patrologia Latina*, volume 122, edited by J.-P. Migne (Paris: Migne, 1857), pp. 125-1244;

Republic of Ireland five-pound note depicting John Scottus Eriugena

"Johannis Scotti Carmina," edited by L. Traube, in *Monumenta Germaniae Historica: Poetae latini aevi Carolini,* volume 3 (Berlin: Weidmann, 1896), pp. 518-556;

Iohannis Scotti Annotationes in Marcianum, edited by Cora E. Lutz (Cambridge, Mass.: Mediaeval Academy of America, 1939);

"Le 'De imagine' de Grégoire de Nysse traduit par Jean Scot Erigène," edited by M. Cappuyns, *Recherches de Théologie ancienne et médiévale,* 32 (1965): 206-262;

Iohannis Scotti Eriugenae Periphyseon (De Diuisione Naturae), 3 volumes, edited by I. P. Sheldon-Williams, *Scriptores Latini Hiberniae,* volumes 7, 9, 11 (Dublin: Dublin Institute for Advanced Studies, 1968, 1972, 1981);

Jean Scot, Homélie sur le Prologue de Jean, edited and translated into French by Edouard Jeauneau, *Sources Chrétiennes,* no. 151 (Paris: Editions du Cerf, 1969);

Jean Scot: Commentaire sur l'évangile de Jean, edited and translated into French by Jeauneau, *Sources Chrétiennes,* no. 180 (Paris: Editions du Cerf, 1972);

Iohannis Scotti Eriugenae Expositiones in Ierarchiam coelestem, edited by J. Barbet, *Corpus Christianorum: Continuatio Mediaevalis,* volume 31 (Turnhout: Brepols, 1975);

Iohannis Scotti De divina praedestinatione liber, edited by Goulven Madec, *Corpus Christianorum: Continuatio Mediaevalis,* volume 50 (Turnhout: Brepols, 1978);

Maximi Confessoris Quaestiones ad Thalassium, volume 1: *Quaestiones 1-55, una cum latina interpretatione Iohannis Scotti Eriugenae iuxta posita,* edited by Carl Laga and Carlos Steel, *Corpus Christianorum: Series Graeca,* volume 7 (Turnhout: Brepols & Louvain University Press, 1980);

Maximi Confessoris Ambigua ad Iohannem iuxta Iohannis Scotti Eriugenae latinam interpretationem, edited by Jeauneau, *Corpus Christianorum: Series Graeca,* volume 18 (Turnhout: Brepols & Louvain University Press, 1988).

EDITIONS IN ENGLISH: "On the Division of Nature," translated by Richard McKeon, in *Selections from Medieval Philosophers,* volume 1: *Augustine to Albert the Great* (New York: Scribners, 1929), pp. 106-141;

Periphyseon: On the Division of Nature: John the Scot (Joannes Scotus Eriugena), translated by Myra L. Uhlfelder, with summaries of the untranslated portions by Jean A. Potter, Library of Liberal Arts, no. 157 (Indianapolis: Bobbs-Merrill, 1976);

The Division of Nature Periphyseon, translated by I. P. Sheldon-Williams, revised by John J. O'Meara (Montreal: Bellarmin / Washington, D.C.: Dumbarton Oaks, 1987).

John Scottus Eriugena was the most original synthetic thinker between the time of Augustine and that of Thomas Aquinas. He is certainly the greatest Irish philosopher of all time. In recognition of this preeminent status, an idealized portrait of Eriugena graces the five-pound note of the Republic of Ireland. But close attention of the kind paid to other major medieval thinkers has, in general, rarely been paid to Eriugena, and much of his work remains inaccessible to readers of English. The reasons for this neglect are three: the difficult and complex character of his thought has appealed to only the more dedicated students of medieval philosophy; his influence on medieval thought has seemed slight; and his major work was less than orthodox. Some nineteenth-century scholars turned to the study of Eriugena precisely for these reasons, seeing in him a lonely and misunderstood figure. They characterized him as a thinker outside his time, with no intellectual equals, no schools of followers, and no friends in the church. It has fallen to twentieth-century scholars to undo this romantic image by setting Eriugena's thought in the context of his time, by editing his works, and by interpreting his complex system of thought. Since 1933 there has been an explosion of interest in Eriugena.

The range of Eriugena's works and ideas is almost dizzying, but his thought developed in two essential stages. The first was prior to 860, when his sources were the traditional Latin texts of Augustine and Martianus Capella; during the second, which lasted from 860 until his death, he both translated and was deeply influenced by the writings of the Greek Fathers. In the first stage of his career Eriugena wrote two chief works, the *De Diuinae Praedestinatione Liber* (Book on Divine Predestination, circa 850-851) and *Annotationes in Marcianum* (Annotations on Martianus Capella, circa 859-860), both of which need to be seen in the context of the so-called Carolingian renaissance. In them Eriugena reveals himself as a bold thinker and teacher who was prepared to place great emphasis on reason in understanding theological and philosophical matters. In the culminating stage of his career Eriugena began by translating the works of Pseudo-Dionysius and Maximus the Confessor from Greek into Latin. These thinkers exposed him to Neoplatonic doctrines different from those contained in the works of Augustine, in essence moving him indirectly from the influence of Plotinus to that of Proclus. Nevertheless, Eriugena's masterwork, the *Periphyseon* (About Nature, circa 864-866), does not slavishly ape Greek sources but rather seeks an original synthesis of Latin and Greek patristic thought on the nature of the universe. In the end its teachings about God, the primordial causes, Creation, and the return of all things to God are distinctly Eriugenian.

It is generally assumed that Eriugena was born in Ireland circa 810. His name in the full form in use since early modern times, Johannes Scottus Eriugena, literally means "John the Irishman, native of Erin" (the second and third names are frequently spelled *Scotus* and *Erigena*). While "John the Scot" has had some currency, it is misleading to a modern audience. In the early Middle Ages, the epithet *Scottus* denoted an Irishman, whereas later it came to designate someone from Scotland (as can be seen in the example of John Duns Scotus). The name Eriugena, meaning Irish by birth, the philosopher invented for himself and employed as his authorial name at the beginning of the translation of the Pseudo-Dionysian corpus.

Eriugena's original Irish name is unknown, but then virtually all of the philosopher's early career in Ireland is obscure. Even the issue of whether he learned Greek in Ireland has been hotly debated. It seems probable that while Eriugena may have received some instruction in the Greek language in his homeland, his study of Greek only seriously advanced later, on the Continent, since it was fifteen years after he departed Ireland before he began his translations. It was certainly in Ireland that Eriugena learned Latin and was exposed to classical Latin authors such as Virgil and to Christian authors such as Isidore and Augustine. Proof of the formative character of his early Irish education may well exist in his distinctive Irish script, which scholars believe they have identified and which stands in sharp contrast to the regular Caroline script employed on the Continent. Moreover, after only a few years on the Continent Eriugena was already regarded as an extremely learned man, a recognition that could not have come about had he learned nothing in Ireland.

Why Eriugena left his homeland is not a mystery, if his life followed the pattern of other ninth-century Irish scholars. The Vikings repeatedly attacked Ireland and sacked its monasteries in the first half of the ninth century, seriously undermining its ancient civilization. Many learned Irishmen found their way early in the century to Charlemagne's court. Around 845, if not earlier,

Eriugena must have boarded a boat—perhaps an Irish curragh, a leather-covered bark of the kind Saint Brendan was said to have sailed—destined for Gaul. His works contain some striking nautical imagery; for instance, he likens the act of interpreting the Bible to crossing a wave-tossed sea full of rocks and dangerous straits.

Whether Eriugena immediately made his way to the court of Charles the Bald or spent some time elsewhere in the Carolingian empire, as some think, is not clear. What seem to be his earliest extant writings testify to his Irish background and the context of his teaching on the Continent. The *Glossae Diuinae Historiae* (Biblical Glosses, circa 845-850) on the Old Testament, convincingly attributed to Eriugena, contains Old Irish words for such things as the flora and fauna of Ireland, its building materials, and its legal procedures. The glosses are, for the most part, fairly rudimentary and contain little sustained use of Greek, but they were probably designed to instruct Irish students on the Continent. To make matters clear to these students Eriugena occasionally had recourse to their shared native tongue, as when he provided the Latin and Old Irish equivalents for such things as *seagull* and *epileptic*. These sparse glosses reflect Eriugena's first experience at translating cultures, here from Irish into Latin; later he would translate from Greek into Latin. He was certainly connected with some Continental communities of Irish, though whether he ever lived at Laon, where one such community gathered, is not certain. Martin Hiberniensis, who was at Laon, preserved some of the Greek words from Eriugena's poems in his Greek-Latin glossary, which still survives in the municipal library of Laon. In an elegiac couplet Eriugena complained, no doubt for the amusement of his countrymen on the Continent that in the midst of a summer heat wave Bacchus, the god of wine, had deserted the Irish, forcing them to fill their bellies with putrid water. William of Malmesbury, a twelfth-century monastic historian who did much to create a false tradition about Eriugena, connected a well-known joke on the theme of drinking to Eriugena: Eriugena was seated opposite King Charles at the dinner table and apparently offended the king with his table manners. The angry king demanded to know what separated a Scot from a sot, whereupon Eriugena answered, "Only the table." Though William's joke is apocryphal, the philosopher is known to have had a sharp sense of humor. Of Hincmar—either the bishop of Laon or his uncle, the archbishop of Reims—Eriugena said that the only decent thing he had ever done was to die; but he made this remark while both Hincmars were still alive. In a short poem he quipped that should a surgeon dare to cut open one's veins, his hand had best not tremble. It has been suggested that this verse, along with a reference to a physician named John in a charter of 845, may mean that Eriugena began his career on the Continent with an interest in medicine.

Eriugena seems to have been associated with the court of Charles the Bald by 846, since Prudentius of Troyes, who was at court during 845-846, would later refer to Eriugena in familiar terms. The first unequivocal mention of Eriugena comes in the context of the Carolingian predestination controversy. Pardulus, the bishop of Laon, explained to the church of Lyons how he and Hincmar, the archbishop of Reims, had sought out "that Irishman, John by name, who is in the palace of the King" to compose something for them on the subject of predestination. A dispute on this issue had arisen in the late 840s and was ultimately to divide Carolingian intellectuals and ecclesiastical authorities into separate camps.

The Saxon Gottschalk (or Gottescalc), the main sower of doctrinal dissension, had been given as an oblate to the monastery of Fulda by his noble father but had denied his monastic vows in 829 and moved to Orbais, where he was irregularly ordained. He then set off on a voyage to Rome, northern Italy, Dalmatia, and parts east. In Italy Gottschalk taught a doctrine of double predestination: that God, in his foreknowledge and justice, predestined the elect to eternal life or heaven and the reprobate to everlasting death or hell. For Gottschalk, God's foreknowing and predestining were identical; they were also absolutely fixed and unchanging. One sees in Gottschalk a sensitive reader of the anti-Pelagian tracts of Augustine, and his Carolingian supporters understood him in these terms. But the implications of his doctrine for the institutional church were perceived to be too radical and threatening. He taught, for instance, that the blood of Christ redeemed only the elect, not the reprobate, thus calling into question the efficacy of the sacraments. Gottschalk emphasized the unlimited power of God to dispose of humans, thus effectively bypassing the intercessory role of the earthly church. In 848 Gottschalk returned to Mainz, where his teachings were condemned and he was handed over to Hincmar of Reims.

At Quierzy in 849 he was tried, beaten, forced to burn a copy of his teachings, and condemned to perpetual silence in a cell at the monastery of Hautvilliers, where he died twenty years later.

In the midst of these events, Pardulus and Hincmar called on Eriugena to compose his *De Diuinae Praedestinatione Liber*. The bishops received more than the simple refutation of Gottschalk that they had desired, for Eriugena's treatise in nineteen chapters contained a strikingly original position. When he identifies, in Augustinian fashion, true philosophy with true religion in the opening chapter, he immediately reveals himself as a thinker whose aim is to analyze questions logically, rationally, and abstractly. In his discussion of what can and cannot be said of God, Eriugena recognizes the inadequacy of human descriptions of God. What humans perceive are the accidents of his creation, a multiplicity of effects; but God is utterly simple and lacks all multiplicity. There can, therefore, be no division associated with God. To speak, then, of double predestination is a deficiency of human talk about God. The very terms *predestination* and *foreknowledge*, he argues, are misleading, since God exists outside time in eternity and precedes the things he creates.

Eriugena is careful in the *De Diuinae Praedestinatione* to preserve the idea of free will, which human beings possess in God's image and which remains after the Original Sin, and to dissociate God from human sinning. Free will is a good given to humans by God so that they might seek the blessed life, but it can be corrupted. Evil, for Eriugena as for Augustine, is a lack of good and is nothing in itself: since God, who created everything, did not create evil, then evil must not exist; it must be nothing. Thus sin, which arises from the abuse of free will, and the punishment for sin are to be located in humans themselves, not in God. Sin shuts itself up in its own prison of iniquity and punishes itself, for the absence of blessedness is the greatest punishment of all. It follows that there could be no hell, filled with fire and corporeal punishment, where the damned would be eternally tortured. God's house is like a splendid mansion where all people will gather, some to rejoice in the vision of its magnificence, others to be tormented by greed at the sight of unattainable wealth. In this way Eriugena made sin and its punishment entirely the business of humanity, freeing God from any causal responsibility.

As might be imagined, given the boldness of Eriugena's arguments on predestination, free will, sin, and hell, critics pounced almost immediately on his tenets. Hincmar, who frequently reminded his parishioners of the real torments of hell, at first simply ignored the book. Prudentius of Troyes claimed to see in Eriugena's tract a revival of the errors of Pelagius and Origen and too great a reliance on reason in matters already resolved by authority. In a series of letters and a treatise by Florus, the church of Lyons attacked not only Eriugena's novelty but also his use of Scripture. Two church councils within the next ten years rejected Eriugena's position on predestination; other councils simply disregarded it. Predestination was an issue that had become politicized in the divided Carolingian empire, but it was to fade in importance after 860. Seventeenth-century Europe, however, living in the shadow of the predestination doctrines of Martin Luther and John Calvin, would rediscover and read with renewed interest the Carolingian treatises of Gottschalk and Eriugena.

Between 851 and 860 little was heard from Eriugena, perhaps as a consequence of the continuing controversy over predestination. Hincmar of Reims and Charles the Bald, whatever they may have thought of his teaching on the subject, did not abandon the scholar. Charles frequented several palaces during these years, but his scholars and artists may have settled at an important monastery, such as Saint-Médard of Soissons or Saint-Denis outside Paris, and later at the favored palace of Compiègne, whence they were called to Charles at specific times during the year. In 858 Charles's half-brother Louis the German invaded his kingdom, but he was driven out early the next year. Eriugena, who was also something of a royal poet, wrote a verse of celebration on Charles's return to power. His poem on Charles and his queen, Ermintrude, probably dates from these years as well. The poem depicts the queen praying, reading, and weaving the jewel-encrusted robes of her husband. The domesticity of the portrait suggests Eriugena's familiarity with the court and its personalities. He regularly wrote poems praising the king and his royal lineage. It was Christ, thought the poet, from whom the king gained his authority, and neither a faithless brother nor other invaders should deprive him of what had been justly bestowed.

Eriugena had fled Ireland to escape the Vikings, but between 856 and 859 they attacked Rouen, Paris, Saint-Denis, Chartres, Noyons,

Amiens, and Beauvais—precisely the parts of the kingdom where the philosopher was most likely resident. In one of his poems he asks Christ to drive away the "pagan prows" and describes in another "the uncivilized pagan surging forth from the North Pole." In the poem on Queen Ermintrude he implores Christ to overthrow, convert, and teach obedience to the enemies of the king and queen. If they resist, he implores Christ to "Drown in the deeps of the sea the pagan pirates who, / Devoted totally to the sword, are ravaging the world's kingdoms; / Let them be cast here and there on various sandbanks by southwinds, / To perish there in the surging tides of the Ocean." Let bountiful peace, he beseeches Christ, flourish among all Christians and lead the faithful to the heavenly bodies beyond the ethereal choirs. Eriugena understood historical disorder as an attack on reason itself, and he thought of himself and his king as seekers after truth and the fixed order of things. The poet held forth reason as the wind that would blow away the shadows and allow people to enter into the higher truth; for in a fragile and transient life, harassed all around by perilous hardships such as the Viking attacks, theological truth offered the palm of victory to all.

In these difficult years Eriugena continued his work as a teacher of the liberal arts. At Charlemagne's court Alcuin had thought of the seven liberal arts as the seven columns on which the temple of Christian wisdom rested; three, the so-called Trivum (grammar, rhetoric, and dialectic), concerned words, while the other four, the Quadrivium (arithmetic, geometry, music, and astronomy), treated things. The cultivation of the liberal arts by the Carolingians reinforced a tradition stretching back to late antiquity. Eriugena found himself in the midst of an educational reform that, although limited in the number of people it reached, was to be tremendously influential. From it came Caroline minuscule, that reformed script of small, regular, and economical form in which books are printed today. Associated with the movement in Charlemagne's day were Alcuin, Angilbert, and Theodulf of Orléans; in Louis the Pious's time, Rabanus Maurus, Walafrid Strabo, and Einhard; and in Charles the Bald's, Lupus of Ferrières, Paschasius Radbertus, Ratramnus of Corbie, and Nithard. Among them were humanists, controversialists, historians, biographers, and poets. All of them would have received a grounding in the liberal arts at monasteries or at royal courts. Charlemagne had urged the clerics of his realm to pursue their study of the liberal arts, for correct speech and writing would insure that God's nature was not the subject of crude talk and less-than-pious prayer. Eriugena thus took his place in the palace of Charles the Bald as a teacher of the liberal arts and as a representative of the continuing Carolingian renaissance.

Although the textual history of the *Annotationes in Marcianum* is complex and controversial, there can be no doubt about Eriugena's interest in Martianus or in his authorship of some work on him. In a short letter attributed to him, Eriugena asked a certain Lord Winibert to lend him the copy of Martianus's work that they had failed to correct completely when they had been together. In the *Annotationes in Marcianum* Eriugena explains the difficult vocabulary and passages of Martianus—sometimes fully, as when he discusses the harmony of the spheres, sometimes briefly, as when he explains who the gods and goddesses were or states rather obviously that a distich is two lines of verse while a monostich is one. Readers faced with Martianus's difficult but essential text in the course of their education must have been thankful for Eriugena's efforts, even if his explanations were occasionally fanciful and idiosyncratic. He employed a wide range of sources, basically Latin, in this work, including Pliny the Elder, Virgil, Macrobius, and Isidore. To Martianus's encyclopedic treatment of the arts Eriugena added a Carolingian explanation, one reflecting to a lesser degree his Irish background and to a greater his burgeoning interest in Greek. The text of his commentary is important for what it reveals about the state of Carolingian education and about the direction of Eriugena's thought. Though its philosophical content may not rank highly, its cultural information is extensive. The *Annotationes in Marcianum* continued to be influential in Carolingian education, and Remigius of Auxerre at the end of the ninth century would use Eriugena's glosses in his own synthetic treatment of Martianus. Moreover, the *Annotationes in Marcianum* stands near the beginning of a tradition of glosses on classical texts that would dominate Western education for the next three hundred years.

Until 860 Eriugena's work, for all of its creativeness and boldness, was still bound by the typical features of early medieval thought, particularly its reliance on authors such as Martianus and Augustine. If he had given indications in the *Annotationes in Marcianum* and even in the *De*

Diuinae Praedestinatione of a desire to explore Greek sources, he had as yet made no sustained study of them. But the Carolingian royal courts after Charlemagne's imperial coronation in 800 were, despite the localizing features of the early Middle Ages, decidedly cosmopolitan. Foreign ambassadors frequented the royal palaces, often bearing gifts, sometimes expecting them. Contacts were opened up in particular with Constantinople and the Byzantine Empire. In 827 the Byzantine ambassadors of the emperor Michael the Stammerer visited Compiègne and presented Louis the Pious with a copy of the works of the Pseudo-Dionysius, a Byzantine Neoplatonist who was mistakenly identified with Paul's convert, Dionysius the Areopagite (Acts 17:34), and also with the founder of the Abbey of Saint-Denis. Once the monastery had solemnly installed the codex (which still survives in Paris), the abbot Hilduin either translated or commissioned a translation of the Pseudo-Dionysian writings. While it was a considerable achievement given the general lack of knowledge of Greek at the time, the translation was largely literal and often incomprehensible. Thus Charles the Bald, the royal patron of Saint-Denis, turned to his precocious Irish scholar and demanded a new translation of the works of Pseudo-Dionysius. Eriugena produced one, although he claimed that he was but a raw recruit in the study of Greek. Although Eriugena's translation was an improvement on Hilduin's, it was in many places just as incomprehensible.

Eriugena worked under difficult circumstances: his glossaries or dictionaries were unsophisticated and were surely incapable of assisting him in understanding the difficult vocabulary of Pseudo-Dionysius. Moreover, he can have had no training in Greek paleography, and the Saint-Denis manuscript lacked punctuation and accents. He was unable, for instance, to distinguish between the Greek words for *therefore* and *therefore not*, thus occasionally providing a translation exactly opposite to the meaning intended. Anastasius, the librarian of the Holy See, wrote to Charles the Bald confessing amazement that a barbarian from the very ends of the civilized world was able to make any translation at all of the work; but he lamented that Eriugena had taken Dionysius further away from Latin understanding, burying his meaning in deep caverns where it must await another translation. Despite the criticism, Eriugena's translation, later emended, was for three hundred years the basis for study of the Pseudo-Dionysius.

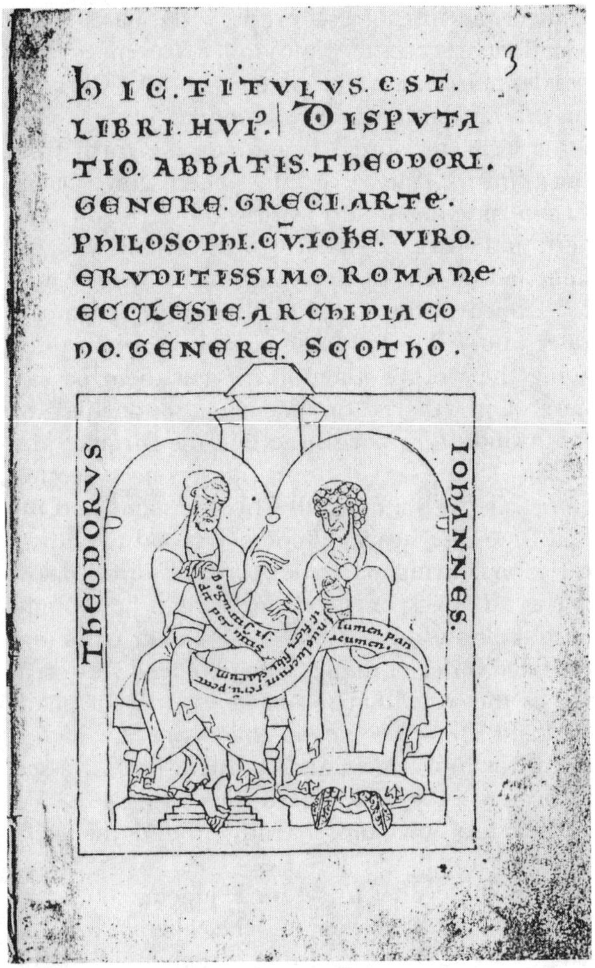

Illustration from a twelfth-century manuscript for a work by Honorius Augustodunensis, depicting Eriugena (right) and Theodore of Tarsus, a seventh-century archbishop of Canterbury (Paris, Bibliothèque Nationale, lat.6734, fol. 3r)

Anastasius indirectly worked to open up yet other horizons for Eriugena. In his letter criticizing the translation, he had enclosed corrections and glosses by Maximus the Confessor that he thought would cast light on the meaning of Pseudo-Dionysius. Charles once again commissioned Eriugena to undertake a translation, this time of the *Ambigua ad Iohannem* (Ambigua to John, translated circa 862-864) of Maximus. Although it was a much longer text, the translator seems to have worked with more confidence, and he also found a striking continuity between the two Greek authors. He regretted that he had not known Maximus's work earlier, since it laid bare so much of the perplexity that had surrounded Pseudo-Dionysius's meaning. Eriugena or perhaps scholars under his direction translated other Greek works: Gregory of Nyssa's *De Imagine* (On the Making of Man, translated circa

862-864); Maximus's *Quaestiones ad Thalassium* (Questions to Thalassius, translated 864-866); and Epiphanius's work *On Faith* (translation lost or unidentified). Eriugena's accomplishment in translating these works was remarkable, particularly if he did so in the six years (860 to 866) usually assigned to this period of his career. For all their flaws, they show that he had a gift for grasping the essential meaning of a Greek passage. Other medieval philosophers, such as Aquinas, ordered translations of Greek texts from expert translators; Eriugena was forced to make his own. He had been encouraged in his Greek studies by Charles the Bald, at whose court Greek became fashionable. Eriugena even wrote a few verses in Greek to praise the ruler who loved the Greeks as much as he did.

For Eriugena the translation of these Greek texts was more than mere fashion; it was the pivotal event in the development of his thought. The Greek Fathers unfolded for him a dazzling array of ideas that had been largely unknown in the West. Although Eriugena would not abandon Latin texts, he would thenceforth place them alongside those of the Greek Fathers. Much of his effort was designed to bring Pseudo-Dionysius and Augustine, with their different strains of Neoplatonism, into harmony. Where Augustine, drawing on Plotinus, had emphasized the interiority and immediacy of the divine presence in the human mind, Pseudo-Dionysius, under the influence of Proclus, had painted a picture of a hierarchical universe in which the Divine Light spread downward through a series of intermediate agents to humanity and the lower orders. In Pseudo-Dionysius, Eriugena also encountered what is known as apophatic or negative theology: the position that when speaking of God negation is superior to affirmation, for it is better to say what God is not than what he is. On both of these points Eriugena tried to reconcile Augustine and Pseudo-Dionysius, thus fashioning a fresh Eriugenian Neoplatonism for the Middle Ages.

The influence of Pseudo-Dionysius on Eriugena was reinforced and enriched by Maximus the Confessor. In the letter to Charles the Bald he prefixed to the translation of the *Ambigua ad Iohannem,* Eriugena drew the king's attention to the main doctrines of Maximus. For Maximus, God was the cause of all things, being at once simple and multiple. He taught the procession of divine goodness into all things, from the highest to the lowest, descending from being in general to the most specialized species. All would be regathered in the return of divine goodness to that simple unity of everything which is in God and is God. According to Maximus, the less multiplied or divided a thing was, the greater its virtue. In Maximus, Eriugena observed a reconciliation of the positive and negative theologies: human beings could only know *that* God is, not *what* he is. Though his translations of Maximus were not widely circulated in the Middle Ages, Maximus may well have made the most impact on the development of Eriugena's work. Maximus provided the Irish thinker with a richer theological vocabulary, one that not only explained the difficult doctrines of Pseudo-Dionysius but drew on a lesser-known Aristotelian tradition. Throughout the *Periphyseon* the influence of Maximus is evident, frequently in the form of direct quotations.

Finally, Eriugena employed Gregory of Nyssa's *De Imagine* to fashion his anthropological ideas and to provide a counterweight to Augustine's notion of a historical, terrestrial paradise. Eriugena (or one of his revisers), having mistakenly conflated Gregory of Nyssa with another Byzantine theologian, Gregory of Nazianzen, would argue that Gregory was the preeminent authority among the Greeks just as Augustine was among the Latins. He stressed Gregory's authority in order to deny the Augustinian position that Paradise was a literal reality with definite spatial and temporal boundaries. For Eriugena, the Fall lay outside time and, therefore, outside history; Genesis was to be understood allegorically. Given Augustine's dominant position in the West as an interpreter of Genesis, Eriugena would need all the support he could muster. In Gregory's short treatise he was also exposed to important ideas about the division of the sexes; the implicit rejection of a corporeal hell; humanity as an image of God, an image preserved despite the Fall; the human being as a microcosm; and the ascent of the soul toward the divine.

By the mid 860s Eriugena must have been one of the most learned men in Europe. Though deeply influenced by the doctrines he had encountered, Eriugena shaped what he had received into something new. He was not to remain a mere translator of or commentator on the texts of others but was to write his own masterwork.

Although this work is often referred to in English by the title *On the Division of Nature*, it is correctly known as the *Periphyseon.* At the end of the work Eriugena names Wulfad, the abbot of Saint-

Médard of Soissons who became the archbishop of Bourges in 866, as his colleague in the pursuit of wisdom, thanks him for the encouragement given at the outset of the project, and promises to make the corrections suggested by him. (In the list of books in Wulfad's library that is contained in one of Wulfad's manuscripts, two books or copies of the *Periphyseon* are listed.) The work, divided into five books, is a dialogue between a Disciple and his Master. The younger interlocutor often serves as a foil for the teacher; unlike Platonic dialogues, in which it is often difficult to distinguish Plato's own thought from those of his speakers, Eriugena's dialogue is sufficiently one-sided to allow for some certainty about the author's ideas. Still, the Disciple reveals himself to be clever.

According to some scholars, the *Periphyseon* began as a much shorter and less ambitious text over which Eriugena and his students layered several stages of corrections and substantial additions. The 1853 edition by H. J. Floss, which served for many years as the standard text, failed to distinguish the various stages of recension. It has been charged that even the edition of the first three books by I. P. Sheldon-Williams (1968, 1972, 1981) was compromised by the editor's failure to separate two different sets of early Irish corrections, one of which may be in the handwriting of Eriugena himself. Edouard Jeauneau has begun a critical edition of the *Periphyseon*, but much critical work remains to be done on the text of his magnum opus before Eriugena will assume his rightful place as one of the western world's major thinkers.

The *Periphyseon*, which presents a sweeping and systematic view of God and Creation and how they relate to each other, begins with a series of definitions, divisions, and distinctions. Nature is defined as the general name for all things, both those that are and those that are not. But being and nonbeing are susceptible of five modes of interpretation. In the first, things perceptible to the senses exist, while things not perceptible, such as God and the Platonic Ideas, do not. The second mode of interpretation is based on the order of things in the hierarchy descending from God to creation: thus, the affirmation of a higher being is the negation of a lower and vice versa. In the third, things are said to be when they come into being or are generated; thus an unborn human is not, even though its potentiality already exists in the first man created by God, and a seed is said not to be until it sprouts. In the fourth mode only intellectual and eternal things are real, while things that suffer material change and dissolution are not. In the fifth mode, which belongs to humanity alone, being is judged according to its adherence to the divine image; in sin humans lost their being, but it is restored by the grace of Christ. Not all of these ways of speaking about or identifying being and nonbeing can be applied at the same time or to the same things.

The Master sets out a more fundamental division of Nature into four aspects: "first into that which creates and is not created, secondly into that which is created and also creates, thirdly into that which is created and does not create, while the fourth neither creates nor is created." These divisions characterize, in succession, God the Creator, the primordial causes that emanate from him, the material universe including humanity, and God again as the End. Creation proceeds in a process of division from God through the primordial causes to a multitude of things and then returns through resolution to God.

Perhaps when he began Eriugena thought that he would write four books, one for each division of Nature; but the scheme could not hold the weight of his reflections and quickly broke down. Thus, while book 1 treats that which creates and is not created (God the Creator) and book 2 that which is created and creates (the primordial causes), book 3 continues the discussion of the primordial causes. Eriugena is, moreover, unable to complete the discussion of the third division—that which is created and does not create (material creation)—in book 3, which takes up a systematic examination of the six days of creation from Genesis but breaks off its exegesis at the fifth day (Gen. 1:21). The fourth book begins where the third leaves off and considers the fifth and sixth days of creation, then turns to the return of all things to that which neither creates nor is created. The fifth book completes the circle that leads from God back to God.

In the first book Eriugena considers the problem of predication: what can one say about God? Rejecting the applicability of Aristotle's ten categories to God, he employs the negative and positive theologies of Pseudo-Dionysius and Maximus the Confessor. If one says that the divine nature is essence, one has made an affirmation that is not entirely true of God, while the statement that the divine nature is nonessence is a negation that does not so much deny that the divine nature is an essence as it denies the affirmative predication. Best of all, thought Eriugena, was to say that the divine nature is superessential, which appears to be an affirmation but is in reality a negation meaning "beyond essence" or "more than essence." To affix the prefix *super* to the things properly said of God in no way limits or defines him, for they say not *what* he is, but *that* he is. In this way Eriugena proposed to marry the negative and positive theologies in a superior form of predication.

Creatures could know that God exists but would never know just what he is, for God is not a "what" to be known. Even the angels comprehend only the theophanies, or manifestations, of God, and these appearances are present in creation. Eriugena employs an etymology of the Greek word for *God*: God is he who runs throughout all things. Thus, God is in some sense present in created things.

The second and third books chiefly treat the first stage of creation. God creates in order to know himself; he does not know himself before he begins to manifest himself to himself in creating the primordial causes. In addition, he does not know evil, nor things whose reasons he does not know eternally in himself, nor the experiential reality of things not yet manifest but whose invisible reasons he knows, nor does he know himself as part of the things he has made. The Creator first fashioned an intelligible world in such primordial causes or divine ideas as Goodness, Essence, Life, Reason, Intellect, Wisdom, Power, Blessedness, Truth, and Eternity. These ideas are achieved in the Word or Son, who is coeternal with the Father. Out of the intelligible world of the primordial causes comes the externalized world of perceptible and sensible things; the latter is fully contained in the former.

To demonstrate the procession of creation downward into sensible things Eriugena turns to Maximus's fivefold division into the uncreated and the created, the intelligible and sensible, heaven and earth, paradise and the world, and male and female. Just as the division of the sexes marked the end of the procession, so their reunification at the resurrection will begin the return to God. Human beings are wonderfully placed at the center or conjunction of things, since they have bodies in material creation and souls in the intelligible. The whole universe, in this sense, is contained in humanity and will return in it to God. Eriugena's anthropology, with its dependence on Gregory of Nyssa, grants a distinct dignity to humanity as the linchpin of the linked movements of procession and return. The physical world seeks, in humanity, to rise to the intelligible world; and humanity itself reaches toward the divine intellect.

In books 4 and 5 the return of all things to God is systematically discussed, as the Master continues to expound on the creation narrative of Genesis. In the return, the stages of the downward division will be reversed. In human beings the return proceeds through five steps: the body will be dissolved into the four elements of which it was made; at the resurrection each person will recover his or her sexually undifferentiated body from the common mass of elements; the body will change to spirit; the spirit will return to the primordial causes that have always existed in God; finally, Nature and its causes will return to God, who will be all in all. In the return different essences and different substances will retain their identities; they will be united, but distinct, as when a piece of iron heated in fire glows like the fire but remains metal.

Echoing his views from the *De Diuinae Praedestinatione*, Eriugena says that there will be no hell of physical punishment where wrongdoers will be eternally tormented. God cannot have created evil, and therefore human nature cannot be evil. Rather, since the Fall of humanity was brought about by an abuse of free will, punishment will consist in the inability of the perverse will to satisfy its longings: the sinner will "burn" in his own wicked desires. But all will participate in the return to God: the saints and the just will share in theophanies of God, while the unjust will suffer from false fantasies of things they can never possess. While the reprobate will suffer the absence of a knowledge of truth, the just will enjoy deification, a blessed state of perfect peace and joy shared with the angels, in which they will be pure intellect absorbed into God.

Thus, the return consists of seven steps but is a union of eight things. The earthly body will change into vital motion, vital motion into sense, sense into reason, and reason into intellect. These first four steps describe the union of human nature into a single thing, as the lower is always taken up into the higher. Next, the intellect crosses over to a knowledge of all things but God, knowledge passes into wisdom or into the intimate contemplation of the truth that is granted to creatures, and finally the most purified souls are supernaturally placed in God himself. They fall into a darkness of incomprehensible and inaccessible light, in the shadows of which the causes of things are hidden. Night will then become as day, for the secret and divine mysteries will be ineffably revealed to blessed and enlightened intellects.

Eriugena ends with a mystical discussion of the number eight as a supernatural cube: just as the five parts of human nature will return first, to be followed by three stages of ascent within God, so the pentad of Creation will join with the triad of the Creator. Humanity, moreover, awaits the eighth day, which will succeed the seven of Creation and which Christ mystically signified by his resurrection on the eighth day (the day after the Sabbath). After a plea to the readers of the *Periphyseon* for understanding, Eriugena concludes with an invocation: "Let each man flourish in his own understanding until the coming of that light which turns to darkness the light of those falsely philosophizing and transforms into light the darkness of those who rightly know." One emerges from reading the *Periphyseon* with the impression that Eriugena was sure that he had unlocked the pattern of the universe and that he was one of those who rightly know.

The *Periphyseon* was the most ambitious book to have been written in the western world since Augustine's *De Civitate Dei* (The City of God, 426). No sketch can do justice to its wealth of themes, for Eriugena, while he was a systematic thinker, engaged in constant digression, here reflecting on angelic nature, the liberal arts, and the procession of the Holy Spirit, there on planetary motions, reptiles, and grasses. Like all great works, the *Periphyseon* can be read on several levels: as an exegetical treatment of the Creation story of Genesis, as Neoplatonic theology, as properly philosophical in some of its particular concerns such as the ten categories, and as a comprehensive description of everything (both that which is and that which is not). Its subject is truly metaphysical: the universal order of all things. As a modern physicist or astronomer might in contemplating the Big Bang, Eriugena re-creates in his mind the creation of the universe. He has talked, to the degree that humans can, about God—the first cause of all things—and about the perfect ideas or primordial causes that reside eternally in the divine mind. The flow of the universe, or, as he would have said, its division from simpler to more complex and from higher to lower, is reconstructed. Not until Aquinas would another medieval thinker dare to write a book with such synthetic sweep.

The difficulties in reading the *Periphyseon* are ones which Eriugena fully recognized and with which he attempted to deal in the dialogue form of the work. Modern readers are not unlike the Disciple, who gropes his way clumsily toward the truth in his discussion with the Master, who already knows. Between the Master and the Disciple there is not always complete understanding—or, rather, different degrees of understanding exist. But both surpass the understanding of many others: they agree, for instance, on the stupidity of those who think substance is corporeal. But the relationship of the student and the teacher also falls within the pattern of the world perceived by Eriugena: of lower striving toward higher, of humanity seeking through knowledge to come to superior intellect, and of the refining nature of true knowledge. It is the Disciple who, in his concluding speech, offers up a marvelous philosophical prayer:

> O Lord Jesus, I ask of you no other reward, no other happiness, no other delight than to understand, purely and without any error of false speculation, your words, which were inspired by your Holy Spirit. This is the sum of bliss for me and the end of perfect contemplation: for even the purest rational soul will find nothing beyond this, since there is nothing beyond this. As you are sought nowhere else more clearly than in them. There you live, and there you bring those who seek and love you; there you prepare for your elect spiritual banquets of true knowledge. And coming, you minister to them.
>
> And what, O Lord, is that coming of yours but an ascent through the infinite steps of your contemplation? For you always come to the intellects of those who seek and find you. You are sought by them always, and are found always, and are always not found. You are found indeed in your theophanies, in which in many different ways, as though in certain mirrors, you encounter the minds of those who understand you in the way in which you allow yourself to be understood—not what you are, but what you are not, and that you are. But you are not found in your superessence, by which you surpass and excel all intellect wishing and ascending to comprehend you. You give to your followers your presence in an ineffable manner of appearance; you pass from them in the incomprehensible height and infinity of your being.

This prayer, shot through with the language of the Bible, Augustine, Pseudo-Dionysius, Maximus, and Gregory of Nyssa, is the student's synthesis of the Master's teaching. It alludes in cryptic fashion to the lessons laboriously learned by the Disciple throughout the five books of the

Periphyseon: to the negative theology, to the soul's ascent in contemplation, to the vision of God, and to the final return. The student has made these teachings part of his knowledge, and thus his prayer stands witness to Eriugena's own accomplishment in the *Periphyseon*: the ascent of an individual human mind toward the divine.

Though few can have hoped to absorb Eriugena's complex thought as the Disciple eventually did the Master's, Eriugena had students and the *Periphyseon* readers in the late ninth century. The most important readers were his powerful patrons: Wulfad, Charles the Bald, and Hincmar of Reims. A series of ninth-century manuscripts of Eriugena's works were copied in Wulfad's monastery of Saint-Médard of Soissons; Wulfad's scriptorium did much to disseminate and keep alive the work of Eriugena for subsequent generations. Charles the Bald had commissioned the translations without which there would have been no *Periphyseon*, and in the years when Eriugena must have been writing his great work he was still a royal scholar who occasionally composed panegyrics for the king. Hincmar, the archbishop of Reims, had been the copatron of the *De Diuinae Praedestinatione*, and he may have stimulated interest in Eriugena's work at Reims. The oldest surviving manuscript of the *Periphyseon*, which was produced at Saint-Médard of Soissons in 875 and which contains corrections that may be in Eriugena's own handwriting, ended up in Reims. Thus Eriugena did not lack for powerful friends and protectors; he was, in this sense, truly the son of the Carolingian renaissance.

He also had students, some of whom worked closely with him. Eriugena's productivity in the 860s was so immense that it has long been assumed that he had help. In addition to the Caroline scripts in which his works have been copied, one finds Irish corrections, annotations, and additions in different hands. Martin Hiberniensis, the Irish master of Laon, may not have worked with Eriugena at court, but his glossary indicates that he read the *Periphyseon*. Lastly, Heiric of Auxerre, who studied at Soissons between 863 and 865 while Eriugena was at work on the *Periphyseon*, became familiar with a series of Eriugena's writings and probably with the philosopher himself. At certain points in his life of Saint Germanus (circa 875) and in one of his homilies Heiric almost outdoes Eriugena with his own Eriugenism, coming close to a caricature of Eriugena's thought. Thus Eriugena's influence on his own time was not negligible; but the *Periphyseon* suffered the fate of Carolingian culture in general: tied to a royal court and royal patronage, it would not prosper during the decentralized tenth century, when these courts effectively ceased to exist. Whatever influence Eriugena might have exerted had these courts continued was, thus, broken off.

The monastery of Cluny, which inherited so much of the Carolingian legacy, was to possess many works of Eriugena in its vast library, including the *Periphyseon*; but Eriugena's teachings, without the intense focus a court school could bring to bear on them, seem to have been neglected. The Cluniac monk and historian Raoul Glaber, an eccentric reader of odd texts just after the millennium, would, however, base his notion of the divine quaternities on Eriugena's translation of the *Ambigua ad Iohannem* of Maximus. In the twelfth century, though many may have been intrigued by Eriugena, few seem to have read the *Periphyseon* with any deep understanding. Honorius Augustodunensis, who may have been a monk in Germany early in the twelfth century, excerpted passages freely from the *Periphyseon*, but he was a collector of all sorts of random reflections by philosophers. In one of his manuscripts there is a stylized drawing of Eriugena seated beside Theodore, the archbishop of Canterbury. Other twelfth-century writers, such as William of Saint-Thierry, Hugh of Saint-Victor, and William of Malmesbury, chiefly knew of Eriugena and his great work by reputation, but the legends were most often false. In the early thirteenth century the *Periphyseon* fell under a cloud: it was connected with Amaury of Bène and David of Dinant, whose doctrines were condemned for their apparent pantheism, and in 1225 William of Auvergne, the bishop of Paris, secured Pope Honorius III's condemnation of the work. In 1684 Thomas Gale's first edition of the *Periphyseon* was placed on the *Index of Forbidden Books*, where it languishes still. Much of the official suspicion of Eriugena has been based on simple misunderstanding and ignorance of the complex *Periphyseon*. One must wonder what weight this official disapprobation carried when one sees that Nicholas, the great bishop of Cusa in the fifteenth century, could not only own and read the *Periphyseon* but absorb its teachings in his own *De Docta Ignorantia* (On Learned Ignorance, 1440). Not since the late ninth century, however, has the *Periphyseon* been read and studied as intensely as in the late twentieth.

Illumination from the Codex Aureus *of Saint-Emmeram depicting Eriugena's patron, Charles the Bald, on his throne, surrounded by his attendants. The* Codex Aureus *is a book of the four Gospels that was produced for Charles by his court school of artists (Bayerische Staatsbibliothek, Munich).*

Eriugena's career did not cease after the composition and circulation of the *Periphyseon,* but it would take no radical new turns. He improved and polished his translation of the Pseudo-Dionysian corpus and explained (circa 865-870) the perplexities of the *De Caelesti Hierarchia* (The Celestial Hierarchy, circa 500), by the same author. Among Eriugena's last works are a homily on the prologue of John (circa 870-872) and a commentary on the Gospel according to John (circa 875-877). The latter is incomplete, and the manuscript of the unique copy housed in Laon is damaged, but it has the virtue of possessing corrections in one of the Irish scripts closely associated with Eriugena himself. Eriugena was attracted to the Gospel of John because of its symbolic richness, a theme he explores throughout the commentary. For Eriugena, John was the greatest theologian of the four Evangelists, for it was he who achieved the most ethereal or theological sense of Scripture.

Eriugena's homily on the Prologue of John, titled *Vox Spiritualis Aquilae* . . . (The Voice of the Mystical Eagle . . . , 870-872), has been called by its editor the jewel of early medieval rhetoric and philosophy. Although short, it is packed with allusions to the profound doctrines laid out at great length in the *Periphyseon*: the primordial causes, ascent to God, division of the sexes, and theophanies. Here also are to be found the influence of Eriugena's favorite authors—Augustine, Pseudo-Dionysius, and Maximus the Confessor. Eriugena presents his sermon in almost poetic prose so as to lift the minds of his listeners to profound contemplation through the musicality of his voice and the profundity of Sacred Scripture.

He begins the homily with an arresting image: "The voice of the mystical eagle [the eagle was the standard symbol of John] throbs against the hearing of the church." The exterior sense gathers in the fleeting sound and the interior spirit penetrates its enduring meaning. The flight of the eagle carries him with the rapidly beating wings of theology to the highest contemplation of the things that are and are not. The things that are are the things, created by the unique cause of all things, which do not escape entirely from human and angelic understanding. The things that are not are those beyond the power of all intelligence to understand. John, in his mystic flight, is transported to the heart of reality, which surpasses understanding. The ineffable soaring of his spirit carries him to the mysteries of the beginning of all things, where he perceives the superessential unity and supersubstantial distinction of the beginning and the Word—that is, of the Father and Son—both incomprehensible. Hence the opening words of John are: "In the beginning was the Word."

The mystical eagle flies over the mountain of theology, where he gazes on the eternal truths of the generation of the Word in the bosom of the Trinity and the creation of the primordial causes of all things in the Word. The light from the mountain of theology filters down to the valley of history, the place temporal reality inhabits. Eriugena enters this world by means of the four senses of Scripture and studies the coming of the light by way of the precursor John the Baptist. In the valley of history the world of human nature is illumined, and the Incarnation is the price paid for its deification.

In an age in which most sermons were moralistic in tone, Eriugena's homily is profoundly speculative. The fortune of the homily in the Middle

Ages was considerable, but it circulated under the names of other authors such as Origen, Gregory of Nazianzen, and John Chrysostom. The list of the homily's readers through the centuries includes Gilbert of Poitiers in the twelfth, Robert Grosseteste and Aquinas in the thirteenth, Meister Eckhart in the fourteenth, Nicholas of Cusa in the fifteenth, and Erasmus in the sixteenth. (It was Erasmus who finally denied the authorship to Origen, but he could not restore it to Eriugena.) Still, the *Vox Spiritualis Aquilae* . . . was one channel through which Eriugena influenced the Middle Ages.

If Eriugena's birth and early years in Ireland after 810 are wrapped in a mist that refuses to lift, so too are his last years and his demise about 877 in northern France. William of Malmesbury could not resist completing his fictive biography with another fiction: Eriugena, he said, had departed from France late in life under a cloud of controversy and had traveled to England at the invitation of Alfred the Great. Having settled at the monastery of Malmesbury, Eriugena was murdered by his students, who stabbed him to death with their pens. While it makes for a colorful story and one much appreciated by students, it is not true. Eriugena appears to have remained at the court of Charles the Bald, who also died in 877. The philosopher seems to have been occupied in his last years with his works on the Gospel according to John and might have died before completing the commentary.

The last dated composition of Eriugena is a Latin poem apparently written to celebrate the dedication of Charles the Bald's new chapel at Compiègne in May 877. Since this church was designed in the shape of an octagon, Eriugena begins with praise of the number eight, which had figured so prominently in the mystical speculations at the end of the *Periphyseon*. After an investigation of the quadripartite and octave natures of the seasons, signs of the zodiac, and history of Salvation, the poet reflects on the octagonal church. The king is seen on a high throne, wearing a golden crown and bearing golden scepters, and he gazes on the resplendent church he has constructed. Imagery and language similar to this poem of one hundred hexameters are to be found in the *Codex Aureus*, a manuscript of the four Gospels made for Charles the Bald in 870, which survives today in Munich as one of the most precious books of the Middle Ages. The lines of Eriugena's poem are reworked in the verses that run around the portrait of Christ in Majesty:

> Christ, the very life of men, the greatest glory of the superior world,
> Balances with wonderful division the fourfold world.

Christ is, as the painting so splendidly reveals, the ruler of the fourfold world of the four Prophets and four Evangelists. The meaning of the image deepens when one connects it to the *Periphyseon* and the *Vox Spiritualis Aquilae* . . . , where Eriugena contemplated the parallelism of the tetragonal worlds—material, sensible, intellectual, and spiritual—indwelling in humanity.

Though he was not, in a formal sense, a rationalist, no thinker of the early Middle Ages extended to reason the latitude that Eriugena did. In the *Vox Spiritualis Aquilae* . . . Eriugena describes how Peter and John had run to the tomb of Christ: Peter stood for faith, John for intelligence, and the tomb for Scripture. Though John had arrived first at the tomb and both would enter, it was Peter who entered first. According to the Bible, one needed, said Eriugena, to believe in order to understand. After the Fall human reason was clouded, but Christ provided humanity with an infallible source of truth. The starting point for all speculation is Sacred Scripture; but the treatment of Scripture may be exceedingly rational, as in the *Periphyseon*. Moreover, Eriugena could be most discriminating when weighing his patristic authorities, here reconciling Augustine and Pseudo-Dionysius, there preferring Gregory of Nyssa over Augustine. He critically considered received opinion to arrive at his own, often original points of view. The claim that his position on faith and reason must remove him from the company of philosophers does violence to the concept of philosophy in the Middle Ages. For Eriugena there was no final contradiction between reason and faith, for, as he said in the *De Diuinae Praedestinatione*, true religion and true philosophy were one and the same. Even Plato was a religious thinker who cloaked difficult doctrine in metaphor and myth. Moreover, if Scripture was for Eriugena the given from which speculation must begin, in the return the final truth would be the beatific vision itself, when knowledge would pass into wisdom and the secrets of the universe would be revealed to purified souls and blessed intellects.

In the end, it would seem best to call Eriugena a Christian metaphysician, though few philosophers have made the pursuit of knowledge and the contemplation of truth as integral to the nature of the universe as he. His thought was formed in the midst of the Carolingian renaissance by a half century of reflection on the Bible, the liberal arts, and the Latin and Greek Fathers of the church. But Eriugena's Europe in the mid ninth century suffered from severe political disruption: the fragmentation of Charlemagne's empire, resistance to central royal authority within the kingdom, and invasion by the Vikings from without. This historical context informs Eriugena's work, particularly the poems and the *Periphyseon*, where Eriugena recognized the dangers faced by the kingdom and his king and patron, Charles the Bald. In his distinctive way Eriugena responded to the ninth century's need for reassurance about the nature of the divine purpose. Beyond a disturbed and ever changeable present there would be, he argued, a return to the immutable and divine. Reversals of fortune in this world did not matter; he urged his king and fellow Christians to fix their eyes on the unalterable truth of a divine design that would catch them all up in a majestic return to God.

The sheer range of Eriugena's intellectual endeavors is breathtaking: he was not only a systematic and synthetic thinker but also a glossator, controversialist, poet, annotator, translator, commentator, and homilist. If his philosophical bent of mind requires a label, Neoplatonist surely fits; but it was a Neoplatonism of his own making, which married the divergent traditions of East and West. The *Periphyseon* remains a remarkable synthesis of his thought, surely the most ambitious and adventurous intellectual undertaking of the early Middle Ages. As the pieces of the Eriugenian puzzle continue to fall into place in the late twentieth century and early twenty-first, appreciation of Eriugena's genius is bound to grow and the pure excitement of reading him is bound to build. Certainly the depth of his digressive and enfolding thought has as yet found no bottom.

Bibliographies:

I. P. Sheldon-Williams, "A Bibliography of the Works of Johannes Scottus Eriugena," *Journal of Ecclesiastical History*, 10 (1959): 198-224;

Sheldon-Williams, "A List of the Works Doubtfully or Wrongly Attributed to Johannes Scottus Eriugena," *Journal of Ecclesiastical History*, 15 (1964): 76-98;

Edouard Jeauneau, *Jean Scot, Homélie sur le Prologue de Jean, Sources Chrétiennes*, no. 151 (Paris: Editions du Cerf, 1969), pp. 171-198;

Mary Brennan, "A Bibliography of Publications in the Field of Eriugenian Studies, 1800-1975," in *Studi Medievali*, third series 18, no. 1 (1977): 401-447;

Brennan, *A Guide to Eriugenian Studies (1930-1987)*, Vestigia, 5 (Fribourg, Switzerland: Editions universitaires / Paris: Editions du Cerf, 1989).

References:

G. H. Allard, ed., *Jean Scot Ecrivain: Actes du IVe Colloque international: Montréal 28 août-2 septembre 1983*, Cahiers d'études médiévales; cahier spécial 1 (Montréal: Bellarmin, 1986; Paris: Vrin, 1986);

Allard, ed., *Johannis Scoti Eriugenae Periphyseon: Indices générales* (Montréal: Institut d'études médiévales, 1983; Paris: Vrin, 1983);

Werner Beierwaltes, ed., *Eriugena Redivivus: Zur Wirkungsgeschichte seines Denkens im Mittelalter und im Übergang zur Neuzeit: Vorträge des V. Internationalen Eriugena-Colloquiums, Werner-Reimers-Stiftung Bad Homburg 26.-30. August 1985* (Heidelberg: Winter, 1987);

Beierwaltes, ed., *Eriugena: Studien zu seinen Quellen. Vorträge des III. Internationalen Eriugena-Colloquiums, Freiburg im Breisgau, 27.-30. August 1979* (Heidelberg: Winter, 1980);

Mary Brennan, "Materials for the Biography of Johannes Scottus Eriugena," *Studi Medievali*, third series 27 (1986): 412-460;

Maïeul Cappuyns, "Les *Bibli Vulfadi* et Jean Scot Erigène," *Recherches de Théologie ancienne et médiévale*, 33 (1966): 137-139;

Cappuyns, *Jean Scot Érigène, sa vie, son oeuvre, sa pensée* (Louvain: Abbaye du Mont César, 1933; Paris: Desclée, de Brouwer, 1933; reprinted, Brussels: Culture et Civilisation, 1964);

John J. Contreni, "The Biblical Glosses of Haimo of Auxerre and John Scottus Eriugena," *Speculum*, 51 (July 1976): 411-434;

Contreni, *The Cathedral School of Laon from 850 to 930: Its Manuscripts and Masters*, Münchener Beiträge zur Mediävistik und Renaissance-Forschung, 29 (Munich: Arbeo-Gesellschaft, 1978);

Contreni, "Masters and Medicine in Northern France during the Reign of Charles the Bald," in *Charles the Bald: Court and Kingdom. Papers Based on a Colloquium Held at London in April 1979*, edited by Margaret Gibson and Janet Nelson (Oxford: BAR International Series, 1981), pp. 333-350;

Paul Edward Dutton, "Raoul Glaber's 'De diuina quaternitate': An Unnoticed Reading of Eriugena's Translation of the *Ambigua* of Maximus the Confessor," *Mediaeval Studies*, 42 (1980): 431-453;

Dutton and Edouard Jeauneau, "The Verses of the *Codex Aureus* of Saint-Emmeram," *Studi Medievali*, third series 24, no. 1 (1983): 75-120;

Stephen Gersh, *From Iamblichus to Eriugena: An Investigation of the Prehistory and Evolution of the Pseudo-Dionysian Tradition* (Leiden: Brill, 1978);

Etienne Gilson, *History of Christian Philosophy in the Middle Ages* (New York: Random House, 1955);

Edouard Jeauneau, "La bibliothèque de Cluny et les oeuvres de l'Érigène," in *Pierre Abélard, Pierre le Vénérable: Les courants philosophiques, littéraires et artistiques en occident au milieu du XIIe siècle. Colloque international du CNRS* (Paris: Centre national de la recherche scientifique, 1975), pp. 703-725;

Jeauneau, "Dans le sillage de l'Érigène: Une homélie d'Héric d'Auxerre sur le prologue de Jean," *Studi Medievali*, third series 11 (1970): 937-955;

Jeauneau, *Etudes Erigéniennes* (Paris: Etudes Augustiniennes, 1987);

Jeauneau, "Guillaume de Malmesbury, premier éditeur anglais du *Periphyseon*," in *"Sapientiae Doctrina": Mélanges de théologie et de littérature médiévales offerts à Dom Hildebrand Bascour O.S.B.*, special issue of *Recherches de Théologie ancienne et médiévale* (1980): 148-179;

Jeauneau, "Pseudo-Dionysius, Gregory of Nyssa, and Maximus the Confessor in the Works of John Scottus Eriugena," in *Carolingian Essays: Andrew W. Mellon Lectures in Early Christian Studies*, edited by Uta-Renate Blumenthal (Washington, D.C.: Catholic University of America Press, 1983), pp. 137-149;

M. L. W. Laistner, *Thought and Letters in Western Europe, A.D. 500 to 900*, second edition (Ithaca & London: Cornell University Press, 1957);

John Marenbon, *Early Medieval Philosophy (480-1150): An Introduction* (London: Routledge & Kegan Paul, 1983);

Marenbon, *From the Circle of Alcuin to the School of Auxerre: Logic, Theology, and Philosophy in the Early Middle Ages* (Cambridge: Cambridge University Press, 1981);

Marenbon, "Wulfad, Charles the Bald and John Scottus Eriugena," in *Charles the Bald: Court and Kingdom. Papers Based on a Colloquium Held at London in April 1979*, edited by Margaret Gibson and Janet Nelson (Oxford: BAR International Series, 1981), pp. 375-383;

Dominic J. O'Meara, ed., *Neoplatonism and Christian Thought* (Albany: State University of New York Press, 1981);

John J. O'Meara, *Eriugena*, Irish Life and Culture, 17 (Cork: Cultural Relations Committee of Ireland, 1969);

O'Meara, *Eriugena* (Oxford: Clarendon Press, 1988);

O'Meara and Ludwig Bieler, eds., *The Mind of Eriugena: Papers of a Colloquium, Dublin 14-18 July 1970* (Dublin: Irish University Press, 1973);

René Roques, ed., *Jean Scot Erigène et l'histoire de la philosophie: Actes du Colloque No. 561 du CNRS à Laon, du 7 au 12 juillet 1975* (Paris: Centre national de la recherche scientifique, 1977);

I. P. Sheldon-Williams, "The Greek Christian Platonist Tradition from the Cappadocians to Maximus and Eriugena," in *The Cambridge History of Later Greek and Early Medieval Philosophy*, edited by A. H. Armstrong (Cambridge: Cambridge University Press, 1967), pp. 421-533;

Brian Stock, "Observations on the Use of Augustine by Johannus Scottus Eriugena," *Harvard Theological Review*, 60 (1967): 213-220;

Stock, "The Philosophical Anthropology of Johannes Scottus Eriugena," *Studi Medievali*, third series 8 (1967): 1-57;

J. M. Wallace-Hadrill, *The Frankish Church* (Oxford: Clarendon Press, 1983).

Manuscripts:

Several important manuscripts that can be directly associated with Eriugena and his circle survive. The most significant is Reims, Bibliothèque municipale 875, which contains the first extant versions of the first four books of the *Periphyseon*. Scholars now think that this manuscript was Eriugena's working copy of his masterpiece. Caroline scribes wrote out an early version of the work, to which corrections and substantial additions were made by scribes working under the author's supervision. Two of these scribes wrote in an Irish minuscule script and, hence, have been called i^1 and i^2. It has long been suspected that one of these scribes might be identified with Eriugena himself, and a study of the entire question is being prepared for inclusion in the series *Autographa Medii Aevi*. If Reims 875 represents the first two extant stages of the *Periphyseon*, then Bamberg, Staatsbibliothek, Philos. 2/1 represents the next extant stage. This manuscript of the first three books of the *Periphyseon* contains a copy of the enlarged Reims version with some new additions and corrections entered by i^2.

Al-Farabi
(Abu Nasr Muhammad ibn Muhammad ibn Tarkhan ibn Uzalagh al-Farabi)

(circa 870 - 950)

Deborah L. Black
Pontifical Institute of Mediaeval Studies, Toronto

PRINCIPAL WORKS: *Al-Tawti'ah, aw Al-Risalah Allati Suddira bi-hi al Mantiq* (Introduction, or Prefatory Treatise to Logic, written circa 900);

Al-Fusal al-Khamsah (The Five Chapters [on Logic], written circa 900);

Kitab Iysaghuji ay Al-Madkhal (Short Commentary on Porphyry's *Isagoge* [Introduction], written circa 900);

Kitab Qataghuriyas ay Al-Maqulat (Short Commentary on Aristotle's *Categories*, written circa 900);

Kitab Bari Arminiyas ay Al-'Ibarah (Short Commentary on Aristotle's *On Interpretation*, written circa 900);

Kitab al-Qiyas (Commentary on Aristotle's *Prior Analytics*, written circa 900);

Kitab al-Qiyas al-Saghir (Short Commentary on Aristotle's *Prior Analytics*, written circa 900);

Kitab al-Tahlil (Book of Analysis, written circa 900);

Kitab al-Amkinah al-Mughlitah (Book of Sophistical Topics, written circa 900);

Kitab al-Jadal (Book of Dialectic [Commentary on Aristotle's *Topics*], written circa 900);

Kitab al-Burhan (Book of Demonstration [Commentary on Aristotle's *Posterior Analytics*], written circa 900);

Kitab Shara'it al-Yaqin (On the Conditions of Certitude, written circa 900);

Kitab al-Khatabah (Book of Rhetoric, written circa 900);

Didascalia in Rhetoricam Aristotelis (Lessons on Aristotle's *Rhetoric*, written circa 900);

Kitab al-Shi'r (Book of Poetry, written circa 900);

Qawanin al-Shi'r (Canons of Poetry, written circa 900);

Sharh li-Kitab Aristutalis fi al-'Ibarah (Long Commentary on Aristotle's *On Interpretation*, written circa 900);

Kitab al-Tanbih 'ala Sabil al-Sa'adah (Indication of the Way of Happiness, written circa 900);

Kitab al-Alfaz al-Musta'malah fi al-Mantiq (Book of Utterances Employed in Logic, written circa 900);

Risalah Fi Ma Yanbaghi Qabla Ta'allum al-Falsafah (Treatise on What Must Precede the Study of Philosophy, written circa 900);

Kitab al-Musiqa al-Kabir (Great Book on Music, written circa 900);

Al-Radd 'ala Yahya al-Nahwiy (Refutation of John the Grammarian, written circa 900);
Fi-ma Yasihhu wa-ma La Yasihhu min Ahkam al-Nujum (On What Is Sound and Unsound in the Science of Astrology, written circa 900);
Ihsa' al-'Ulum (Catalogue of the Sciences, written circa 900);
Kitab al-Huruf (Book of Letters or Book of Particles, written circa 900);
Fi Aghrad al-Hakim fi Kull Magalah min al-Kitab al-Mawsum Bi-al-Huruf (The Aims of Aristotle's *Metaphysics*, written circa 900);
Talkhis Nawamis Aflatun (Commentary on Plato's *Laws*, written circa 900);
Kitab al-Millah (Book of Religion, written circa 900);
Kitab al-Jam' Bayn Ra'yay al-Hakimayn Aflatun al-Ilahiy wa-Aristutalis (The Harmonization of the Opinions of the Two Sages, the Divine Plato and Aristotle, written circa 900);
Risalah fi al'Aql (Letter Concerning the Intellect, written circa 900);
Falsafah Aflatun (The Philosophy of Plato, written circa 900);
Falsafah Aristutalis (The Philosophy of Aristotle, written circa 900);
Tahsil al-Sa'adah (The Attainment of Happiness, written circa 900);
Al-Fusal al-Muntaza'ah (Selected Aphorisms or Aphorisms of the Statesman, written circa 900);
Al-Siyasah Al-Madaniyah (The Political Regime, written circa 900);
Mabadi' Ara' Ahl al-Madinah al-Fadilah (Principles of the Opinions of the People of the Virtuous City, written circa 942; revised, 948).

EDITIONS: *Alfarabi's philosophische Abhandlungen*, edited by Friedrich Dieterici (Leiden, Netherlands: Brill, 1890);
Rasa'il al-Farabi (Hyderabad, India: 1927);
Alfarabius De Platonis Philosophia, edited by Franz Rosenthal and Richard Walzer (London: Warburg Institute, 1943);
Risalah fi al-'Aql, edited by Maurice Bouyges (Beirut: Imprimerie Catholique, 1948);
Compendium Legum Platonis, edited by Francesco Gabrieli (London: Warburg Institute, 1952);
"Kitab al-Shi'r li-Abi Nasr al-Farabi," edited by Muhsin Mahdi, *Shi'r*, 3 (1959): 91-96;
Sharh al-Farabi li-Kitab Aristutalis fi al-'Ibarah, edited by Wilhelm Kutsch and Stanley Marrow (Beirut: Imprimerie Catholique, 1960);
Kitab al-Jam' Bayn Ra'yay al-Hakimayn Aflatun al-Ilahiy wa-Aristutalis, edited by Albert Nader (Beirut: Imprimerie Catholique, 1960);
Falsafah Aristutalis, edited by Madhi (Beirut: Dar Majal-lat Shi'r, 1961);
Alfarabi's Political Regime: Al-Siyasa al-Madaniyya also Known as The Treatise on the Principles of Being, edited by Fauzi M. Najjar (Beirut: Imprimerie Catholique, 1964);
Kitab al-Musiqa al-Kabir, edited by Ghattas Khashabah (Cairo: Dar al-Katib al-Arabi, 1967);
Kitab al-Alfaz al-Musta'malah fi al-Mantiq, edited by Mahdi (Beirut: Dar el-Mashreq, 1968);
Ihsa' al-'Ulum, edited by Uthman Amin (Cairo: Librarie Anglo-Egyptienne, 1968);
Kitab al-Millah wa-Nusus Ukhra, edited by Mahdi (Beirut: Dar el-Mashreq, 1968);
Al-Farabi's Book of Letters (Kitab al-Huruf): Commentary on Aristotle's "Metaphysics," edited by Mahdi (Beirut: Dar el-Mashreq, 1969);
Al-Farabi: Deux ouvrages inédits sur la réthoriques, edited and translated by Jacques Langhade and Marion Grignaschi (Beirut: Dar el-Mashreq, 1971);
Al-Farabi's Fusul Muntaza'ah, edited by Najjar (Beirut: Dar el-Mashreq, 1971);
"The Arabic Text of Alfarabi's Against John the Grammarian," edited by Mahdi, in *Medieval and Middle Eastern Studies in Honor of Aziz Suryal Atiya*, edited by Sami A. Hanna (Leiden, Netherlands: Brill, 1972), pp. 268-284;
Tahsil al-Sa'adah, edited by Jafar Al Yasin (Beirut: Al-Andaloss, 1981);
Al-Mantiq 'inda al-Farabi, 4 volumes, edited by Rafiq al-'Ajam and Majid Fakhry (Beirut: Dar el-Mashreq, 1986-87);
Kitab al-Tanbih 'ala Sabil al-Sa'adah, edited by Al Yasin (Beirut: Dar al-Manahel, 1987);
Risalat Falsafiyat, edited by Al Yasin (Beirut: Dar al-Manahel, 1987).

EDITIONS IN ENGLISH: "Farabi's Canons of Poetry," edited and translated by A. J. Arberry, *Rivista degli Studi Orientali*, 17 (1938): 266-278;
"Al-Farabi's Introductory Sections on Logic," edited and translated by D. M. Dunlop, *Islamic Quarterly*, 2 (1955): 264-282 [translation of *Al-Fusul al-Khamsah*];
"Al-Farabi's *Eisagoge*," edited and translated by Dunlop, *Islamic Quarterly*, 3 (1956): 117-138;
"Al-Farabi's Introductory *Risalah* on Logic," edited and translated by Dunlop, *Islamic Quar-*

terly, 3 (1957): 224-235 [translation of *Al Tawti'ah*];

"Al-Farabi's Paraphrase of the *Categories* of Aristotle," edited and translated by Dunlop, *Islamic Quarterly*, 4 (1958): 168-197; 5 (1959): 21-54;

Fusul al-Madani: Aphorisms of the Statesman, edited and translated by Dunlop (Cambridge: Cambridge University Press, 1961);

"The Political Regime," translated by Fauzi M. Najjar, and "Summary on Plato's *Laws*," translated by Muhsin Mahdi, in *Medieval Political Philosophy: A Sourcebook*, edited by Mahdi and Ralph Lerner (Ithaca, N.Y.: Cornell University Press, 1963), pp. 31-57, 83-94;

Al-Farabi's Short Commentary on Aristotle's "Prior Analytics," translated by Nicholas Rescher (Pittsburgh: Pittsburgh University Press, 1963);

"Alfarabi against Philoponus," translated by Madhi, *Journal of Near Eastern Studies*, 26 (1967): 233-260;

Alfarabi's Philosophy of Plato and Aristotle, translated by Madhi (Ithaca, N.Y.: Cornell University Press, 1969);

"The Letter Concerning the Intellect," translated by Arthur Hyman, in *Medieval Philosophy: The Christian, Islamic, and Jewish Traditions*, edited by Hyman and James J. Walsh (Indianapolis: Hackett, 1973), pp. 215-221;

Al-Farabi's Commentary and Short Treatise on Aristotle's "De Interpretatione," edited and translated by F. W. Zimmermann (Oxford: Oxford University Press, 1981);

Al-Farabi on the Perfect State: Abu Nasr al-Farabi's Mabadi' Ara' Ahl al-Madina al-Fadila, edited and translated by Richard Walzer (Oxford: Clarendon Press, 1985).

Al-Farabi's importance in the history of Islamic philosophy may be gathered from the epithet commonly applied to him by later philosophers. Known as the "Second Teacher"—second, that is, only to Aristotle—al-Farabi in many ways set the course for developments in later Islamic philosophy. While greatly admiring Aristotle and adopting an Aristotelian approach to logic and epistemology, al-Farabi consciously and creatively supplements the Stagirite's teachings with the emanative cosmology and metaphysics of Neoplatonism and with the political philosophy of Plato.

Despite his importance and the esteem in which he was held, knowledge of al-Farabi's life is rather scant, and few of his writings can be dated with any certainty or even ordered chronologically. The son of a military officer, he was born around 870 in the village of Wasij of the district of Farab in Turkestan. He was educated in Damascus and later in Baghdad, where he lived and taught until 942. In the ninth century the school of Alexandria, an important center of philosophical and medical scholarship, settled at Baghdad after a series of peregrinations. During that century it had become the headquarters of several well-known Christian scholars; al-Farabi was one of its first Islamic students, studying with such noted logicians as Yuhanna ibn Haylan and Abu Bishr Matta. The logician and translator Yahya Ibn 'Adi is said to have been al-Farabi's pupil.

Al-Farabi appears to have held none of the medical, administrative, or religious appointments that provided the financial means for other illustrious Islamic philosophers. Instead, he is reported to have led a humble and even ascetic life, working as a laborer in the gardens and vineyards of Damascus, sustained by a meager diet, and studying philosophy by the light of the night watchmen's lamps. While not a Sufi, he is reported to have dressed in simple, brown Sufi garb, a mark of his intellectual independence and unwillingness to compromise philosophical ideals for political patronage and recognition. In 942, however, al-Farabi seems to have mitigated these scruples, accepting the invitation of the Shiite prince Sayf al-Dawlah to reside at his court in Aleppo. Most of al-Farabi's writings appear to date from his Damascus and Baghdad periods. What is believed to be his last work was composed just before his departure to Aleppo and was later revised.

In 948 al-Farabi is reported to have taken a trip to Egypt. Most scholars believe he returned to Aleppo and died there in 950 at the age of eighty, but some medieval biographers say that he died a violent death at the hands of highwaymen on the road from Damascus to Ashkelon.

The full extent and content of the Farabian corpus is unclear: the medieval Arabic biographers list more than one hundred works under his name, but many of these are lost. The works that are available vary in style and purpose: some are introductory texts in logic and philosophy, some are comprehensive philosophical commentaries on ancient texts, others are original philosophical discussions, and still others appear to be popular treatises aimed at an educated but nonspecialist audience. By later medieval philosophers al-Farabi was especially noted for his logical expertise, and many of the extant texts address logical concerns. But the area on which al-Farabi's thought had the most influence in both Jewish and Muslim circles, and on which most modern scholarship has centered, is political philosophy—in particular, the relations between philosophy and religion.

The interpretation of al-Farabi's thought is difficult, in part because of the large quantity of lost writings but also because of problems in the writings that are available. Al-Farabi's metaphysical teachings, for example, were long misunderstood because of the false attribution to him of treatises now generally believed to have been written by a follower of Avicenna. But even with the resolution of this problem, difficulties remain. In some works al-Farabi espouses the Neoplatonic teaching of emanation; in others he shies away from all discussion of divine and metaphysical matters. And while al-Farabi was clearly interested in showing that religion and philosophy were compatible, his deliberate ambiguity has made it difficult to determine the extent to which his view of religion is purely political and expedient. Still, some elements of al-Farabi's philosophical outlook are constant and unquestionable. Perhaps most characteristic is his intense interest in the nature of language and his conviction that linguistic analysis is essential in any effort to arrive at philosophical distinctions. Equally pervasive is his commitment to a balance between theoretical and practical pursuits within philosophy: every philosopher, he says, has the obligation to engage in political activity if he is able; and every adequate political theory, in turn, must be based on a sound theoretical grasp of the nature of things.

Al-Farabi's logical writings are principally commentaries on the Aristotelian logical treatises, or *Organon,* and reflect in part his historical links to the school of Alexandria. Many of the texts are directed to the beginning student, but a few represent more detailed and sophisticated discussions of Aristotelian logic for advanced readers.

Among the former group are the *Al-Tawti'ah, aw Al-Risalah Allati Suddira bi-hi al-Mantiq* (Introduction, or Prefatory Treatise to Logic, circa 900) and *Al-Fusul al-Khamsah* (The Five Chapters [on Logic], circa 900), which introduce the reader to the study of logic and define basic logical terms. Despite their introductory character, these treatises present themes that are central to al-Farabi's overall logical perspective. Logic is treated as an instrumental science, whose role is to safeguard the mind from error. It includes both syllogistic and nonsyllogistic branches, and it culminates in the study of demonstrative science, which al-Farabi often identifies as the method of philosophy itself. He also addresses the relationship between grammar and logic, a thorny issue in his day and a point of controversy between the philosophers and Arabic grammarians. Al-Farabi treats logic as a kind of universal grammar, providing the rules that govern thought and reasoning and are thus common to all languages. Grammar, by contrast, is restricted to the study of the rules and conventions of language itself and so varies according to the variety of linguistic groups: "Thus the relation of the science of grammar to the language and the expressions is as the relation of the science of logic to the intellect and the intelligibles, and just as grammar is the touchstone of language where there is the possibility of an error in language in regard to the method of expression, so the science of logic is the touchstone of the intellect where there is the possibility of an error in regard to the intelligibles."

Al-Farabi's commentaries on Aristotelian logic, including the *Isagoge* (Introduction) of Porphyry, are neither mere summaries of the original texts nor line-by-line exegeses. Rather, like many of his commentaries, they use Aristotle's writings as a point of departure to present al-Farabi's interpretations of Aristotelian logic and the school tradition that had evolved around it, a tradition that sometimes incorporated non-Aristotelian elements such as those of the logic of the Stoics. Particularly important are al-Farabi's efforts to apply Aristotle's principles in an Arabic context, a feature of the commentaries on *On Interpretation* and *Prior Analytics*. In the latter commentary, for example, while declaring his total fidelity to the canons of Aristotle's syllogistic, al-Farabi vows to "strive to express these matters, as much as possible, by means of words familiar to people who use the Arabic language," so as to lessen any ambiguities that may arise.

Also falling within the scope of al-Farabi's logical writings are his discussions of the arts of rhetoric and poetics. In the Alexandrian tradition Aristotle's *Rhetoric* and *Poetics* were included in the *Organon,* and al-Farabi accordingly treats them as works of logic. In the case of rhetoric, al-Farabi left two writings, one of which survives only partially and in Latin translation, the *Didascalia in Rhetoricam Aristotelis* (Lessons on Aristotle's *Rhetoric*, circa 900). It consists of a preface and the first few pages of what was to have been a close textual commentary. The preface presents al-Farabi's own views of the nature and subject matter of rhetoric. Of particular interest is his rather curious effort to explain the relationship of the *Rhetoric* to the rest of the *Organon*, using his own version of Plato's allegory of the cave in the *Republic*: the study of logic is viewed as a gradual ascent from the study of the most general concepts used in human discourse about the material world, concepts that are shared by philosophers and nonphilosophers alike. These concepts are discussed in Aristotle's *Categories*, which represents the lowest level of logical understanding, analogous to the understanding of those in Plato's cave who view only the shadows of things. The student of logic, in his gradual ascent out of the cave, studies in succession the *Categories*, *On Interpretation*, and *Prior Analytics*, until he reaches the summit of logical instruction, the *Posterior Analytics*, which enables him to view directly the realities in the world outside the cave. But like Plato's allegory, Aristotle's logic also implies a descent back into the cave to communicate to those who still view only the shadows. This descent is accomplished through the remaining logical arts, which are treated in the *Topics*, *Sophistical Refutations*, *Rhetoric*, and finally the *Poetics*, the lowest of the logical arts. While this strange allegory presents a more pejorative view of dialectic, rhetoric, and poetics than is usually the case in al-Farabi's writings, it does give colorful expression to a pervasive theme in the Second Teacher's philosophy: the treatment of rhetoric and poetics as the tools of religion and politics, best suited for communicating in popular and imaginative terms the truths that are known scientifically through philosophical demonstration.

Al-Farabi's second treatment of rhetoric is his *Kitab al-Khatabah* (Book of Rhetoric, circa 900), a work quite different in character from the *Didascalia in Rhetoricam Aristotelis* and much broader in scope. Perhaps the most important feature of this work is its detailed discussion of the epistemological status of rhetoric, which occupies almost all of the first half of the text. In the course of this discussion al-Farabi offers some of his most sophisticated considerations of epistemological topics whose significance extends well beyond the study of rhetorical argument, such as the distinction between opinion and certitude, the nature of doubt and opposition, and the notions of necessity and possibility. The text also considers the formal side of rhetorical argumentation, discussing in detail the various types of enthymeme and the argument from example, as well as the nature of rhetorical signs and proofs.

On the topic of poetics al-Farabi left two short discussions. The *Qawanin al-Shi'r* (Canons of Poetry, circa 900) appears to draw on Alexandrian discussions of logic and deals with such issues as the place of poetics in the study of logic and the differences between the intentions of poetry and those of sophistry. It also contains an unusual classification of Greek poetic genres, probably based on now-lost texts of literary criticism of late Greek origin. This classification departs greatly from that in Aristotle's *Poetics*, and its use by al-Farabi was to leave its mark on later commentaries on the *Poetics*, such as that of Avicenna. Al-Farabi's *Kitab al-Shi'r* (Book of Poetry, circa 900) is a somewhat more original consideration of poetics and focuses on the notion of "imaginative evocation" (*takhyil*), a concept that became identified in later Arabic philosophy as the goal of poetic imitation.

The *Kitab al-Alfaz al-Musta'malah fi al-Mantiq* (Book of Utterances Employed in Logic, circa 900) is aimed at beginning logic students and focuses, as do many of al-Farabi's logical writings, on defining and classifying the technical terms used in logic. Apparently the work was meant to be preceded by an ethical treatise, the *Kitab al-Tanbih 'ala Sabil al-Sa'adah* (Indication of the Way of Happiness, circa 900), and to be followed by a series of short commentaries on the *Organon*, thus providing a total program of study for the novice philosopher.

Al-Farabi's writings outside the realm of logic were many and varied, although most are now lost. Some works, such as the brief *Risalah Fi Ma Yanbaghi Qabla Ta'allum al-Falsafah* (Treatise on What Must Precede the Study of Philosophy, circa 900), are basic introductions to the divisions, history, and proper course of study of philosophy. Al-Farabi is also known as a practitioner and theorist of music, his most comprehensive treatment of the topic being his *Kitab al-Musiqa al-Kabir* (Great Book on Music, circa 900). Of some interest to philosophers is al-Farabi's attempt in this work to apply the Aristotelian conception of a science, as outlined in the *Posterior Analytics*, to the study of harmonics. Also extant are some of al-Farabi's shorter treatises devoted to topics in the physical sciences. *Al-Radd 'ala Yahya al-Nahwiy* (Reformation of John the Grammarian, circa 900) is a refutation of the Greek Christian philosopher of the sixth century John Philoponus, who opposed Aristotle's teaching on the eternity of the world.

Al-Farabi also wrote a treatise on the nature of the vacuum, and a brief discussion, in reply to the request of an astrologer, Abu Ishaq Ibrahim ibn ‘Abdullah al-Baghdadi, outlining the limits of astrology in predicting the future. That the heavenly bodies exert a causal influence on human affairs is a tenet of al-Farabi's own cosmology; but he notes that human science can attain only limited knowledge of the causal sequences that lead to particular events.

Al-Farabi's *Ihsa' al-'Ulum* (Catalogue of the Sciences, circa 900) was widely used by Arabic authors as an introduction to philosophical study and was twice translated into Hebrew. Also translated into Latin in the twelfth century by Gerard of Cremona, it had an important influence on the development of the Aristotelian conception of the sciences in the West in the twelfth and thirteenth centuries. The preface offers a classification of all the recognized sciences, or branches of learning, their parts, and their contents. Al-Farabi identifies five major sciences: grammar, logic, mathematics, the science of physics and metaphysics, and political science, which includes the Islamic religious disciplines of jurisprudence (*fiqh*) and dialectical theology (*kalam*). The preface concludes with some remarks on the purpose and utility of such an enumeration: it will indicate the proper beginning and order of the study of the sciences and will orient the student to the study he is about to undertake; it will show him the relative value of various disciplines; and it will alert him to those who profess expertise in some or all of the sciences but who are in fact charlatans.

Al-Farabi's discussion of logic and grammar in this treatise reflects the conviction that grammar provides the rules for language use within a particular linguistic group, whereas logic provides the rules for thought as manifested in any language whatsoever. Grammar includes the understanding of the meaning of vocabulary items, the knowledge of syntax and morphology, the rules of pronunciation, the principles of metrical composition, and calligraphy. Al-Farabi's logic is thoroughly Aristotelian and is organized around the books of the *Organon*, including the *Rhetoric* and the *Poetics*. The purpose of logic is to provide rules "whose role is to rectify the intellect and to show humans the way to the correct path and to the truth, in everything among the intelligibles about which it is possible to err." Mathematics has seven subdivisions: arithmetic, geometry, optics, astronomy, music, the science of weights and measures, and mechanics. For the fourth science al-Farabi groups physics and metaphysics together and defines the former as the science "which studies natural bodies and the accidents which subsist in them," as well as their causes and effects and the laws that govern them. Al-Farabi's conception of physics revolves around such Aristotelian principles as the four causes, and its divisions are marked by the various physical treatises within the Aristotelian corpus. Theology, or divine science, is assigned three principal divisions, all of which are contained, according to al-Farabi, in Aristotle's *Metaphysics*. The first division corresponds to ontology and is described as the investigation of "existents and their accidents, insofar as they are existents"—that is, the study of being as being. The second division includes the metaphysical investigation of the first principles of demonstration pertaining to the particular theoretical sciences, reflecting the Aristotelian claim that no science can investigate or prove its own first principles. The final branch of metaphysics is that which gives it its Arabic name of divine science, or theology, namely, the investigation of beings that are neither bodies nor in bodies. Al-Farabi makes no mention here of the theory of emanation or of any other metaphysical treatises apart from Aristotle's *Metaphysics*, whereas in some of his other writings the non-Aristotelian doctrine of emanation has a prominent role.

In the final section of the *Ihsa' al-'Ulum* al-Farabi considers political science, which comprises ethics and the religious sciences of *fiqh* and *kalam*. The theme that unites these sciences is that of voluntary action, its direction and goals. For texts al-Farabi lists Aristotle's *Politics*, which was known only by reputation, and Plato's *Republic*. The inclusion of the religious sciences of Islam as a part of political science is original to al-Farabi and reflects his creative efforts to apply Greek philosophy within an Islamic context. Al-Farabi's decision to conclude his discussion of the sciences with a consideration of political philosophy reflects his conviction that a sound political order must rest on a sound metaphysical understanding of the nature and place in the world of the human being.

No area of al-Farabi's philosophy is more difficult to interpret than his metaphysical views. In the case of the *Kitab al-Huruf* (Book of Letters or Book of Particles, circa 900) there is disagreement among scholars as to its character and purpose, and even whether it is intended as a metaphysical tract. When a manuscript of the work was discovered in the twentieth century, its editor, Muhsin Mahdi, identified it as a loose commentary on Aristotle's *Metaphysics*, in part because of its title: the books of the *Metaphysics* are known by their Greek letters, rather than by numbers. More recently, however, the connection between the *Kitab al-Huruf* and the *Metaphysics* has been questioned, for the Farabian text makes no reference to the *Metaphysics*, while frequently drawing from and expanding on the *Categories*. What is clear about this text is that it is highly original and reflects al-Farabi's fundamental interest in language and its relation to philosophy. The text is divided into three parts, all of them centered around the philosophical meanings of various particles. The first part is closely tied to the ten Aristotelian categories and offers a discussion of the various meanings of the Arabic particles used to signify them. As is his custom, Al-Farabi considers not only the technical philosophical use of the terms he is investigating but also their common, everyday meaning and the relation between the popular and specialized meanings. Part 2 of the text is the most studied and read; it presents al-Farabi's views of the historical relations between religion and philosophy, his theory of the origin of language, and an account of the historical development of philosophy among the Greeks. Here and elsewhere al-Farabi argues for the puzzling historical thesis that philosophy is temporally prior to religion, basing his claim on the assertion that philosophy employs religion as its tool for communicating with the mass of humanity: "For philosophy as a whole precedes religion, in the same way that the user of tools precedes the tools in time." The final part of the *Kitab al-Huruf* is devoted to the consideration of interrogative particles and the kinds of philosophical questions to which these particles are addressed. Al-Farabi's approach is idiosyncratic and curiously modern in its attitude to the relations between language and philosophy. Whatever its ultimate theme was intended to be, in the *Kitab al-Huruf* al-Farabi shows himself to be a master of linguistic analysis and keenly aware of the inseparability of philosophy and language.

While the relationship between the *Kitab al-Huruf* and the *Metaphysics* remains unclear, al-Farabi did compose a brief treatise dedicated explicitly to clarifying the aims of the *Metaphysics*. In his autobiography Avicenna, not one generally noted for his intellectual modesty, tells of his struggle to understand the *Metaphysics*, a struggle that even forty readings of the text could not overcome. Then he chanced on a copy of al-Farabi's *Fi Aghrad al-Hakim fi Kull Magalah min al-Kitab al-Mawsum Bi-al-Huruf* (The Aims of Aristotle's *Metaphysics*, circa 900) at a bookseller's stall and finally was able to comprehend the Stagirite's purpose.

In al-Farabi's view, much of the difficulty that faces readers of the *Metaphysics* stems from the erroneous belief that Aristotle's text is focused on the study of God, soul, intellect, and related matters—that is, that it is primarily a work of theology, or divine science. When they discover how little attention Aristotle actually devotes to divine matters, they become confused as to his actual purpose. In fact, notes al-Farabi, divine science is but one part of the study of metaphysics. Metaphysics derives its primacy, then, not from its lofty subject matter but from the greater generality and comprehensiveness of the explanations it offers, explanations that apply to all beings and not merely to one class or genus of things.

While most of al-Farabi's commentaries are on Aristotle, he also wrote *Talkhis Nawamis Aflatun* (Commentary on Plato's *Laws*, circa 900). The introduction offers another of al-Farabi's colorful allegorical statements of his basic methodological principle that the same modes of discourse and reasoning are not suitable to all people, and that those who cannot understand philosophy must be presented its findings in symbolic rather than literal form. Al-Farabi tells the tale of a famous ascetic who wished to flee his city but feared its tyrannical ruler. The ascetic dresses in the clothes of a beggar and pretends to be drunk. When he reaches the city's gates, the guard asks him who he is; he replies truthfully, but owing to his disguise he is not believed. The moral, al-Farabi says, is that this ascetic "saved himself without having lied in what he said." The method of speaking through symbols and images, so well understood by Plato, works much like the ascetic's clever ploy. If one speaks figuratively often enough, one may on occasion speak the truth openly and literally and have it taken as symbolic by those who do not know better. The *Laws*, he contends, is a rare literal presentation of Plato's political views.

In the *Kitab al-Millah* (Book of Religion, circa 900) al-Farabi defines religion as "the beliefs and actions determined and limited by the conditions which their first ruler ordains for the community, seeking to bestow, by their use of [these beliefs and actions], a determinate goal for them, either about or by means of them." He offers an alternative to rule by a philosopher-king, rule which he insists in other works is necessary for a virtuous political order. Here he suggests that the laws laid down by a philosopher-king may be sufficient to maintain a virtuous religion and society even if subsequent leaders are not themselves philosophers, providing that they respect the law and apply it correctly in new situations. Thus, in the absence of a philosopher-ruler, the onus of maintaining the fabric of a virtuous society rests on the lawyers.

In *Kitab al-Jam' Bayn Ra'yay al-Hakimayn Aflatun al-Ilahiy wa-Aristutalis* (The Harmonization of the Opinions of the Two Sages, the Divine Plato and Aristotle, circa 900) al-Farabi asserts the identity of Platonic and Aristotelian philosophy, using as evidence the emanationist teachings of the pseudo-Aristotelian *Theology of Aristotle*. Until recently, scholars assumed that this work showed that al-Farabi was unaware of the deep differences separating Plato and Aristotle because of his erroneous belief that the *Theology of Aristotle*—which is in fact a paraphrase of Plotinus's *Enneads* 4-6—was genuinely Aristotelian. Al-Farabi himself, however, notes the disputed authenticity of the *Theology of Aristotle*; and in his *Falsafah Aristutalis* (The Philosophy of Aristotle, circa 900) Neoplatonic doctrines, particularly the doctrine of emanation, are conspicuously absent.

Al-Farabi's care in the interpretation of Aristotelian texts is also evident in his short *Risalah fi al-'Aql* (Treatise on the Intellect, circa 900), in which he analyzes the various meanings of the term *intellect* in both popular and technical contexts. He isolates six basic uses of the term: its use in common parlance to designate someone who is practically wise; its use by theologians to designate the faculty which dictates religious laws; the intellect that is the source of the first principles of demonstration according to Aristotle's *Posterior Analytics*; the faculty of practical reason (*phronesis*) discussed in book 6 of Aristotle's *Nicomachean Ethics*; the faculty of intellect as discussed in book 3 of Aristotle's *On the Soul*; and the First Intellect and mover of the universe of Aristotle's *Metaphysics*, book lambda. It is the fifth, psychological meaning of *intellect* to which al-Farabi devotes the most attention in this treatise. This sense of intellect, however, is also multiple, consisting of the potential intellect, the pure capacity for abstracting immaterial forms that exists in the human soul; the intellect in act, which has already realized its capacity to think; the acquired intellect, the stage reached when the intellect has made itself an object of thought and becomes like one of the separate intellects; and the Agent Intellect, a separate substance that acts as the efficient cause of human intellection. Some of these doctrines, such as that of the acquired intellect, derive from Aristotelian commentators, most notably Alexander of Aphrodisias. Aristotle himself is rather vague on these matters in *On the Soul*, but al-Farabi views his own systematization as consonant with Aristotle's explicit teachings. Most important, perhaps, al-Farabi scrupulously avoids assigning any emanative function to the Agent Intellect, suggesting his recognition that this theory is a non-Aristotelian development of the Neoplatonic tradition.

Al-Farabi's ability to differentiate his own philosophical views from those of his Greek masters without undermining his tremendous respect for them is especially evident in the trilogy of writings known as Falsafat Aflatun wa-Aristutalis (The Philosophies of Plato and Aristotle). The trilogy begins with al-Farabi's statement of his own philosophical views, *Tahsil al-Sa'adah* (The Attainment of Happiness, circa 900), followed by an account of his reading of Plato's and Aristotle's views on the same matters. At the end of *Tahsil al-Sa'adah* al-Farabi says: "Both [Plato and Aristotle] have given us an account of philosophy, but not without giving us also an account of the ways to it and of the ways to re-establish it when it becomes confused or extinct. . . . So let it be clear to you that, in what they presented, their purpose is the same, and that they intended to offer one and the same philosophy." All three philosophies, he contends, are variations on a single theme.

Al-Farabi's own presentation of the true philosophy emphasizes methodological questions and questions of the practical and political realization of what the true philosophy teaches. His Aristotelian inspiration is reflected in his concern with logical and epistemological distinctions and their role in the effort to understand in what human perfection truly consists; but in political matters al-Farabi is more Platonic, emphasizing the philosopher's responsibility in political as well as theoretical matters. Expressing this conviction in terms applicable to his own Islamic culture, he claims that the concepts of philosopher, legislator, and imam are different facets of a single idea. Thus, the philosopher who chooses not to realize his theoretical perfection in political action is a "vain philosopher."

In the final two parts of his trilogy al-Farabi presents Plato's and Aristotle's ultimate conceptions of philosophy and human perfection as the same. As in his *Kitab al-Huruf*, however, al-Farabi sees a historical progression within philosophy, with Aristotle completing some of the tasks that Plato was not able to finish. Al-Farabi's Plato is a curious figure, in part because al-Farabi seems to have had to rely on summaries of many dialogues which were not known to him directly. In general, he presents the Platonic dialogues as a series of systematic investigations into the nature of human perfection and the best means of attaining it, with each dialogue examining various popular visions of happiness and delineating their limitations.

The presentation of Aristotle's philosophy in the final part of the trilogy is equally exhaustive: all of the works of Aristotle known to al-Farabi are surveyed, and many are summarized in some detail. But no mention is made of any emanationist teachings, suggesting again al-Farabi's awareness of the non-Aristotelian character of emanation. In the closing pages of this work al-Farabi suggests that metaphysics remained an incomplete science for Aristotle and for the philosophers of al-Farabi's own day; the exact point of these cryptic remarks is not entirely clear.

The philosophy that al-Farabi develops in *Tahsil al-Sa'adah* is given systematic expression in a series of closely related metaphysical-political treatises that seems to be his latest writing. *Al-Fusul al-Muntaza'ah* (Selected Aphorisms or Aphorisms of the Statesman, circa 900) is a collection of brief philosophical statements of the principles of political philosophy. *Al-Siyasah al-Madaniyah* (The Political Regime, circa 900), a text whose alternative titles reflect al-Farabi's conviction that metaphysics and political philosophy are inseparable, was held in high regard by philosophers of the medieval Islamic and Jewish traditions; Moses Maimonides remarked that while all of al-Farabi's writings were of unparalleled excellence, this treatise in particular was one of his best. Al-Farabi's last work, in many ways similar to the *Al-Siyasah al-Madaniyah*, is *Mabadi' Ara' Ahl al-Madinah al-Fadilah* (Principles of the Opinions of the People of the Virtuous City, circa 942; revised, 948). The Arabic biographers relate that this work was begun by al-Farabi in Baghdad just before he left to take up residency in the court of Sayf al-Dawlah in Aleppo; it was revised and reorganized in Egypt, two years before al-Farabi's death.

In both this text and *Al-Siyasah al-Madaniyah* al-Farabi outlines his views on a wide range of philosophical topics: the nature of God and his role as first cause of the universe; cosmology and physics; the physiological and psychological composition of human beings; the theoretical explanation of prophecy; the relations between philosophy and religion; and the nature of the perfect political association and the various corruptions that it may undergo.

In these works al-Farabi freely accepts the Neoplatonic theory of emanation. The theory attempts to fuse together a metaphysical conception of the nature of God with geocentric cosmology, according to which the earth is at the center of a series of concentric spheres—five representing the orbits of the then-known planets, plus the sphere of the fixed stars and an outermost sphere, the First Heaven. The theory of emanation relies on Aristotle's notion that the eternal motion of the heavens is governed by celestial intelligences which act as movers of their particular spheres, and on Aristotle's conception of God as thought thinking itself. In al-Farabi's metaphysics God is the cause both of the being and of the motion of the universe; in contrast, for Aristotle God is only a first mover. The emanational process is eternal: as a result of God's contemplation of himself, there overflows from him the existence of a first intelligence. This intelligence has two objects of thought: its own essence and God. The act of thinking each of these objects causes a dyadic emanation: the emanation of a second intelligence through the thinking of God and the emanation of a heavenly body through the intelligence's self-contemplation. (This dyadic conception of the process appears to be a Farabian innovation: the usual Neoplatonic model was triadic, including an intellect, a heavenly body, and a rational soul.) The process of emanation continues according to this dyadic pattern, culminating in the emanation of the earth from the last celestial mind, the Agent Intellect. In this way al-Farabi combines psychology and epistemology with cosmology: the same Agent Intellect posited by Aristotle as the cause of the actualization of human knowledge is also the cause of the existence of the sublunar world through the process of emanation.

Another link between al-Farabi's cosmological and psychological teachings in his mature works occurs in his theory of prophecy. According to al-Farabi the prophet is a philosopher whose imaginative faculty is especially keen and is able to receive the overflow or emanation of the Agent Intellect. As a result of this unique link between intellect and imagination, the prophet is able not only to express his knowledge conceptually but also to imitate it through images, symbols, and depictions. Prophecy and revelation thus represent for al-Farabi a particularized, imaginative copy of the abstract conceptual truths grasped intellectually by philosophers. And since those capable of abstract philosophical thinking are, in al-Farabi's view, limited in number, prophecy serves the important political function of allowing the general populace to grasp, in the only way it can, the truth about the nature and the place of human beings in the world.

Al-Farabi's cosmological and psychological teachings provide the basis for his political philosophy and his resolution of the relationship between religion and philosophy, themes that occupy the latter halves of both the *Al-Siyasah al-Madaniyah* and the *Mabadi' Ara' Ahl al-Madinah al-Fadilah.* His view that the human being is a microcosm explains his penchant for prefacing his political theories with a theory of the hierarchical ordering of the universe. The political order that will best ensure human flourishing will be that which best reflects the ordering of the cosmos, and it will be similarly governed by a rational principle in the form of a philosopher-cum-statesman and prophet. Such a political order will ensure the harmony of philosophy and religion, while simultaneously providing for the perfection of all its citizens. But, like Plato in the *Republic,* al-Farabi does not merely explain the ideal conditions that must obtain for the flourishing of the virtuous city; he also analyzes the various corruptions of that ideal and attempts to explain the causes of those corruptions.

The *Al-Siyasah al-Madaniyah* identifies three basic types of corruptions: ignorant cities, immoral cities, and errant cities. There are six kinds of ignorant cities: indispensable cities, in which the citizens join together solely to meet the needs of subsistence; vile cities, which are concerned only with the acquisition of wealth; base cities, which seek mere sensual gratification; timocratic cities, which are concerned with the pursuit of honor; tyrannical cities; and democratic cities. What all these cities have in common is their ignorance of the true nature of humanity and its place in the cosmos, and hence of the true path to happiness. The other forms of nonvirtuous political association are more properly corruptions: in them some knowledge of the truth is, or was once, possessed but is ignored or forsaken by the citizens or their leadership. In immoral cities knowledge of true happiness is deliberately forsaken for some baser goal; in errant cities the leader possesses the requisite knowledge but leads his people astray so that they remain ignorant. Al-Farabi also discusses what he calls the "weeds" in the virtuous city itself: members of the city who do not truly participate in its virtuous goals.

Al-Farabi crowns his attempt to interweave political and metaphysical themes by making the political theory outlined in these texts the basis for an eschatological account of reward and punishment in the afterlife. Citizens in the ignorant cities are simply annihilated at death, since their ignorance has prevented the actualization of their intellectual capacities—the only basis for the soul's survival apart from the body. The fate of those in the immoral cities is harsher: since they turn away from the truth voluntarily, their souls suffer eternal punishment through their continued desire for goals which are no longer available in their disembodied state. In the case of the erring city the citizens, who remain ignorant, perish after death, whereas their corrupt leader receives his just punishment.

The scope and variety of al-Farabi's philosophical endeavors are undeniably impressive. Despite the many interpretive difficulties and despite the many aspects of his literary output that remain unknown, the picture of al-Farabi that emerges is one of a careful and systematic thinker able to appropriate creatively elements from the Greek tradition and convey the results of his efforts effectively to a variety of audiences. These qualities no doubt explain al-Farabi's appeal to subsequent philosophers in the medieval Islamic and Jewish traditions, an appeal that is evident even when his followers take issue with him. Avicenna and Moses Maimonides openly acknowledge their debt to the Second Teacher, and Averroës often defers to al-Farabi's authority, particularly in logical matters, and considers it a matter of some gravity to have to disagree with al-Farabi in psychology as well as in logic. Many lesser-known figures in Jewish and Islamic philosophy could be added to this list, as could medieval Christian philosophers; many of al-Farabi's works were translated into Latin, albeit to a lesser extent than those of Avicenna and Averroës. The breadth of al-Farabi's appeal is also evident in the various approaches to his work taken by modern scholars. His logical teachings and his sophisticated linguistic approach to philosophical issues have attracted the attention of historians working in the analytic tradition. But his political and social teachings—in particular, his concern with the nature and purpose of religion—have also attracted a large following in the realm of political philosophy.

Bibliography:

Nicholas Rescher, *Al-Farabi: An Annotated Bibliography* (Pittsburgh: University of Pittsburgh Press, 1962).

Biography:

Moritz Steinschneider, *Al-Farabi: Des arabischen Philosophen Leben und Schriften* (St. Petersburg: Commissionnaires de l'Académie impériale des Sciences, 1869; reprinted, Amsterdam: Philo Press, 1966).

References:

Shukri B. Abed, *Aristotelian Logic and the Arabic Language in Alfarabi* (Albany: State University of New York Press, 1991);

William F. Boggess, "Alfarabi and Rhetoric: The Cave Revisited," *Phronesis*, 15 (1970): 86-90;

Charles E. Butterworth, "The Rhetorician and His Relationship to the Community: Three Accounts of Aristotle's *Rhetoric*," in *Islamic Theology and Philosophy: Studies in Honor of George F. Hourani*, edited by Michael Marmura (Albany: State University of New York Press, 1984), pp. 111-136;

Hans Dauber, *The Ruler as Philosopher: A New Interpretation of al-Farabi's View* (Amsterdam & New York: North Holland, 1986);

Herbert A. Davidson, "Alfarabi and Avicennna on the Active Intellect," *Viator*, 3 (1972): 109-178;

Thérèse-Anne Druart, "Al-Farabi and Emanationism," in *Studies in Medieval Philosophy*, edited by John F. Wippel (Washington, D.C.: Catholic University of America Press, 1987), pp. 23-43;

Druart, "Al-Farabi's Causation of the Heavenly Bodies," in *Islamic Philosophy and Mysticism*, edited by Parviz Morewedge (Delmar, N.Y.: Caravan Books, 1981), pp. 35-46;

Druart, "Substance in Arabic Philosophy: Al-Farabi's Discussion," *Proceedings of the American Catholic Philosophical Association*, 61 (1987): 88-97;

Miriam Galston, "Al-Farabi on Aristotle's Theory of Demonstration," in *Islamic Philosophy and Mysticism*, edited by Morewedge, pp. 23-34;

Galston, *Politics and Excellence: The Political Philosophy of Alfarabi* (Princeton: Princeton University Press, 1990);

Galston, "A Re-examination of al-Farabi's Neoplatonism," *Journal of the History of Philosophy*, 15 (January 1977): 13-32;

Fuad Haddad, *Alfarabi's Theory of Communication* (Beirut: American University, 1989);

Salim Kemal, *The Poetics of Alfarabi and Avicenna* (Leiden, Netherlands: Brill, 1991);

Jacques Langhade, "Grammaire, logique, études linguistiques chez al-Farabi," *Historiographia Linguistica*, 8, no. 2/3 (1981): 365-377;

Ibrahim Madkour, *La place d'al-Farabi dans l'Ecole Philosophique Musulmane* (Paris: Librairie d'Amerique et d'Orient, 1934);

Muhsin Mahdi, "Al-Farabi and the Foundation of Philosophy," in *Islamic Philosophy and Mysticism*, edited by Morewedge, pp. 3-22;

Mahdi, "Alfarabi on Philosophy and Religion," *Philosophical Forum*, 4 (Fall 1972): 5-25;

Mahdi, "Remarks on Alfarabi's *Attainment of Happiness*," in *Essays on Islamic Philosophy and Science*, edited by George F. Hourani (Albany: State University of New York Press, 1975), pp. 47-66;

Mahdi, "Science, Philosophy, and Religion in Alfarabi's *Enumeration of the Sciences*," in *The Cultural Context of Medieval Learning*, edited by John Emery Murdoch and Edith Dudley Sylla (Dordrecht, Netherlands & Boston: Reidel, 1975), pp. 113-147;

Shlomo Pines, "The Limitations of Human Knowledge According to Al-Farabi, ibn Bajja, and Maimonides," in *Studies in Medieval Jewish History and Literature*, edited by Isadore Twersky (Cambridge, Mass.: Harvard University Press, 1972), pp. 82-109;

Erwin I. J. Rosenthal, "The Place of Politics in the Philosophy of al-Farabi," *Islamic Culture*, 29 (1955): 157-178;

Leo Strauss, "Farabi's Plato," in *Louis Ginzberg: Jubilee Volume on the Occasion of His Seventieth Birthday* (New York: American Academy for Jewish Research, 1945), pp. 357-393;

Strauss, "How Farabi Read Plato's *Laws*," in *Mélanges Lous Massignon* (Damascus: Institut Français de Damas, 1957), III: 357-393;

Richard Walzer, "Al-Farabi's Theory of Prophecy and Divination," in *Greek into Arabic: Essays on Islamic Philosophy* (Oxford: Cassirer, 1962), pp. 206-219;

F. W. Zimmermann, "Some Observations on Al-Farabi and the Logical Tradition," in *Islamic Philosophy and the Classical Tradition: Essays Presented to Richard Walzer*, edited by S. M. Stern, Albert Hourani, and Vivian Brown (Columbia: University of South Carolina Press, 1972), pp. 517-546.

Richard Fishacre

(circa 1205 - 1248)

R. James Long
Fairfield University

PRINCIPAL WORKS: *Postillae in Ps. I-LXX* (Commentary on Psalms 1-70, written circa 1240); not extant;

In IV Libros Sententiarum Petri Lombardi (Commentary on the Four Books of the *Sentences* of Peter Lombard, written 1241-1245);

Sermones (Sermons, written circa 1241-1248);

In Parabolas Salomonis (On the Parables of Solomon, written circa 1245);

De Poenitentia (On Penance, written circa 1245); not extant;

Quaestio de Ascensione Christi (Question on the Ascension of Christ, written circa 1245-1248);

Adnotationes in S. Augustini De Haeresibus (Notations on Saint Augustine's Treatise on Heresies, written circa 1245-1248);

De Fide, Spe, et Caritate (On Faith, Hope, and Charity, written circa 1245-1248).

EDITIONS: "Der Liber propugnatorius des Thomas Anglicus und die Lehrunterschiede zwischen Thomas von Aquin und Duns Scotus, Teil II: Die Trinitarisichen Lehrdifferenzen," edited by Michael Schmaus, in *Beiträge*, 29 (Münster: Aschendorffschen, 1930), pp. 107-116;

"The Science of Theology according to Richard Fishacre: Edition of the Prologue to his *Commentary on the Sentences*," edited by R. James Long, *Mediaeval Studies*, 34 (1972): 71-98;

"Richard Fishacre's *Quaestio* on the Ascension of Christ: An Edition," edited by Long, *Mediaeval Studies*, 40 (1978): 30-55;

"The Virgin as Olive Tree: A Marian Sermon of Richard Fishacre and Science at Oxford," edited by Long, *Archivum Fratrum Praedicatorum*, 52 (1982): 77-87;

"Two Versions of a Sermon by Richard Fishacre OP for the Fourth Sunday of Lent on the Theme: 'Non enim heres erit filius ancille cum filio libere,'" edited by Maura O'Carroll, *Archivum Fratrum Praedicatorum*, 54 (1984): 113-141;

"The Moral and Spiritual Theology of Richard Fishacre: Edition of Trinity Coll. MS O.1.30," edited by Long, *Archivum Fratrum Praedicatorum*, 60 (1990): 5-175.

The friar Richard Fishacre deserves serious attention because he was the first among the Dominicans at Oxford who left behind a substantial body of writings. More important, he was the first to have composed a commentary on the *Libri Quatuor Sententiarum* (Four Books of Sentences, 1157-1158), by the twelfth-century bishop of Paris Peter Lombard. Lombard's work had become at Paris and would subsequently become at Oxford a required text for anyone proceeding to a degree in theology. Given this privileged status, it was widely commented on, developing into the preeminent locus for speculative theologizing in the thirteenth and fourteenth centuries. As the first commentator, Fishacre set the tone for much of the Oxonian theological and philosophical speculation that was to follow and exerted an influence on his successors that is only now beginning to be properly assessed.

Fishacre seems never to have ventured from his native England. The city of his birth appears to have been Exeter, in Devonshire. The name Fishacre was prominent among the gentry of that region from the twelfth through the fifteenth centuries; there were also several Fishacres among the clergy, including a prior (Robert), a prioress (Jane), and the rector of a church (Peter). Although the year of Fishacre's birth is unknown, he probably entered the Order of Preachers within the first decade following their arrival in England in 1221. Showing intellectual promise, he was sent to Oxford for higher studies. There he came under the tutelage of Robert Bacon, the first Dominican regent master in theology at the young university and uncle of the better-known Roger. Shortly before 1240 Fishacre incepted in theology, the first Dominican to do so at Oxford, and began his rather brief career there as teacher and scholar.

The work on which Fishacre's reputation rests is *In IV Libros Sententiarum Petri Lombardi* (Commentary on the Four Books of the *Sentences* of Peter Lombard, 1241-1245). Although commenting on Lombard's compilation was required of all candidates for the degree of master of theology, and although it later became the custom for such works to have been composed before inception, the evidence suggests that Fishacre's commentary was the work of a master. He writes the work under obedience, he says in the prologue, even though infirm in mind and body—a protestation more credible coming from a master than a student. Furthermore, his reference to his work on the "other part of theology" (Scripture) is probably to his commentary on the Psalms (1240); though no extant copy has been discovered, this work was published, whereas the fruits of the *cursor biblicus* (student lecturing on Scripture) were rarely published. The most telling piece of evidence is provided by a letter from Pope Innocent IV to the bishop of Lincoln and chancellor of Oxford University, Robert Grosseteste, which refers to Fishacre's lectures on the *Sentences* as "ordinary." In the academic terminology of the time this designation identifies them as the lectures of a master; students lectured "cursorily." The letter also mentions a dispute at Oxford to which Fishacre was a party.

Earlier in the century masters of theology at Paris had gradually adopted a more specialized approach to their theologizing, concentrating in their Scripture lectures on textual exegesis and moral exhortation and relegating the more speculative and philosophical questions to their lectures on the *Sentences*. Fishacre greets such a division with approval in the prologue to his commentary. Of the two parts of theology, asserts Fishacre, one pertains to the practical intellect and deals with moral instruction; the other pertains to the speculative intellect and concerns itself with difficult questions regarding the articles of faith. Although both parts are contained indistinctly in sacred Scripture, the "modern masters," he says, treat them separately.

Such espousal of methodological novelties aroused the ire of the formidable bishop of Lincoln. In a 1246 letter to the regent masters of Oxford, Grosseteste required that the only textbooks in theology be the Old and New Testaments. The support of the papacy for the Parisian system, however, spelled the end of the "old theology" at Oxford, though its demise did not come without a struggle. Richard Rufus, an Oxford Franciscan and Fishacre's principal adversary, continued to be vigorously opposed to the new methodology: the *Sentences* were useful for elucidation, he said, but simply were not theological. A full two decades later Roger Bacon was still urging the integration of all theological questions with the interpretation of sacred Scripture.

If Fishacre's commentary provides virtually the only witness to the philosophical activities of the Dominicans at Oxford before midcentury, it does not allow their thought to be identified as distinctly "Dominican"; in fact, a study of his commentary leads one to the conclusion that Fishacre, like his Franciscan and secular colleagues at Oxford, can most readily be identified with the Christian Neoplatonism first forged by Augustine.

Later in the century the Augustinians resisted the inroads of Aristotelianism, especially as interpreted by Averroës; it would be unfair, however, to label Fishacre's thought reactionary or conservative. On the contrary, he was engaged in a bold effort to understand and absorb into his theological speculation the newly translated natural philosophy of Aristotle. And if he failed to integrate the metaphysics of Aristotle (or if he failed even to understand it fully), he was more successful in making use of the Stagirite's scientific writings: the *Physics*, *On the Heavens*, *On Generation and Corruption*, *On Animals*, the *Short Works on Nature*, the *Meteors*, even the falsely attributed *On Plants*. In the same prologue wherein he espouses the Parisian methodology, Fishacre argues for the propaedeutic value of the natural sciences for the aspiring theologian. While such a rationale for the study of the sciences had become commonplace, the analogy Fishacre finds to illustrate the relationship was novel: the tale of Abraham, who had to sleep with the maidservant, Hagar, before his wife, Sarah, could conceive—the former representing science, the latter theology.

As was the case with others of his generation, Fishacre sought help in understanding the pagan Aristotle in the commentaries of the Muslims Avicenna and Averroës. Although the former had a more pervasive influence on his thought, his use of Averroës, who was already generally referred to as "the Commentator," was among the earliest at Oxford and the earliest yet identified in a theological context. In addition to the Arabs, Fishacre was influenced by older contemporaries at Paris, such as William of Auvergne, Alexander of Hales, William of Auxerre, and the Dominican Hugh of Saint Cher. The extent of Grosseteste's influence on Fishacre has not yet been fully documented.

Fishacre's Augustinian leanings can be seen in the discussion of God in the first book of the commentary on the *Sentences*. His ten arguments for the existence of God all presuppose Augustine's metaphysics of participation and exemplarism, whereby every hierarchical order of perfection leads the human mind to posit the existence of a greatest. Three of the arguments are variations on the so-called Ontological Argument of Anselm's *Proslogion* (An Address of the Mind to God, 1077-1078). Anyone thinking of God must affirm his existence, says Fishacre like Anselm, for the same reason first articulated by Augustine: whoever sees something in the presence of light, sees the light more than the object; if God is the light of every intelligible object, as sensible light is of every visible object, whoever sees anything with the intellect also sees God. Thus the atheist is simply not comprehending what he is saying when he repeats the words "God is something than which nothing greater can be thought."

In addition to Augustine's teaching on Divine Illumination, Fishacre also embraces the bishop of Hippo's theory of seminal natures (*rationes seminales*): the explanation of physical change must include an active potency in matter. These *rationes* become actualized either through the instrumentality of some physical agent, producing what Aristotle called a natural change, or through divine intervention, resulting in a miracle. These seminal natures were infused into primordial matter by God at the instant of creation. Here Fishacre is following Augustine but believes that he is also in conformity with Aristotle.

Indeed, Fishacre uses the Aristotelian language of matter and form, potency and act, and nature and action but adjusts these terms to fit a mental world that was still Augustine's. In his philosophy of human nature, for instance, Fishacre quotes with approval Aristotle's definition of the soul as the form of the body, yet is eager to preserve the Platonic-Augustinian understanding of the soul as an independent, spiritual, and hence immortal substance. Here Fishacre finds help in a compromise first proposed by Avicenna and later adopted by Albert the Great: the soul is both substance, when considered in itself as an essence, and form, when considered in its activity with respect to the body. This awkward truce, which ultimately proved untenable, is typical of the struggle between two conflicting philosophical systems which Fishacre and others of his generation were trying to mediate.

Another teaching which characterized the so-called Augustinian school in the thirteenth century was that of the plurality of forms. This doctrine, traceable to the eleventh-century Spanish Jew Solomon Ibn Gabirol, holds that for every essential perfection in the individual there is a corresponding form. The various powers of the human composite, therefore, are derived from distinct forms, arranged in a hierarchical order, with the form of rationality in the sovereign position. Although in describing the contemporary positions with respect to the issue Fishacre typically refuses to decide in favor of any of them, in practice the texts reveal him to be a pluralist.

According to Fishacre, light, the noblest of bodies, acts as a bond (*vinculum*) between the soul and the human body. It is through light that the soul performs its operations in the body. This "light metaphysics" is clearly borrowed from Grosseteste, who exploits the idea in several of his writings. The soul has a natural appetite for the body; if the soul eternally lacked a body, it would be eternally miserable. Even if, for instance, the soul of Adam had had foreknowledge of the Fall and its results, it would still have chosen to enter a body rather than be eternally disembodied. It is this appetite for a body—in fact, for a particular body—that distinguishes the soul from the angel, both of which are otherwise of the same species.

The other stock-in-trade "Augustinian" teaching, also derived from Ibn Gabirol, was universal hylomorphism, the view that matter-form composition extended to spiritual substances (that is, angels and human souls). The nobler the creature, the less it has of matter, says Fishacre. The human soul, as the noblest of creatures, has the least amount of matter; if it were outside the human body, it would occupy only a point. Both parts of the "most famous twosome" (*binarium famosissimum*), the plurality of forms and universal hylomorphism, were reaffirmed in the Condemnations of 1277 after Thomas Aquinas and other Aristotelians had taken issue with them.

A more complete assessment of the first two books of the commentary on the *Sentences*, as well as of the teaching on Christ and the virtues in book 3 and the sacramentology in book 4, must await a critical edition of the entire work. Only then will Fishacre's place in the intellectual history of the High Middle Ages be properly established.

Of the remaining works which survive and have been identified, none alters dramatically the portrait that has emerged from the piecemeal studies of the commentary on the *Sentences*. *Adnotationes in S. Augustini De Haeresibus* (Notations on Saint Augustine's Treatise on Heresies, circa 1245-1248) displays Fishacre's interest in a topic that had from the beginning been a professional concern of the Order of Preachers. Fishacre's point of departure is Augustine's catalogue, or handbook, composed at the end of his life, which lists and describes eighty-eight (ninety by Fishacre's reckoning) heresies of the early church. Trained in academic disputation, the Dominican undertakes to provide what he feels is lacking in Augustine's handbook: rational refutations of the listed heresies. Fishacre, however, presents detailed arguments on only six of the heresies in Augustine's catalogue and mentions another four in passing. Possibly the project proved too much for him and he abandoned it; or he may have died before he could complete it.

The *Quaestio de Ascensione Christi* (Question on the Ascension of Christ, circa 1245-1248), which is found uniquely in the same Vatican manuscript as the *Adnotationes in S. Augustini De Haeresibus*, provides a good example of the theological methodology suggested in the prologue of the commentary on the *Sentences*: the mining of the secular sciences for truths that might illustrate the sacred science revealed in the Scriptures. Using concepts such as natural place, natural motion, gravity, levity, and velocity from Aristotle's *Physics* and *On the Heavens*, Fishacre attempts to explicate the theological doctrine of the Ascension. Did Jesus ascend gradually or instantaneously, and by what power and in what direction did he ascend? (Christ's ascension was gradual, according to Fishacre, and it took place by the power of his soul. Since he ascended straight up from Jerusalem, which according to the geography of the day was the midpoint between east and west, the direction depended on one's location vis-à-vis Jerusalem.) The doctrine of the Ascension must have suggested itself to Fishacre as a test case for the adequacy of the new science: do Aristotelian concepts illuminate a truth that is known only through divine revelation?

In his Latin sermons, probably delivered to academic congregations, Fishacre borrows liberally from the new Aristotelian science to elucidate his texts: from cosmology to explain the density of hell's atmosphere; from optics to illustrate the clarity of the heavenly realm; and from botany to clarify the Psalm text comparing Mary to an olive tree. Further study of the fifteen to twenty-five sermons attributed to Fishacre will undoubtedly uncover further indications of the unity of his thought.

Neither of the Scripture commentaries attributed to Fishacre has been identified; nor has a treatise on penance also attributed to him. They may yet be located among the uncatalogued collections of medieval manuscripts. A treatise on the theological virtues that was once tentatively assigned to Fishacre is now known to have been written by Richard of Wetheringsett around 1220.

If one can take as evidence his protestations in the prologue to his commentary on the *Sentences*, Fishacre seems to have suffered from a weak constitution. Adding to this impression is a colophon in one of the Sorbonne manuscripts containing the commentary which urges prayers for his spiritual and bodily strength so that he can finish the work. He seems to have been relatively young, certainly under fifty, when death claimed him in 1248. His beloved teacher and colleague Robert Bacon died in the same year, and both were buried in the new Dominican priory at Oxford.

A final judgment regarding Fishacre's influence will have to await the edition of his commentary on the *Sentences*. From the evidence now available, however, it is safe to assert that his mark on his and the following generation of theologians at Oxford was significant. The Dominicans Simon of Hinton, who succeeded him in the chair of theology at Oxford, and Robert Kilwardby, Fishacre's best-known pupil, as well as the little-known Magister R. de Stanington all show traces of his influence. He is cited extensively in the *Speculum Iuniorum*, a pastoral manual composed about 1250 by a Magister Galienus, who is yet to be further identified, as well as several other works composed at midcentury. In addition, an intriguing marginal gloss in a work by Bernard Gui, which is otherwise unsubstantiated, attests to Thomas Aquinas's desire to have a copy of Fishacre's commentary. Further testimony to his importance is that Fishacre provoked the opposition not only of Grosseteste but also of the Franciscan Rufus. The latter's opposition was on specific points of doctrine as well as on general methodological grounds.

The chronicler Matthew of Paris, who generally wasted little love on the friars, extended to Fishacre and his master Bacon a rare encomium when recording their deaths: they had in theology and in the other sciences no superiors nor equals alive, he wrote; they lectured eminently in the same faculty for many years, and to the people they preached the word of God gloriously.

References:

Stephen F. Brown, "Richard Fishacre on the Need for Philosophy," in *A Straight Path: Studies in Medieval Philosophy and Culture (Essays in Honor of Arthur Hyman)*, edited by R. Link-Salinger, Jeremiah Hackett, M. S. Hyman, R. James Long, and C. H. Manekin (Washington, D.C.: Catholic University of America Press, 1988), pp. 23-36;

Richard C. Dales, "The Influence of Grosseteste's 'Hexaemeron' on the 'Sentences' Commentaries of Richard Fishacre, O.P. and Richard Rufus of Cornwall, O.F.M.," *Viator*, 2 (1971): 271-300;

L.-B. Gillon, "L'espirit 'partie' de l'univers: Autour d'un texte de Richard Fishacre," in *Studi tomistici*, volume 1, edited by Antonio Piolanti (Rome: Pontificia Accademia romana di S. Tommaso d'Aquino; Cittá nuova, 1974), pp. 210-222;

Joseph Goering and R. James Long, "Richard Fishacre's Treatise *De fide, spe, et caritate*," *Bulletin de philosophie médiévale*, 31 (1989): 103-111;

R. James Long, "Richard Fishacre," in *Dictionnaire de Spiritualité*, volume 13 (Paris: Beauchesne, 1987), pp. 509-512;

Long, "Richard Fishacre and the Problem of the Soul," *Modern Schoolman*, 52 (March 1975): 263-270;

Long, "Richard Fishacre's Way to God," in *A Straight Path: Studies in Medieval Philosophy and Culture (Essays in Honor of Arthur Hyman)*, pp. 174-182;

Franz Pelster, "Der älteste Sentenzenkommentar aus der Oxforder Franziskanerschule," *Scholastik*, 1 (1926): 50-80;

Pelster, "Die Bedeutung der Sentenzenvorlesung für die theologische Spekulation des Mittelalters: Ein Zeugnis aus der ältesten Oxforder Dominikanerschule," *Scholastik*, 2 (1927): 250-255;

Pelster, "Eine Handschrift mit Predigten des R. Fishacre und anderer Oxforder Lehrer," *Zeitschrift für katholische Theologie*, 57 (1933): 614-617;

Pelster, "Das Leben und die Schriften des Oxforder Dominikanerlehrers R. Fishacre," *Zeitschrift für katholische Theologie*, 54 (1930): 518-553;

Walter H. Principe, "Richard Fishacre's Use of Averroes with Respect to Motion and the Human Soul of Christ," *Mediaeval Studies*, 40 (1978): 349-360;

D. E. Sharp, "The Philosophy of Richard Fishacre (d. 1248)," *New Scholasticism*, 7 (1933): 281-297;

David M. Solomon, "The Sentence Commentary of Richard Fishacre and the Apocalypse Commentary of Hugh of St. Cher," *Archivum Fratrum Praedicatorum*, 46 (1976): 367-377;

Leo Sweeney and Charles J. Ermatinger, "Divine Infinity according to Richard Fishacre," *Modern Schoolman*, 35 (March 1958): 191-212.

Manuscripts:

Thirteen manuscripts contain Richard Fishacre's commentary on Peter Lombard's *Sentences*. Two contain only the fourth book, which circulated independently under the title *De Sacramentis* (On the Sacraments); only four contain the work in its entirety. The most significant of the witnesses, and those that should be given first consideration in the preparation of a critical edition, are the five that contain line numberings. These numberings, in increments of five, run down the center of the page and appear for the first time in the Fishacre codices. These manuscripts, Bologna Univ. MS 1546, Cambridge Gonville and Caius College MS 329/1410, Oxford New College MS 112, Paris Bibliothèque Nationale MS lat. 15754, and Vatican Ottob. lat. MS 294, are fully described by R. James Long in "The Science of Theology according to Richard Fishacre: Edition of the Prologue to his *Commentary on the Sentences*," *Mediaeval Studies*, 34 (1972): 75-77. Although incomplete, the Vatican manuscript is possibly the earliest copy of Fishacre's commentary. Directly copied from it was a second Paris manuscript, Bibliothèque Nationale MS lat. 16389, which ends at the third distinction of book 2 but which also contains a colophon that shows that the writer obviously believed Fishacre still to be alive. One can, therefore, argue that the Vatican manuscript was also produced during Fishacre's lifetime, that is, circa 1205-1248. The Vatican manuscript is also significant in that it contains the only known copies of Fishacre's question on the Ascension of Christ and the treatise on heresies, the only other extant works from Fishacre's pen.

Gersonides (Levi ben Gerson)

(1288 - 20 April 1344)

T. M. Rudavsky
Ohio State University

PRINCIPAL WORKS: *Sefer Ha-heqesh Ha-yashar* (On Valid Syllogisms, written 1319); translated into Latin as *Liber Syllogismi Recti*;

Sefer Ma'aseh Hoshev (The Work of a Counter, written 1321);

Perush 'al Sefer Iyob (Commentary on Job, written 1325);

Sefer Milhamot Ha-Shem (The Wars of the Lord, written 1329);

Perush 'al Sefer Ha-Torah (Commentary on the Pentateuch, written 1329-1338).

EDITIONS: *Perush 'al Ha-Torah* (Mantua: Abraham ben Solomon Conat, circa 1476; Venice, 1547; Jerusalem, 1967);

Perush 'al Sefer Iyob (Ferrara, 1477);*Milhamot Ha-Shem* (Riva di Trento, 1560; Leipzig, 1866; Berlin, 1923);

Sefer Maassei Choscheb: Die Praxis des Rechners. Ein hebraisch-arithmetisches Werk des Levi ben Gerschom aus dem Jahre 1321, edited and translated into German by Gerson Lange (Frankfurt am Main: Golde, 1909).

EDITIONS IN ENGLISH: *The Commentary of Levi ben Gerson on the Book of Job*, translated by Abraham L. Lassen (New York: Bloch, 1946);

"The Problem of Prophecy in Gersonides," translated by David W. Silverman, Ph.D. dissertation, Columbia University, 1973;

Providence and the Philosophy of Gersonides, translated by David Bleich (New York: Yeshiva University Press, 1973);

Gersonides' The Wars of the Lord. Treatise Three: On God's Knowledge, translated by Norbert M. Samuelson (Toronto: Pontifical Institute of Mediaeval Studies, 1977);

The Creation of the World According to Gersonides, translated by Jacob Staub (Chico, Cal.: Scholars Press, 1982);

The Wars of the Lord, 2 volumes published, translated by Seymour Feldman (Philadelphia: Jewish Publication Society of America, 1984-).

Perhaps no other medieval Jewish philosopher has been so maligned over the centuries as Gersonides. Indeed, his major philosophical

Title page for an edition of Gersonides' major philosophical work, Sefer Milhamot Ha-Shem, *printed in Riva di Trento in 1560*

work, *Sefer Milhamot Ha-Shem* (The Wars of the Lord, 1329), was called "Wars against the Lord" by one of his opponents. At the same time, his biblical commentaries have been highly regarded. Despite the vilification of his position, Gersonides emerges as one of the most insightful and comprehensive thinkers in the medieval Jewish tradition. He has been constantly quoted (even if only to be criticized), and, through the works of Hasdai Crescas and others, Gersonides' ideas influenced such thinkers as Gottfried Wilhelm Leibniz and Benedict de Spinoza.

Gersonides left few letters and does not talk about himself in his writings; nor is his life discussed at great length by his contemporaries. Hence, what is known of his biography is sketchy at best. Levi ben Gerson was born in 1288 in Provence and may have lived for a time in Bagnols-sur-Ceze. It is probable that his father was Gershom ben Salomon de Beziers, a notable mentioned in medieval histories. Gersonides may have married a distant cousin; it is not known whether he had any offspring.

Gersonides spoke Provençal; his works, however, are all written in Hebrew, and all his quotations from Averroës, Aristotle, and Moses Maimonides are in Hebrew as well. He may have had a reading knowledge of Latin; he appears to manifest an awareness of contemporary Scholastic discussions. He might, however, have learned of such discussions in oral conversations with his Christian contemporaries.

Apart from several trips to Avignon, Gersonides most likely resided his entire life in Orange. There is some evidence that he may have followed the traditional occupation of his family, moneylending. He died on 20 April 1344.

With the decline of Spanish Judaism in the thirteenth century, Provence quickly became the cultural center for Jewish intellectual activity. The popes in Avignon had a lenient policy toward the Jews, whose creative life flourished, particularly in philosophy and theology. Jewish philosophers did not have direct access to the works of Aristotle, but Provençal Jews learned of Aristotle through the commentaries of Averroës, the twelfth-century Spanish Muslim philosopher. By the end of the thirteenth century these commentaries had been translated from Arabic into Hebrew, and Averroës' thought, as well as that of Aristotle, was being integrated into the mainstream of Jewish philosophy.

In addition to Averroës and Aristotle, Gersonides was influenced by Moses Maimonides, his greatest Jewish philosophical predecessor. Gersonides' works can be seen as an attempt to integrate the teachings of Aristotle, as mediated through Averroës and Maimonides, with those of Judaism. In *Milhamot Ha-Shem* he laid down the general rule that "the Law cannot prevent us from considering to be true that which our reason urges us to believe." His adherence to this principle is reflected throughout his work. Gersonides' scientific works comprise mathematics and astronomy. His *Sefer Ma'aseh Hoshev* (The Work of a Counter, 1321) is concerned with arithmetical operations and uses of a symbolic notation for numerical variables. Gersonides' major scientific contributions were in astronomy; his works were known by his contemporaries and were influential on later astronomers. His astronomical writings are contained primarily in book 5, part 1 of *Milhamot Ha-Shem.* In 136 chapters Gersonides reviews and criticizes astronomical theories of the day, compiles astronomical tables, and describes one of his astronomical inventions. This instrument, which he called *Megalle 'amuqqot* (Revealer of Profundities) and which was called *Bacullus Jacob* (Jacob's staff) by his Christian contemporaries, was used to measure the heights of stars above the horizon. The astronomical parts of *Milhamot Ha-Shem* were translated into Latin during Gersonides' lifetime. One of the craters of the moon, Rabbi Levi, is named after him.

Gersonides was well known as a *Halakhist*, one who deals with the intricacies of Jewish law. By far his greatest contribution to Judaica was in the area of biblical commentary. His commentary on the Book of Job, completed in 1325, proved to be one of his most popular works and was one of the earliest Hebrew books to be published (in Ferrara, 1477). The commentary, which complements book 4 of *Milhamot Ha-Shem*, is concerned with the problem of divine providence. Each of the characters in the Book of Job represents a different theory of divine providence; Gersonides' own position is a restatement of Elihu's theory that providence is not directed to particulars but rather to groups of individuals, or universals.

Gersonides also wrote a philosophical treatise, *Sefer Ha-heqesh Ha-yashar* (On Valid Syllogisms, 1319), in which he examines problems associated with Aristotle's modal logic as developed in the *Posterior Analytics*. This treatise was translated into Latin at an early date; Gersonides' name was not attached to it.

Gersonides' major philosophical work, *Milhamot Ha-Shem*, was completed in 1329; it had been twelve years in the making. In 1317 Gersonides began an essay on the problem of creation. This problem, which has vexed Jewish philosophers since Philo Judaeus, had recently received elaborate treatment by Maimonides. Gersonides was dissatisfied with Maimonides' discussion and proposed to reopen the issue. This project was soon laid aside, however, for he felt that it could not be adequately discussed without proper grounding in the issues of time, motion, and the infinite. By 1325 his manuscript had developed to include discussion not only of creation but also of immortality, divination, and prophecy. By 1328 it included a chapter on providence as well. Books 5 and 6 were completed, by Gersonides' own dating, by 1329.

As Isaac Husik has pointed out, Gersonides "has no use for rhetorical flourishes and figures of speech . . . the effect upon the reader is monotonous and wearisome." His style has been compared to that of Thomas Aquinas and even of Aristotle in its use of a precise, technical vocabulary which eschews examples. In contradistinction to Maimonides, who introduced allegory, metaphor, and imprecise language into his work to convey the ambiguity of the subject matter, Gersonides saw it as his function to elucidate the issues as clearly as possible. Gersonides is the first Jewish philosopher to use this analytic, Scholastic method.

In his introduction Gersonides specifies six questions which he hopes to examine: Is the rational soul immortal? What is the nature of prophecy? Does God know particulars? Does divine providence extend to individuals? What is the nature of astronomical bodies? Is the universe eternal or created? Each question occupies a separate book. Gersonides attempts to reconcile traditional Jewish beliefs with what he feels are the strongest points in Aristotle's philosophy. Although a synthesis of these systems is his ultimate goal, the philosophy often wins out at the expense of theology.

Gersonides' discussion of immortality of the soul in book 1 must be understood against the backdrop of a notoriously difficult passage in *On the Soul*, book 3, chapter 5. In this passage Aristotle seems to postulate the existence of an active intellect which is separable from the passive intellect and which is primarily responsible for the intellectual activities of the human mind. But what is the relation between the active and passive intellects, and which, if either, is immortal? Gersonides summarizes and criticizes four representative positions on this question. His own view is a version of that of Alexander of Aphrodisias, according to whom the active intellect is associated with the eternal "Agent Intellect"—that is, God—and is to some extent immortal. Gersonides agrees with Alexander that immortality of the soul consists in the perfection of the human intellect, but he disagrees with Alexander over the precise nature of this intellectual attainment. Unlike Alexander, who emphasized the process of conjunction between the human intellect and the Agent Intellect, Gersonides argues that the content rather than the process of knowledge is what matters. When the content of the human intellect mirrors that of the Agent Intellect, immortality is achieved. This knowledge, according to Gersonides, is of the complete ordering of particulars in the sublunary universe.

Books 2 to 4 focus on the relation between God and the world. The general problem is whether God's knowledge is limited to necessary states of affairs or extends to the domain of contingency as well. If the former, then God could not be said to have knowledge of humans, and so divine providence would not be efficacious. But if God does know contingents—in particular, future contingent events—then it would appear that human freedom is curtailed by God's prior knowledge of human actions.

The problem of the apparent conflict between divine omniscience and human freedom was discussed by many medieval philosophers. Gersonides does not follow the majority opinion on this issue: rather than claim that God does know particulars and that this knowledge somehow does not affect human freedom, Gersonides argues that God knows particulars only in a certain sense. In an apparent attempt to mediate between the view of Aristotle, who said that God does not know particulars, and that of Maimonides, who said that he does, Gersonides holds that God knows particulars only insofar as they are ordered. That is, God knows that certain states of affairs are particular, but he does not know in what their particularity consists. God knows individual persons, for example, only through knowing the species humanity.

Whereas Maimonides claimed that God's knowledge does not render the objects of his knowledge necessary, Gersonides maintains that divine knowledge precludes contingency. To retain the domain of contingency, he adopts the one option open to him: namely, that God does not have prior knowledge of future contingents. According to Gersonides, God knows that certain states of affairs may or may not be actualized. But insofar as they are contingent states, he does not know which of the alternatives will be the case. For if God did know future contingents prior to their actualization, there could be no contingency in the world.

In book 2, in an attempt to explain how prophecies are possible in a system which denies the possibility of knowledge of future contingents, Gersonides claims that the prophet does not receive knowledge of particular future events; rather his knowledge is of a general form, and he must instantiate this knowledge with particular facts. What distinguishes prophets from ordinary persons is that the former are more attuned to receive these universal messages and are in a position to apply them to particular circumstances.

A further dilemma surrounds the doctrine of divine providence. If God does not have knowledge of future contingents, how can he be said to bestow providence on his creatures? This problem is discussed by Gersonides both in his commentary on Job and in book 4 of *Milhamot Ha-Shem*. In both texts he argues that providence is general in nature; it primarily appertains to species and only incidentally to particulars of the species. God, for example, does not know the particular individual Levi ben Gerson and does not bestow particular providence on him. Rather, inasmuch as Levi ben Gerson is a member of the species humanity and the species philosopher, he is in a position to receive the providential care accorded to those groups.

Finally, book 6 concerns the original issue that interested Gersonides, the creation of the universe. The question of whether the universe was created or had existed from eternity had been treated by Maimonides in an ambiguous manner; scholars still disagree over whether Maimonides ultimately upheld an Aristotelian, Platonic, or scriptural doctrine of creation. Gersonides' position is unambiguously Platonic.

Gersonides argues that the world was created outside of time by a freely willing agent. He must then decide whether the world was engendered ex nihilo or out of a preexistent matter. Arguing that ex-nihilo creation is incompatible with physical reality, he adopts a model drawn from Plato's *Timaeus*. Gersonides interprets the opening of Genesis to refer to two types of matter. *Geshem* is the primordial matter out of which the universe was created; not capable of motion or rest, it was characterized by negation and was inert and chaotic. This matter is identified with the primeval waters described in Genesis. *Homer* is prime matter, in the Aristotelian sense of a substratum always aligned with form. It contains within itself the potentiality to receive forms but is not an ontologically independent entity. Gersonides compares this matter to darkness: just as darkness is the absence of light, this matter represents the absence of form or shape. On this basis Gersonides argues that the world was created out of an eternally preexistent matter.

Gersonides' philosophical ideas went against the grain of traditional Jewish thought. Whereas his commentaries occupied a central place in Jewish theology, his philosophical work was rejected. Jewish philosophers such as Hasdai Crescas and Isaac Abrabanel, however, felt obliged to subject his works to lengthy criticism. Only in recent years has Gersonides received his rightful place in the history of philosophy. As scholars have rediscovered his thought and have made his corpus available to a modern audience, Gersonides is once again appreciated as an insightful, ruthlessly consistent philosopher.

Bibliography:

Menahem M. Kellner, "R. Levi Ben Gerson: A Bibliographical Essay," *Studies in Bibliography and Booklore*, 12 (1979): 13-23.

References:

Joseph Carlebach, *Levi ben Gerson als Mathematiker: Ein Beitrag zur Geschichte der Mathematik bei den Juden* (Berlin: Lamm, 1910);

Seymour Feldman, "Gersonides on the Possibility of Conjunction with the Agent Intellect," *American Jewish Society Review*, 3 (1978): 99-120;

Feldman, "Gersonides' Proofs for the Creation of the Universe," *Proceedings of the American Academy for Jewish Research*, 35 (1967): 113-137;

Bernard R. Goldstein, *The Astronomical Tables of Rabbi Levi ben Gerson*, Transactions of the Connecticut Academy of Arts and Sciences, volume 45 (Hamden, Conn.: Shoestring Press, 1975);

Isaac Husik, "Studies in Gersonides," *Jewish Quarterly Review*, new series 7 (1916-1917): 553-594; 8 (1917-1918): 113-156, 231-268;

Menahem M. Kellner, "Maimonides and Gersonides on Mosaic Prophecy," *Speculum*, 52 (1977): 62-79;

Shlomo Pines, "Scholasticism after Thomas Aquinas and the Teachings of Hasdai Crescas and his Predecessors," *Proceedings of the Israel Academy of Sciences and Humanities*, 1 (1967): 1-101;

Tamar M. Rudavsky, "Creation, Time and Infinity in Gersonides," *Journal of the History of Philosophy*, 26 (January 1988): 25-44;

Rudavsky, "Divine Omniscience and Future Contingents in Gersonides," *Journal of the History of Philosophy*, 21 (October 1983): 513-536;

Norbert Samuelson, "Gersonides' Account of God's Knowledge of Particulars," *Journal of the History of Philosophy*, 10 (October 1972): 399-416;

Charles Touati, *La pensée philosophique et théologique de Gersonide* (Paris: Les Editions de Minuit, 1973);

Isidore Weil, *Philosophie religieuse de Levi-ben-Gerson* (Paris: Ladrange, 1868).

Al-Ghazali
(Algazel)
(Abu Hamid Muhammad ibn Muhammad al-Tusi al-Ghazali)
(1058 - 1111)

Michael E. Marmura
University of Toronto

PRINCIPAL WORKS: *Maqasid al-Falasifah* (The Aims of the Philosophers, written circa 1093);
Tahafut al-Falasifah (The Incoherence of the Philosophers, written circa 1094);
Mi'yar al-'Ilm (The Standard for Knowledge, written circa 1094);
Fada'ih al-Batiniyya (Scandals of the Esoterics, written circa 1094);
Al-Iqtisad fi al-I'tiqad (Moderation in Belief, written circa 1095);
Ihya' 'Ulum al-Din (The Revivification of the Sciences of Religion, written between 1096 and 1105);
Al-Maqsad al-Asna Fi Sharh Ma'ani Asma' Allah al-Husna (The Highest Goal in Explaining the Meanings of the Beautiful Names of God, written circa 1106);
Mishkat al-Anwar (The Niche of Lights, written circa 1107);
Al-Qistas al-Mustaqim (The Just Balance, written circa 1107);
Faysal al-Tafriqa Bayna al-Islam wa al-Zandaqa (Distinguishing between Islam and Unbelief, written circa 1108);
Al-Munqidh min al-Dalal (The Deliverer from Error, written circa 1108);
Al-Mustasfa min Usul al-Din (The Choice Essentials of the Principles of Religion, written 1109).

EDITIONS: *Al-Mustazhiri*, edited by I. Goldziher (Leiden: Brill, 1916);
Tahafut al-Falasifah, edited by M. Bouyges, Bibliotheca Arabica Scholasticorum, 2 (Beirut: 1927);
Al-Mustasfa min Usul al-Din, 2 volumes (Cairo: Tijariyya Press, 1937);
Ihya' 'Ulum al-Din, 15 volumes (Cairo: Lajnat Nashr al-Thaqafa al-Islamiiyya, 1937-1939);
Al-Munqidh min al-Dalal, edited by J. Saliba and K. Ayyad (Damascus: Matba' at al-Jami'a al-Suriyya, 1956);
Al-Qistas al-Mustaqim, edited by V. Chelhot (Beirut: Catholic Press, 1959);
Faysal al-Tafriqa Bayna al-Islam wa al-Zandaqa, edited by S. Dunya (Cairo: Isa Babi al-Halabi, 1961);
Maqasid al-Falasifa, edited by Dunya (Cairo: Dar al-Ma'arif bi Misr, 1961);
Mi'yar al-'Ilm, edited by Dunya (Cairo: Dar al-Ma'arif bi Misr, 1961);
Al-Iqtisad fi al-I'tiqad, edited by I. A. Çubuçku & A. Atay (Ankara: Nur Matbassi, 1962);
Mishkat al-Anwar, edited by A. A. Affifi (Cairo: Al-Dar al-Qawymiyya li al-Tiba'a wa al-Nashr, 1964);
Fada'ih al-Batiniyya, edited by A. Badawi (Cairo: Al-Dar al-Qawmiyya li al-Tiba'a wa al-Nashr, 1964);
Al-Maqsad al-Asna Fi Sharh Ma'ani Asma' Allah al-Husna, edited by F. Shehadi (Beirut: Librairie Orientale, 1971).

EDITIONS IN ENGLISH: *The Alchemy of Happiness by Mohammad al-Ghazzali, the Mohammedan Philosopher, Translated from the Turkish*, translated by Henry A. Homes (Albany, N.Y.: Munsell, 1837);
The Alchemy of Happiness; or, The Key to Eternal Bliss: An Exposition of Islamic Theology, translated by K. F. Mirza (Lahore: Islamia Press, 1894);
"Emotional Religion in Islam as Affected by Music and Singing, Being a Translation of a Book of the Ihya 'Ulum ad-Din of al-Ghazzali,' " translated by Duncan B. Macdonald, *Journal of the Royal Asiatic Society* (1901): 195-252, 705-748; (1902): 1-28;

The Confessions of al-Ghazzali, Translated for the First Time into English, translated by Claud Field (London: Murray, 1909);

The Alchemy of Happiness by al Ghazzali, Translated from the Hindustani, translated by Field (London: Murray, 1910);

Some Religious and Moral Teachings of al-Ghazzali, Being Brief Extracts from His Ihya-u-ulum-id-din, Freely Rendered into English, translated by Syed Nawab Ali (Baroda: Widgery, 1921);

Al-Ghazzali's Mishkat al-Anwar ("The Niche for Lights"): A Translation with Introduction, translated by W. H. T. Gairdner (London: Royal Asiatic Society, 1924);

Worship in Islam: Being a Translation, with Commentary and Introduction, of al-Ghazzáli's Book of the Ihya on the Worship, translated by the Reverend Edwin Elliot Calverley (Madras: Christian Literature Society for India, 1925);

"Al-Ghazali on Penitence," translated by C. G. Naish, *Moslem World*, 16 (1926): 6-18;

O Youth, Being a Translation of al-Ghazzali's Ayyuha 'l-walad, translated by the Reverend George H. Scherer (Beirut: American Press, 1933);

"Al-Risalat al-Laduniyya," translated by Margaret Smith, *Journal of the Royal Asiatic Society* (1938): 177-200, 353-374;

"Al-Ghazzali's Epistle of the Birds, a Translation of the Risalat al-Tayr," translated by Nabih Amin Faris, *Moslem World*, 34 (1944): 46-53;

Al-Ghazali, the Mystic, translated by Smith (London: Luzak, 1944);

The Faith and Practice of al-Ghazzali, translated by W. Montgomery Watt (London: Allen & Unwin, 1953);

Our Beginning in Wisdom, translated by Isma 'il R. el Faruqi (Washington, D.C.: American Council of Learned Societies, 1953);

Al-Ghazali's Tahafut al Falasifah (Incoherence of the Philosophers), translated with an introduction by Sabih Ahmad Kamali (Lahore: Pakistan Philosophical Congress, 1958);

The Concept of Man in Islam, in the Writings of al-Ghazali, translated by Ali Issa Othman (Cairo: Dar al-Maaref, 1960);

Some Moral and Religious Teachings of al-Ghazzali, translated by Ali (Lahore: Ashraf, 1960);

Al-Ghazali's Book of Fear and Hope, translated by William McKane (Leiden: Brill, 1962);

The Book of Knowledge, Being the English Translation of Kitab al 'Ilm, translated by Faris (Lahore: Ashraf, 1962);

The Foundations of the Articles of Faith, translated by Faris (Lahore: Ashraf, 1963);

Book XX of al-Ghazali's Ihya' 'Ulum al-Din, edited and translated by L. Zolondek (Leiden: Brill, 1963);

Ghazali's Book of Counsel for Kings, Translated by F. R. C. Bagley from the Persian Text Edited by Jalal Huma'i and the Bodleian Arabic Text Edited by H. D. Isaacs, with Introduction, Notes, and Biographical Index (London: Oxford University Press, 1964);

"Al-Ghazali's Tract on Dogmatic Theology," edited and translated by A. L. Tibawi, *Islamic Quarterly*, 9 (1965): 65-112;

The Mysteries of Almsgiving, Translation of Kitab Asrar al-Zakah, translated by Faris (Beirut: American University Press, 1966);

The Mysteries of Purity: Kitab Asrar al-Taharah of al-Ghazzali's Ihya' 'Ulum al-Din, translated by Faris (Lahore: Ashraf, 1966);

Freedom and Fulfillment: An Annotated Translation of al-Ghazali's al-Munqih min al-Dalai and Other Relevant Works, translated by R. J. McCarthy (Boston: Hall, 1980).

Medieval Islam's great lawyer, theologian, and mystic, al-Ghazali is known to Muslims as *hujjat al-Islam*, "the proof of Islam." The appellation refers to his role in defending "orthodox" Islam and to his refutation of doctrines he regarded as contrary to Islamic teaching. His refutations include *Tahafut al-Falasifah* (The Incoherence of the Philosophers, circa 1094), an incisive critique of Islamic philosophy, particularly that of Avicenna. This work, which had repercussions in medieval and Renaissance European thought, questioned basic tenets of Islamic Aristotelianism, including the concept of necessary causal connection. It also leveled a devastating logical criticism on Islamic Neoplatonic emanative philosophy as developed by Avicenna. At the same time, al-Ghazali admired Avicenna's logic, which he regarded as a philosophically neutral tool of knowledge. He wrote several excellent expositions of it, recommending it to his fellow theologians and lawyers. His writings also include important works on Islamic law. Al-Ghazali, however, is particularly noted for his conversion to Sufism (Islamic mysticism) and his endeavor to reconcile it with traditional Islamic belief.

A few years before his death in 1111 al-Ghazali wrote *Al-Munqidh min al-Dalal* (The Deliverer from Error, circa 1108), a short autobiography that is a literary masterpiece. It tells the story of his intellectual and spiritual search after epistemological uncertainty, the period of doubt he experienced, his encounters with philosophy and with heterodox doctrine, and finally his adoption of the Sufi way of life. The work's emphasis is on his intellectual and spiritual journey; it is not devoid of factual information about the more mundane events in his life, but such information tends to be tantalizingly sparse. For example, the autobiography tells little about his childhood and early youth. For this information, as well as to fill in other gaps in his account, one has to examine critically other medieval Arabic sources.

Abu Hamid Muhammad ibn Muhammad al-Tusi al-Ghazali was born in 1058 in the town or district of Tus, in northeast Persia (present-day Iran)—hence one of his names, "the Tusite." Abu Hamid, which means "the father of Hamid," is his honorific title or *kunya* and does not mean that he had a son named Hamid. (As far as is known, he had daughters but no sons.) The name al-Ghazali in all probability relates him to his birthplace, Ghazala, a village in the environs of Tus. Sometimes his name is spelled al-Ghazzali; the derivation here would be from *Ghazzal*, "spinner of wool." Those who defend this spelling advocate the theory that his father or another ancestor was a wool spinner. There is no evidence, however, that his father pursued this occupation, and there are indications that his family belonged to the class of traditional Islamic religious scholars rather than that of tradesmen.

Al-Ghazali had a brother, Ahmad, who also became a scholar and a Sufi, and several sisters. Before their father died he left some funds with a Sufi friend, entrusting him to use them to educate the two sons. There is no reason to believe that the Sufi did not fulfill his obligation, but it seems that the fund was exhausted before their education was complete. The two orphans were then sent to *madrasas*, religious schools or colleges, that emphasized the study of Islamic law. These colleges were endowed institutions that provided the students with room and board. Al-Ghazali studied in Tus and then for a short period in Jurjan, at the southeast end of the Caspian Sea. In 1077 he went to a major *madrasa* in Neyshabur, where he was taught by Imam al-Haramayn al-Juwayni, a noted doctor of Islamic law and the leading theologian (*mutakallim*) of the school of speculative theology (*kalam*) founded by Abu al-Hasan al-Ash'ari in the tenth century.

By the eleventh century the Ash'arite school was becoming the dominant school of *kalam* in Islam. It viewed the material world as consisting of transient atoms and held that all temporal existents and events were the direct creation of the divine voluntary act. What appear as sequences of natural causes and effects are actually nothing more than concomitant events whose regular association is the arbitrary decree of the divine will; there is no real causal interaction between them. Their regularity is not necessary and is disrupted without contradiction when God creates a miracle. Al-Ghazali subscribed to this view and ardently defended it on epistemological and logical grounds. Although he had some reservations about *kalam* as such, the evidence is overwhelming that the theoretical framework in which he formulated his teaching remained Ash'arite.

After the death of al-Juwayni in 1085 al-Ghazali seems to have remained in Neyshabur for some six years, becoming known as a brilliant scholar and author on Islamic law. In 1091 he was appointed by the vizier, Nizam al-Mulk, as professor of law in the *Nizamiyya* at Baghdad. The Nizamiyyas were instituted in various Islamic cities by Nizam al-Mulk (hence their name) for the teaching of Islamic law according to the school of Abu 'Abd Allah al-Shafi'i.

In the second half of the eleventh century the Islamic world was divided, with two counter-caliphates, the Shiite Fatimid caliphate in Cairo and the Sunnite Abbasid caliphate in Baghdad. The caliph in Baghdad wielded moral and religious authority, rather than actual political power. Real power rested with the Seljuk Turks, nomadic warriors who had been converted to Sunni Islam and who occupied Baghdad. Nizam al-Mulk was the vizier of the Seljuk sultan, and the *madrasas* he instituted were meant in part to train scholars to counter the religious propaganda of the Egyptian Fatimids. Al-Ghazali's appointment to this most prestigious of academic chairs made him part of the Seljuk-Abbasid establishment.

Around this time al-Ghazali underwent a period of skepticism. He examined the various sciences that he had attained but found them to fall short of yielding absolutely certain knowledge. Nor could the senses provide certainty. In his autobiography he wrote: "How can there be confidence in the things attained by the senses? The strongest [of the senses] is the sense of sight. But [this faculty] looks at the shadow and sees it static, not moving, and makes the judgment denying [its] motion. But then through observation and experiment, after an hour, it knows that the shadow moves, that it did not move all at once, but gradually, atom by atom, so that it would never have had a static state. [This faculty] would [also] look at the star and would see it small, the size of a dinar, but then astronomical proofs would show that it is greater in magnitude than the earth."

This skepticism extended itself to reason; for if the senses can deceive us, so could reason. He thus began to doubt the bases of all reasoning, the self-evident logical truths. He remained in this "illness," he says, for two months, until God restored to him belief in reason.

His professorship at Baghdad lasted until 1095, during which time he annually taught three hundred students. For two years during this period, despite his many duties, he applied himself to the study of the Islamic philosophers; he spent a third year going over what he studied. The result was a series of important works on philosophy, the foremost being *Tahafut al-Falasifah.* He also wrote *Maqasid al-Falasifah* (The Aims of the Philosophers, circa 1093), a work of exposition that was mistakenly taken in the Latin West to be an expression of al-Ghazali's own philosophy. In introducing it, and again at the end, he says that he wrote it to explain the philosophers' theories before refuting them in the *Tahafut al-Falasifah.* It is curious, however, that not once in the *Tahafut al-Falasifah* does he refer back to this work. A possible explanation is that he initially wrote it to summarize for himself the theories of the philosophers he had studied, and that he only decided to publish it after the *Tahafut al-Falasifah* was already written and published. Another work, *Mi'yar al-'Ilm* (The Standard for Knowledge, circa 1094), was written as an appendix to the *Tahafut al-Falasifah.* An exposition of Avicenna's logic, it is the most comprehensive of the logical expositions that al-Ghazali wrote. Al-Ghazali suggests in it how he would reinterpret Aristotelian demonstrative theory in terms of his Ash'arite doctrine that the uniformities in nature are created at will by God.

Another work belonging to this period is *Al-Iqtisad fi al-I'tiqad* (Moderation in Belief, circa 1095). The expressed purpose of the *Tahafut al-Falasifah* is to refute the Islamic philosophers, not to affirm doctrine; the affirmation of doctrine is given in this work of *kalam.* To this period also belongs *Fada'ih al-Batiniyya* (Scandals of the Esoterics, circa 1094), a work refuting the Batinis, Ismaili Shiites who upheld the doctrine of esoteric knowledge. This work was written at the request of the Abbasid caliph, indicating again al-Ghazali's association with the political powers in Baghdad.

His works on logic and *kalam* raise the question of his attitude toward these two disciplines. His attitude toward logic is clear: it is a philosophically neutral tool of inquiry. The logic used by the philosophers does not differ basically from that used by the theologians, but it is more refined and elaborate and uses a different technical vocabulary. He writes in his autobiography:

> As for [the philosophers'] logical sciences, none of these relates to religion either by way of denial or affirmation. They are no more than the study of the methods of proof and standards for reasoning, the conditions of the premises of demonstration and the manner of their ordering, the conditions of correct definition and the manner of its construction.
>
> They simply affirm that knowledge is either conception, arrived at through definition, or assent, arrived at through demonstration. Nothing of this ought to be denied. It is the same kind of thing the theologians and the religious speculative thinkers mention in their treatments of proofs. The philosophers differ from them only in their expressions and idioms and their more exhaustive definitions and classifications.

The main purpose of *kaIaml*, al-Ghazali says in the autobiography, is to protect true belief against the distortions of heretical innovators. To this extent it is good and serves a religious purpose, but it did not satisfy him in his quest for certitude.

In 1095 al-Ghazali left his prestigious chair of law in Baghdad to follow the Sufi way of life. He underwent a severe spiritual crisis that came to a head in July of that year when for a period of time he lost his ability to speak. Part of the reason for this illness, he says, is that he realized that his motivation in pursuing his career was worldly success and prestige rather than authentic religious impulse. But he also hints at a deeper reason, a dissatisfaction with the purely doctrinal and rational approaches to religion that for him bypassed the heart of the matter, namely, that which is directly experiential in religion, the *dhawq* (a Sufi term that literally means "taste"). He had read the works of the Sufis, and he desired to follow their practice, which meant seclusion and a life of mystical devotion unencumbered by worldly concerns. To leave Baghdad without opposition from the authorities, he gave as his reason for traveling the intent to go on the pilgrimage to Mecca. After making arrangements for the welfare of his family, he went to Syria and secluded himself in a mosque in Damascus. He then went to Palestine, where he secluded himself in prayer at the Dome of the Rock in Jerusalem and also visited Hebron. Ultimately he did go to Mecca and Medina.

It was during the eleven-year period of travel that he wrote his magnum opus, the voluminous *Ihya' 'Ulum al-Din* (The Revivification of the Sciences of Religion, written between 1096 and 1105). This work strives to reconcile traditional Muslim belief with Sufism; it also attempts to reconcile Islamic theological principles and the Aristotelian doctrine of the golden mean with the virtues expounded by the Sufis, the highest of which is the love of God. It also gives an interpretation of the goal the Sufis strove for. The ultimate end is not, as some Sufis had expressed it, annihilation (*al-fanā'*) of the self in the divine essence. Such a statement, taken in a literal sense, is unacceptable to the traditional Muslim. Rather, the mystical end is "closeness" (*qurb*) to God, a closeness to the eternal divine attributes, which for the Ash'arites are "additional" to the divine essence.

Finally, in 1106, under pressure from the Seljuk authorities, he resumed the teaching of law. He returned to Neyshabur and then to Tus, where he taught until his death in 1111. During this period he wrote his major work on Islamic law, *Al-Mustasfa min Usul al-Din* (The Choice Essentials of the Principles of Religion, 1109), which begins with a succinct exposition of Avicenna's logic. To this period also belongs his autobiography; his mystical work *Mishkat al-Anwar* (The Niche of Lights, circa 1107); and *Al-Maqsad al-Asna Fi Sharh Ma'ani Asma' Allah al-Husna* (The Highest Goal in Explaining the Meanings of the Beautiful Names of God, circa 1106), an important work on the divine attributes that raises the question of the knowability of God. These works are all of philosophical interest; nonetheless, al-Ghazali's work on philosophy par excellence is the *Tahafut al-Falasifah*. This work had an immense influence on subsequent Islamic theological and philosophical thought and was also influential in the Latin West during the medieval period and the Renaissance. It continues to be of intrinsic philosophic interest, as it probes and analyzes perennial philosophical questions. What it says about causality, for example, remains relevant today. Its sequel, the Ash'arite theological treatise *Al-Iqtisad fi al-I'tiqad*, is not as well known as the *Tahafut al-Falasifah* but is essential for understanding al-Ghazali's real position on causality.

Al-Ghazali gives the purpose of the *Tahafut al-Falasifah* in its religious preface and four short introductions. His intention, he stresses, is simply to refute the Islamic philosophers al-Farabi and Avicenna, whom he regards as the best representatives of Aristotelianism in Islam. His main concern, he says, is with those of their theories that contravene "the principles of religion." He has no quarrel with their mathematical and astronomical sciences, and certainly not with their logic. He will show that, contrary to what they claim, these philosophers have not demonstrated their metaphysical theories: "We will make it clear that in their metaphysical sciences they have been able to fulfill none of the conditions they set down for the truth of the matter of the syllogism [that is, its premises] in the section of demonstration in logic, none of the conditions they set down for the form of the syllogism in the *Book of the Syllogism*, and none of the postulates they set down in the *Isagoge* and the *Categories* which are parts of logic, constituting its preliminaries." Underlying this statement is the criterion of demonstrability, which is also part of his theory of scriptural interpretation: a theory which has been demonstrated is necessarily true and has to be accepted; if such a theory happens to contradict the literal sense of a scriptural utterance, then the utterance must be interpreted metaphorically. Conversely, unless a scriptural utterance can be demonstrably proved to be impossible, then it must be accepted literally. Hence, any metaphysical theory whose truth has not been rigorously demonstrated and which also opposes the literal truth of religious utterances must be rejected as false.

His purpose in the *Tahafut al-Falasifah* is to refute the philosophers, to demolish their theories, not to affirm his own doctrine. "I do not enter into [argument] objecting to them," he writes, "except as one who demands and denies, not as one who claims and affirms." This statement in one of the introductions is expanded on at the end of the First Discussion, devoted to refuting the philosophers' proofs that the world existed from eternity. Imagining a possible criticism of his method of refuting the philosophers, he writes:

> If it is said, "in all the objections, you have resorted to opposing difficulties with [other] difficulties and have not resolved the difficulties [the philosophers] brought forth," we say:
>
> Objection inescapably shows the falsity of what is said and the problematic facet of the diffi-

> culty [they raise] is resolved by what is implied in the objection and by what is being asked. In this book we have committed ourselves only to rendering their doctrine murky and the modes of their proofs dusty wherewith we show their incoherence.
>
> We have not endeavored to defend a particular doctrine and as such have not departed from the objective of this book. We will not argue exhaustively for the doctrine of the temporal origination [of the world], since our purpose is to refute their claim of knowing [its] pre-eternity.
>
> As for the true doctrine, we will write a book concerning it after completing this one—if success, God willing, comes to our aid—and will name it "The Principles of Belief." We will engage in it in affirmation, just as we have devoted ourselves in this book to destruction.

In his *Tahafut al-Tahafut* (The Incoherence of the Incoherence, circa 1180), a reply to al-Ghazali's *Tahafut al-Falasifah*, the Islamic Aristotelian Averroës repeatedly refers to arguments used by al-Ghazali as Ash'arite. To a large extent, Averroës is correct: one can show, more often than not, that al-Ghazali is arguing from an Ash'arite theological base, and he makes categorical statements that are Ash'arite. But the intention remains to refute, rather than to establish a position. At the same time, however, there are instances where he defends non-Ash'arite positions. But he defends them simply for the sake of argument, as a means of refuting the philosophers, not because he actually subscribes to them. His primary purpose in the *Tahafut al-Falasifah* continues to be to refute, not to construct and develop doctrine.

In his statement that after completing the *Tahafut al-Falasifah* he intends to write a book in which he will affirm true doctrine, the title given poses a minor problem of identification. The title is *Qawa'id al-'Aqa'id* (The Principles of Belief). An Ash'arite work bearing this title forms one of the books of his magnum opus, the *Ihya' 'Ulum al-Din,* which he wrote during his eleven years of travel. The work that best fulfills the purpose stated in the *Tahafut al-Falasifah,* however, is the more detailed *Al-Iqtisad fi al-I'tiqad* written shortly after the *Tahafut al-Falasifah*. Significantly, he says in this work that its concern is "*qawa'id al-'aqa'id*" (the principles of beliefs), although he does not use this phrase as the title. The *Al-Iqtisad fi al-I'tiqad* refers directly to the *Tahafut al-Falasifah* and is close to it in idiom, spirit, and the issues it discusses. There can be little doubt that the *Al-Iqtisad fi al-I'tiqad,* rather than the *Qawa'id al-'Aqa'id,* is the sequel to the *Tahafut al-Falasifah.*

In the *Tahafut al-Falasifah* al-Ghazali undertakes to refute twenty of the philosophers' theories. Seventeen of these, he says, are heretical innovations. Three, however, are utterly contrary to Islamic teaching; those who uphold these theories are infidels. The three theories are the world's pre-eternity, Avicenna's doctrine that God knows particulars "in a universal way," and his doctrine that affirms the individual immortality of the human soul but denies bodily resurrection. Al-Ghazali's method of refutation is to present the opponent's theory clearly and in its strongest form. He then raises objections to it, gives possible answers to his objections, presents his own answers to the answers, and so on, until the theory is refuted. The first of the two theories he rejects as irreligious are metaphysical. The doctrine denying bodily resurrection, however, belongs to the natural sciences because it is concerned with psychology. The section on the natural sciences also includes his famous Seventeenth Discussion on miracles, in which he objects to the Islamic philosophers' denial of the literal truth of certain miracles. This denial is based on their theory that natural existents have natural powers that, when the causal conditions are fulfilled, produce their effect necessarily. Al-Ghazali does not consider this theory necessarily irreligious; he says that it is identical with the doctrine of generated acts of the Mu'tazilite theologians, a theory which he rejects but which in itself does not contravene the principles of religion.

In arguing for the doctrine of bodily resurrection in the *Tahafut al-Falasifah*, al-Ghazali offers a refutation of ten of Avicenna's standard proofs for the immateriality of the human soul. Nonetheless, he tries to show that even if one adopts a doctrine of an immaterial soul, one can still uphold bodily resurrection. His argument in the *Tahafut al-Falasifah* is so convincing that one is left with the impression that al-Ghazali in fact subscribes to a doctrine of an immaterial soul. When one turns to the *Al-Iqtisad fi al-I'tiqad* one finds that al-Ghazali subscribes to the Ash'arite doctrine of a material soul, according to which life is a transient accident God creates in the body, animating it. In defending the doctrine of bodily resurrection in the *Al-Iqtisad fi al-I'tiqad* he writes:

> We have treated this problem in detail in the *Incoherence of the Philosophers*, adopting in it refut-

> ing the philosophers' doctrine the view that affirms the immortality of the soul—which according to them has no position in space—and that allows the resumption of its management of the body, regardless of whether or not such a body is the same as the original human body.
>
> This, however, is a consequence [we made logically incumbent on them to accept] that does not agree with what we believe. For that book was written for the purpose of refuting their doctrine, not for the purpose of establishing true doctrine.

In other words, al-Ghazali defends a theory in the *Tahafut al-Falasifah* simply for the sake of refuting the opponent, not because he holds the theory to be true. All indications in the *Tahafut al-Falasifah* suggest strongly that he fully subscribes to the Ash'arite position that temporal events and existents are the direct creation of God, that there is no real causal interaction between them. Nonetheless, in the Seventeenth Discussion, after forcefully arguing that observation shows only concomitance, not necessary causal connection in nature, he introduces an alternative causal theory which, he argues, allows for the possibility of those miracles the philosophers deem impossible. First he brings up a possible response to his denial of necessary causal connection: "This leads to the commission of repugnant impossibilities; for if one denies that the effects follow necessarily from their causes and relates them to the will of the Creator, the will having no specific designated course—[a course] that can vary and become multifarious—then let each of us allow the possibility of his being in the presence of ferocious beasts, raging fires, high mountains, or enemies ready with their weapons to kill him, but he does not see them because God does not create for him vision [of them]. . . ." In reply, al-Ghazali maintains that this conclusion does not follow. These events would be possibilities; God, however, creates the knowledge in us that such absurdities would not occur. Hence the objection of the opponent is not a real argument and amounts to sheer vilification. Nonetheless, one can avoid being subject to such vilification by adopting another causal theory that would still allow for the possibility of those miracles rejected by the philosophers. According to this theory, which is perhaps best described as a modified Aristotelian causal theory (although one can also consider it as a modified Ash'arite theory), natural things possess causal powers that produce necessary effects. But the act of the omnipotent God, which is always a voluntary act not necessitated by his essence, can intervene in the natural causal chain to create a new natural cause that produces an uncommon event, the miracle. Al-Ghazali says that both causal theories, the Ash'arite and the modified Aristotelian, are possible, and each is capable of explaining miraculous happenings; but they are mutually exclusive, one denying causal efficacy in natural things, the other affirming it. Hence the question arises as to which of the two causal theories al-Ghazali actually subscribes. The *Al-Iqtisad fi al-I'tiqad* provides the answer, for in this work the modified Aristotelian theory is never mentioned. Al-Ghazali's position on causality becomes clear from two related discussions. The first is his discussion of divine power, in which he rejects the Mu'tazilite theory of the generated act, a theory which in the *Tahafut al-Falasifah* he had identified with the Islamic philosophers' causal theory. The second is in his discussion of *al-ajal*, a religious term signifying an individual's appointed time of death.

In the discussion of divine power al-Ghazali reaffirms the Ash'arite point that the attribute of divine power is "additional" to the divine essence. If God's power and essence were identical, then God's actions would be necessitated by his essence; in this case, God would lack will. He then argues that the divine attribute of power is universally pervasive; that is, it is one power, not many powers each producing an event. For future events (unlike past events) can be infinite; if each of these possible events requires an individual power to produce it, then the divine power would be fragmented. Moreover, should these events actually be infinite, the divine productive powers would be numerically infinite, which is not possible. Hence, there is only one divine power that is the direct cause of each and every event: "All temporal things, their substances and accidents, those occurring in the entities of the animate and inanimate, come about through the power of God, exalted be He. He alone holds the sole prerogative of inventing them. It is not the case that some creatures come about through some others. Rather, all come about through [divine] power."

In the discussion of *al-ajal*, the question raised is: if a person is decapitated, for example, is his death due to the decapitation or to his *ajal*, the predetermined time of his death? Al-Ghazali argues that the action of the sword represents a series of accidents that at one point become concomitant with the event, death. Death is not caused by the action of the sword, but by God:

> Killing means the cutting of the neck. This reduces to accidents that are motions of the hand of the striker, accidents that are the separations in the parts of the neck of the one struck, another accident being associated with these, namely death.
>
> If there is no bond between the cutting and death, the denial of death would not follow necessarily from the denial of cutting. For these are created together, connected in accordance with habit [*al-'ada*], there being no bond between one and the other. They are similar to two separate things that are habitually connected.

Al-Ghazali maintains that "death is a thing which the Lord, exalted be He, alone invented with the cutting. . . . Hence, it does not follow from the supposition of the negation of cutting, the negation of death. And this is the truth." In resolving the causal question, over which, as he says, there has been so much dispute, he refers the reader to the rule "we have mentioned regarding the universal pervasiveness of the power of God, exalted be He, and the negation of generation": "On this is based the statement that with respect to the individual killed, it ought to be said that he died by his *ajal, ajal* meaning the time which God creates in him his death, regardless of whether this occurs with the cutting of the neck, the occurrence of a lunar eclipse, or the falling of rain. For all these things are for us associated things, not generated acts, except that with some their connection is repeated according to habit, but with some they are not repeated."

The *Al-Iqtisad fi al-I'tiqad* shows conclusively that the modified Aristotelian theory in the *Tahafut al-Falasifah* does not represent al-Ghazali's view; he merely presents it to demonstrate that one can account for miracles even if causal efficacy in things is allowed. The opening of the Seventeenth Discussion of the *Tahafut al-Falasifah* is a statement of what he actually believes:

> According to us, the connection between what is habitually believed to be the cause and what is habitually believed to be the effect is not necessary. But in the case of two things, neither of which is the other and where neither the affirmation nor the negation of the one entails the affirmation or negation of the other, the existence or nonexistence of the one does not necessitate the existence or nonexistence of the other; for example the quenching of thirst and drinking, satiety and eating, burning and contact with fire, light and the rising of the sun, death and decapitation, recovery and the taking of medicine, the bowel movement and the taking of a laxative and so on to the inclusion of all observed connections in medicine, astronomy, arts and crafts.
>
> The connection of these things is due to the prior decree of God, who creates them side by side, not to any inherent necessity in these things that would render their separation from each other impossible. On the contrary, it is within God's power to create satiety without eating, death without decapitation, to prolong life after decapitation and so on in the case of all concomitant things.

The many cogent arguments and denunciations in the *Tahafut al-Falasifah* put Islamic philosophy on the defensive. Ironically, however, the work also helped to spread philosophical knowledge in the Islamic world. To refute the Islamic philosophers, al-Ghazali had to explain their theories. The clarity of his expositions made these theories better known in Islam and certainly made them much more accessible to those not trained in philosophy. They also became better known because al-Ghazali, in effect, initiated a new theological tradition. After the *Tahafut al-Falasifah*, any Islamic theologian worth his salt had to discuss philosophical doctrine. Thus *kalam* itself became more philosophical, without ceasing to be *kalam*. Moreover, his criticisms evoked responses, the most comprehensive being that of Averroës in his *Tahafut al-Tahafut*, which blunts the edge of many of al-Ghazali's arguments even if it does not totally refute them. Averroës' work is a philosophical classic in its own right, and al-Ghazali was responsible for its existence.

Al-Ghazali was a versatile, intense, deeply religious thinker. Strictly speaking, he was not a philosopher but a lawyer, theologian, and Sufi. But the philosophical impulse is ever present in his writings and manifests itself in what is known of his life. His autobiography indicates that he was primarily motivated by the need for epistemological certainty. After a long search, he found certainty in the literal sense of scriptural language, as long as this language did not involve the acceptance of what is demonstratively impossible. He used reason to defend the religious certitude he had attained. He was not a mere literalist; religious language, for the most part, has to be taken in its literal sense, he maintained. But it is also symbolic, its symbols serving as road signs for the Sufi's spiritual journey as he seeks proximity to the attributes of the divine.

Bibliographies:

W. Montgomery Watt, "The Authenticity of the Work Attributed to al-Ghazali," *Journal of the Royal Asiatic Society* (1952): 23-45;

Maurice Bouyges, *Essai de chronologie des oevres d'al-Ghazali (Algazel)*, edited by Michael Allard (Beirut: Imprimerie Catholique, 1959);

George F. Hourani, "A Revised Chronology of Ghazali's Writings," *Journal of the American Oriental Society*, 104 (April-June 1984): 289-302.

References:

Georges H. Bousquet, ed., *Ih'ya 'ouloûm ed-din; ou, Vivification des sciences de la foi* (Paris: Besson, 1953);

Majid Fakhry, *Islamic Occasionalism* (London: Allen & Unwin, 1958);

George F. Hourani, "The Dialogue between al-Ghazali and the Philosophers on the Origin of the World," *Muslim World*, 48 (July 1958): 183-191; (October 1958): 308-314;

Hourani, "Ghazali on Ethical Action," *Journal of the American Oriental Society*, 91 (January-March 1976): 69-98;

Hourani, "A Revised Chronology of Ghazali's Writings," *Journal of the American Oriental Society*, 104 (April-June 1984): 289-302;

Farid Jabre, *La Notion de la certitude selon Al-Ghazali dans son origine psychologique et historique* (Paris: Urin, 1958);

Michael E. Marmura, "Al-Ghazali On Bodily Resurrection and Causality in the Tahafut and the Iqtisad," *Aligarth Journal of Islamic Thought*, 2 (1989): 46-75;

Marmura, "Ghazali and Demonstrative Science," *Journal of the History of Philosophy*, 3, no. 2 (1965): 183-204;

Marmura, "Ghazali on Ethical Premises," *Philosophical Forum*, new series 1 (Spring 1969): 393-403;

Fadlou Shehadi, *Ghazali's Unique Unknowable God* (Leiden: Brill, 1964);

Mohammed Ahmed Sherif, *Ghazali's Theory of Value* (Albany: State University of New York Press, 1975);

M. Sinaceur, *Ghazali: La Raison et la Miracle* (Paris: Maisonneuve & Larose, 1987);

W. Montgomery Watt, "The Authenticity of the Work Attributed to al-Ghazali," *Journal of the Royal Asiatic Society* (1952): 23-45;

Watt, *Muslim Intellectual: A Study of al-Ghazali* (Edinburgh: Edinburgh University Press, 1963);

Arent J. Wensinck, *La pensée de Ghazali* (Paris: Adrien-Maisonneuve, 1940);

Harry Austryn Wolfson, "Niclaus of Autrecourt and Ghazali's Argument against Causality," *Speculum*, 44 (April 1969): 234-238.

Giles of Rome
(Aegidius Romanus, Egidius Colonna)

(circa 1243 - 22 December 1316)

Thomas A. Losconcy
Villanova University

PRINCIPAL WORKS: *In De Generatione et Corruptione* (Commentary on [Aristotle's] *On Generation and Corruption*, written 1263-1274);

De Mensura Angelorum (On the Motion of Angels, written 1270-1272);

De Cognitione Angelorum (On the Knowledge of Angels, written 1270-1272);

Rhetorica (Rhetoric, 1270-1272);

Tractatus de Plurificatione Intellectibus Possibilis (Treatise on the Multiplication of the Possible Intellect, written 1272-1275);

De Materia Coeli contra Averroistas (On Celestial Matter, against the Averroists, written 1272-1275);

Theoremata de Corpore Christi (Theorems on the Body of Christ, written 1276);

De Formatione Corporis Humani in Utero (On the Formation of the Human Body in the Womb, written circa 1276);

Metaphysicales Quaestiones (Metaphysical Questions, written 1276);

In Physica (Commentary on [Aristotle's] *Physics*, written 1277);

Liber contra Gradus et Pluralitates Formarum (Book against the Grades and Plurality of Forms, written 1277-1278);

De Regime Principium (On the Rule of Princes, written circa 1277 or 1282);

Theoremata XXII de Esse et Essentia (Twenty-two Theorems on Being and Essence, written 1278-1286);

Expositio de Liber de Causis (Exposition of the *Book of Causes*, written circa 1279);

Exposition in Aristotelis Libros De Anima (Exposition of Aristotle's Book *On the Soul*, written circa 1280);

De Differentia Rhetoricae, Ethicae, et Politicae (On the Differences among Rhetoric, Ethics, and Politics, written circa 1285);

Quaestiones de Esse et Essentia (Questions on Being and Essence, written 1285-1287);

Quodlibeta VI (Six Quodlibetal Questions, written 1285-1291);

Commentarius in Libros Sententiarum (Commentary on the *Sentences* [of Peter Lombard], written 1285-1309);

De Renunciatione Papae (On the Renunciation of the Papacy, written 1294);

De Ecclesiastica Potestate (On Ecclesiastical Power, written 1302);

Contra Exemptos (Against the Templars, written 1310);

De Divina Influencia in Beatos (On Divine Influence on Beatitude, written after 1312).

EDITIONS: *In Aristotelis De Anima Commentum* (Pavia: C. de Canibus for H. de Durantibus, 1491);

Expositio Egidii Romani super Libros De Anima cum Textu (Venice: Octavianus Scotus, 1496);

Egidius Romanus De Esse et Essentia. De Mensura Angelorum. Et de Cognitione Angelorum (Venice: Printed by Simon de Luerc for Andreas Torresanus, 1503);

Tractatus de Plurificatione Intellectus Possibilis (Venice, 1552);

De Ecclesiastica Potestate, edited by Richard Scholz (Weimar: Böhlau, 1929);

Aegidii Romani Theoremata de Esse et Essentia, edited by Edgard Hocedez (Louvin, 1930).

Giles of Rome was probably born at Rome around 1243; no exact date is recorded for his birth, and the estimate is based on his likely ages at various stages of his career. He entered the Augustinian Hermits shortly before his fifteenth birthday at the monastery of Santa Maria del Populo in Rome. Sometime after completing his novitiate in 1259 he was sent to the new Augustinian foundation at Paris at the direction of the general of the order, Clement de Osimo. His early academic career remains relatively unknown, but the surmised dates of his early works and their pro-

Illumination in a manuscript for Giles of Rome's commentary on the Sentences *of Peter Lombard, dated 1301 (Innsbruck, Universitätsbibliothek Cod. 41, fol.* 1ra*)*

fusion indicate considerable work and ability. Thomas Aquinas was among the masters under whom he studied or, at least, whose lectures he attended while Thomas was at Paris from 1269 to 1272.

The first period of Giles's literary output corresponds to the period during which he was a student and young teacher at Paris (1263 to 1278). The subjects of his works represent his academic progress. Except for the *De Mensura Angelorum* (On the Motion of Angels, 1270-1272) and the *De Cognitione Angelorum* (On the Knowledge of Angels, 1270-1272), the early 1270s are marked by a series of logical works. Other original works of this period include the *Tractatus de Plurificatione Intellectibus Possibilis* (Treatise on the Multiplication of the Possible Intellect, 1272-1275), *De Materia Coeli contra Averroistas* (On Celestial Matter, against the Averroists, 1272-1275), and the *Rhetorica* (Rhetoric, 1270-1272). Works of a philosophical and scientific character in the form of commentaries on Aristotle, such as those on *On Generation and Corruption* (1263-1274) and on *Physics* (1277), also occur.

The commentaries on Aristotle, especially the commentary on *On Generation and Corruption*, reflect their early dates of composition in their style. The commentaries are frequently strings of paraphrases with little explanation. In the commentary on the *Physics*, however, Giles adopts what becomes a frequent practice, the use of *dubitarets*—paragraphs or short essays presenting possible or real objections, and his responses. In these early works Giles displays a strong interest in natural philosophy and the empirical sciences. His lengthy discussion of time and his treatment of matter as possessing certain dispositions ("modalities," in other works) but remaining simply matter or pure potency, in the Aristotelian sense, are major features of his thinking at this time.

Giles's treatment of time in his commentary on the *Physics* in many particulars closely follows Averroës' commentary on the same work. Other passages are taken nearly verbatim from Aquinas's commentary on the *Physics*. Such a combination makes sense in one who has just finished his studies of Aristotle's writings with Averroës' commentaries at hand and under the direction of Aquinas.

Giles first raises three points about the relationship between time and motion: time is not the same as motion; time does not exist without motion; and time is conjoined to motion. Time's roots lie in the material realm of change, but time retains its distinct being. This distinction, he claims, follows Averroës as to the material and formal relation time bears to motion: materially, time is identical with motion, but formally, it is distinct. Every encounter with motion—physical and external, or the succession of images or thoughts in the soul—produces an awareness of time. Conversely, awareness of time is always an awareness of motion. Time, like motion, is continuous. The awareness of time springs from the diversification of motion into prior and posterior, for "between any two points there cannot be any intermediary except a line; so when we grasp two *nows*, one of which is prior and the other posterior, and when we grasp that between the two *nows* there is something serving as an intermediary, at that moment we grasp time."

In a quite unusual step, as regards his contemporaries' approach, Giles adds that time exists in a specific fashion in its unique subject, the movement of the first heaven. Giles's objective here is to ground time materially in a universal and unending motion, enabling him to maintain a kind of medieval counterpart to present-day Greenwich time. Everywhere time is one and the same as residing in one subject, the primary motion. Only one measure supersedes that of time: eternity. Eternity, however, is twofold. God is measured by absolute eternity; separate intelligences (angels) and human souls are measured by a participated eternity.

As a measure of motion, time is a cause of corruption in the material world. Generation—the movement toward the perfection of a thing's nature and the realization of its form—is owed primarily to the generating agent. On the other hand, motion is primarily a movement away from a thing's form.

Giles counters the claim by Aristotle and Averroës that the world existed from eternity by pointing out that in contrast to finite things composed of potency and act, God is pure and absolute act. Beings beneath the divine level cause motion and becoming, but God effects the existence (*esse*) of things outside himself. Secondary causes presuppose a prior cause and motion, but divine causation operates without preceding motion or becoming. In immediately communicating *esse*, God produces things apart from the conditions of natural generation. Since God's immediate production of *esse* does not require a prior motion, time has a beginning, and the world need not have existed from eternity.

The debate over the eternity of the world raged on, and in his commentary (1285-1309) on the *Sentences*, by Peter Lombard, Giles again addressed the problem. He says that the mind can travel along one of three possible roads on this question: the philosophers insist that a world run by natural causes has to be eternal; certain great theologians present arguments that purport to demonstrate a creation in time; and faith informs us that the world began in time. Giles holds that neither the proposition that the world had a beginning nor its contradictory is provable by demonstration. He presents twenty-two arguments (thirteen from Aristotle, seven from Averroës, and two from Avicenna) for an eternal world. He insists that all fail by reason of assuming that the divine agent operates along the same lines as natural agents. He surveys seventeen arguments from theologians, including Bonaventure and Henry of Ghent, and counters all of them. He leans toward the reasons of the theologians as establishing the probability of a temporal creation but insists that neither side is capable of demonstration.

Giles carried out a wide range of empirical studies. He taught that the speed of a falling body increases as the distance from the beginning of the fall, and he conducted experiments with a vacuum in which he displays an understanding of air as a material substance capable of keeping water in an inverted vessel. Perhaps his most remarkable achievement in this area is his *De Formatione Corporis Humani in Utero* (On the Formation of the Human Body in the Womb, circa 1276), which rejects Galen's two-seed theory of conception and claims to be more Aristotelian in attributing the active power in conception to the male seed. Giles discusses the period of gestation, the development of the human fetus and its membranes, and the question of sex determination and hereditary resemblances.

Giles's short but powerful *Liber contra Gradus et Pluralitates Formarum* (Book against the Grades and Plurality of Forms, 1277-1278) provides some details about what was transpiring at the University of Paris. Some theologians were borrowing from the philosophers in taking the pluralist position that there are two substantial forms in the human being. This development, Giles says, was caused by difficulties raised in relation to Christ's having a human body and by the need to account for the twofold agency—God and man—responsible for the production of the human being. Giles endeavors to show that the pluralists fail to achieve what they hope to gain and, moreover, that their thesis is simply untenable. He argues that if there is more than one substantial form in a composite, then all substantial change will be eliminated; in any change some substantial form will remain and will make substantial change impossible. Therefore, if there is more than one substantial form in things, then no generation or destruction, which are substantial changes, can occur. Once there exists a permanent bodily form or "form of corporeity" in things, all other forms can only be added as accidents, since they do not replace the original form. Giles charges the pluralists with denying true generation of the human composite and making it impossible for the human soul to have an essential relation to the body. Furthermore, since the intellect's relation to the body would be merely accidental, the pluralists end up justifying Averroës' position that there is only one possible intellect in all people. Giles holds, in opposition to the pluralists that the human being is composite, that the being that enlivens the composite is the single intellectual soul, that the intellectual soul is intermediate between the immaterial and the material and participates in both realms of being.

To demonstrate the "composite being" of the human person Giles invokes the Aristotelian methodology for comprehending the nature of things which are not artifacts but products of the natural world. One must proceed from the functions of such beings to an enumeration of their proper powers in order to assess the kind of nature responsible for them. Employing this approach, Giles finds that the human soul clearly belongs in the world of matter inasmuch as any faulty sense power, or the deprivation of any sense power, severely or entirely affects the range of knowledge humans can attain.

This relation of soul and body is so integral that it carries over into the domain of generation and procreation. If matter is well disposed to receive as its proper substantial form an intellectual soul, one will find a highly refined sense of touch in the resulting individual. Such heightened sensitivity will be, in turn, a stimulus to a more intellectual life. Only a specific animate body can fulfill the need of a given soul. The soul can only affect the body on which it directly depends; it must move other bodies through its proper body: "If the nature of the soul were not dependent on a proper body, then it would never be so determined to that body that it would not be able to move another body except through the motion of its own body." Moreover, it cannot be compatible with any body lower than the human body, as such a body would be inadequate. The soul informs the body as a totality; it is wholly in the body and in all of its parts, but to separate a part of the body from the whole is not to disrupt the soul in any way. Humans contribute properly disposed matter to the existence of a new human being, and God contributes the intellectual soul. The capacities of the human soul extend beyond activities which are simply material to include immaterial intellectual functions. Among the many activities that indicate the human's difference from other animate beings are the pursuit of science for its own sake, while other animate beings do little more than act to survive; the use of language; and the abstracting of a universal idea from particular things of a given kind, an activity which necessitates an immaterial agent. The human soul encompasses most of the capabilities of living beings of lower species; and what mankind does not include naturally it is able to provide through human ingenuity. This intellectual capacity conveys to humanity dominion over the material world.

The human soul is different from the intelligences (angels) that are wholly separate from matter; it exists at a level intermediate between purely material beings and purely immaterial beings. The soul does not unite with just any body but requires a definite kind of body in order to exercise its powers and functions; the separate substances, on the other hand, are known to have appeared in many bodies and human shapes. If such substances were like human souls they could not function fully and freely in different sorts of bodies but would be constrained to operate via one particular body.

Furthermore, the human soul must always move other bodies through the use of its own body as a medium. Even self-movement requires the use of one's own body. Because of this requirement, the soul develops in its body the various muscles adapted for movement and experiences fatigue resulting from the exercise of these bodily members. Giles holds that separate substances experience nothing like these conditions and that true physical motion cannot be attributed to them.

Giles also discerns some major distinctions between human intellectual souls and separate intelligences in their acquisition of knowledge. An intellectual soul commences its existence devoid of all knowledge; it must acquire its knowledge from the sensible world by means of the body. By contrast, separate intelligences have no need to abstract their intelligible species (ideas) from things of the sensible world; they have full possession of their intelligible species, as derived from the divine ideas, from the first instant of their being.

Self-knowledge also distinguishes human intellectual souls from separate intelligences. An intellectual soul's ability to reflect on its knowing activity necessitates its prior knowledge of other beings. Separate intelligences, however, are created wholly intelligible to themselves and in possession of their intelligible species. Through these species they proceed to a knowledge of other beings and so act in reverse fashion to intellectual souls.

Even in terms of the content of their respective ideas the intellectual soul and separate intelligences differ. Just as a wiser human being can grasp more ideas, in a more thorough fashion, under fewer concepts, so too a separate intelligence comprehends more notions under a single concept and knows these notions more intensely than do human souls. In addition, intellectual souls are compelled to derive their ideas from sensible images, whereas separate intelligences know the singular without recourse to images. Giles's account of knowledge is on Aristotelian lines; he does not subscribe to any form of Augustinian divine illumination.

Giles's earliest political writing appears to be the *De Regime Principium* (On the Rule of Princes, circa 1277 or 1282). The work was written for the instruction of the future Philip IV (the Fair) at the request of Philip's father. This work marked the beginning of an amiable relationship in which Giles would represent the university at Philip's coronation in 1285 and Philip would assist Giles in gaining property for his Augustinians and sponsor his appointment to the see of Bourges.

The *De Regime Principium* is likely Giles's best-known work. Thirty-five dated manuscripts were produced between 1282 and 1484, and at least twenty-eight editions appeared between 1473 and 1911 in various languages. The work is of a type known in antiquity, the Middle Ages, and Renaissance as *specula regum* or *specula principis*—"mirrors" intended to reflect a true image of royal virtue for the emulation of kings and princes. It is remarkable among medieval writings of its type because it contains no treatment at all of the place of the church within the prince's realm, and no assertion of ecclesiastical rights and prerogatives.

In *De Differentia Rhetoricae, Ethicae, et Politicae* (On the Differences among Rhetoric, Ethics, and Politics, circa 1285), a treatise written in letter form to a Dominican friar in Anjou named Oliverius, Giles first turns to the issue of how rhetoric differs from politics and ethics. He disagrees with Cicero's claim that rhetoric is part of politics; rather, Giles believes, it is properly tied to dialectics. They both take human acts as their special matter. Still, Giles does not wish to give rhetoric over totally to dialectics; it is a distinct science that can work in the realm of dialectics as regards opinion, but it can also belong to the science of politics as regards persuasion. Since one is to be persuaded to do the "good," rhetoric must be informed by the morality of politics if it is to avoid mere sophistry.

Giles then undertakes the differentiation of ethics from politics. First, ethics is about those things which pertain to the governance of the individual, while politics concerns the governance of the entire state. And since the good of the people is more divine than the good of the individual, politics is superior to ethics. Second, in ethics one is moved by love of the good, whereas in politics one is moved to the good from a fear of pain. Third, ethics is directed to the "good in general," but politics is directed to some specific good pinpointed by the law. The proper subject of law is human action which the law labels just or unjust according to whether the action is done from the appropriate or inappropriate passions. True laws will be made by politicians who have the art or skill of drafting legislation in accordance with sound morals. Legislators who enact laws without the requisite moral Giles calls "vulgar and political idiots."

The commentary on Aristotle's *Rhetoric* enlarges on some of the issues found in the *De Differentia Rhetoricae, Ethicae, et Politicae* and adds its own issues. It gives a thorough analysis of the relation of rhetoric to dialectics and politics; the conclusion is that rhetoric, in the hands of politics, is meant to persuade, that is, to move one's appetites for good; dialectic's use of rhetoric involves, instead, a purely intellectual aim, to show the truth of something. Following a long and involved examination of the differences between a sign and an example, Giles decides rhetoric, in the service of politics, will use examples so as to keep things simple and appeal to the senses. Giles adds a detailed account of the passions and how the soul is moved, discusses the differences between the concupiscible and irascible appetites, and explores the distinction between passion and pleasure. In these works Giles's Aristotelian bent is clearly evident, and his approaches to morality and politics are not noticeably different from those of his contemporaries.

The position that each being contains a single substantial form was condemned in 1277 by Stephen Tempier, the bishop of Paris. When Giles refused to retract his position, he was expelled from the city. His main metaphysical writings can be dated from the period of his exile from Paris. He lived for a year in Bayeux, France; then he traveled to Rome, where he remained until his reinstatement in the university in 1285.

He began work on the *Theoremata XXII de Esse et Essentia* (Twenty-two Theorems on Being and Essence) in 1278, completing it in 1285 or 1286. Between 1285 and 1287 he wrote *Quaestiones de Esse et Essentia* (Questions on Being and Essence), and in the late 1270s or about 1280 he wrote the *Expositio de Liber de Causis* (Exposition of the *Book of Causes*). Metaphysics receives further attention in his *Quodlibeta VI* (Six Quodlibetal Questions, 1285-1291).

In his metaphysics Giles repeatedly states his abhorrence of the necessitarianism in the Avicennian account of the origin of the universe. His objective in countering such an account of the universe's origin is to defend the uniqueness of the divine being as simple, immutable, and independent. Giles asks questions similar to those of Aquinas, uses a similar vocabulary, and even appears to reach similar conclusions at times. Yet his framing of the problem, his reasoning, and his principles reflect a philosophical bent that is decidedly unlike that of Aquinas in vital ways. The result of this curious relation of Giles's writings with Aquinas's and the fact that he had studied under Aquinas for a brief time was to produce confusion for centuries of commentators on Aquinas's thought. Attacks on Giles's metaphysics were, at times, mistaken for attacks on Aquinas.

In God, Giles says, being and essence are identical. Thus, to know something of God's being is simultaneously to know something of God's essence. Giles constructs four proofs of God's existence based on the created universe. The first of these proofs proceeds from the mutability and contingency of all creatures; the second argues from the conservation, governance, and providence evident in the universe; the third is from motion; and the fourth is from final causality as ruling out chance and fortune.

In terms of God's efficient causality, Giles invokes the principle that every cause acts insofar as it has being. Thus, God, to whom belongs all being, is to be assigned all act. This means that God is the cause of a thing's whole being.

The converse of God's being is the universe of participated being. All beings which participate have some potency in them and are not pure act. Their being is from another, is that of an effect, and flows from being that is pure, existing in itself, and infinite.

After establishing the universality of the creative act as causing all beings, Giles turns to the issue of creature causality. Secondary causes are viewed as transforming or moving agents. They do not cause existence but rather act on a presupposed existing subject. They do not cause being as such but are the cause of the type of being that is caused. Thus, God, who is being itself, is the efficient cause of being in every created being, while secondary "creative" causes determine the "whatness" of created beings.

It is in his account of secondary causality that Giles introduces metaphysical views that are distinctly his. He affirms the existence of modalities, powers that are potential or latent in matter. Thus, the essences created by God have inherent requirements which serve as laws of nature. The being God creates is always fitted to the requirements of a particular essence. This receptivity of matter for specific essences makes secondary causes to be genuine causes in the natural world. Giles reflects the influence of Neoplatonism in his efforts to allot to creatures their proper causality. Although he maintains that God causes the being and the essence of creatures, he posits diversity as the function of creatures. Giles's willingness to accept some potential demands of matter places a real distinction between his metaphysics and Aquinas's.

Giles's third period of writing commenced with his appointment as master at the University of Paris in 1285. By this time Giles was the recognized leader of the Augustinian Hermits, and in May 1287 the general council of the order at Florence passed a decree imposing his teachings on the whole order. It was during this period that he presented his six *Quodlibetal Questions*, which were held annually and finished in 1291.

In 1289 Giles dedicated his *Quodlibet IV* to Cardinal Benedict Caetani. The cardinal had concurred with Philip IV in allowing Giles to acquire certain properties which he sold to gain living quarters closer to the university for his Augustinian charges. On 6 January 1292 Giles was elected prior general of the order at the general chapter held in Rome in the convent of Santa Maria del Populo, where he had first entered the order as a boy. His election officially marked the close of his teaching days, although not of his literary efforts.

The years 1292 to 1295 saw Giles engaged in affairs of the order—seeing to quarters for students at Paris, arranging the course requirements for graduation, and so on. When Cardinal Caetani became Pope Boniface VIII in 1294 and was accused of wrongly acquiring his office, Giles wrote *De Renunciatione Papae* (On the Renunciation of the Papacy) on the pope's behalf. On 5 April 1295 he was elevated to archbishop of Bourges by Boniface. This appointment was met with complaints about preferring foreigners, but both the pope and Philip IV supported Giles.

Between 1296 and 1303 Boniface VIII and Philip IV became bitter combatants over two issues, taxation of the clergy and the subjection of the clergy to secular courts. Giles could no longer maintain his two friendships. He rushed to the support of Boniface with his treatise *De Ecclesiastica Potestate* (On Ecclesiastical Power, 1302). The work is verbose, hastily pieced together, and short on organization and order; nevertheless, it was the dominant influence on Boniface's bull *Unam Sanctam* (1302).

In 1305 Giles decided to press claims for the see of Bourges over the see of Bordeaux. Bertrand de Got, the archbishop of Bordeaux, resisted Giles's claims. Giles then urged Gauthier de Bruges, Archbishop of Poitiers, to publish Giles's excommunication of de Got. Gauthier complied. But on 5 June 1305 de Got was elected Pope Clement V. After his coronation Clement had the archbishop of Poitiers removed from his see and confined to a Franciscan convent until he died in 1307. Giles was confined to his quarters at Bourges, deprived of most of his revenues, and forced to pay a fine to Rome in 1306.

Giles regained his freedom in 1310 by helping the pope with the suppression of the Templars, wrote the treatise *Contra Exemptos* against them, and even gained their house at Bourges for his Augustinian Hermits. He drew up two wills: one gave his property to the diocese of Soana and his library to the Augustinian house in Paris; the second bequeathed his precious vessels and ornaments for divine service to the houses in Bourges and Rome.

He died on 22 December 1316 at Avignon and was buried in the Augustinian church there. His body was later taken to the convent of the Grand Augustins in Paris and reinterred before the high altar. Thus ended the career of a remarkable Scholastic, a diligent student of and commentator on the works of Aristotle, a major player in the crises of his age, and a leading Augustinian spokesman.

References:

William Ernest Carlo, "The Role of Essence in Existential Metaphysics: A Reappraisal," *International Philosophical Quarterly*, 2 (December 1962): 557-590;

Carlo, *The Ultimate Reducibility of Essence to Existence in Existential Metaphysics* (The Hague: Nijhoff, 1966);

Pawel Czartoryski, "Quelques éléments nouveaux quant au commentaire de Gilles de Rome sur la Politique," *Mediaevalia Philosophica Polonorum*, 11 (1964): 43-48;

Stephen D. Dumont, "Giles of Rome and the *De rerum principio* attributed to Vital du Four," *Archivum franciscanum historicum*, 77 (1984): 81-109;

Richard Egenter, *Die Erkenntnisphyschologie des Aegidius Romanus* (Regensburg: Habbel, 1925);

Egenter, "Vernunft und Glaubenswahrheit im Aufbau der theologischen Wissenschaft nach Aegidius Romanus," in *Philosophia Perennis: Festschrift für Joseph Geyser*, edited by F.-J. von Rintelen (Regensburg: Habbel, 1930);

I. Eichinger, "Individuum und Gemeinschaft bei Aegidius Romanus," *Divus Thomas*, 13 (1935): 160-166;

Barbara Faes de Mottoni, "*Mensura* im Werk De mensura angelorum des Aegidius Romanus," in *Mensura, Mass, Zahl, Zahlensymbolik im Mittelalter*, edited by Albert Zimmermann (Berlin & New York: De Gruyter, 1983/1984), pp. 86-102;

Palémon Glorieux, "Les premiers écrits de Gilles de Rome," *Recherches de Théologie ancienne et médiévale*, 41 (1974): 204-208;

M. Anthony Hewson, *Giles of Rome and the Medieval Theory of Conception: A study of the De formatione corporis humani in utero* (London: Athlone Press, 1975);

Otto Hieronimi, *Die allgemeine Passionenlehre bei Aegidius von Rom* (Würzburg: Mayr, 1934);

Edgar Hocedez, "La Condamnation de Gilles de Rome," *Recherches de Théologie ancienne et médiévale*, 4 (1932): 34-58;

Hocedez, "Gilles de Rome et Henri de Gand sur la distinction réelle," *Gregorianum*, 8 (1927): 358-384;

Hocedez, "Gilles de Rome et Saint Thomas," in *Mélanges Mandonnet* (Paris: Vrin, 1930), I: 385-409;

R. Kuiters, "Aegidius Romanus and the Authorship of 'In utramque partem' and 'De ecclesiastica potestate,'" *Augustiniana*, 8 (1958): 267-280;

Carey J. Leonard, "A Thirteenth Century Notion of the Agent Intellect: Giles of Rome," *New Scholasticism*, 37 (1963): 327-358;

Theodorus Servus Makaay, *Der Traktat des Ägidius Romanus Uber die Einzigkeit der substantiallen Form* (Würzburg: St. Rita, 1924);

Pierre Mandonnet, "La Carrière scolaire de Gilles de Rome (1276-1291)," *Revue des Sciences Philosophiques et Thélogigues*, 4 (1910): 480-499;

Ugo Mariana, *Il "de Regimine Principum" e le Teorie Politiche di Egidio Romano* (Florence: Olschkie, 1926);

Friedrich Merzbacher, "Die Rechts-Staats und Kirchenzuffassung des Aegidius Romanus," *Archiv für Rechts- und Sozialphilosophie*, 41 (1954): 88-97;

Ernest A. Moody, "Ockham and Aegidius of Rome," *Franciscan Studies*, 9 (1949): 417-442;

Peter W. Nash, "The Accidentality of Esse according to Giles of Rome," *Gregorianum*, 38 (1957): 103-115;

Nash, "Giles of Rome: A Pupil but Not a Disciple of Thomas Aquinas," in *Readings in Ancient and Medieval Philosophy*, edited by James Collins (Westminster, Md., 1960), pp. 251-257;

Nash, "Giles of Rome and the Subject of Theology," *Mediaeval Studies*, 18 (1956): 61-92;

Nash, "Giles of Rome, Auditor and Critic of St. Thomas," *Modern Schoolman*, 28 (1950): 1-20;

Nash, "Giles of Rome on Boethius' 'Diversum est esse et id quod est,'" *Mediaeval Studies*, 12 (1950): 57-91;

Kieran Nolan, *The Immortality of the Soul and the Resurrection of the Body according to Giles of Rome* (Rome: Studium Theologicum Augustinianum, 1967);

J. R. O'Donnell, "The Commentary of Giles of Rome on the Rhetoric of Aristotle," in *Essays in Medieval History Presented to Bertie Wilkinson*, edited by T. A. Sandquist and M. R. Powicke (Toronto: University of Toronto Press, 1969), pp. 139-156;

Jean Paulus, "Les Disputes d'Henri de Gand et de Gilles de Rome sur la Distinction, de L'Essence et de L'Existence," *Archives d'Histoire doctrinale et Littéraire du Moyen Âge*, 13 (1940-1942): 323-358;

F. Pelster, "Thomistische Streitschriften gegen Aegidius Romanus und ihre Verfasser: Thomas von Sutton und Robert von Oxford, O.P.," *Gregorianum*, 24 (1943): 135-170;

Jan Pinborg, "Diskussionen um die Wissenschaftstheorie an der Artistenfakultät," in *Die Auseinandersetzungen an der Pariser Universität im XIII. Zahrhundert*, edited by Albert Zimmermann (Berlin & New York: De Gruyter, 1976), pp. 240-268.

Gregory of Rimini

(circa 1300 - November 1358)

Jeremiah Hackett
University of South Carolina

PRINCIPAL WORKS: *Tractatus de Imprestantiis Venetorum et de usura* (The Tract on the Lending Practices of the Venetians and on Usury, written 1340-1358);

Tractatus de Intensione et Remissione Formarum Corporalium (Tract on the Intension and Remission of Corporeal Forms, written 1342-1344);

De Quatuor Virtutibus Cardinalibus (On the Four Cardinal Virtues, written 1342-1358);

Epistolarum Divi Augustini Tabula (The List of the Letters of Saint Augustine, written 1342-1358);

In Omnes Divi Pauli Epistolas (Commentaries on all the Epistles of Saint Paul, written 1342-1358);

In Divi Jacobi Epistolas (On the Epistles of Saint James, written 1342-1358);

Lectura super Primum et Secundum Librum Sententiarum (Lectures on the First and Second Books of the Sentences, written 1343-1347);

Registrum Epistolarum sui Generalatus (The Register of the Letters from His Generalate, written 1357-1358).

EDITIONS: *Lectura in Primum et Secundum Librum Sententiarum*, edited by Guglielmus Militis (Paris: Louis Martineau, 1482);

In Secundo Libro Sententiarum Expositio, edited by Francisus Busti (Milan: Uldericus Scinzenzeler, for Petrus Antonius de Castellano, 1494);

Lectura super Primum Librum Sententiarum, edited by Juan Verdú (Valencia: Christof Kaufmann, 1500);

Super Primum et Secundum Sententiarum (Venice: Printed by L. de Giunta, 1522; photographically reprinted, Saint Bonaventure, N.Y.: Franciscan Institute, 1955);

Tractatus de Imprestantiis Venetorum et de Usura (Reggio Emilia, 1522);

Tractatus de Imprestantiis Venetorum et de Usura (Reggio Emilia, 1622).

CRITICAL EDITION: *Lectura super Primum et Secundum Sententiarum*, 6 volumes, edited by Damasus Trapp and Venicio Marcolino, Spätmittelalter und Reformation, Texte und Untersuchungen, volume 6 (Berlin & New York: De Gruyter, 1979-1984).

In 1961 historian of medieval philosophy Gordon Leff had an article published titled "Gregory of Rimini: A Fourteenth-Century Augustinian." It was followed the same year by his *Gregory of Rimini: Tradition and Innovation in Fourteenth-Century Thought.* Since then, no book in English on Gregory has appeared. Between 1979 and 1984, however, the leading scholar on Gregory, Damasus Trapp, together with Venicio Marcolino, edited Gregory's magnum opus, the *Lectura super Primum et Secundum Librum Sententiarum* (Lectures on the First and Second Books of the Sentences [of Peter Lombard], 1343-1347). The product of Gregory's teaching years at the University of Paris, the *Lectura* is an outstanding witness to the central debates on philosophy and theology at the university in the fourteenth century. The lack of a presentation of Gregory's philosophical position, or a downplaying of that position in modern textbooks and histories of philosophy, has led to a distorted view of medieval philosophy. Most students, when introduced to medieval philosophy, confront the problem of universals; and the texts have used such generalizations as "extreme realist," "moderate realist," and "nominalist" to describe the various positions on the issue. The difficulty is that positions such as those of William of Ockham, on the one hand, and of Gregory of Rimini, on the other, are not so easily pigeonholed. Masterpieces of analytic thinking, they are nuanced and thorough.

Gregory of Rimini was born around 1300. His scholarly career seems to have begun in 1323 at the University of Paris, where he studied as a bachelor for six years. These were significant years for philosophy, during which William of

Ockham and Meister Eckhart were called to the papal court at Avignon to defend their views; both were condemned.

In 1329 Gregory returned from Paris to his native Italy and became *lector* (reader) at Bologna until 1338, then at Padua and Perugia. He returned to Paris in 1341, and from 1343 to 1347 he lectured on the *Libri Quatuor Sententiarum* (Four Books of Sentences, 1157-1158) of Peter Lombard, the normal task of a regent master in theology. By 1345 he was known as *magister cathedraticus*. In 1347 he became lecturer at Padua. In 1351 he was named master of studies and prior of the Augustinian *studium* (house of studies) at Rimini. He remained there until he was elected prior general (head) of the Augustinian order in 1357. He was involved in travel and administrative duties from that time until his death in November 1358 at Vienna.

Gregory can be seen as a representative of the new "linguistic" turn in fourteenth-century thought after the manner of William of Ockham. He used Ockhamist methods to retrieve and defend traditional Augustinian metaphysics and philosophical psychology. On the important issue of the *potentia absoluta Dei* (absolute power of God), Gregory held that the power of God to do whatever he pleased (short of a logical contradiction) was limited by virtue of God's being the summum bonum (highest good).

Gregory's doctrine of the *complexe significabile* (complex significable) was developed as a direct answer to the semantics of William of Ockham and his followers. Ockham had developed the "terminist" view of logic, which owed its origins to William of Sherwood, Roger Bacon, and others in the thirteenth century, to its extremes. Terminism held that the meaning of a proposition had to be determined on the basis of the meaning of each term taken singly; thus, it was not the proposition as a whole which was the locus of meaning. Apart from terminist theories of meaning, there was another medieval tradition, going back to Boethius, which has been called "dictism." Here, a proposition was seen as an expression which signifies what is true or not true. Terms are not mere sounds or marks on paper. Rather, a term signifies a thought, which in turn indicates the actual things which are the subject of thought.

Gregory recognized that single words can signify beings, but he held that the terminist view ignored the central role of the proposition. Single words are not on the same level as the proposition, which signifies in a holistic manner: it is a *complexe significabile*, something which no word or grouping of words without affirmative or negative force can be.

Over and above the linguistic expression and the extramental reality, Gregory recognizes the existence of an objective realm of meaning. The *significatum* (that which is meant) of a proposition is not the linguistic expression itself, nor is it a piece of the world: it is an object in a realm of objective meaning. It does not exist in the sense that physical things and linguistic expressions exist, but it is still real. For Gregory, the primary objects of belief and knowledge are these meaningful entities. Meaning bridges the gap between the sign (word or proposition) and the thing; sign and object share in a world of meaning. Gregory of Rimini's theory of the proposition as *complexe significabile* has similarities to certain theories of such modern philosophers as Gottlob Frege, Edmund Husserl, Ludwig Wittgenstein, and Martin Heidegger.

For Ockham, a rigorous empiricist, all knowledge begins with a direct sensory intuition of the sensible object. The role of species, or mental representations, as mediators between the external world and the knower is curtailed. The term denotes the existing thing itself, not the mental concept. In Gregory's epistemology, on the other hand, the species retains its role as a mediating element in knowledge. Furthermore, knowledge, for Gregory, is not limited to the perception of a present object: there is also memory of past objects and projection of future ones. Thus, whether or not an object exists in reality, it can be present to consciousness as a meaningful object. In brief, while Gregory is as rigorous as Ockham about empirical knowledge of the external world, he differs from Ockham in recognizing a world of meaning which is not circumscribed by the empirical.

For Ockham, the object of knowledge in science is the conclusion of a demonstration. Gregory rejects Ockham's account: in addition to knowing the conclusion, one must know whether or not that which the conclusion signifies is the case. The conclusion of a demonstrative proof could be shown by experience to be false.

Gregory held fast to Augustine's moral vision. He could not accept a view in which God was seen as having an inscrutable will which could confuse good and evil. Gregory's God was that of Augustine—a God of absolute goodness, whose will was circumscribed by goodness, justice, and love. The tradition which Gregory of Rimini handed on stressed the primacy of love over knowledge; it defended the primacy of good over truth and of will over understanding. This tradition was different from that of Aquinas (Thomism), which stressed the primacy of truth; and it differed from Ockhamism in that its doctrine of the sovereignty of the good recognized limits to the will of God. For these Augustinian thinkers, theology was not a speculative science in competition with philosophy; rather, it was an affective science of the heart.

A major consequence of this view of theology is the marked tendency in Augustinian thinkers to limit the domain of philosophy in favor of theology. This is the great enigma of the Augustinian tradition: beginning with Augustine, it presented a powerful philosophical anthropology replete with significant metaphysical, psychological, and ethical insights; but because of its emphasis on the primacy of love, it always had within it the tendency to subordinate reason to action.

Gregory of Rimini used reason—that is, Aristotelian argument; he valued it highly in his philosophical semantics. In subordinating reason to faith, or the creature to the Creator, he was recognizing that philosophy, like all other human things, is contingent and finite; he was arguing that philosophy should not claim to have a God's-eye view of all things. (Neither should theology make such a claim.) Philosophy, for Gregory, found its completion in the theological virtues of faith, hope, and love.

Letters:

Gregorii de Arimino O.S.A. Registrum Generalatus, 1357-1358, edited by Albericus de Meijer, Fontes Historiae OSA, no. 1 (Rome: Augustinianum, 1976).

References:

Willigis Eckermann, O.S.A., *Wort und Wirklichkeit: Das Sprachverständnis in der Theologie Gregors von Rimini und sein Weiterwirken in der Augustinerschule*, Cassiciacum, volume 33 (Würzburg: Augustinus-Verlag, 1978);

Hubert Elie, *Le complexe significabile* (Paris: Vrin, 1936);

Norman Kretzmann, "Medieval Logicians on the Meaning of the Propositio," *Journal of Philosophy*, 67 (22 October 1970): 767-787;

Gordon Leff, "Gregory of Rimini: A Fourteenth-Century Augustinian," *Revue des études augustiniennes*, 7, no. 2 (1961): 153-170;

Leff, *Gregory of Rimini: Tradition and Innovation in Fourteenth-Century Thought* (Manchester, U.K.: Manchester University Press, 1961);

Eliseo García Lescún, *La theología trinitaria de Gregorio de Rimini: Contribución a la historia de la escolástica tardía* (Burgos: Ediciones Aldecos, 1970);

André de Muralt, *L'Enjeu de la philosophie médiévale: Etudes thomistes, scotistes, occamiennes et grégoriennes*, Studien und Texte zur Geistesgeschichte des Mittelalters, volume 24 (Leiden, New York, Copenhagen & Cologne: Brill, 1991), pp. 127-167, 265-266;

Gabriel Nuchelmans, *Theories of the Proposition: Ancient and Medieval Bearers of Truth and Falsity* (Amsterdam & London: North Holland Publishing Co., 1973), pp. 227-272;

Heiko A. Obermann, ed., *Gregor von Rimini: Werk und Wirkung bis zur Reformation*, Spätmittelalter und Reformation-Texte und Untersuchungen, volume 20 (Berlin & New York: De Gruyter, 1981);

Martin Schüler, *Prädestination, Sünde und Freiheit* (Stuttgart: Kohlhammer, 1934);

Friedrich Stegmüller, "Gratia Sanans," in *Aurelius Augustinus*, edited by Martin Grabmann and Joseph Mausbach (Cologne: Bachem, 1930), pp. 395-409;

Paul A. Streveler, "Gregory of Rimini and the Black Monk on Sense and Reference: An Example of Fourteenth-Century Philosophical Analysis," *Vivarium*, 18 (May 1980): 67-78;

Katherine H. Tachau, *Vision and Certitude in the Age of Ockham: Optics, Epistemology and the Foundations of Semantics 1250-1345*, Studien und Texte zur Geistesgeschichte des Mittelalters, volume 22 (Leiden, New York, Copenhagen & Cologne: Brill, 1988);

Damasus Trapp, "Augustinian Theology in the Fourteenth Century: Notes on Editions, Marginalia, Opinions, and Book Lore," *Augustiniana*, 6 (1956): 146-274;

Trapp, "Gregory of Rimini: Manuscripts, Editions and Additions," *Augustiniana*, 8 (1958): 425-443;

Trapp, "A New Approach to Gregory of Rimini," *Augustinianum*, 2 (1962): 425-443;

Trapp, "Peter Ceffons of Clairvaux," *Recherches de théologie ancienne et médiévale*, 24 (1957): 101-154;

Paul Vignaux, *Justification et prédestination au XIVe siècle: Duns Scot, Pierre d'Auriole, Guillaume d'Occame, Grégoire de Rimini*, Bibliothèque de

l'Ecole des Hautes Etudes: Sciences religieuses (Paris: Leroux, 1934);
Vignaux, *Nominalisme au 14e siècle* (Paris: Vrin, 1948);
Joseph Würsdörfer, *Erkennen und Wissen nach Gregor von Rimini* (Münster: Aschendorff, 1917).

Robert Grosseteste

(circa 1160 - 8 October 1253)

Jeremiah Hackett
University of South Carolina

PRINCIPAL WORKS: *De Unica Forma Omnium* (On the Unity of All Forms, written circa 1214-1235);
De Intelligentiis (On the Intelligences, written circa 1214-1235);
De Statu Causarum (On the Status of Causes, written circa 1214-1235);
De Potentia et Actu (On Potency and Act, written circa 1214-1235);
De Veritate (On Truth, written circa 1214-1235);
De Veritate Propositionis (On the Truth of Propositions, written circa 1214-1235);
De Scientia Dei (On the Knowledge of God, written circa 1214-1235);
De Ordine Emanandi Causatorum a Deo (On the Order of Causes Emanating from God, written circa 1214-1235);
De Libero Arbitrio (On the Freedom of the Will, written circa 1214-1235);
De Utilitate Artium (On the Usefulness of the Arts, written circa 1214-1235);
De Generatione Sonorum (On the Generation of Sounds, written circa 1214-1235);
De Sphaera (On the Sphere, written circa 1214-1235);
De Computo (On Computation, written circa 1214-1235);
De Generatione Stellarum (On the Generation of the Stars, written circa 1214-1235);
De Cometis (On Comets, written circa 1214-1235);
De Impressione Aeris (On Atmospheric Impressions, written circa 1214-1235);
De Lineis, Angulis et Figuris (On Lines, Angles, and Figures, written circa 1214-1235);
De Natura Locorum (On the Nature of Places, written circa 1214-1235);
De Iride (On the Rainbow, written circa 1214-1235);
De Colore (On Colors, written circa 1214-1235);
De Calore Solis (On the Heat of the Sun, written circa 1214-1235);
De Differentiis Localibus (On the Differences of Places, written circa 1214-1235);
De Impressionibus Elementorum (On the Impressions of the Elements, written circa 1214-1235);
De Motu Corporali (On the Movement of Bodies, written circa 1214-1235);
De Motu Super-caelestium (On Supracelestial Movement, written circa 1214-1235);
De Finitate Motus et Temporis (On the Finitude of Motion and Time, written circa 1214-1235);
Quod Homo Sit Minor Mundus (That the Human Being is a Microcosm, written circa 1214-1235);
De Fluxu et Refluxu Maris (On the Tides, written circa 1214-1235);
Commentarius in Posterium Analyticorum Libros (Commentary on [Aristotle's] *Posterior Analytics*, written circa 1214-1235);
Commentarium in VIII Libros Physicorum (Commentary on the Eight Books of [Aristotle's] *Physics*, written circa 1214-1235);
Hexaëmeron (Commentary on Genesis, written circa 1214-1235);
De Cessatione Legalium (On Setting Aside the Law, written circa 1214-1235);
De Decem Mandatis (On the Ten Commandments, written circa 1214-1235);
De Poenetencia (On Penitence, written circa 1214-1235);

Robert Grosseteste as depicted in a detail of an illumination in a late-fourteenth-century manuscript of his works (British Museum, MS Roy. 6. E. V, fol. 6r)

Le Chasteau d'Amour (The Castle of Love, written circa 1214-1235);

Confessioun (Confession, written circa 1214-1235);

Le Mariage des neuf Filles du Diable (The Marriage of the Nine Daughters of the Devil, written circa 1214-1235);

De Luce (On Light, written circa 1225-circa 1241).

TRANSLATIONS: Aristotle, *Ethica Nicomachea* (Nichomachean Ethics, circa 1235-1253);

Aristotle, *De Caelo et Mundo* (On the Heavens and the Earth, circa 1235-1253);

Testamentum XII Patriarcharum (Testament of the Twelve Patriarchs, circa 1235-1253);

John Damascene, *Dialectica* (Dialectic, circa 1235-1253);

John Damascene, *De Hymno Trisagio* (On the Hymn of Threefold Wisdom, circa 1235-1253);

John Damascene, *Introductio Dogmatum Elementaris* (Introduction to Elementary Doctrine, circa 1235-1253);

John Damascene, *Disputatio Christiani et Saraceni* (Dispute between a Christian and a Saracen, circa 1235-1253).

EDITIONS: "Le Mariage des neuf Filles du Diable," edited by Paul Meyer, *Romania*, 29 (1900): 61-72;

Die philosophischen Werke des Robert Grosseteste, Bischofs von Lincoln, edited by Ludwig Baur (Münster: Aschendorff, 1912);

Le château d'amour de Robert Grosseteste, évêque de Lincoln, edited by Jessie Murray (Paris: Champion, 1918);

"The Text of Grosseteste's *De Cometis*," edited by S. Harrison Thomson, *Isis*, 19 (April 1933): 19-25;

"Mediaeval Versions of Aristotle, *de Caelo*, and of the Commentary of Simplicius," edited by D. J. Allan, *Mediaeval and Renaissance Studies*, 2 (1950): 82-120;

"Un ineditio di Roberti Grossetesta," edited by E. Franceschini, *Rivista di filosofia neo-scolastica*, 44 (1952): 1-11;

John Damascene, *Dialectica*, translated by Grosseteste, edited by Owen A. Colligan (St. Bonaventure, N.Y.: Franciscan Institute, 1953);

"Grosseteste's *Questio de Calore, De Cometis*, and *De Operacionibus Solis*," edited by Thomson, *Medievalia et Humanistica*, 11 (1957): 34-43;

Roberti Grosseteste Commentarius in VIII libros Physicorum Aristotelis, edited by Richard C. Dales (Boulder: University of Colorado Press, 1963);

"Robert Grosseteste's Treatise 'De Finitate Motus et Temporis,'" edited by Dales, *Traditio*, 19 (1963): 245-266;

"Traces of God in Nature according to Robert Grosseteste with the Text of the Dictum 'Omnis creatura speculum est,'" edited by Servus Gieben, *Franciscan Studies*, 24 (1964): 144-158;

The Middle English Translation of Robert Grosseteste's "Chateau d'Amour," edited by Kari Sajavaara (Helsinki: Uusfilologinen yhdistys, 1967);

"Robert Grosseteste's Treatise on Confession, 'Deus est,'" edited by S. Wenzel, *Franciscan Studies*, 30 (1970): 218-193;

"An Edition of Three Unpublished Translations by Robert Grosseteste," edited by M. Holland, M.A. thesis, Harvard University, 1980;

Commentarius in Posteriorum analyticorum libros, edited by Pietro Rossi, Corpus Philosophorum Medii Aevi, 2 (Florence: Olschki, 1981).

CRITICAL EDITIONS: *Hexaëmeron*, edited by Richard C. Dales and Servus Gieben (London: Published for the British Academy by Oxford University Press, 1982);

"The *Meditaciones* of Robert Grosseteste," edited by J. Goering and F. A. C. Mantello, *Journal of Theological Studies*, new series 36 (1985): 118-128;

De Cessatione Legalium, edited by Dales (London: Published for the British Academy by Oxford University Press, 1986);

De Decem Mandatis, edited by Edward B. King (Oxford & New York: Published for the British Academy by Oxford University Press, 1987).

Robert Grosseteste belonged to a generation of Anglo-Normans who benefited greatly from the enlightened high-school education of twelfth-century England. Coming from a family of serfs, he rose through the ranks to become *magister scholarum* (master of the scholars) at Oxford; lector to the Franciscans; one of the first chancellors of Oxford University in the thirteenth century; and finally, in his late sixties, bishop of Lincoln, head of one of the most important ecclesiastical centers in medieval England. He seems to have been born around 1160. He is recorded as a member of the household of Bishop William de Vere at Hereford in 1190. He was commended for his legal and medical knowledge, and sometime after the death of de Vere in 1198 he began teaching at Oxford. During the suspension of the clerks from 1209 to 1214, when the university ceased to exist on account of a murder case, Grosseteste went to Paris to study theology. From 1214 to 1229 he taught at Oxford, becoming chancellor of the university by 1225. He left the university in 1229 and devoted his time to teaching the young Franciscan friars at Oxford. This connection had major consequences for the future of studies in England and in Europe. Grosseteste's example and practice led to the humanities becoming a major ingredient in the education of the friars so that they could read and interpret sacred Scripture in a critical manner. On 27 March 1235 he was elected bishop of Lincoln, the largest diocese in England. A younger man might have faltered under the burden, but not Grosseteste. He launched into a vigorous reforming campaign. He organized a team of translators to provide the Latin world with clear and precise translations of Greek and Hebrew works. He set out to learn Greek; toward the end of his life, he began to learn Hebrew. He died on 8 October 1253.

Much of the modern research on Robert Grosseteste centers on his philosophical, scientific, and theological works written from about 1214 to 1235 and his translations and works of pastoral care written between 1235 and 1253. Considerable controversy exists concerning the dating of the works, especially the scientific and theological ones. According to a chronology developed by James McEvoy in 1983, although Grosseteste was acquainted with scientific matters while at Hereford—the twelfth-century center for scientific and theological knowledge—he did not write down any of his ideas on these matters until after 1225. In 1986, however, Richard Southern argued that some of these works should be dated to the period before 1225. One thing is clear: Grosseteste did many things concurrently. During the course of his reading of Scripture, he was inspired to study the nature of phenomena such as rainbows and comets.

Regardless of the chronology of his works, it is clear that Grosseteste produced a scientific, philosophical, and theological synthesis of the greatest importance for the Middle Ages. It could be argued that he and William of Auvergne were the truly seminal minds of the early thirteenth century. Everyone who came after—Albert the Great, Roger Bacon, Thomas Aquinas, Bonaventure—lived in the universe which came to be in the work of Grosseteste and William. The way for Aquinas's synthesis of reason and faith was paved by Grosseteste, who first showed the possibility of a synthesis of science and theology. That synthesis was, perhaps, his greatest achievement. But he was an eminently gifted man: a great administrator and a fearless social reformer who defended the rights of the clergy when kings and popes stepped beyond the limits of legal practice and who defended his own rights as a bishop. It is small wonder that lesser minds in the Reformation and Counter-Reformation fought over his patrimony.

Grosseteste's reform of studies and of society was based on a deep vision of the interplay of science, philosophy, religion, and poetry. He respected and used logic, but he was no pedant. He expressed a truly universalist interpretation of the world. And yet he devoted much of his time to the minute, scientific, empirical study of nature.

Among the contemporary witnesses to the life of Grosseteste are Matthew Paris, Roger Bacon, and a member of Grosseteste's household, Friar Hubert. The witness of Bacon was traditionally dismissed on account of the alleged exaggerations in his work; but it is becoming increasingly clear that, even when one allows for Bacon's invective, there is much of historical value to be learned from his reports. In the *Opus Maius* (Major Work, 1267), Bacon remarks: "Boethius alone, the first translator, had full mastery of languages, and Master Robert Grosseteste, recently Bishop of Lincoln, was the only one who knew the sciences. Certain other translators like Gerard of Cremona, Michael Scot, Alfred the Englishman, Hermann the German, whom we saw in Paris, have failed greatly in both languages and sciences, since the same Hermann admitted this about himself and others, and their translations make this obvious." Bacon had devised a major plan for the renewal of studies in the West. The basis of this was the study of languages and sciences, and for this program Bacon raised the name Grosseteste as his emblem.

In 1232 Grosseteste, by then in his early or mid seventies, began his study of Greek. He organized a group of translators in his household that included native Greek scholars such as Nicolas Graecus. Grosseteste's aim was to provide translations of the Greek Christian writers such as John Damascene, Pseudo-Dionysius, and Origen; he also attempted translations of and commentaries on works by Aristotle. It would seem, however, that Bacon is correct when he says that only in his late old age did Grosseteste himself master Greek.

In theology, the most outstanding translations were those of Pseudo-Dionysius and John Damascene. These works opened up a world of Greek theology which with the exception of John Scottus Eriugena had been a closed book for the Western mind. They also provided other scholars with the riches of pagan Neoplatonism.

In philosophy, Grosseteste's greatest achievement was his translation of the major work in Western ethics, the *Nicomachean Ethics* of Aristotle. This translation was fundamental for all later medieval and modern interpretations of Aristotelian ethics. Just a few years after its production it was being used in the Dominican studium (house of studies) in Cologne by Albert the Great and his pupil Aquinas. Through their works and their commentaries on the *Nicomachean Ethics*, a new vision of human life became possible for medieval and Renaissance humanity.

The translation work in Grosseteste's household was not limited to Greek; there were also translations from Hebrew. Grosseteste was clearly interested in having at hand a reliable text of the Bible. The extent to which this work influenced Grosseteste's commentaries on Scripture is still a matter of scholarly discussion.

The translation work also extended to the sciences. Among the many obiter dicta of Bacon one finds the following: "Robert, formerly bishop of Lincoln of blessed memory, neglected the books of Aristotle and their arguments and, by using his own experience and other authors and other means of learning, he worked his way into the wisdom of Aristotle and came to know and write about the subjects of Aristotle's works a hundred thousand times better than those who used only the perverted translations of these works. You can see this in his treatises on Rainbows, on Comets, and other works which he wrote." Grosseteste challenged facile translations of Aristotelian scientific works; his own scientific works are attempts to rewrite Aristotle's treatises.

Between the time of Grosseteste's birth and 1235, when he became bishop of Lincoln, a massive change took place in Western learning as Greek science, transmitted through Arabic commentators, became available to Western readers. Prominent among the translators of this learning were Adelard of Bath, Daniel of Morley, and Alfred of Shareshill. These scholars, and others such as Robert of Chester, actively pursued the new knowledge by going to Spain to learn it. By the end of the twelfth century English scientists and philosophers were becoming aware of a new world, one which was different from and wider than that of traditional Latin culture. Adelard of Bath conveys the spirit of these scholars. Speaking to his students in Laon, he says: "I left you in Laon, so that I could give my full attention to the work done by the Arabs, while you no less zealously imbibed the changing opinions of the French. . . . It is difficult for me to discuss the nature of animals with you, because I learnt from my masters, the Arabs, to follow the light of reason, while you are led by the bridle of authority; for what other word than 'bridle' can I use to describe authority?" One can, therefore, speak of an English scientific tradition before Grosseteste; indeed, he is the culmination of that tradition. And as Bacon pointed out, he was able to bring so many scientific developments together on account of his long life. The contrast between the careful Scholastic, logical analysis of received knowledge in grammar, logic, theology, and law, and the search for essentially new knowledge in the revival of ancient learning, was noted by Roger Bacon in his *Opus Maius*. The lawyers and theologians, he said, were satisfied to elaborate received knowledge; the naturalists, such as Adelard of Bath, went in search of two sources of new knowledge: astronomy and Aristotle.

The study of nature by medieval writers up to Grosseteste's time was a means of moral and mystical ascent to the Creator. Nature was seen as a book in which moral allegories could be read. When one goes from early medieval works on nature such as those by Rhabanus Maurus or Isidore to Grosseteste, one goes from one world into another. Aristotle would, in time, show the methods by which knowledge of the natural things could be acquired.

In astronomy, progress was faster. As Southern puts it: "Here the development is substantially different from that . . . in the study of natural objects; the role of symbolism is much reduced, the practical applications are more extensive and urgent, and the flow of new material and of new scientific techniques is much more rapid and revolutionary." The astrolabe had come into use by the twelfth century; in England, especially at Worcester, Malvern, and Hereford, efforts were made to translate and adapt Arabic star-tables. Scholars such as Robert of Ketton, Robert of Chester, Roger of Hereford, Daniel of Morely, and Alfred of Shareshill were motivated by the practical applications of astronomy; in other words, they were what today would be called astrologers. In Daniel of Morley's account, "Since the astronomer knows about future events, he can repel or avoid disasters such as civil wars or famine, earthquakes, conflagrations, floods, and general pestilences of men and beasts. Even if he cannot altogether escape them, he can prepare for them in advance, which will make them more tolerable than they are to those who are overtaken unawares. I interject this to refute the errors of those who malign the studies of astronomers."

The failure, however, to predict individual human events gradually led scholars to see the limits of this study. Early in his career Grosseteste would have accepted the view of Robert of Marseilles that astrologers can use the conjunctions of the stars and planets to know "not only the present, but the past and the future." But as he came to write more mature works, such as the *Hexaëmeron* (Commentary on Genesis), he retained the notion of predictability in regard to atmospheric conditions while limiting its application to human events. Thus, he advocated astronomy as a mathematical discipline, but he opposed a deterministic science of astrology in regard to human action.

Most of the scholars in the twelfth century discovered Aristotle's works through Arabic commentators. It was difficult to separate the authentic Aristotle from an Aristotle who had been assimilated by Arabic sciences, including Arabic astrology with its deterministic tendencies. Grosseteste's long rumination on Aristotle and astronomy involved the purification of views which were incompatible with those of the real Aristotle. By the 1230s Grosseteste had assimilated many central texts in Arabic science and philosophy, and he had come to know the texts of Aristotle. As a result, in the *Hexaëmeron* he wholeheartedly condemned the errors of the astrologers insofar as they claimed to predict human action. A great development took place between Grosseteste's youth and old age: a world of myth, fable, and magic gave way to one in which natural science gave access to the truth about nature and the human being.

By the time Grosseteste wrote his scientific treatises, *De Sphaera* (On the Sphere), *De Cometis* (On Comets), and *De Iride* (On the Rainbow), the *Almagest* of Ptolemy had replaced the *De Natura Rerum* (On the Nature of Things) of Bede as the basic work in astronomy. Grosseteste, however, held that one need not be a slave to what one reads in books: when book knowledge conflicted with his experiences of nature, Grosseteste put aside book knowledge and looked for a new solution to the problem at hand.

The notion of experimental verification in these texts has to do mainly with the use of mathematics, especially geometry, in astronomy and astrology. In *De Sphaera*, for example, Grosseteste says:

> However, that all the aforesaid bodies are spheres is shown by natural reasons and the experiments of astronomy.
>
> We also known by experiment that the earth is round.

Also in *De Sphaera*, Grosseteste mentions that Thabit ben Qura had shown *per certa experimenta* (by certain experiments) that the movement of the fixed stars differed from the account given by Ptolemy. Finally, in *De Iride* Grosseteste says: "The visual ray penetrating through several transparent substances of diverse natures is refracted at their junctions, and its parts, in different transparent media existing at those junctions, are joined at an angle. This is revealed by that experiment in the book *De Speculis*." In the *De Natura Locorum* (On the Nature of Places) Grosseteste considers the view found in the Pseudo-Aristotelian *De Vegetabilibus* (also know as *De Plantis*) and in Averroës that at the poles the heat of the sun burns the material of animals and plants. He responds that "this is contrary to the truth, since these regions are inhabitable because of the cold, as can be proved by the experiments and reasons of Aristotle, Ptolemy and other authors." (It should be noted, however, that the text of Ptolemy to which Grosseteste explicitly refers in *De Natura Locorum* is *De Dispositione Sphaerae* [On the Disposition of the Spheres]. This work, which was also known in the Middle Ages as *Liber Introductorium in Almagesti Ptolomaei* [Introduction to the *Almagest* of Ptolemy], is not by Ptolemy. It is, in fact, the *Eisagoge in Astronomiam* [Introduction to Astronomy] of Geminus, translated into Arabic and then translated into Latin by Gerard of Cremona. It is the kind of useful summary of astronomy which a scholar like Grosseteste would have found helpful, and he made wider use of this text than is generally recognized.) Although Grosseteste's notion of experimental natural science lacked the controlled experiments and quantitative sophistication of post-Cartesian science, it did lay out the essentials of scientific methodology. As medieval science, it was novel and progressive.

Much more important, however, was Grosseteste's qualification of the notion of experience in the light of Aristotle's *Posterior Analytics*. This work was so difficult that John of Salisbury in the twelfth century held it to be impenetrable. Grosseteste eventually mastered it, and he wrote a commentary which was to have much influence on the later interpretations of the *Posterior Analytics* in the Middle Ages.

Grosseteste distinguishes bare experience—sensation—from the experience which is at the basis of science. Animals share with humans a bare sensation of, for example, heat; but humans alone are capable of formulating a concept of heat. The concept, which is universal, is the key to science; it is the means by which human beings can understand individual instances as belonging to a certain kind. From the repetition of many sensations, a memory is formed; and from many memories, a universal is created. Grosseteste elaborates on Aristotle's image of an army in retreat: there is total disorder until one soldier, then another and yet another stand and hold the line so that an army exists where disarray existed before.

The wide chasm between twelfth-century science and the new vision opened up by the *Posterior Analytics* can be seen by comparing the *Didascalicon* of Hugh of St. Victor with the ideas developed by Grosseteste. In Hugh's work one finds a model of knowledge which is entirely conservative: knowledge consists of the recollection, restoration, and reorganization of all previous knowledge so that the creature can rise to a knowledge of the Creator. There is an absence of discovery, novelty, and direct knowledge of nature.

It was in the *Posterior Analytics* that Grosseteste found the crucial distinction on which to base a scientific methodology: the distinction between a knowledge of the proper and proximate cause of a fact and a knowledge of the bare fact. Many observers see an eclipse, but only the scien-

Objects found in Grosseteste's tomb in 1782: (left to right) episcopal ring, chalice, paten, and the metal ring that attached the staff to the head of the bishop's crosier (Lincoln Cathedral)

tist can offer the reason for the occurrence of the eclipse. Science, therefore, consists in a knowledge of causes. Further, by means of resolution and composition, a scientist can mentally take a phenomenon apart and put it together again, thereby reconstructing in his mind the basic structure of the thing. In geometry, this method provides certitude; but in physics, it leads only to probable knowledge. Thus, in physics one needs verification by experience. Grosseteste's model of scientific procedure laid the foundations for science in the Western world. When Grosseteste finds that Aristotle's accounts of physical phenomena do not match what he discovers in ordinary experience or in the accounts in other writers, he argues out the position for himself. He does not remain a slave to the text of Aristotle but attempts to think out what Aristotle must have meant. In place of Aristotle's reflection theory of the rainbow in the *Meteorologies*, book 3, for example, Grosseteste proposed an account based on refraction. Where Aristotle said that the twinkling of the stars resulted from the visual ray becoming weakened by excessive length, Grosseteste held that the phenomenon is due to the "diminishing angle of vision." Grosseteste also contradicted Aristotle's positions on the cause of thunder, the nature of sound, falling leaves, and the irrigation of the earth. In all cases he provided a combination of good reasons and more detailed experiences. Later writers who commented on the *Posterior Analytics* had more advanced texts to work with; the sheer difficulty of the Latin translation available to him forced Grosseteste to come up with his own solutions to difficult problems in Aristotle.

Grosseteste realized that the work of individual scholars can vanish quickly. For knowledge to grow and develop, one needs institutions of knowledge. As chancellor of Oxford University Grosseteste made the study of languages and of the sciences the foundation of the curriculum. This institutionalization of natural science and language study at Oxford saved the West from disaster, since the University of Paris, with its overemphasis on theology, had forbidden the study of natural science—especially that of Aristotle and his commentators—in the early thirteenth century.

Much of Grosseteste's doctrine on angels is taken from Augustine. Angels are bearers of light; if the process of creation is an illumination, as it was for Augustine and Grosseteste, then the angels play a role in the preservation of the cosmos. The angels are described by Grosseteste "as an image of the eternally active and generative light which is God." Light, for Grosseteste, is synonymous with creative being; it transcends the dichotomy of spirit and matter. Grosseteste's account of angels has some parallels with the cosmology of Avicenna; but for Grosseteste, the angels do not play a role as "intermediaries" in creation as they do in Avicenna's account. Like human beings, they are created light. In his short treatise *De Luce* (On Light) Grosseteste combines a Christian doctrine of creation with the system of the universe found in Aristotle's *On the Heavens*. The key to this synthesis is his doctrine of light. For Grosseteste, the first form of body (corporeity) is light. Through the unity of matter and form, light in its instantaneous self-diffusion brings about a world. Light, when infinitely multiplied, brings about a world of finite dimensions.

The metaphysics of light finds its remote origins in early Greek philosophy. This tradition was complemented by the Wisdom tradition of the Old Testament, and light imagery can be found in the Logos doctrine of Saint John and in Philo Judaeus. The high point of the development of the Greek metaphysics of light was the founder of Neoplatonic philosophy, Plotinus. Plotinus presented a cosmogony in which there was a hierarchical devolution of being from the transcendent, self-sufficient One, the source of all being, through *Nous* (mind) and soul down to the visible universe. The metaphor of emanation or radiation gave a visual image of this relationship between the One and the remainder of reality. The light metaphor was developed in Western philosophy by Augustine, Basil, Pseudo-Dionysius, and Eriugena among Christian philosophers; by the Arab philosopher al-Kindi in his *De Radiis* (On Radiation); and by the Jewish philosopher Solomon Ibn Gabirol in his *Fons Vitae* (The Fountain of Life).

In *De Luce* Grosseteste does not describe the creation of a finite universe by an infinite Creative Light, but he presupposes it. Rather, he describes the creation of a point of created finite light. In the beginning, God created a point of light and imposed it on matter; both the light and the matter were devoid of extension. It is the nature of light to self-diffuse instantaneously in all directions. As the original point of light did so, it drew the matter with it and thus gave rise to the great sphere of the world-machine (*machina mundi*). This process of the diffusion of light continued outward until the outermost sphere in the firmament, consisting of first matter and first form, was generated. The sphere, in turn, diffused its light back toward the center of the universe. Through this process the nine celestial spheres and the four elemental spheres were produced.

In his work *De Lineis, Angulis et Figuris* (On Lines, Angles, and Figures) Grosseteste, following al-Kindi, works out a theory of radiation for sublunary things: "A natural agent multiplies its power from itself to the recipient, whether it acts on sense or on matter. This power is sometimes called species, sometimes a likeness, and it is the same thing whatever it may be called, and the agent sends the same power into sense and into matter, or into its own contrary, as heat sends the same thing into the sense of touch and into a cold body. . . . But the effects are diversified by the diversity of the recipient, for when this power is received by the senses, it produces an effect that is somehow spiritual and noble; on the other hand, when it is received by matter, it produces a material effect. Thus, the sun produces different effects in different recipients by the same power, for it cakes mud and melts ice." For Grosseteste, radiation and causation are the same thing. And, he says, "every natural action is varied in strength and weakness according to variation of lines, angles, and figures." Thus, geometry can be used to analyze the operation of natural forces.

With the arrival of Aristotle's *On the Soul* in the Latin West, Grosseteste had to face the task of linking up Aristotle's doctrine of the soul with that of Augustine. Grosseteste had to rely on Avicenna's interpretation of Aristotle's doctrine of the soul, and that interpretation had Platonic overtones.

According to Grosseteste the intellectual part of the soul comes from outside; it is not generated from matter. This element in the theory is Platonic; but a significant Aristotelian addition can be seen in his account of knowledge: the soul cannot arrive at knowledge in this life without sensation. Thus, the soul has to be both a self-mover in the Platonic sense and the form of an organic body in the Aristotelian sense. Both views sit side by side, almost unconsciously, in Grosseteste. In the late 1260s Aquinas would attempt to resolve these difficult issues.

The soul, according to Grosseteste, maintains its freedom in responsible action; although the stars might influence the body, they could not compel the soul to act. Grosseteste subordinates the Aristotelian account of the soul to the Augustinian-Platonic account: spirit has a superiority and rule over matter. The vegetative, sensitive, and rational powers of the soul are integrated and perfected in the intellectual. The intellectual part of the soul is divided into reason, intellect, and intelligence. Reason has to do with demonstration, intellect with grasp of first principles. Both are subordinated to intelligence or higher reason. The latter is the ability of the mind to transcend all created beings and approach the One in a mystical intuition. This theory is Neoplatonism as mediated by Augustine, who subdivided the intellect into memory, intelligence, and love. The trinitarian structure of the human mind is analogous to the Trinitarian structure of God. Grosseteste adopted the Augustinian doctrine of divine illumination of the mind as the center of his theory of knowledge: we know things in the light of the eternal light. The doctrine of illumination enables Grosseteste to take a "naturalistic" system of knowledge like that of Aristotle and subordinate it to a concept of revealed knowledge such as that of Augustine. Wisdom is superior to mere knowledge.

For Grosseteste, the human being was a *minor mundus* (microcosm) which reflected the splendor of the world, God's creation. Grosseteste was highly influenced by the School of Chartres, in which the notion of a world-soul had gained much support. Here again, Greek cosmic religion showed its influence, despite strong criticism from some theologians. Grosseteste is the crucial figure in the move from this religious cosmos to the more Aristotelian scientific cosmos of the thirteenth century; by the 1260s, the belief in a world-soul was looked on as a piece of folk psychology.

In Grosseteste the human being is at the center, halfway between the divine and the worldly. Humanity is an *imago Dei* (image of God); *image* here has the connotation of a reflection of light. The human being is the place where the mundane and the divine are united. In the human being, intelligence and materiality are present in a dynamic unity. Further, the human being is the final cause of all lower beings, while it in turn leads all beings toward the ultimate final cause, God. The human being, as the end and center of creation, is the way to a recovery of all things in God. Grosseteste is thus a representative of a theme which the Renaissance would take up again, the theme of microcosm.

It is difficult for modern readers truly to enter the world of Grosseteste's time. The notion of sacral order is especially distant from modern democratic and nontheocratic ideas. In the world of Grosseteste, the king, the bishops, and the priests all had sacral offices. All sovereign power came from God. The spheres of influence were distinct, but, inevitably, questions of jurisdiction and interaction arose. Grosseteste was a jealous defender of the rights of the church, the king, and the whole feudal system. He was in his mid sixties when he became bishop of Lincoln. He was a compromise candidate; people did not expect much from him. And yet he launched a great campaign for reform of religious houses, parishes, and schools. He was concerned that all orders and estates in society should have access to true religion and learning, and he wanted to see that the law was administrated justly.

Grosseteste was fearless in his defense of his prerogatives as bishop. In 1245 and again in 1250 he traveled to Lyons to confront Pope Innocent IV on matters of doctrine and practice. He insisted that the government of the church, which he believed to be corrupt and self-serving, was detrimental to the well-being of both church and society. Secular searching for power had corrupted the ideal of Christian living.

At the end of his life, Grosseteste faced the supreme challenge to his beliefs when the pope appointed his own nephew to be a canon of Lincoln Cathedral, Grosseteste's church. Grosseteste rejected this nepotism; the pope, in his view, was overstepping his limits.

Grosseteste had a major influence on the philosophy and theology of the Middle Ages. He brought the wisdom of antiquity—above all, that of Aristotle—to Christian Europe. Others after him, such as Albert the Great and Thomas Aquinas, would develop this wisdom.

Letters:

Roberti Grosseteste episcopi quondam Lincolniensis Epistolae, edited by Henry R. Luard (London: Her Majesty's Stationery Office, 1861; New York: Kraus Reprint, 1965).

Bibliographies:

S. Harrison Thomson, *The Writings of Robert Grosseteste, Bishop of Lincoln, 1235-1253* (Cambridge, Mass.: Harvard University Press, 1940);

Servus Gieben, "Bibliographica universa Robert Grosseteste, 1474-1969," *Collectanea Franciscana,* 39 (1969): 362-418.

Biographies:

Francis S. Stevenson, *Robert Grosseteste, Bishop of Lincoln: A Contribution to the Religious, Political and Intellectual History of the Thirteenth Cen-*

tury (London: Macmillan, 1899; New York: Macmillan, 1899);

Richard Southern, *Robert Grosseteste: The Growth of an English Mind in Medieval Europe* (Oxford: Clarendon Press, 1986; New York: Oxford University Press, 1986).

References:

Franco Alessio, "Storia e teoria nel pensiero scientifico di Roberto Grossatesta," *Rivista critica di storia della filosofia*, 12 (1957): 251-292;

R. L. Benson and G. Constable, eds., *Renaissance and Renewal in the Twelfth Century* (Cambridge, Mass.: Harvard University Press, 1982);

L. E. Boyle, "Robert Grosseteste and Pastoral Care," *Mediaeval and Renaissance Studies*, new series 8 (1979): 3-51;

Daniel A. Callus, "Introduction of Aristotelian Learning to Oxford," *Proceedings of the British Academy*, 29 (1943): 229-281;

Callus, "The Oxford Career of Robert Grosseteste," *Oxoniensia*, 10 (1945): 42-72;

Callus, ed., *Robert Grosseteste: Scholar and Bishop. Essays in Commemoration of the Seventh Centenary of His Death* (Oxford: Clarendon Press, 1955);

J. I. Catto, ed., *History of the University of Oxford*, volume 1: *The Early Oxford Schools* (Oxford: Clarendon Press, 1984);

M.-D. Chenu, *La Théologie comme science au XIIIe siècle*, Bibliotheque thomiste, 33 (Paris: Vrin, 1957);

Alistair C. Crombie, *Robert Grosseteste and the Origins of Experimental Science, 1100-1700* (Oxford: Clarendon Press, 1953);

Richard C. Dales, "Adam Marsh, Robert Grosseteste and the Treatise on the Tides," *Speculum*, 52 (October 1977): 900-901;

Dales, "The Authorship of the *Questio de fluxu et refluxu maris* Attributed to Robert Grosseteste," *Speculum*, 37 (October 1962): 582-588;

Dales, "A Medieval View of Human Dignity," *Journal of the History of Ideas*, 37 (October-December 1977): 557-572;

Dales, "Robert Grosseteste's Scientific Works," *Isis*, 52 (September 1961): 381-402;

Bruce S. Eastwood, "Grosseteste's 'Quantitative' Law of Refraction: A Chapter in the History of Non-experimental Science," *Journal of the History of Ideas*, 28 (July-September 1967): 403-414;

Eastwood, "Mediaeval Empiricism: The Case of Robert Grosseteste's Optics," *Speculum*, 43 (April 1968): 306-321;

Eastwood, "Robert Grosseteste's Theory of the Rainbow: A Chapter in the History of Non-experimental Science," *Archives internationales de l'histoire des sciences*, 19 (1966): 313-332;

Ulderico Gamba, ed., *Il commento di Roberto Grossatesta al "De Mystica Theologia" del Pseudo-Dionigi Areopagita*, Orbis Romana, Biblioteca di testi medievali, 15 (Milan: Vita e pensiero, 1942);

Klaus Hedwig, *Sphera Lucis: Studien zur Intelligibilität des Seinden im Kontext der mittelalterlichen Lichtspekulation* (Münster: 1980);

Richard William Hunt, "Manuscripts Containing the Indexing Symbols of Robert Grosseteste," *Bodleian Library Record*, 4 (1952-1953): 241-255;

Andrew George Little, "The Franciscan School at Oxford in the Thirteenth Century," *Arvhivium Franciscanum Historicum*, 19 (1926): 803-874;

Little, *The Grey Friars in Oxford* (Oxford: Printed for the Oxford Historical Society at the Clarendon Press, 1892);

Little, *Studies in English Franciscan History*, Ford Lectures, 1916 (Manchester, U.K.: Manchester University Press, 1917; London: Longmans, Green, 1917);

Lawrence E. Lynch, "The Doctrine of Divine Ideas and Illumination in Robert Grosseteste, Bishop of Lincoln," *Mediaeval Studies*, 3 (1941): 163-173;

Frank A. C. Mantello, "Letter CXXX of Bishop Robert Grosseteste: A Problem of Attribution," *Mediaeval Studies*, 36 (1974): 144-159;

Steven P. Marrone, *William of Auvergne and Robert Grosseteste: New Ideas of Truth in the Early Thirteenth Century* (Princeton: Princeton University Press, 1983);

James McEvoy, "The Chronology of Robert Grosseteste's Writings on Nature and Natural Philosophy," *Speculum*, 58 (July 1983): 614-655;

McEvoy, "La connaissance intellectuelle selon Robert Grosseteste," *Revue philosophique de Louvain*, 75 (1977): 5-48;

McEvoy, "Medieval Cosmology and Modern Science," in *Philosophy and Totality*, edited by McEvoy (Belfast: Queen's University of Belfast, 1977), pp. 91-110;

McEvoy, *The Philosophy of Robert Grosseteste* (Oxford: Clarendon Press, 1982; New York: Oxford University Press, 1982);

McEvoy, "The Sun as *res* and *signum*: Grosseteste's Commentary on Ecclesiasticus ch. 43, vv 1-5," *Recherches Theologie Ancienne et Medievalle*, 41 (1974): 38-91;

J. T. Muckle, "The *Hexameron* of Robert Grosseteste: The First Twelve Chapters of Part Seven," *Mediaeval Studies*, 6 (1944): 151-174;

F. M. Powicke, *Robert Grosseteste and the Nicomachean Ethics* (London: Milford, 1930);

Pietro Rossi, "Trace della versione latino di un commento greco dai Secondi Analitici nel *Commentarius in Posteriorum Analyticorum* Libros di Roberto Grossatesta," *Rivista filosofica neo-scholastica*, 70 (1978): 433-439;

Francis Ruello, "La *Divinorum Nominum Reseratio* selon Robert Grosseteste et Albert le Grand," *Archives D'Histoire Doctrinale et Litteraire Du Moyen Âge*, 26 (1959): 99-197;

Josiah C. Russell, "Hereford and Arabic Science in England about 1175-1200," *Isis*, 18 (July 1932): 14-25;

Russell, "Phases of Grosseteste's Intellectual Life," *Harvard Theological Review*, 43 (1950): 93-116;

S. Harrison Thomson, "A Note on Grosseteste's work of Translation," *Journal of Theological Studies*, 34 (1933): 48-52;

Thomson, "The 'Notule' of Robert Grosseteste on the *Nicomachean Ethics*," *Proceedings of the British Academy*, 19 (1933): 195-218;

B. Tierney, "Grosseteste and the Theory of Papal Sovereignty," *Journal of Ecclesiastical History*, 6 (April 1955): 1-17;

Colin M. Turbayne, "Grosseteste and an Ancient Optical Principle," *Isis*, 50 (December 1959): 467-472.

Manuscripts:

The manuscripts of Robert Grosseteste's works are in libraries all over Europe, from Oxford to Erfurt.

Henry of Ghent

(circa 1217 - June 1293)

B. B. Price
York University

PRINCIPAL WORKS: *Summa Theologica* (Summary of Theology, written 1276-1292);

Quodlibeta (Quodlibetal Questions, written 1276-1292).

EDITIONS: *Quodlibeta Magistri Henrici Goethals a Gandavo Doctoris Solenis: Et Archidiaconi Tornacensis Theologica cum Duplici Tabella*, 2 volumes (Paris: Iodocus Badius Ascensius, 1518; reprinted, Louvain: Bibliothèque S.J., 1961);

Summa Quaestionum Ordinariarum Theologi, 2 volumes (Paris: Ioducus Badius Ascensius, 1518; reprinted, Saint Bonaventure, N.Y.: Franciscan Institute, 1953);

Aurea Quodlibeta, 2 volumes (Venice: Apud Iacobum de Franciscis, 1613);

Summa Quaestionum Ordinariarum Theologiae, 3 volumes, edited by A. R. P. M. Hieronymus Scarparius (Ferrara: Franciscum Succium, 1646);

Opera Omnia, 46 volumes projected, edited by Raymond Macken and others (Leuven: Leuven University Press, 1979-).

Henry of Ghent is mainly remembered for serving on the theological commission of the bishop of Paris, Stephen Tempier, in 1277. He also held the position of archdeacon at Bruges and at Tournai and was in attendance at the Council of Lyons in 1274 and at the Synods of Sens, Montpellier, Cologne, and Compiègne. A secular theologian in vociferous opposition to the mendicant orders, Henry of Ghent has been slow in gaining widespread scholarly attention. As regent master in theology in Paris he lived in the foremost intellectual center of the late thirteenth century, asserting himself among his colleagues and students in teaching and disputing. Henry was both theologically outspoken and philosophically innovative.

Henry was born either at Ghent or Tournai in present-day Belgium. After studying at the cathedral school of Tournai, where he was appointed canon in 1267, he entered the faculty of arts at the University of Paris, probably becoming master of arts by 1271. He then undertook study at the Parisian faculty of theology. It is likely that Henry studied under Geoffrey of Bar, regent master in the faculty of theology around 1274, and also under many of the fifteen masters of theology who would be asked in 1282 for their opinions in the mendicant controversy. During his student years Henry was undoubtedly exposed to the thought of Plato, Aristotle, Augustine, Avicenna, and Averroës, all of whom influenced his own ideas.

Henry became regent or teaching master of theology in Paris in 1276; all his extant works date from that point forward. That same year he was named archdeacon of Bruges. In Advent of 1276 he presented his first quodlibetic disputation to the students and guild of masters of theology. Some of the ideas Henry attacked in his first quodlibet were shortly to be put under censure by Bishop Tempier, whose commission Henry joined in early 1277; Henry may have destroyed his earliest works at that time. In formulating his second quodlibet, in the Advent of 1277, Henry obviously had Tempier's sentiments in mind. He alludes to his own opposition to 4 of the 219 Averroist teachings that the commission condemned: article 219, "the substance of incorporeals [separate substances] is said to be the reason for their being in place"; article 96, "God is not able to multiply several individuals of one species without matter"; article 191, "Forms do not receive division save through matter, unless it is understood that forms are educed from the potency of matter"; and article 81, "since intelligences do not have matter, God is not able to make several of the same species." The absence of any works by Henry dating from before 1276 might also be explained by the possibility, however, that Henry simply incorporated into later works whatever he deemed worth saving from his earliest writings and abandoned the rest.

Henry taught in the faculty of theology at the University of Paris from 1276 to 1292. He became archdeacon of Tournai in 1278; thus, from 1278 until 1292 he divided his time between Paris and Tournai. He is known to have rented quarters in Paris as early as 1271 from Master Phillipe de Louans in the front part of a house, probably at 21 rue Coupe Gueule, which was owned by a Benedictine chapter. Henry knew Robert de Sorbon in Paris, and his residence came under the ownership of Robert's college, the Sorbonne, at the beginning of the fourteenth century. Whenever Henry was in Tournai he lived in a house next to Nôtre Dame Cemetery. In 1289 he donated money for commemorative masses and obituary vigils to be said annually in Tournai for his parents and his sister, Catherine.

Henry's writing follows the late-thirteenth-century formats of quodlibetal disputations and of formal university lectures on theology: they are highly concise and woven with ideas drawn from authoritative theological and philosophical sources. Although the Aristotelian Christianity of Thomas Aquinas was receiving condemnation in Henry's day, some of Aquinas's ideas concerning the relation of faith and reason as distinct but compatible spheres were adopted by Henry. His primary focus was a concept which would become fundamental in fourteenth-century theology and metaphysics: the omnipotence of God. God's omnipotence, for Henry, essentially meant divine freedom of creation. Possible essences (*res a ratitudine*) proceed from God by an eternal and necessary emanation, but God does not act according to necessity: divine creation is a free act of the will of God.

In his lectures to students of theology, beginning in 1276, Henry formulated the ideas which would culminate in his *Summa Theologica* (Summary of Theology, written 1276-1292). There is some indication that at least from 1277 to 1281 Henry gathered his students somewhere in Paris in quarters that he probably rented himself. There he confidently presented his own ideas on theology and philosophy. He died before finishing the complete course in theology he had announced in the prologue of his *Summa Theologica*. He intended to treat both God and creatures, as had the most comprehensive thirteenth-century summae. He may have realized that his initial plan could not be completed, and therefore he frequently referred to his *Summa Theologica* as *Quaestiones Ordinariae*. Nonetheless, he neither revised his prologue nor rejected the title of *Summa Theologica* for the first university exemplar of the work, which appeared in 1289. The *Summa Theologica* circulated in three parts: articles 1-20 on the nature of theological knowledge, articles 21-52 on the one God, articles 53-75 on the Trinity.

Although his sympathy for an Augustinian theory of knowledge through divine illumination was clearly revealed from his early years of teaching, Henry's adherence to a purely Augustinian epistemology becomes less secure in later articles of the *Summa Theologica*. The only major component of Augustine's theory Henry steadfastly adhered to was the conviction that God is the first object of knowledge; he could not remain loyal to a strict theory of *illustratio divina*, whereby God's "light" implants ideas in the human mind. Instead of the ultimate knowledge being afforded by such illumination, Henry believed that understanding of God could be acquired through analogy. While divine being and created being are fundamentally distinct and without commonality, human beings can, through "natural knowledge" (a posteriori abstraction from sense experience of created being) and "rational knowledge" (a priori notion of the conceivable), come to know the divine being.

Being was the concept of greatest importance in Henry's thought. He distinguished three kinds of being. Imaginary being is anything the mind can imagine (*res a reor reris* or *res absoluta*). There are two kinds of genuine being: actual being, which includes anything that has actually existed (*res existens in actu*); and possible being, which comprises anything that can be conceived and can possibly come to be (*res a ratitudine*). For Henry, God is being itself and creatures are contingent beings; yet he saw his metaphysics of being as bridging the gap between God and humanity. The essential being (*esse essentiae*) of humanity consists in being thought by God, its existential being (*esse existentiae*) in depending on God as creative cause.

As a product of divine creativity, every *esse existentiae* is also related to God individually. Individuation is thus not the result of the addition of matter to the intelligible essence; the source of individuation is the individual relation of creature to Creator. No concrete distinction existed for Henry between *esse essentiae* and *esse existentiae*; thus knowledge of any genuine thing is accessible to the human mind, and the mind can have all the knowledge of the divine that the relation of exemplified to exemplar affords.

Henry's exposition of his concept of being did not prove to be transparently clear either to his contemporaries or to scholars since; his revisions of the *Summa Theologica* reveal many changes in exposition and a desire that some sections be deleted. Henry provided some explication of his ideas on being in his quodlibetal disputations. Although occasionally he expressed his ideas in the *Quodlibeta* (Quodlibetal Questions, written 1276-1292) using a slightly different vocabulary, he included most of the contents of the first and second parts of the *Summa Theologica* in his disputations. Henry seemed to wish to clarify his ideas on being at least in part due to his justified opinion that they were and would continue to be misunderstood. John Duns Scotus, for example, criticized Henry for teaching that necessary and created being had absolutely nothing in common, and that therefore no argument from creatures of God could be valid.

The *Quodlibeta* reflect the intellectual concerns of academe between Advent of 1276 and Lent of 1292, when Henry gave his last disputation. For each question, Henry's response follows the current quodlibetal literary genre in a format of five parts: the presentation of the question, the arguments pro and con, the solution, and his answers to the arguments pro and con. When authors such as Aristotle or Boethius are cited against his positions, he often tries to show that what those authors "really" meant is not so different from his own point of view. Comparisons of contemporary quodlibeta reveal Henry to have been at odds with most other intellectuals of his time; he was frequently labeled "quarreling" and "argumentative."

In 1290 Henry's vociferous opposition to the confessional privilege of the mendicant orders was quieted by a reprimand from Cardinal Benedict Caetani, the future Pope Boniface VIII. As a result of the censure against him, Henry incurred on all his fellow regent masters a ban against their accepting in their disputations any questions concerning confessional privilege.

Giles of Rome, a somewhat younger contemporary, carried on a running controversy with Henry, especially on the subjects of essence and existence and of the primacy of human will over human intellect. Godfrey of Fontaines, who was Henry's student between 1276 and 1285, entered this discussion espousing a pronounced intellectualism, and the Franciscan John de Murro rose to debate on the side of what Henry considered a position of exaggerated voluntarism. Henry's response to the flurry of opinions was to admit both the influence of the judgments of the intellect on the will, which the intellectualists stressed, and the influence of the emotions on the will, as emphasized by the voluntarists. He nonetheless maintained that the last word belonged to the will, not to the intellect or the emotions. As time went on Henry stressed ever more the active, autonomous character of the will.

Godfrey of Fontaines, like Giles, rejected Henry's distinction between *esse essentiae* and *esse existentiae*. Siger of Brabant initially attacked Henry's theory of "indirect intellection" but seems later to have come to accept it. Duns Scotus tried to counter what he considered skeptical consequences of Henry's theory of divine illumination. Later, William of Ockham, James of Metz, and Durandus of Saint-Pourçain all considered Henry worthy of attack.

Henry of Ghent also had admirers. His quodlibetal questions of moral and pastoral importance were extracted and copied for circulation. When Henry was suspended from university teaching in 1290 because of his outspokenness, a long parade of professors and students made their way in protest to the house of the papal legates and bargained for the lifting of the suspension. So impressed with his thought was the sixteenth-century Servite order of friars that they chose him as their official theologian. His writings were widely read well through the eighteenth century.

In addition to the *Summa Theologica* and *Quodlibeta*, many works have been attributed to Henry of Ghent. Among those more possibly of Henry's authorship are *Lectura Ordinaria super Sacram Scripturam* (Ordinary Lectures on Sacred Scripture), *Syncategoremata* (Syncategorematic Terms), *Quaestiones in VIII Libros Physicorum Aristotelis* (Questions on the Eight Books of Aristotle's *Physics*), and *Summa de Poenitentia* (Summary on Penance). *Lectura Ordinaria super Sacram Scripturam* comprises an introduction to the study of Scripture and of Genesis in particular, and a commentary on the first three chapters of Genesis. It is definitely a work dating from the early career of a master of theology of Henry's time, and many of its points are in keeping with Henry's own philosophical teaching. The clarity of the *Syncategoremata*, a grammatical work, has led it to be cited as exemplary for Henry's period.

Henry continued to travel between Paris and Tournai until 1292. In Paris, his last decade was punctuated by his participation with other Parisian masters in collective opposition to the university chancellor, Philip of Thory. In 1290 Henry was threatened with suspension and official censure. He died in June 1293.

During his lifetime Henry was called *Doctor Solemnis* (Solemn Doctor), *Doctor Reverendus* (Reverend Doctor), *Doctor Digressivus* (Digressive Doctor), and *Summus Doctorum* (Supreme Doctor). None of his readers can fail to notice his intellectual sophistication; some have been able to see nothing but the difficulty it presents, and no doubt much criticism derives from confusion in understanding him. Twentieth-century surveys of Henry's work conclude that his two fundamentally distinct notions of being and his restricted conception of divine illumination offer no firm basis for a metaphysical theology; that his notion of knowledge by analogy was a "misconception"; that he provided no solid argument for a conception of God as necessary Being; and that he failed to blend his diverse influences into a fully coherent system. On the other hand, the independence of his ideas from both the Aristotelian and Augustinian traditions is striking; and his novel approach to divine freedom, to the role of sense experience, and to individuation, as well as his anticipation of certain critical attitudes of the fourteenth century, recommend his work to further analysis. Henry himself felt that a master of theology ought to be "a major light in the Church," speaking both to burning questions of his day and to issues of lasting principles. He seemed to have fulfilled that role. In his extensions and refinements of later medieval Platonism, he lit a philosophical path delicately drawn between contemporary Aristotelianism, as espoused by Siger of Brabant, and the varieties of Augustinianism of William de la Mare, Richard of Middleton, Bonaventure, and Matthew of Aquasparta. Historians centuries apart agree that as "a powerful thinker" and "the most adventurous of theologians" of the late thirteenth century "Henry of Ghent had everything needed to evoke the admiration of posterity."

References:

Paul Bayerschmidt, *Die Seins- und Formmetaphysik des Heinrich von Gent in ihrer Anwendung auf die Christologie*, Beitrage zur Geschichte der Philosophie des Mittelalters, volume 36, nos. 3-4 (Munster: Aschendorff, 1941);

Lucien Bellemare, "Authenticité de deux commentaires sur la Physique attribués à Henri de Gand," *Revue philosophique de Louvain*, 63 (1965): 545-571;

Jerome V. Brown, "Abstraction and the Object of the Human Intellect according to Henry of Ghent," *Vivarium*, 11 (May 1973): 80-104;

Brown, "Divine Illumination in Henry of Ghent," *Recherches de théologie ancienne et médiévale*, 41 (1974): 177-199;

Brown, "John Duns Scotus on Henry of Ghent's Theory of Knowledge," *Modern Schoolman*, 56 (November 1978): 1-29;

Brown, "Sensation in Henry of Ghent: A Late Medieval Aristotelian-Augustinian Synthesis," *Archiv fur Geschichte der Philosophie*, 53, no. 3 (1971): 238-266;

Maurice de Wulf, *Etudes sur Henri de Gand* (Louvain: Uystpruyst-Dieudonné / Paris: Alcan, 1894);

Palémon Glorieux, *La littérature Quodlibétique de 1260 à 1320*, volume 2, Bibliothèque thomiste, no. 21 (Paris: Vrin, 1935);

Glorieux, *Répetoire des maitres en théologie de Paris au XIIIe siècle* (Paris: Vrin, 1933);

J. Gomez-Caffarena, "Cronologica de la 'Suma' de Enrique de Gante por relacion a sus 'Quodlibeta,'" *Gregorianum*, 38 (1957): 116-133;

F. Huet, *Recherches historiques et critiques sur la vie, les ouvrages et la doctrine de Henri de Gand* (Ghent: Librarie générale de Leroux, 1838);

Norman Kretzmann, "Syncategoremata, Exponibilia, Sophismata," in *The Cambridge History of Later Medieval Philosophy: From the Rediscovery of Aristotle to the Disintegration of Scholasticism*, edited by Kretzmann and others (Cambridge: Cambridge University Press, 1982), pp. 211-245;

Raymond P. Macken, "Les corrections d'Henri de Gand à sa 'Somme,'" *Recherches de théologie ancienne et médiévale*, 44 (1977): 55-100;

Macken, "Les corrections d'Henri de Gand à ses 'Quodlibets,'" *Recherches de théologie ancienne et médiévale*, 40 (1973): 5-51;

Macken, "Le 'De potentia' d'Henri de Gand retrouvé?," *Recherches de théologie ancienne et médiévales*, 36 (1969): 184-194;

Macken, "Heinrich von Gent im Gespräch mit seinen Zeitgenossen über die menschliche Freiheit," *Franziskanische Studien*, 59 (1977): 125-182;

Macken, *Henri de Gand (+1293), maitre en théologie à l'Université de Paris, archidiacre de l'éveché de Tournai: Dates et documents*

(Leuven: Leuven University Press, forthcoming);

Macken, "Human Friendship in the Philosophy of Henry of Ghent," *Franziskanische Studien*, 70 (1988): 176-184;

Macken, "La liberté humaine dans la philosophie d'Henri de Gand," in *Regnum Hominis et Regnum Dei*, 2 volumes, edited by Camille Bérubé, Studia scholastico-scotistica, nos. 6-7 (Rome: Societas Internationalis Scotistica, 1978), pp. 577-584;

Macken, "Les sources d'Henri de Gand," *Revue Philosophique de Louvain*, 76 (February 1978): 5-28;

Macken, "Le statut de la matière première dans la philosophie d'Henri de Gand," *Recherches de théologie ancienne et médiévale*, 46 (1979): 130-181;

Macken, "Synderesis and Conscience in the Philosophy of Henry of Ghent," *Franziskanische Studien*, 70 (1988): 185-195;

John Marenbon, *Later Medieval Philosophy (1150-1350): An Introduction* (London & New York: Routledge & Kegan Paul, 1987);

S. P. Marrone, "Matthew of Aquasparta, Henry of Ghent and Augustinian Epistemology after Bonaventure," *Franziskanische Studien*, 65 (1983): 252-290;

Marrone, *Truth and Scientific Knowledge in the Thought of Henry of Ghent* (Cambridge, Mass.: Medieval Academy of America, 1985);

Jean Paulus, "Les disputes d'Henri de Gand et de Giles de Rome sur la distinction de l'essence et de l'existence," *Archive d'histoire doctrinale et littéraire du moyen age*, 13 (1940-1942): 323-358;

Paulus, *Henri de Gand: Essai sur les tendences de sa métaphysique* (Paris: Vrin, 1938);

Anton C. Pegis, "Henry of Ghent and the New Way to God (III)," *Mediaeval Studies*, 33 (1971): 158-179;

Pegis, "A New Way to God: Henry of Ghent (II)," *Mediaeval Studies*, 31 (1969): 93-116;

Pegis, "Toward a New Way to God: Henry of Ghent," *Mediaeval Studies*, 30 (1968): 226-247;

Karl Werner, *Heinrich von Gent, als Repräsentant des christlichen Platonismus im dreizehnten Jahrhundert* (Vienna: Holzhaus, 1878);

John F. Wippel, "The Relationship between Essence and Existence in Late-Thirteenth-Century Thought: Giles of Rome, Henry of Ghent, Godfrey of Fontaines, and James of Viterbo," in *Philosophies of Existence—Ancient and Medieval* (New York: Fordham University Press, 1982), pp. 131-164;

John P. Zwaenepoel, *Les Questiones in librum de Causis attribuées à Henri de Gand*, Edition critique (*Philosophes médiévaux* XV) (Louvain: Publications Universitaires, 1974).

William Heytesbury
(Guillelmus Hentisberus)

(circa 1310 - 1372 or 1373)

André Goddu
Stonehill College

PRINCIPAL WORKS: *Regulae Solvendi Sophismata* (Rules for Resolving Sophisms, written 1335);

Sophismata XXXII (Thirty-two Sophisms, written circa 1335);

Insolubilia (Insoluble Sentences, written circa 1335);

Tractatus Consequentiarum (Treatise on Consequences, written circa 1335);

De Veritate et Falsitate Propositionis (On the Truth and Falsity of a Proposition, written circa 1335);

Casus Obligatorii (On Logical "Obligations," written circa 1335);

De Sensu Composito et Diviso (On the Composite and Divided Sense, written circa 1335);

De Probationibus Conclusionum Tractatus Regularum Solvendi Sophismata (On the Proofs of Conclusions from the Treatise of Rules for Resolving Sophisms, written circa 1335);

Termini Naturales (Natural Terms, written circa 1335);

Tractatus de Eventu Futurorum (Treatise on Future Contingents, written circa 1335).

EDITIONS: *Regulae Solvendi Sophismata*, edited by Ioannes Petrus de la Porta (Pavia, 1481);

Sophismata (Pavia, 1481);

Probationes Conclusionum Tractatus Regularum Solvendi Sophismata Guillelmi Heytesberi, edited by Nicholas of Girardengis (Pavia, 1483);

Quaedem Consequentie Subtiles (N.p., circa 1490);

De Sensu Composito et Diviso (Venice: Joannes & Gregorius de Gregoriis, de Folvino, 1491);

De Veritate et Falsitate Propositionis, edited by Johannes Mapellus (Venice, 1494);

Regulae Solvendi Sophismata, edited by Gaetano de Thienis (Venice, 1494).

EDITIONS IN ENGLISH: *William Heytesbury on "Insoluble" Sentences: Chapter One of His* Rules for Solving Sophisms, translated by Paul Vincent Spade, Mediaeval Sources in Translation, 21 (Toronto: Pontifical Institute of Mediaeval Studies, 1979);

William Heytesbury: On Maxima and Minima. Chapter 5 of Rules for Solving Sophismata, *with an Anonymous Fourteenth-Century Discussion*, translated by John Longeway (Dordrecht, Boston & Lancaster: Reidel, 1984).

The appellation "Merton Calculators" is an artificial designation referring principally to four individuals who were students or masters at Merton College, Oxford, in the fourteenth century. Their real link derives from their common interest in developing techniques for solving a variety of logical dilemmas and mathematical problems applicable to natural philosophy and theology. "Calculator" was the name given apparently by fifteenth-century Italian Schoolmen to the chronologically last of these authors, Richard Swineshead, and it has been applied retrospectively to the others. The other principal "Calculators" were William Heytesbury, Thomas Bradwardine, and John of Dumbleton.

Heytesbury's date of birth is a matter of pure conjecture; it must have been before 1313, as he was a doctor in theology by July 1348. He is thought to have been born in Wiltshire in the diocese of Salisbury. He was a fellow at Merton College in 1330, a bursar at Merton in 1338, and apparently a foundation fellow at Queen's College in 1340, at which time he would have been a student in theology. But his name reappears among the fellows at Merton. He may have been chancellor of the university in 1353-1354 and again in 1371.

All of his known works were probably written between 1331 and 1339, and an Erfurt manuscript dates his *Regulae Solvendi Sophismata* (Rules for Resolving Sophisms) as having been composed in 1335. His most important and influential work, the treatise contributes significantly to the understanding and treatment of problems involving quantitative change. Heytesbury linked discussions and traditions that emerged out of the topical and sophistical literature of the twelfth and thirteenth centuries with more recent developments in natural philosophy and mathematics. He based his discussions on foundations that derive from distinctions and techniques of logic and more explicitly on ontologically reductive assumptions in natural philosophy. Logical and linguistic analysis is meant to make discourse more precise by distinguishing and arranging the various senses in which terms are understood; the goal is to expose all conceivable misunderstandings and ambiguities in assertions and arguments. Among the techniques developed in the Middle Ages for accomplishing this goal were the doctrines of the supposition of terms (how terms stand for things or other terms in propositions), of the exponibility of terms (how propositions with terms that taken by themselves have no signification, for example, the preposition *with*, require exposition), and of the distinction between composite and divided senses (involving fallacies arising from interpreting terms conjointly that should be understood separately, or interpreting terms separately that should be understood conjointly).

Denomination refers to the application of these logical techniques to contexts involving change and motion: denomination is the determination of how and what to name a subject undergoing change and how to characterize the change. The medieval philosophers who developed these techniques were not describing actual measurements and did not develop techniques of empirical measurement. In that sense it is correct to say that the analyses do not derive from real cases, nor are the results applicable to real cases. On the other hand, their intentions were not purely speculative. From a Scholastic-Aristotelian point of view, what was revealed in experience as perceivable by way of the senses and as "reproduced" in ordinary speech constituted the referents from which hypothetical cases were abstracted and to which the results could be subsequently applied. One may wonder why they did not bother to develop empirical techniques of measurement and actually take precise measurements. A plausible answer lies in the context of the discussions, which did not call for more precise measurement but for more precise analysis of the data that they possessed. What would more accurate measurements have given them, they may have implicitly assumed, than the same fundamental problems that they were trying to address, namely, the conditions for relating complex changes to ordinary experience and to ordinary discourse? These were complex problems involving paradoxes arising out of ordinary experience, such as the liar paradox, the problem of defining the beginning or end of a change, the question of the divisibility of a continuum, and so forth.

The evidence in support of such a reading of Heytesbury is primarily of two kinds: that his discussions are concerned with fundamental principles of analysis, and that the rules generated are always applied by way of example to the sorts of questions or assertions that students encountered in natural-philosophical or theological contexts. In other words, the resolution of fundamental problems requires a discussion of terms before one can decide questions about the things to which the terms are applied. The exercises in which students engaged were intended to provide them with examples of how to resolve analytical problems in philosophy and theology.

Heytesbury's principal contribution to the kinematical analysis of local motions is the Merton mean-speed rule: a moving body acquiring or losing velocity uniformly over a given period will traverse a distance equal to the distance it would traverse if it were moved continuously in the same period at its mean velocity. The rule was not applied to bodies falling from rest, nor was there any effort to test it experimentally. Starting from Scholastic-Aristotelian assumptions and distinctions, Heytesbury constructed an account that seemed to meet the demands of logical coherence and conceptual clarity and that referred to commonly experienced cases for confirmation. Because modern mathematical physics is so readily associated with empirical measurement and experimental confirmation, it is confusing and misleading—indeed, a category mistake—to characterize fourteenth-century efforts as being or not being mathematical physics. The denial may be less misleading than the affirmation, but denial implies that there was no advance at all with significance for the history of science, a conclusion that is odd in the face of achievements such as the Merton mean-speed rule. In *De Probationibus Conclusionum Tractatus Regularum Solvendi Sophismata* (On the Proofs of Conclusions from the Treatise of Rules for Resolving Sophisms, circa 1335), Heytesbury proves from the mean-speed

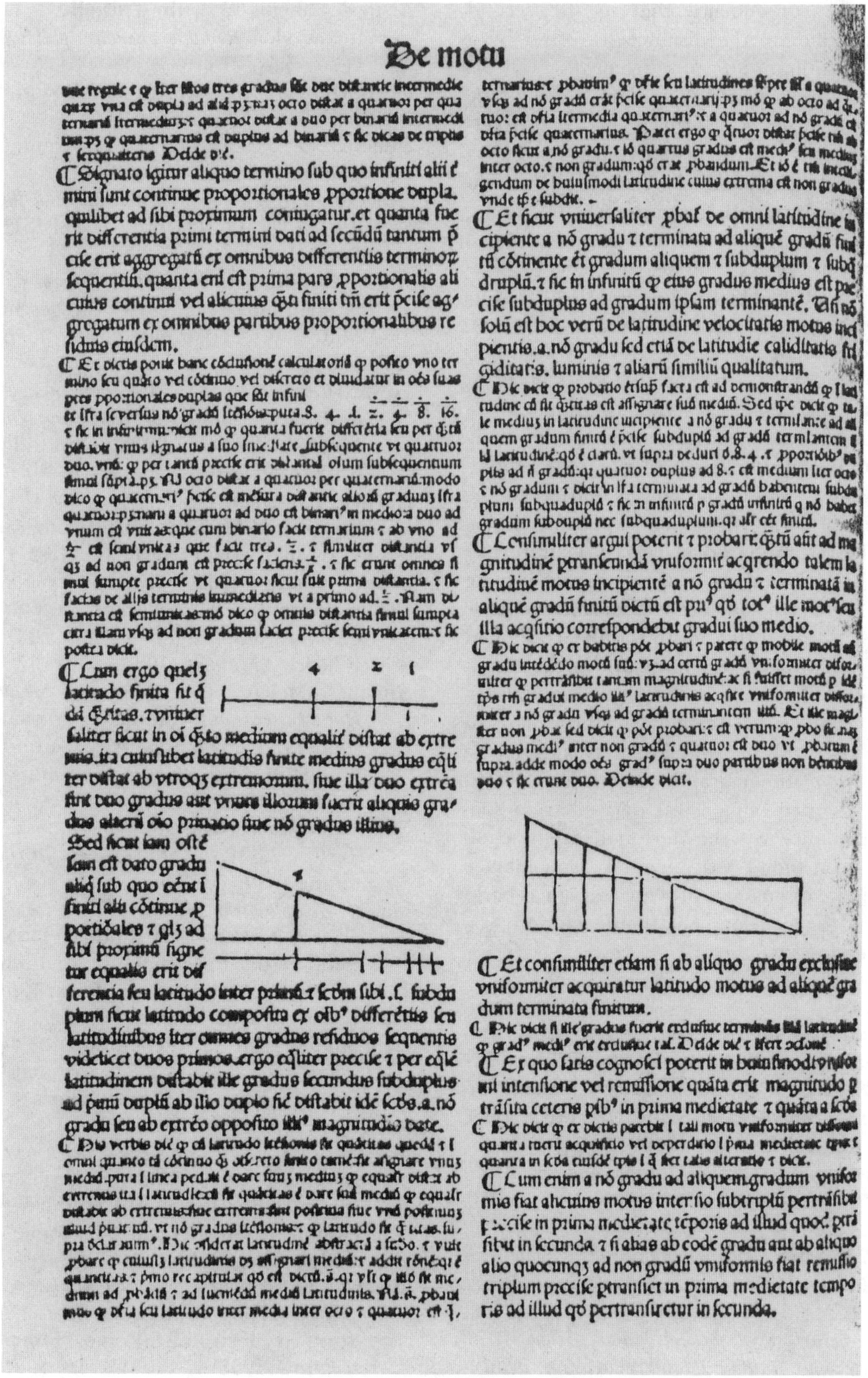

De motu

Page from a 1494 Venice edition of Heytesbury's Regulae Solvendi Sophismata, *including a discussion of the Merton mean-speed rule. The comments in smaller type are by the editor, Gaetano de Thienis.*

theorem the consequence that in the second equal time interval the distance traversed by a body accelerating uniformly from rest will be three times the distance that it traverses in the first interval. A general form of this result states that in each interval the distances traversed by a body accelerating uniformly from rest will increase as the series of odd numbers beginning from unity, that is, 1, 3, 5, 7, and so forth.

There is evidence that Heytesbury influenced later writers. The first to assert that the Merton theorem is applicable to free fall was Domingo de Soto in 1555; and Curtis Wilson has drawn attention to the possible influence of Heytesbury on Thomas Harriot. In a manuscript from around 1600, Harriot discusses projectile motion and explicitly refers to the 1494 edition of Heytesbury's works and commentaries. In the manuscript Harriot describes experimental results of the assumption that free fall is uniformly accelerated with respect to time, thus indicating that the Merton mean-speed theorem may have been used to prove that in uniformly accelerated motion from rest the distances are in the duplicate ratios of the times, that is, that the total distance traversed is proportional to the square of the time of the fall. Although it is improbable that Galileo's mathematical characterization of naturally accelerated motion was derived from specific acquaintance with the Merton theorem, scholars have concluded that general acquaintance with medieval discussions probably served as background to the development of the modern science of motion.

References:

Vern Bullough, "Medical Study at Mediaeval Oxford," *Speculum*, 36 (1961): 600-612;

Stefano Caroti, ed., *Studies in Medieval Natural Philosophy*, Biblioteca di Nuncius, Studi e Testi, 1 (Florence: Olschki, 1989);

Marshall Clagett, *Giovanni Marliani and Late Medieval Physics* (New York: Columbia University Press, 1941);

Clagett, *The Science of Mechanics in the Middle Ages* (Madison: University of Wisconsin Press, 1959);

William Courtenay, *Schools and Scholars in Fourteenth-Century England* (Princeton: Princeton University Press, 1987);

A. C. Crombie, "Quantification in Medieval Physics," *Isis*, 52 (1961): 143-160;

Alain de Libera, "Bulletin d'histoire de la logique médiévale," *Revue des sciences philosophiques et théologiques*, 71 (1987): 590-634;

Pierre Duhem, *Etudes sur Léonard de Vinci*, third series (Paris: Hermann, 1913);

Duhem, *Le Système du Monde*, volumes 7-10 (Paris: Hermann, 1956-1959);

A. B. Emden, *A Biographical Register of the University of Oxford* (Oxford: Oxford University Press, 1957), II: 927-928;

André Goddu, *The Physics of William of Ockham*, Studien und Texte zur Geistesgeschichte des Mittelalters, 16 (Leiden & Cologne: Brill, 1984);

Edward Grand and John Murdoch, eds., *Mathematics and Its Application to Science and Natural Philosophy in the Middle Ages* (Cambridge: Cambridge University Press, 1987);

Norman Kretzmann, ed., *Infinity and Continuity in Ancient and Medieval Thought* (Ithaca, N.Y. & London: Cornell University Press, 1982);

Christopher Lewis, *The Merton Tradition and Kinematics in Late Sixteenth and Early Seventeenth Century Italy*, Saggi e Testi, 15 (Padua: Editrice Antenore, 1980);

Anneliese Maier, *An der Grenze von Scholastik und Naturwissenschaft*, Studien zur Naturphilosophie der Spätscholastik, 3, second edition, Studie e Testi, 41 (Rome: Storia e Letteratura, 1952);

Maier, *Ausgehendes Mittelalter*, 3 volumes, Studie e Testi, 97, 105, 138 (Rome: Storia e Letteratura, 1964-1977);

Maier, *Metaphysische Hintergründe der spätscholastischen Naturphilosophie*, Studien zur Naturphilosophie der Spätscholastik, 4, Studi e Testi, 52 (Rome: Storia e Letteratura, 1955);

Maier, *Die Vorläufer Galileis im 14. Jarhhundert*, Studien zur Naturphilosophie der Spätscholastik, 1, second expanded edition, Studi e Testi, 22 (Rome: Storia e Letteratura, 1966);

Maier, *Zwei Grundprobleme der scholastischen Naturphilosophie*, Studien zur Naturphilosophie der Spätscholastik, 2, third expanded edition, Studi e Testi, 37 (Rome: Storia e Letteratura, 1968);

Maier, *Zwischen Philosophie und Mechanik*, Studien zur Naturphilosophie der Spätscholastik, 5, Studi e Testi, 69 (Rome: Storia e Letteratura, 1958);

Alfonso Maierù, ed., *English Logic in Italy in the 14th and 15th Centuries*, History of Logic, 1 (Naples: Bibliopolis, 1982);

Maierù, *Terminologia logica della tarda scolastico*, Lessico intellettuale europeo, 8 (Rome: Edizioni dell'Ateneo, 1972);

Jürgen Miethke, "Zur sozialen Situation der Naturphilosophie im späteren Mittelalter," in *Lebenslehren und Weltentwürfe im Übergang vom Mittelalter zur Neuzeit*, edited by Hartmut Boockmann and others, Abhandlungen der Akademie der Wissenschaften in Göttingen, Philologisch-Historische Klasse, third series 179 (Göttingen: Vandenhoeck & Ruprecht, 1989), pp. 249-266;

A. George Molland, "The Geometrical Background to the 'Merton School,'" *British Journal for the History of Science*, 4 (1968): 108-125;

John Murdoch, "From Social into Intellectual Factors: An Aspect of the Unitary Character of Late Medieval Learning," in *The Cultural Context of Medieval Learning*, edited by Murdoch and Edith Sylla, Boston Studies in the Philosophy of Science, 26, Synthese Library, volume 76 (Dordrecht & Boston: Reidel, 1975), pp. 271-339;

Murdoch, "Geometry and the Continuum in the Fourteenth Century," Ph.D. dissertation, University of Wisconsin, 1957;

Murdoch, *"Rationes Mathematice": Un aspect du rapport des mathématiques et de la philosophie au moyen âge* (Paris: Palais de la Découverte, 1962);

Murdoch, "Scientia Mediantibus Vocibus: Metalinguistic Analysis in Late Medieval Natural Philosophy," *Sprache und Erkenntnis im Mittelalter, Miscellanea Mediaevalia*, 13, no. 1 (1981): 73-106;

F. M. Powicke, *The Medieval Books of Merton College* (Oxford: Oxford University Press, 1931);

Paul Vincent Spade, "William Heytesbury's Position on 'Insolubles': One Possible Source," *Vivarium*, 14 (November 1976): 114-120;

Edith Sylla, "Medieval Concepts of the Latitudes of Forms: The Oxford Calculators," *Archives d'histoire doctrinale et littéraire du moyen âge*, 40 (1973): 223-283;

Sylla, "Medieval Quantifications of Qualities: The 'Merton School,'" *Archive for History of Exact Sciences*, 8 (1971): 9-39;

James Weisheipl, "Early Fourteenth Century Physics of the Merton 'School' with Special Reference to Dumbleton and Heytesbury," Ph.D. dissertation, Oxford University, 1956;

Weisheipl, "Ockham and Some Mertonians," *Mediaeval Studies*, 30 (1968): 163-213;

Weisheipl, "Repertorium Mertonense," *Mediaeval Studies*, 31 (1969): 174-224;

Curtis Wilson, *William Heytesbury: Medieval Logic and the Rise of Mathematical Physics* (Madison: University of Wisconsin Press, 1956).

Manuscripts:

A preliminary checklist of manuscripts of Heytesbury's works has been compiled by James Weisheipl in "Repertorium Mertonense," *Mediaeval Studies*, 31 (1969): 212-217. Most of the manuscripts are located in Cambridge, Erfurt, Munich, Oxford, Paris, the Vatican, and Venice. A critical edition of the *Regulae Solvendi Sophismata* under the general editorship of Paul Vincent Spade has been announced. To the manuscripts of *Regulae Solvendi Sophismata* listed by Weisheipl should be added Milan, Ambrosiana C 23 superior. Also, Weisheipl's entry for the London manuscript of *Termini Naturales* should be corrected to London, B. M. Royal 8. A. XVIII. Discussion of the authenticity of the works attributed to Heytesbury by Weisheipl is provided by Curtis Wilson, "Heytesbury, William," *Dictionary of Scientific Biography*, volume 6 (New York: Scribners, 1972), pp. 379-380, where Wilson attributes to Heytesbury the *Tractatus de Eventu Futurorum* in only one manuscript: Venice, San Marco, fa. 300 (X, 207), folios 78-79.

Ibn Bajja
(Avempace)
(Abu Bakr Muhammad ibn Yahya ibn al-Sayigh al-Tujibi al-Andalusi al-Saraqusti)

(circa 1077 - 1138)

Thérèse-Anne Druart
Catholic University of America

PRINCIPAL WORKS: *'Ilm al-Nafs* (On the Soul, written circa 1100);

Tadbir al-Mutawahhid (The Rule of the Solitary, written circa 1100).

EDITIONS: *El Régimen del Solitario*, edited and translated into Spanish by Miguel Asín Palacios (Madrid & Granada, 1946);

Ibn Bajjah's 'Ilm al-Nafs, edited by M. Saghir Hasan Ma'sumi (Karachi: Pakistan Historical Society, 1960);

Ibn Bajjah's Opera Metaphysica, edited by Majid Fakhry (Beirut: Dar al-Nahar, 1968);

Rasa'il Falsafiyya, edited by Jamal al-Din al-'Alawi (Beirut: Dar al-Thaqafa, 1983).

EDITIONS IN ENGLISH: "Ibn Bajjah's 'Tadbiru l-Mutawahhid' (Rule of the Solitary)," edited and translated by D. M. Dunlop, *Journal of the Royal Asiatic Society* (1945): 61-81;

Ibn Bajjah's 'Ilm al-Nafs, translated by M. Saghir Hasan Ma'sumi (Karachi: Pakistan Historical Society, 1961);

"The Governance of the Solitary," excerpts translated by Lawrence Berman, in *Medieval Political Philosophy*, edited by Ralph Lerner and Muhsin Mahdi (Ithaca, N.Y.: Cornell University Press, 1963), pp. 122-133;

"Ibn Bajjah on the Human Intellect," translated by Ma'sumi, *Islamic Studies*, 4 (1965): 121-136.

Known in the Latin West as Avempace, the ill-fated philosopher Ibn Bajja remains somewhat mysterious. It is not known exactly when and where he was born, and there are gaps in his biography. He had an extensive knowledge of medicine and in 1109 became vizier or minister of Ibn Tafalwit, the Almoravid governor of Zaragoza. When he was sent as an ambassador to the Huds, they threw him into prison for several months. In 1118, after Ibn Tafalwit's death, he was again imprisoned. In 1135 he was engaged in study with the governor of Seville. He died in 1138 in Fez, Morocco, probably of poison.

Ibn Tufayl, another twelfth-century Spanish philosopher, explains why Ibn Bajja's thought is as elusive as its author: "There was none among [this generation of Spanish philosophers] of a finer genius, of a greater understanding, or of a truer insight than [Ibn Bajja]. Yet, the things of this world kept him busy until death overtook him before the treasures of his science could be brought to light and the secrets of his wisdom made available. The greatest part of his extant writings are in imperfect state and incomplete, such as *'Ilm al-Nafs* (On the Soul [circa 1100]) and *Tadbir al-Mutawahhid* (The Rule of the Solitary [circa 1100]), as well as his books on logic and physics. As for his finished works, they include only concise books and hastily written treatises." Ibn Bajja's fame rests on his position on the material intellect, which he construed as a disposition in the imaginative faculty of the soul. Yet Averroës, who at first followed him, later confessed that it was Ibn Bajja who misled him in his earlier interpretations of Aristotle on this point.

In political philosophy, probably because of the political upheavals of his time, Ibn Bajja does not describe the rule of the philosopher in the perfect state. Rather, he speaks of the role of the philosopher in a truly imperfect state and advises him to become a solitary.

Bibliography:

Jamal al-Din al-'Alawi, *Mu'allafat Ibn Bajjah* (Beirut: Dar al-Nashr, 1983);

Charles Butterworth, "The Study of Arabic Philosophy Today," and "Appendix (1983-87)," in *Arabic Philosophy and the West: Continuity and Interaction,* edited by Thérèse-Anne Druart (Washington, D.C.: Center for Contemporary Arabic Studies, Georgetown University, 1988), pp. 77-80, 129-130.

Biography:

D. M. Dunlop, "Remarks on the Life and Works of Ibn Bajjah (Avempace)," in *Proceedings of the 22th Congress of Orientalists,* volume 2, edited by Z. V. Togan (Leiden, Netherlands: Brill, 1957), pp. 188-196.

References:

Alexander Altmann, "Ibn Bajja on Man's Ultimate Felicity," in *H. A. Wolfson Jubilee Volume* (Jerusalem: American Academy for Jewish Research, 1965), pp. 47-87;

Michael Blaustein, "Aspects of Ibn Bajja's Theory of Apprehension," in *Maimonides and Philosophy,* edited by Shlomo Pines and Y. Yovel (Dordrecht, Netherlands: Nijhoff, 1986), pp. 202-212;

Ibn Tufayl, "Hayy the Son of Yaqzan," translated by George N. Atiyeh, in *Medieval Political Philosophy,* edited by Ralph Lerner and Muhsin Mahdi (Ithaca, N.Y.: Cornell University Press, 1963), p. 139;

Oliver Leaman, "Ibn Bajja on Society and Philosophy," *Der Islam,* 57 (1980): 109-119;

M. S. H. Ma'sumi, "Avempace—The Great Philosopher of Andalus," *Islamic Culture,* 36 (1962): 35-53, 85-101;

Erwin I. J. Rosenthal, "The Place of Politics in the Philosophy of Ibn Bajja," *Islamic Culture,* 25 (1951): 187-211.

Manuscripts:

Manuscripts of Ibn Bajja's texts are few. Berlin National Library, 5060 WE 87 disappeared at the end of World War II. Pococke 206 at the Bodleian Library, Oxford University, is difficult to read. Escurial 609 contains only logical works. Various texts have been found in Tashkent and in Istanbul and Ankara, Turkey.

Solomon Ibn Gabirol
(Avicebron or Avicebrol)
(circa 1021 - circa 1058)

T. M. Rudavsky
Ohio State University

PRINCIPAL WORKS: *Anak* (Poem on Hebrew Grammar, written circa 1040);

Tikkun Middot ha-Nefesh (On the Improvement of Moral Qualities, written 1045);

Mekor Hayyim (Fountain of Life, date of composition unknown);

Keter Malkhut (The Royal Crown, date of composition unknown).

EDITIONS: *Tikkun Middot ha-Nefesh* (Riva di Trento: Joseph Ottolengo, 1562);

Avencebrolis (Ibn Gebirol) Fons vitae ex arabico in latinum translatus ab Iohanne Hispano et Dominico Gundissalino: Ex codicibus Parisinus, Amploniano, Columbino, 3 volumes, edited by Clemens Baeumker, Beiträge zur Geschichte der Philosophie des Mittelalters, volume 1, parts 2-4 (Münster: Aschendorff, 1892-1895).

EDITIONS IN ENGLISH: *The Improvement of the Moral Qualities: An Ethical Treatise of the Eleventh Century by Solomon ibn Gabirol, Printed from an Unique Arabic Manuscript, Together with a Translation and an Essay on the Place of Gabirol in the History of the Development of Jewish Ethics*, translated by Stephen S. Wise (New York: Columbia University Press, 1901; reprinted, New York: AMS Press, 1966);

Selected Religious Poems of Ibn Gabirol, Translated into English Verse by Israel Zangwill from a Critical Text Edited by Israel Davidson (Philadelphia: Jewish Publication Society of America, 1923; reprinted, New York: Arno Press, 1973);

Fountain of Life, Translated from Clemens Baeumker's Edition of the Latin Version of Johannes Hispanus and Dominicus Gundissalinus, Published in Beiträge zur Geschichte der Philosophie des Mittelalters, *Münster, 1892-1895*, translated by Alfred B. Jacob (Philadelphia: Dropsie College, 1954);

The Kingly Crown, translated by Bernard Lewis (London: Vallentine-Mitchell, 1961);

The Fountain of Life, Fons Vitae, by Solomon ibn Gabirol (Avicebron): Specially Abridged Edition, translated by Harry E. Wedeck (New York:

Solomon ibn Gabirol; statue by Reed Armstrong in Málaga, Spain

Philosophical Library, 1962; London: Owen, 1963);

"The Kingly Crown," translated by Raphael Loewe, in his *Ibn Gabirol* (New York: Grove Weidenfeld, 1990).

In an early poem Solomon ben Judah ibn Gabirol called himself a sixteen-year-old with the heart of an eighty-year-old. If metaphysics is the domain of those experienced in wisdom and years, then Ibn Gabirol's self-assessment is not far off the mark. For although Ibn Gabirol lived—by some accounts—barely forty years, he is known primarily for his metaphysical writings: his major philosophical work, *Mekor Hayyim* (Fountain of Life, date of composition unknown), is a metaphysical treatise which presents a rigorously worked-out Neoplatonic cosmology. But Ibn Gabirol was a metaphysical and religious poet as well. A product of the flourishing of Jewish intellectual life in Andalusia under the enlightened reign of the Umayyad caliphate, Ibn Gabirol was one of the first Jewish philosophers in Spain to benefit from the intellectual ferment of this golden age.

Of Ibn Gabirol's life little is known. He was born in Málaga, Spain, in 1021 or 1022. From his poetry it can be inferred that he was orphaned young and relied on patronage for support. In one of his poems he describes himself as "small, ugly, and sickly, and of a disagreeable disposition"; in another he gives an account of the terrors of his recurrent skin diseases. At sixteen Ibn Gabirol was already writing poetry and came under the protection of Yekutiel ben Ishaq ibn Hasan, a Jewish dignitary at the court of the king of Zaragoza. In 1045, it is thought, Ibn Gabirol composed his ethical treatise *Tikkun Middot ha-Nefesh* (On the Improvement of Moral Qualities). But Ibn Gabirol was known for his arrogant, sometimes virulent temper, and on the death of his patron he was forced out of Zaragoza to Granada, and finally to Valencia. It is not clear exactly when he died: his near contemporaries place his death anywhere from 1054 to 1070. It is most likely, however, that he died in 1057 or 1058.

Living during the height of the Muslim reign in southern Spain, Ibn Gabirol was influenced by the rich Judeo-Arabic interaction which colored Spanish intellectual life during the eleventh century. Much of his work was written in Arabic, and many of his ideas and poetic styles reflect Arab intellectual and stylistic components. Ibn Gabirol boasted of having written more than twenty philosophical works, but only *Mekor Hayyim* and *Tikkun Middot ha-Nefesh* are extant. Several other works have been attributed to him—for example, *Mibhar Peninim* (Choice of Pearls), a collection of 610 proverbs, maxims, and parables—but with little evidence. Two other philosophical treatises which Ibn Gabirol mentions in *Mekor Hayyim* are not extant, and it is not clear whether they ever really existed. Ibn Gabirol did, however, write hundreds of poems; these poems have been scattered throughout the Jewish liturgical and literary corpus and have not yet been fully collected. In fact, although Ibn Gabirol's philosophy has endured throughout the ages, it is through his poetry that he made his most original contributions.

Ibn Gabirol's poetry falls into two divisions that might be termed the secular and philosophical genres. His secular output represents one of the first attempts in Hebrew literature to write a purely nonreligious poetry, unconnected to Scripture or liturgical themes. Ibn Gabirol's knowledge of Hebrew is reflected in *Anak* (The Necklace), a four-hundred-verse exposition of Hebrew grammar written when he was nineteen. He also wrote elegies, love poems, and panegyrics.

Ibn Gabirol's major literary contribution, however, comprises what may be termed his "wisdom poetry." Here his work most clearly spans the interface between poetry and philosophy. In these poems Ibn Gabirol is obsessed with the search for knowledge. He depicts himself as devoting his life to knowledge in order to transcend the worthlessness of bodily existence. The underlying motif of these poems, reflected in his philosophical works as well, is that the purpose of our temporary sojourn on this earth is to acquire knowledge and ultimate felicity. The mystical undercurrents are akin to Muslim Sufi poetry, as well as to themes in earlier Cabalistic literature.

The best-known and most elegant example of this philosophical poetry is Ibn Gabirol's masterpiece *Keter Malkhut* (The Royal Crown, date of composition unknown), which to this day forms the text for the Jewish Day of Atonement service. It comprises forty songs of unequal lengths and is divided into three parts. Part 2 of the poem is cosmological; it describes the sublunar elements, the throne of glory, angels, and human corporeal existence.

In *Tikkun Middot ha-Nefesh*, which is primarily a treatise on practical morality, the qualities and defects of the soul are described, with particular emphasis on the Aristotelian doctrine of virtue as a mean between extremes of excess and defect which constitute vices. This doctrine is supported by biblical references as well as by quotations from Greek philosophers and Arab poets. Ibn Gabirol describes humans as representing the pinnacle of creation; inasmuch as the final purpose of human existence is perfection, they must overcome their passions and detach themselves from this base existence in order to attain felicity of the soul.

Many of these standard elements can be readily found in classical Jewish Neoplatonism. As Jacques Schlanger has pointed out, however, Ibn Gabirol introduces an original element into his work: the connection between the moral and physiological makeup of the human. Each of twenty personal traits is correlated to one of the five senses. Hence, the body as well as the soul must participate in the person's aspirations toward felicity: "In the actions of the senses as well as in the moral actions, one must reside in the mean and not fall into excess or defect," Schlanger points out. Ibn Gabirol delineates a complete parallel between the microcosm, represented by the human being, and the macrocosm.

This contrast between the microcosm and the macrocosm finds its fullest expression in Ibn Gabirol's most comprehensive philosophical work, *Mekor Hayyim*. Written in Arabic, the work has survived in a twelfth-century Latin translation, *Fons Vitae*, by John of Spain in collaboration with Dominicus Gundissalinus; the author's name was given as "Avicebrol" or "Avicebron." Latin Scholastics reading the *Fons Vitae* had no idea that this work was written by a Spanish Jew; the author was thought to be a Muslim. Extracts of the original Arabic poem were translated into Hebrew in the thirteenth century by Shem Tov ben Josef ibn Falaquera.

In 1859 a French scholar, Salomon Munk, edited and translated the Hebrew extracts into French. Comparing passages in the Hebrew translation by Falaquera with quotations from the Latin version in works of Albert the Great, Munk realized that the appellations "Avicebron," "Avencebrol," and "Avicebrol" referred to Ibn Gabirol. *Mekor Hayyim* is unique among Jewish medieval works in that it contains virtually no references to any other Jewish texts, ideas, or sources: it is wholly lacking in Jewish content. Medieval readers thus had no reason to suspect that the author was the noted Jewish poet Ibn Gabirol.

Mekor Hayyim is a dialogue between a teacher and his disciple, a style popular in Arabic

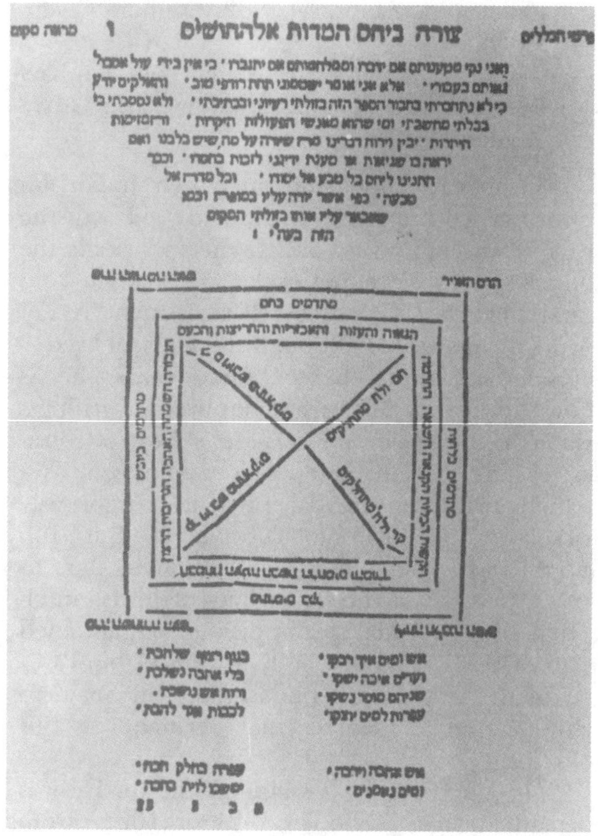

Page from a 1562 edition of Ibn Gabirol's Tikkun Middot ha-Nefesh. *The diagram shows the relationships of the basic traits of human nature.*

philosophical literature of the period. Unlike most such dialogues, in which the student contributes to the argument, Ibn Gabirol's interlocutor functions primarily as a literary device. The work comprises five books, of which the third is the longest (more than three hundred pages in the Latin edition). A succinct summary of the work is given by Ibn Gabirol in his introduction: "Inasmuch as we propose to study universal matter and universal form, we must explain that whatsoever is composed of matter and form comprises two elements: composed corporeal substance and simple spiritual substance. The former further subdivides into two: corporeal matter which underlies the form of qualities; and spiritual matter which underlies corporeal form. . . . And so in the first treatise we shall treat universal matter and universal form; in the second we shall treat spiritual matter. This will necessitate subsequent treatises as well. In the third we shall treat the reality of simple substances; in the fourth, the search for knowledge of matter and form of simple substances; and in the fifth universal matter and form in and of themselves."

The work has several basic themes: science or knowledge is the ultimate aim of human life; knowledge of oneself (the microcosm) contains the science of everything (the macrocosm); the world was created by and is dependent on divine will; to return to the world of spirit, the soul must purify itself of the pollutions of this base world; the purpose of human existence is the knowledge of being; being comprises matter and form, God, and will. Ibn Gabirol's most creative contribution is his hylomorphism. All substances, both spiritual and corporeal, are composed of matter and form. Types of matter are ordered in a hierarchy which extends downward from most to least simple: general spiritual matter, general corporeal matter, general celestial matter, general natural matter, particular natural matter, individual matter, and prime matter, which lies at the very limits of being.

On the question of how form and matter are interrelated Ibn Gabirol presents two alternative answers. On the one hand, he argues that form and matter are differentiated only according to one's perspective; both are aspects of simple substance. On the other hand, he emphasizes the complete opposition between matter and form, suggesting that they possess mutually exclusive properties which render impossible a reduction of one to the other.

In book 2 the question arises: are the ultimate constituents of reality divisible or indivisible? Ibn Gabirol answers that extension and indivisibility pertain to two different kinds of being: the former is associated with matter, the latter with spirit. It is impossible to reduce one to the other. Hence, matter cannot be composed of indivisible, spaceless atoms (*minimae partes*); any indivisible unit must be of a spiritual nature. "It is now clear to me that the smallest part in question is not non-divisible, for we cannot find an indivisible part; and it is clear as well that the part in question . . . is composed of substance and accident." Although one can imagine ultimate indivisible units of matter, such entities are theoretical and not actual. Material reality, therefore, is a seamless whole: "the parts of the totality of the body are joined, continuous, and have no separation among themselves." Atomism leads to the untenable thesis that reality is ultimately disconnected or disjointed.

Creation takes place outside of time: "It is necessary that the First Author achieve its work outside of time." Reflecting the discrepancies in his account of matter and form, Ibn Gabirol's discussion of creation is also inconsistent. He argues in some places that matter was created bereft of form, for which it yearns. In other contexts, he asserts that matter subsists not even for an instant without form. Additionally, Ibn Gabirol offers two accounts of the actual process of creation. In one, universal matter comes from the essence of God, and form comes from the divine will; but according to the other account, both were created by the divine will.

In his conception of matter, Ibn Gabirol has incorporated both Aristotelian and Stoic elements, the latter possibly from Galen. It has been suggested that his notion of spiritual matter may have been influenced by Proclus's *Elements of Theology*, a fifth-century Neoplatonic work that was translated into Arabic. Unlike Ibn Gabirol, however, Proclus did not maintain that universal form and matter are the first simple substances after God and will. It is more likely that on this point Ibn Gabirol was influenced by Pseudo-Empedocles and Isaac Israeli, both of whose views on matter and form are similar to his.

Ibn Gabirol's influence on Jewish philosophy was limited. Jewish philosophers steeped in Aristotelianism had little interest in his work. Abraham Ibn Daud in the twelfth century attacked *Mekor Hayyim* on several grounds: that it was aimed toward all religions, and not Judaism alone; that it developed a single subject to excessive length; that it lacked scientific method; and that it seduced Jews into error. *Mekor Hayyim* was, however, influential on several Jewish Neoplatonists, such as Ibn Zaddik and Moses Ibn Ezra, as well as on important Cabalistic figures such as Ibn Latif.

With respect to the Christian world, the story is quite different. Many Scholastics, Thomas Aquinas included, were affected by Ibn Gabirol's conception of matter. While Aquinas subjected Ibn Gabirol's theory of spiritual matter to virulent criticism, others, most notably Franciscans such as Bonaventure and John Duns Scotus, accepted some of his views. It might even be argued that the Franciscan notion of universal matter is directly indebted to Ibn Gabirol's hylomorphism. Thus Solomon ben Judah ibn Gabirol, the Spanish Jew, came to influence fourteenth-century Scholasticism under the pseudonym Avicebron, his true identity concealed as a result of his efforts to systematize the basic principles of Jewish thought without recourse to religious dogma.

References:

Fernand Brunner, *Platonisme et aristotelisme: La Critique d'Ibn Gabirol par St. Thomas d'Aquin* (Louvain: Publications universitaires de Louvain, 1965);

T. M. Rudavsky, "Conflicting Motifs: Ibn Gabirol on Matter and Evil," *New Scholasticism*, 52 (Winter 1978): 54-71;

Jacques Schlanger, *La Philosophie de Salomon ibn Gabirol* (Leiden: Brill, 1968);

Colette Sirat, *A History of Jewish Philosophy in the Middle Ages* (Cambridge: Cambridge University Press, 1985), pp. 68-85.

John of Dumbleton (Johannes de Dumbleton)

(circa 1310 - circa 1349)

André Goddu
Stonehill College

PRINCIPAL WORKS: *Expositio Capituli Quarti Bradwardini De Proportionibus* (Exposition of the Fourth Chapter of Bradwardine's *De Proportionibus*, written circa 1332);

Summa Logicae et Philosophiae Naturalis (Summary of Logic and Natural Philosophy, written circa 1349).

EDITION: "Compendium sex conclusionum," edited by James Weisheipl in his "Early Fourteenth Century Physics of the Merton 'School' with Special Reference to Dumbleton and Heytesbury," Ph.D. dissertation, Oxford University, 1956, pp. 392-399.

The appellation "Merton Calculators" refers primarily to four men who were students or masters at Merton College, Oxford, in the fourteenth century. They never formed an actual "school" or movement but shared an interest in developing techniques for solving a variety of logical dilemmas and mathematical problems applicable to natural philosophy and theology. "Calculator" was the name given apparently by fifteenth-century Italian Schoolmen to the chronologically last of these authors, Richard Swineshead, and it has been applied retrospectively to John of Dumbleton, Thomas Bradwardine, and William Heytesbury.

Born probably around 1310, John was a native of the village of Dumbleton in Gloucestershire in the diocese of Worcester. He was a fellow of Merton College in 1338. In the *Merton Muniments* of 1338-1339 he is mentioned along with Heytesbury, John Ashinden, William Sutton, Simon Bredon, and Thomas Buckingham. In the founder's statutes of 10 February 1340 he is named as a fellow of Queen's College, from which it is surmised that he had completed his necessary regency in arts and begun the study of theology. In 1344-1345 he was again a fellow of Merton College, and he was still at Merton in 1347-1348. As far as can be ascertained, he was a bachelor of theology at the time of his presumed death in 1349. Since all of the manuscripts of his *Summa Logicae et Philosophiae Naturalis* (Summary of Logic and Natural Philosophy) are incomplete, he may still have been working on the text at the time of his death. The rejection by Dumbleton of views found in Heytesbury's *Regulae Solvendi Sophismata* (Rules for Resolving Sophisms, 1335) indicates that Dumbleton began his *Summa Logicae et Philosophiae Naturalis* after 1335. The work was to have contained ten parts, with the last on universals and signification, but no extant manuscript contains part 10; even the most complete manuscripts break off in part 9.

It is unfortunate that the one author among the Merton Calculators who wrote a comprehensive text and commentary on natural philosophy from their mathematical perspective apparently did not live to complete it. In addition, whether because of its incompleteness, length, lack of concise concentration on mathematical problems and applications, or some other reason, Dumbleton's *Summa Logicae et Philosophiae Naturalis* evidently had neither the impact nor distribution that the works of other Calculators enjoyed. The number of manuscripts from the fourteenth century suggests that it had some influence, but it seems to drop out of sight in the fifteenth century.

Contrary to the assumptions made by many scholars that the Calculators possessed philosophical principles that were contrary to the principles of William of Ockham, Dumbleton, like Heytesbury, seems to have been a disciple of both Ockham and Bradwardine. More than Heytesbury, however, Dumbleton adheres openly to Ockham's doctrines, even though Dumbleton never cites Ockham by name. Heytesbury's influence is shown in Dumbleton's own proof of the Merton mean-speed theorem, first devised by Heytesbury: a body uniformly accelerating from rest over a given period of time will traverse a distance equal to the distance it would traverse if it moved in the same period at a constant velocity that is one-half of the final velocity of its uniformly accelerated motion. Dumbleton's proof is remarkable for its ingenuity. It is a reductio ad absurdum argument. If one assumes that the velocity equivalent to a uniform acceleration is either greater or less than its mean velocity, the result will be absurd. If the uniform velocity is greater than the mean velocity (that is, its velocity at the middle instant of time), then the velocity equivalent to the uniform acceleration through the first half of the time must be greater than its mean; if applied to ever smaller fractions of time, this result has the absurd consequence that the velocity equivalent to the uniform acceleration is equal to the final velocity of the acceleration. If the uniform velocity is less than the mean velocity, then the velocity equivalent to the uniform acceleration through the first half of the time must be less than its mean; if applied to ever smaller fractions of time, this result has the absurb consequence that the velocity equivalent to a uniform acceleration is equal to the initial velocity of the acceleration, that is, zero velocity. Since two of three possibilities have been eliminated as logically absurd, it follows that the velocity equivalent to a uniform acceleration is the mean velocity of a body traversing an equal space in an equal time.

Another ingenious innovation by Dumbleton is his use of a geometrical analogy to explain the decrease in intensity of a light at different distances from the source: he refers to a pyramid, evidently meaning a cone. Using a triangular figure to represent a uniform decrease to zero degree constitutes one of the earliest suggestions known for using geometry to analyze problems discussed in verbal or algebraic terms.

Part 1 of the *Summa Logicae et Philosophiae Naturalis* is concerned largely with certitude and with the psychology of logic. It is divided into articles dealing with the signification of terms and "insolubilia," questions of more and less in knowledge, the principles of knowledge, and the increase of credulity and science.

Parts 2 through 9 represent the only extensive commentary by the Calculators on Aristotle's *Physics* and present an entire philosophy of nature. Parts 2 and 3 correspond roughly to the first six books of the *Physics*, part 2 focusing on matter and form and on first principles, part 3 concentrating on change, alteration and augmentation, and motion and time. In part 3 Dumbleton also takes up Bradwardine's dynamics in detail. Bradwardine's theorem that velocity increases arithmetically as the ratio of force to resistance increases geometrically is expressed by Dumbleton as "the proportion of proportions," thus clarifying the mathematical function that the ratio of two velocities is treated as the exponent of the ratio of force to resistance $[F_2/R_2 = F_1/R_1^{(V_2/V_1)}]$. In addition, Dumbleton considers the relation between changes in the ratio of force to resistance as a function of time differences; but he does not explicitly draw the further consequence that a constant ratio of force to resistance produces a uniformly accelerated motion.

Parts 4 through 6 correspond primarily to Aristotle's *On the Heaven and the Earth* and to part of the eighth book of the *Physics*. Part 5 is on "spiritual action" and on questions such as whether light belongs to some element. Part 6 treats such topics as active potency, natural action and the end of forms, motion and rest, heavenly motions, and the first mover. In part 6 Dumbleton also discusses such questions as whether a form is properly mobile and how natural bodies are quantitatively determined. Part 7 corresponds to the two books of Aristotle's *On Generation and Corruption* and to books 7 and 8 of the *Physics*.

Parts 8 and 9 are devoted to the generation of living creatures and the operation of the senses and the intellect. They correspond to the problems treated in Aristotle's *On the Soul* and *Parva Naturalia*. Part 9 deals with the five senses before breaking off. According to Dumbleton's own description, part 10 was to deal with universals and signification; perhaps it was his intention to return to central logical and cognitive issues and to address some of the criticisms that had been leveled against Ockhamist natural philosophy.

One of the crucial but still relatively little-researched questions broached by the Calculators is whether mathematical demonstrations can provide demonstrative knowledge of physical phenomena. The Mertonians tended to regard mathematical entities as abstractions from real things; such a reduction helped to direct attention to the measure of quantified realities in the physical world rather than to questions about act and potency. This result has often been exaggerated by characterizing Mertonian efforts as a form of mathematical physics. The so-called Calculators did not measure or calculate about actually existing things or phenomena, but they did engage in conceptual analysis of commonly experienced physical things and events and, to that extent, provided some foundation for a more mathematical approach to the physical world.

One area in which such discussions contributed to conceptual development is the notion of quantity of matter. The expression *quantitas materiae* derives from the thirteenth century and by the seventeenth century becomes the Latin equivalent for the modern concept of mass. No one in the fourteenth century developed a concept equivalent to the modern concept of mass. Medieval discussions of such questions were complicated by fundamental disagreements over the ontological status of matter, over the finite or infinite divisibility of a continuum, and over the explanation of condensation and rarefaction. Ockham and Dumbleton held that a given body had a *quantitas materiae*, a finite and in principle denumerable number of parts. They explained condensation and rarefaction as the contraction and expansion, respectively, in space of the constant number of parts of the body: that is, without loss or addition of parts, the same number of parts could occupy different volumes. The explanation of rarefaction and condensation, then, involves the local motion of the parts.

Dumbleton devotes considerable attention to the question of the velocity of condensation and rarefaction. He says that a proportional increase of volume depends on matter and density taken together, that an increase of rarity depends on matter and volume taken together, and that bodies possess "natural" rarities or densities. These notions were introduced, however, by philosophers who continued to think of weight as a property of "heavy" bodies only. Furthermore, they regarded continuous, permanent entities as infinitely divisible in principle. Because they lacked a concept of molecules, it was difficult for them to reconcile their acceptance of infinite divisibility with their intuition that a given elemental body possesses a constant number of finite, denumerable parts. Finally, the lack of actual measurement and experimentation for all of this speculation lends it an air of imaginative theorizing without empirical support.

The first five parts of the *Summa Logicae et Philosophiae Naturalis* suggest that their forcefully argued conclusions were drawn from disputations, whereas the later parts have the character of commentaries on authoritative texts. Dumbleton apparently had little time for revision and was possibly distracted by other studies or obligations. As it stands, his style is unpolished. Some arguments are presented clearly and concisely; others are prolix and obscure.

Where one scholar insists that the Mertonians' work was totally divorced from any consideration of real physical problems, another insists that Dumbleton, above all, had concrete physical problems in mind and, indeed, that Dumbleton's mathematics was taken as descriptive of physical objects and processes. Although the second of these two opinions is closer to the truth, as generalizations both views are invalid. For instance, in astronomy Dumbleton believed that the geometry should reflect the actual motions of the heavenly bodies, but in optics he regarded geometry as useful for calculation and not as representing the motion or existence of any objects. Dumbleton was following Ockham's lead in the effort to reconcile perspectivist optics with the Aristotelian account of light and vision, without the assumption of "species" (the forms of objects) or other superfluous entities. To Ockham and Dumbleton, the conclusion that visual rays are real entities does not square with Aristotle's qualitative analysis of light. On the other hand, it would be wrong to conclude that geometry has no function to perform in the analysis of light and vision. Dumbleton's basically Aristotelian conception of mathematical abstraction did not commit him to the view that all mathematical descriptions are referential or that they are all referential in the same way; some mathematical descriptions, like some concepts, are purely functional and utilitarian. Like Ockham, Dumbleton held views that are more complex and more comprehensive than is usually thought. The qualifications made by such a subtle thinker must be noted carefully, and generalizations must be formulated cautiously.

Likewise, claims about Dumbleton's later influence must be asserted cautiously. In the late fourteenth century, Mertonian scholars seem to have paraphrased Dumbleton's works and codified them in the form of elementary handbooks. Dumbleton's ingenious proof of the mean-speed theorem reappears in the work of the fifteenth-century philosopher Giovanni Marliani at Pavia, but it is possible that Marliani arrived at the idea of using the reductio ad absurdum method of proof independently of Dumbleton. Scholars have not found any evidence of Dumbleton's influence on natural philosophy after the middle of the fifteenth century.

References:

Stefano Caroti, ed., *Studies in Medieval Natural Philosophy*, Biblioteca di Nuncius, Studi e Testi, 1 (Florence: Olschki, 1989);

Marshall Clagett, *Giovanni Marliani and Late Medieval Physics* (New York: Columbia University Press, 1941);

Clagett, *The Science of Mechanics in the Middle Ages* (Madison: University of Wisconsin Press, 1959);

William Courtenay, *Schools and Scholars in Fourteenth-Century England* (Princeton: Princeton University Press, 1987);

A. C. Crombie, "Quantification in Medieval Physics," *Isis*, 52 (1961): 143-160;

Alain de Libera, "Bulletin d'histoire de la logique médiévale," *Revue des sciences philosophiques et théologiques*, 71 (1987): 590-634;

Pierre Duhem, *Etudes sur Léonard de Vinci*, third series (Paris: Hermann, 1913);

Duhem, *Le Système du monde*, volumes 7 and 8 (Paris: Hermann, 1956-1958);

A. B. Emden, *A Biographical Register of the University of Oxford* (Oxford: Oxford University Press, 1957), I: 603;

André Goddu, *The Physics of William of Ockham*, Studien und Texte zur Geistesgeschichte des Mittelalters, 16 (Leiden & Cologne: Brill, 1984);

Edward Grant and John Murdoch, eds., *Mathematics and Its Application to Science and Natural Philosophy in the Middle Ages* (Cambridge: Cambridge University Press, 1987);

Norman Kretzmann, ed., *Infinity and Continuity in Ancient and Medieval Thought* (Ithaca, N.Y. & London: Cornell University Press, 1982);

Christopher Lewis, *The Merton Tradition and Kinematics in Late Sixteenth and Early Seventeenth Century Italy*, Saggi e Testi, 15 (Padua: Editrice Antenore, 1980);

Anneliese Maier, *An der Grenze von Scholastik und Naturwissenschaft*, Studien zur Naturphilosophie der Spätscholastik, 3, second edition, Studi e Testi, 41 (Rome: Storia e Letteratura, 1952);

Maier, *Ausgehendes Mittelalter*, 3 volumes, Studi e Testi, 97, 105, 138 (Rome: Storia e Letteratura, 1964-1977);

Maier, *Metaphysische Hintergründe der spätscholastischen Naturphilosophie*, Studien zur Naturphilosophie der Spätscholastik, 4, Studi e Testi, 52 (Rome: Storia e Letteratura, 1955);

Maier, *Die Vorläufer Galileis im 14. Jahrhundert*, Studien zur Naturphilosophie der Spätscholastik, 1, second expanded edition, Studi e Testi, 22 (Rome: Storia e Letteratura, 1966);

Maier, *Zwei Grundprobleme der scholastischen Naturphilosophie*, Studien zur Naturphilosophie der Spätscholastik, 2, third expanded edition, Studi e Testi, 37 (Rome: Storia e Letteratura, 1968);

Maier, *Zwischen Philosophie und Mechanik*, Studien zur Naturphilosophie der Spätscholastik, 5, Studi e Testi, 69 (Rome: Storia e Letteratura, 1958);

Alfonso Maierù, *Terminologia logica della tarda scolastico*, Lessico intellettuale europeo, 8 (Rome: Edizioni dell'Ateneo, 1972);

Maierù, ed., *English Logic in Italy in the 14th and 15th Centuries*, History of Logic, 1 (Naples: Bibliopolis, 1982);

Jürgen Miethke, "Zur sozialen Situation der Naturphilosophie im späteren Mittelalter," in *Lebenslehren und Weltentwürfe im Übergang vom Mittelalter zur Neuzeit*, edited by Hartmut Boockmann and others, Abhandlungen der Akademie der Wissenschaften in Göttingen, Philologisch-Historische Klasse, third series 179 (Göttingen: Vandenhoeck & Ruprecht, 1989), pp. 249-266;

A. George Molland, "The Geometrical Background to the 'Merton School,'" *British Journal for the History of Science*, 4 (1968): 108-125;

John Murdoch, "From Social into Intellectual Factors: An Aspect of the Unitary Character of Late Medieval Learning," in *The Cultural Context of Medieval Learning*, edited by Murdoch and Edith Sylla, Boston Studies in the Philosophy of Science, 26, Synthese Library, volume 76 (Dordrecht & Boston: Reidel, 1975), pp. 271-339;

Murdoch, "Geometry and the Continuum in the Fourteenth Century," Ph.D. dissertation, University of Wisconsin, 1957;

Murdoch, *"Rationes Mathematice": Un aspect du rapport des mathématiques et de la philosophie au moyen âge* (Paris: Palais de la Découverte, 1962);

Murdoch, "Scientia Mediantibus Vocibus: Metalinguistic Analysis in Late Medieval Natural Philosophy," in *Sprache und Erkenntnis im Mittelalter*, edited by Albert Zimmerman, Miscellanea Mediaevalia, 13, no. 1 (Berlin & New York: De Gruyter, 1981), pp. 73-106;

F. M. Powicke, *The Medieval Books of Merton College* (Oxford: Oxford University Press, 1931);

Edith Sylla, "Medieval Concepts of the Latitudes of Forms: The Oxford Calculators," *Archives d'histoire doctrinale et littéraire du moyen âge*, 40 (1973): 223-283;

Sylla, "Medieval Quantifications of Qualities: The 'Merton School,'" *Archive for History of Exact Sciences*, 8 (1971): 9-39;

Sylla, "The Oxford Calculators and Mathematical Physics: John Dumbleton's *Summa logicae et philosophiae naturalis, Parts II and III*," in *Physics, Cosmology, and Astronomy, 1300-1700: Tension and Accommodation*, edited by Sabetai Unguru, Boston Studies in the Philosophy of Science, volume 126 (Dordrecht & Boston: Kluwer, 1991);

Thomas Tanner, *Bibliotheca Britannico-Hibernica* (N.p., 1748; reprinted, Tucson, Ariz.: Audax Press, 1963), p. 237;

James Weisheipl, "Early Fourteenth Century Physics of the Merton 'School' with Special Reference to Dumbleton and Heytesbury," Ph.D. dissertation, Oxford University, 1956;

Weisheipl, "Ockham and Some Mertonians," *Mediaeval Studies*, 30 (1968): 163-213;

Weisheipl, "The Place of John Dumbleton in the Merton School," *Isis*, 50 (1959): 439-454;

Weisheipl, "Repertorium Mertonense," *Mediaeval Studies*, 31 (1969): 174-224.

Manuscripts:

A preliminary checklist of manuscripts of John of Dumbleton's works has been compiled by James Weisheipl in "Repertorium Mertonense," *Mediaeval Studies*, 31 (1969): 210-211. The manuscripts are located in Cambridge, Dubrovnik, London, Munich, Oxford, Padua, Paris, Prague, the Vatican, Venice, and Worcester. None of the existing manuscripts contains a complete text of the *Summa Logicae et Philosophiae Naturalis*; some contain only fragments. A substantial part of MS Cambridge, Peterhouse 272 has been transcribed by Edith Sylla, but so far only selective citations and translations have appeared in print. The text of MS Oxford, Merton College 306 is preceded on folios $1\text{-}7^v$ by a text ascribed to Dumbleton: *Liber de Insolubilibus, de Significatione et Suppositione Terminorum, et de Arte Obligatoria cum aliis incidentibus* (Book on Insolubles, the Signification and Supposition of Terms, the Art of Logical "Obligation" with Other Related Treatises). The authenticity of this text has been questioned on the grounds that the author regards intentions of the soul as signifying naturally, although Dumbleton elsewhere says that no term signifies naturally. There is, in fact, no contradiction between these two claims. Intentions of the soul are concepts, and concepts signify naturally whereas terms signify by imposition. That the text is not inauthentic on these grounds, however, is not proof of its authenticity. The *Expositio Capituli Quarti Bradwardini De Proportionibus* is extant in only one copy: MS Paris, B. N. Nouv. Acq. lat. 625, folios $70^v\text{-}71^v$.

Robert Kilwardby

(circa 1215 - 10 September 1279)

P. Osmund Lewry, O.P.
Blackfriars, Oxford, and Pontifical Institute of Mediaeval Studies, Toronto

PRINCIPAL WORKS: *In Libros Priorum Analyticorum Expositio* (Commentary on [Aristotle's] *Prior Analytics*, written circa 1240);

Sophismata Logicalia (Logical Sophismata, written circa 1240);

In Priscianum de Constructione Commentarius (Commentary on Priscian's *On Construction*, written circa 1240);

In Barbarismum Donati (Commentary on Donatus's *Barbarism*, written circa 1240);

Sophismata Grammaticalia (Grammatical Sophismata, written circa 1240);

De Ortu Scientiarum (On the Beginnings of the Sciences, written circa 1250);

De Natura Relationis (On the Nature of Relation, written circa 1252-1261);

De Tempore (On Time, written circa 1252-1261);

De Spiritu Fantastico (On the Fantastic Spirit, written circa 1252-1261);

Quaestiones in Libri Sententiarum (Questions on the *Sentences* [of Peter Lombard], written circa 1256);

De Necessitate Incarnationis (On the Necessity of the Incarnation, written circa 1256-1261);

Sermo in Capite Ieiunii (Sermon for Ash Wednesday, written circa 1256-1272);

Sermo in Dominica in Passione (Sermon for Passion Sunday, written circa 1256-1272);

De XLIII Quaestionibus (Response to the Forty-three Questions [of John of Vercelli], written 1271).

EDITIONS: *In Libros Priorum Analyticorum Expositio,* attributed to Giles of Rome (Venice, 1516; reprinted, Frankfurt am Main: Minerva, 1968);

"Der Brief Robert Kilwardbys an Peter von Conflans und die Streitschrift des Ägidius von Lessines," in *Vermischte Untersuchungen zur Geschichte der mittelalterlichen Philosophie,* edited by Alexander Birkenmajer, Beiträge zur Geschichte der Philosophie und Theologie des Mittelalters, volume 20, part 5 (Münster: Aschendorff, 1922), pp. 36-69;

The Injunctions of Archbishop Kilwardby (on His Visitation of the University of Oxford in 1276), edited by H. W. Garrod (Oxford: Privately printed, 1929);

"Sermo in Capite Ieiunii," edited by Ellen M. F. Sommer-Seckendorff, in her *Studies in the Life of Robert Kilwardby O.P.,* Dissertationes Historicae, 8 (Rome: Instituto Storico Domenicano, S. Sabina, 1937), pp. 163-176;

"La Question *De necessitate incarnationis* de Robert Kilwardby, O.P.," edited by A. Dondaine, *Recherches de théologie ancienne et médiévale,* 8 (1939): 97-100;

"Epistola Roberti Kilwardby Archiepiscopum Corinthi," edited by Franz Ehrle, in *Gesammelte Aufsätze zur englischen Scholastik,* edited by Franz Pelster (Rome: Edizioni di Storia e Letteratura, 1970), pp. 18-54;

De ortu scientiarum, edited by Albert G. Judy, Auctores Britannici Medii Aevi, 4 (London & Toronto: British Academy & Pontifical Institute of Mediaeval Studies, 1976);

"Le *De 43 quaestionibus* de Robert Kilwardby," edited by H.-F. Dondaine, *Archivum Fratrum Praedicatorum,* 47 (1977): 5-50;

De natura relationis, edited by Lorenz Schmücker (Brixen: Weger, 1980);

"A Passiontide Sermon of Robert Kilwardby OP," edited by P. Osmund Lewry, *Archivum Fratrum Praedicatorum,* 52 (1982): 89-113;

Quaestiones in librum tertium Sententiarum, 1. Christologie, edited by Elisabeth Gössmann, Veröffentlichungen der Kommission für die Herausgabe ungedruckter Texte aus der mittelalterlichen Geisteswelt, 10 (Munich: Bayerische Akademie der Wissenschaften, 1982);

In Donati Artem Maiorem III, edited by Schmücker (Brixen: Weger, 1984);

Quaestiones in librum tertium Sententiarum, 2. Tugendlehre, edited by Gerhard Leibold, Veröffentlichungen der Kommission für die Herausgabe ungedruckter Texte aus der mittelalterlichen Geisteswelt, 12 (Munich:

Bayerische Akademie der Wissenschaften, 1985);

Quaestiones in librum primum Sententiarum, edited by Johannes Schneider, Veröffentlichungen der Kommission für die Herausgabe ungedruckter Texte aus der mittelalterlichen Geisteswelt, 13 (Munich: Bayerische Akademie der Wissenschaften, 1986);

On Time and Imagination, edited by Lewry, Auctores Britannici Medii Aevi, 9 (Oxford: Oxford University Press for The British Academy, 1987).

Robert Kilwardby played an important part in the development of philosophy and theology in the thirteenth century. His lecture courses on logic, grammar, and ethics represent the most complete collection of works by one author that has survived to witness to what was taught in the faculty of arts at the University of Paris in the first half of that century. "Robert" was still being cited as an authority in grammar in the fourteenth century. His treatise *De Ortu Scientiarum* (On the Beginnings of the Sciences, circa 1250), written when he was a student of theology at Oxford, was widely read, as is clear from its existence today in some twenty manuscripts dating from the thirteenth to the fifteenth century; the son of Christopher Columbus purchased a copy in Spain in 1531. Kilwardby's *Quaestiones in Libri Sententiarum* (Questions on the *Sentences*, circa 1256), based on Peter Lombard's standard text in theology, are only the second surviving work of that kind by an Oxford Dominican and are remarkable for their synthesis of the Parisian teaching of Bonaventure with the earlier teaching of the Oxford schools. Concern for synthesis is also evident in his treatises *De Tempore* (On Time, circa 1252-1261) and *De Spiritu Fantastico* (On the Fantastic Spirit, circa 1252-1261), where Kilwardby seeks to reconcile his knowledge of Aristotle, acquired in Paris, with his more extensive reading of Augustine in Oxford. This reading led him to the preparation of tools for the preacher, summaries, indexes, and a concordance primarily to the writings of Augustine. Augustinianism, which had always been a strain in his thought, eventually predominated; his Oxford condemnations of 1277 fought a rear-guard action for positions Kilwardby associated with Augustine, in the face of the increasing influence of the thought of Thomas Aquinas among the Dominicans. These positions were to have more enduring support among the Franciscan students of Bonaventure.

The first firm date in Kilwardby's life is 1261, when he was elected prior provincial of the English Dominicans. Supposing that he went to Paris as a student in arts in 1231, when the suspension of teaching ended, he would perhaps have been born in Yorkshire around 1215 and have become a master in arts around 1237. He probably continued teaching in Paris until around 1245. He then entered the Order of Friars Preachers (Dominicans), most likely in England, and after studies in theology at Oxford was a master in the faculty of theology there from about 1256 to 1261.

In his *In Libros Priorum Analyticorum Expositio* (Commentary on the *Prior Analytics*, circa 1240) of Aristotle, Kilwardby says that logic provides a general methodology for all the sciences and that the study of the syllogism is the main part of logic. Kilwardby displays an early interest in empty terms and negative expressions such as *nonman*. (His commentary may have been printed in 1516 because it was wrongly thought to be by Giles of Rome.)

Grammar at Paris around 1240 was not so much a study of the rules for writing and speaking Latin as a philosophical account of meaningful speech. The principal text was *Priscian Minor*, which dealt with grammatical constructions thought to be valid for all languages. Kilwardby's commentary on the work—*In Priscianum de Constructione Commentarius* (Commentary on Priscian's *On Construction*, circa 1240)—holds that there is a universal grammar for the essential features of language, such as the noun and verb, even though some features, such as the article, belong only to particular languages. His *In Barbarismum Donati* (Commentary on Donatus's *Barbarism*, circa 1240) treats grammatical mistakes and figurative speech.

After entering the Dominican order, probably after returning to England around 1245, Kilwardby became a student of theology at Blackfriars, the Dominican priory in Oxford. It was there, around 1250, that he composed *De Ortu Scientiarum* at the request of his superiors. He makes a division between divine and human science, saying that he is not yet competent to talk about theology. His basic division is between things created by God and those made by human beings. The first division comprises speculative philosophy, divided, as Aristotle divides it, into physics, mathematics (which embraces geometry, astronomy, arithmetic, and music), and metaphysics; the second division comprises practical philosophy—that is, ethics, politics, the mechanical arts (where he places agriculture, the making of food and drink, medicine, the making of clothes and armor, architecture, and commerce)—and the linguistic sciences of grammar, logic, and rhetoric. Kilwardby characterizes each branch according to its subject matter, defines it, and relates it to the whole of human knowledge. It is clear, however, that Kilwardby's major interest is in logic, as this is the branch that receives most attention.

Around 1256 Kilwardby became a master in theology at Oxford. At this time he may have prepared for publication discussions of questions on selected topics from Lombard's *Sentences*. Clearly, he was reacting to the Parisian teaching of Bonaventure and that of his Oxford predecessors, particularly Richard Fishacre, an English Dominican master. As was Lombard's, Kilwardby's work is strongly influenced by the writings of Augustine; but his synthesis reflects a close acquaintance with Aristotle. In book 1 much space is devoted to there being three, and only three, Persons in the one God. The influence of Augustine and Bonaventure is evident in the importance given to vestiges of the Trinity in creation, especially in human psychology. Divine ideas are models for what has been created. Book 2 describes angels as composed of unique intellectual forms and spiritual matter. There is some discussion of the creation of matter, light, and the heavenly bodies; Kilwardby rejects the notion of matter as pure potentiality and adopts the Augustinian account of "seminal reasons," latent principles of development in the created world. The principal concerns, however, are the creation of the human being in the image of God, Original Sin, and grace. Book 3 opens with questions on the Incarnation of Christ, a subject also discussed in Kilwardby's *De Necessitate Incarnationis* (On the Necessity of the Incarnation, circa 1256-1261), and continues with a long discussion of Christian worship, including the veneration of images, before considering Christ's sonship, human knowledge, and Passion. The book also includes a lengthy treatment of the Christian moral life. In his account of the theological virtues Kilwardby finds a place for implicit faith among simple folk before and after Christ; in his exposition of the moral virtues he reveals his knowledge of all ten books of Aristotle's *Nicomachean Ethics*, with their Greek commentaries (translated by Robert Grosseteste before 1250), and the teaching of Augustine. The latter leads Kilwardby to stress the affective aspect of the virtues and the gifts of the Holy Spirit; prudence, for instance, is not merely a cognitive disposition but love directing a discerning choice, and wisdom is related to delight in divine objects of knowledge. Justice is the supreme moral virtue, and the theological virtue of charity is the form of all the virtues, the condition of a gracious life and the primary ordination to God. The treatment of the sacraments in book 4 remains general. Apart from a discussion of Lombard's definition, which sees them as visible forms of the invisible grace which they signify and cause, Kilwardby's principal concern is with the efficacy of Jewish rites and the way in which they anticipate the Christian rites of the New Testament.

As a master Kilwardby would have conducted public disputations; the fruit of some of these disputations may be reflected in several treatises in which the question form is used. *De Natura Relationis* (On the Nature of Relation, circa 1252-1261) goes back to Kilwardby's Parisian interest in the categories of Aristotle but includes a more theological interest in the relationship between God and creatures. *De Tempore* tries to justify Aristotle's objective account, in terms of a measure of change in the physical world, with the more subjective account of Augustine. Here, too, the theological interest is evident in the discussion of the relationship of time to the duration of the spiritual life of the angels and to God's eternity.

The treatise *De Spiritu Fantastico* is an effort to harmonize the teaching of Aristotle on the imagination with that of Augustine. Kilwardby's purpose is to show that images are not innate but are acquired through the senses and retained by the imagination. He also attempts to reconcile Aristotle's teaching with contemporary medical opinion on the relative functions of the brain and the heart in regard to the acquisition and retention of images.

Besides teaching and disputing, a master was expected to preach. Kilwardby's sermons display the typical form of a Scholastic sermon, with elaborate divisions, arguments, and a parade of authorities. *Sermo in Capite Ieiunii* (Sermon for Ash Wednesday, circa 1256-1272) develops reasons for fasting and ritual ablution; an unusual source is the work on pharmacy by the Islamic writer Avicenna.

Kilwardby was elected prior provincial of the Dominican order in England in 1261. During the years he was provincial, he is known to have written a letter to the English Dominican novices defending the mitigated poverty of their order against the more extreme views of the Franciscans and commending to them their vocation as preachers. The letter evoked a response from the Franciscan John Peckham. Kilwardby also wrote letters interceding on behalf of the Jews. The only philosophical work that is clearly from this period is his *De XLIII Quaestionibus* (Response to the Forty-three Questions [of John of Vercelli], 1271). The master of the Dominican order had addressed these questions from the lector of Venice to the three most celebrated theologians of the order—Thomas Aquinas, Albert the Great, and Kilwardby. Aquinas replied briefly and quickly on 2 April 1271, Albert and Kilwardby at greater length and, presumably, after a longer interval. Aquinas and Albert ascribe the movement of the heavenly bodies to angels or superhuman intelligences; Kilwardby, in a more rationalistic spirit, attributes it to an inherent natural inclination.

In 1272 Kilwardby was reelected provincial. On 11 October of that year Pope Gregory X named him archbishop of Canterbury, the first friar to fill that position. He was consecrated on 26 February 1273; the following year he performed the coronation of King Edward I. Kilwardby attended the General Council of Lyons in 1274; an interest in conversion of non-Christians, fostered by that event, may have led to a correspondence with Abgar, Great Khan of the Persian Tartars, which has not survived. In 1276 he bought Baynard's Castle as a new site for the London Blackfriars; it was to become an important house of studies in the fourteenth century. His letters show him initially sympathetic to Llywelyn, Prince of Wales, and still willing to act as a mediator when the latter had become a rebel in the eyes of the king.

A continuing interest in the affairs of Oxford is evident in his correspondence with Walter de Merton and the injunctions that resulted from his visitation at Merton College in 1276. He enjoins the appointment of a subwarden, three bursars, and three deans; attempts to regulate the finances—although financial matters were not a strong point of his archbishopric; and makes provision for fellows' books to go to the library.

On 18 March 1277 Kilwardby, with the consent of the Oxford masters, condemned four propositions in grammar, ten in logic, and sixteen in natural philosophy. The propositions in grammar relate to an approach in which considerations of completeness and congruity of expression were sacrificed to the meaning of the words, allowing such expressions as "I runs." Those in logic include contraries being true together, syllogisms being regarded as invalid because of their subject matter rather than their form, a confusion of reference and meaning, demonstration being only of existent realities, true propositions about the future being necessary, terms with a verb in the present tense covering every time, and affirmative statements with an infinite predicate (such as *non-man*) following from negatives with a finite predicate (such as *man*). Only the last was clearly maintained by an Oxford Dominican: Thomas Sutton, a supporter of Aquinas. It is clearer with the propositions in natural philosophy that the influence of Aquinas is being opposed. All involve the claim that there is only one form in a human being, that of the intellectual soul; this doctrine was taught by Aquinas and rejected by Kilwardby in favor of an "Augustinian" (in fact, the source is the *Fons Vitae* [Fountain of Life], by the Jewish Neoplatonist Solomon Ibn Gabirol) pluralism of vegetative, sensitive, and intellective forms. Later in 1277, responding to the criticisms of the Dominican archbishop of Corinth, Peter Conflans, Kilwardby maintained that a form cannot be corrupted into pure nothingness, since such annihilation would make it impossible for a body at the Last Judgment to rise with the same form it had in life; that there is an active power in matter and that future development is latent in the beginnings of creation; and that, both in the embryo and after birth, the vegetative, sensitive, and intellective are not just powers of one simple form, the intellectual soul, but that the complexity of the human being requires a plurality of forms.

On 4 April 1278 Pope Nicholas III named Kilwardby cardinal bishop of Porto, and Kilwardby resigned his see of Canterbury. He took with him to the papal court in Italy his archiepiscopal register of letters, now lost. The only correspondence that survives from this time is with his king. On 10 September 1279 he died at Viterbo, where he was buried in the Dominican church.

The grammatical and logical writings of Roger Bacon show a dependence on those of Kilwardby, so it is not unlikely that Bacon was his student at Paris. Albert the Great also depends on Kilwardby in his logic, so Kilwardby's influence spread to Germany. At Oxford, Kilwardby's logic was excerpted by Nicholas of Cornwall in the thirteenth century and by the Scottish master Brichemore in the fourteenth. Kilwardby's successor as archbishop of Canterbury, the Franciscan Peckham, in 1284 renewed the condemnations of 1277 in an effort to promote Augustinianism, but by the fourteenth century they had become a dead letter. The views of Aquinas on the unity of form won the day. *De Ortu Scientiarum* proved more durable; it was adapted for a Dominican study house by Dante's teacher, Remigio dei Girolami, and was read at least down to the sixteenth century.

Biography:

Ellen M. F. Sommer-Seckendorff, *Studies in the Life of Robert Kilwardby O.P.*, Dissertationes Historicae, 8 (Rome: Istituto Storico Domenicano, 1937).

References:

Alexander Birkenmajer, "Der Brief Robert Kilwardbys an Peter von Conflans und die Streitschrift des Ägidius von Lessines," in his *Vermischte Untersuchungen zur Geschichte der mittelalterlichen Philosophie*, Beiträge zur Geschichte der Philosophie und Theologie des Mittelalters, volume 20, no. 5 (Münster: Aschendorff, 1922), pp. 36-65;

Daniel A. Callus, *The Condemnation of St. Thomas at Oxford*, The Aquinas Society of London, Aquinas Paper no. 5 (Oxford: Blackfriars, 1955);

Callus, "New Manuscripts of Kilwardby's *Tabulae super originalia Patrum*," *Dominican Studies*, 2 (1949): 38-45;

Callus, "The *Tabulae super originalia Patrum* of Robert Kilwardby O.P.," in *Studia mediaevalia in honorem Adm. Rev. Patris Raymundi Josephi Martin Ordinis Praedicatorum . . . LXXum natalem diem agentis* (Bruges: De Tempel, 1948), pp. 243-270;

M.-D. Chenu, "Le *De spiritu imaginativo* de Robert Kilwardby O.P. (+ 1279)," *Revue des sciences philosophiques et théologiques*, 15 (1926): 507-517;

Chenu, "Les réponses de S. Thomas et de Kilwardby à la consultation de Jean de Verceil (1271)," in *Mélanges Mandonnet*, 2 volumes, Bibliothèque Thomiste, volumes 13-14 (Paris: Vrin, 1930), I: 191-222;

Chenu, "Le traité *De tempore* de R. Kilwardby," in *Aus der Geisteswelt des Mittelalters*, 2 volumes, edited by Albert Lang, Joseph Lechner, and Michael Schmaus, Beiträge zur Geschichte der Philosophie und Theologie des Mittelalters, Supplementband, 3 (Münster: Aschendorff, 1935), II: 855-864;

A. Dondaine, "Le *De tempore* de Robert Kilwardby O.P.," *Recherches de théologie ancienne et médiévale*, 8 (1930): 94-97;

Franz Ehrle, "Der Augustinismus und der Aristotelismus in der Scholastik gegen Ende des 13. Jahrhunderts," in *Gesammelte Aufsätze zur Englischen Scholastik*, edited by Franz Pelster, Storia e Letteratura, 50 (Rome: Edizioni di Storia e Letteratura, 1970), pp. 3-57;

L.-B. Gillon, "L'amour naturel de Dieu d'après Robert Kilwardby," *Angelicum*, 29 (1952): 371-379;

Gillon, "Structure et genèse de la foi d'après Robert Kilwardby," *Revue Thomiste*, 55 (1955): 629-636;

Martin Grabmann, "Die *Sophismata logicalia et grammaticalia* des Robert Kilwardby," in *Die Sophismataliteratur des 12. und 13. Jahrhunderts*, Beiträge zur Geschichte der Philosophie und Theologie des Mittelalters, volume 26, no. 1 (Münster: Aschendorff, 1940), pp. 41-50;

Ludwig Hödl, "Über die averroistische Wende der lateinische Philosophie des Mittelalters im 13. Jahrhundert," *Recherches de théologie ancienne et médiévale*, 39 (1972): 171-204;

P. Osmund Lewry, "The Commentary on *Priscianus maior* Ascribed to Robert Kilwardby: The Problem of Authorship," *Cahiers de l'Institut du moyen-âge grec et latin*, 15 (1975): 12-17;

Lewry, "The Oxford Condemnations of 1277 in Grammar and Logic," in *English Logic and Semantics from the End of the Twelfth Century to the Time of Ockham and Burleigh*, edited by H. A. G. Braakhuis, C. H. Kneepkens, and L. M. de Rijk, Artistarium Supplementa, 1 (Nijmegen: Artistarium, 1981), pp. 235-278;

Lewry, "Robert Kilwardby on Imagination: The Reconciliation of Aristotle and Augustine," *Medioevo*, 9 (1983): 1-42;

Lewry, "Robert Kilwardby on Meaning: A Parisian Course on the *Logica vetus*," in *Sprache und Erkenntnis im Mittelalter*, 2 volumes, edited by A. Zimmermann, Miscellanea mediaevalia, 13 (Berlin & New York: De Gruyter, 1981), I: 376-384;

Lewry, "Robert Kilwardby's Commentary on the *Ethica nova* and *vetus*," in *L'homme et son univers au moyen âge*, 2 volumes, edited by Christian Wenin, Philosophes médiévaux, 26, 27 (Louvain-la-Neuve: Editions de l'Institut supérieur de philosophie, 1986), II: 799-807;

Lewry, "Robertus Anglicus and the Italian Kilwardby," in *English Logic in Italy in the 14th and 15th Centuries*, edited by A. Maierù, History of Logic, 1 (Naples: Bibliopolis, 1982), pp. 33-51;

Raymond-M. Martin, "Quelques 'premiers' maitres dominicains de Paris et d'Oxford et la soi-disant école dominicaine augustinienne (1229-1279)," *Revue des sciences philosophiques et théologiques*, 9 (1920): 556-580;

Michael Schmaus, "Augustins psychologische Trinitätserklärung bei Robert Kilwardby OP," in *Sapientiae procerum amore*, edited by Theodor Wolfram Köhler, Studia Anselmiana, 63 (Rome: Editrice Anselmiana, 1974), pp. 149-209;

D. E. Sharp, "The Condemnation of 1277," *New Scholasticism*, 9 (1934): 306-318;

Sharp, "The *De ortu scientiarum* of Robert Kilwardby (d. 1279)," *New Scholasticism*, 8 (1932): 1-30;

Sharp, "Further Philosophical Doctrines of Kilwardby," *New Scholasticism*, 9 (1935): 39-55;

Friedrich Stegmüller, "Les questions du commentaire des Sentences de Robert Kilwardby," *Recherches de théologie ancienne et médiévale*, 6 (1934): 55-79, 215-228;

Stegmüller, "Der Traktat des Robert Kilwardby O.P. *De imagine et vestigio Trinitatis*," *Archives d'histoire doctrinale et littéraire du moyen âge*, 10 (1936): 324-407;

Ivo Thomas, "Kilwardby on Conversion," *Dominican Studies*, 6 (1953): 56-76;

Thomas, "Maxims in Kilwardby," *Dominican Studies*, 7 (1954): 129-146;

S. Harrison Thomson, "Robert Kilwardby's Commentaries *In Priscianum* and *In Barbarismum Donati*," *New Scholasticism*, 12 (1938): 52-65;

Leland E. Wiltshire, "Were the Oxford Condemnations of 1277 directed against Aquinas?," *New Scholasticism*, 48 (1964): 125-132.

Papers:

Most of Robert Kilwardby's writings remain unedited in manuscript copies widely distributed throughout the world. Important codices are found at Oxford, Cambridge, and London. The listing by Charles H. Lohr, "Medieval Latin Aristotle Commentaries, Authors: Robertus—Wilgelmus," *Traditio*, 29 (1973): 108-113, includes many manuscripts of works wrongly attributed to Kilwardby, as does that by Palémon Glorieux, *La faculté des arts et ses maitres au XIII-siècle*, Etudes de philosophie médiévale, 59 (Paris: Vrin, 1971), pp. 332-337.

Moses Maimonides
(Rabbi Moshe ben Maimon; acronym: Rambam)

(1138 - 13 December 1204)

Idit Dobbs-Weinstein
Vanderbilt University

PRINCIPAL WORKS: *Millot ha-Higayyon* (Treatise on Logic, written circa 1154);

Ma'amar ha-Ibbur (Treatise on Astronomy and the Jewish Calendar, written circa 1158);

Mishnah 'im Perush (Commentary on the Mishnah, written circa 1158-1168);

Ma'amar Kiddush ha-Shem (An Essay on the Sanctification of God's Name); also known as *Iggeret ha-Shemad* (Epistle Concerning Apostasy, written circa 1160);

Sefer ha-Mitzvot (Book of Commandments, written circa 1169);

Iggeret Teiman (Epistle to Yemen, written 1172);

Mishneh Torah (Code of the Torah, written 1180);

Dalalat al-Ha'irin (Guide of the Perplexed, written 1190); translated from Arabic into Hebrew by Samuel Ibn-Tibbon as *Moreh Nevukhim* (1204);

Ma'amar Tehiyyat ha-Metim (Treatise on Resurrection, written 1191).

EDITIONS: *Mishneh Torah* (Italy, 1480);

Mishneh Torah (Soncino: Gerson ben Moses Soncino, 1490);

Mishneh Torah, 3 volumes (Constantinople: David & Samuel Nachmias, 1509); edited by Saul Liebermann (Jerusalem: Orekh Marav Kuk, 1964);

Le Guide des égarés, 3 volumes, edited and translated into French by Salomon Munk (Paris: Franck, 1856-1866);

"Ma'amar Tehiyyat ha-Mettim," with Samuel Ibn-Tibbon's Hebrew translation, edited by Joshua Finkel, *Proceedings for the American Academy for Jewish Research*, 9 (1939): 61-105;

Sefer ha-Mitzvot, edited by Joseph Kafih (Jerusalem: Mosad ha-Rav Kuk, 1958);

Mishnah 'im Perush Rabenu Mosheh ben Maimon, 7 volumes, edited by Kafih (Jerusalem: Mosad ha-Rav Kuk, 1963-1968).

EDITIONS IN ENGLISH: *The Reasons of the Laws of Moses, from the "Moreh Nevochim" of Maimonides, with Notes, Dissertations, and a Life of the Author*, translated by James Townley (London: Longman, Rees, Orme, Brown & Green, 1827);

The Main Principles of the Creed and Ethics of the Jews, Exhibited in Selections from the Yad Hachazakah of Maimonides, with a Literal English Translation, translated by Herman Hedwig Bernard (Cambridge, U.K.: Smith, 1832);

The Laws of the Hebrews Relating to the Poor and the Stranger, Written in Hebrew in the 12th Century by the Celebrated Rabbi, M. Maimonides, translated by J. W. Peppercorne (London: Richardson, 1838);

Book of the Precepts; or, The Affirmative and Prohibitive Precepts, Compiled by Rabbi Moses Maimonides out of the Books of Moses, with a Life of the Author, translated anonymously (Edinburgh: Young, 1849?);

Moses Maimonides: Yad-Hachazakah, or Mishne Torah, Containing Ethical, Theological, and Philosophical Instructions, Translated from the Hebrew into English by Several Learned Writers, edited by Elias Soloweyczik (London: Nicholson, 1863);

The Guide of the Perplexed of Maimonides, 3 volumes, translated by M. Friedländer (London: Trübner, 1881-1885);

"Maimonides on the Jewish Creed," translated by J. Abelson, *Jewish Quarterly Review* (London), 19 (October 1906): 24-58;

The Eight Chapters of Maimonides on Ethics (Shemonah Perakim): A Psychological and Ethical Treatise, edited and translated by Joseph I. Gorfinkle (New York: Columbia University Press, 1912);

"Maimonides' Treatise on Poisons," translated by Louis J. Bragman, *Medical Journal and Record*, 124 (1926): 103-107, 169-171;

Depiction of Moses Maimonides on a medallion; this engraving appears at the end of the first volume of Ugolinus's Thesaurus Antiquitatum Sacrarum *(1744). The banners surrounding the medallion say that the portrait is "from an old picture," but it is not known whether any such picture existed.*

Book of Mishnah Torah, Yod ha-Hazakah, by Our Master Moses Son of Maiman . . . with RABD's Criticism and References, translated by Simon Glazer (New York: Maimonides Publishing Co., 1927);

The Teachings of Maimonides, translated by Abraham Cohen (London: Routledge, 1927);

"A Letter by Maimonides to the Jews of South Arabia Entitled 'The Inspired Hope,'" translated by Sabato Morais, *Jewish Quarterly Review,* new series 25 (1934-1935): 330-369;

The Mishneh Torah by Maimonides: Book I, Edited According to the Bodleian (Oxford) Codex, with Introduction, Biblical and Talmudical References, Notes, and English Translation, translated by Moses Hyamson (New York: Bloch, 1937);

Maimonides' Treatise on Logic (Makalah fi-Sina'at al-Mantik): The Original Arabic and Three Hebrew Translations, Critically Edited on the Basis of Manuscripts and Early Editions, and Translated into English, translated by Israel Efros (New York: American Academy for Jewish Research, 1938);

The Book of Divine Commandments (the Sefer ha-Mitzvoth of Moses Maimonides), Translated from the Hebrew, translated by Charles B. Chavel (London: Soncion Press, 1940);

The Code of Maimonides, 14 volumes published to date, translated by various translators, edited by Julian Obermann and Leon Nemoy (New Haven: Yale University Press, 1949-);

Epistle to Yemen: Arabic Original and the Three Hebrew Versions, edited by Abraham S. Halkin, translated by Boaz Cohen (New York: American Academy for Jewish Research, 1952);

The Guide of the Perplexed, translated by Chaim Rabin (New York: Farrar, Straus / London: East and West Library, 1952);

The World of Moses Maimonides, with Selections from His Writings, translated by Jacob Samuel Minkin (New York: Yoseloff, 1957);

The Preservation of Youth: Essays on Health, translated by Hirsch L. Gordon (New York: Philosophical Library, 1958);

Maimonides on Sexual Intercourse, translated and edited by Morris Gorlin (Brooklyn, N.Y.: Rambash, 1961);

The Mishneh Torah by Maimonides, Book II: The Book of Adoration, Edited According to the Bodleian (Oxford) Codex, 2 volumes, translated by Hyamson, with Talmudical references and Hebrew footnotes by Chaim M. Brecher (Jerusalem: Boys Town, 1962);

The Guide of the Perplexed, translated by Shlomo Pines (Chicago: University of Chicago Press, 1963);

Treatise on Asthma, edited and translated by Suessman Muntner (Philadelphia: Lippincott, 1963);

The Degrees of Jewish Benevolence, by Moses ben Maimon and Israel ibn al-Nakawa, translated by Abraham Cronbach (New York: Society for Jewish Bibliophiles, 1964);

Two Treatises on the Regimen of Health, translated and edited by Ariel Bar-Sela, Hebbel E. Hoff, and Elias Faris (Philadelphia: American Philosophical Society, 1964);

Treatise on Poisons and Their Antidotes, edited and translated by Muntner (Philadelphia: Lippincott, 1966);

The Commandments: Sefer ha-Mitzvoth of Maimonides, 2 volumes, translated by Chavel (London & New York: Soncino Press, 1967);

Mishneh Torah, edited and translated by Philip Birnbaum (New York: Hebrew Publishing Co., 1967).

The controversies generated by his major philosophical work, *Dalalat al-Ha'irin* (Guide of the Perplexed, 1190), from the time of its appearance in the late twelfth century to the present, attest to the preeminent position held by Moses Maimonides in the Jewish philosophical and theological tradition. Whether or not Maimonides was the greatest Jewish philosopher of all time, he is, without a doubt, the Jewish thinker best known by non-Jewish philosophers; the one best respected as a philosopher by the Christian tradition, on which he exerted a significant influence; and the one most worthy of the designation *Jewish philosopher*, as distinct from simply *philosopher* or *Jewish theologian*. Although he was not the first Jewish philosopher to attempt a reconciliation between pagan philosophy and revealed religion, Maimonides' specific formulation of the problems central to such an undertaking and his resolution of the apparent conflicts between the two traditions influenced subsequent Christian and Jewish philosophical attempts to address the question of the compatibility of faith and reason. Despite the fact that there is a difference between his philosophical and religious works, and despite the fact that both Maimonidean scholars and adherents can be sharply distinguished into philosophers and theologians, it would be an anachronistic mistake, furthest from Maimonides' own enterprise, to attribute to him the view that the pursuit of philosophy and that of faith are incompatible or even divisible. Like many medieval thinkers, especially in the Islamic and Mediterranean Jewish cultural traditions, Maimonides was a sage (hakim) who had mastered and practiced all the sciences of his day; and all of the sciences informed his writings to some degree, depending on the requirements of the subject. Consequently, examples drawn from medicine, which he practiced, are equally evident in his philosophical writings as those from jurisprudence; the influence of Galen is acknowledged in addition to that of the Sages of the Talmud and the philosophers.

Studies of documents from Cairo have made it evident that previously accepted information about Maimonides' life is inaccurate; even his date of birth, which was believed to have been 30 March 1135, is now set at 1138. He was born in Cordova, the flourishing Andalusian court city first of the Umayyad and then of the Almoravid caliphate and one of the prominent centers of Jewish culture and learning until its conquest by the Almohads. His father, Maimon, a rabbinic judge as well as a mathematician and astronomer, was a descendant of a line of Talmudists. It is most likely that Maimonides' early education in the Torah, the Talmud, mathematics, and astronomy was guided by his learned father, whereas his instruction in the natural sciences, medicine, and philosophy was directed by Arab masters. In 1148, when the intolerant Almohads conquered Andalusia and immediately embarked on the persecution and forced conversion of all non-Muslims, the Maimon family fled from their home. They wandered throughout Spain until 1161, when they arrived in North Africa and settled in Fez. It has been suggested that the family settled in Almería for three years until it too was overtaken by the Almohads in 1151, and that during this period they were offered refuge by Averroës. According to Islamic sources, the family was forced to convert; the claim has been made about many Jewish scholars and is difficult to validate or refute.

In any case, the forced conversions by the Almohads certainly aroused a profound concern for their victims in the Maimon family, a concern that was articulated in writing by both father and son. While still wandering in Spain, Maimonides' father wrote the *Iggert ha-Nehamah* (Letter of Consolation, circa 1160) to those Jews who had been forced to convert; he argued that saying one's prayers and performing good actions sufficed for remaining Jewish. Around 1160 Maimonides too wrote an unusually tolerant, consoling letter to the persecuted Jews of Morocco; it is known by two different titles: *Ma'amar Kiddush ha-Shem* (An Essay on the Sanctification of God's Name) and *Iggeret ha-Shemad* (Epistle Concerning Apostasy). In the letter, apart from the practical advice to

Jews to emigrate from countries where they are forced to transgress the Torah, Maimonides criticizes those who chastised the ones who converted and argues on the basis of the Talmud for the innocence of those who conformed in speech only, and not in deed. The distinction between public speech and private acts, between appearance and reality, informs all of Maimonides' works and is responsible for much of the misunderstanding and controversy associated with his name.

Before the appearance of the letter Maimonides had completed his first philosophical and his first "traditional" works. It is claimed that his *Millot ha-Higayyon* (Treatise on Logic, circa 1154), an unoriginal work in Arabic which is most notable for making manifest his early training in Peripatetic Arabic logic, was written when he was sixteen. His *Ma'amar ha-Ibbur*, a mathematical and astronomical work on the Jewish calendar, written in Hebrew, was completed by 1158. In the same year, at age twenty, Maimonides is said to have commenced his first significant original work, the *Mishnah 'im Perush* (Commentary on the Mishnah), which was completed ten years later. Apart from providing a clear explanation of the Mishnah to render it more accessible to the simple reader and providing halakhic decisions in cases where the Tannaim (the Sages of the Mishnah) disagreed, in the commentary Maimonides also develops a more intellectual approach to the Torah in general and to the Oral Law in particular in comprehensive philosophical introductions to some of the tractates. Of the introductions, the one to Avot, known under the title "Shemonah Perakim" (Eight Chapters), and that to Sanhedrin 10:1, known under the title "Pereq Heleq" (Chapter on the Portion in the World to Come), are of great philosophical significance. The latter discussion includes Maimonides' formulation of the thirteen fundamental principles of Judaism, which was later incorporated into the siddur.

In 1165 an inquisition was initiated in Fez, and execution was instituted as the penalty for relapsing from Islam. The Maimon family escaped by boat to Palestine; they remained for six months, first settling in Acre and then traveling to Jerusalem and other holy sites. But, owing to the sparsity and relative poverty, both material and intellectual, of the Jewish community in Palestine, they left for Egypt. After a short stay in Alexandria they settled in Al-Fustat (Cairo), where Maimonides was to remain until his death on 13 December 1204. Although Maimonides' date of arrival in Egypt is uncertain, it is clear that by 1168 the family was well established there. Documents dating from 1169 which refer to Maimonides as "*ha-Rav ha-Gadol*" (the Great Rav [authority on religious law and spiritual matters; a title of merit, in contrast to the hereditary "Rabbi"]) show that by this time he was recognized by the Jewish community as an authority. He was deeply involved not only with the well-being and spiritual life of the Jewish community in Egypt but also with those of other Jewish communities; documents and fragments in which Maimonides solicits contributions for the ransoming of Jewish captives survive from this period. Around 1169 appeared *Sefer ha-Mitzvot* (Book of Commandments), in which Maimonides enumerates his own version of the 613 commandments and criticizes his predecessors' enumerations. According to Maimonides, *Sefer ha-Mitzvot* was meant to serve as an introduction to the *Mishneh Torah* (Code of the Torah, 1180).

In 1171, at the request of the community, Maimonides was officially nominated by the government as head of the Jews (*Ra'is al-Yahud*); he was ousted from the post five years later for about twenty years, then resumed it for the rest of his life.

Such spiritual authority, including its busy practical execution, did not commonly carry a remuneration; Maimonides was vehemently opposed to any violation of this principle, denouncing the acceptance of pay in several letters. He also opposed simony, arguing that it was contrary to Jewish Law. Maimonides earned his living from the family's engagement in commerce until the business collapsed after the death of his brother David. Thereafter, in addition to some personal engagement in business, he earned his living primarily from the practice and teaching of medicine. In 1185 he was chosen as court physician to Salah-al Din's vizier, al-Fadil. His son Abraham, born in 1186, would become head of the Egyptian Jewish community after Maimonides' death. Throughout his life Maimonides was engaged in extensive correspondence with the Jewish communities throughout the world as he responded to legal, theological, and philosophical inquiries.

Of Maimonides' legal-theological works, the most significant and influential is the *Mishneh Torah*. Unlike his other important books, which were written in Judeo-Arabic, the *Mishneh Torah* was written in Hebrew, each of the fourteen volumes examining a distinct category of Jewish

Law. The purpose of the *Mishneh Torah*, as stated in the introduction, is to give a clear, brief systematic exposition of the entire Oral Law in order to make it fully accessible to all Jews, irrespective of their intellectual capacity. But since Maimonides believed that the entire Torah was intended to lead to proper—that is, intellectual—human perfection, the *Mishneh Torah* includes preliminary discussions of some of the significant philosophical questions which were later investigated at length in the *Dalalat al-Ha'irin*. The immediate reaction to the appearance of the *Mishneh Torah* was extremely critical. In addition to the charge that Maimonides deliberately omitted citations of his sources in order to replace them with his own authoritative interpretation and thereby discourage study of the Talmud itself, he was also accused of denying the resurrection of the body. In response to the latter allegation Maimonides wrote the *Ma'amar Tehiyyat ha-Metim* (Treatise on Resurrection, 1191), in which he reaffirms the doctrine of resurrection; the doctrine constitutes the last of the thirteen principles in the commentary on the Mishnah.

The common practice of philosophers and theologians since the thirteenth century has been to divide Maimonides' works into exoteric, popular ones addressed to the "vulgar" and esoteric, philosophical ones addressed to the intellectual elite. The general tendency in Maimonidean scholarship is to draw a sharp distinction between legalistic and religious writings, such as the *Mishneh Torah*, the "Responsa" (a technical term in Jewish jurisprudence referring to a source of legal precedent), and the commentary on the Mishnah, on the one hand, and the *Dalalat al-Ha'irin*, on the other. The legalistic works are understood to represent exoteric explanations of authoritative traditional writings, meant to safeguard the stability of the community but to be devoid of true meaning, whereas the *Dalalat al-Ha'irin* is understood as an esoteric philosophical work containing teachings which often conflict with the exoteric doctrines. Moreover, it is suggested that the *Dalalat al-Ha'irin* itself is composed of two conflicting types of discourse, exoteric and esoteric, a strategy adopted by Maimonides owing to the danger inherent in candid speech. The subjects in the *Dalalat al-Ha'irin* most commonly identified with Maimonides' true opinions are those designated by him as "Secrets of the Torah." Among the theologians, some view Maimonides' work as heterodox and deliberately inconsistent, whereas others refuse to recognize inconsistencies between and within his works, let alone impiety in them. The controversies between scholars today are almost as heated as those most prevalent throughout the thirteenth century. This diversity in reading Maimonides is neither unwarranted nor readily resolvable; the formal and substantial differences between the legal and philosophical works, as well as the style of the *Dalalat al-Ha'irin*, are, to a great extent, responsible for the problem. The difficulty is compounded by Maimonides' failure to elaborate a systematic methodology by means of which his interpreters can account for the differences between the two types of works.

Nevertheless, Maimonides does indicate the relation between the exoteric and esoteric modes of discourse by means of a parable depicting an apple of gold encased in a silver filigree: the outer layer of a proper mode of discourse must implicitly hint at its inner, more philosophically subtle substance without rendering itself useless or meaningless. Both the "Sefer ha Madd'a" (Book of Knowledge), the preface to his most legalistic (hence "exoteric") *Mishneh Torah*, and the "Eight Chapters" in the commentary on the Mishnah deal with philosophical questions in a preliminary manner, proportionate to the prior preparation of the readers to whom the works are addressed. In the "Book of Knowledge" Maimonides discusses subjects that are properly philosophical and that were to be explained later, in detail, in the *Dalalat al-Ha'irin*: the unity, simplicity, and incorporeality of God; composition; the four elements; the soul as the form of the human being; the celestial spheres; and so forth. Likewise, in the "Eight Chapters" Maimonides provides a preliminary discussion of the soul, the moral virtues, the relation between moral and intellectual perfection, and human freedom. Although these discussions are prephilosophical or propaedeutic, it is possible to argue that the accounts of the same subjects in the *Dalalat al-Ha'irin* are incomplete without them: without the explanation of the constitution of the soul or of the difference between moral and theoretical perfection in the "Eight Chapters," the *Dalalat al-Ha'irin* is philosophically incomplete.

Maimonides' writings, thus, must be understood as proportionate to the intellectual capabilities of their intended audiences, capabilities which are to be developed through proper instruction. Proper instruction, in turn, must befit the subject matter and must recognize the changes in circumstances and in idiom that occur over time. Repeating a saying of the sages, Maimonides says

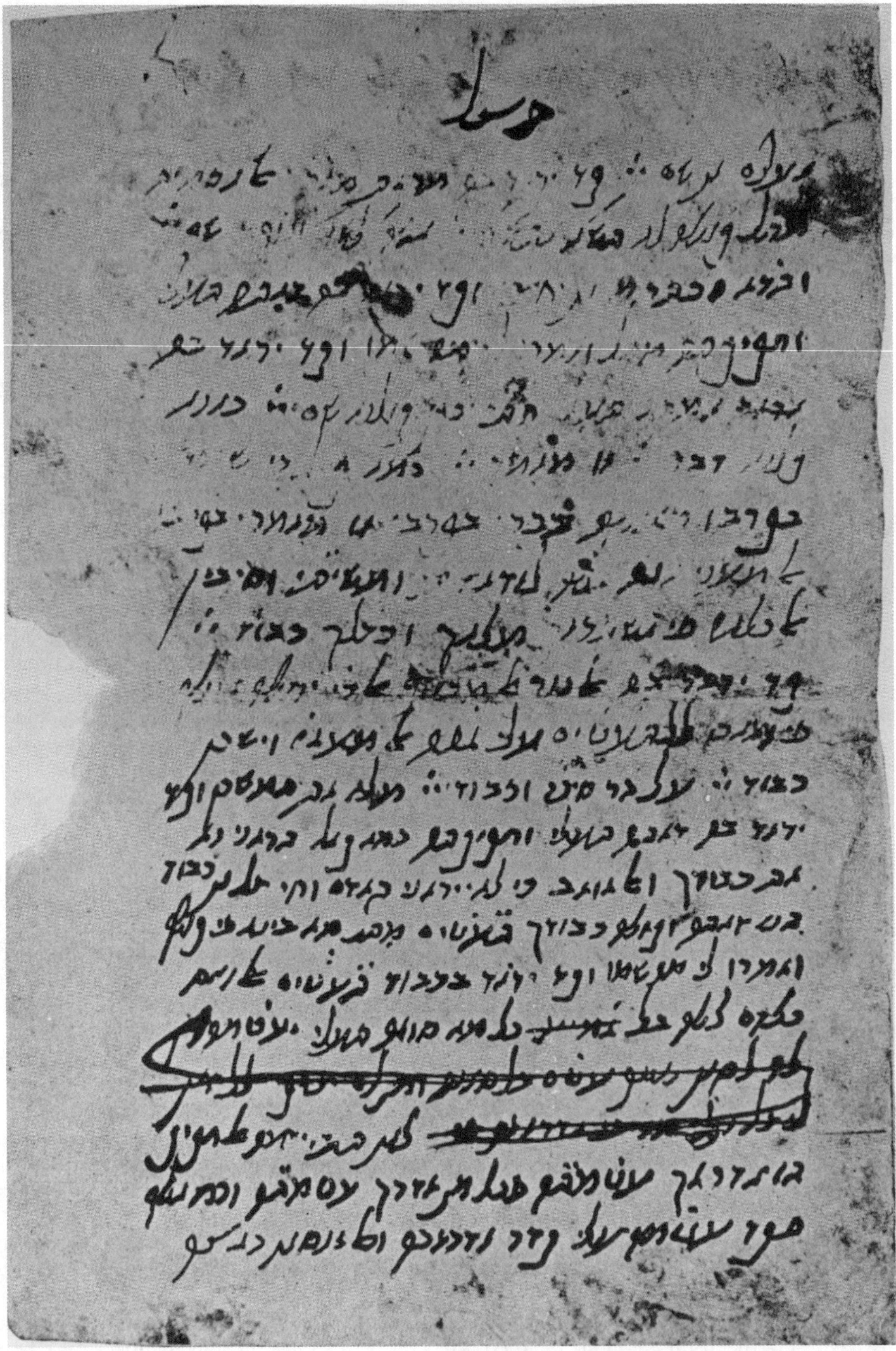

Page from a draft, in Maimonides' handwriting, for the Dalalat al-Ha'irin *(Taylor-Schechter Collection, Cambridge University Library)*

that "the Torah speaks the language of the children of Adam." Thus, when Maimonides' text is a commentary on another difficult text or texts, as is the case with his legalistic works as well as with the large segments of the *Dalalat al-Ha'irin* which address the teachings of the Bible, both Maimonides as writer, and the modern reader, have to exercise great caution in interpretation. And as the preface and introduction to the *Dalalat al-Ha'irin* make clear, Maimonides considers one of his primary tasks as "guide" to be instruction in the practice of interpretation.

The preface is written as a personal communication to an absent student, Joseph, whom Maimonides had instructed previously in person, and hence whose preparation for advanced instruction he could assess. By explicitly stating the conditions prerequisite to the study of the *Dalalat al-Ha'irin,* Maimonides not only delimits its audience and informs the generic "student" about the nature of the work, but he also counsels caution; he criticizes undue haste and disordered procedure as sources of perplexity. In so doing he indirectly rebukes both Joseph and Joseph's former teachers for lack of prudence. Joseph's natural capacity for intellectual perfection as well as Maimonides' repeated counsel to him should have curbed his unruly desire for knowledge. The preface indicates that prior to seeking Maimonides' help Joseph has studied the Torah and the Talmud, and hence already has attained the rank of "jurist" and holds true opinions on the basis of authority; he has also studied *Kalam* (dialectical theology). This preparation would not in itself have qualified Joseph for further study had he not exhibited a strong desire for speculative knowledge. But strong desire for knowledge is not necessarily proportionate to the capacity for it and hence must be tested through instruction in the preliminaries to the natural sciences, first in mathematics and then in astronomy and logic, although these studies do not suffice as preparation for instruction in divine subjects. The progressive mastery of these subjects, accompanied by a strong desire for additional knowledge, are the "tools" prerequisite to reading the *Dalalat al-Ha'irin.* But they do not necessarily lead to perplexity and thus are not the principal reasons for its composition. Rather, inordinate haste, untimely pursuit, and improper instruction in divine matters are the principal causes for the type of perplexity that occasioned the composition of the *Dalalat al-Ha'irin.*

Maimonides, as a prudent teacher, begins by dissolving minor doubts and establishing primary principles for inquiry into more obscure subjects. The introduction to book 1 and the lexicographical chapters that comprise most of the first book constitute the preparatory stages for overcoming the perplexity which is consequent on the first confrontation between philosophy and revelation.

Since the perplexity in question occurs only to the potentially wise, the resolution of apparent difficulties must proceed in a manner proportionate to their intellectual capacity. Since the intellectually inept, the vulgar, may chance upon the book, however, it is necessary to proceed with greater caution than had the instruction taken place in private; the inability of the vulgar to grasp abstract and complex concepts may be detrimental to them. If, on the other hand, caution is exercised, the vulgar too will benefit from the work. Thus, like the commentary on the Mishnah and the *Mishneh Torah,* the *Dalalat al-Ha'irin* contains preparatory as well as advanced discourses even within a single topic. Moreover, since perplexity arises out of the nature of biblical speech, and since biblical speech proceeds in a nonlinear fashion, the *Dalalat al-Ha'irin* will resolve difficulties best by proceeding in a similar manner. This method is pedagogically most expedient because it follows both biblical prudence, which counsels great caution in disclosing divine matters, and philosophical prudence, which teaches by developing the capacity for such pursuit in the student rather than by indoctrinating true opinion.

After explaining that much of the truth contained in prophecy cannot be expressed clearly by recourse to the methods of the natural sciences, Maimonides mentions the limitations of human reason for apprehending divine science—that is, the intellectual instruction contained in the Torah, as distinct from its moral teachings. At the same time, he assures the reader not only that divine and natural science are in harmony but also that knowledge of the latter is necessary for knowledge of the former. Thus, although by means of revelation the believer may possess true opinions about divine subjects, he can understand these subjects only after he has gained knowledge of natural science. That is why, according to Maimonides, the Bible commences with the "Account of the Beginning," and the philosophers begin their study with physics. Initially, there is no difference between the vulgar and the learned; neither group is able to perceive the apparent contradictions within the Bible, or those between philosophy and revelation, occasioned by the Bible's parabolic form of speech. But the vulgar are content with the letter of the Bible, whereas the potentially wise are prompted to the pursuit of additional knowledge. It is only after study of the natural sciences that the learned experience perplexity and seek to gain true understanding of the Torah.

Maimonides' major principle of interpretation, laid down in the preface and repeated throughout the *Dalalat al-Ha'irin*, also exhibits his debt to Aristotle, the pagan philosopher whom he held in the highest esteem and with whose writings he was most familiar. Following Aristotle's dictum in the *Nicomachean Ethics* that "it is the mark of an educated man to look for precision in each class of things just so far as the nature of the subject admits," Maimonides does not seek demonstrative proofs in divine science and in subjects which derive their principles from it. The less a subject admits of demonstration, the greater the disagreement it engenders. Thus, the greatest disagreements are encountered in metaphysics, lesser ones in natural science, and none in mathematics. (A letter to Samuel Ibn-Tibbon, who translated the *Dalalat al-Ha'irin* into Hebrew as *Moreh Nevukhim* in 1204, consists of Maimonides' evaluations of previous philosophers. In addition to expressing great approbation of all of Aristotle's works, which, according to Maimonides, are a manifestation of the utmost natural human perfection, he commends the commentaries on Aristotle by Alexander of Aphrodisias, Themistius, and Averroës. With similar praise, he endorses the logical writings of al-Farabi, whose Platonic political philosophy also exerted great influence upon him, although the letter does not indicate it. The works of Avicenna and Ibn Bajja are also praised by Maimonides, albeit with some reservations. He expresses disapproval of other philosophers, dismissing the writings of al-Tayyib, Yahya Ibn-'Adi, Yahya al-Bitriq, al-Razi and Isaac Israeli as philosophically insignificant.)

Since the expressed purpose of his writings is the resolution of perplexity occasioned by errors, Maimonides' primary foci are questions which are most susceptible to mistaken interpretations. The bulk of the inquiry is devoted to refutation of these misinterpretations, and only subsequently does Maimonides articulate his own position. In this sense, the *Dalalat al-Ha'irin* is polemical and does not shy away from criticisms of other Jewish thinkers, often proposing the teachings of the philosophers, especially of Aristotle, as superior to those of Maimonides' coreligionists. It is not surprising, therefore, that Maimonides aroused the wrath of many leaders of Jewish communities, both before and after his death, who misinterpreted his writings as presenting philosophical teachings as superior to revelation. The elimination of errors or of obstacles necessary for attaining perfection, according to Maimonides, is most critical with respect to the subjects of divine incorporeality, creation, Providence, divine law, and human perfection. Whereas concerning the first subject the philosophical and revealed teachings are in complete agreement, apparent disagreement being the result of vulgar misunderstanding of revelation, with respect to the following four there are disagreements between the two traditions; some of these disagreements are apparent, others real. When the disagreements between philosophical and revealed teachings manifest real conflicts, Maimonides' position is always an adaptation of the revealed tradition which is philosophically reasonable, although often indemonstrable.

The proper understanding of God's incorporeality, according to Maimonides, is the primary purpose of the entire Torah, since true human perfection is impossible without such an understanding. Hence, despite the great difficulty in obtaining such an understanding and despite the esoteric nature of the subject, all Jews must attain some understanding of God's incorporeality and must deny its contrary. On this issue Maimonides adopts a radical, uncompromising position, adhering to a strict negative theology: he insists on a figurative interpretation of the Torah and of the tradition in every instance that may indicate corporeality. In so doing, Maimonides is challenging both the beliefs of most Jews and the teachings of some of his predecessors, most notably Yehudah ha-Levi. Unlike many Jewish thinkers who considered anthropomorphic language to be necessary for the religious instruction of the majority, even if they denied the ultimate veracity of such language, Maimonides considers all anthropomorphisms to be conducive to idolatry. (He also discusses divine incorporeality in the commentary on the Mishnah and the *Mishneh Torah* and bases five of the thirteen principles necessary for gaining immortality on the affirmation of divine incorporeality.) Conversely, Maimonides insists that the belief in corporeality, and thus the literal understanding of biblical verses implying it, leads to exclusion from the community of Israel and

נגמר ספר שני בעזרת שדי

הלכות קרית שמע

הלכות תפלה

הלכות תפלין ומזוזה וספר תורה

הלכות ציצית

הלכות ברכות

הלכות מילה

הוגה מספרי אני משה ברבי מימון ז״ל

Page from a manuscript for Maimonides' Mishneh Torah, *with an inscription at the bottom in Maimonides' hand attesting that the manuscript has been corrected from his own copy: "It had been corrected from my book; I, Moses, son of Rabbi Maimon of blessed memory" (Bodleian Library, Oxford University, MS. Huntington 80, fol. 165r)* from the world to come. Consequently, most of book 1 of the *Dalalat al-Ha'irin* is devoted to the explanation of anthropomorphic biblical terms, leading to the denial of any meaning to positive divine attributions and of any positive knowledge of God by analogy, however remote. Even attributes of action—that is, attributes designating God's effects in the created world—which are permissible are, properly speaking, untrue. These attributes are acceptable because they are the best exemplars to be imitated in human actions, but they do not articulate anything true about God. The most adequate knowledge of God accessible to human reason is the understanding of what he is not, of the radical distinction between God and humanity. Thus, Aristotle, "prince of the philosophers," could demonstrate that God exists but no more. Following Aristotle and the Islamic philosophical tradition, Maimonides provides four demonstrative proofs for the existence of God, all of them causal: beginning from observed physical phenomena, he concludes that since an infinite regress of causes is impossible there must be an uncaused first cause or prime mover of the entire chain of causality. Following Avicenna, Maimonides identifies the prime mover of Aristotle with the singular necessary being whose existence is identical with his essence, unlike all other beings whose existence is distinct from their essence and is possible rather than necessary. But departing from Avicenna, who posited creation as a necessary emanation, Maimonides denies that causal necessity extends to God; God is the cause of necessity in the universe but is not bound by it.

Because Aristotle recognized the limitations of natural human reason, Maimonides can use revelation to challenge some of his teachings about subjects inaccessible to demonstrative reason. Thus, on subjects which Maimonides considered to constitute the foundations of faith, such as creation and providence, subjects on which the doctrines of Aristotle and the teachings of revelation disagree, Maimonides seeks to establish the greater probability of revealed over philosophical knowledge. He first exposes the weaknesses of the philosophical position and then attempts to show that revealed teachings are not only more likely but either that they are more congruent with the requirements of logic, insofar as they do not violate any of its principles, or that they provide better explanations of sensible experience.

In his investigation of creation Maimonides outlines three main positions that can be upheld: that of the Torah, that of Plato, and that of Aristotle. The first affirms creation ex nihilo by an act of God's will; the second affirms creation of the world out of a prime matter coeternal with God; the third affirms a prime mover who emanates the world eternally from the necessity of his nature. Maimonides argues that even though the Platonic position does not undermine the foundation of the Torah while the Aristotelian position destroys it, the two philosophical positions can be refuted as if they were one. The conflation of the two distinct philosophical positions and Maimonides' admission that neither the philosophical nor the revealed positions are demonstrable have led scholars to speculate that Maimonides is hiding his true opinion, which is contrary to that of the Torah—that is, that he believes in the eternity of the world. But it is possible to explain Maimonides' position in a way that would be philosophically more cogent than such speculation allows. That is, he may have held that although the Platonic position does not destroy the foundations of the Torah for nonphilosophical believers, it restricts divine power and so compromises the revealed notion of God. The coeternal existence of anything prior to creation, and its necessity for the act of creation, restricts the creative act insofar as it determines to some extent (however small) what God can or cannot do. The simple believers cannot recognize the difference between creation ex nihilo and one out of coeternal prime matter; hence, for them, the Platonic position is consistent with the Torah's affirmation of creation. But the perplexed philosophers, the audience of the *Dalalat al-Ha'irin*, can recognize the difference. Moreover, the Platonic position is attractive to the believing philosophers since it allows them simultaneously to affirm creation and explain it, whereas the Torah's position places creation beyond explanation. By adopting the Platonic position, however, the religious philosophers must admit a principle of change and corruption independent of the divine will, an admission with grave consequences for the possibility of human perfection.

The central question, thus, is whether or not the origin of the world is demonstrable. Since Aristotle attempted to resolve the question philosophically, while Plato proposed his doctrine as a myth only, it is Aristotle's teachings which pose a real threat to the Torah. If they are shown to be based on conjecture rather than demonstration, then the position of the Torah can be proposed as at least equally possible. Maimonides takes great pains to show that whereas with respect to sublunar physics Aristotle's teachings are true, with respect to celestial physics, let alone metaphysics, they are uncertain, contradict Ptolemy's physics, and also violate some of Aristotle's own logical teachings. Moreover, he points out many times that Aristotle himself concluded that the question of the origin of the world exceeds the domain of demonstration and that it is only the later Aristotelians who believed in its demonstrability. To underscore this conclusion, Maimonides argues for the indemonstrability not only of unobserved unique metaphysical events but of all unobserved phenomena. Once the philosophical position proves to be doubtful and the position of the Torah is accepted as equally likely, all the teachings of the Torah, including miracles and prophecy, can be shown to be philosophically reasonable.

The denial of causal necessity pertains only to divine acts; it is not meant to undermine natural, necessary teleology but rather to limit it to the created universe without excluding the possibility of free, undetermined divine intervention in that universe. This possibility, according to Maimonides, is made immanent in nature in virtue of the creative act: that is, a miraculous event does not constitute a disruption of the natural order; rather, miracles form a constitutive part of the original plan of creation. Likewise, it is precisely because of the cognitive and voluntary nature of the act of creation, precisely insofar as it is not necessitated, that God can be said to be a provident omniscient God, rather than one who, as argued by Aristotle, is indifferent with respect to the sublunar world. God's knowledge of the world of corruption is general, whereas his knowledge of potentially immortal things—of human beings insofar as they are intellects and thus in the image of the divine intellect—is particular. The sublunar extension of particular providence solely to human beings is neither merely a concession to the Torah nor the result of excessive intellectualism (two opposed accusations brought against Maimonides). Rather, this schema is the only one that can be held consistently once both free voluntary creation and natural causality are affirmed. Beings which are subject to the laws of necessary causality are known only as species, since only as species do they possess permanence. On the other hand, intellectual beings who do not act necessarily actualize their proper perfection and thus attain their permanence insofar as they choose to act or refrain from action, and thus they can be known as distinct individuals rather than identical members of a species. Human beings were given the Law, by means of which they can act according to the intellect (the divine intellect as well as their own) and which they can choose, or refrain from choosing, to make their own. Whereas irrational creatures attain their proper perfection by the necessary universal laws of their nature, human beings are free to attain their perfection through the "intellectual" revealed law. Failure to do so is a willed corruption of their natural perfection which reduces them to a rank of being lower than the rational.

Insofar as human beings belong to two realms, the natural-corruptible and the intellectual-permanent, their full perfection must encompass both domains. For Maimonides, the human soul is at the same time a corporeal entity belonging to the realm of change and a potentially immortal one, so that the tensions between the two domains are constitutive of the soul itself. All the faculties of the soul must be perfected and perfectly ordered if the soul is to attain its proper perfection, which is intellectual. All faculties other than the intellect are corruptible. Insofar as the perfection of the body must precede that of the intellect, is easily attainable by almost all individuals, and is immediately gratifying, it is not only preferred by the many but is also confusedly identified by them with ultimate perfection. In addition, the limitation of natural human knowledge itself is a hindrance to the acquisition of full perfection since one of its manifestations is the intellect's inability to recognize itself as limited. The limitation of human knowledge is twofold, namely, corporeal and intellectual. As natural, human knowledge depends on sensible objects, which are first possessed as material particulars by the imagination (a corporeal, corruptible faculty of the soul) before they can become objects of intellection; thus, it has as its source the changeable rather than the permanent. But even as intellects, human beings occupy the lowest rank in the order of intellects, and hence they are limited in their capacity to apprehend certain things. Of the intellectual perfections, the practical or moral is the most difficult to attain, since practical reason deliberates about the particular rather than the universal and hence cannot reach demonstrative certainty. In the "Eight Chapters" Maimonides maintains that even Moses, the most perfect human being, did not persist in moral perfection. Because Maimonides holds that moral perfection is a near impossibility for human beings, irrespective of the degree of their theoretical perfection, he is philosophically consistent in arguing that prophecy is not natural. Were it natural, the morally imperfect but theoretically perfect man could reach conjunction with the agent intellect and so receive prophetic illumination. But human reason, even at its height of natural perfection, requires divine aid or revelation to become fully perfect. For Maimonides, aside from prophecy, Mosaic law is the most excellent means to acquire full human perfection.

The end of divine law, according to Maimonides, is the acquisition of the two perfections belonging to humanity, "the welfare of the soul and the welfare of the body"; the acquisition of the latter is a prerequisite for the acquisition of the former, and it is possible only in a well-ordered, or law-abiding, society. But law-abiding societies are not all equally excellent. Rulers who are prophets and those who possess only natural perfection promulgate different classes of laws. True divine law aims at the perfections of both body and soul, whereas *nomos* (conventional law) aims only at the perfection of the body. Since the perfection of the body is not the perfection proper to a human being, laws which do not aim first and foremost at perfection of the soul cannot be understood as laws proper to humanity.

The limitations of human reason explain people's inability to know by natural reason the true reality of their proper perfection and hence explain their inability to legislate the means to attain it without divine aid. Thus, since reason does not possess legislative power, obedience to law cannot be consequent on rational assent; rather, rational assent must follow on obedience, or on the understanding of the limitations of human reason. Consequently, obedience to divine commandments is the necessary condition for understanding the inherent rationality of the law.

Maimonides devotes twenty-four chapters of the *Dalalat al-Ha'irin* to establishing the inherent rationality of the law, which becomes manifest after some of the reasons for distinct classes of commandments are understood. Commandments aiming at intellectual perfection communicate the end for which they aim; conventional commandments communicate necessary rules for acquiring moral perfection, guaranteeing stable political organization. The former, according to Maimonides, not only communicate true opinions necessary for intellectual perfection but also point to the necessity for acquiring the theoretical sciences as the only means to ultimate perfection. The call to intellectual perfection is contained in the commandment to love God. Thus, the distinction drawn by Maimonides between intellectual and conventional commandments touches the very core of the tension between the two human perfections, since the perfection of the body is motivated by fear of punishment or desire for reward, whereas the perfection of the intellect is motivated only by love.

The tension between the two kinds of motivation may lead to dangerous perplexity in the potentially perfect man. Although the commandments cannot be derived by rational demonstration, the utility of some conventional commandments becomes evident after they have been inculcated and become habitual through fear. As soon as reason perceives the rational foundation for some commandments, however, doubt may arise with respect to other commandments, whose external meaning does not manifest their utility. The possibility of rational dissent pertains only to the elite; the multitude, whose rational faculty is most defective, does not seek the causes of things and obeys all the commandments out of fear. They neither seek nor acquire ultimate perfection but only possess perfection of the body. The possible disobedience which may be consequent on dangerous doubt pertains only to those who are capable of desiring and attaining true perfection. Once fear is overcome and reason gains autonomy, these people are devoid of a principle of obedience to the seemingly irrational commandments, since, lacking moral perfection, they still lack intellectual perfection as well. Unless the perplexed recognize the limitations of natural reason, which become evident through proper guidance in divine science, they cannot become morally perfect and so cannot become intellectually perfect. For Maimonides, intellectual perfection is identical with love of God. The good conventional or positive law must be an interpretation and adaptation of divine law. Divine law can never be superseded or abrogated, because the abrogation of a single commandment will undermine the law as a whole.

In addition to their great impact on Jewish thought since the twelfth century, Maimonides' writings exerted great influence on Christian philosophy. In both traditions his writings met with opposition to, as well as approbation of, their strictly intellectual nature. The *Dalalat al-Ha'irin* engendered a tradition of full commentaries as well as of treatises devoted to particular philosophical questions. The best known among the for-

Maimonides' tomb in Tiberias, Israel

mer are those of Profiat Duran, Shem Tov ben Shem Tov, Hasdai Crescas, and Isaac Abrabanel, which are often published with Samuel Ibn-Tibbon's Hebrew translation of the *Dalalat al-Ha'irin.* Among the latter, the most notable works are Ibn-Kaspi's *Ammudei Kesef* (Pillars of Silver) and *Maskiyyot Kesef* (Filigrees of Silver) and Ibn-Tibbon's *Ma'amar Yikavu ha-Mayyim* (The Declaration "Let the Water be Gathered"). Despite their reverence for Maimonides, the early Maimonideans contributed to the animus of the controversies surrounding his name by often presenting his teachings as fully congruent with those of Averroës, whose thought has aroused the ire of many Jewish, Christian, and Muslim thinkers. The most notable of the modern Jewish thinkers to have been influenced by Maimonides are Salomon Maimon, Moses Mendelssohn, and Hermann Cohen. In addition to his great influence on Albert the Great and Thomas Aquinas, who often refer to him as Rabbi Moyses and exhibit great respect for him even when they disagree with his position, Maimonides' works exerted influence, both positive and negative, on such other notable scholastic thinkers as Alexander of Hales, William of Auvergne, and Giles of Rome. Of the later secular thinkers who responded to Maimonides, Baruch (Benedict) de Spinoza is the most important and the most critical.

Letters:

"Translation of an Epistle Addressed by R. Moses Maimonides to R. Samuel ibn Tibbon," translated by H. Adler, *Miscellany of Hebrew Literature,* 1 (1872): 219-228;

Iggrot ha-Rambam, edited by David Baneth (Jerusalem: Mezike Nirdanim, 1946);

"Maimonides' Letter on Astrology," translated by Ralph Lerner, *History of Religions,* 8 (November 1968): 143-158;

Letters of Maimonides, edited and translated by Leon D. Stitskin (New York: Yeshiva University Press, 1977);

Crisis and Leadership: Epistles of Maimonides, translated by Abraham S. Halkin (Philadelphia: Jewish Publication Society of America, 1985).

Biographies:

David Yellin and Israel Abrahams, *Maimonides: His Life and Works,* revised edition, with supplement by Jacob I. Dienstag (New York: Herman Press, 1972);

Shelomoh D. Goitein, "Moses Maimonides, Man of Action: A revision of the Master's Biography in Light of the Geniza Documents," in *Hommage a Georges Vajda: Etudes d'histoire et de pensee juives,* edited by Gerard Nahon and Charles Touati (Louvain: Editions Peeters, 1980), pp. 156-167.

References:

Alexander Altmann, "Free Will and Predestination in Saadia, Bahya and Maimonides," "Maimonides' 'Four Perfections,'" and "Maimonides and Thomas Aquinas: Natural or Divine Prophecy?," in his *Essays in Jewish Intellectual History* (Hanover, N.H.: Published for Brandeis University Press by University Press of New England, 1981), pp. 35-96;

Altmann, "Maimonides on the Intellect and the Scope of Metaphysics," in his *Von der mittelalterlichen zur modernen Aufklarung,* Texts and Studies in Medieval and Early Modern Judaism, 2 (Tübingen: Mohr, 1987), pp. 60-129;

Samuel Atlas, "The Contemporary Relevance of the Philosophy of Maimonides," *Central Conference of American Rabbis Yearbook,* 1 (1954): 186-213;

Atlas, "Maimon and Maimonides," *Hebrew Union College Annual,* 23 (1950-1951): 517-547;

Atlas, "Moses in the Philosophy of Maimonides, Spinoza and Salomon Maimon," *Hebrew Union College Annual,* 25 (1954): 369-400;

M. Beit-Arie, "A Maimonides Autograph in the Rylands Gaster *Genizah* Collection," *Bulletin of the John Rylands Library,* 57 (Autumn 1974): 1-6;

Stephen D. Benin, "Maimonides and Scholasticism: Sacrifice as Historical Hermeneutic," in *Proceedings of the Eighth World Congress of Jewish Studies, Jerusalem, August 16-21, 1981* (Jerusalem: World Union of Jewish Studies, 1982), pp. 41-46;

Lawrence V. Berman, "Maimonides on Political Leadership," in *Kinship and Consent: The Jewish Political Tradition and Its Contemporary Uses,* edited by Daniel J. Elazar (Ramat Gan, Israel & Philadelphia: Turtledove, 1981), pp. 113-125;

Berman, "Maimonides on the Fall of Man," *Association for Jewish Studies Review,* 5 (1980): 1-15;

Berman, "Maimonides, the Disciple of Alfarabi," *Israel Oriental Studies,* 4 (1974): 154-178;

Berman, "A Reexamination of Maimonides' Statement on Political Science," *Journal of the American Oriental Society,* 89 (1969): 106-111;

Berman, "Some Remarks on the Arabic Text of Maimonides' *Treatise on the Art of Logic,*" *Journal of the American Oriental Society,* 88 (1968): 340-342;

Berman, "The Structure of Maimonides' *Guide of the Perplexed,*" in *Proceedings of the Sixth World Congress of Jewish Studies* (Jerusalem: World Union of Jewish Studies, 1977), pp. 7-13;

Berman, "The Structure of the Commandments of the Torah in the Thought of Maimonides," in *Studies in Jewish Religious and Intellectual History: in Honor of Alexander Altmann,* edited by Siegfried Stein and Raphael Loewe (University: University of Alabama Press / London: Institute of Jewish Studies, 1977), pp. 51-66;

Kalman P. Bland, "Moses and the Law According to Maimonides," in *Mystics, Philosophers and Politicians: Essays in Jewish Intellectual History in Honor of Alexander Altmann,* edited by Jehuda Reinharz and Daniel Swetschinski, Duke Monographs in Medieval and Renaissance Studies, 5 (Durham, N.C.: Duke University Press, 1982), pp. 49-66;

Harry Blumberg, "The Problem of Immortality in Avicenna, Maimonides and St. Thomas Aquinas," in *Essays in Medieval Jewish and Islamic Philosophy,* edited by A. Hyman (New York: Ktav, 1977), pp. 95-115;

David R. Blumenthal, "Maimonides' Intellectualist Mysticism and the Superiority of the Prophecy of Moses," in *Approaches to Judaism in Medieval Times,* edited by Blumenthal (Chico, Cal.: Scholars Press, 1984), pp. 27-51;

Blumenthal, "Maimonides on Genesis," *Jewish Quarterly Review,* 2 (1982): 223-225;

Aryeh Botwinick, "Maimonides' Messianic Age," *Judaism,* 33 (1984): 418-425;

Fred Gladstone Bratton, *Maimonides, Medieval Modernist* (Boston: Beacon Press, 1967);

S. Daniel Breslauer, "Philosophy and Imagination: The Politics of Prophecy in the View of Moses Maimonides," *Jewish Quarterly Review,* 70 (1979-1980): 153-171;

Alexander Broadie, "Maimonides on Negative Attribution," *Transactions of the Glasgow University Oriental Society*, 25 (1976): 1-17;

Ferdinand Brungel, "Maimonides' Agnosticism and Scholasticism," *Central Conference of American Rabbis Yearbook*, 19 (1972): 65-68;

Joseph A. Buijis, "Comments on Maimonides' Negative Theology," *New Scholasticism*, 49 (Winter 1975): 87-93;

Buijis, "Negative Language and Knowledge About God: A Critical Analysis of Maimonides' Theory of Divine Attributes," Ph.D. dissertation, University of Western Ontario, 1976;

Buijis, "The Philosophical Character of Maimonides' Guide—A Critique of Strauss' Interpretation," *Judaism*, 27 (1967/1968): 448-457;

David Burrell, *Knowing the Unknowable God: Ibn Sina, Maimonides, Aquinas* (Notre Dame, Ind.: University of Notre Dame Press, 1986);

Burrell, "Maimonides, Aquinas and Gersonides on Providence and Evil," *Religious Studies*, 20 (September 1984): 335-351;

Richard C. Dales, "Maimonides and Boethius of Dacia on the Eternity of the World," *New Scholasticism*, 56 (Spring 1982): 306-319;

Herbert Davidson, "Maimonides' Secret Position on Creation," in *Studies in Medieval Jewish History and Literature*, edited by Isadore Twersky (Cambridge, Mass.: Harvard University Press, 1979), pp. 16-40;

Davidson, "Maimonides' *Shemonah Peraqim* and Alfarabi's *Fusul Al-Madani*," *Proceedings of the American Academy for Jewish Research*, 31 (1963): 33-50;

Jacob I. Dienstag, "Biblical Exegesis of Maimonides in Jewish Scholarship," in *Samuel K. Mirsky Memorial Volume: Studies in Jewish Law, Philosophy, and Literature*, edited by Gersion Appel (New York: Yeshiva University Press, 1970), pp. 151-190;

Dienstag, "Christian Translators of Maimonides' *Mishneh Torah* into Latin," in *Salo Wittmayer Baron Jubilee Volume on the Occasion of his 80th Birthday*, 3 volumes, edited by Saul Lieberman (Jerusalem: American Academy for Jewish Research / New York: Columbia University Press, 1974), I: 287-309;

Dienstag, ed., *Studies in Maimonides and St. Thomas Aquinas*, Biblioteca Maimonidica, 1 (New York: Ktav, 1975);

Idit Dobbs-Weinstein, "The Concept of Providence in the Thought of Moses Maimonides and St. Thomas Aquinas," Ph.D. dissertation, University of Toronto, 1987;

William Dunphy, "Maimonides and Aquinas on Creation: A Critique of Their Historians," in *Graceful Reason: Essays in Ancient and Medieval Philosophy Presented to Joseph Owens*, edited by Lloyd P. Gerson (Toronto: PIMS, 1983), pp. 361-379;

Israel Efros, *Philosophical Terms in Moreh Nebukhim* (New York: Columbia University Press, 1924);

Efros, *Studies in Medieval Jewish Philosophy* (New York: Columbia University Press, 1974);

Isidore Epstein, ed., *Moses Maimonides, 1135-1204: Anglo-Jewish Papers in Connection with the Eighth Centenary of His Birth* (London: Soncino Press, 1935);

Emil Fackenheim, "The Possibility of the Universe in Alfarabi, Ibn Sina, and Maimonides," *Proceedings of the American Academy for Jewish Research*, 16 (1946-1947): 39-70;

José Faur, "Freedom and Linguistic Expression in Maimonides," *Semiotica*, 46, no. 1 (1983): 61-77;

Faur, "Maimonides on Freedom and Language," *Helios*, 9 (Winter 1982): 73-95;

Marvin Fox, "The Doctrine of the Mean in Aristotle and Maimonides," in *Studies in Jewish Religious and Intellectual History in Honor of Alexander Altmann*, edited by Siegfried Stein and Raphael Loewe (University: University of Alabama Press / London: Institute of Jewish Studies, 1977), pp. 93-120;

Isaac Franck, "Maimonides and Aquinas on Man's Knowledge of God: A Twentieth Century Perspective," *Review of Metaphysics*, 38 (March 1985): 591-615;

Daniel H. Frank, "The End of the Guide: Maimonides on the Best Life for Man," *Judaism*, 34 (1985): 485-495;

Amos Funkenstein, "Maimonides: Political Theory and Realistic Messianism," *Miscellanea Medievalia*, 11 (1977): 81-103;

Miriam Galston, "Philosopher-King vs. Prophet," *Israel Oriental Studies*, 8 (1978): 204-218;

Galston, "The Purpose of the Law According to Maimonides," *Jewish Quarterly Review*, 4 (1978): 27-51;

David Hartman, *Maimonides: Torah and Philosophic Quest* (Philadelphia: Jewish Publication Society of America, 1976);

Warren Zev Harvey, "The Return of Maimonideanism," *Jewish Social Studies*, 42 (Summer-Fall 1980): 249-268;

Harvey, "A Third Approach to Maimonides' Cosmogony-Prophetology Puzzle," *Harvard Theological Review*, 74 (July 1981): 287-301;

Joseph Heller, "Maimonides' Theory of Miracles," in *Between East and West*, edited by Alexander Altmann (London: East and West Library, 1958), pp. 112-127;

Robert A. Herrera, "An Episode in Medieval Aristotelianism: Maimonides and St. Thomas Aquinas on the Active Intellect," *Thomist*, 47 (July 1983): 317-338;

Herrera, "Saint Thomas and Maimonides on the Tetragrammaton: The 'Exodus' of Philosophy," *Modern Schoolman*, 59 (1981/1982): 179-193;

Roger E. Herst, "Where God and Man Touch: An Inquiry into Maimonides' Doctrine of Divine Overflow," *Central Conference of American Rabbis Yearbook*, 23 (1976): 16-21;

Arthur Hyman, "Interpreting Maimonides," *Gesher*, 6 (1976): 46-59;

Hyman, "Maimonides' 'Thirteen Principles,'" in *Jewish Medieval and Renaissance Studies*, edited by Alexander Altmann (Cambridge, Mass.: Harvard University Press, 1967), pp. 119-144;

Hyman, "A Note on Maimonides' Classification of Law," *Proceedings of the American Academy for Jewish Research*, 46-47 (1979/1980): 323-343;

Hyman, "Some Aspects of Maimonides' Philosophy of Nature," in *La filosofia della natura nel Medioevo: Atti del terzo Congresso internazionale di filosofia medioevale* (Milan: Società Editrice Vita e Pensiero, 1966), pp. 209-218;

Alfred L. Ivry, "Maimonides on Creation," in *Creation and the End of Days: Judaism and Scientific Cosmology. Proceedings of the 1984 Meeting of the Academy for Jewish Philosophy*, edited by David Novak and Norbert Samuelson (Lanham, Md: University Press of America, 1986), pp. 185-213;

Ivry, "Maimonides on Possibility," in *Mystics, Philosophers, and Politicians: Essays in Jewish Intellectual History in Honor of Alexander Altmann*, edited by Reinharz and Swetschinski, pp. 67-84;

Ivry, "Providence, Divine Omniscience and Possibility: The Case of Maimonides," in *Divine Omniscience and Omnipotence in Medieval Philosophy: Islamic, Jewish and Christian Perspectives*, edited by Tamar Rudavsky (Boston: Dordrecht, 1985), pp. 143-159;

Lawrence Kaplan, "Maimonides on the Miraculous Element in Prophecy," *Harvard Theological Review*, 70 (July-October 1977): 233-356;

Menachem M. Kellner, "Maimonides and Gersonides on Mosaic Prophecy," *Speculum*, 52 (January 1977): 62-79;

Kellner, "Maimonides's Thirteen Principles and the Structure of the 'Guide of the Perplexed,'" *Journal of the History of Philosophy*, 20 (January 1982): 76-84;

Lottie H. Kendzierski, "Maimonides' Interpretation of the 8th Book of Aristotle's Physics," *New Scholasticism*, 30 (1956): 37-48;

Robert S. Kirschner, "Maimonides' Fiction of Resurrection," *Hebrew Union College Annual*, 52 (1981): 163-193;

Joel L. Kraemer, "Alfarabi's *Opinions of the Virtuous City* and Maimonides' Foundations of the Law," in *Studia Orientalia Memoriae D. H. Baneth Dedicata* (Jerusalem: Magnes Press, Hebrew University, 1979), pp. 107-153;

Kraemer, "On Maimonides' Messianic Posture," in *Studies in Medieval Jewish History and Literature*, volume 2, edited by Isadore Twersky (Cambridge, Mass.: Harvard University Press, 1984), pp. 109-142;

Jeffrey Macy, "The Rule of Law and the Rule of Wisdom in Plato, al-Farabi and Maimonides," in *Studies in Islamic and Judaic Traditions*, edited by W. D. Brinner and S. D. Ricks (Atlanta: Scholars Press, 1986), pp. 205-232;

C. Miller, "Maimonides and Aquinas on Naming God," *Journal of Jewish Studies*, 28 (1977): 65-71;

Henry D. Morris, "Interpretation and Reinterpretation in Maimonides and Spinoza," in *Jewish Civilization: Essays and Studies*, edited by Ronald A. Brauner (Philadelphia: Reconstructionist Rabbinical College, 1979), pp. 75-88;

A. L. Motzkin, "On the Interpretation of Maimonides," *Independent Journal of Philosophy*, 2 (1978): 39-46;

Michael Nutkiewicz, "Maimonides on the Ptolemaic System: The Limits of our Knowledge," *Comitatus*, 9 (1978): 63-72;

Shlomo Pines, "Ibn Khaldun and Maimonides," *Studia Islamica*, 32 (1970): 265-274;

Pines, "The Limitations of Human Knowledge according to Al-Farabi, Ibn Bajja, and Maimonides," in *Studies in Medieval Jewish History and Literature*, volume 1, edited by Isadore

Twersky (Cambridge, Mass.: Harvard University Press, 1979), pp. 82-109;

Pines, "Notes on Maimonides' Views Concerning Human Will," *Scripta Hierosolymitana*, 6 (1960): 195-198;

Pines, "Some Traits of Christian Theological Writing in Relation to Moslem *Kalam* and to Jewish Thought," Appendix II: "Adam's Disobedience in Maimonides' Interpretation and a Doctrine of John Philoponus," *Proceedings of the Israel Academy of Sciences and Humanities*, 5 (1971-1976): 105-125;

Pines and Yirmiiahu Yovel, eds., *Maimonides and Philosophy: Papers Presented at the Sixth Jerusalem Philosophical Encounter* (Boston: Dordrecht, 1986);

Charles Raffel, "Maimonides' Theory of Providence," Ph.D dissertation, Brandeis University, 1983;

Simon Rawidowicz, "Knowledge of God: A Study in Maimonides' Philosophy of Religion" and "On Maimonides' Sefer-ha-Mada," in *Studies in Jewish Thought*, edited by Rawidowicz (Philadelphia: Jewish Publication Society of America, 1974), pp. 269-304, 317-323;

Alvin J. Reeies, "Maimonides' Concept of Miracles," *Hebrew Union College Annual*, 45 (1974): 234-285;

Reeies, "Maimonides' Concept of Mosaic Prophecy," *Hebrew Union College Annual*, 40-41 (1969-1970): 125-152;

Reeies, "Maimonides' Concepts of Providence and Theodicy," *Hebrew Union College Annual*, 43 (1972): 169-206;

Norbert M. Samuelson, "Comments on Maimonides' Concept of Mosaic Prophecy," *Central Conference of American Rabbis Yearbook*, 18 (1971): 187-195;

Samuelson, "On Knowing God: Maimonides, Gersonides and the Philosophy of Religion," *Judaism*, 18 (1969): 64-67;

Samuelson, "Philosophic and Religious Authority in the Thought of Maimonides and Gersonides," *Central Conference of American Rabbis Yearbook*, 16 (1969): 31-43;

Samuelson, "The Problem of Free Will in Maimonides, Gersonides, and Aquinas," *Central Conference of American Rabbis Yearbook*, 17 (1970): 3-13;

Daniel J. Silver, *Maimonidean Criticisms and the Maimonidean Controversy, 1180-1240* (Leiden: Brill, 1965);

Silver, "Who Denounced the *Moreh*?," *Jewish Quarterly Review*, Seventy-Fifth Anniversary Volume (1967): 498-514;

H. Soloveitchik, "Maimonides' Iggeret ha-Shemed: Law and Rhetoric," in *Rabbi Joseph H. Lookstein Jubilee Volume*, edited by Leo Landman (New York: Ktav, 1979), pp. 1-39;

Shubert Spero, "Is the God of Maimonides Truly Unknowable?," *Judaism*, 22 (1973): 66-78;

Spero, "Maimonides and Our Love of God," *Judaism*, 32 (1983): 321-330;

Kenneth Stein, "Exegesis, Maimonides, and Literary Criticism," *Modern Language Notes*, 88 (December 1973): 1134-1151;

Leo Strauss, "The Literary Character of the *Guide for the Perplexed*," in his *Persecution and the Art of Writing* (Westport, Conn.: Greenwood Press, 1952), pp. 38-94;

Strauss, "Maimonides' Statement on Political Science," in his *What is Political Philosophy?* (Glencoe, Ill.: Free Press, 1959), pp. 155-169;

Strauss, "Notes on Maimonides' *Letter on Astrology*," "Note on Maimonides' *Treatise on the Art of Logic*," and "Notes on Maimonides' Book of Knowledge," in *Studies in Mysticism and Religion Presented to Gershom G. Scholem on His Seventieth Birthday by Pupils, Colleagues and Friends*, edited by Efraim E. Urbach, Raphael J. Zwi Werblowsky, and Chaim Wirszubski (Jerusalem: Magnes Press, Hebrew University Press, 1967), pp. 205-207, 208-209, 269-283;

Strauss, "On the Plan of *The Guide of the Perplexed*," in *Harry Austryn Wolfson Jubilee Volume on the Occasion of his Seventy-fifth Birthday*, volume 2, edited by Saul Lieberman (Jerusalem, 1965), pp. 775-792;

Isadore Twersky, "The Beginnings of Mishneh Torah Criticism," in *Biblical and Other Studies*, edited by Alexander Altmann (Cambridge, Mass.: Harvard University Press, 1963), pp. 161-183;

Twersky, *Introduction to the Code of Maimonides (Mishneh Torah)* (New Haven: Yale University Press, 1980);

Twersky, "The Mishneh Torah of Maimonides," *Proceedings of the Israel Academy of Sciences and Humanities*, 5 (1971-1976): 265-296;

Twersky, "Some Non-Halakic Aspects of the *Mishneh Torah*," in *Jewish Medieval and Renaissance Studies*, edited by Alexander Altmann (Cambridge, Mass.: Harvard University Press, 1967), pp. 95-118;

Joshua Weinstein, *Maimonides, the Educator* (New York: Pedagogic Library, 1970);

Raymond L. Weiss, "Language and Ethics: Reflections on Maimonides' 'Ethics,'" *Journal of the History of Philosophy*, 9 (October 1971): 425-433;

Weiss, "Some Notes on Twersky's *Introduction to the Code of Maimonides*," *Jewish Quarterly Review*, 74 (July 1983): 61-79;

Weiss, "Wisdom and Piety: The Ethics of Maimonides," Ph.D. dissertation, University of Chicago, 1966;

Harry Austryn Wolfson, "Maimonides and Gersonides on Divine Attributes as Ambiguous Terms" and "Maimonides on the Unity and Incorporeality of God," in *Studies in the History and Philosophy of Religion*, volume 2, edited by Wolfson (Cambridge, Mass.: Harvard University Press, 1977), pp. 231-246, 433-457;

Wolfson, "Maimonides on Modes and Universals," in *Studies in Rationalism, Judaism and Universalism in Memory of Leon Roth*, edited by R. Loewe (London: Routledge & Kegan Paul, 1966; New York: Humanities Press, 1966), pp. 311-321;

Martin Yaffe, "Providence in Medieval Aristotelianism: Moses Maimonides and Thomas Aquinas on the Book of Job," *Hebrew Studies*, 20-21 (1979-1980): 62-74.

Marsilius of Padua (Marsiglio dei Mainardini)

(circa 1275 - circa 1342)

Bernard Cullen
Queen's University of Belfast

PRINCIPAL WORKS: *Defensor Pacis* (The Defender of Peace, written circa 1324);

De Translatione Imperii (On the Transfer of the Empire, written circa 1324-1325);

Tractatus super Divorcio Matrimonii (Treatise on the Dissolution of Marriage, written circa 1339-1342);

Defensor Minor (Short Defender, written circa 1339-1342).

EDITIONS: *Defensor Minor*, edited by C. K. Brampton (Birmingham, U.K.: Cornish Brothers, 1922);

"Tractatus consultacionis per Marcilium de Padua editus super divorcio matrimonii," edited by Carlo Pincin, in his *Marsilio* (Turin: Pubblicazioni dell'Istituto di scienze politiche dell'Università di Torino, 1967), pp. 268-283;

Marsile de Padoue: Oeuvres Mineures, edited and translated into French by Colette Jeudy and Jeannine Quillet (Paris: Editions du Centre National de la Recherche Scientifique, 1979).

CRITICAL EDITIONS: *Defensor Pacis*, edited by C. W. Previté-Orton (Cambridge: Cambridge University Press, 1928);

Defensor Pacis, 2 volumes, edited by Richard Scholz (Hannover: Hahn, 1932-1933).

EDITIONS IN ENGLISH: *The Defence of Peace, Lately Translated out of Laten into Englysshe*, translated by William Marshall (London: Printed by Robert Wyer, 1535);

The Defender of Peace, translated by Alan Gewirth (New York: Columbia University Press, 1956).

In the summer of 1324 a book began to circulate in Paris that was to send shock waves throughout Christendom. It was a long book, published anonymously under the simple title *Defensor Pacis* (The Defender of Peace), and its main thesis was that the chief impediment to civil peace was the papal claim to supreme jurisdiction in all things. The discussion of the struggle for sovereignty between the secular and ecclesiastical powers, between *regnum* and *sacerdotium*, which had dominated medieval political writing for centuries, had reached a high point with the flood of polemical literature occasioned by the battle for supremacy between Pope Boniface VIII and Philip the Fair of France around the turn of the fourteenth century. The *Defensor Pacis*, the climax of this long literary tradition, was written to refute the partisans of papal "plenitude of power," who claimed that the authority of the papacy was supreme in temporal as well as spiritual matters. According to the papalists, secular rulers, no matter how elevated, were completely subject to the pope and could be deposed by him at any time. The *Defensor Pacis*, by contrast, argued that the papacy and the ecclesiastical hierarchy must be wholly subordinate to the secular government, which derives its authority from the people as a whole. This doctrine was itself fairly explosive in its democratic implications; but what made the work even more subversive was the author's determination not just to write a polemic tract but to prove the truth of his teachings using the philosophical methods of Aristotle, whose works had come to exercise enormous influence within the universities.

The author of the *Defensor Pacis* was Marsilius of Padua, a physician and master of arts who had been rector of the University of Paris. When his authorship became known he fled to the court of the emperor-elect, King Ludwig of Bavaria, who had been excommunicated in 1324 by Pope John XXII for refusing to submit to papal authority. At Ludwig's court Marsilius immediately assumed a position of considerable political influence and set about putting the central ideas of his book into practice. Not only was he condemned by the pope as a heretic in 1327, but long after his death his "evil" doctrines were claimed, by those anxious to uphold the established order, to be responsible for the heretical teachings of John Wycliffe, Jan Hus, Martin Luther, and many others. In the history of political and ecclesiological ideas he has been hailed as the great prophet of modern times and as the intellectual forerunner of just about every subsequent political theorist of note, from Niccolò Machiavelli through Thomas Hobbes and Jean-Jacques Rousseau to Karl Marx. Marsilius of Padua, in short, was probably the most influential political theorist of the later Middle Ages, and his subversive influence has reverberated down to the present.

He was born Marsiglio dei Mainardini sometime between 1275 and 1280, son of Bonmatteo dei Mainardini, notary to the University of Padua. The details of his early life are sketchy; the main source for them is a metrical epistle by Albertino Mussato, the Paduan poet and historian, addressed to "Marsilius, master, scientist [*physicum*], reproaching him for his inconstancy." Mussato reports that his friend Marsilius had sought his guidance as to whether to study law, theology, philosophy, or medicine, and had acted on Mussato's advice to study medicine. It is likely that Marsilius studied medicine at the University of Padua. Soon, however, he joined the armed forces of Cangrande della Scala, ruler of Verona, and Matteo Visconti of Milan. He later returned to his studies of "nature" (*physis*) under an "egregious doctor," who might have been William of Brescia, Peter of Abano, or John of Jandun. Mussato provides no dates for these episodes, and little information as to locations.

Marsilius eventually made his way to Paris, then the center of the European intellectual world, and it was probably there that he developed close associations with leading Averroist philosophers such as John of Jandun and Peter of Abano and with prominent advocates of the Spiritual Franciscans such as Michael of Cesena and Ubertino da Casale. (Peter of Abano, however, had taught at Padua before his spell as master in Paris, and had returned to Padua in 1310; Marsilius might well have studied with him in Padua before he went to Paris.) It is known that Marsilius was master of arts and rector of the University of Paris on 12 March 1313; he probably held the position from December 1312 until March 1313. It is uncertain whether he had already attained the degree of master at Padua or if he did so after his arrival in Paris. Three short philosophical works, thought to have been composed about this time, have been attributed to Marsilius: *Questions on Aristotle's Metaphysics Books I-VI* and two *Sophismata*, or studies of logical fallacies.

Marsilius was one of the witnesses to the profession of faith by Peter of Abano, which took place in Padua on 24 May 1315. In John of Jandun's commentary on a work of Peter of Abano that is thought to have been composed in 1315 and which Marsilius had apparently brought to Paris for John from Padua, Marsilius is referred to as "my dear friend." Pope John XXII promised Marsilius a canonry in Padua in a communication dated 14 October 1316; the pope also reserved for him the first vacant benefice in Padua in a communication dated 15 April 1318. In a letter of John XXII dated 29 April 1319 Marsilius is referred to as an emissary in the service of the Ghibelline leaders of Verona and Milan who was offering leadership of the Ghibelline League to the French prince Charles, Count of La Marche. There is no indication of when Marsilius first embarked on these diplomatic activities; but it is widely surmised that when the mission failed, probably in 1320, he returned to Paris, where he seems to have given lectures on natural philosophy and probably engaged in medical research and practice.

It is not known when Marsilius began work on his monumental *Defensor Pacis*, but he says in the final lines that he completed it on 24 June 1324. The work circulated anonymously in Paris, permitting its author to continue to study and teach unhindered. Although there is no direct evidence concerning the subjects he studied and taught, his servant Francis of Venice reported in May 1328 (to a court of inquisition in Avignon, before which he had to defend himself against charges of complicity in the authorship and distribution of the *Defensor Pacis*) that in 1326 his master had been about to offer a course of lectures on theology. Such a course could only have been seriously contemplated by Marsilius if he had already completed several years of theological studies.

Several strong influences are evident in the *Defensor Pacis*: the *Politics* of Aristotle, with its insistence that people are essentially political or social beings; "political Averroism," understood as the rational autonomy of political theory; Marsilius's medical training, which encouraged him to see the political world as an organism and to dissect it and diagnose its ills with a clinical eye; and the radical Franciscans' condemnation of the wealth of the clergy. But perhaps the greatest contribution was made by Marsilius's experience of growing up and studying in Padua. The intelligent son of a notary could not but be affected by the social and political problems of his native city. The Padua in which Marsilius probably spent the first twenty-five or thirty years of his life was a prosperous trading and manufacturing city with a fundamentally republican constitution. The many institutional similarities between the Padua he knew and the "city or state" (*civitas sive regnum*) elaborated in the *Defensor Pacis* are striking. Even the "peace" which Marsilius's ruler defends—"the good disposition of the city or state whereby each of its parts will be able perfectly to perform the operations belonging to it in accordance with reason and its establishment"—is modeled on the constitutions and the socioeconomic goals of the North Italian cities. One of his declared reasons for writing his treatise is his concern for the serious problems then besetting his homeland: Italy, he says, "is once again battered on all sides because of strife and is almost destroyed, so that it can easily be invaded by anyone who wants to seize it and who has any power at all."

The treatise is divided into three "discourses" (*dictiones*), the third of which is a brief summary of conclusions. The first and second discourses are concerned with the causes of civil peace and strife, since the civil authority cannot enable its citizens to attain "the sufficient life" without concord and peace. The first discourse, which leans heavily on the *Politics*, discusses the principles and institutions of good government. According to Marsilius's radically democratic theory, "the whole body of the citizens or the weightier part thereof" makes the laws and elects the ruler, who must govern in accordance with the laws and can be deposed and punished by the citizens for his failure to do so. The first discourse also considers the "general" causes of strife enumerated and, according to Marsilius, dealt with adequately by Aristotle. The second discourse is devoted to a "singular" cause of discord: the papal claim to plenitude of power. "For the Roman bishops have gradually seized one jurisdiction after another, especially when the imperial seat was vacant; so that now they finally say that they have total coercive temporal jurisdiction over the Roman ruler. Most recently and most obviously, the present bishop has written that he has supreme jurisdiction over the ruler of the Romans, both in the Italian and the German provinces, and also over all the lesser rulers, communities, groups, and individuals of the aforesaid provinces, of whatever dignity and condition they may be, and over all their fiefs and other temporalities. This bishop openly ascribes to himself the power to give and transfer their governments, as all can clearly see from certain writings of this bishop, which he calls 'edicts' or 'sentences.' This wrong opinion of certain Roman bishops, and also perhaps their perverted desire for rulership, which they assert is owed to them because of the plenitude of power given to them, as they say, by

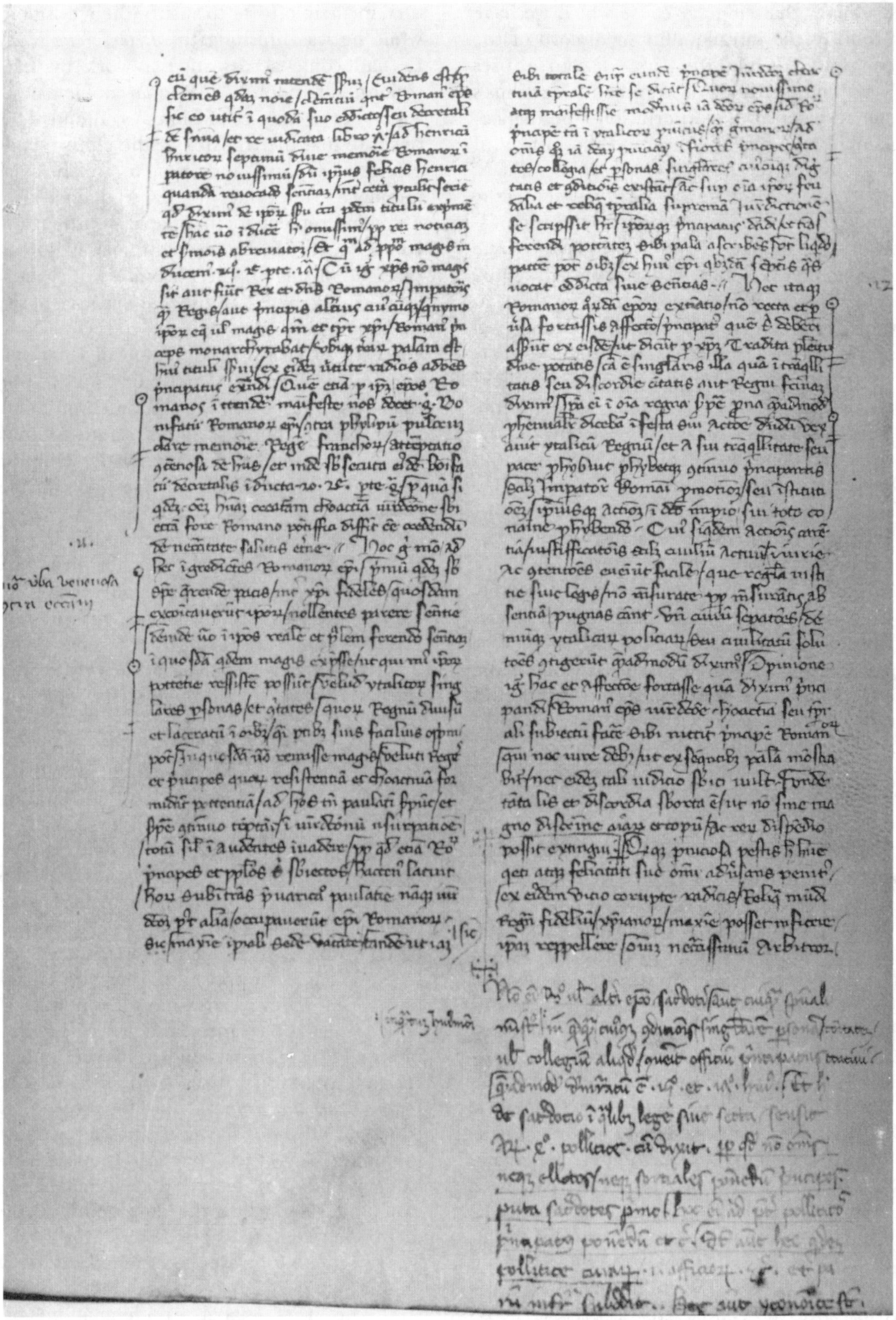

Page from a manuscript for Marsilius of Padua's landmark work of political philosophy, the Defensor Pacis. *This transcription was probably made within a few years of Marsilius's completion of the work, circa 1324 (Tortosa Cathedral Chapter, MS. 141, fo. 22r)*

Christ—this is that singular cause which we have said produces the intranquillity or discord of the city or state." While the first discourse uses purely rational methods of argument, Marsilius's arguments against "this pernicious pestilence" are mainly based on Scripture and the history of the early Church.

He concludes that the jurisdiction of the pope and the priests is to be limited to the administration of the sacraments and the teaching of the divine law; and even these rights are bestowed by the secular power, which may withdraw them at any time. The clergy may exercise no coercion whatsoever within the state, and specifically may not use the sacraments (especially the sacrament of penance) as political weapons. One of the most revolutionary of Marsilius's teachings is the doctrine of the equality of priests, with its implicated rejection of the idea of a clerical hierarchy. All priests have received from Christ or the Apostles, or from their successors, exactly the same clerical authority; bishops are not in any significant way different from other priests and certainly have no greater powers than the latter. He draws a conclusion that lays down a direct challenge to the power of the pope: "no particular one of the bishops who are the successors of the apostles has any authority or power . . . over his fellow bishops or priests, and this, rather than the opposite, is what can be proved by the words of Scripture." (With his extreme antipathy to popes, Marsilius can scarcely ever bring himself to use the word *papa*; he usually refers instead to "the so-called bishop of the Romans" [*vocatus Romanorum episcopus*].) Finally, in all ecclesiastical matters, including the correct interpretation of Scripture, the principal authority is the General Council, a democratic assembly of priests and laypeople. The General Council retains the powers of excommunication, bestowal and revocation of benefices, and appointment to ecclesiastical offices, including the election of the pope himself.

Toward the end of the *Defensor Pacis*, in a brief discussion of the transfer of the Roman Empire from the Byzantines to the Germans, Marsilius promises that "in a separate treatise we are going to discuss this transfer with respect to how it in fact proceeded." The reference is to the treatise *De Translatione Imperii* (On the Transfer of the Empire), which Marsilius probably composed just after he completed the *Defensor Pacis*: that is, in late 1324 or early 1325. In the interminable struggles for supremacy between the papacy and the empire, both sides had often turned to history in their efforts to justify their position; and while he was finishing the *Defensor Pacis* Marsilius had come across such a work by Landolfo Colonna. Landolfo, a Roman nobleman and a canon of the chapter of Chartres, intended to demonstrate that the transfer of the empire had been effected by papal authority, to which, as a consequence, imperial power remained subject. Marsilius replied to this papalist propaganda by composing his own history of the Holy Roman Empire "according to the chronicles and the histories." He shows how the imperial authority was in fact passed down from the Greeks to the Gauls or Franks (in the person of Charlemagne) and finally "from the Franks or Gauls to the Teutons or Germans" without the intervention of any pope, thereby buttressing the claims to universality and independence made by the Holy Roman Emperor-elect Ludwig of Bavaria. While the *Defensor Pacis* sought to establish the supremacy of the people, who are represented by the emperor, by the use of reason in the first discourse and by the use of revelation in the second discourse, the *De Translatione Imperii* seeks to support the same conclusion by reference to history. The work seems to have had a wide readership, since at least seventeen manuscript copies are still extant.

That Marsilius was the sole author of the *Defensor Pacis*, without the active participation of his friend and colleague John of Jandun, has been argued most persuasively by Alan Gewirth: criteria neither of content nor of style, he says, support the supposition of joint authorship. (Ludwig Schmugge, however, continues to harbor serious reservations about Marsilius's sole authorship, based on his own detailed comparison of relevant texts.) Such a supposition, however, seems to have been widespread almost from time of the book's first appearance; and when, in the summer of 1326, Marsilius and John were publicly associated as authors of the *Defensor Pacis*, they fled together to Nuremberg and took refuge at the court of Ludwig of Bavaria, who had been excommunicated by the Avignon pope. Although Ludwig's advisers feared that acceptance of the two would jeopardize the developing rapprochement between the pope and the monarch, Marsilius and John were welcomed into Ludwig's entourage.

The first papal condemnation of the *Defensor Pacis* came in the bull *Quia Iuxta Doctrinam* of 3 April 1327, in which Ludwig was castigated for giving protection to Marsilius and

John, "two good-for-nothings, sons of perdition" (*duos viros nequam, perditionis filios*) who had brought the king a book full of errors and heresies which they had not dared to publish in Paris; although there had been learned men in Ludwig's court who had warned him against taking under his protection heretics who should really have been punished, he had persisted in welcoming and honoring them. On 9 April 1327 Marsilius and John had all their benefices removed and were suspended from all their official posts. Under threat of excommunication, they were ordered to appear in Avignon within four months to purge their errors. They refused. On 23 October 1327, in the bull *Licet Iuxta Doctrinam*, the pope declared six articles of the *Defensor Pacis* heretical, and Marsilius and John were branded as "manifest and notorious heretics or rather heresiarchs" (*praedictos quoque Marsilium et Johannem ut haereticos manifestos et notorios immo ut haeresiarchas potius reprobamus et sententialiter condemnamus*). The texts of the various bulls make it clear that the knowledge the pope and the papal curia had of the contents of the *Defensor Pacis* was derived entirely from informants at Ludwig's court, who forwarded to Avignon extracts of the offending work, and eventually a copy of the book itself. The other contemporary sources seem to derive all their information about the affair from the condemnatory bulls.

Marsilius quickly became an influential member of Ludwig's entourage, as well as the king's personal physician. He clearly grasped that the circumstances surrounding the Bavarian king provided an outstanding opportunity to put into practice some of the central ideas of the *Defensor Pacis*. Ludwig had been in open dispute with John XXII since 8 October 1323. In 1322 he had won an eight-year struggle against the Hapsburg Frederick of Austria for the crown of the Holy Roman Empire, following which his accession to the imperial throne was acknowledged by the seven prince-electors. The pope, however, had insisted that papal supervision and confirmation of the election was required before his accession could be considered valid. Ludwig had refused to submit to papal authority and had been excommunicated on 23 March 1324. The tension between king and pope had reached a new pitch after Ludwig took the side of the radical Franciscans in their dispute with the curia over the issue of evangelical poverty. If Marsilius saw in Ludwig's quarrel with the pope the perfect testing ground for his political and ecclesiological theories, the king also seized the opportunity to cultivate the support of an author whose doctrines he could use in his challenge to papal authority.

Marsilius urged Ludwig to embark on a triumphal expedition to Rome, there to be crowned emperor regardless of the opposition of the pope; he represented the king at a preparatory meeting with Ghibelline leaders in Trent in March 1327. At Whitsuntide of that year Ludwig was crowned in Milan with the iron crown of Henry VII. On 7 January 1328, on the invitation of the people's representatives, the German army entered Rome. Ten days later Ludwig was crowned Holy Roman Emperor by Sciarra Colonna, delegate of the Roman people. Marsilius, who was appointed the emperor's spiritual vicar (*vicarius in spiritualibus*), clearly played a leading role in orchestrating these and subsequent events. On 18 April 1328, following a public trial, John XXII was declared a heretic by Ludwig and deposed "by our authority together with the entire clergy and Roman people." On 12 May Ludwig had the Franciscan Peter of Corvara elected Pope Nicholas V by the Roman people.

Marsilius played energetically his role as chief spiritual official in the service of the elected ruler of "the people"; he thus followed practically to the letter the model set forth in the *Defensor Pacis*, according to which the priesthood functions as an integral organ of the state. In early 1328, presumably on the advice of Marsilius, Ludwig appointed new bishops to the sees of Cremona, Como, Castello, and Ferrara (Marsilius's friend John of Jandun), having deposed the sitting prelates, supporters of John XXII, for the crime of treason (*lesae maiestatis*). This action was in full accordance with the teaching of the *Defensor Pacis*: the emperor, the people, and the clergy are the competent authorities within a diocese; the papacy has neither authority nor influence. All spiritual offices within the diocese are to be filled through election by the people and the clergy; the bishop has the power only to confirm these appointments, while the monarch remains the authority of ultimate appeal. The latter has the right to rescind any measures or regulations promulgated by a bishop, and ultimately to remove the bishop from office. Marsilius certainly endeavored to make these theories a reality in the first half of 1328. The likelihood, however, that these imperial appointments and concomitant removals from office were not actually given practical effect (certainly not in the case of John of Jandun's "election" to the see of

Ferrara) makes it difficult to concur with Gewirth's contention that Marsilius "energetically persecuted" the clergy who maintained allegiance to the Avignon pope.

In the face of an attack by Robert of Anjou and an insurrection within the city, Ludwig's forces lost military control of Rome. Ludwig, his army, and his entourage were forced to leave the city during the night of 4 August 1328 and retreat via Pisa and Milan. By February 1330 Marsilius was at the court of Ludwig in Munich, where he was joined by William of Ockham and other dissident Franciscans.

Although information again becomes scanty, Marsilius seems to have spent the remainder of his life in Munich as counselor and personal physician to Ludwig. A steady stream of letters continued to emanate from the papal headquarters at Avignon urging bishops, archbishops, King John of Bohemia, and Duke Otto of Austria, among many others, to publicize as widely as possible the papal condemnation of Ludwig, Marsilius, and John of Jandun (even though the last had died at Montalto, near Pisa, in September 1328). In an edict dated 30 May 1329 the pope called on the authorities of the University of Paris, the birthplace of the *Defensor Pacis*, to do all that was in their power, and as quickly as possible, to publicize the condemnation of the book and the two writers so that nobody could remain ignorant of their heresies. This papal campaign undoubtedly did much to spread the notoriety, but also the influence, of the *Defensor Pacis*.

When Benedict XII was elected successor to John XXII in 1334, Ludwig immediately entered into correspondence with the pontiff with a view to bringing to an end the long conflict which had blighted his relations with Benedict's predecessor. Benedict did not affirm the supremacy of the papal over the imperial power, but he did insist that the king banish from his court his most important counselors, among them Marsilius, Ockham, and Michael of Cesena, and that he renounce the heresies of Marsilius. In the diplomatic messages sent with his legates to the curia on 5 March and 28 October 1336 Ludwig, anxious for a settlement, agreed to this demand and proceeded to distance himself from the teachings of the *Defensor Pacis*. The negotiations might have continued to a satisfactory conclusion if Benedict had not been persuaded by Ludwig's rival, King Philip VI of France, to exercise extreme caution in his dealings with the emperor. Benedict broke off the negotiations in 1337.

Relations quickly soured. In 1338 and 1339 Ludwig gathered together at Frankfurt the prince-electors and representatives of the nobility and the cities, who on both occasions affirmed their unanimous conviction that the election of Ludwig as emperor had been legitimate. At the height of this controversy William of Ockham, still resident at the court of Ludwig in Munich, wrote the third part of his *Dialogus*, in the course of which, while borrowing strongly from the arguments of the *Defensor Pacis*, he strongly criticized Marsilius's ecclesiology. The Paduan responded to Ockham's criticisms by composing the *Defensor Minor* (Short Defender).

Around the same time, Ludwig became embroiled in the fate of Margaret Maultasch, Countess of the Tyrol. Since about 1340 Margaret had made no secret of her desire to divorce John Henry, son of the king of Bohemia, whom she had married in 1330, when she was twelve and he was ten. She expelled him from the Tyrol on 2 November 1341. Ludwig took a special interest in the affair, since he wanted to marry Margaret to his own son, Ludwig of Brandenburg, thereby acquiring the Tyrol. There were two obstacles in the way: Margaret was already married; and she was already related to Ludwig of Brandenburg, her grandmother and his grandfather being sister and brother. Not wishing to approach the pope directly on the issue, Ludwig turned to his resident advisers, Ockham and Marsilius.

The affair produced four surviving texts. First, there are two undated judgments, in the name of the emperor: the *Forma Divortii*, granting Margaret a divorce, and the *Forma Dispensationis super Affinitatem Consanguinitatis*, granting her a dispensation to marry her cousin. There are also the responses of Ockham and Marsilius to Ludwig's request for advice on the issues. Marsilius's response, *Tractatus super Divorcio Matrimonii* (Treatise on the Dissolution of Marriage, circa 1339-1342), corresponds in large measure to chapters 13, 14, and 15 of the *Defensor Minor*; the *Forma Dispensationis*, obviously written by him even though it was promulgated under Ludwig's name, appears as chapter 16 of the same book. The emperor gratefully accepted his counselors' advice, which was to the effect that only the monarch has jurisdiction in the realm of human law; since the dissolution of a marriage and the granting of a dispensation to marry in spite of consanguinity are matters of human law, only the monarch is competent. Margaret and the younger Ludwig were married on 10 February 1342.

The date of composition of the *Defensor Minor* remains an open question: C. K. Brampton, its first editor, claimed that it was written after the marriage of Margaret and Ludwig; while a later editor, Jeannine Quillet, argues that Marsilius began work on it, in response to Ockham's criticisms, as early as 1339 and finished it at the end of 1340 or the beginning of 1341, at the height of the controversy surrounding Margaret's marriage.

The *Defensor Minor* recapitulates the main themes of Marsilian ecclesiology as contained in the second *dictio* of the *Defensor Pacis*, especially his bitter critique of the papal claim to plenitude of power. Much of the argumentation is directed against Ockham's more moderate position, which grants the papacy much more jurisdiction than Marsilius will allow. The latter's restatement of his teaching is markedly sharper than was the original version: the clergy, he insists, has no coercive power at all; only the secular authority has coercive power, which has been conferred on it either by the whole of the citizens (*universitas civium*) or its weightier part (*valentior pars*). The clergy may exhort and admonish, but it may exercise no coercion or constraint on its flock.

Marsilius offers in the *Defensor Minor* a scathing attack on the practice of granting indulgences. He points out that this power is nowhere to be found in Scripture. The clergy (even the bishop of Rome) has no power whatsoever to grant or refuse sinners remission of suffering in the next life for their sins in this one in connection with fasts or with pilgrimages, "which in most cases are simply an opportunity to visit distant or foreign parts, rather than to exercise the devotion required in such matters." Distributing the money spent on such pilgrimages among the poor (or even using it to defend the republic should the need arise) would be more in keeping with the spirit of the Gospel, "since we can find in Scripture no counsel or precept about making pilgrimages, while the counsel to give alms and distribute goods and money to the poor is clearly formulated in the old law as well as the new."

Another topic which receives extensive treatment in the *Defensor Minor* is the problem of vows. A vow or an oath, a promise freely made to God, cannot be revoked by a pope or a priest. One can release oneself from the terms of a vow to achieve a greater good or to avoid a greater evil. But, more tellingly, because the breaking of vows can have consequences on the level of human relations, it is legitimate for the secular power to exercise its coercive authority in such a case; and the secular power is also competent to absolve someone of a vow: a vow may be retracted with the agreement of "the human legislator" (the emperor) or the prince who represents him. This teaching on the retraction of vows clearly had immediate political relevance in connection with the divorce of Margaret Maultasch: only the secular power, Marsilius is saying, has the authority to release Margaret from her marriage vows.

Quillet emphasizes the originality and importance of the *Defensor Minor*, which has tended to be somewhat overlooked by most students of Marsilius. Essentially a recapitulation of his great work, it is devoted even more passionately to the total destruction of the doctrine of the papal plenitude of power. The mood has become darker, and Marsilius's ideas have hardened, not only in response to the continuing condemnation of him (sometimes quite hysterical) by the papacy and its supporters but also in response to those supporters of the emperor, such as Ockham, whose criticisms of papal pretensions he regarded as half-hearted. The central role of the emperor as the sole and ultimate authority in all matters, whether civil, political, or religious, now receives greater emphasis. But even Ludwig himself seemed to be eager to make peace with the papacy for political reasons. Marsilius must have been a lonely and isolated man at the court in his last years. No information is available concerning the date, place, or circumstances of his death; but an edict of Pope Clement VI, dated 10 April 1343, mentions that Marsilius ("One of the worst heretics we have ever read") is dead.

His infamy lingered in the papal curia long after his death: in 1377, in a letter to King Edward III of England, Pope Gregory XI complained that the erroneous teachings of Wycliffe bore a marked resemblance to the condemned heresies of Marsilius of Padua. His great work, the *Defensor Pacis*, continued to be widely read, even though copies were continually seized by inquisitors. It exercised a profound influence on the conciliar movement and the leaders of the Protestant Reformation. William Marshall prepared an English translation in 1535, deleting the work's democratic kernel so as to make it a useful propaganda weapon for Henry VIII. Even as it was influential, so was it feared, and so was Marsilius reviled by those who sought to defend the politico-religious established order.

While the novelty of Marsilius has sometimes been exaggerated, he was the first to expound democratic theories of civil and ecclesiastical government with such clarity and vigor. In some respects he was a typical product of that generation of philosophers, based in Paris, who read Aristotle through the interpretive lens of Averroës; but he used his knowledge of Aristotelian philosophy and his training as a physician to dissect clinically the political power of the papacy in a unique way. Marsilius was the great demystifier of the papal claim to plenitude of power: only after 1324 could the political activities of the papacy be analyzed with the same soberness as those of any Italian state. But allied to his razor-sharp intellect was a passionate determination to apply the results of his philosophical analysis so as to make the world a better place.

In Marsilius, philosophy spoke with a new self-confidence, demanding the integration of the church, which had for many centuries dominated philosophy, into the fabric of the state as the first precondition of peace. This new self-confidence is perhaps seen most vividly in his insistence that no bishop or priest has the right to confer or remove a license to teach. Because he does not fit comfortably into the traditional picture of medieval Scholastic philosophy (a picture dominated by Anselm, Albert the Great, Thomas Aquinas, Bonaventure, and John Duns Scotus), he has often been seen primarily as a forerunner of various modern political theories. But this picture should be modified, and Marsilius should be regarded as one of the outstanding philosophers of the fourteenth century, one who adapted the philosophical teachings of Aristotle so as to analyze the political situation of contemporary Europe and the outstanding impediment to peace and tranquillity—the political pretensions of the papacy and the clergy—as a prelude to the establishment of "civil happiness, which seems the best of the objects of desire possible to man in this world, and the ultimate aim of human acts."

References:

C. Francisco Bertelloni, " 'Constitutum Constantini' y 'Romgedanke': La donación constantiniana en el pensamiento de tres defensores del derecho imperial de Roma: Dante, Marsilio de Padua y Guillermo de Ockham," *Patristica et Mediaevalia*, 3 (1982): 21-46; 4-5 (1983-1984): 67-99; 6 (1985): 57-78;

D. R. Carr, "The Prince and the City," *Medioevo*, 5 (1979): 279-291;

Aldo Checchini and Norberto Bobbio, eds., *Marsilio da Padova: Studi Raccolti nel VI Centenario della Morte* (Padua: Cedam, 1942);

Marino Danuato, *"Plenitudo potestatis" e "Universitas civium" in Marsilio da Padova* (Florence: Edizioni "Studi Francescani," 1983);

Alan Gewirth, "John of Jandun and the *Defensor Pacis*," *Speculum*, 23 (April 1948): 267-272;

Gewirth, *Marsilius of Padua and Medieval Political Philosophy* (New York & London: Columbia University Press, 1951);

M. Grignaschi, "Le rôle de l'aristotélisme dans le 'Defensor Pacis' de Marsile de Padoue," *Revue d'histoire et de philosophie religieuses*, 35 (1955): 301-340;

Horst Kusch, "Friede als Ausgangspunkt der Staatstheorie des Marsilius von Padua," *Das Altertum*, 1 (1955): 116-125;

Georges de Lagarde, *La naissance de l'esprit laïque au déclin du Moyen-âge*, revised edition, volume 3: *Le "Defensor Pacis"* (Louvain & Paris: Nauwelaerts, 1970);

E. Lewis, "The 'positivism' of Marsiglio of Padua," *Speculum*, 38 (1963): 541-582;

Medioevo, two volumes devoted to studies of Marsilius, 5 (1979) and 6 (1980);

G. Piaia, ed., "Marsilio, ieri e oggi: Simposio su Marsilio da Padova nel VII centenario della nascita," *Studia Patavina*, 27 (1980): 257-363;

Carlo Pincin, *Marsilio* (Turin: Pubblicazioni dell'Istituto di scienze politiche dell'Università di Torino, 1967);

C. W. Previté-Orton, "Marsilius of Padua," *Proceedings of the British Academy*, 21 (1935): 137-183;

Friedrich Prinz, "Marsilius von Padua," *Zeitschrift für bayerische Landesgeschichte*, 39 (1976): 39-77;

Jeannine Quillet, *La philosophie politique de Marsile de Padoue* (Paris: Vrin, 1970);

Marjorie Reeves, "Marsiglio of Padua and Dante Alighieri," in *Trends in Medieval Political Thought*, edited by Beryl Smalley (Oxford: Blackwell, 1965), pp. 86-104;

Nicolai Rubinstein, "Marsilius of Padua and Italian Political Thought of His Time," in *Europe in the Late Middle Ages*, edited by J. R. Hale and others (London: Faber & Faber, 1965), pp. 44-75;

Ludwig Schmugge, *Johannes von Jandun (1285/89-1328): Untersuchungen zur Biographie und Sozialtheorie eines Lateinischen Averroisten* (Stuttgart: Hiersemann, 1966);

Richard Scholz, "Marsilius und Dante: Reichs- und Staatsgedanke in Italien um 1300," *Deutsches Dante-Jahrbuch*, 24 (1942): 159-174;

Hermann Segall, *Der "Defensor Pacis" des Marsilius von Padua: Grundfragen der Interpretation* (Wiesbaden: Steiner, 1959);

Dolf Sternberger, *Die Stadt und das Reich in der Verfassungslehre des Marsilius von Padua* (Wiesbaden: Steiner, 1981);

Cesare Vasoli, "Introduzione," *Il Difensore della Pace di Marsilio da Padova* (Turin: Unione Tipografico-Editrice Torinese, 1960; revised, 1975);

Vasoli, "Marsilio da Padova," *Storia della cultura veneta: Il Trecento* (Vicenza: Pozza, 1976), pp. 207-237;

Vasoli, "La *Politica* di Aristotele e la sua utilizzazione da parte di Marsilio da Padova," *Medioevo*, 5 (1979): 237-257;

Michael Wilks, "Corporation and Representation in the *Defensor Pacis*," *Studia Gratiana*, 15 (1972): 251-292.

Nicholas of Cusa
(Nicolaus Cusanus, Niclas Krebs, Niclas von Cusse)

(1401 - 11 August 1464)

Donald F. Duclow
Gwynedd-Mercy College

PRINCIPAL WORKS: *De Concordantia Catholica* (On Universal Concord, written 1433);

De Docta Ignorantia (Of Learned Ignorance, written 1440);

De Coniecturis (Conjectures, written 1443);

De Deo Abscondito (The Hidden God, written 1444);

De Quaerendo Deum (On Seeking God, written 1445);

De Filiatione Dei (Divine Sonship, written 1445);

De Dato Patris Luminum (The Gift of the Father of Lights, written 1446);

De Genesi (On Genesis, written 1447);

Apologia Doctae Ignorantiae (A Defense of Learned Ignorance, written 1449);

Idiota (The Layman, written 1450);

De Pace Fidei (The Peace of Faith, written 1453);

De Visione Dei (The Vision of God, written 1453);

Complementum Theologicum (The Theological Complement, written 1453);

De Beryllo (The Beryl, written 1458);

De Aequalitate (On Equality, written 1459);

De Principio (The Principle, written 1459);

Trialogus de Possest (On Actualized-Possibility, written 1460);

Cribratio Alcorani (A Scrutiny of the Koran, written 1461);

Directio Speculantis seu de Non Aliud (On Not-Other, written 1462);

De Venatione Sapientiae (The Hunt of Wisdom, written 1463);

De Ludo Globi (The Game of Spheres, written 1463);

Compendium (The Compendium, written 1463);

De Apice Theoriae (The Summit of Contemplative Vision, written 1464).

EDITIONS: *Opera* (Strasbourg: Martin Flach, 1488); reprinted, 2 volumes, edited by Paul Wilpert (Berlin: De Gruyter, 1967);

Opera (Cortemaggiore: Benedetto Dolcibelli, 1502);

Opera, 3 volumes, edited by Jacques Le Fèvre d'Etaples (Paris: J. Bade, 1514; reprinted, Frankfurt am Main: Minerva, 1962);

Opera (Basel: Henri Petrus, 1565);

Nicolaus von Cues: Texte seiner philosophischen Schriften, edited by A. Petzelt (Stuttgart: Kohlhammer, 1949);

De Pace Fidei, edited by Raymond Klibansky and H. Bascour (London: Warburg Institute, 1956);

Philosophisch-theologische Schriften, 3 volumes, edited by Leo Gabriel, translated into German by Wilhelm and Dietlind Dupré (Vienna: Herder, 1964-1976).

CRITICAL EDITION: *Nicolai de Cusa Opera Omnia*, 21 volumes projected, 19 volumes published, edition authorized by the Heidelberg Academy of Letters (Leipzig & Hamburg: Meiner, 1932-).

EDITIONS IN ENGLISH: *The Single Eye, Entituled The Vision of God, Wherein Is Infolded the Mistery of Divine Presence*, translated by Giles Randall (London: Printed for John Streater, 1646);

The Idiot, in Four Books, the First and Second of Wisdome, the Third of the Minde, the Fourth of Statick Experiments or Experiments of the Ballance, translated anonymously (London: Printed for William Leake, 1650; reprinted, San Francisco: California State Library, 1940);

The Vision of God, translated by Emma Gurney Salter (London: Dent, 1928; New York: Dutton, 1928; reprinted, New York: Ungar, 1960);

Of Learned Ignorance, translated by Germain Heron (New Haven: Yale University Press, 1954; London: Routledge & Kegan Paul, 1954);

Unity and Reform: Selected Writings of Nicholas of Cusa, edited by John Patrick Dolan (Notre Dame, Ind.: University of Notre Dame Press, 1962);

"On Actualized-Possibility," translated by Jasper Hopkins, in his *A Concise Introduction to the Philosophy of Nicholas of Cusa* (Minneapolis: University of Minnesota Press, 1978), pp. 63-153;

The Layman: About Mind, translated by Clyde Lee Miller (New York: Abaris Books, 1979);

Nicholas of Cusa on God as Not-other: A Translation and an Appraisal of De Li Non Aliud, translated by Hopkins (Minneapolis: University of Minnesota Press, 1979);

Nicholas of Cusa on Learned Ignorance: A Translation and an Appraisal of De Docta Ignorantia, translated by Hopkins (Minneapolis: Banning Press, 1981);

Nicholas of Cusa's Debate with John Wenck: A Translation and an Appraisal of De Ignota Litteratura and Apologia Doctae Ignorantiae, translated by Hopkins (Minneapolis: Banning Press, 1981);

"The Gift of the Father of Lights," translated by Hopkins, in his *Nicholas of Cusa's Metaphysic of Contraction* (Minneapolis: Banning Press, 1983), pp. 113-131;

Nicholas of Cusa's Dialectical Mysticism: Text, Translation, and Interpretative Study of De Visione Dei, translated by Hopkins (Minneapolis: Banning Press, 1985);

De ludo globi (The Game of Spheres), translated by Pauline M. Watts (New York: Abaris Books, 1986);

The Layman on Wisdom and the Mind, translated by Mark L. Führer (Ottawa: Dovehouse, 1989);

Nicholas of Cusa's De Pace Fidei; and Cribratio Alkorani, translated by Hopkins (Minneapolis: Banning Press, 1990);

"On the Peace of Faith," translated by H. Lawrence Bond, in his and James Biechler's *Nicholas of Cusa on Interreligious Harmony* (Lewiston, N.Y.: Mellin Press, 1990), pp. 2-63.

Nicholas of Cusa was a leading churchman, philosopher, and theologian of the fifteenth century. His career as canon lawyer, conciliarist, papal advocate, cardinal, and reformer placed him at the center of the political turmoil of his age. One of the era's most independent thinkers, he wrote extensively, first on political theory and later on speculative philosophy and theology. His political career and his treatise *De Concordantia Catholica* (On Universal Concord, 1433) have attracted the attention of historians and political scientists, while philosophers and theologians have focused on his speculative writings. Of the latter, *De Docta Ignorantia* (Of Learned Ignorance, 1440) is most familiar. Because this work focuses on human subjectivity and knowledge, Ernst Cassirer and others have considered it a decisive turn toward modernity. Yet, for all its novelty, Nicholas's thought remains deeply rooted in the medieval world. Of particular importance to his philosophy are the Neoplatonic thinkers, such as Proclus and Pseudo-Dionysius, whom he cites often and freely. Innovative yet traditional, Nicholas's work thus marks a turning point between the medieval and modern worlds.

Nicholas was born in Kues—now Bernkastel-Kues—on the Moselle River, near Trier, in 1401. His Latinized name, Cusanus, reflects his place of birth. He was one of four children of

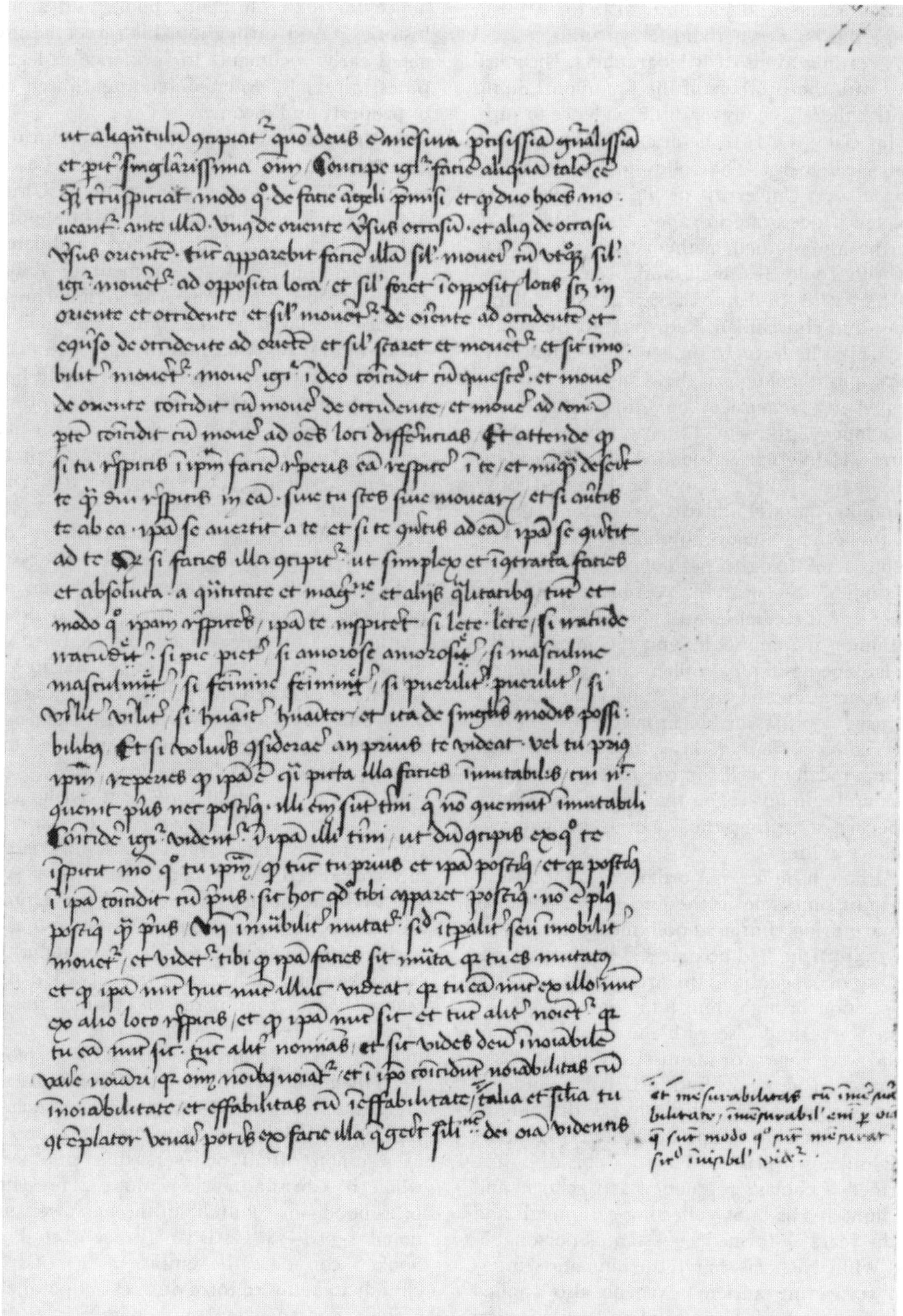

Page from a manuscript for chapter 12 of Nicholas of Cusa's Complementum Theologicum. *The marginal corrections at bottom right are in his handwriting (Brussels, Bibliothèque Royale, cod. 11479-84, fol. 77r).*

Katharina Römer and Johann Cryfftz (or Krebs), a prosperous boat owner and ferryman.

According to his early biographers, Nicholas studied with the Brothers of the Common Life in Deventer; there is, however, little evidence to support this claim. In 1416 he attended the University of Heidelberg. The following year he enrolled at the University of Padua, where he completed a doctorate in canon law in 1423. At Padua he also studied mathematics and the sciences with Paolo Toscanelli and began a lasting friendship with Giuliano Caesarini, the brilliant canonist and churchman. Returning to Germany, in 1425-1426 he lectured on law and studied philosophy and theology at the University of Cologne, where Heimericus de Campo continued the teaching of the school's early master, Albert the Great. Heimericus befriended Nicholas and introduced him to the works of Pseudo-Dionysius and Raymond Lull, two Neoplatonic thinkers who became major influences on his later thought. The Cologne period concluded Nicholas's studies, and—with the possible exception of his brief stay at Heidelberg—included his only formal training in philosophy and theology. Unlike many late-medieval philosophers, he was emphatically not an academic; in 1428 and again in 1435 he refused a professorship in law at the University of Louvain. Rather, his education in canon law prepared him well for the career in church politics and administration that he was to follow. His speculative writings thus emerge within an engaged, active life.

Although he was not ordained to the priesthood until sometime in the late 1430s, Nicholas began acquiring church appointments as early as 1426. By 1427 he had become secretary to his patron Otto of Ziegenhain, the archbishop of Trier. This position brought him into contact with the Roman Curia, and also with the Italian humanists who were eager for manuscripts of lost classical works that he might find in German libraries. After a two-year wait and several disappointments, Nicholas sent Poggio Bracciolini twelve previously unknown plays by Plautus. This discovery confirmed Nicholas's reputation as a scholar and book hunter. His book collecting continued, and over the years he formed a substantial personal library. While Nicholas shared the humanists' interest in recovering ancient texts, he also applied manuscript research to political and ecclesiastical issues. For example, he challenged the Middle Ages' most politically influential forgery, the Donation of Constantine, when he found no evidence for it in "authentic books and approved histories." And throughout his career he investigated early documents for evidence in legal disputes, especially when defending church claims to property and income.

Nicholas came to prominence during the Council of Basel. When he arrived at Basel early in 1432 his task was to present Ulrich of Manderscheid's claim to the archbishopric of Trier; Ulrich, the locally elected candidate, was contesting the papal appointment of Raban of Helmstadt to the position. Although Nicholas lost this case in May 1434, the council provided a useful forum for his work and thought. He strengthened his ties with leading churchmen and humanists, including Caesarini, the council's president. Nicholas also worked effectively for reconciliation with the Hussites and the Bohemian church and became a leading spokesman for the conciliar movement.

Conciliarism asserted the authority of a general church council over the papacy. The issue became especially urgent after 1378, when schism produced two and even three rival popes. The Council of Constance finally resolved the schism in 1417 and elected a single pope, Martin V, thus unifying the church and demonstrating the superiority of a council to divisive papal claims. In its first years the Council of Basel appeared to continue Constance's achievements. Hence, it was with confidence and hope that Nicholas presented his treatise *De Concordantia Catholica* to the council in November 1433. This work is generally considered to be conciliarism's most systematic and thorough defense. Rich in canon law and history, it also announces a theme that came to dominate Nicholas's speculative thought: the relation between unity and diversity. He defines *concordantia* as "that by reason of which the catholic church agrees [*concordat*] in one and in many, in one Lord and many subjects." This harmony reflects the infinite concord of the Trinity and the hierarchical order of creation. Book 1 sketches this theological background and discusses the church as a union of all believers that embraces the whole of Christian society. Book 2 presents the priesthood—or "church" in the narrower, institutional sense—as Christian society's soul, while book 3 considers the empire as its body. The church and empire form distinct but parallel hierarchies, governed by common principles of consent, authority, and concord. All legitimate authority rests on the consent of the governed, whom the ruling powers of church and empire represent. Concord describes both the agreement that underlies this order and the unity that results from it; indeed, a unanimous consensus signals the Holy Spirit's guiding presence.

Nicholas sets clear limits to papal powers. The pope's primacy is a practical, administrative one, and in all other respects he is the equal of other bishops. A universal council represents the church more clearly and infallibly than does the pope alone, and it can depose him for heresy or poor administration. With a hint of nationalistic humor, Nicholas emphasizes the Council of Basel's authority by suggesting that it could transfer the papacy to his home diocese of Trier, whose bishop would then become pope. Yet Nicholas's ideal remains one of unified, orderly action between pope and council, for as a rule the pope convenes and participates in a universal council. In addition, conflict indicates an absence of concord, and when dissent marks a council's deliberations, it ceases to be a true council.

Nicholas's early activities at Basel reflect his ecclesiology. In 1433-1434 he sided with the council against Pope Eugenius IV's attempt to dissolve it, and he denied a papal legate's authority to preside over the council. But the conflict between Eugenius and Basel later intensified and produced increasing division within the council itself. As political reality receded from his ideal of concord, Nicholas's allegiance shifted from the council to the papacy. The turning point in his loyalties was the controversy over the location for a council of reunion with the Eastern church: the promise of broader church unity contrasted sharply with the factional strife of Basel. This contrast, plus the Greeks' insistence that the pope approve the council site, influenced Nicholas's turn toward the papacy as the best hope for concord. In December 1436 he voted with Basel's minority to allow Eugenius to decide where the new council should take place. The following May, Nicholas was one of three delegates commissioned by the minority party to visit Constantinople. With the pope's approval, they set sail from Venice in late summer and returned on 4 February 1437 with the Greek emperor and the patriarch and other representatives of the Eastern church. The voyage was a major success for Nicholas, especially when the ensuing Council of Florence proclaimed union—however fragile and short-lived—between the churches in July 1439.

The voyage also completed Nicholas's turn from conciliarism to the papal cause. On his return he took up the pope's defense against those

Copy, on a tapestry, of a self-portrait of Roger van der Weyden. The original, now destroyed, was in the Brussels town hall, where Nicholas saw it. In De Visione Dei *he uses the portrait, whose eyes seem to look at the viewer no matter where the latter stands, to illustrate the all-seeing vision of God (Bern Museum).*

who remained at Basel and who in 1439 deposed Eugenius and named an antipope, Felix V. Faced with renewed schism, Nicholas traveled in Germany for the next ten years. At local and imperial diets in Mainz, Frankfurt, and elsewhere he worked to persuade the German nobility to support Eugenius. Partly as a result of Nicholas's efforts the Concordat of Vienna (1448) aligned Germany with Eugenius and led to the end of both the schism and the conciliar movement. Nicholas's energy and success earned him Aeneas Sylvius's epithet, "Hercules of Eugenians," as well as elevation to the cardinalate in 1449. Nicholas had come far from his bourgeois German roots, and he took pride in his achievements. In an autobiographical note he says that his appointment as cardinal shows that the church does not respect status or place of birth, but generously rewards virtue.

Yet Nicholas's conversion to the papal cause remains the most controversial move in his career. Because he says nothing about the motives behind this shift, commentators have been free to identify several: loss of Ulrich's case before the council, personal ambition, concern over Basel's factionalism, and desire for reunion with the Greek church. Edmond Vansteenberghe's 1920 biography stresses the first reason; current opinion generally emphasizes the last two and notes that Nicholas's change of loyalties is consistent with the respect for the papacy and emphasis on ecclesial unity displayed in *De Concordantia Catholica.* But others, especially among his contemporaries who remained loyal to Basel, have been less kind. They see his move as an opportunist's reach for prominence—a view that his elevation to the cardinalate did little to diminish. This estimate fuels both Gregor Heimburg's *Invectiva* (1461) against Nicholas and Johann Kymeus's Reformation tract *Des Bapsts Hercules wider die Deutschen* (The Pope's Hercules against the Germans, 1538). Kymeus's title page portrays Nicholas standing before the kneeling, submissive German nation, while the Roman hierarchy stands behind him and the pope holds the reins to his cardinal's hat.

However Nicholas's actions during this period are judged, one point is clear: the shift to the papal cause not only advanced his ecclesiastical career but also marked a new direction for his literary work. Having abandoned his conciliar commitments, he ceased writing about political theory and ecclesiology and began to compose works of speculative philosophy and theology.

De Docta Ignorantia decisively announces this turn. It is Nicholas's best-known work and outlines the program that his later writings would develop. He completed the work in Kues in February 1440. In the dedication to Cardinal Caesarini he artfully apologizes for offering the classically trained humanist this product of Germanic folly but hopes that the book's paradoxical title will recommend it to the cardinal's inquiring mind.

Nicholas presents learned ignorance, the book's central insight, as a revelation. He was sailing back from Constantinople, he says, when, "by what I believe was a supreme gift of the Father of Lights from Whom is every perfect gift (James 1:17), I was led in the learning that is ignorance to grasp the incomprehensible; and this I was able to achieve not by way of comprehension but by transcending those perennial truths that can be reached by reason." Learned ignorance is both a divine gift and a speculative method that goes beyond reason. Significantly, Nicholas's discovery occurred while he was accompanying Greek church officials and theologians to Italy; from this point on, whenever he discusses learned ignorance he appeals to Pseudo-Dionysius the Areopagite, the Eastern church father who describes mystical union as "unknowing." Nicholas's description of his revelation echoes Dionysius in another way: the quote from James's epistle also begins Pseudo-Dionysius's *Celestial Hierarchy,* which describes the gift of lights descending through the ranks of angels. Nicholas returns to the same biblical text in his treatise *De Dato Patris Luminum* (The Gift of the Father of Lights, 1446).

Learned ignorance expresses Nicholas's concern for human knowledge and divine unknowability. We naturally desire to know the truth; yet God, who is the absolute or "precise" truth, cannot be known as he is. But if we recognize that we cannot know God, our very ignorance becomes learned. Nicholas explores the dynamics of knowing to develop this theme. Learning and rational inquiry are based on proportion, as we compare what we seek to understand and what we judge to be certain. As long as the objects compared are similar, we can establish proportions between them and grow in knowledge. Yet there are clear limits to this process. For proportion requires number, and therefore occurs only in the finite region where comparisons of "more and less" are possible. But when we approach the infinite, comparison becomes impossible because "there is no proportion of the infinite to the finite." While we cannot comprehend the infinite, we nevertheless can approach it indirectly through symbols. As Nicholas's use of proportion, number, and infinity suggest, he especially prizes mathematical signs "on account of their indestructible certitude." One such symbol, a polygon inscribed within a circle, represents the mind's relation to truth. As the polygon's angles multiply, it becomes more like the circle; but unless the polygon is reduced to identity with the circle, multiplying its angles will never produce equality between them. The circle remains the measure and goal that the polygon approximates but never attains. Similarly, the finite mind never attains infinite truth but approaches it without limit. Therefore, learned ignorance both recognizes knowledge's limits and begins an unending symbolic inquiry.

Nicholas develops mathematical symbolism throughout the discussion of God as absolute maximum in book 1 of *De Docta Ignorantia.* As infinite, the maximum stands beyond comparison in two respects. The first emphasizes transcendence, since the maximum is not the greatest within a comparative series; rather, it is absolute—that is, free from distinctions of "more and less." The second is a typically Cusan theme, the coincidence of opposites: the maximum enfolds all contrasts and differences within its unity. Nicholas illustrates both points by analyzing an infinite line, which would be at once a straight line, a circle, a triangle, and a sphere. His discussion of the straight line and circle indicates the direction of his thought: as a circle expands, its circumference becomes less curved; hence, at infinity the circle's arc becomes a straight line. The infinite line thus transcends and measures the straight and curved lines and enfolds their distinctions within its unity. Similarly, the maximum transcends and enfolds finite being and its distinctions within itself, so that "in God all things are God." For these reasons, Nicholas prefers negative to affirmative theology. Whereas affirmations posit restricted, symbolic proportions between God and creatures, negations suggest divine infinity by denying all limits to God.

Book 2 contains Nicholas's cosmology, which historians of science have seen as breaking through the closed spheres of the medieval cosmos. Nicholas again centers his argument around infinity and the maximum. Because the universe reflects God or the absolute maximum, he describes it as a "contracted maximum" that is "neither finite nor infinite." The universe cannot be infinite, because God could have created a greater universe and because matter cannot expand without limit; yet neither can the universe be finite, because it includes all things, and therefore no physical or spatial boundaries enclose it. Nicholas thus describes the universe as unbounded or "privatively infinite," in contrast to positive divine infinity. Drawing novel conclusions from this insight, Nicholas says that the earth is not the cosmic center and that the fixed stars do not circumscribe an unbounded universe. He also claims that the earth moves and is a noble star shining in the heavens. Learned ignorance notes the absence of precise measures—and hence of circles and centers—in nature and suggests instead a symbolic geometry. To describe God's relation to the universe Nicholas uses the Neoplatonic image of an infinite sphere whose "center is everywhere and whose circumference is nowhere"; as the universe's center and circumference, God is at once everywhere and nowhere, immanent and transcendent. Alexandre Koyré and others have drawn attention to Nicholas's originality in extending this image from metaphysics to cosmology.

Book 3 concludes *De Docta Ignorantia* with a Christology that brings together themes from the previous two books. At once divine and human, Christ is "the maximum in limitation"—that is, the perfect expression of the divine in an individual creature. As such, he unites the absolute and contracted maximum. Nicholas locates this union in the intellect and describes it with a familiar image: "It is as though a polygon inscribed in a circle were human nature and the circle were the divine nature. If the polygon were to become the maximum than which no greater could exist, it could never exist by itself in finite angles, but only as a circular figure." In book 1 this image represents the mind's dynamic movement toward God; here it indicates that movement's completion in Christ, who perfectly assimilates the human intellect to the divine and thus becomes the goal of learned ignorance's quest. With this central point established, Nicholas comments at length on Christ's Incarnation, Passion, Resurrection, Ascension, and Final Judgment of the living and the dead. The work ends by discussing faith and the church. Faith and learned ignorance converge and carry us into the unknowable darkness of Christ's divinity. The church unites the many believers in Christ—a union that springs from his own "maximal union of natures." As in *De Concordantia Catholica*, Nicholas invokes the image of the mystical body, but here he says nothing of church structure and government. Although these were matters of intense practical concern at the time of its composition, *De Docta Ignorantia* remains on the higher ground of metaphysics, theology, and individual faith.

De Docta Ignorantia was the first in an impressive series of speculative works that Nicholas composed during the 1440s as he traveled and worked on the papacy's behalf in Germany. Principal among these works is *De Coniecturis* (Conjectures, 1443), a companion piece to *De Docta Ignorantia.* Here Nicholas develops his methodology and the anthropology that underlies it. *Conjecture* means neither skepticism nor guesswork, but inquiry and knowledge based on learned ignorance. Nicholas defines *conjecture* as "a positive assertion that in otherness participates in truth as it is." While truth in its infinite precision cannot be

Detail from Nicholas's monument, sculpted by Andrea Bregno in 1456, at the Church of Saint Peter-in-Chains, Rome. Nicholas is depicted at left, kneeling before Saint Peter.

known, it can still be expressed indirectly in the "otherness" of image, metaphor, and concept. *De Coniecturis*, for example, uses diagrams and mathematical progressions to analyze human knowing. Nicholas distinguishes four "unities" within the mind: a "divine" unity and those of intellect, soul, and body. The first unity is not God himself but his image, from which the other unities descend and to which they return in continuous motion. As this movement unfolds, the mind constructs a cultural world of likenesses and thereby mirrors God's creation of the actual world. Embracing all within its unity and unfolding its own creative power, humanity becomes a "human god" and microcosm. As Pauline M. Watts notes, in this work Nicholas presents the first major Renaissance discussion of human dignity and creativity.

Recognition of knowledge as conjecture energizes inquiry. For since truth is infinite, there can be no limit to the symbols and concepts that seek to express it. Consequently, Nicholas continually creates new conjectures, as his other writings of the 1440s illustrate. These writings include his first philosophical dialogues, beginning with *De Deo Abscondito* (The Hidden God, 1444), and his only work to survive in the vernacular, a commentary on the Lord's Prayer (*Sermon* 24, 1441). *De Filiatione Dei* (Divine Sonship, 1445) connects sonship with the Eastern church's understanding of "deification" (*theosis*) and says that both take place in the intellect as in a living mirror. Images of light and seeing figure prominently in *De Quaerendo Deum* (On Seeking God, 1445) and dominate *De Dato Patris Luminum*, where Nicholas uses light symbolism to explore God's relation to creation and the intellect. In the dialogue *De Genesi* (On Genesis, 1447) Nicholas's taste for metaphysically probing wordplay emerges when he proposes "the same" (*idem*) as a new name for God that—like "absolute maximum"—points to a unity beyond opposites.

Shortly after becoming a cardinal in 1449 Nicholas replied to the strong criticisms of the Heidelberg theologian John Wenck. Wenck had attacked *De Docta Ignorantia* in his own treatise, *De Ignota Litteratura* (On Unknown Learning, 1442-1443). This work comments on ten theses and their corollaries drawn from *De Docta Ignorantia*. For Wenck, learned ignorance is a delusion, because by seeking to "see God as he is" in this life, Nicholas "vanishes amid thoughts" instead of glorifying God for creation's beauty. Wenck singles out the coincidence of opposites as Nicholas's basic mistake, since it "destroys the fundamental principle of all knowledge"—Aristotle's principle of noncontradiction—and thus makes all learning impossible. By blurring distinctions at every level, coincidence entails serious errors. It confounds knowledge and ignorance and abolishes "the individual existence of things within their own genus." But most serious are its consequences in theology, where distinctions disappear between the Trinitarian Persons and between God and creation, and the "individuality of Christ's humanity" is destroyed. These errors justify the shrill alarm of Wenck's rhetoric, as he places Nicholas among late-medieval "false prophets" and heretics—"Waldensians, Eckhartians and Wycliffites." *De Ignota Litteratura* thus goes well beyond academic criticism and bluntly accuses Nicholas of heresy.

Nicholas answered Wenck in *Apologia Doctae Ignorantiae* (A Defense of Learned Ignorance, 1449), combining the forms of letter and dialogue to distance himself from his accuser while simultaneously responding to his charges. He presents the work as a letter from one of his devoted students to a like-minded friend. The student, outraged by Wenck's attack, has overcome Nicholas's weary reluctance to discuss his criticisms and reports their conversation to his friend. With the eager student leading and reporting the conversation, Nicholas appears to stand above the fray. From this comfortable distance he impugns his adversary's motives, intelligence, and learning. The Heidelberg theologian speaks "out of passion," and his animus stems from the Council of Basel, which he continued to defend after Nicholas turned to the papal cause. When the student calls Wenck "a lying and conceited man who knows no theology," Nicholas replies "that with someone who is mad we ought to deal sparingly rather than heaping insults upon him." In addition, Wenck has read little and understood less. He falsifies texts and meanings and thus distorts Nicholas's teaching.

The *Apologia Doctae Ignorantiae* corrects Wenck's misinterpretations. For example, Wenck misunderstands Nicholas's views on God and creation. The radical lack of proportion between God and creatures precludes a simple identity between them. Only insofar as creatures remain enfolded within God's unity is he all things; but insofar as they unfold into distinct, created beings they are not one with God. On this and other issues Wenck's errors stem from his commitment to the "Aristotelian sect," which considers the coincidence of opposites to be heretical. Nicholas thus agrees with his critic in tracing their disagreement to the logics of coincidence and noncontradiction. To Wenck's claim that Nicholas does not know logic, he replies, "Deliver us, O Lord, from the dialecticians," and notes that "chattering logic" can harm theology. Aristotle's is a logic of discursive reason that moves among finite contrasts and oppositions and is therefore inadequate for seeing God's infinite simplicity. But intellect stands above reason's discursive motion, embraces opposites in unity, and has a distinctive logic of coincidence that is more appropriate to the vision of God. Nicholas links coincidence with mystical theology's "unknowing" ascent into divine unity. This ascent begins when we recognize learned ignorance's root: "that God cannot be known as he is." Predictably, Nicholas appeals to Pseudo-Dionysius's authority on these issues and with obvious pride cites his own copy of Ambrose Traversari's new translation of the Pseudo-Dionysian corpus. He thus answers Wenck by shifting the context for their dispute from academic Aristotelianism to the negative theology of Pseudo-Dionysius.

Wenck replied to the *Apologia Doctae Ignorantiae* with *De Facie Scolae Doctae Ignorantiae* (The Pretense of the School of Learned Ignorance). This text has not survived, nor does it seem to have come to Nicholas's attention. As a result, his *Apologia Doctae Ignorantiae* remains the final document in this controversy.

After ten years' work in Germany on behalf of the papacy Nicholas arrived in Rome, where he formally received the cardinal's hat on 11 January 1450. He enjoyed comparative leisure in Italy until the year's end, and during the summer he composed three dialogues featuring an "*Idiota*," an unlettered layman or citizen who becomes an ideal spokesman for learned ignorance. The uneducated layman whose piety surpasses the learned clergy's was a commonplace figure in late medieval religion. Nicholas uses this figure to explore the nature and limits of knowledge. His Layman is a fifteenth-century Socrates who serves no academic authority and freely acknowledges his ignorance. The Layman engages a professionally trained Orator and a Philosopher in conversation and proves wiser than either of them. As the Layman becomes the teacher of the Orator and Philosopher, Nicholas challenges two prevailing educational models: the rhetorical education of Renaissance humanism and the dialectical tradition of the universities. Schooling, authorities, and books matter less than desiring and assimilating wisdom itself.

The two books of the first dialogue, *Idiota de Sapientia* (The Layman on Wisdom), concern wisdom, which "cries out in the very streets and her cry is how she dwells in the highest." The Layman connects wisdom with the activity of measuring. For wisdom's cry is heard in the marketplace, where all weighing and money changing presume one, or unity, as their basic measure. When the Layman turns toward "the highest," this unity symbolically leads to divine wisdom itself, the infinite One that underlies all diversity and is sought in all inquiry. In *Idiota de Mente* (The Layman on Mind) the Layman derives the term *mind* (*mens*) from *measure* (*mensura*). God is the absolute measure, and the human mind, made in God's image, participates in his measuring. Numbering and measuring are essential activities, since the mind—like a living compass—takes the measure of things and conforms itself to its divine standard. *Idiota de Staticis Experimentis* (The Layman on Experiments with Weights) applies measuring to the sciences and medicine. The Layman praises the balance scale's precision and sketches experiments for its use; physicians, for example, may assess urine more accurately "by weight and color than by color alone." Measuring thus unifies the dialogues' discussions of wisdom, mind, and scientific experiments.

The discussion of mind in *Idiota de Mente* highlights another of Nicholas's central themes: human creativity. As in *De Coniecturis*, he links creativity to human nature as made in the image of God. Since "all human crafts are images, as it were, of the infinite and divine craft," we create culture as God creates the world. Language, work, and the arts illustrate this theme. For example, the Layman boasts that the wooden spoon that he carves imitates no natural form but derives from an original human concept; and so his art is closer to divine creativity than are the imitative arts of the painter or sculptor. But later in the dialogue, painting illustrates the mind as God's image. The Layman describes an artist who paints two self-portraits: one that is a better likeness but "dead," and another that is a poorer likeness but "alive" and capable of appearing ever more like the artist. The mind resembles the second painting because it, too, is an "imperfect image which has the power of corresponding more and more without limit to its unreachable original." The divine exemplar remains beyond our reach but is open to unlimited participation and assimilation. This process occurs in work, creativity, and the measuring activity of knowledge. Nicholas's Layman discusses and dramatically enacts each of these activities.

Detail of the portrait of Nicholas and his brother John on the altar panel in the chapel of Saint Nicholas Hospital in Bernkastel-Kues, Germany

The first book of *Idiota* suffered the strangest fate of any of Nicholas's works. Late in the fifteenth century it was combined with other materials into *On True Wisdom* and attributed to Petrarch. Despite clear differences of style, it circulated under the Florentine humanist's name into the twentieth century.

Early in 1450 Pope Nicholas V named Nicholas bishop of Brixen in the Tirol. The appointment was, however, contested because the cathedral chapter had elected one of its own members, Leonard Wismayer. The situation was ironic, since at Basel Nicholas had defended the locally elected candidate for bishop of Trier against a papal appointee. He succeeded to the bishopric of Brixen, but before taking up residence in his new diocese he undertook another mission.

Pope Nicholas V declared 1450 a year of jubilee, with special indulgences for pilgrims to Rome. In late December he commissioned Nicholas as legate to Germany and the Low Countries. His tasks included reforming church affairs and dispensing the jubilee indulgences to those unable to visit Rome. Departing on 31 December

1450, he traveled to Salzburg, Nuremberg, northern Germany, the Netherlands, Trier, and Mainz. The legation ended on Easter 1452 when he arrived in Brixen. Along his route he had met with clergy in local synods where he proclaimed the jubilee and issued edicts against simony, clerical concubinage, superstitious veneration of "bleeding hosts," and other abuses. He had also visited monastic houses and had regularly preached to lay audiences in German. Latin versions of these sermons are his only extant literary works from the period of the legation; they emphasize orthodox faith and the sacraments, which Nicholas praises as more valuable than the indulgences that he himself was dispensing. The legation's reform efforts yielded mixed results. Where local communities and their leaders supported Nicholas's aims, his reforms were often embraced and implemented. But where political and economic pressures worked against change, the legate's decrees encountered resistance and appeals to Rome—with the pope occasionally reversing Nicholas's abortive reforms and threats of excommunication.

Nicholas's years in Brixen were marked by serious and occasionally violent conflict. From the first, the local nobility viewed him with suspicion as a bourgeois outsider and papal agent, and his strong-willed administration of the diocese only confirmed their doubts. As bishop he undertook two major projects: restoring the diocese's independence from secular control and reforming the clergy and monasteries. The Germanic bishops were not exclusively spiritual leaders but also rulers with their own territories and powers. In Brixen, however, the bishop's authority had long been weakened to the benefit of the dukes of Austria. Using neglected archives and strict management, Nicholas reclaimed sources of income and restored the diocese's financial strength. With this wealth he was soon lending money to Archduke Sigismund, and in 1456 he bought back Taufers castle from Sigismund. But Nicholas's very success threatened Sigismund's authority: as the bishop's claims to property increased, so did the duke's wariness of his ambitions and strong ties to powers beyond the Tirol, especially to the papacy.

Nicholas's program for monastic reform was less successful than his financial administration. Among the first communities targeted for reform was the small convent at Sonnenberg, whose abbess, Verena von Stuben, repeatedly appealed to Sigismund, the pope, and others against Nicholas's measures. The escalating conflict brought the eviction of the nuns, their excommunication, and the slaughter of their mercenaries by a peasant band. Resolution came only in 1459, when Verena resigned as abbess; but by then the conflict had further soured relations between Nicholas and Sigismund and slowed the pace of reform throughout the diocese. Nicholas's fierce insistence on purifying Sonnenberg contrasts with another incident: in 1456 he compelled the cathedral chapter, under threat of excommunication, to favor his nephew Simon Wehling's claim to a prebend in the diocese. There were, it seems, limits to Nicholas's zeal for genuine reform.

Amid continuing disputes over reform and land rights, Sigismund and Nicholas met at Wilten Abbey near Innsbruck in late June 1457. But along the route and at Wilten, rumors and troop movements led Nicholas to fear that the duke's agents were about to kill him. Although Sigismund denied any such plot, Nicholas retreated to Andraz castle near the diocese's southern border. There he remained until August 1458, when he departed for Rome. Apart from a brief, disastrous meeting with Sigismund at Bruneck in 1460, Nicholas never again entered his diocese.

During these troubled years in Brixen, Nicholas continued to preach and write. Indeed, preaching was integral to his pastoral role and reform efforts, and more than a hundred sermons survive from this period. He also composed several works on mathematics and on philosophy and theology. Of the latter, two are especially noteworthy: *De Pace Fidei* (The Peace of Faith, 1453) and *De Visione Dei* (The Vision of God, 1453).

By July 1453 the problems of Nicholas's bishopric were already apparent, but the pope denied his request to resign the position. While struggling with his local difficulties, Nicholas heard that Constantinople had fallen to the Turks. His contemporaries generally responded to the Muslim advance with fear and rage; Nicholas composed *De Pace Fidei*. In this, one of the first Renaissance works on universal religion, Nicholas returns to his conciliar mood and presents a "vision" of a heavenly council on world religions. A Platonic rule guides the discussion: "There is only one religion in a variety of rites." Since every "rite" participates in the one "religion," they need not conflict and can achieve concord. All seek the one truth or wisdom that underlies their faiths; these faiths, like so many conjectures, express this truth partially and symbolically. A basic tolerance thus governs the conversation, although Christianity holds a privileged place as the fullest, most precise revelation of the true religion. Nicholas underlines Christianity's leading role by having the divine Word, Peter, and Paul lead the conversation. With surprising ease, representatives from the nations—Greek, Italian, Arab, Indian, Jew, Bohemian, and others—accept God's unity, the Trinity, the Incarnation, Resurrection, and the Christian sacraments. With this concord achieved "in the heaven of reason," Nicholas proposes a conference in Jerusalem to secure everlasting peace and praise of God.

De Pace Fidei is remarkable in many ways. In one sense it seems an exercise in escapism, since its visionary optimism and simplicity contrast so sharply with contemporary political and military realities. More in line with the times—and with Pope Nicholas's wishes—was Nicholas's Regensburg appeal for a crusade against the Turks in May 1454. But, in another sense, Nicholas might have been better off if he had heeded his own advice and respected the differing customs and "rites" within his diocese. His actions as bishop and the conflicts they provoked confirm that "to seek exact conformity in all things is to disturb the peace." Finally, though, the visionary quality of *De Pace Fidei* may be its greatest strength, because it reflects an exceptional tolerance toward Islam in fifteenth-century Europe. Nicholas supported his friend John of Segovia's proposal for a conference of Christians and Muslims, and at Pope Pius II's request wrote *Cribratio Alcorani* (A Scrutiny of the Koran, 1461). Based on careful reading of translations of the Koran and related texts, this work marks out considerable common ground between Muslims and Christians. Although Nicholas sharply criticizes particular teachings, he generally opens the way for clarification and mutual understanding. Lacking the naive optimism of *De Pace Fidei* concerning Muslim-Christian relations, *Cribratio Alcorani* still considers Islam appreciatively and critically rather than vengefully—a noteworthy achievement amid Europe's near hysteria after Constantinople's fall.

Nicholas's other major work of 1453, *De Visione Dei*, was written for the monks of Tegernsee Abbey. Not all of Nicholas's efforts went unappreciated during his stay in Brixen: he found a receptive audience for both his speculative and practical activities in the reforming monasteries of Bavaria, which assisted his attempts at wider monastic reform and were also responsible for several early collections of his writings. Especially important was the Benedictine community at Tegernsee, whose prior, Bernard of Waging, visited Sonnenburg on Nicholas's behalf and wrote *Laudatorium Doctae Ignorantiae* (The Praise of Learned Ignorance, 1451). Nicholas found this abbey so hospitable that in February 1454 he asked that a cell be set aside where he could retire to the contemplative life. While he never withdrew to Tegernsee, he corresponded with Bernard and with Abbot Gaspard Aindorffer, and at their request composed *De Visione Dei* and *De Beryllo* (The Beryl, 1458). These letters and treatises concern learned ignorance's implications for mystical theology. *De Beryllo* considers intellectual vision and the coincidence of opposites, and *De Visione Dei* is Nicholas's literary masterwork.

Nicholas sent *De Visione Dei* to the monks with an accompanying painting and asked that they meditate with him on this "icon of God." The treatise comments on the painting and reflects Nicholas's interest in both the Eastern church, where icons are privileged revelations of the divine, and Renaissance art, with its concern for visual perspective. The portrait is "all seeing"—that is, its eyes seem to meet the viewers' regardless of where they stand. Nicholas refers to several such paintings, including one by Roger van der Weyden and another of Christ's face on Veronica's veil in his own chapel at Koblenz.

De Visione Dei promises "an easy way unto mystical theology." Its title suggests both God's seeing of humanity and humanity's seeing of God. To emphasize this mutual vision Nicholas directs the monks to look at the portrait; each will find it gazing directly at him, no matter where he stands or moves. The all-seeing icon represents God's absolute sight, while the monks' individual perspectives illustrate the restricted character of human seeing. The treatise then probes these ways of seeing in a carefully crafted series of prayers. Because the divine nature is hidden, "None can see Thee [Lord] save insofar as Thou grantest a sight of Thyself, nor is that sight aught else than Thy seeing him that seeth Thee." Here God's self-disclosure is primary, and his vision is ontological and creative: "Since Thy look is Thy being, I am because Thou dost look at me, and if Thou didst turn Thy glance from me I should cease to be." The mind, created in God's image, freely turns toward its divine source and exemplar: "O Lord, . . . Thou hast left me free to be mine own self, if I desire. Hence, if I be not mine own self, Thou art not mine, for Thou dost make freewill needful, since Thou canst not be mine if I be not mine own." The vision of God thus confirms human freedom and identity.

Yet our seeing remains perspectival and partial, so that when we look toward God in love we see a loving God; in anger, a wrathful God. Nicholas develops a dialectic of vision that moves between our restricted perspectives and God's absolute vision. From the story of the Fall in Genesis he takes the image of the wall of paradise and describes its three elements: the enclosed garden where God dwells, the wall where opposites coincide, and the outside region of exile where reason makes its distinctions and perspectives vary. The mind moves among these three, going in and out of the garden, from creatures to God and back again. As we move through the wall of coincidence, we "see" what we cannot know: "I behold Thee in the garden of Paradise and I know not what I see, for I see naught visible. This alone I know, that I know not what I see, and never can know." For God is infinite and hence beyond both opposites and their coincidence. Learned ignorance thus completes Nicholas's dialectic of vision.

De Visione Dei then discusses God's unity, the Trinity, and Christ. The last, intensely devotional chapters concern Christ, "the final and entirely perfect Image of God." Having begun by considering the all-seeing portrait, the treatise ends by focusing on Christ, who is the ultimate icon of God. It is tempting to think that the portrait represents Christ, for these final chapters would then renew and intensify the opening meditation on the painting. But regardless of the portrait's subject, *De Visione Dei* illustrates more clearly and concretely than any of Nicholas's other works the central role that he accords symbol and image in the intellectual and spiritual life.

During his last years in Italy Nicholas remained active in church administration. He advised Pope Pius II in many matters, including the dispute with Duke Sigismund over Brixen. In 1459 he ably governed the Papal States as vicar general while the pope attended a congress in Mantua. He lived simply and continued to support church reform, this time within the papal court itself, and again encountered frustration. Late in 1461 he complained to Pius II, "I like nothing which goes on in this Curia. Everything is corrupt. No one does his duty. Neither you nor the cardinals have any care for the Church. . . . All are bent on ambition and avarice. If I ever speak in a consistory about reform, I am laughed at. I do no good here. Allow me to withdraw. I cannot endure these ways. I am an old man and I need rest." He then burst into tears. The pope rebuked him and refused his resignation.

Whatever Nicholas's practical frustrations during these years, he produced an extraordinary series of speculative works. His reading of Proclus's commentary on Parmenides led to *De Principio* (The Principle, 1459), published in early editions as the sermon "Tu Quis Es?" (Who Are You?); it begins with this question and Jesus' reply that he is "the principle" (John 8:25) but quickly becomes a Neoplatonic commentary on the one, self-subsisting principle. *De Aequalitate* (On Equality, 1459) similarly starts with a biblical text, "The life was the light of men" (John 1:4); here the symbol of equality guides Nicholas's analyses of the mind's relation to the divine Word, its light and life-giving principle. At Pope Pius's request he completed *Cribratio Alcorani. Compendium* (1463) is a sustained reflection on language and signs; Nicholas again emphasizes that knowledge is symbolic and approximative and that language's expressive power reflects the divine, creative Word.

In his late dialogues Nicholas no longer creates typical characters like the Layman but presents himself in conversation with friends. These concretely portrayed discussions highlight the personal—indeed, biographical—character of these late works. In *De Ludo Globi* (The Game of Spheres, 1463), for example, Nicholas expresses his delight in speaking with the sons of his friend Albert, Count Palatine and Duke of Bavaria. The contrast between their youth and the cardinal's age colors this informal work as they playfully explore a ballgame as a symbolic focus for cosmology, metaphysics, the soul, and mystical theology.

Nicholas also leads the conversations in *Trialogus de Possest* (On Actualized-Possibility, 1460), *Directio Speculantis seu de Non Aliud* (On Not-Other, 1462), and *De Apice Theoriae* (The Summit of Contemplative Vision, 1464). These works use reflective wordplay to propose new approaches to naming God. *Directio Speculantis seu de Non Aliud* is Nicholas's most self-consciously academic dialogue. He presents himself as a student of Pseudo-Dionysius, while his friends have been studying Plato's *Parmenides*, Proclus, and Aristotle. Their discussion concerns the Neoplatonic dialectic of unity and difference as they explore the tautology that "Not-other is not other than not-other." By defining itself, the "not-other" precedes the distinction between definition and what is defined. Moreover, it defines all otherness, since "the other is not other than the other"—for example, "the heavens are not other than the heavens." Every definition thus derives from the "not-other," yet it alone defines itself. For this reason, it provides direction to the mind's contemplation of God, whose unity likewise grounds and transcends all created difference and otherness.

In *Trialogus de Possest* Nicholas notes that "God alone is what [he] is able to be," while no creature is all that it can be. Since actual being and possibility or power coincide only in God, Nicholas fuses *posse* (can-be) and *esse* (to be) into the single divine name "*Possest.*" This term carries so wide a range of meanings that it defies translation into English. By rendering it "Actualized-Possibility" Jasper Hopkins captures its meaning as possibility but slights the more dynamic notions of potency and omnipotence that Nicholas's Latin also suggests. Nicholas accents these notions in his last work, *De Apice Theoriae*, where God is described as omnipotent, as the power of all powers. Nicholas here telescopes the dialectic of *posse* and *est* into the simple declaration that God is "*posse ipsum*," the absolute, active capacity or power which appears in all restricted powers and modes of being. It is what we seek in every inquiry, and its disclosure perfects the mind's power of seeing.

In June 1461 Nicholas suffered an intestinal illness so critical that he prepared his will. He retired to Orvieto, where he recovered during the summer. After this illness he began to consolidate his speculative achievements. He commissioned a manuscript of his philosophical and theological writings, which he corrected in his own hand and which survives in his personal library at Kues. In 1463 he composed an overview of his thought, *De Venatione Sapientiae* (The Hunt of Wisdom). In the prologue he says that since his sixty-first year has passed, he does not know whether much time remains for him to recount his speculative career. He describes philosophy as "the hunt for wisdom" and uses Diogenes Laertius's *Lives of the Philosophers* to set his thought in historical context. He claims that all philosophers agree on one principle that Aristotle expressed clearly: "what is impossible to become, does not come to be" (*quod impossibile fieri non fit*). Here too Nicholas explores the dynamics of becoming and creation. For the capacity to become is not self-sufficient but requires a prior, active principle that—like the *Possest* and *Posse ipsum*—both is all that it can be and makes this capacity actual. Philosophy seeks wisdom and this principle through the three "regions" of time, the perpetual, and the eternal. Nicholas reviews his own hunt for wisdom in ten "fields": learned ignorance, *Possest*, not-other, light, praise, unity, equality, connection, limit or goal, and order. By surveying major themes from his writings, *De Venatione Sapientiae* becomes Nicholas's philosophical testament.

On 11 August 1464 he died at Todi, en route to Ancona to assist Pius's preparations for a crusade against the Turks. As he wished, his body was buried at Saint Peter-in-Chains, his titular church in Rome, and his heart lies beneath the chapel floor at Saint Nicholas Hospital in Bernkastel-Kues. He had established this hospital to house thirty-three poor older men. In 1450 he had received permission to fund the hospital with his benefice income, and over the next eight years he had collaborated with his brother John on its construction and organization. The brothers are portrayed as donors on the fifteenth-century altar panel in the hospital chapel. After Nicholas's death many of his books were installed in the hospital's library. The hospital has expanded but retains its original buildings along the Moselle and continues to function as its founders intended. Although Nicholas himself never saw the hospital, he seems intimately present in this simple, generous place where his heart lies buried and his library opens to the visitor.

Following his death, Nicholas was remembered as both churchman and thinker. Indeed, considering the reversals and frustrations of his ecclesiastical career, his greatest legacy is philosophical and theological. The biographer Vespasiano da Bisticci and Giovanni Andrea de'Bussi, Nicholas's personal secretary and friend, praised him as a leading Platonic thinker of the age. Their high estimate finds confirmation in the early printed editions of his collected works in Strasbourg (1488), Cortemaggiore (1502), Paris (1514), and Basel (1565). English versions of individual works first appeared in the seventeenth century, when Giles Randall translated *De Visione Dei* as *The Single Eye* (1646) and William Leake published the *Idiota* dialogues as *The Idiot, in Four Books* (1650).

Nicholas exerted little direct influence on modern philosophy. It was largely through Giordano Bruno, who praised and cited him freely, that Nicholas came to the attention of

Gottfried Wilhelm Leibniz and later philosophers. A rediscovery of Nicholas in his own right began in German universities during the nineteenth century, first at Tübingen and later at Marburg. In Marburg's Neo-Kantian milieu, Ernst Cassirer encountered Nicholas, who became central to his classic *Individuum und Kosmos in der Philosophie der Renaissance* (1927; translated as *The Individual and the Cosmos in Renaissance Philosophy*, 1963). Thirty years later Karl Jaspers devoted a major section of *Die großen Philosophen* (1957; translated as *The Great Philosophers*, 1962) to Nicholas. For Cassirer and Jaspers, Nicholas's approach to knowledge, mind, and symbol appeared strikingly modern. But while acknowledging Nicholas's originality, one should also recognize the contexts and sources that shaped his thought.

Nicholas led a complex and often turbulent life. He moved among humanists and churchmen, monks and lords. Perhaps more intensely than any of his contemporaries, he engaged the Eastern Christian and Islamic traditions. Canon law and mathematics, as well as philosophy and theology, were among his intellectual concerns. His book collecting reflects this breadth, from his early discovery of classical texts to his close reading of Pseudo-Dionysius and his critical survey of the Koran. In so rich a life, scholars have identified several contexts for Nicholas's speculative work—Renaissance humanism, mystical theology, and nominalism. But underlying these varied emphases, the consensus is that Nicholas stands within the medieval Platonic tradition. This tradition, well represented in his works and library, includes Proclus, Pseudo-Dionysius, John Scottus Eriugena, Thierry of Chartres, Raymond Lull, Albert the Great, and Meister Eckhart. Viewing these thinkers as companions in wisdom's hunt, Nicholas uses their writings with freedom and originality even when citing them as authorities.

Nicholas's Platonism—with its focus on the one and the many—suggests a perspective for viewing his life and work as a whole. In his deeds and writings can be seen a continuing effort to reconcile differences into unity. His conciliarism, voyage to Constantinople, papal politics, and reform activities all sought a more perfectly united Christendom. His practical efforts yielded important successes, such as union with the Eastern church and Germany's alignment with the papacy; they also yielded the disastrous failures in Brixen. In *De Pace Fidei* he expands his integrating vision beyond Christianity to world religions. Beginning with *De Docta Ignorantia*, he sought a metaphysical and theological unity. He noted the rift between the finite and infinite and used Platonism's resources to approach infinite unity through the coincidence of opposites and a long series of conjectures. What seems "modern" in Nicholas is the way that he connects knowledge with human creativity, symbolism, and an unending approximation to a truth whose precision can never be expressed. What remains "medieval" is the direction of this entire process toward a vision in which the unknowable God is nevertheless "seen." For Nicholas, philosophy finally becomes mystical theology. Both the modern and medieval features of Nicholas's thought derive from his novel reading of the Platonic tradition, which exalts both transcendent unity and humanity's participation in that unity. Nicholas represents one of this tradition's most creative and powerful voices, one who, as his many current commentators suggest, addresses issues that remain vital today.

Letters:

"Correspondence de Nicolas de Cues avec Gaspard Aindorffer et Bernard de Waging," edited by Edmond Vansteenberghe, in *Autour de la docte ignorance: Beiträge zur Geschichte der Philosophie des Mittelalters*, volume 14 (Münster: Aschendorff, 1915), pp. 107-162;

Briefwechsel des Nikolaus von Kues, edited by Josef Koch (Heidelberg: Winter, 1944);

Das Brixener Briefbuch des Kardinals Nikolaus von Kues, edited by F. Hausmann (Heidelberg: Winter, 1952);

Das Vermächtnis des Nikolaus von Kues: Der Brief an Nikolaus Albergati nebst der Predigt in Montoliveto (1463), edited by Gerda von Bredow (Heidelberg: Winter, 1955).

Biographies:

Edmond Vansteenberghe, *Le Cardinal Nicolas de Cues (1401-1464): L'action—la pensée* (Paris: Champion, 1920; Geneva: Slatkine Reprints, 1974);

Henry Bett, *Nicholas of Cusa* (London: Methuen, 1932; Merrick, N.Y.: Richwood, 1976);

Erich Meuthen, *Nikolaus von Kues, 1401-1464: Skizze einer Biographie* (Münster: Aschendorff, 1979).

References:

American Catholic Philosophical Quarterly, special

Nicholas of Cusa issue, edited by Louis Dupré, 64 (Winter 1990);

James E. Biechler, "Christian Humanism Confronts Islam: Sifting the Qur'an with Nicholas of Cusa," *Journal of Ecumenical Studies*, 13 (Winter 1976): 1-14;

Biechler, *The Religious Language of Nicholas of Cusa* (Missoula, Mont.: Scholars Press, 1975);

Ernst Cassirer, *Individuum und Kosmos in der Philosophie der Renaissance* (Leipzig & Berlin: Teubner, 1927); translated by M. Domandi as *The Individual and the Cosmos in Renaissance Philosophy* (Oxford: Blackwell, 1963);

Gerald Christianson and Thomas M. Izbicki, eds., *Nicholas of Cusa: In Search of God and Wisdom* (Leiden: Brill, 1991);

The Commentaries of Pius II, Books VI-IX, translated by Florence A. Gragg, Smith College Studies in History, 35 (1951);

F. Edward Cranz, "Saint Augustine and Nicholas of Cusa in the Tradition of Western Christian Thought," *Speculum*, 28 (April 1953): 297-316;

Donald F. Duclow, "The Analogy of the Word: Nicholas of Cusa's Theory of Language," *Bijdragen*, 38 (September 1977): 282-299;

Mark L. Führer, "The Metaphysics of Light in the *De dato patris luminum* of Nicholas of Cusa," *International Studies in Philosophy*, 14 (1986): 17-32;

Führer, "Wisdom and Eloquence in Nicholas of Cusa's *Idiota de sapientia* and *de mente*," *Vivarium*, 16 (November 1978): 142-155;

Maurice de Gandillac, *La philosophie de Nicolas de Cues* (Paris: Editions de Montaigne, 1942);

Karsten Harries, "The Infinite Sphere: Comments on the History of a Metaphor," *Journal of the History of Philosophy*, 13 (January 1975): 5-15;

Karl Jaspers, *Die großen Philosophen* (Munich: Piper, 1957); edited by Hannah Arendt and translated by Ralph Manheim as *The Great Philosophers* (New York: Harcourt, Brace & World, 1962);

Alexandre Koyré, *From the Closed World to the Infinite Universe* (Baltimore & London: Johns Hopkins University Press, 1957);

Luis Martínez Gómez, "From the Names of God to the Name of God: Nicholas of Cusa," *International Philosophical Quarterly*, 5 (February 1965): 80-102;

Jacob Marx, *Verzeichnis der Handschriften-Sammlung des Hospitals zu Cues* (Trier: Privately printed, 1905);

Thomas P. McTighe, "Nicholas of Cusa's Theory of Science and its Metaphysical Background," in *Nicolò Cusano agli Inizi del Mondo Moderno* (Florence: Sansoni, 1970), pp. 317-338;

Erich Meuthen and Hermann Hallauer, eds., *Acta Cusana: Quellen zur Lebensgeschichte des Nikolaus von Kues*, 2 fascicles of volume 1 published (Hamburg: Meiner, 1976-);

Clyde Lee Miller, "Nicholas of Cusa's *The Vision of God*," in *An Introduction to the Mystics of Europe*, edited by Paul Szarmach (Albany: State University of New York Press, 1984);

Mitteilungen und Forschungsbeiträge der Cusanus-Gesellschaft (Mainz: Matthias-Grünewald, 1961-);

Paul E. Sigmund, *Nicholas of Cusa and Medieval Political Thought* (Cambridge, Mass.: Harvard University Press, 1963);

Donald Sullivan, "Nicholas of Cusa as Reformer: The Papal Legation to the Germanies, 1451-1452," *Mediaeval Studies*, 36 (1974): 382-428;

Pardon E. Tillinghast, "Nicholas of Cusa vs. Sigmund of Hapsburg: An Attempt at Post-conciliar Church Reform," *Church History*, 36 (December 1967): 371-390;

Morimichi Watanabe, "Nicholas of Cusa and the Tyrolese Monasteries: Reform and Resistance," *History of Political Thought*, 7 (Spring 1986): 53-72;

Watanabe, *The Political Ideas of Nicholas of Cusa with Special Reference to his De concordantia catholica* (Geneva: Librairie Droz, 1963);

Pauline M. Watts, *Nicolaus Cusanus: A Fifteenth-Century Vision of Man* (Leiden: Brill, 1982).

Manuscripts:

In his *Verzeichnis der Handschriften-Sammlung des Hospitals zu Cues* Jacob Marx describes three major manuscripts of Nicholas's writings in the library of Saint Nicholas Hospital in Bernkastel-Kues. Two (Cod. Cusanus 218 and 219) include nearly all of his speculative works; they were commissioned by Nicholas in 1462 and corrected in his own hand. The third (Cod. Cusanus 200) is an autograph manuscript containing *De Deo Abscondito* and many sermons, with notations on when and where they were preached. The Vatican Library has two manuscripts of Nicholas's sermons (Cod. Vaticanus Latinus 1244 and 1245);

Nicholas also commissioned and corrected these manuscripts. Information on other manuscripts can be found in the introductions to the Heidelberg Academy's critical edition of Nicholas's works.

William of Ockham
(Guillelmus de Ockham)

(circa 1285 - 1347)

André Goddu
Stonehill College

PRINCIPAL WORKS: *Quaestiones in Librum Quartum Sententiarum* (Commentary on the Fourth Book of the *Sentences*, written circa 1317);

Quaestiones in Librum Secundum Sententiarum (Commentary on the Second Book of the *Sentences*, written circa 1318);

Quaestiones in Librum Tertium Sententiarum (Commentary on the Third Book of the *Sentences*, written circa 1318);

Quaestiones Variae (Various Questions, written circa 1318);

Scriptum in Librum Sententiarum Ordinatio (Commentary on the *Sentences*, Ordinatio, written circa 1319-1321);

Summulae Philosophiae Naturalis (Summary of Natural Philosophy, written circa 1319-1324);

Expositio in Libros Artis Logicae (Commentaries on Logical Works, written circa 1321-1322);

Expositio super Libros Elenchorum Aristotelis (Commentary on Aristotle's *Sophistical Refutations*, written circa 1321-1322);

Expositio in Libros Physicorum Aristotelis I-IV (Commentary on Aristotle's *Physics*, Books 1-4, written 1322);

Summa Logicae (Summary of Logic, written 1322);

Expositio in Libros Physicorum Aristotelis V-VIII (Commentary on Aristotle's *Physics*, Books 5-8, written 1322);

Brevis Summa Libri Physicorum (A Short Summary of the *Physics*, written circa 1322-1323);

Quodlibeta Septem (Quodlibetal Questions, written 1322-1327);

Tractatus de Quantitate (Treatise on Quantity, written 1323);

William of Ockham, as depicted in the Franciscan Window of All Saints Church at Ockham, England. The window was designed by Lawrence Lee.

Tractatus de Corpore Christi (Treatise on the Body of Christ, written 1323);

Quaestiones in Libros Physicorum Aristotelis (Questions on Aristotle's *Physics*, written 1324);
Opus Nonaginta Dierum (Work of Ninety Days, written 1332);
Dialogus de Potestate Papae I (Dialogue on the Power of the Pope, Part 1, written 1332-1334);
Epistola ad Fratres Minores (Letter to the Friars Minor, written May 1334);
Dialogus de Potestate Papae II, also known as *De Dogmatibus Johannis XXII* (Dialogue on the Decrees of John XXII, written 1335);
Tractatus contra Johannem XII (Treatise against Pope John XII, written 1335);
Venerandorum Virorum (Of Men Worthy of Veneration, written 1335-1338);
Tractatus contra Benedictum XII (Treatise against Pope Benedict XII, written 1337);
Compendium Errorum Papae (Compendium of the Errors of the Pope, written 1337-1338);
An Princeps (On the Right of Kings, written 1338-1339);
Octo Quaestiones (Eight Questions, written 1340-1342);
Breviloquium de Principatu Tyrannico (Brief on Tyrannical Government, written 1341-1342);
Consultatio de Causa Matrimoniali (Advice on the Right of the Emperor to Dispense from an Impediment of Consanguinity, written 1341-1342);
Dialogus de Potestate Papae III (Dialogue on the Power of the Pope, Part 3); also known as *De Gestis circa Fidem Altercantium Orthodoxam* (On the Actions of Those Contesting the Orthodox Faith, written 1341-1346);
Tractatus de Imperatorum et Pontificum Potestate (Treatise on Imperial and Pontifical Power, written 1347).

EDITIONS *Libri Septem Primae Partis Dyalogorum* (Paris, 1476);
Scriptum super Primum Librum Sententiarum (Strasbourg, 1483);
Quodlibeta Septem, edited by Cornelius Oudenijk (Paris: Pierre le Rouge, 1487);
Tractatus Logicae (Paris: Johannes Higman, 1488);
Tractatus de Sacramento Altaris (Paris, circa 1490);
Opera Plurima, 4 volumes, edited by John Trechsel (Lyons, 1494-1496; reprinted, London: Gregg Press, 1962);
Summulae in Libros Physicorum, edited by Mark of Beneveto (Bologna; 1494);
Expositio Aurea, edited by Mark of Benevento (Bologna, 1496; reprinted, Ridgewood, N.Y.: Gregg Press, 1964);
Imperatoris Ludovici IIII Bavariae Ducis Sententia separationis . . . Cum consultationibus et responsis doctissimorum eius aevi virorum Marsilii de Padua et Guilhelmi Occami, edited by Marquard Freher (Heidelberg, 1598);
Monarchia Sancti Romanii Imperii, 3 volumes, edited by Melchior Goldast (Hannover: Conrad Biermann, 1611-1614; reprinted, Graz: Akademische Druck, 1960);
The De Imperatorum et Pontificum Potestate of William of Ockham, edited by C. Kenneth Brampton (Oxford: Clarendon Press, 1927);
Epistola ad Fratres Minores, edited by Brampton (Oxford: Blackwell, 1929);
Breviloquium de Potestate Papae, edited by Léon Baudry (Paris: Vrin, 1937);
Guillelmi de Ockham Opera Politica, 3 volumes published (volume 1, edited by J. G. Sikes and H. S. Offler, Manchester, U.K.: Manchester University Press, 1940; revised, 1974; volume 3, edited by Offler, Manchester, U.K.: Manchester University Press, 1956; volume 2, edited by Sikes, Offler, and R. F. Bennett, Manchester, U.K.: Manchester University Press, 1963);
The Tractatus de Praedestinatione et de Praescientia Dei et de Futuris Contingentibus of William of Ockham, edited by Philotheus Boehner (Saint Bonaventure, N.Y.: Franciscan Institute, 1945);
Expositio in Libros Artis Logicae Prooemium, Expositio in Librum Porphyrii De Praedicabilibus, edited by Ernest Moody (Saint Bonaventure, N.Y.: Franciscan Institute, 1965);
Opera Theologica, 10 volumes, edited by Gedeon Gál and others (Saint Bonaventure, N.Y.: Franciscan Institute, 1967-1986);
Opera Philosophica, 6 volumes, edited by Boehner and others (Saint Bonaventure, N.Y.: Franciscan Institute, 1974-1985).

EDITIONS IN ENGLISH: *The De Sacramento Altaris of William of Ockham: Latin Text and English Translation*, edited by T. Bruce Birch (Burlington, Iowa: Lutheran Literary Board, 1930);
Ockham: Studies and Selections, translated by Stephen Chak Tornay (La Salle, Ill.: Open Court, 1938);
Philosophical Writings: A Selection, edited and translated by Philotheus Boehner (Edinburgh &

New York: Nelson, 1957); revised and corrected by Stephen Brown (Indianapolis & Cambridge: Hackett, 1990);

Predestination, God's Foreknowledge, and Future Contingents, translated by Marilyn McCord Adams and Norman Kretzmann (New York: Appleton-Century-Crofts, 1969);

"William of Ockham's Commentary on Porphyry: Introduction and English Translation," translated by Eike-Henner W. Kluge, *Franciscan Studies*, 33 (1973): 171-254; 34 (1974): 306-382;

"Ein Selbstzeugnis Ockhams zu seinem *Dialogus*," edited by Jürgen Miethke, in *From Ockham to Wyclif*, edited by Anne Hudson and Michael Wilks (Oxford: Oxford University Press, 1987), pp. 19-30;

A Short Discourse on Tyrannical Government, edited by A. S. McGrade (Cambridge: Cambridge University Press, 1992);

Ockham's Theory of Terms, translated by Michael J. Loux (Notre Dame, Ind.: University of Notre Dame Press, 1974);

Ockham's Theory of Propositions, Part II of the Summa Logicae, translated by Alfred J. Freddoso (Notre Dame, Ind.: University of Notre Dame Press, 1980);

Ockham on Aristotle's Physics, translated by Julian Davies (Saint Bonaventure, N.Y.: Franciscan Institute, 1989);

Quodlibetal Questions, 2 volumes, translated by Freddoso and Francis E. Kelley (New Haven: Yale University Press, 1991).

William of Ockham holds the distinction of being the most rejected but influential philosopher-theologian of the fourteenth century. His ideas have been the subject of revisionist assessments ever since that time. In some circles he continues to be a bête noire, in others a harbinger of modern advances in the philosophical analysis of language, nature, and society.

William was born around 1285 in the town of Ockham (probably modern-day Woking) in Surrey. Around the age of twelve he entered the Franciscan friary, probably at London. He would have spent his first year in novitiate, and then he would have undertaken his eight-year study of philosophy. In 1306 he was ordained subdeacon at Southwark, London, in the archdiocese of Winchester. Probably around 1306-1307 he began the study of theology at Oxford. His first six years would have been spent attending lectures on the Bible and the *Libri Quatuor Sententiarum* (Four Books of *Sentences*, 1157-1158) of Peter Lombard; during the next three years he would have engaged in theological disputations and responsions. In 1318 he was presented to the bishop of Lincoln for permission to hear confessions. Ockham had begun his lectures on the *Sentences* in 1317 and completed them in 1319, at which time he was recognized as an "inceptor," the Oxford equivalent of a Parisian bachelor of theology and the reason for references to him as the "Venerable Inceptor." Because of his youth and because only one bachelor could go on in theology at Oxford, he was unable to complete his theological education at this time.

In 1321 Ockham may have returned to the London friary to teach philosophy, or he may have remained in Oxford. In 1324, as the result of charges of heresy brought by the former chancellor of Oxford, John Lutterell, Ockham was summoned to Avignon to face a theological commission. He remained in Avignon for four years while the commission investigated the charges. Although no formal action was taken, Ockham's academic career was at an end: he did not serve a term as a regent master, and he was never promoted to master of theology.

It seems probable that Ockham's nonpolemical treatises were composed between 1317 and 1327: Commentaries on the *Sentences* (1317-1321), *Summulae Philosophiae Naturalis* (Summary of Natural Philosophy, circa 1319-1324), *Expositio in Libros Artis Logicae* (Commentaries on Logical Works, circa 1321-1322), *Expositio super Libros Elenchorum Aristotelis* (Commentary on Aristotle's *Sophistical Refutations*, circa 1321-1322), *Expositio in Libros Physicorum Aristotelis I-IV* (Commentary on Aristotle's *Physics*, Books 1-4, 1322), *Summa Logicae* (Summary of Logic, 1322), *Expositio in Libros Physicorum Aristotelis V-VIII* (Commentary on Aristotle's *Physics*, Books 5-8, 1322), *Brevis Summa Libri Physicorum* (A Short Summary of the *Physics*, circa 1322-1323), *Tractatus de Quantitate* (Treatise on Quantity, 1323), *Tractatus de Corpore Christi* (Treatise on the Body of Christ, 1323), *Quaestiones in Libros Physicorum Aristotelis* (Questions on Aristotle's *Physics*, 1324), and *Quodlibeta Septem* (Quodlibetal Questions, 1322-1327). On the basis of these works one may conclude that several issues were of burning moment to Ockham as early as 1317: traditional debates about substantial and accidental forms, the traditional doctrine of intelligible and sensible species, concern with contextual features of language, and the problems of necessity and of the indepen-

First page of a manuscript for Ockham's Summa Logicae, *dated 1341 (Gonville & Caius College MS 464/571 f.1r; published with permission of the Master and Fellows of Gonville & Caius College, Cambridge)*

dent existence of acts and relations. On these issues he was likely influenced at least indirectly by such thinkers as Robert Grosseteste, Roger Bacon, Peter John Olivi, John Duns Scotus, and Walter Burley. Ockham recognized that many debates centered around "entities" whose existence could be doubted without loss of explanatory power. He seems to have regarded theoretical completeness alone as an insufficient warrant for assuming the existence of particular entities. This is the principle of parsimony now known as "Ockham's razor." Nowhere, however, does Ockham refer to a razor, nor does the adage usually attributed to him—"Entities should not be multiplied without necessity"—occur in his works. Ockham does say: "It is useless to do with more what can be done with fewer"; "Plurality should not be assumed without necessity"; "When a proposition is verified of things, if two things suffice for its truth, it is superfluous to assume a third"; "No plurality should be assumed unless it can be proved by reason, experience, or infallible authority." The one significant exception that Ockham makes in the application of this principle is in theology, where he maintains that God does many things with more that he could do with fewer, especially in matters concerning salvation: God's freedom is not restricted by the principle of parsimony. Ockham attempted to incorporate the ideas of his predecessors into a comparatively reductionist doctrine of form and matter; but his efforts were certainly not successful in the *Summulae Philosophiae Naturalis*, and reactions to his more expanded efforts provide abundant evidence that he was misunderstood. Some of Ockham's ideas were premature.

What distinguishes Ockham stylistically from his many prolix predecessors and successors is his occasionally excessive talent for uncovering the central issues and critiquing them incisively. His own solutions, when he offers them at all, are often sketchy and disappointing. He possessed the mind of a gadfly; his mission was to provoke inquiry and suggest the limits for correct solutions, not provide solutions himself. If the Commentaries on the *Sentences* and his early philosophical works provide any indication of Ockham's procedure in the classroom, one can well imagine that some students found him refreshing and brilliant while others were perplexed and dismayed.

Ockham was an individual of extraordinary self-confidence and ambition, and of some arrogance. His boldness and abrasiveness are startling as he dismisses an argument of no less a figure than Thomas Aquinas as puerile, rejects the theory of impetus summarily and derisively, and rarely misses an opportunity to expose a howler in the logic of an opponent. On the other hand, Ockham often shows himself flexible enough to change his mind, revise an argument, or confess to a dilemma in the face of a telling criticism.

Still, it is the abrasive, and occasionally abusive, Ockham who stands out from the text, and one can speculate that this was the Ockham who so incensed Lutterell that the latter went to Avignon and presented to the papacy a list of Ockham's allegedly heretical views that was so slovenly in its execution that the commission appointed to examine his complaint had to put it into some kind of intelligible order. Ockham's views were known by his contemporaries primarily from his early treatises; it is virtually certain that the versions of texts that he took with him to Avignon and his final version of the *Quodlibeta Septem* were unknown to his English, French, and probably Italian contemporaries, and perhaps not known in the fourteenth century at all; the *Quodlibeta Septem* began to influence the presentation of Ockham's philosophical and theological views for the first time in the twentieth century. Hence there are at least two Ockhams: the Ockham known in the fourteenth century and the complete Ockham. In his nonpolemical treatises through 1327 Ockham remained basically Aristotelian in his ontology. His deviations from Aristotle are occasionally striking and significant, but they are often efforts to reconcile the Aristotelian text, as Ockham understood it, with contemporaneous learning or belief.

Theology, Ockham says, is not a demonstrative science. Though not demonstrable, traditional theological beliefs are true, certain, and necessary. Theologians bent on proving the rationality of faith endanger both reliance on revealed truth and the integrity of demonstrative science. Reliance on revealed truth has to do in part with receptivity to the divine will and divine commands, with humility, and with a corresponding sensitivity to the human capacity for self-deception, arrogance, and lust for power. Ockham cites texts in Scripture (Abraham and Isaac, the simple faith of Jesus' mother) that challenge humanity's deepest natural beliefs and defy common sense. Such texts, he says, do not support the conclusion that religious faith is irrational, but they do constitute serious challenges for theologians.

Ockham believed that certain knowledge can be derived from Scripture, but he displayed admirable caution over the human capacity to arrive at natural knowledge about God. Like all orthodox medieval Christian philosopher-theologians he allowed his theological commitments to restrict his philosophical principles.

According to Ockham's account of knowledge, cognitions are caused partly by the intellect and the senses and partly by objects. Intuitive cognitions cause existential and other contingent judgments; abstractive cognitions are the source of general and universal knowledge. Perfect intuitive cognition is of an existent and is naturally caused by the existent, or is of a nonexistent and is supernaturally caused (with God as partial cause) by the nonexistent (that is, it is cognition that the "object" does not exist), or is of an absent existent and is supernaturally caused by the absent existent (that is, it is cognition that the object exists but is not present). Imperfect intuitive cognition is of a past existent causing assent that something did exist, or a future existent causing assent that something will exist.

Ockham's "empiricism" is revealed in his tolerance for incompleteness in explanation as well as in his commitment to the principle of parsimony. He regarded even the tendency to superfluity as fatal, perhaps because it engenders bad habits—jumping to conclusions, achieving closure prematurely, relaxing critical tests, and the like. The danger in inflationary accounts lies in their dissipation of the energy that is generated by genuine problems. Ockham's account of perception exemplifies both his empiricist inclinations and his effort at a synthesis of standard accounts. In his theory of vision, for example, Ockham tried to mediate between the Aristotelian and "perspectivist" accounts. In the Aristotelian account, a source of illumination such as fire or the sun instantaneously actualizes a potentially transparent medium. The perspectivist account, on the other hand, posited the multiplication of species (forms of objects) along three-dimensional lines of radiation joining a point in the visual field with a point in the eye. Ockham denied the existence of visual species and, accordingly, denied their multiplication through the medium. Ockham's causal account of vision permitted him to explain perceptual errors, illusions, doubts, and the like.

There is hardly a text where Ockham's effort to reduce talk about particular existing things to individual substances and qualities does not generate severe problems in ontology, logic, and semantics. One of the clearest examples occurs in Ockham's refutation of Zeno's paradoxes of motion. The consequence of the refutation is that motions are neither substances nor qualities; and yet motions are not nonexistent. There are many conditions, states, and relations in which things exist. Propositions that assert such conditions, states, and relations do not assert the existence of any *thing* beyond the substance or quality, but they do assert *ways* in which substances and qualities exist. Ockham resisted thinking of ways or modes of being as real things distinct from their subjects; he treated them syntactically, as adverbs, or by way of circumlocution. He says that time and place, for example, do not exist, and yet that it is not correct to say without qualification that they do not exist. The attribution of existence to time and place is mind-dependent in ways that the judgment of the existence of an object is not. The existence of an object is a partial cause of the apprehension of the object, while the existence of a place is not apprehended directly but is inferred: when we conceive a physical object, we conceive it as extended in space and hence as occupying a place. There is no time without measure, and measuring requires the mind to make comparisons and hence to do more than simply apprehend. The cognitions of place and time, then, are abstractive and dependent on the intuitive apprehensions of existing things. While the judgment that place and time are accidents inhering in things may seem innocuous, the implication that they are distinct from the things in which they inhere has philosophical consequences that Ockham considered pernicious. In those theological cases where he accepts the real distinction of accidents from subjects, Ockham's view is that this distinction would not be known without revelation. To allow such revelation into philosophy would violate the integrity of philosophy and its independence from theology.

Ockham's ethical theory has also been the subject of vigorous debate. Some have attributed to Ockham a radical form of voluntarism that leaves ethical choice without any rational foundation at all, whether in natural law or in right reason. According to this line of reasoning, Ockham held an authoritarian divine-command theory that attributes to God a completely arbitrary power to dictate right and wrong and that God can exercise his arbitrary power at any time he chooses. Others have argued in behalf of a more Aristotelian reading of Ockham's ethical theory.

The fortress-palace of the popes at Avignon. Ockham spent four years in Avignon while a theological commission investigated charges of heresy that had been brought against him.

According to this reading, Ockham adopted an Aristotelian right-reason theory modified by a divine-legislation theory of eternal destiny. Such an account emphasizes some limitations on God's power, but the result seems to be little different from a modified divine-command theory. The Aristotelian reading has refuted the radical voluntarist interpretation, but in doing so it has not produced a satisfactory account of Ockham's emphasis on divine freedom. This interpretation also has the consequence that it minimizes Ockham's emphasis on the distinction between God's absolute power and God's ordained power. In several texts Ockham adopts a clearly unmodified divine-command theory. When God commanded Abraham to sacrifice Isaac, did he not command Abraham to act against his deepest inclinations? Is the point of this story that God stayed the hand of Abraham, or that Abraham was willing to obey a command from God even in such an extreme case? Ockham maintains the absoluteness of God's power to dictate right and wrong. But Ockham also recognizes God's self-limiting actions and generosity. When God stayed the hand of Abraham, he did so out of generosity. Similarly, God's covenants (including conformity to right reason) are the result of his generosity, actions that fall under God's ordained power. Accordingly, it is much more in conformity with Ockham's emphasis and distinctions to attribute to him an unmodified divine-command theory considered from the point of view of God's absolute power, and a modified divine-command theory considered from the point of view of God's ordained power.

Ockham distinguishes three kinds of natural law: absolute, unchanging natural law in conformity with infallible natural reason; natural law as it obtained prior to the Fall; and natural law *ex suppositione*, that is, a law which arises in response to a violation of natural law or as a recognition of or concession to a contingent state of affairs. Natural laws of the first kind appear to be unchangeable except through an intervention by God himself. There is an order to which human reason conforms; this order seems immune to change without an essential change in human nature. That is, even prior to the Fall, fornication and lying were wrong. As matters now stand after the Fall, private property seems to conform to natural law. But Ockham's view is that natural law prior to the Fall dictated common ownership of property. Even though it was the Fall that led to private property, Ockham acknowledges the apparent conformity of private property with natural law by distinguishing what natural law permits from what natural law dictates. Natural law permits private property; it does not dictate it. It is this permissive sense of natural law that Ockham designates as natural law of the second type. By contrast, natural laws of the third type include concessions to fallen human nature, such as the right of self-defense, and positive laws because they address contingent circumstances or local needs. The right of self-defense is a law of the third kind because it conforms to natural reason as a response to an unjust use of violence. The procedure for the election of a pope is also a law of the third type because it is a recognition of a contingent state of affairs, the selection of Rome as the see of Saint Peter. Laws addressing contingent circumstances or local needs should not be extended to the whole of humankind.

The distinction between God's absolute and ordained powers provokes questions about God's identity, unity, simplicity, and attributes. The divine attributes cannot refer to anything really distinct in God, for God is absolutely simple. With the exception of the Persons of the Trinity, there are no distinctions in God. God's knowledge is identical with his essence.

A cause, according to Ockham, is that which posited, all else destroyed, the effect follows, and which not posited, whatever else posited, the effect does not follow. The exclusive total sufficient cause of an effect is that which can produce an effect and without which the effect cannot be produced. An essential cause is that which, if posited, the effect *could* follow. An accidental cause acts by means of an essential cause of which it is a part. If an accidental cause is posited, the effect occurs; but if it is not posited the effect could still occur as long as the essential cause remains. Finally, by prior cause Ockham means some thing or condition that obtains before an effect occurs without causing the effect; a prior cause, then, is not a true cause but indicates a reason why an effect does *not* occur. A cause sine qua non is a necessary condition for an effect to be produced, but it is not a true cause because it is not productive of an effect: a cause sine qua non is a hindrance which must be removed before the true cause can act effectively. Theological or sacramental causes are sine qua non because they express a necessary condition for the production of grace, but the true cause of that effect is God himself. Ockham sometimes speaks of natural causes as sine qua non; for example, he regards the illuminated medium as a cause sine qua non. In such cases, however, he does not regard them as true causes. Theological causes are *only* sine qua non and, hence, are never true causes.

In his commentary on book 3, question 7 of the *Sentences* Ockham considers the problem of the responsibility of the will in the face of certain natural inclinations. Sin is excused in a case where the inclination is like that of weight downwards. Since, however, Ockham found the supposition of a will that is totally caused by a created cause inconsistent with the freedom of the will, he concluded that the act is caused partially by the habit and partially by the will. Ockham allowed one exception to the principle that freedom and compulsion are compatible: God could cause such an act totally, and the implication is that God could do it without compromising the freedom of the will.

In 1328 Ockham's superior, Michael of Cesena, minister general of the Franciscans, asked him to examine three papal constitutions. Ockham denounced them as containing assertions that were "heretical, erroneous, foolish, ridiculous, fantastic, senseless, defamatory, and equally contrary and patently adverse to the orthodox faith, sound morality, natural reason, certain experience, and fraternal charity." Pope John XXII had condemned the doctrine of the absolute poverty of Jesus and the apostles and had threatened to dissolve the legal distinction between use and ownership, all of which had been confirmed by Pope Nicholas III, approved by Bonaventure, and accepted by the most moderate Franciscans. The commission examining his own works had completed its task, and it regarded some of Ockham's views as heretical and potentially dangerous. Ockham's defense apparently involved the standard strategy of showing that he had been misquoted, providing more extensive texts, denying that some of the questioned statements represented his views, and attacking the logical competence of his accusers. The defense seems to have been ineffective.

Perhaps anticipating an unfavorable outcome, on the night of 26 May 1328 Ockham left Avignon with Michael of Cesena, Bonagratia of Bergamo, and, apparently, Francis of Ascoli. A ship, sent in all likelihood by Genoese Ghibellines, picked up the group at Aigues-Mortes and took them to Pisa. Ludwig of Bavaria had been engaged for some time in an effort to secure his position as Holy Roman emperor. Unable to hold Rome, he retreated northward in August and met with Michael of Cesena and his group in Pisa. Ludwig greeted these new opponents of the pope with open arms. In September, Ludwig extended his protection officially to the Franciscans. For the time being this relationship was a marriage of necessity; only later did the rebellious Franciscans become ideological supporters of the emperor. The pope removed Michael from his position as minister general and also removed all of the provincial ministers suspected

Sketch of a monk, with an inscription indicating that it is Ockham who is depicted, on the last page of a manuscript of Ockham's Summa Logicae *(Gonville & Caius College MS 464/571 f.69r; published with permission of the Master and Fellows of Gonville & Caius College, Cambridge)*

of sympathizing with him. Michael, Ockham, Bonagratia, and Francis were charged with apostasy and excommunicated.

By 1330 Ockham was settled at the Franciscan friary in Munich. For the next seventeen years the dispute that had begun over Franciscan poverty and questions about the pope's orthodoxy expanded into original analyses of the nature of the church, of the relation of church and state, and of natural law. Ockham apparently viewed his excommunication as invalid; he continued to profess himself a faithful Catholic, indicating his willingness to recognize legitimate authority. In his polemical treatises he carefully studied papal documents, assessed their use of Scripture and their logical validity, and proposed solutions consistent with tradition as he understood it. In view of Ockham's sharp wit, his often terse dismissal of his opponents' views in his nonpolemical works, and his assessment of John XXII's legal and theological opinions, one would hardly expect him to be reserved in his polemical works. But while the earliest polemical works, written in a state of agitation, are at times insulting—once Ockham refers to John XXII as a quarrelsome lawyer—by comparison with the polemics of others Ockham's texts are remarkable for their objectivity. The massive *Dialogus de Potestate Papae* (Dialogue on the Power of the Pope, 1332-1346), especially part 3, is a model of academic neutrality, reasoned argumentation, prudential moderation and restraint.

The political works include *Opus Nonaginta Dierum* (Work of Ninety Days, 1332), *Epistola ad Fratres Minores* (Letter to the Friars Minor, May 1334), *Tractatus contra Johannem XXII* (Treatise against Pope John XXII, 1335), and *Venerandorum Virorum* (Of Men Worthy of Veneration, 1335-1338). Except for the last text (if it is authentic), there was a pause between 1335 and 1337. The reason was John XXII's death in 1334 and Ockham's hope for reconciliation with the new pope, Benedict XII. The war between England and France that erupted in 1337 complicated the negotiations between the emperor and the pope, which broke down early in that year. Ockham's political treatises resumed in 1337: *Tractatus contra Benedictum XII* (Treatise against Pope Benedict XII, 1337), *Compendium Errorum Papae* (Compendium of the Errors of the Pope, 1337-1338), *An Princeps* (On the Right of Kings, 1338-1339), *Octo Quaestiones* (Eight Questions, 1340-1342), *Breviloquium de Principatu Tyrannico* (Brief on Tyrannical Government, 1341-1342), *Consultatio de Causa Matrimoniali* (Advice on the Right of the Emperor to Dispense from an Impediment of Consanguinity, 1341-1342), and *Tractatus de Imperatorum et Pontificum Potestate* (Treatise on Imperial and Pontifical Power, 1347).

Ockham's early political works are in the disputative style, but he quickly adopted the far more subtle dialogue form. The *Dialogus de Potestate Papae* makes a self-conscious break with its polemical antecedents by virtue of its systematic, comprehensive, and definitive character. Like the nonpolemical works—but to an even higher degree—it and the last treatise present a comprehensive arrangement of options with their logical limits clearly outlined. In addition to the external dialectic of the contemporary sociopolitical scene, Ockham leads the reader through a process of internal dialectic that will drive him to his own view, within limits carefully delineated by

Ockham. Although Ockham's views are clear from other treatises, the dialectical procedure does generate some uncertainty; here one encounters the penetration and sensitivity of a mind convinced of the correctness of its own conclusions but ever alert to the tension between truth as goal and truth as apprehended. Whereas the former is whole, eternal, and unchanging, the latter is partial, time-dependent, and evolutionary. In this distinction one may find the import of Ockham's academic and objective deportment, on the one hand, and the engaged controversialist who consistently opposed doctrinaire authoritarianism, on the other.

Ockham died in 1347 and was buried in the cemetery of the Franciscan friary at Munich, which is now the site of the Bavarian National Theater. At the bottom of the stairs to the garage nearest the front entrance of the theater there is a plaque commemorating Ockham and others.

When Ockham died, a few months prior to Ludwig's death, the cause to which he had committed himself—the struggle against the pretensions of the papacy to universal secular power—appeared desperate if not lost. In retrospect it can be seen that the church had already lost that battle for all practical purposes, but at the end of his life Ockham saw his decision to carry on the struggle and warn Christians of the likely outcome of papal authoritarianism as a solemn obligation. Ockham concluded on behalf of his fellow Franciscans that their silence would have left them open to the reproach that "the 'word of God is bound' [2 Tim. 2: 9] in their mouths, 'they are dumb dogs unable to bark' " [Isa. 56:10].

Bibliographies:

Franz Federhofer, "Ein Beitrag zur Bibliographie und Biographie des Wilhem von Ockham," *Philosophisches Jahrbuch*, 38 (1925): 25-48;

Valens Heynck, "Ockham-Literatur 1919-1949," *Franziskanische Studien*, 32, no. 1/2 (1950): 164-183;

James Reilly, "Ockham Bibliography, 1950-1967," *Franciscan Studies*, 28 (1968): 197-214.

Biography:

León Baudry, *Guillaume d'Occam: Sa vie, ses oeuvres, ses idées sociales et politiques*, volume 1: *L'homme et les oeuvres*, Etudes de Philosophie Médiévales, 39 (Paris: Vrin, 1949).

References:

Marilyn McCord Adams, *William Ockham*, 2 volumes (Notre Dame, Ind.: University of Notre Dame Press, 1987);

Otl Aicher, Gabriele Greindl, and Wilhelm Vossenkuhl, *Wilhelm von Ockham: Das Risiko modern zu denken* (Munich: Callwey, 1986);

Philotheus Boehner, *Collected Articles on Ockham*, edited by Eligius Buytaert (Saint Bonaventure, N.Y.: Franciscan Institute, 1958);

Stephen Brown, "A Modern Prologue to Ockham's Natural Philosophy," in *Sprache und Erkenntnis im Mittelalter*, edited by Albert Zimmermann, Miscellanea Mediaevalia, 13, no. 1 (Berlin: DeGruyter, 1981): 107-129;

Stefano Caroti, ed., *Studies in Medieval Natural Philosophy*, Biblioteca de Nuncius, Studi e Testi, 1 (Florence: Olschki, 1989);

Alfred B. Emden, *A Biographical Register of the University of Oxford to A.D. 1500*, volume 2 (Oxford: Clarendon Press, 1958) pp. 1384-1387;

Lucan Freppert, *The Basis of Morality according to William Ockham* (Chicago: Franciscan Herald Press, 1988);

Gedeon Gál, "William of Ockham Died 'Impenitent' in April 1347," *Franciscan Studies*, 42 (1982): 90-95;

Alessandro Ghisalberti, *Guglielmo di Ockham* (Milan: Università Cattolica del Sacro Cuore, 1972);

André Goddu, *The Physics of William of Ockham*, Studien und Texte zur Geistesgeschichte des Mittelalters, 16 (Leiden & Cologne: Brill, 1984);

Johannes Hofer, "Biographische Studien über Wilhelm von Ockham OFM," *Archivum Franciscanum Historicum*, 6 (1913): 209-233, 439-465, 654-669;

Helmar Junghans, *Ockham im Lichte der neueren Forschung*, Arbeiten zur Geschichte und Theologie des Luthertums, 21 (Berlin & Hamburg: Lutherisches Verlagshaus, 1968);

Wilhelm Kölmel, *Wilhelm Ockham und seine kirchenpolitischen Schriften* (Essen: Ludgerus, 1962);

Gottfried Martin, "Ist Ockhams Relationstheorie Nominalismus?," *Franziskanische Studien*, 32 (1950): 31-49;

Martin, *Wilhelm von Ockham* (Berlin: De Gruyter, 1949);

Arthur S. McGrade, *The Political Thought of William of Ockham*, Cambridge Studies in Medieval Life and Thought, third series 7 (Cambridge: Cambridge University Press, 1974);

Jürgen Miethke, *Ockhams Weg zur Sozialphilosophie* (Berlin: De Gruyter, 1969);

Calvin Normore, "Ockham on Mental Language," in *Historical Foundations of Cognitive Science*, edited by J.-C. Smith (Dordrecht: Kluwer, 1990), pp. 53-70;

Claude Panaccio, *Connotative Terms in Ockham's Mental Language*, Cahiers d'épitémologie, no. 9016 (Montreal: University of Quebec, 1990);

Rolf Schönberger and Wilhelm Vossenkuhl, eds., *Die Gegenwart Ockhams* (Mannheim: VCH, 1990);

Paul Vincent Spade, "Ockham's Distinctions between Absolute and Connotative Terms," *Vivarium*, 13 (May 1975): 55-76.

Manuscripts:

The oldest and most reliable manuscripts of Ockham's nonpolemical treatises are found in Florence, Paris, Rome, Oxford, Cambridge, and Munich. The manuscripts of the political works are somewhat rarer, some preserved in only one extant copy. The most important of these manuscripts are in the Bibliothèque Nationale at Paris, in the Vatican, at Oxford University, Avignon, Basel, Bremen, Frankfurt am Main, Koblenz, and Ulm. Two manuscripts of the *Dialogus de Potestate Papae* are Paris, BN lat. 14313 and Rome, Vatican lat. 4115.

Peter of Spain (Petrus Hispanus)

(circa 1205 - 20 May 1277)

John Longeway
University of Wisconsin—Parkside

PRINCIPAL WORKS: *Tractatus* (Treatise, written circa 1230);

Tractatus Syncategorematum (Treatise on Syncategorematic Terms, written circa 1230?);

Expositio Libri Sancti Dionysii (Exposition of the Books of Saint [Pseudo-] Dionysius the Areopagite, 1246-1250?);

In De Anima (Commentary on [Aristotle's] *On the Soul*, written before 1258);

Expositio Libri De Anima et Parva Naturalia (Exposition of the Book *On the Soul* and the Smaller Natural Treatises, written before 1258);

Scientia Libri De Anima (The Science of the Books *On the Soul*, written before 1258);

Thesaurus Pauperum (Treasury for the Poor, written 1272);

Summa de Conservanda Sanitate (On the Preservation of Health, date of composition unknown);

Liber de Morbis Oculorum (On Diseases of the Eye, date of composition unknown).

EDITIONS: *Textus Summularum* (Alosti: Joannes de Westphalia & Theodoricus Martini, 1474);

Tractatus et Tractatus Exponibilium cum Commento (Antwerp, 1487);

Thesaurus Pauperum (Antwerp: T. Martin, 1497);

Die Ophthalmologie des Petrus Hispanus mit deutscher Übersetzung und Kommentar, edited by Albrecht Maria Berger (Munich: Lehmann, 1899);

Pedro Hispano: Obras filosóficas, 3 volumes, edited by Manuel Alonso (Madrid: Consejo Superior de Investigaciones Científicas, Instituto de Filosofico "Luis Vives," 1941-1952);

Petri Hispani Summulae Logicales quas e codice manuscripto Reg. lat. 1205, edited by Innocentius M. Bocheński (Turin: Marietti, 1947);

Exposição sobre os livros do Beato Dionisio Areopagita, edited by Alonso (Lisbon: Instituto de alta cultura, 1957);

Tractatus, Called Afterwards Summule logicales, edited by L. M. de Rijk (Assen: Van Gorcum, 1972);

Obras Medicas de Pedro Hispano, edited by Maria Helena da Rocha Pereira (Coimbra por ordem da Universidade de Coimbra, 1973).

EDITIONS IN ENGLISH: *The Summulae Logicales of Peter of Spain*, translated by Joseph P. Mullally, Publications in Medieval Studies, 8 (Notre Dame, Ind.: University of Notre Dame Press, 1945);

Peter of Spain: Tractatus Syncategorematum and Selected Anonymous Treatises, translated by Mullally and Roland Houde, Medieval Philosophical Texts in Translation, 13 (Milwaukee: Marquette University Press, 1964);

Peter of Spain on Composition and Negation, edited and translated by Joke Spruyt (Nijmegen, Netherlands: Ingenium, 1989);

Peter of Spain: Language in Dispute. An English Translation of Peter of Spain's Tractatus Called Afterwards Summulae Logicales, translated by Francis P. Dinneen (Philadelphia: Benjamins, 1990).

Peter of Spain was born in Lisbon, Portugal, probably around 1205, or a bit earlier. It is likely that his father, Rebolo Julianus, was a nobleman and a man of some wealth. Peter studied the arts at the University of Paris "for many years," by his own report, presumably for a longer time than required by the curriculum. He was probably at Paris from about the age of fifteen, when one usually began attendance at the university in those days. It has been pointed out that he promised himself a long pontificate when elected pope in 1277, which might seem to count against such an early birth; but the basis of this expectation was his medical skill, not his youth.

Generally six years were required to finish the arts curriculum, so he would have taken up theology in 1226 if he were on schedule; but it seems possible that he was late beginning his theological studies and commenced or completed them somewhere outside Paris. Some scholars have supposed that he might have studied under Thomas Aquinas, but both the dates of his stay at Paris and Peter's doctrine count decisively against this assumption. The view that Peter was influenced in his logic by William of Sherwood is certainly to be rejected, too: certain fundamental views of the two logicians are at variance, reflecting the different traditions at Paris and Oxford; and Peter was at Paris too early to be influenced by William, who would have been there, if he was ever there at all, around 1240-1248. (The earlier error of Carl Prantl, making Peter of Spain's work a Latin translation of a Greek compendium of logic by the Byzantine Michael Psellos, was decisively refuted by Valentin Rose, Charles Thurot, and Richard Stapper. In fact, Psellos's work is a translation of Peter's.) Peter might have studied logic under John Pagus and Hervaeus Brito, the great masters at Paris in the 1220s. In theology he may have studied under Alexander of Hales, one of the first to teach the *Sentences* of Peter Lombard (approved for study by the Lateran Council in 1215), and under William of Auxerre and William of Auvergne.

Peter left Paris in 1229 and spent the next four years or so in the north of Spain. He no doubt left Paris with the general exodus of masters and pupils that year, in protest against the punishment by the civil authorities of certain innocent students for crimes known to have been committed by their companions. The other members of the university did not return to the city until the beginning of 1231.

Peter became professor of medicine at the new university in Siena in 1245. It can be surmised that he studied medicine outside Paris between 1235 and 1245. The Universities of Montpellier and Salerno had the most notable medical schools at this time. An additional clue to Peter's presence in the south of France in these years is the fact that the two earliest commentaries on his *Tractatus* (Treatise, circa 1230) were produced in the 1240s by Robert Anglicus at Montpellier and William Arnaldus at Toulouse. These commentaries were the outcome of teaching the text, and it seems quite possible that Robert Anglicus was lecturing on the *Tractatus* at Montpellier as Peter himself studied or taught medicine at the same university.

From 1250 to 1272 Peter lived mostly in Lisbon, enjoying various preferments and offices and attending the Cortes (Parliament) of Guimarães in the north of Portugal in 1250 and 1258 and the Cortes of Leiria in 1254. He made brief visits to Italy in 1260 and 1261 to attend the papal court. In 1263 he became *magister scholarum* of the cathedral school at Lisbon.

It was while he was in Salerno or Portugal, certainly before 1258, that Peter wrote his works

Illustration by Giovanni di Paolo from a mid-fifteenth-century manuscript for Canto XII of Dante's Paradiso, *in which Saint Bonaventure mentions "Peter of Spain, who down below shines in twelve books." In the picture, Bonaventure is shown hovering at the top, speaking to Dante and Beatrice; the figure at the far right is thought to be Peter of Spain (British Museum, Yates Thompson MS. 36, f. 151r)*

on the soul. They betray a deeply biological interest in the topic. One question considered is why the soul, in itself a unity and the form of the body, gives rise to a variety of organs. The answer, Peter holds, is that the soul has a variety of powers, and although these powers can be held in a unity immaterially, they require different organs if they are to be realized in matter. Thus the sensitive power of an animal soul requires sense organs, the power of ruling the body (*virtus regitiva*) requires limbs and muscles, and the vital power requires a heart and organs of respiration. The pattern of Peter's argument could easily have been founded on Robert Grosseteste's rather Neoplatonic notion of scientific demonstration in his commentary (circa 1230) on the *Posterior Analytics* of Aristotle, for Grosseteste argues that the highest sort of demonstration proceeds from the unity of a form, deducing how its powers and properties can be realized in an extended, complex structure or series of events in the natural world.

Peter's place in the dispute over the potential and agent intellects is typical of Augustinian scholars of the first half of the thirteenth century, and is, again, reminiscent of Grosseteste. The dispute arose because Aristotle, in an obscure passage in book 3, chapter 5 of his *On the Soul*, was thought by Arabic interpreters to have argued that the intellect must be divided into a potential intellect within the soul, which receives the immaterial conception of whatever it is brought to understand, and the agent intellect, which places that form in the potential intellect but is separate from the individual soul and enjoys an eternal existence. Avicenna held that the potential intellect was the highest part of the human soul, a spiritual substance accidentally joined to the body as its form, while the agent intellect was a single intelligence that contained all forms within it and transmitted them into those individual potential intellects that were disposed by their circumstances to receive them. The view is fundamentally Neoplatonist, positing a realm of forms which acts on individual human intellects. Christian thought absorbed this Avicennian view at first but repudiated the opinion of Averroës, who placed both agent and potential intellect outside the soul. The Averroist position suggested that the individual human soul was not in its nature immortal, since the standard arguments, ultimately rooted in Plato's *Phaedo*, depend on the presence in the soul of an intellect that participates in the eternity of the forms it apprehends. In the thirteenth century Avicenna was rejected as well as Averroës, and it came to be insisted that both the agent and the potential intellects are present in the individual human soul. This view is generally associated with the position, characteristic of Thomas Aquinas, that the human intellect is capable by its own nature of abstracting forms from sensible intuitions of individuals, without assistance from an outside agent intellect.

Peter of Spain's view in his *Scientia Libri De Anima* (The Science of the Books *On the Soul*, before 1258), which represents his most mature

The papal lodge at Viterbo. Peter, who by then had become Pope John XXI, died here on 20 May 1277, six days after the roof of his apartment fell on him.

thought, is that the agent intellect within the soul is adapted only to the understanding of forms as they occur in nature and cannot free itself from the material conditions under which these forms must realize themselves in nature, so that a second agent intellect external to the soul is required for scientific knowledge. This separate agent intellect is God. Using a simile rooted in Augustine and also to be found in Grosseteste, Peter argues that just as light makes the colors of material things to be actually visible, so that they can act on the passive power of vision, so an intellectual light is needed to make the forms of natural objects "visible" to the potential intellect. The agent intellect within the soul has the function of separating out the intelligible form of a natural object from the complex of sensitive perception in which it is embedded, so that the potential intellect may see it. The separated agent intellect then illuminates the intelligible form so that it is actually seen. When the soul is separated from the body after this life, the agent intellect outside the soul (God) acts on the soul directly, producing a vision of the forms as they are prior to their realization in the natural world; but such a direct vision is impossible in this life, and it is only through sensory experience of objects illumined by the separated agent intellect that the soul is able to grasp a natural form and gain knowledge of a thing.

The soul is an incorporeal substance joined to and providing life to a body. Its incorporeal nature is evident from its intellective grasp of immaterial things and of the forms of material things in their immaterial aspect, prior to their being realized as material particulars. The soul's intellective power is not a product of natural processes but is created directly by God. Some powers of the soul, being entirely material, could be generated naturally. The development of the fetus before the soul is infused into it is a preparation for life; as soon as the body is suited to receive the soul, it does so, in that instant becoming actually, and not merely potentially, a human body for the first time. During this development toward life the purely bodily powers of the soul are present potentially, though by a potency closer to actuality than before the fetus was formed, and are awaiting subordination to the intellectual soul. The body, Peter says, is rather like a machine, which is only potentially what it is before it is actually used by someone. Peter's views, then, are of the Neoplatonic, Augustinian-Avicennian sort prevalent in the first half of the thirteenth century. Although he shows no awareness of the controversy, he would no doubt have been unhappy with the radical Aristotelian insistence on the unicity of substantial forms, in particular of the human soul, and the suspicion such views would cast on the adequacy of his own view of the unity of the human soul and its status as the form of the body.

In 1272 Peter was summoned to Viterbo to become court physician to Pope Gregory X. It was probably in that year that he wrote the *Thesaurus Pauperum* (Treasury for the Poor), a medical handbook that established itself as a standard work for centuries afterward. (The attribution of this work to Peter has been contested.) The *Thesaurus Pauperum* was intended for students who could not afford the expensive books from which its teachings are extracted. It is a handbook of illnesses affecting various parts of the body, beginning with the head and working down to the feet, along with their cures. Peter was elected archbishop of Braga in 1273; Gregory X appointed him cardinal of Tusculum later in the same year. Gregory died on 10 January 1276, and his successors Innocent V and Adrian V enjoyed only the briefest of reigns. Peter of Spain was elected Pope John XXI on 18 August 1276, after the seat had been vacant for twenty-six days. The new pope was not only aged but a scientist absorbed by his studies and relatively innocent in politics and the management of men. The Dominican historian Ptolemy of Lucca remarks that "although he was great in science, he was mediocre in distinction; for he was impetuous in speech, and too mild in his manner, which was the more apparent because he was easily approached, and thus his faults were open to all." Peter was no doubt a compromise candidate, an apolitical man on whom all parties could agree when called to fill the vacant see a third time within a year, thereby putting off a little longer the coming showdown between the French and the Italians.

John XXI was responsible for one of the most important actions of the papacy in regard to philosophy in the Middle Ages, the two Bulls of 1277 addressed to Bishop Stephen Tempier of Paris. In the first he ordered Tempier to begin an inquiry into the errors (for the most part associated with radical Aristotelianism) taught at the University of Paris; and in the second, *Flumen atque vive*, he ordered Tempier to bring the teaching of false and heretical doctrines at Paris to an end. Tempier's resulting condemnation of 219 articles in theology and natural philosophy emphasized God's absolute power to do whatever he will, short of a logical contradiction. Thus, Article 147 condemns the opinion "That the absolutely impossible cannot be done by God or any other agent, if 'impossible' is understood [as impossible] according to nature." Thinkers after 1277 became accustomed to the contemplation of physical possibilities outside the range of what Aristotle might allow, and to thinking of natural laws as contingencies that hold only because of God's free decision to uphold them.

To ensure that he was not interrupted in his studies, John XXI had ordered a private apartment added to the palace at Viterbo. On 14 May 1277 the roof of this apartment collapsed on him, and he died on 20 May.

There is a tradition from as early as the 1280s that the Peter of Spain who wrote the *Tractatus* became a Dominican friar, perhaps after completing his logical work. This view was stubbornly defended by H. D. Simonin in the 1930s, but there was already stronger evidence that the Peter who had produced the logical treatise became Pope John XXI. Certainly that pope was highly regarded as a logician, and as the details of his life fell into place, it had become clear that the tradition that he was the author of the *Tractatus* and notable physician, Peter of Spain, had to be credited. But the evidence of Ptolemy of Lucca that Pope John XXI was a secular (a member of no order) is irrefutable. He says not only that John XXI was a secular but that "he did not much like members of religious orders, and hence it is, as some believe, that he came to a bad end. For the histories relate that at the time when the apartment fell upon his head he was fulminating against the religious." Peter of Spain, then, cannot have been a Black Friar.

As a philosopher Peter of Spain is known chiefly for the *Tractatus*, which became a standard introductory textbook in logic for the later Middle Ages. Peter's eminence as a logician in his own day is clear from Dante's mention of him in *The Divine Comedy* (completed 1321), where he is referred to by Saint Bonaventure as the author of twelve books (the twelve chapters of the *Tractatus*).

The *Tractatus* begins with a review of logic organized along lines established in the twelfth century and based ultimately in Aristotle's *Organon*.

Sarcophagus of John XXI in the cathedral at Viterbo

It covers both the "old logic" (the *Categories*, Porphyry's *Isagoge* [Introduction to the *Categories*], and the *On Interpretation*), which had been taught in the eleventh century, and most of the "new logic" (the *Prior Analytics, Topics*, and *Sophistical Refutations*, but not the *Posterior Analytics*), which was introduced into the curriculum with the recovery of Aristotle's works in the twelfth century. Peter, following the usual practice, used book 1 of Boethius's *De Syllogismo Categorico* (On Categorical Syllogisms, 505-506), which is based on Aristotle's *On Interpretation*, as his direct source for his first tract, "De Introductionibus" (On Introductory Matters). Here are treated the parts of a proposition and such matters as conversion, modal propositions, and squares of opposition. The second treatise, "De Praedicabilibus" (On Predicables), is, again following tradition, based on twelfth- and thirteenth-century discussions of Boethius's commentaries on Porphyry's *Isagoge*. The third treatise, "De Praedicamentis" (On the Categories), is drawn almost verbatim from Boethius's commentary (509-510) on Aristotle's *Categories* and from the *Liber Sex Principiorum* (Book of Six Principles) wrongly attributed to Gilbert de la Porrée. In the beginning of this treatise is inserted a discussion of the senses in which a thing may be in something, drawn from Aristotle's *Physics*, and a list of four manners in which things can be opposites. The fourth treatise, "De Syllogismis" (On Syllogisms), is drawn indirectly from Boethius's *De Syllogismo Categorico* via some other introductory text of the twelfth or thirteenth century. Here one finds rules for assessing the validity of syllogisms and the mnemonic rhyme "*Barbara celarent.*" The fifth treatise, *De Locis* (Concerning Commonplaces), is taken from Boethius's *De Topicis Differentiis* (On the Different Topics, before 523), with a few additions from Aristotle's *Topics*. Peter treats a locus as a rule confirming the validity of an argument. The seventh treatise concerns fallacies and is developed from Aristotle's *Sophistical Refutations*. In copies of the *Tractatus* produced after the 1280s this treatise was often replaced with a shorter treatment not by Peter, and in Italy Thomas Aquinas's tract on fallacies frequently took its place.

But Peter of Spain's work is important not so much for his treatment of these traditional matters as for his development of the theory of supposition and the other properties of terms in the sixth treatise, "De Suppositionibus" (On Supposition), and the last five treatises, "De Relatives" (On Relational Terms), "De Ampliationibis" (On Ampliation), "De Appellationibus" (On Appellation), "De Restrictionibus" (On Restriction), and "De Distributionibus" (On Distribution). This logical theory, developed in the twelfth century especially in connection with treatments of fallacy, was the common property of all medieval thinkers and constitutes one of the period's chief claims to fertility and originality of philosophical thought. The theory of supposition and the other properties of terms concerns the kinds of reference and signification terms can have and the way in which these are influenced by the term's context in the proposition. In Peter's version of the theory, drawn perhaps from the twelfth-century treatise *Summulae Antiquorum* (Summaries "of the Ancients"), the signification of a term belongs to the term in itself, regardless of its use in a particular context. Thus *man* signifies the universal man and signifies this same thing in every occurrence. Supposition, on the other hand, belongs to an occurrence of a term in a particular context. An occurrence of *man*, for example, may supposit for an individual man (discrete supposition), as in "that man is happy," or for several men (common supposition). Every occurrence suppositing for several men will have the same natural supposition—the term will supposit naturally for every man—past, present, or future—that is, every individual that falls under its signification, the universal man. The accidental supposition of a universal term, however, depends entirely on its context. The term *man* may accidentally supposit for the species man (simple supposition), as in "man is a species"; for some unspecified individual selected from the natural supposition of the term (personal determinate supposition), as in "some man is running"; or for all individual men in such a way that what is said of the term is taken to be said of each man (personal confused supposition), as in "every man is an animal." Peter admits in the last example that the predicate term *animal* also has personal confused supposition, but, he says, its supposition is "immobile," whereas that of *man* is "mobile." That is, one can descend from the universal to the particular with *man*, since it follows from "every man is an animal" that "this man is an animal," but not with *animal*, for it does not follow that "every man is this animal." Appellation, ampliation, and restriction are additional sorts of supposition. The first restricts personal supposition to presently existing instances, as would usually occur in a present-tense sentence. The second extends appellation to other instances than the present tense of the verb might suggest, as in "some man can be the Antichrist." Here *man* clearly supposits for both present and future men. Restriction occurs when the supposition of a term is restricted by an adjectival phrase, as in "a white man is running," in which *man* covers only men who are white, or by the tense of a verb, as when the statement is restricted to present or past men.

It is noteworthy that Peter's theory makes the signification of a term its central property and explains supposition (or reference to individuals) in terms of signification. In virtue of its signification, a common term has a natural capacity to supposit for what is signified taken in itself (the universal considered absolutely, without reference to what falls under it), or for whatever has fallen, will fall, or does fall under what it signifies (its natural supposition). Within some sentential contexts this capacity is limited, thus giving rise to the different sorts of supposition, ampliation, and so on. His theory, in brief, is friendly to moderate realism, which takes it that universals can be thought and spoken of independently of any reference to individuals. Connected with this position is his treatment in the *Tractatus Syncategorematum* (Treatise on Syncategorematic Terms, circa 1230?) of the copula *is* in such sentences as "A man is an animal." Peter takes it that the copula carries no existential implication and no signification of its own but only provides the connection between subject and predicate. Thus, in "*Homo est animal*" ("Man is an animal" or "A man is an animal") the connection is made between the significata of the two terms (the universals man and animal considered absolutely), and the sentence is true in virtue of this connection, even if no man actually exists.

The rather different tradition developed at Oxford, witnessed in the *Introductiones in Logicam* (Introductions to Logic, circa 1250?) of William of Sherwood, treated supposition syntactically, the supposition of a term (or of the thought or concept associated with it) being the ordering of other terms (or thoughts or concepts) under it. Moreover, William asserts that the supposition of a common term such as *man*, standing by itself, can only be existing men, not future or past men; for although the term signifies a form, it only signifies it as it actually occurs in existing reality, not as considered absolutely. Thus, the proposition "*Homo est animal*" is not true if no man actually exists at the time the sentence is uttered. This view is a precursor of the nominalism of William of Ockham and the "terminist" tradition of logic after him.

Bibliography:

"Bibliografia sobre Pedro Hispano," *Revista Portuguesa de Filosofia*, 8 (1952): 233-248.

References:

Cassiano Abranches, "Pedro Hispano e as 'Summulae Logicales,'" *Revista Portuguesa de Filosofia*, 8 (1952): 243-259;

J. Morais Barbosa, "O legado do 'Corpus Areopagiticum' no Occidente: A 'expositio in librum de mystica theologia' de Pedro Hispano," *Cultura, História e Filosofia*, 1 (1982): 25-44;

Otto Bird, "The Tradition of the Logical Topics: Aristotle to Ockham," *Journal of the History of Ideas*, 23 (July-September 1962): 307-323;

Philotheus Boehner, *Medieval Logic: An Outline of its Development from 1250 to c. 1400* (Chicago: University of Chicago Press, 1952);

Leonard E. Boyle, "Pierre Dubois and the *Summulae Logicales* of Peter of Spain," *Mediaeval Studies*, 34 (1972): 468-470;

H. A. G. Braakhuis, "Peter of Spain on Propositional Composition," in *Logos and Pragma: Essays in the Philosophy of Language in Honour of Professor Gabriel Nuchelmans*, Artistarium Supplementa, volume 3, edited by Braakhuis and L. M. de Rijk (Nijmegen, Holland: Ingenium, 1987), pp. 99-21;

Braakhuis, "The Views of William of Sherwood on Some Semantical Topics and Their Relation to Those of Roger Bacon," *Vivarium*, 15 (November 1977): 111-142;

Tomás y Joaquín Carreras y Artau, *Historia de la Filosofía Española*, volume 1 (Madrid: Real academia de ciencias exactas, físicas y naturales, 1939), pp. 101-144;

Carreras y Artau, "Rectificación historica, La nacionalidad portuguesa de Pedro Hispano," *Las Ciencias* (1934): 378-384;

Ettore Carrucio, "La logica nel pensiero di Dante," *Physis*, 8 (1966): 233-246;

Amândio Coxito, "Las doctrinas de la significatio y de la suppositio in Pedro Hispano," *Pensamiento*, 45 (1989): 227-237;

Francesco Cristofori, "Di Pietro Ispano ricordato da Dante e dell'identitá di lui con il papa Giovanni XXI provata," *Nuovo Giornale Arcadico*, 3 (1890);

J. M. da Cruz Pontes, *A Obra Filosófica de Pedro Hispano Portugalense: Novos Problemas Textuais* (Coimbra: Universidade de Coimbra, 1972);

Cruz Pontes, "La division du texte dans le ms. inédit des *Quaestiones super libro de animalibus* de Petrus Hispanus Portugalensis," *Bulletin de la Societé Internationale pour l'Étude de la Philosophie Médiévale*, 4 (1962): 118-126;

Cruz Pontes, "L'intérêt philosophique de deux commentaires inédites sur le 'De animalibus' et le problème de leur attribution à Pierre Hispane," in *La Filosofia della Natura nel Medioevo: Atti del Terzo congresso internazionale di Filosofia Medioevale* (Milan: Società Editrice Vita e Pensiero, 1966), pp. 493-501;

Cruz Pontes, "Un nouveau manuscrit des *Qaestiones libri de anima de Petrus Hispanus Portugalensis*," *Recherches de théologie ancienne et médiévale*, 43 (1976): 167-201;

Cruz Pontes, "Para situar Pedro Hispano na historia da filosofía," *Revista Portuguesa de Filosofia*, 24 (1968): 21-45;

Cruz Pontes, *Pedro Hispano Portugalense e as Controvérsias Doutrinais do Século XIII a Origem de Alma* (Coimbra: Universidade de Coimbra, 1964);

Cruz Pontes, "Les *Quaestiones libri de anima* de Petrus Hispanus Portugalensis d'aprés le codex 726 de la Biblioteka Uniwersytetu Jagiellońskiego de Kraków et le codex Lat. Z.253 de la Biblioteca Nazionale Marciana de Venezia," *Mediaevalia Philosophica Polonorum*, 19 (1974): 127-139;

Cruz Pontes, "As traducões dos tratados zoológicos aristotelicos e as inéditas *Quaestiones super libro de animalibus* de Pedro Hispano Portugalense," *Revista Portuguesa de Filosofia*, 19, fasc. 3 (1963): 243-263;

Vicente Muñoz Delgado, "La logica de Bernardo Jordan: Estudio de su *Explanatio in Petrum Hispanarum* (Florence 1914)," *Ciudad de Dios*, 185 (1972): 459-462;

João Ferreira, "A relevância de Pedro Hispano na filosofia medieval," *Bracara Augusta*, 16-17 (1964): 80-93;

Ferreira, "As 'Súmulas logicais' de Pedro Hispano e os seus Comentadores," *Collectânea de Estudos*, 3 (September 1952): 360-394;

Ferreira, "Esbocio sumário das ideias antropológicas de Pedro Hispano," *Itinerarium*, 4, no. 21 (1958): 326-341; published in French as "L'homme dans la doctrine de Pierre d'Espagne," in *L'homme et son destin d'après le penseurs der moyen âge: Actes du Premier Congrés international de Philosophie médiévale* (Louvain: Nauwelaerts, 1960), pp. 445-461;

Ferreira, "Os estudos de Pedro Hispano," *Collectânea de Estudos*, 5 (September 1954): 195-210;

Ferreira, "Um grande portugues nas Cortes de Leiria de 1254: Mestre Pedro Hispano (d.

1277)," *Revista Filosófica*, 6 (May 1954): 92-97;

Ferreira, "Importáncia histórico-filosófica de Pedro Hispano no contexto da escolástica," *Leopoldianum*, 11, no. 32 (1984): 99-110;

Ferreira, "Introducião ao estudo do *Liber de anima* de Pedro Hispano," *Revista Filosofica*, 3 (1953): 177-198;

Ferreira, "Presença do augustinismo avicenizante na teoria dos intellectos de Pedro Hispano," *Itinerarium* (1959): 29-68;

Ferreira, "O problema de Deus em Pedro Hispano," *Filosofia*, 2 (October-December 1955): 146-176;

Ferreira, "Temas de cultura filosofica portuguesa: Sobre a posicião doutrinal de Pedro Hispano," *Colectânea de Estudos*, 5 (January 1954): 48-56;

F. da Gama Caeiro, "Novos elementos sobre Pedro Hispano: Contribuicião para o estudo da sua biografia," *Revista Portuguesa de Filosofia*, 22 (1966): 157-163;

Bernhard Geyer, "Zu den *Summulae logicales* des Petrus Hispanus und Lambert von Auxerre," *Philosophische Jahrbuch*, 50 (1937): 511-513;

Martin Grabmann, "Die Lehre vom Intellectus Possibilis und intellectus agens im liber de Anima des Petrus Hispanus des späteren Papstes Johannes XXI," *Archives d'histoire doctrinale et littéraire du moyen âge*, 12-13 (1937-1938): 167-208;

Edward Grant, "The Effects of the Condemnation of 1277," in *The Cambridge History of Later Medieval Philosophy*, edited by Norman Kretzmann, Anthony Kenny, and Jan Pinborg (Cambridge: Cambridge University Press, 1982), pp. 536-539;

Johann Tobias Köhler, *Vollständige Nachricht von Pabst Johann XXI* (Göttingen, 1760);

Johann Kohlmeier, "Vita est actus primus: Ein Beitrag zur Erhellung der Geschichte der Philosophie der ersten Hälfte des 13. Jahrhunderts anhand der Lebens metaphysik des Petrus Hispanus," *Freiburger Zeitschrift für Philosophie und Theologie*, 16, no. 1 (1969): 40-91; no. 2 (1969): 287-320;

Norman Kretzmann, John Longeway, Eleonore Stump, and John Van Dyk, "L. M. de Rijk on Peter of Spain," *Journal of the History of Philosophy*, 16 (July 1978): 325-333;

Kretzmann, Longeway, Stump, and Van Dyk, Review of L. M. de Rijk's edition of Peter of Spain's Tractatus, *Philosophical Review*, 84 (October 1975): 560-567;

M.-H. Laurent, "Maître Pierre d'Espagne fut-il Dominicain?," *Divus Thomas*, 39 (1936): 35-45;

Alain de Libera, "The Oxford and Paris Traditions in Logic," in *The Cambridge History of Later Medieval Philosophy*, edited by Kretzmann, Kenny, and Pinborg (Cambridge: Cambridge University Press, 1982), pp. 174-187;

Peter Mack, "Valla's Dialectic in the North: A Commentary on Peter of Spain by Gerardus Listrius," *Vivarium*, 21 (May 1983): 58-72;

Jim Mackenzie, "Confirmation of a Conjecture of Peter of Spain Concerning Question-Begging Arguments," *Journal of Philosophical Logic*, 13 (February 1984): 35-45;

Alfonso Maierú, *Terminologia logica della scolastica*, Lessico intelletuale Europeo, 8 (Rome: Edizioni dell'Ateneo, 1972);

Diamantino Martins, "O *De Anima* de Pedro Hispano," *Revista Portuguesa de Filosofia*, 8 (1952): 260-294;

M. Martins, "Os Commentarios de Pedro Hispano au Pseudo-Dionisio Areopagita," *Revista Portuguesa di Filosofia*, 8 (1952): 295-314;

Joseph Moreau, "Un pape portugais: Jean XXI dénommé Pierre d'Espagne," *Teoresi*, 34 (1979): 391-407;

Moreau, "Pedro Hispano et la problème de la connaissance de l'áme," *Arquivos de Historia de Cultura Portuguesa*, 1 (1967);

Artur Moreira de Sá, "O Papa João XXI: Filosofo e politico," *Boletin Cultural da Câmara Municipal do Porto*, 12 (1949): 262-279;

Moreira de Sá, "Pedro Hispano e a crise de 1277 da Universidade de Paris," *Boletin da Biblioteca da Universidade de Coimbra*, 22 (1954): 1-21;

Moreira de Sá, "Pedro Hispano, prior da Ingreja de Santa Maria de Guimarães e arcebispo da Sé in Braga," *Biblos*, 30 (1955): 1-24;

Moreira de Sá, "Um grande filósofo europeu, Arcebispo eleito da Sé de Braga, que ocupou a cadeira de S. Pedro," *Bracara Augusta*, 6 (1956): 3-16;

Giovanni Battista Petella, "Les connaissances oculistiques d'un médecin philosophe devenu pape," *Janus: Archives internationales pour l'histoire de la médecine et pour la* géographie médicale, 2 (1897-1898): 405-420, 570-596;

Petella, "Sull' identità de Pietro Ispano, medico in Siena e poi pap col filosofo dantesco," *Bolletino Senese di Storia Patri*, 6 (1899): 277-329;

Jan Pinborg, ed., "Anonymi quaestiones in Tractatus Petri Hispani I-III traditae in codice Cracoviensi 742 (anno fere 1350)," *Cahiers de l'Institut du Moyen Âge Grec et Latin*, 41 (1982): 1-170;

Celestino Pires, "Logica et methodus apud Petrum Hispanum," in *Arts libéraux et philosophie au moyen âge* (Berlin: De Gruyter, 1969), pp. 895-900;

Pires, "Petrus Hispanus et problema metaphysicae," in his *Die Metaphysik im Mittelalter, ihr Ursprung und ihre Bedeutung: Vorträge des II. Internationalen Kongresses für Mittelalterliche Philosophie*, edited by Paul Wilpert (Berlin: De Gruyter, 1963), pp. 154-160;

Carl Prantl, *Geschichte der Logik im Abendlande*, volume 3 (Leipzig: Hirzel, 1867; reprinted, Graz: Akademische Druk, 1955), pp. 33-75;

Prantl, *Michael Psellus und Petrus Hispanus: Eine Rechtfertigung* (Leipzig: Hirzel, 1867);

Arthur N. Prior, "The *Parva Logicalia* in Modern Dress," *Dominican Studies*, 5 (1952): 78-87;

David Riesman, "A Physician in the Papal Chair," *Annals of Medical History*, 5 (1923): 291-300;

L. M. de Rijk, "The Development of Suppositio Naturalis in Mediaeval Logic," *Vivarium*, 9 (November 1971): 71-107;

Rijk, *Logica Modernorum: A Contribution to the History of Early Terminist Logic*, 2 volumes (Assen: Van Gorcum, 1962, 1967);

Rijk, "On the Genuine Text of Peter of Spain's *Summule logicales*, I: General Problems concerning Possible Interpolations in the Manuscripts," *Vivarium*, 6 (May 1968): 1-34; "II: Simon of Faversham (d. 1306) as a Commentator of the Tracts I-V of The *Summulae*," *Vivarium*, 6 (November 1968): 69-101; "III: Two Redactions of a Commentary upon the *Summulae* by Robertus Anglicus," *Vivarium*, 7 (May 1969): 8-61; "IV: The *Lectura Tractatum* by Guillelmus Arnaldi, Master of Arts at Toulouse (1235-44)," *Vivarium*, 7 (November 1969): 120-162; "V: Some Anonymous Commentaries on the *Summulae* dating from the Thirteenth Century," *Vivarium*, 8 (May 1970): 10-55;

Rijk, "On the Life of Peter of Spain, the Author of the *Tractatus* Called Afterwards *Summule logicales*," *Vivarium*, 8 (1970): 123-154;

Rijk, "Significatio y suppositio en Pedro Hispano," *Pensamiento*, 25 (1969): 225-234;

Oswaldo Robles, "Fray Tomas de Mercado O.P., Traductor de Aristoteles y comendador de Pedro Hispano en la Nueva España del siglo XVI," *Revista de Filosofía*, 9 (1950): 541-559;

Manuel Augusto Rodriguez, "O pensamente teologico e mistico de Pedro Hispano, interprete e comentador do Pseudo-Dionisio Areopagita," *Biblos*, 56 (1979): 95-150;

Valentin Rose, "Pseudo-Psellus und Petrus Hispanus," *Hermes: Zeitschrift für classische Philologie*, 2 (1867): 146-147;

Francis Ruello, "Un commentaire dionysien en quête d'auteur: Le commentaire attribué à Pierre d'Espagne," *Archives d'histoire doctrinale et littéraire du moyen âge*, 19 (1952): 141-181;

Manuel Sánchez del Bosque, "Pedro Hispano, 'Vita fluit ab anime substantia,' " *Cuadernos Salmantinos de Filosofía*, 15 (1988): 59-72;

Heinrich Schipperges, "Grundzüge einer scholastischen Anthropologie bei Petrus Hispanus," *Aufsätze zur portugiesischen Kulturgeschichte*, 7 (1967): 1-51;

Schipperges, "Der Stufenbau der Natur im Weltbild des Petrus Hispanus," *Gesnerus*, 17 (1960): 14-29;

Schipperges, "Zur Psychologie und Psychiatrie des Petrus Hispanus," *Confinia Psychiatrica*, 4, nos. 3-4 (1961): 137-157;

Lucio Craveiro da Silva, "Pedro Hispano (1277-1977) a luz dos ultimos estudos," *Revista Portuguesa de Filosofia*, 33 (1977): 113-123;

H. D. Simonin, "Magister Petrus Hispanus O.P.," *Archivum Fratrum Praedicatorum*, 5 (1935): 340-343;

Simonin, "Les *Summulae logicales* de Petrus Hispanus," *Archives d'histoire doctrinale et littéraire du moyen âge*, 5 (1930): 267-278;

Richard Stapper, *Papst Johannes XXI: Ein Monographie* (Münster: Schoningh, 1898);

Stapper, "Pietro Hispano (Papa Giovanni XXI) ed il suo soggiorno in Siena," *Bulletino Senese di Storia Patria*, 5, fasc. 3 (1898): 424-429;

Stapper, "Die *Summulae logicales* des Petrus Hispanus und ihr Verhaltnis zu Michael Psellus," in *Festschrift zum elfhundertjährigen Jubilaum des deutschen Campo Santo in Rom* (Freiburg: Herder, 1897), pp. 130-138;

Karl Sudhoff, "Petrus Hispanus, richtiger Lusitano, Professor der Medizin und Philosophie, schliesslich Papst Johann XXI: Eine Studie," *Die medizinische Welt*, 24 (1934): 1-10;

Lynn Thorndike, *A History of Magic and Experimental Science*, volume 3 (New York & London: Columbia University Press, 1923), pp. 488-516;

Charles Thurot, "De la logique de Pierre d'Espagne," *Revue archéologique*, new series 5 (1864): 267-281;

John Versor, *Petrus Hispanus Summulae cum Versorii Parisiensis clarissima expositione* (Venice, 1572; photographic reprint, Hildesheim & New York: Olms, 1981);

Graziella Federici Vescovini, "Le quaestioni dialettichi di Biagio Palacani da Parma sopra i trattati de logica di Pietro Ispana," *Medioevo*, 2 (1976): 253-287.

Manuscripts:

Manuscripts for Peter of Spain's *Tractatus* and *Tractatus Syncategorematicum* can be found in the Biblioteca del Palacio Arzobispal, Tarragon, Spain; the Biblioteca Apostolica Vaticana, the Vatican; the Biblioteca Ambrosiana, Milan; the Biblioteca Capitolave, Ivrea, Italy; and the Biblioteca del Excellentissimo Cabildo, Córdoba. Other manuscripts are in the Bibliotheque Nationale, Paris; the Royal Library, London; the Library of Corpus Christi College, Oxford University; and the Biblioteca Nacional, Madrid.

Pseudo-Dionysius the Areopagite

(floruit circa 500)

J. C. Marler
Saint Louis University

PRINCIPAL WORKS: *Peri Theiōn Onomatōn*; Latin: *De Divinis Nominibus* (The Divine Names, written circa 500);

Peri Mustikēs Theologias; Latin: *De Mystica Theologia* (The Mystical Theology, written circa 500);

Peri tēs Ouranias Hierarchias; Latin: *De Caelesti Hierarchia* (The Celestial Hierarchy, written circa 500);

Peri tēs Ekklēsiastikēs Hierarchias; Latin: *De Ecclesiastica Hierarchia* (The Ecclesiastical Hierarchy, written circa 500).

EDITIONS: *Tade Enestin en Tēdē tē Biblō tou Hagiou Dionusio*, edited by Phillip Junta (Florence, 1516);

Opera S. Dionysii Areopagitae cum scholiis s. Maximi et paraphrasi Pachymerae, edited by Balthasar Cordier (Antwerp, 1534); reprinted in *Patrologiae cursus completus, series graeca*, volume 3, edited by J.-P. Migne (Paris: Lutetiæ Parisiorum, 1857);

La hiérarchie céleste, edited by René Roques and others (Paris: Editions du Cerf, 1958).

EDITIONS IN ENGLISH: "The Mystical Theology of Dionysius the Areopagite," translated by John Everard, in his *Some Gospel Treasures Opened; or, The Holiest of All Unvailing in Several Sermons . . . Whereunto Is Added the Mystical Divinity of Dionysius* (London, 1653; reprinted, Germantown, Pa.: Sower, 1757), pp. 767-779;

"The Epistle of S. Dionysius the Areopagite to S. Timothy, Translated from an Ethiopic Manuscript," translated by S. C. Malan, in his *The Conflicts of the Early Apostles: An Apocryphal Book of the Early Eastern Church* (London: Nutt, 1871), pp. 230-243;

The Works of Dionysius the Areopagite, Now First Translated into English from the Original Greek, 2 volumes, translated by John Parker (London: Parker, 1897-1899);

Mysticism: Its True Nature and Value, with a Translation of the "Mystical Theology" of Dionysius and of the Letters to Caius and Dorotheus, translated by A. B. Sharpe (London: Sands, 1910; Saint Louis: Herder, 1910);

"A Cosmological Tract by Pseudo-Dionysius in the Syriac Language," edited and translated by Giuseppe Furlani, *Journal of the Royal Asiatic Society* (1917): 245-272;

Dionysius the Areopagite: On the Divine Names and The Mystical Theology, translated by C. E. Rolt (London: Society for the Propagation of Christian Knowledge, 1920; New York: Macmillan, 1920);

The Mystical Theology of Dionysius the Areopagite, with Elucidatory Commentary by the Editors of the Shrine of Wisdom, and Poem on the Superessential Radiance of the Divine Darkness by St. John of the Cross (London: Shrine of Wisdom, 1923);

Dionysius the Pseudo-Areopagite: The Ecclesiastical Hierarchy, translated and annotated by Thomas S. Campbell (Washington, D.C.: Catholic University of America Press, 1955);

Cosmic Theology: The Ecclesiastical Hierarchy of Pseudo-Denys, translated with commentary by Denys Rutledge (London: Routledge & Kegan Paul, 1964);

A Letter of Private Direction, by the Author of the "Cloud of Unknowing," Rendered into Modern English with an Introduction, translated by James Walsh (London: Burns & Oates, 1965);

Pseudo-Dionysius: The Complete Works, translated by Colm Luibheid and Paul Rorem (New York: Paulist Press, 1987).

Dionysius the Areopagite is the nom de plume of the unknown author of the theological treatises and epistles that came to light in western Syria during the controversies provoked among Christians by the definition of the faith proclaimed in 451 by the Council of Chalcedon. The collection of his works, known to scholars as the *Corpus Dionysiacum*, the *Corpus Areopagiticum*, or the *Dionysiaca*, originated in Greek, was rendered into Syriac, and later came to be translated into Latin and the vernacular languages of medieval Europe. In the Christian Near East, east of the Anatolian Plateau, and in the Caucasus it appeared in Arabic and Armenian.

The tractates included in the Latin version of the *Corpus Dionysiacum* are *De Divinis Nominibus* (The Divine Names), *De Mystica Theologia* (The Mystical Theology), *De Caelesti Hierarchia* (The Celestial Hierarchy), and *De Ecclesiastica Hierarchia* (The Ecclesiastical Hierarchy); it also contains ten letters. Nothing is known of the author of those texts. It is certain, however, that he was an accomplished forger and that as a theologian his eminence is unsurpassed either by Thomas Aquinas or by Gregory Palamas, both of whom considered his works to be authoritative. Pseudo-Dionysius influenced many of the best minds of the Middle Ages and the Renaissance. Today the effects of the *Dionysiaca* are most prominent among the pastors and expositors of Christianity in the East.

It is most likely that the existence of the *Corpus Dionysiacum* was first publicized around 514 by Severus, the patriarch of Antioch, at the Synod of Tyre, to defend the Monophysite doctrine that Christ's nature remains altogether divine against the Chalcedonian thesis of the union of divinity and humanity in Christ. Pseudo-Zacharias Rhetor, in his chronicle of the synod, commends the patriarch for his mastery not only of the Scriptures but of what had been taught by such Christian authorities as Dionysius, Hierotheus, Ignatius, and Clement of Alexandria, but he gives no details. If, however, René Roques has correctly identified 510 as the date of a letter from Severus to John Higoumenos in which the *Dionysiaca* are an object of explicit reference, the Synod of Tyre would not have been the instance of their earliest citation. But the letter cannot be dated with certainty; and because Pseudo-Zacharias has omitted the particulars of the debate at Tyre, Pseudo-Dionysius cannot now be proven to have been cited earlier than in the polemical narrative *Adversus Apologiam Juliani* which Severus wrote between 518 and 528.

In any case, on the second day of the conference which the emperor Justinian summoned in 533 at Constantinople between the Severians and the defenders of Chalcedonian orthodoxy, the writings attributed to Dionysius the Areopagite were offered in support of the Monophysite reduction of two natures in Christ to one. By that time the *Corpus Dionysiacum* was well known to the Monophysite bishops in attendance. Though the Chalcedonian party, led at Constantinople by Hypatius of Ephesus, protested them as a forgery, they were soon admitted as authentic on all sides.

In the Acts of the Apostles, Paul of Tarsus, while visiting the synagogue at Athens, is invited by the Stoics and Epicureans to address the citizens gathered at the Areopagus (Hill of Ares) to debate questions of public good. Paul devotes his sermon to the "unknown god" (*agnōstos theos*) whose votive altar he had seen on his way through the city, and, for rhetorical effect among the Athenians, he is careful to include passages from Aratus and Pseudo-Epimenides, both of whom were familar to Greek men of learning. Even so, his words seem not to have carried the majority of his audience; but "certain men clave unto him, and believed: among the which was Dionysius the Areopagite, and a woman named Damaris, and certain others with them." Of this Dionysius nothing further is said anywhere in the New Testament. The silence of history is broken only by the report of Dionysius of Corinth, cited by Eusebius of Caesarea, that he was the first bishop of Athens.

That Dionysius the Areopagite was a philosopher is a possible inference from the circumstances under which he and Paul met at Athens. It is on the basis of such an inference that the mysterious author of the *Dionysiaca* constructed his literary forgery.

In *De Divinis Nominibus* Pseudo-Dionysius borrows from Ignatius of Antioch—martyred at Rome in 107—with full credit to its source, the passage "my love is crucified." He seems thereby to have deliberately invited suspicion against the authenticity of his text: to have been acquainted with what Ignatius was to publish, the Dionysius converted by Paul would have to have survived to a prodigious old age. Further misgivings are aroused by his reference in *De Ecclesiastica Hierarchia* to the Credo sung at mass, a liturgical innovation made by Peter the Fuller no earlier than 476. In the early history of modern philology, with recovery in the West of Greek literature from late antiquity, doubts were cast on the Pseudo-Dionysian corpus by Lorenzo Valla, the scholarly fifteenth-century confrere of Erasmus; misgivings continued to be voiced in scholarship until, at the close of the nineteenth century, Josef Stiglmayr and Hugo Koch independently demonstrated considerable portions of the *Dionysiaca* to have been appropriated from Proclus, the scholarch of the Platonic Academy revived in Athens by Plutarch in the fifth century A.D. Later, L. H. Grondijs showed that it is likely that Pseudo-Dionysius was influenced not only by Proclus but also by Damascius, the last known of the Platonic *diadochoi* (successors), who had charge of the school in Athens when the emperor Justinian decreed the closure of institutes devoted to pagan learning in 529.

Since Proclus died in 485, the literary career of Pseudo-Dionysius probably occurred between that date and the time at which Severus cited the *Dionysiaca* in opposition to Chalcedon. Pseudo-Dionysius, therefore, was a contemporary of Severus.

The intellectual culture of Greco-Roman paganism survived for more than a century after Chalcedon. In the great cities on which the empire depended for commerce, schools could be found where those unreconciled to Christian practice and precept were tolerated and, in some instances, were openly sponsored by the municipal authorities. Athens, Alexandria, and Beirut were notable, respectively, for philosophy, rhetoric, and law, and in each of these locales extensive communication was possible between Christians and pagans devoted to ancient learning. The school of Proclus is known to have admitted both pagans and Christians; Marinus, who was Proclus's successor as leader of the school, was a Jewish convert to Christianity.

The knowledge of Proclus which can be gathered from the *Corpus Dionysiacum* is detailed and exact; and it is at least as considerable, if not indeed more so, as what the author shows of Christian Scripture. In all probability, then, Pseudo-Dionysius was a student of Proclus; some, at least, of his studies were pursued in Athens; and among his interests was the conservation of a philosophy which, by accommodating polytheism, bore the risk of extinction under Christianity.

Throughout his works, but in *De Divinis Nominibus* especially, Pseudo-Dionysius is full of praise for a certain Hierotheus, who, he says, was his teacher before Paul and was the author of *Theological Elements* and *Hymns of Divine Love*. Except for Pseudo-Dionysius, there is no source for the life of Hierotheus; nothing prevents the discerning reader from identifying Hierotheus with Proclus, who wrote *Elements of Theology* and, in celebration of his gods, several hymns.

Ronald F. Hathaway suggested in 1969 that Pseudo-Dionysius may have intended to remove the grounds for dispute not primarily between Monophysites and Chalcedonians but between Christians and pagans. In part, Hathaway defended his thesis by noting the parallel between Pseudo-Dionysius's report in his letter to Polycarp of visiting Heliopolis—whether the Egyp-

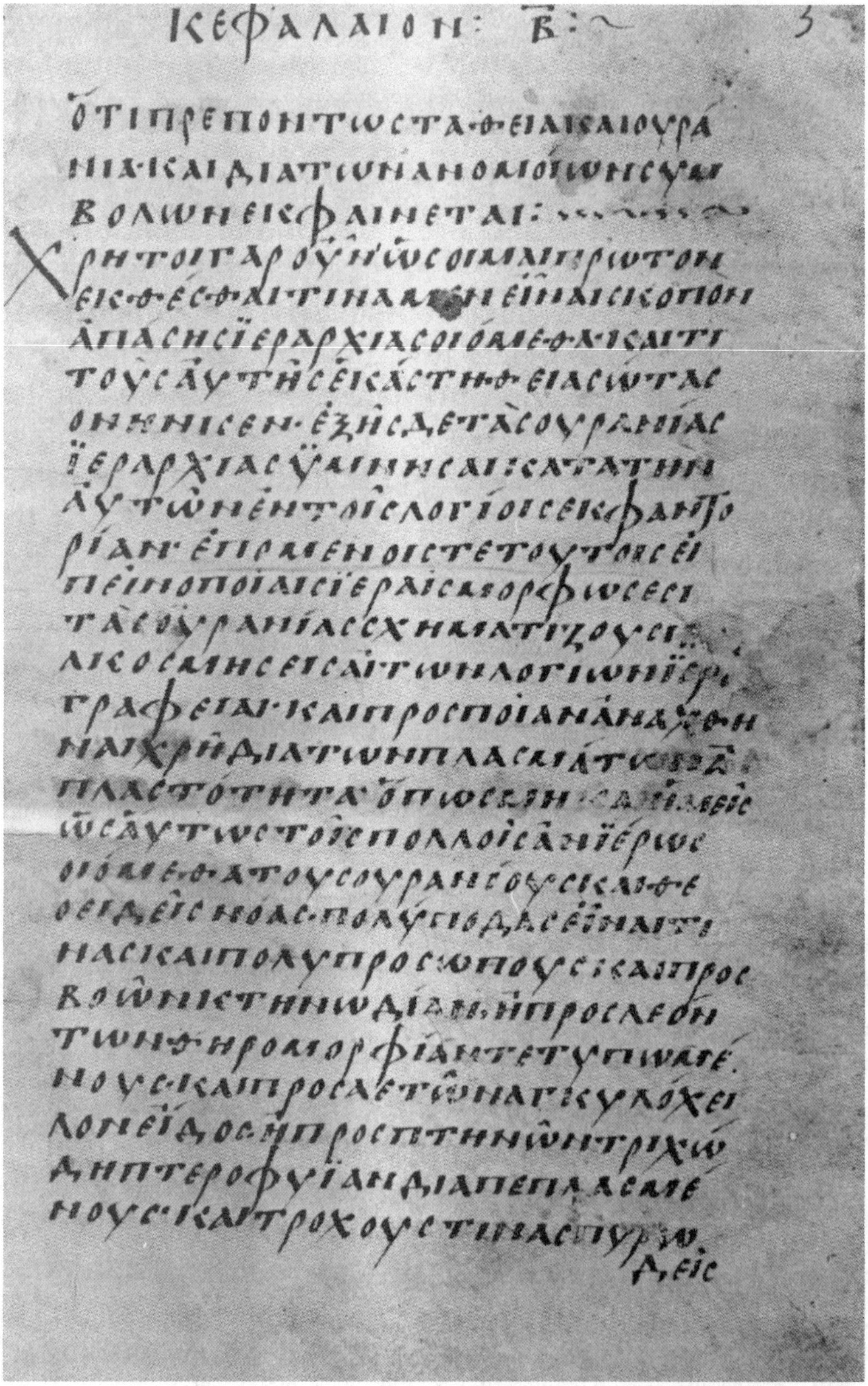
ΚΕΦΑΛΑΙΟΝ: Β:~ 3
ὅτι πρεπόντως τὰ θεῖα καὶ οὐρα
νια καὶ διὰ τῶν ἀνομοίων συμ
βόλων ἐκφαίνεται:
Χρὴ τοιγαροῦν ὡς οἶμαι πρῶτον
ἐκθέσθαι τίνα μὲν εἶναι σκοπὸν
ἁπάσης ἱεραρχίας οἰόμεθα καὶ τί
τοὺς αὐτῆς ἑκάστης θιασώτας
ὀνίνησιν· ἑξῆς δὲ τὰς οὐρανίας
ἱεραρχίας ὑμνῆσαι κατὰ τὴν
αὐτῶν ἐν τοῖς λογίοις ἐκφαντο
ρίαν· ἑπομένοις τε τούτοις εἰ
πεῖν ὁποίαις ἱεραῖς μορφώσεσι
τὰς οὐρανίας σχηματίζουσι τά
ξεις ὁσίως αἱ τῶν λογίων ἱερο
γραφίαι· καὶ πρὸς ποίαν ἀναχθῆ
ναι χρὴ διὰ τῶν πλασμάτων ἁ
πλότητα· ὅπως μὴ καὶ ἡμεῖς
ὡσαύτως τοῖς πολλοῖς ἀνιέρως
οἰόμεθα τοὺς οὐρανίους καὶ θε
οειδεῖς νόας πολύποδας εἶναί τι
νας καὶ πολυπροσώπους καὶ πρὸς
βοῶν κτηνωδίαν ἢ πρὸς λεόν
των θηριομορφίαν τετυπωμέ
νους καὶ πρὸς ἀετῶν ἀγκυλόχει
λον εἶδος ἢ πρὸς πτηνῶν τριχώ
δη πτεροφυΐαν διαπεπλασμέ
νους· καὶ τροχούς τινας πυρώ
δεις

Page from an early-ninth-century transcription of a work by Pseudo-Dionysius. This manuscript was once owned by Louis the Pious of France (Bibliothèque Nationale, Paris, Cod. Paris gr. 437, fol. 3r).

tian or the Syrian city known by that name is not clear—and what Damascius recounted in his *Life of Isidore* (circa 500) of his own experiences at Baalbek, the Heliopolis in Syria. Since, in the first quarter of the sixth century, only Pseudo-Dionysius and Damascius are known to have employed the "superunknown" (*hyperagnōstos*) as an epithet for the ultimate principle of their philosophies, and since the *Life of Isidore* is among the sources of the *Dionysiaca*, the most likely field in which to seek the pretended convert of Paul seems the retinue of Damascius. Of the companions of Damascius, Hathaway was inclined to link Pseudo-Dionysius with Heraïscus, an Egyptian theologian who had studied under Proclus and whom the latter had acknowledged to be his superior in learning. In his *Dubitationes et Solutiones de Primis Principiis* (Problems and Solutions Regarding First Principles) Damascius mentions Heraïscus as belonging to the tradition of those who celebrated the first principle of the universe as an "unknowable darkness." Since Damascius gives no account sufficient to prove any doctrinal relationship between Heraïscus and Pseudo-Dionysius, Hathaway infers the possibility of their being one and the same person on the basis of an exceedingly cryptic passage in the *Life of Isidore* which can be understood to mean that during some interval of his career Heraïscus affected a Christian identity. On the other hand, Damascius portrays Heraïcus as having been enshrouded after his death with the Osirian robe worn customarily by the priests of Isis. If, then, as Hathaway has averred, Heraïscus became a Christian, his sense of religious commitment must have been highly equivocal. Heraïscus is also named in the Syriac *Life of Severus*, by Zacharias Scholasticus, as an influence of note among the scholars at Alexandria, where the future patriarch of Antioch studied grammar. Certainly, of those associated with Damascius, none may seem more promising as Pseudo-Dionysius than Heraïscus; but without better evidence, his claim to authorship of the *Dionysiaca* remains undemonstrated.

To identify Pseudo-Dionysius with the Egyptian student of Proclus is to date the *Corpus Areopagiticum* between 476 and 500. Otherwise, if Pseudo-Dionysius could not have known, except from the *Life of Isidore*, of the pilgrimage Damascius had made to Baalbek, his works can be dated no earlier than 500 and no later than 528. How, or from whom, Severus acquired the *Dionysiaca*, history does not say.

For Pseudo-Dionysius, the fundamental antinomy in theology is that of holiness and profanity. By their participation in holiness, an enlightened few, who alone are privy to divine mysteries, are isolated from the profane and vulgar multitudes (*amuētoi*) who persist in ignorance of higher truths. Those initiated (*mustai*) into the mysteries are able to recognize the extent to which no image of divinity, whether sensible or intelligible, bears any resemblance to its paradigm; thus, the privileged minority does not need to contemplate God under the limitation of symbols. In contrast to the initiates—for whom, it is apparent, Pseudo-Dionysius is writing—the vulgar are inclined to mistake images for the paradigm and to fall into controversy and confusion over such fragments of divinity as the symbols can embrace.

Believing that the multitudes are irremediably attached to and misled by images of God in preference to the divinity beyond symbols, Pseudo-Dionysius enjoins the vulgar from all access to the mysteries. And because truth is one and not many, he advises theologians never to take sides in arguments regarding their subject matter.

De Divinis Nominibus, *De Mystica Theologia*, *De Caelesti Hierarchia*, and *De Ecclesiastica Hierarchia* are all addressed by their pretended author to his "compresbyter" Timothy, the better known among the Greeks corresponding with Paul. Four of the letters of the corpus are addressed to the "monk" Gaius, mentioned by Paul in Romans 16:23 and 1 Corinthians 1:14, in Acts 19:29 and 20:14, and in 3 John. The fifth letter is written to Dorotheus, said to be a deacon; the sixth to Sosipater, a priest; the seventh to Polycarp, called a "hierarch"; the eighth to Demophilus, another "monk"; the ninth to Titus, also the correspondent of Paul and, like Polycarp, a "hierarch"; and the tenth to the apostle John, in exile on Patmos. Other titles mentioned by Pseudo-Dionysius—*Theological Representations*, *Symbolic Theology*, *Properties and Ranks of Angels*, *Divine Hymns*, *On the Intelligible and the Sensible*, *On Justice and Divine Judgment*, and *On the Soul*—are believed to be fictitious.

The word *hierarchy* (*hierarchia*) was coined by Pseudo-Dionysius from *hierarch* (*hierarchēs*), meaning high priest or bishop. Narrowly construed, it denotes the relation of a bishop to those of lesser rank; but in its widest application it refers to the ordering of all being under the principle of transcendent unity.

In *De Ecclesiastica Hierarchia* Pseudo-Dionysius says that the love of God is the commanding terminus of every hierarchy and that, as originating from God, all hierarchies participate in "the One itself, as far as possible." In the church, the clerical order is made up of bishops, priests, and deacons; the ranks subordinate to them consist of monks, the "holy people," and a lowest grade populated by catechumens, the "possessed" (energumens), and penitents. Of the sacraments, Pseudo-Dionysius acknowledges baptism, communion, and unction. The sacraments are among the mysteries to be witnessed only by the initiates; other mysteries are sacerdotal consecration, tonsure, and a ritual for the dead.

The mysteries are essential to the theurgical universe in which the church operates under Jesus, the divine mind from whom every hierarchy originates. *Theurgy* (*theourgia*) refers to the divine acts facilitating the return of things, and especially of the soul, to the unity of their ultimate source. At its lowest level, theurgy pertains to the rituals by which divinity is united with physical objects; at its highest, to the union of immaterial being with the singular cause of all being and divinity.

In *De Caelesti Hierarchia* Pseudo-Dionysius schematizes three triads of angelic choirs; each triad constitutes a hierarchy within a hierarchy. In the highest are seraphim, cherubim, and thrones; in the second, virtues, dominations, and powers; in the lowest, principalities, archangels, and angels. The structure of the angelic hierarchy is not derived from Scripture but, as the author says, from Hierotheus, his "sacred initiator." The seraphim are the immediate recipients of the divine light, which they retransmit to the cherubim, by whom the process is repeated. The light is passed from superiors to inferiors, each receiving and giving according to its own capacity, until the hierarchy terminates in the rank of angels. The lowest triad has direct charge over the human hierarchies.

The beings which constitute the celestial hierarchy are said by Pseudo-Dionysius to be "intelligences" and are the causes of perfection to whatever receives their influence. Except for the seraphim, there is none to which the divine light is given directly. In every further communication of the light from one being to another, something less is revealed and something more is hidden.

The action of hierarchies is based on a Neoplatonic conception of causality as the procession (*proodos*) from unity to plurality and the reversion (*epistrophē*) of plurality to unity. Inasmuch as what is undivided in a cause must be divided throughout its effects, the result of procession must be an increase in number; but in the order of reversions, number is diminished and power is increased.

Like much else in the *Dionysiaca*, the language and treatment of causality are derived from Proclus and adapted to Christian symbols. How far Pseudo-Dionysius distinguishes creation from Neoplatonic emanation, if indeed he does, continues to be a disputed question. Unlike Augustine, he offers no discussion of creation with reference to time.

Pseudo-Dionysius views the symbols to which thought attaches itself as partly revealing and partly concealing; the difference between revelation and concealment is the difference between *kataphasis* and *apophasis*, that is, between the *via affirmativa* and the *via negativa* in theology. Kataphatic (affirmative) theology is based on what can be signified positively concerning God among the finite symbols of which the mind always makes use. Apophatic (negative) theology is based on the transcendence of God, who is unlimited by what can be uttered or thought. (The distinction of kataphatic from apophatic theology did not originate with Pseudo-Dionysius; it is at least as old as the allegorical treatment accorded to Scripture by Philo Judaeus or to Homeric epic by Heracleides Ponticus and, much earlier, as the protest lodged by Xenophanes against the anthropomorphic deities of Greek myth.) Since, in the relation of symbols to the cause of all beings, unlikeness prevails against likeness, apophatic theology is more appropriate to its object and more accurate than kataphatic. God, then, is affirmed primarily by not affirming and known by not knowing.

In *De Divinis Nominibus* Pseudo-Dionysius devotes himself to what can be affirmed and denied concerning the principle of divinity. Reflecting on a multitude of holy names, most of which he obtains from Scripture, he maintains that the most enduring of all the terms applicable to God are *perfect* and *one* and that the highest is *good*. These names can be predicated positively of God as the unqualified cause of perfection, unity, and goodness in all things. The human concepts of perfection, unity, and goodness are drawn, however, only from their created manifestations; and because God is eternally more than what can be said of him, perfection, unity, and goodness are

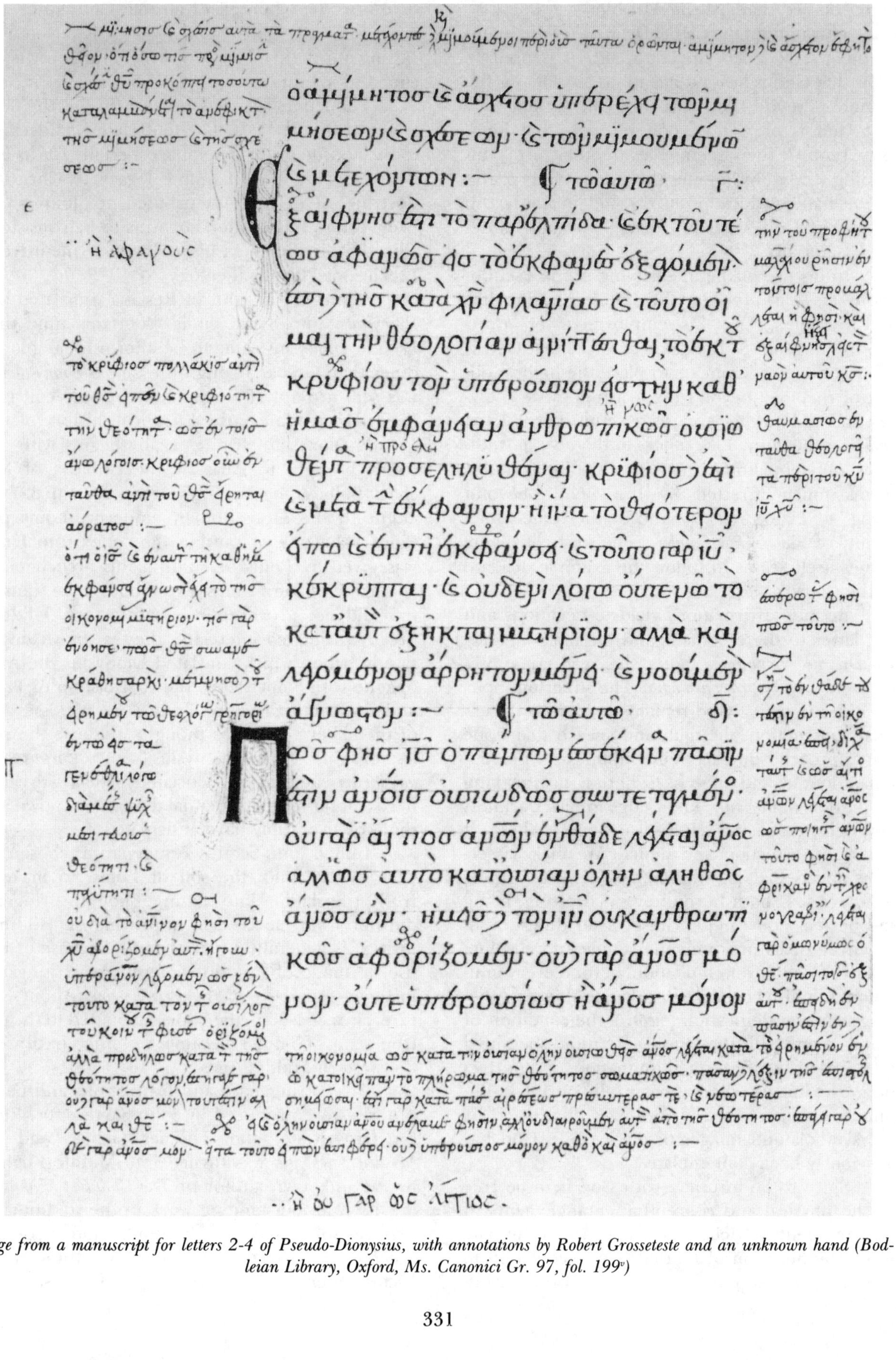

Page from a manuscript for letters 2-4 of Pseudo-Dionysius, with annotations by Robert Grosseteste and an unknown hand (Bodleian Library, Oxford, Ms. Canonici Gr. 97, fol. 199v)

better denied than affirmed of him.

Throughout the *Corpus Dionysiacum* the intensifying prefix *hyper-* (in Latin, *super-*) is used to show that God is beyond negations as well as affirmations. Pseudo-Dionysius thus can say not only that God is or is not good but also that he is "supergood"; the same applies to other terms, including *divine*. By joining the intensifying prefix to the names which positively and properly can be said of God, what is affirmed formally is denied materially.

In his use of the intensifying prefix Pseudo-Dionysius was preceded by Damascius, Proclus, and Syrianus, and his employment of *hyperagnōstos* ties him to Damascius. To say that God is "superunknown" appears to place the highest object of theology beyond the grasp both of knowing and unknowing and, as a result, beyond the reach of theology. Like others in the several traditions of Neoplatonic thought, Pseudo-Dionysius seems much affected by the Good "beyond being" of Plato's *Republic* and by the "One which is not" of Plato's *Parmenides*. (The study of divine names itself seems to follow the example of Plato in the *Cratylus*.)

Because affirmations yield to negations and the latter to the enigmatic and ineffable (*arrētos*), *De Divinis Nominibus* should be read as a prologue to *De Mystica Theologia*. The superluminous darkness in which God remains hidden so far exceeds perception, thought, and speech that none can approach him except in emptiness of perception, thought and speech: "There is no speaking of it, nor name nor knowledge of it. Darkness and light, error and truth—it is none of these. It is beyond assertion and denial. We make assertions and denials of what is next to it, but never of it, for it is both beyond every assertion, being the perfect and unique cause of all things, and, by virtue of its preeminently simple and absolute nature, free of every limitation, beyond every limitation; it is also beyond every denial." Mystical theology aims at deification (*theōsis*), the condition of being at one with the One. Deification is attained by stages of purification, illumination, and perfection. The initiate who has been fully purified, illumined, and perfected is no longer dominated by the symbols and images through which God has previously been contemplated.

Since to be in union with God is to be free of the physical and conceptual entanglements of human identity, deification requires the initiate to be the negation of himself. For assimilation to the one, good, and perfect mystery of God, the initiate is to deny himself of all that God is not; toward this end, *The Mystical Theology* is devoted to casting out the symbols with which humanity is inclined to identify not only God but also itself.

The letters supplement and fill out the doctrines of the treatises. The tenth letter, addressed to the apostle John, is notable especially for its endorsement of the Johannine legacy to Christian doctrine. The works attributed to John were likely found by Pseudo-Dionysius to be consistent with the principles, as he understood them from Proclus, of Platonic theology.

About 536 Sergius of Resaina translated the *Dionysiaca* into Syriac; it is from this time that Pseudo-Dionysius came to be known in languages other than Greek. Though the *Corpus Dionysiacum* was sent around 757 from Rome to the court of Pépin III in France, the European history of the Pseudo-Dionysian writings really begins with the codex brought to Paris by the embassy of Michael Balbus, the Byzantine emperor, in 827 as a gift to the Holy Roman emperor, Louis the Pious. The task of putting the codex into Latin was given by Louis to Hilduin, his archchaplain and abbot of Saint Denis. Even though the translation did not prove entirely satisfactory, Hilduin greatly promoted interest in the text by writing a saintly fiction which conflated Dionysius the Areopagite with Saint Denis, the first bishop of Paris and the protomartyr of France. As a possession of the abbey which was thought to house the relics of this "Denis-Dionysius," the *Corpus Dionysiacum* came to be associated with a Christian hero cult far more influential than its unknown author could possibly have anticipated.

In 858 John Scottus Eriugena was chosen by Charles the Bald, the son of Louis, to make a fresh translation into Latin. Though Eriugena did not always succeed in improving on Hilduin, his text is generally superior; and, because of the use he made of Pseudo-Dionysius in writings of his own, especially in the *Periphyseon* (About Nature, circa 864-866), the books attributed to the patron saint of France became a literary fixture of the western Middle Ages.

After Eriugena, Latin translations and paraphrases were produced by John Sarracenus, Robert Grosseteste, and Thomas Gallus; and *De Mystica Theologia* was turned into Middle English by the unknown author of *The Cloud of Unknowing*, itself an outstanding work in the tradition of mystical spirituality. In philosophy and theology, the *Dionysiaca* were reflected on by Hugh of St. Victor, Peter Lombard, Alexander of Hales, Bonaventure, Albert the Great, Thomas Aquinas, and Meister Eckhart. Toward the close of the Middle Ages and into the Renaissance, the influence of Pseudo-Dionysius can be seen in Dante, Johannes Tauler, Henry Suso, Jean de Gerson, Nicholas of Cusa, Denis the Carthusian, Pico della Mirandola, Marsilio Ficino, and John Colet.

Though Pseudo-Dionysius cannot be said to have shaped medieval worldviews to the exclusion of other sources, his legacy to Europe rivaled that of Augustine. He was esteemed by the Church as its mystical theologian par excellence. His stature both in the East and in the West continues to transcend all the barriers of culture and creed by which Christians so long have been divided.

References:

Hans Urs von Balthasar, "Das Scholienwerk des Johannes von Skythopolis," *Scholastik*, 15 (1940): 16-38;

H. J. Blumenthal, "529 and Its Sequel: What Happened to the Academy?," *Byzantion*, 48 (1978): 369-385;

Alan Cameron, "The Last Days of the Academy at Athens," *Proceedings of the Cambridge Philological Society*, new series 15 (1979): 7-29;

Alb. van den Daele, *Indices Pseudo-Dionysiani* (Louvain: Université de Louvain, 1941);

Alison Frantz, "From Paganism to Christianity in the Temples of Athens," *Dumbarton Oaks Papers*, 19 (1965): 185-206;

W. H. C. Frend, *The Rise of the Monophysite Movement* (Cambridge: Cambridge University Press, 1972);

Stephen E. Gersh, *From Iamblichus to Eriugena* (Leiden: Brill, 1978);

John Glucker, *Antiochus and the Late Academy* (Göttingen: Vandenhoeck & Ruprecht, 1978);

L. H. Grondijs, "The Patristic Origins of Gregory Palamas' Doctrine of God," *Texte und Untersuchungen*, 80 (1962): 323-328;

Grondijs, "Sur la terminologie dionysienne," *Bulletin de l'Association Guillaume Budé*, series 4, no. 4 (1959): 438-447;

Grondijs, "La terminologie métalogique dans la théologie dionysienne," *Nederlands Theologisch Tijdschrift*, 14, no. 6 (1960): 420-430;

Ronald F. Hathaway, *Hierarchy and the Definition of Order in the Letters of Pseudo-Dionysius* (The Hague: Nijhoff, 1969);

Edouard Jeauneau, "Pseudo-Dionysius, Gregory of Nyssa, and Maximus the Confessor in the Works of John Scottus Eriugena," in *Carolingian Essays*, edited by Uta-Renate Blumenthal (Washington, D.C.: Catholic University of America Press, 1983), pp. 137-149;

Hugo Koch, "Proklus als Quelle des Pseudo-Dionysius Areopagita in der Lehre vom Bösen," *Philologus*, 54 (1895): 438-454;

Koch, *Pseudo-Dionysius in seinen Beziehungen Zum Neuplatonismus und Mysterienwesen* (Mayance: Kirchheim, 1900);

Hans Lewy, *Chaldaean Oracles and Theurgy* (Paris: Etudes Augustiniennes, 1978);

R. L. Loenertz, "La légende parisienne de saint Denys l'Aréopagite, sa genèse et son premier témoin," *Analecta Bollandiana*, 69 (1951): 217-237;

John Meyendorff, *Byzantine Theology* (New York: Fordham University Press, 1974);

John M. Rist, "In Search of the Divine Denis," in *The Seed of Wisdom*, edited by William S. McCullough (Toronto: University of Toronto Press, 1964), pp. 118-139;

René Roques, "Rappel de la question dionysienne," in *Dictionnaire de spiritualité*, volume 3, edited by Charles Baumgartner (Paris: Beauchesne, 1957);

Roques, *l'Univers dionysien: Structure hiéarchique du monde selon le pseudo-Denys* (Aubier: Montaigne, 1955);

Paul Rorem, "The Place of the Mystical Theology in the pseudo-Dionysian *Corpus*," *Dionysius*, 4 (1980): 87-97;

H.-D. Saffrey. "New Objective Links between the Pseudo-Dionysius and Proclus," in *Neoplatonism and Christian Thought*, edited by Dominic J. O'Meara (Albany: State University of New York Press, 1982), pp. 64-74;

I. P. Sheldon-Williams, "The Ps.-Dionysius and the Holy Hierotheus," *Texte und Untersuchungen*, 93 (1966): 108-145;

Dom Placid Spearritt, "A Philosophical Enquiry into Dionysian Mysticism," Ph.D. thesis, University of Fribourg, 1968;

Josef Stiglmayr, "Das Aufkommen der Pseudo-Dionysischen Schriften und ihr Eindrigen in die christliche Literatur bis zum Laterankonzil 649," in *IV. Jahresbericht des öffentlichen Privatgymnasiums an der Stella Matutina zu Feldkirch* (Feldkirch, 1895), pp. 3-96;

Stiglmayr, "Der Neuplatoniker Proclus als Vorlage des sogen. Dionysius Areopagita in der Lehre vom Übel," *Historisches Jahrbuch*, 16 (1895): 253-273;

Reinhold Strömberg, "Damascius: His Personality and Significance," *Eranos: Acta philologica suecana*, 44 (1946): 175-192;

G. Théry, "l'Entrée du pseudo-Denys en occident," in *Mélanges Mandonnet II*, Bibliothèque Thomiste, 14 (Paris: 1930), pp. 23-30;

Théry, *Etudes dionysiennes I: Hilduin, traducteur de Denys* (Paris: Vrin, 1932);

Théry, *Etudes dionysiennes II: Hilduin, traducteur de Denys. Edition de sa traduction* (Paris: Vrin, 1937);

Théry, "Recherches pour une édition grecque historique du pseudo-Denys," *New Scholasticism*, 3, no. 4 (1929): 353-442.

Siger of Brabant

(circa 1240 - circa 1284)

James South
Duke University

PRINCIPAL WORKS: *Quaestiones in Tertium De Anima* (Questions on the Third Book of [Aristotle's] *On the Soul*, written 1269-1270);

De Aeternitate Mundi (On the Eternity of the World, written 1271-1272);

Impossibilia (Impossibles, written 1271-1272);

De Necessitate et Contingentia Causarum (Concerning the Necessity and the Contingency of Causes, written 1271-1272);

De Anima Intellectiva (Concerning the Intellective Soul, written 1272-1273);

Quaestiones in Metaphysicam (Questions on [Aristotle's] *Metaphysics*, written 1272-1275);

Quaestiones Naturales (Natural Questions, written 1274);

Quaestiones Morales (Moral Questions, written 1274);

Quaestiones super Librum De Causis (Questions on the *Book of Causes*, written 1276).

EDITIONS: *Siger de Brabant et l'averroisme latin au XIIIe siècle*, 2 volumes, edited by Pierre Mandonnet, Les Philosophes belges, 6-7 (Louvain: Editions de l'Institut Supérieur de Philosophie de l'Université, 1908-1911);

Siger de Brabant d'après ses oeuvres inédites, 2 volumes, edited by Fernand Van Steenberghen, Les Philosophes belges, 12-13 (Louvain: Editions de l'Institut Supérieur de Philosophie de l'Université, 1931-1942);

"De necessitate et contingentia causarum," edited by Joannes Josef Duin, in his *La Doctrine de la providence dans les écrits de Siger de Brabant*, Philosophes médiévaux, 3 (Louvain: Editions de l'Institut Supérieur de Philosophie, 1954), pp. 14-50;

Les Quaestiones super librum De causis de Siger de Brabant, edited by A. Marlasca, Philosophes médiévaux, 12 (Louvain & Paris: Publications universitaires, 1972);

Siger de Brabant: Quaestiones in tertium De anima, De anima intellectiva, De aeternitate mundi, edited by Bernardo C. Bazán, Philosophes médiévaux, 13 (Louvain: Publications universitaires, 1972);

Siger de Brabant: Ecrits de logique, de morale et de physique, edited by Bazán, Philosophes médiévaux, 14 (Louvain & Paris: Publications universitaires, 1974);

Siger de Brabant: Quaestiones in Metaphysicam, edited by William Dunphy, Philosophes médiévaux, 24 (Louvain-la-Neuve: Editions de l'Institut Supérieur de Philosophie, 1981);

Siger de Brabant: Quaestiones in Metaphysicam, edited by Armand Maurer, Philosophes médiévaux, 25 (Louvain-la-Neuve: Editions de l'Institut Supérieur de Philosophie de l'Université, 1983).

One of the most important philosophers of the thirteenth century, Siger of Brabant was a pioneer of a radical return to the philosophy of Aristotle. He said that his main philosophical method was to determine as precisely as possible the authentic teachings of the ancient philosophers. In this process the philosopher given the most attention was Aristotle, and it is Siger's constant concern, especially in his earlier writings, to determine exactly what Aristotle said. This enterprise entailed a radical separation between philosophy and religion.

Siger accepted the truths of the Catholic faith but also realized that philosophy can be carried out independently of faith. Thus, for example, in his *Quaestiones in Tertium De Anima* (Questions on the Third Book of [Aristotle's] *On the Soul*, 1269-1270) and *De Aeternitate Mundi* (On the Eternity of the World, 1271-1272) Siger holds that philosophy demonstrates that the world is eternal. This conclusion, however, must be false, because it is in direct contradiction to the Judeo-Christian belief that the world results from an act of creation by God. Siger never held to a "double truth" theory, in which a proposition would be true for philosophy and its contradictory would be true for theology; he never said that any proposition contrary to faith was true.

Little is known about the early years of Siger's life. It is thought that he was born around 1240. His name shows that he was a native of the Duchy of Brabant, most probably from the Walloon area, which was a fief of the Germanic empire. It was customary at that time to begin the study of the liberal arts at fourteen, so Siger was probably around that age when he was admitted into the Picard nation of the University of Paris. He obtained his master's degree six years later. He was a master of arts in 1266, when his name is first mentioned in documents which have survived: on 27 August the papal legate Simon of Brion issued a decree aimed at ending dissensions in the faculty of arts at the University of Paris; Siger is portrayed in this decree as a young and unscrupulous leader who is employing all means at his disposal to force his views on others.

Siger's earliest known writing, *Quaestiones in Tertium De Anima*, shows that from the beginning of his career he had a disregard for theology and pursued a radical version of Aristotle's thought, unmediated by Christian tradition. On 10 December 1270 Stephen Tempier, the bishop of Paris, published a condemnation of thirteen philosophical propositions. Most of these propositions, including that of the eternity of the world, can be found in Siger's writings. Although Siger moderated his radical Aristotelian views under the influence of Thomas Aquinas, on 23 November 1276 Simon du Val, the inquisitor of France, cited Siger as one of those holding heretical views. Siger had already left France and had apparently appealed to the inquisitor of the pontifical curia in Orvieto. He was declared innocent of the charges of heresy by the papal tribunal but was forced to stay at the curia, where he was allowed to have a secretary. On 7 March 1277 Tempier condemned 219 propositions; many of them were from the writings of Siger, although several were from the writings of Aquinas. This action effectively ended any hope Siger might have had of continuing in an academic career. Nothing is known concerning how Siger spent his remaining years. There is a strong tradition that he was stabbed to death by his secretary, who had gone mad, at the papal curia in Orvieto during the pontificate of Martin IV (formerly the papal legate Simon of Brion) between 1281 and 1285. Siger's death is attested in a letter of John Peckham dated 10 November 1284.

Siger's basic views on metaphysical issues can be obtained from his *Quaestiones in Metaphysicam* (Questions on [Aristotle's] *Metaphysics*, 1273). Siger is adamant that God is not the primary subject of metaphysics, since metaphysics is concerned with what is universal. Since God is a being, however, he falls under the general notion of being and hence may be studied in metaphysics. The existence of God can also be proven in physics, via the argument that there cannot be an infinite regress of moved movers. This conclusion reached in physics can be used in metaphysics to reason about God, since it provides some specific knowledge concerning God. Siger invokes the first three of the five ways of Aquinas to prove the existence of God: the impossibility of an infinite regress of movers, the impossibility of an infinite series of efficient causes, and the argument that the existence of merely possible beings implies the existence of a necessary being.

God has an immediate effect which is unique, eternal, and necessary. This first necessary effect is the first of the separated intelligences or spiritual substances. All the other intelligences proceed from this first intelligence, as do the celestial spheres and the movements of the heavens. Following on this procession, the physical world is produced. So, for Siger, everything originates from the first being through a process of intermediate causes according to a necessary and eternal law. The spiritual substances or intelligences are eternal, simple, and unique in their species and are the movers of the heavenly spheres.

Siger holds that there is no real distinction between essence and existence in creatures; but existence has the mode of act while essence has the mode of potency. Thus all things other than the first being, who alone is simple, recede from the simplicity of the first being insofar as they recede from the actuality of the first being and approach potentiality. Beings participate more in being the more they approach the first being and participate less in being the farther they recede from the first being. No being can ever attain to equality with the first being, which is the measure of all things.

Aquinas argued for the real distinction between essence and existence, in part because there are created things which are not composed of matter and form, such as angels. Siger responds that the distinction is unnecessary. All that is necessary is that such spiritual creatures fall short of the first being in that unlike the first being, who understands himself through himself, all creatures must acquire knowledge by means of intelligible species (mental objects) which are different from themselves. By the time Siger came to write *Quaestiones super Librum De Causis* (Questions on the *Book of Causes*, 1276) his views had undergone some revision. Particularly noteworthy is his move toward a position close to that of Aquinas concerning the relation between essence and existence in creatures. Here Siger claims that essence and existence are constituent parts of creatures, which seems to imply a real distinction between the essence of a thing and its existence.

In *Quaestiones in Tertium De Anima* Siger propounds his early views on philosophical psychology. He argues that the soul is composed of the intellect, on the on hand, and the vegetative and sensitive powers, on the other hand. The intellect is a simple substance that is eternally caused by the first being. It is one for all people and is united to individuals in the manner of an accident; that is, it is united not by its substance but by its activity. This one intellect is divided into two powers: the agent intellect, an active power which abstracts universal concepts from sense experience; and the possible intellect, which receives the universals thus abstracted and uses them to think. Both powers are dependent on the sense images generated in the sensitive part of the soul. According to this theory, we are deceived when we seem to experience that we are thinking: in fact, the one intellect thinks *in* us by using our sense images.

In 1270 Aquinas published a critique of Siger's views. In particular, Aquinas objected to Siger's contention that the possible intellect is only accidentally united to the body and is thus not essential to the body, and that this possible intellect is the same for all people. For Aquinas the intellective soul is the form of the body and so must be united to the body essentially, not accidentally. The intellect, though, operates without a material organ. In this way the intellect can "transcend" matter and can form abstract and universal concepts. What most vexes Aquinas is Siger's apparent disregard for experience: Aquinas claims that it is indisputable that each individual is aware that he, as an individual, thinks. Siger first replied to Aquinas in the now lost *De Intellectu* (Concerning the Intellect), which is known through quotations in the works of the Renaissance philosopher Agostino Nifo. This work seems to have been rushed to completion without Siger really having had time to come to terms with the criticisms of Aquinas.

His next reply to Aquinas was *De Anima Intellectiva* (Concerning the Intellective Soul, 1272-1273). This work is an attempt to determine what Aristotle had to say on these topics; Siger admits that he is not concerned with discovering the truth concerning the soul, which, he believed, can only come from revelation. Siger argues that the intellect, while one for all humans and also separate, is united to the body by its nature; but this union is not to be understood as a substantial one, as Aquinas understood it. If there were a substantial union, abstract and universal knowledge would be impossible, since the activity of a substance cannot be more immaterial than the substance of which it is an activity. Thus, if the intellective soul is in substantial union with the body, it would not be able to have universal knowledge. Siger sees as inadequate Aquinas's distinction between the form and operation of the intellect; instead, Siger argues that each individual knows because the actions of parts of a composite can be considered acts of

Illustration by Giovanni di Paolo from a mid-fifteenth-century manuscript for Canto X of Dante's Paradiso. *The hovering figure holding the staff is Thomas Aquinas; he is introducing Albert the Great to Dante and Beatrice. Siger of Brabant is thought to be one of the two figures on the far right. In the text, Aquinas calls him "Siger, who, lecturing in Straw Street, demonstrated invidious truths" (British Museum, Yates Thompson MS. 36, f. 147r).*

the whole entity. Siger says that he is not sure what Aristotle's position is regarding the multiplicity of agent intellects, and he even repeats some of Aquinas's arguments in favor of the multiplicity of intellects. He concludes that when such philosophical doubt exists, one must accept the multiplicity of intellects on the basis of religious teaching. It was no doubt the arguments of Aquinas as well as the general atmosphere in Paris after 1270 that made Siger moderate his views regarding the soul and intellect. What is most striking, however, is that Siger now abandons the commentaries on Aristotle of Averroës, who was his model for his earlier theory, and argues with Aquinas on the basis of the same sources Aquinas used. Particularly important is the use both authors make of Themistius, the Greek Neoplatonic commentator on Aristotle.

In *Quaestiones super Librum De Causis* Siger says that since Aristotle was human, it is possible that he was wrong. Siger now holds, under the influence of Aquinas, that the intellect is the substantial form of the body; and he admits, partly due to Aquinas's criticism concerning the individual experience of thinking, that human intellects are multiplied and are the forms of individual bodies. The individual intellect requires the body in order to know, since it is dependent on sense experience. Siger still tries to hold on to the unique status of the intellect, however, by claiming that it is not simply material in its essence, as Aquinas held, but rather that some part of it is distinct from the material body. This position is distinguishable from Aquinas's view that it is only the *power* of the intellect which is distinct from the body. The agent intellect abstracts an intelligible species from the sense-image in the imagination, and the possible intellect, by receiving this species, is able to know an intelligible object.

In his earliest writings Siger often expounded views which were contradictory to the Christian faith. For example, in *Quaestiones in Tertium De Anima* he asks whether a separated soul can experience fire, a question that has an obvious reference to the Christian doctrine of Hell. Saying that it is not much of a *philosophical* problem, he does not discuss the teaching of revelation when talking about the issue, which he decides in the negative.

This attitude toward faith and theology was mitigated somewhat after the first criticisms of his views by Aquinas and the condemnation of 1270. In *De Anima Intellectiva*, where he explicitly discusses his philosophical methodology, he says that in treating issues philosophically the goal is to determine what previous philosophers have said, not necessarily to discover the truth. But he became increasingly concerned with determining why philosophy and theology often seem to conflict. In *Quaestiones in Metaphysicam* he is still unsure of how to reconcile reason and revelation and resorts to the rather makeshift explanation that theological truths are true due to a supernatural intervention from God. On other occasions he stresses the weakness of the human intellect in discerning the truth. In his final work, *Quaestiones super Librum De Causis*, however, Siger is able to reconcile philosophy and theology along much the same lines as Aquinas, who worked within the framework of revealed theology. In this work Siger is concerned with the truth and not with the thoughts of the philosophers. Indeed, he explicitly says that faith is superior to reason. Thus, by the end of his career Siger had come to expound a doctrine which can no longer be called radical Aristotelianism. Instead, he is comfortable to work within the confines of revealed theology.

Siger, like most of the radical Aristotelians who gathered around him in the arts faculty at Paris, was more interested in metaphysics and philosophical psychology than in ethics. His *Quaestiones Morales* (Moral Questions, 1274) is concerned with some minor moral issues but has nothing to say about general ethical principles. The five questions are concerned with humility, the formation of habits, the comparison of the intensity of maternal and paternal love, the suitability of the state of virginity for philosophers, and disinterested love.

Of more philosophical concern is his discussion of freedom of the will, a topic he brings up in several of his works. His central teaching is that every cause which influences the will can also be impeded by the will. That is, the will is always free not to act on the basis of an external cause; but if it does act on the basis of this external cause, then the sufficient cause of its action is the external cause alone. Siger is careful to note that this position is not a form of determinism, which was soundly condemned in 1270 and 1277. The passive will, which can impede a cause, is the only way open to him to deny a necessitated will; it entails, however, a disagreement with Aquinas, who thought that the will could move itself. Even in his last work, *Quaestiones super Librum De Causis*, which has a clear Thomistic influence, Siger upholds his view of the will.

Even after the condemnation of 1277, Siger's brand of Aristotelianism continued in Paris. John of Jandun, a follower of Siger, taught on the arts faculty at the university. In Dante's *Divine Comedy* (completed in 1321), Siger is placed in the fourth heaven alongside Aquinas, Albert the Great, Boethius, Solomon, Gratian, and six other major thinkers. He is even introduced to Dante and Beatrice by Aquinas. The works of Jandun and Siger were read and discussed during the Renaissance and were influential at the University of Padua near the end of the fifteenth century. Issues raised by Siger's writings were continually discussed down to the time of René Descartes in the seventeenth century.

References:

Bernardo C. Bazán, "Le dialogue philosophique entre Siger de Brabant et Thomas d'Aquin: A Propos d'un ouvrage récent de E. H. Wéber, O.P.," *Revue Philosophique de Louvain*, 72 (1974): 53-155;

Joannes Josef Duin, *La Doctrine de la providence dans les écrits de Siger de Brabant*, Philosophes médiévaux, 3 (Louvain: Editions de l'Institut Supérieur de Philosophie, 1954);

Roland Hissette, *Enquête sur les 219 articles condamnés à Paris le 7 mars 1277* (Louvain & Paris: Publications universitaires & Béatrice-Naulwelaerts, 1977);

Edward P. Mahoney, "Metaphysical Foundations of the Hierarchy of Being According to Some Late-Medieval and Renaissance Philosophers," in *Philosophies of Existence: Ancient and Medieval*, edited by Parviz Morewedge (New York: Fordham University Press, 1982), pp. 165-257;

Mahoney, "Saint Thomas and Siger of Brabant Revisited," *Review of Metaphysics*, 27 (March 1974): 531-553;

Mahoney, "Sense, Intellect, and Imagination in Albert, Thomas, and Siger," in *The Cambridge History of Later Medieval Philosophy*, edited by Norman Kretzmann, Anthony Kenny, and Jan Pinborg (Cambridge: Cambridge University Press, 1982), pp. 602-622;

Mahoney, "Themistius and the Agent Intellect in James of Viterbo and Other Thirteenth Century Philosophers (Saint Thomas, Siger of Brabant and Henry Bate)," *Augustiniana*, 23 (1973): 422-467;

Armand Maurer, "*Esse* and *Essentia* in the Metaphysics of Siger of Brabant," *Mediaeval Studies*, 8 (1946): 68-86;

Maurer, "A Promising New Discovery for Sigerian Studies," *Mediaeval Studies*, 29 (1967): 364-369;

Maurer, "Siger of Brabant and Theology," *Mediaeval Studies*, 50 (1988): 257-278;

Maurer, "Siger of Brabant on Fables and Falsehoods in Religion," *Mediaeval Studies*, 43 (1981): 515-530;

Maurer, "The State of Historical Research in Siger of Brabant," *Speculum*, 31 (January 1956): 49-56;

Christopher J. Ryan, "Man's Free Will in the Works of Siger of Brabant," *Mediaeval Studies*, 45 (1983): 155-199;

Fernand Van Steenberghen, *Aristotle in the West: The Origins of Latin Aristotelianism*, translated by L. Johnston (Louvain: Naulwelaerts, 1955);

Steenberghen, *Maître Siger de Brabant*, Philosophes médiévaux, 21 (Louvain & Paris: Publications universitaires de Louvain, 1977);

Steenberghen, *La Philosophie au XIIIe siècle*, Philosophes médiévaux, 9 (Louvain & Paris: Publications universitaires de Louvain & Béatrice-Naulwelaerts, 1966);

Steenberghen, *Thomas Aquinas and Radical Aristotelianism* (Washington, D.C.: Catholic University of America Press, 1980);

John F. Wippel, "Essence and Existence," in *The Cambridge History of Later Medieval Philosophy*, edited by Kretzmann, Kenny, and Pinborg (Cambridge: Cambridge University Press, 1982), pp. 385-410.

Richard Swineshead
(Riccardus Suiseth)
(floruit circa 1350)

André Goddu
Stonehill College

PRINCIPAL WORKS: *Tractatus de Motu Locali* (Treatise on Local Motion, written circa 1340);

De Motu (On Motion, written circa 1340);

In Librum De Caelo (Commentary on Aristotle's *On the Heavens*), also known as *Tractatus de Intensione et Remissione Formarum* (Treatise on the Intension and Remission of Forms, written circa 1340);

Liber Calculationum (Book of Calculations, written circa 1350).

EDITIONS: *Opus Aureum Calculationum* (Padua, circa 1477);

"Swineshead on Falling Bodies: An Example of Fourteenth-Century Physics," edited by M. A. Hoskin and A. G. Molland, *British Journal for the History of Science*, 3 (1966): 150-182.

The appellation "Merton Calculators" is a completely artificial one, referring principally to four individuals who were students or masters at Merton College, Oxford, in the fourteenth century. They are linked by their common interest in developing techniques for solving a variety of logical dilemmas and mathematical problems applicable to natural philosophy and theology. "Calculator" was the name given apparently by fifteenth-century Italian Schoolmen to the chronologically last of these authors, Richard Swineshead; it has been applied retrospectively to Thomas Bradwardine, William Heytesbury, and John of Dumbleton.

Confused by even near contemporaries with at least two other Swinesheads of the fourteenth century, Richard Swineshead is recorded as a Merton fellow in 1344 and again in 1355. Other records indicate that he came from Lincoln diocese, and he is mentioned as one of the supporters of John Wylyot in his election as chancellor of the university in 1349. His major work, *Liber Calculationum* (Book of Calculations), was probably completed around 1350. His dates of birth and death are unknown, but his life probably ran its course entirely within the fourteenth century.

In his treatment of three problems, Swineshead's analyses are clearly superior to those of his predecessors. First, according to previous views, the intensity of any quality was measured by its nearness to the maximum degree of that quality or its distance from zero degree; remission was measured by distance from the maximum degree. Swineshead simplifies the analysis

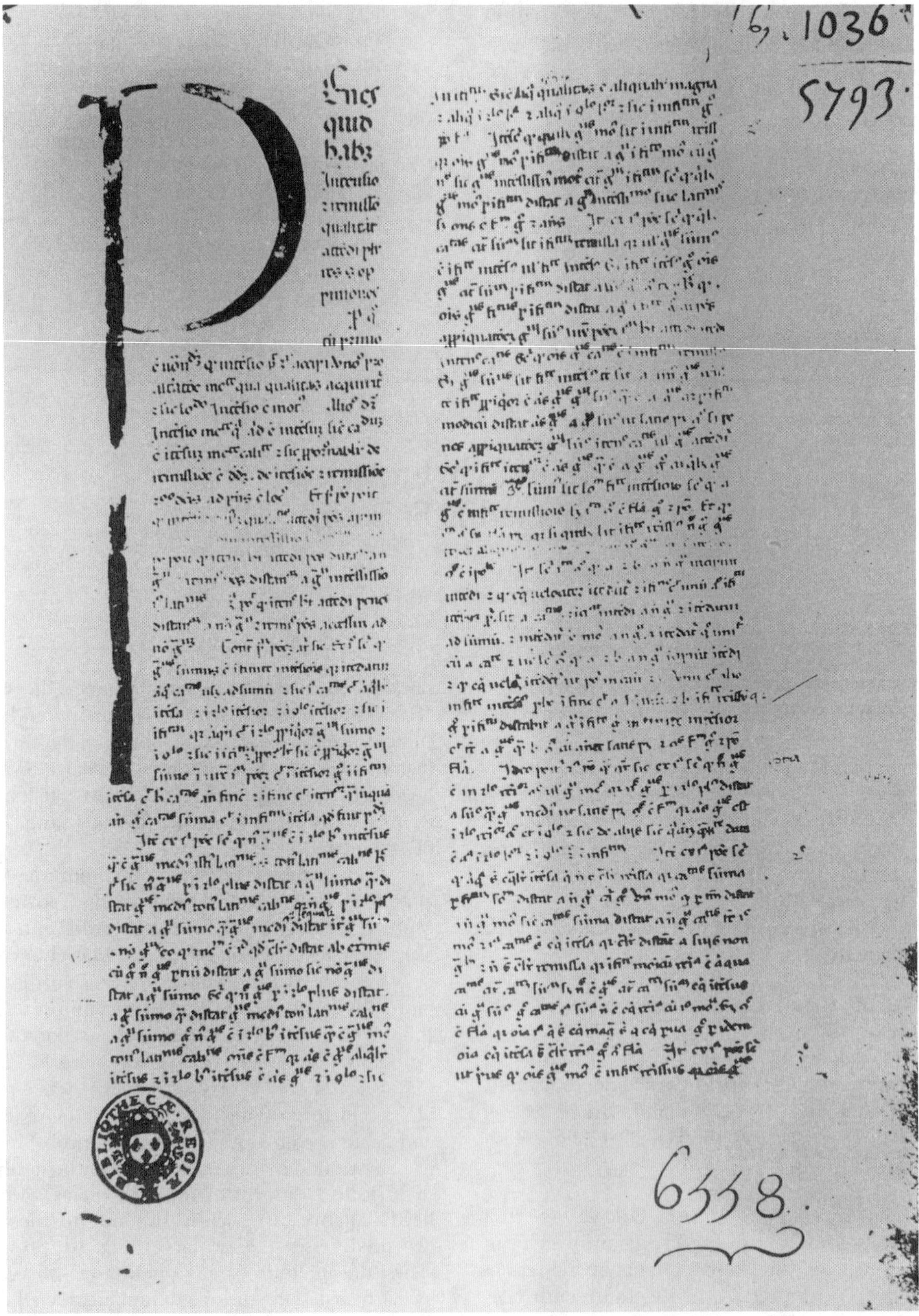

Page from a manuscript of Richard Swineshead's Liber Calculationum, *dated 1375 (Bibliothèque Nationale, Paris, MS Paris, BN lat. 9558, f. Ir)*

by making the intensity of a quality depend on its distance from zero degree and its remission on its nearness to zero degree. Because both intensity and remission are measured from zero degree, he labels the degrees of remission by the same numbers as the degrees of intensity, thus eliminating talk of remission altogether. He thereby removes the cumbersomeness of double measures (intensity and remission) and makes intensities additive—that is, he reduces all measures of the intensities of qualities to additive measures. Although his analysis does not provide a complete basis for actual measurements of qualities, the emphasis on measures of quality that are additive is a starting point.

Second, the additive theory of qualitative increase preferred by Swineshead had consequences that were not consistent with the Aristotelian account of action and passion. Swineshead maintains that the "multitude of form" of a quality is determined by the intensity, extension, and density of the form. If the quality is condensed and the intensity remains the same, the quality will have the same multitude of form. Multitude of form, then, is a measure of the power of a quality; Swineshead adds, however, that the amount of form induced in a subject depends on the amount of matter present. Swineshead understands the quantity of matter to refer to a finite and, in principle, denumerable number of parts. Consistent with the views of his Mertonian predecessors and of William of Ockham, Swineshead asserts that a form could be condensed to a point without its intensity increasing, thus implying that forms can expand and contract without losing or gaining in intensity and without the loss of their essential elemental character. As with Ockham and Dumbleton, the explanation of condensation and rarefaction is, in principle, reducible to the local motion of material parts.

A third and related problem is the relation between action and distance. A paradigm of the problem is illumination. Swineshead maintains that the power of a light source is determined by measuring (or "denominating") its multitude of form. Equal light sources are those that are equal both in intensity and in multitude of form. On the assumption that a light source produces its entire extension in every medium, Swineshead concludes that the illumination varies according to the density of the medium. A uniform medium acts as an impediment subtracting from the intensity of illumination. Hence, the intensity of illumination decreases linearly; it does not vary inversely with the distance from the light source.

Swineshead's treatment of local motion is the most thorough of the Mertonian analyses, considering all possible variations in force, resistance, and velocity that follow from Bradwardine's law that velocity increases arithmetically as the ratio of force to resistance increases geometrically. Although these achievements mark a considerable advance over those of his predecessors, Swineshead fails to exploit some suggestions from his predecessors that might have led to even more interesting developments in the treatment of problems of change and motion and in the use of geometrical representations. The limitations in the Aristotelian approach to problems of motion were corrected by the Mertonians in ways that left the basic principles of Aristotelianism intact. No urgency existed for the resolution of the problems of falling bodies until after the Copernican theory achieved plausibility several decades after its publication in 1543. Furthermore, even when the geometrical analysis is applied to bodies falling freely from rest, producing experiments and using the results to confirm the mathematical analysis requires extraordinary virtuosity in addition to mathematical ability. Measurable results could only be obtained by retarding the speed of a falling body, and Aristotelians could reasonably object that such artificially obtained results cannot be extrapolated to the motion of bodies falling freely from rest. The efforts of the Calculators probably contributed to the formulation of the problems of motion solved in the seventeenth century, but they were not solved in the fourteenth century because the problems did not yet exist in the form provoked by the Copernican theory. The problems of interest to the Calculators remain broadly consistent with Aristotelian natural philosophy and cosmology; that is, the problems are formulated in terms of characteristics of nature apprehended directly by the senses, of quantitative analysis subordinated to a fundamentally qualitative approach to nature, of causal powers and resisting media, and of local motion in an earth-centered cosmos.

Of the logico-mathematical works of the Calculators it was especially those of Heytesbury and Swineshead that were influential in Continental Europe. For example, Angelus of Fossambruno, who received his doctorate in arts at Bologna in 1395, taught at Bologna until 1400, and then began teaching natural philosophy at Padua, cites Swineshead in his *De Reactione* (On Reaction, circa 1402), calling him "the Calculator," the name by which Swineshead was known to Julius Caesar Scaliger, Girolamo Cardano, and Gottfried Wilhelm Leibniz. After its initial publication at Padua around 1477, Swineshead's *Liber Calculationum* was republished at Padua in 1489, at Pavia in 1498, at Venice in 1505, and again at Venice in 1520. There can be no question that Galileo was acquainted with Mertonian kinematics, although its influence on him is unclear.

References:

Stefano Caroti, ed., *Studies in Medieval Natural Philosophy*, Biblioteca di Nuncius, Studi e Testi, 1 (Florence: Olschki, 1989);

Marshall Clagett, *Giovanni Marliani and Late Medieval Physics* (New York: Columbia University Press, 1941);

Clagett, *Nicole Oresme and the Medieval Geometry of Qualities and Motions* (Madison & London: University of Wisconsin Press, 1968);

Clagett, "Richard Swineshead and Late Medieval Physics," *Osiris*, 9 (1950): 131-161;

Clagett, *The Science of Mechanics in the Middle Ages* (Madison: University of Wisconsin Press, 1959);

William Courtenay, *Schools and Scholars in Fourteenth-Century England* (Princeton: Princeton University Press, 1987);

A. C. Crombie, "Quantification in Medieval Physics," *Isis*, 52 (1961): 143-160;

Alain de Libera, "Bulletin d'histoire de la logique médiévale," *Revue des sciences philosophiques et théologiques*, 71 (1987): 590-634;

Pierre Duhem, *Etudes sur Léonard de Vinci*, third series (Paris: Hermann, 1913);

Duhem, *Le Système du Monde*, volumes 7-10 (Paris: Hermann, 1956-1959);

A. B. Emden, *A Biographical Register of the University of Oxford* (Oxford: Oxford University Press, 1957), III: 1836-1837;

André Goddu, *The Physics of William of Ockham*, Studien und Texte zur Geisteschichte des Mittelalters, 16 (Leiden & Cologne: Brill, 1984);

Edward Grant and John Murdoch, eds., *Mathematics and Its Application to Science and Natural Philosophy in the Middle Ages* (Cambridge: Cambridge University Press, 1987);

M. A. Hoskin and A. G. Molland, "Swineshead on Falling Bodies: An Example of Fourteenth-Century Physics," *British Journal for the History of Science*, 3 (1966): 150-182;

Norman Kretzmann, ed., *Infinity and Continuity in Ancient and Medieval Thought* (Ithaca, N.Y. & London: Cornell University Press, 1982);

Christopher Lewis, *The Merton Tradition and Kinematics in Late Sixteenth and Early Seventeenth Century Italy*, Saggi e Testi, 15 (Padua: Editrice Antenore, 1980);

Anneliese Maier, *An der Grenze von Scholastik und Naturwissenschaft*, Studien zur Naturphilosophie der Spätscholastik, 3, second edition, Studi e Testi, 41 (Rome: Storia e Letteratura, 1952);

Maier, *Ausgehendes Mittelalter*, 3 volumes (Rome: Storia e Letteratura, 1964-1977);

Maier, *Metaphysische Hintergründe der spätscholastischen Naturphilosophie*, Studien zur Naturphilosophie der Spätscholastik, 4, Studi e Testi, 97 (Rome: Storia e Letteratura, 1955);

Maier, *Die Vorläufer Galileis im 14. Jahrhundert*, Studien zur Naturphilosophie der Spätscholastik, 1, second expanded edition, Studi e Testi, 22 (Rome: Storia e Letteratura, 1966);

Maier, *Zwei Grundprobleme der scholastischen Naturphilosophie*, Studien zur Naturphilosophie der Spätscholastik, 2, third enlarged edition, Studi e Testi, 37 (Rome: Storia e Letteratura, 1968);

Maier, *Zwischen Philosophie und Mechanik*, Studien zur Naturphilosophie der Spätscholastik, 5, Studi e Testi, 69 (Rome: Storia e Letteratura, 1958);

Alfonso Maierù, *Terminologia logica della tarda scolastico*, Lessico intellettuale europeo, 8 (Rome: Edizioni dell'Ateneo, 1972);

Maierù, ed., *English Logic in Italy in the 14th and 15th Centuries*, History of Logic, 1 (Naples: Bibliopolis, 1982);

Jürgen Miethke, "Zur sozialen Situation der Naturphilosophie im späteren Mittelalter," in *Lebenslehren und Weltentwürfe im Übergang vom Mittelalter zur Neuzeit*, edited by Hartmut Boockmann and others, Abhandlungen der Akademie der Wissenschaften in Göttingen, Philologisch-Historische Klasse, third series 179 (Göttingen: Vandenhoeck & Ruprecht, 1989), pp. 249-266;

A. George Molland, "The Geometrical Background to the 'Merton School,' " *British Journal for the History of Science*, 4 (1968): 108-125;

John Murdoch, "From Social into Intellectual Factors: An Aspect of the Unitary Character of Late Medieval Learning," in *The Cultural Context of Medieval Learning*, edited by Murdoch and Edith Sylla, Boston Studies in the Philosophy of Science, 26, Synthese Library, volume 76 (Dordrecht & Boston: Reidel, 1975), pp. 271-339;

Murdoch, "Geometry and the Continuum in the Fourteenth Century," Ph.D. dissertation, University of Wisconsin, 1957;

Murdoch, *"Rationes Mathematice": Un aspect du rapport des mathématiques et de la philosophie au moyen âge* (Paris: Palais de la Découverte, 1962);

Murdoch, "Scientia Mediantibus Vocibus: Metalinguistic Analysis in Late Medieval Natural Philosophy," in *Sprache und Erkenntnis im Mittelalter*, Miscellanea Mediaevalia, edited by Albert Zimmermann, volume 13, no. 1 (Berlin: De Gruyter, 1981) pp. 73-106;

F. M. Powicke, *The Medieval Books of Merton College* (Oxford: Oxford University Press, 1931);

Edith Sylla, "Medieval Concepts of the Latitudes of Forms: The Oxford Calculators," *Archives d'histoire doctrinale et littéraire du moyen âge*, 40 (1973): 223-283;

Sylla, "Medieval Quantifications of Qualities: The 'Merton School,' " *Archive for History of Exact Sciences*, 8 (1971): 9-39;

James Weisheipl, "Early Fourteenth Century Physics of the Merton 'School' with Special Reference to Dumbleton and Heytesbury," Ph.D. dissertation, Oxford University, 1956;

Weisheipl, "Ockham and Some Mertonians," *Mediaeval Studies*, 30 (1968): 163-213;

Weisheipl, "Repertorium Mertonense," *Mediaeval Studies*, 31 (1969): 174-224.

Manuscripts:

A preliminary checklist of manuscripts of Richard Swineshead's works has been compiled by James Weisheipl in "Repertorium Mertonense," *Mediaeval Studies*, 31 (1969): 219-221; additional manuscripts (with a detailed outline of the contents of the *Liber Calculationum*) are listed by John Murdoch and Edith Sylla in 'Swineshead, Richard," *Dictionary of Scientific Biography*, volume 13 (New York: Scribners, 1976), p. 211. The *Liber Calculationum* is extant in whole or in fragments in fifteen manuscripts in Cambridge, Erfurt, Padua, Paris, Pavia, Perugia, Rome, the Vatican, Venice, and Worcester. It was published several times in the late fifteenth and early sixteenth centuries. *In Librum De Caelo* is extant in two manuscripts: Cambridge, Gonville and Caius 499/268, folios 204^r-211^v; and an incomplete version in Worcester, Cathedral F. 35, folios 65^v-69^v. *De Motu* is known in three manuscripts: Cambridge, Gonville and Caius 499/268, folios 212^r-213^r; Oxford, Bodleian, Digby 154, folios 42^r-44^v; and Seville, Biblioteca Colombina 7-7-29, folios 28^v-30^v. The *Tractatus de Motu Locali* is extant in two manuscripts: Cambridge, Gonville and Caius 499/268, folios 213^r-215^r; and Seville, Biblioteca Colombina 7-7-29, folios 30^v-34^r.

William of Auvergne

(circa 1190 - 30 March 1249)

Roland J. Teske, S.J.
Marquette University

PRINCIPAL WORKS: *De Causis cur Deus Homo* (The Reasons Why God Became Human, written circa 1223);

De Fide (The Faith, written circa 1223);

De Sacramentis (The Sacraments, written circa 1223);

De Trinitate (The Trinity, written circa 1223);

De Virtutibus et Vitiis (The Virtues and Vices, written circa 1223);

De Bono et Malo ([First Treatise] On Good and Evil, written circa 1225);

De Bono et Malo ([Second Treatise] On Good and Evil, written circa 1225);

De Gratia et Libero Arbitrio (Grace and Free Will, written circa 1225);

De Faciebus Mundi (The Faces of the World, written circa 1225);

De Immortalitate Animi (The Immortality of the Soul, written circa 1225);

De Laudibus Patientiae (The Praises of Patience, written circa 1225);

De Missa (The Mass, written circa 1225);

De Passione Domini (The Lord's Passion, written circa 1225);

De Poenitentia Novus Tractatus (The New Treatise on Penance, written circa 1225);

In Cantica Canticorum (Commentary on the Song of Songs, written circa 1225);

In Ecclesiasten (Commentary on Ecclesiastes, written circa 1225);

In Proverbia (Commentary on Proverbs, written circa 1225);

De Collatione et Singularitate Beneficiorum (The Bestowal and Singleness of Benefices, written circa 1228);

Sermones de Tempore et de Sanctis (Sermons on the Season and on the Saints, written 1228-1249);

De Legibus (The Laws, written circa 1230);

De Anima (The Soul, written 1231-1236);

De Universo (The Universe, written 1231-1236);

De Arte Praedicandi (The Art of Preaching, written circa 1240);

De Claustro Animae (The Cloister of the Soul, written circa 1240);

Rhetorica Divina, sive Ars Oratoria Eloquentiae Divinae (Divine Rhetoric; or, The Art of Praying with Divine Eloquence, written circa 1240).

EDITIONS: *De Universo Pars Prima* (Nuremburg: Georgius Stuchs, 1497);

De Trinitate (Strasbourg, 1507);

De Claustro Animae, edited by Henri Estienne (Paris: Henricus Stephanus, 1507);

Opera Omnia (Venice, 1591);

Guilelmi Alverni Episcopi Parisiensis Opera Omnia, 2 volumes, edited by Franciscus Hotot and Blaise Le Feron (Orléans & Paris: Pralard, 1674; photographically reprinted, Frankfurt am Main: Minerva, 1963);

"De immortalitate animae," edited by G. Bülow, in *Des Dominicus Gundissalinus Schrift von der Unsterblichkeit der Seele*, Beiträge zur Geschichte der Philosophie des Mittelalters, volume 2, no. 3 (Münster: Aschendorff, 1897), pp. 39-61;

"De arte praedicandi," edited by A. De Poorter, *Revue néoscholastique de philosophie*, 25 (1923): 191-209;

"Tractatus magistri Guillelmi Alvernensis *De bono et malo*," edited by J. R. O'Donnell, *Mediaeval Studies*, 8 (1946): 245-299;

"Tractatus Secundus Guillelmi Alvernensis *De bono et malo*," edited by O'Donnell, *Mediaeval Studies*, 16 (1954): 219-271;

"Il 'Tractatus de gratia' di Guglielmo d'Auvergne," edited by Guglielmo Corti, *Corona Lateranensis*, 7 (1966): 45-66;

William of Auvergne: De trinitate. An Edition of the Latin Text with an Introduction, edited by Bruno Switalski (Toronto: Pontifical Institute of Mediaeval Studies, 1976).

EDITIONS IN ENGLISH: *William of Auvergne: The Trinity, or The First Principle*, translated

by Francis C. Wade and Roland J. Teske (Milwaukee: Marquette University Press, 1988);
William of Auvergne: The Immortality of the Soul, translated by Teske (Milwaukee: Marquette University Press, 1992).

William of Auvergne is the first of the great philosophical theologians of the thirteenth century; his thought is original, systematic, and vigorous. He was the first medieval theologian to take serious account of the Greek and Arab philosophical works that poured into the West during the last half of the twelfth and beginning of the thirteenth centuries. The translation of nearly all the Aristotelian works, along with those of Arab and Jewish philosophers and theologians, confronted the Christian West for the first time with a rival understanding of the world and of humanity and its destiny. Despite repeated ecclesiastical warnings against Aristotle's writings and Arabic thought in 1210, 1215, and 1231, William continued to study Avicenna and used his metaphysics and psychology to come to an understanding of the Christian faith. Though William rejected the doctrine of Aristotle and Avicenna when it opposed the faith, he used it and expounded it whenever it was in accord with and supportive of the Christian faith. In *De Anima* (The Soul, 1231-1236) he said, "Although in many matters we have to contradict Aristotle, as is truly right and proper, and this holds for all the statements in which he contradicts the truth, still he should be accepted, that is, upheld, in all those statements in which he is found to have held the correct position."

Little is known of William's early life. He was born in Aurillac in the province of Auvergne in south central France, probably about 1190 but perhaps as early as 1180. He became a canon of Nôtre Dame in Paris; he was a master in theology by 1223 and professor of theology at the University of Paris by 1225. For the latter position one ordinarily had to be thirty-five. On 20 October 1227 Bartholomaeus, the bishop of Paris, died. A dispute arose over his successor, and William, still a mere deacon, went to Rome to appeal the election of the dean of the cathedral. He apparently impressed Gregory IX, for on 10 April 1228 the pope wrote to the canons of Nôtre Dame, informing them that he had ordained William a priest, consecrated him a bishop, and appointed him to the See of Paris.

William's works are dated either before or after his ordination, and little further precision seems possible. In some cases different parts of a work stem from before and after 1228. His main work, *Magisterium Divinale et Sapientiale* (The Teaching on God in the Mode of Wisdom), was composed between 1223 and 1240; it encompasses eight or nine of his treatises: *De Causis cur Deus Homo* (The Reasons Why God Became Human, circa 1223), *De Fide* (The Faith, circa 1223), *De Sacramentis* (The Sacraments, circa 1223), *De Trinitate* (The Trinity, circa 1223), *De Virtutibus et Vitiis* (The Virtues and Vices, circa 1223), *De Legibus* (The Laws, circa 1230), *De Anima,* and *De Universo* (The Universe, 1231-1236). *Rhetorica Divina, sive Ars Oratoria Eloquentiae Divinae* (Divine Rhetoric; or, The Art of Praying with Divine Eloquence, circa 1240) may also belong to this vast summa. William's early editors regarded these works as independent treatises, though internal evidence indicates that they form one immense work that begins with God as the first principle, explores the doctrine of the Trinity, and moves to the created universe and especially the human soul. Of the works written prior to 1228, *De Trinitate* is of most interest philosophically.

The prologue to *De Trinitate* introduces the whole of *Magisterium Divinale et Sapientiale.* It explains that the knowledge with which it deals can be acquired in three ways: by the gift of prophecy, by the virtue of faith, and by proof and inquiry. William intends to use only the third way, that of those who philosophize, even though it can only be of help to the learned and it has no merit before God. Later in *De Trinitate* he explains that philosophizing involves combating error and moral depravity while pursuing truth and moral goodness. William claims to provide demonstrative certitude and irrefragable proofs; but his proofs are often theological and patently less than demonstrative.

William's writings are neither in the form of commentaries on texts nor in the *quaestio* format of later Scholastics. His prose is rather a continuous discussion of a problem, often in conscious imitation of the prose of Avicenna's *Daneshname-ye 'Ala'i* (Metaphysics) or *Kitab al-Najat* (The Soul), even to the point of adopting the phraseology of the Latin translations. It is principally through Avicenna that William knew the Greek and Arab tradition, though he may have had some knowledge of the works of Averroës and certainly knew those of the Jewish philosopher Solomon Ibn Gabirol (Avicebron), whom he took to be a Christian.

De Trinitate begins with a treatment of being that is deeply indebted to Avicenna and Boethius. William argues that either a thing is its own being, or something else is being for it. If the latter, we are faced with a causal explanation that moves either in a circle or in a straight line. The circular explanation is contradictory, and the regress in a straight line must end in a being that is its own being. Hence, there must be a being of which being is said essentially. Such a being is uncaused, simple, and without composition; being (*esse*) is its name, while everything created is only *a* being (*ens*). Everything subsequent to the being that is its own being is caused and composed. This primary being is the one root and source of being to which every other being owes the fact that it is. All other things are the outpourings of the first being, which is pure goodness and abounding generosity, filling the possibility of the universe by its outpouring.

Secondary and caused being can be called being in need, possible being, false being, flowing and dependent being. William gives sixteen names for it, and each provides a path to lead inquiry to the first being. Possible being is "that for which, considered in and through itself, nothing is found that excludes its being." The being of a possible being does not belong to it essentially; the thing and its being are really two. Possible being is composite and can be resolved into its possibility and its being. It is only by reason of its participation in the first being, William holds—using language that comes dangerously close to pantheism—that "the first being through itself and alone is primarily and principally the being of all things, and all things are said to be by participation in it." The love of each thing in the universe for being shows that "being is both something other and better than all things that are."

Chapters 8 through 13 deal with the procession of things from God. Against Avicenna, William holds that the possibility of the world before it was made lay in the active potency of the Creator. This first potency cannot be prevented or impeded, and it requires no assistance from anything else. The first being acts through choice and will, which imply knowledge and wisdom.

Since the power, wisdom, and will of the first being are essential to him, the Aristotelians have maintained that the operations of the first being are eternal and, hence, that his effects are eternal. In response, William distinguishes between God's willing that something be without qualification and that something be at a certain time. God wills creatures to be at a certain time and in a certain order. The world, and with it time, must have had a beginning, for the whole of past time could not have elapsed if it were infinite. William agrees with the Aristotelians that there can be no change in God but maintains that in conferring being on what is possible, God need not change.

In giving natures to creatures God gave them the ability to act. The nature of a created agent is not changed, however, in producing an effect; even in the burning bush that was not consumed the fire retained its nature, though by a miracle God prevented its natural effect. William complains that the Aristotelians have attributed more to created natures than such natures can do and that they speak as if God had left natures to themselves. He prefers Augustine's view that creatures are signs or nods by which God expresses his will and points out that Avicenna himself had said that nature acts as a servant dependent on the sign and will of the Lord of all. Though creatures have received certain power, that power is only the will of their maker, and they have no necessity in themselves to operate. He compares the causality of creatures to that of the window admitting the sunlight or to the bed of a stream that carries the water that fills it.

William claims that "the most noble of all philosophers," Ibn Gabirol, realized that creatures do what they themselves are not capable of doing. The flow of the goodness of God is caught in each thing as water in a bucket, and if the creature overflows, producing effects beyond itself, it is due to the outpouring of the first generosity. There is no cause of being aside from the first being, who is a cause in the strict sense; other things are causes only in relation to sense perception. "The whole universe is like a book or tablet written by the marvelousness and beauty of the Creator for those who correctly philosophize to read. . . ." The divine essence is the summation of that book, and the truth of the book of philosophy does not lie in the words of the book of the universe but in the divine essence. William seems to hold that one who has a trained intellect can read the truth in the divine essence.

Chapter 14 begins the properly Trinitarian part of the work. There are two emanations within the divine essence; each is an instance of perfect causality, where the effect is perfectly assimilated to the cause. The Father has the essence primordially and as source; the Son has it by generation, and the Spirit by procession. William links power with the Father, wisdom with the Son, and will or love with the Spirit. William's contribution to Trinitarian theology lies in his rethinking of the Augustinian psychological analogies in terms of the doctrine of intellect he learned from Avicenna. As the human intellect is fertilized by forms that it receives from elsewhere so that it can bring forth knowledge, the first intellect is fruitful in itself and brings forth out of itself knowledge that is equal to itself. In the human intellect the seeds of sense knowledge are sown one by one, and the human intellect brings forth bits and pieces of wisdom. But the first intellect needs no external assistance and brings forth the whole of wisdom all at once. The first intellect speaks itself in the first perfect Word, which is the archetype and exemplar of the universe. The Holy Spirit is the communion of love between the Father and the Son. William describes love as purely gratuitous and as the first of all gifts, arguing that there can be only one love between the first two perfect lovers.

William finds vestiges of the Trinity in each sensible thing, its accidents, and the love between it and its accidents, as well as in matter and form and their mutual love. But he finds clearer images of the Trinity in the human intellect, its knowledge, and its will. He holds "that in everyone who understands, understanding oneself is first and that the power of understanding and its truth comes to it before external things can possibly reach it through their likenesses." Thus intellectual self-knowledge is prior to and independent of sense knowledge; like Avicenna's "floating man," the intellect can know itself and its truth independently of the body and the senses. For other knowledge, sensible forms "act upon the soul through the organs of the senses so that intellectual knowledge might be formed in it."

Life, intellect, and affection are not parts or accidents of the soul; each is the whole soul, and thus they image the three Persons, each of which is the whole divine essence. In the state of glory the human intellect, naturally capable of understanding all things, will actually know all things: "our intellect in its ultimate perfection is a perfect image or perfect exemplification of the first-born Word." God's image is only potentially in the soul as it was created; by philosophizing it is brought to its full actuality.

William's long discussion in chapters 29 to 43 of Trinitarian notions such as paternity, sonship, and active and passive spiration tries to show that all schools of thought on these matters are really in agreement. His solutions are ingenious, but the chapters remain difficult reading. His final chapter, on language used in speaking of God, is of more interest to modern philosophers and theologians.

Also of philosophical interest are William's two treatises titled *De Bono et Malo* (On Good and Evil, both circa 1225). The first explores the problem of good and evil in terms of the doctrine of being: the good is being, evil is the privation of being. Hence, nothing is essentially evil. Within this context William discusses moral goodness and the virtues, as well as the reward of eternal life. The second treatise emphasizes spiritual impoverishment, grace, and moral conduct.

The immense treatise *De Sacramentis,* as well as *De Causis cur Deus Homo,* is purely theological. The former work begins with a treatment of the sacraments in general and then turns to a discussion of each of the seven sacraments in a tone that is more pastoral and devotional than dogmatic. The latter treatise sets forth a series of reasons why the Incarnation was necessary.

Like Louis IX, William exercised a certain independence from Rome; for example, when Gregory IX asked William to send troops to fight Frederick II in 1229, William sent only money. During Carnival in 1229 the queen regent, Blanche of Castille, sent troops to Paris to quell a student riot that originally arose over a tavern bill; some students were killed. When William failed to obtain redress for this violation of their rights, the masters and students left Paris for nearby cities, threatening to strike for six years and appealing to the pope for assistance. Gregory IX, formerly a master of theology at Paris, roared from Rome that he was "so confounded by [William's] action that we are forced to say, . . . 'We regret having made this man.' " Despite such strong language, William soon returned to Gregory's good graces and represented him in 1231 at peace negotiations between France and England. The strike had at least two lasting effects. First, the success of the masters' appeal to the pope marked a major step toward the university's complete independence from the bishop of Paris. Second, during the strike William gave the Dominicans their first chair in the university when he appointed Roland of Cremona to a chair in theology at the university, thus opening the door to the immense influence of the mendicant orders. William also provided the Franciscans with their first chair by allowing

Alexander of Hales to retain his position as a master in theology when he entered the Franciscan order in 1236.

Of William's works written after his consecration as bishop, *De Universo* and *De Anima* are of most interest philosophically. *De Universo* is divided into two principal parts, each of which is subdivided into three parts; the first principal part deals with the corporeal universe, the second with the spiritual universe. William explains that knowledge of the universe can mean either the sum total of all philosophical knowledge or knowledge of how the universe is a universe, that is, of the things that are and how they form a universe. It is in the latter sense, he says, that he will proceed.

In contrast to the calm, systematic development of the argument in *De Trinitate*, *De Universo* is filled with skirmishes with one adversary after another. William begins by arguing against the Manichaean dualism of the Cathars, who posed a serious threat to the church in southern France: the Cathars held that the universe is the battleground of a good and an evil supreme being. He brings both metaphysical and "vulgar" arguments to bear against this dualism, then turns to a consideration of the unity of the universe. He rejects the doctrine that there is another world—such as that of the classical Elysian fields or the sensual paradise of the Muslims—and argues that there cannot be a plurality of worlds separated by a vacuum. He argues that God creates out of his goodness as an artisan produces a work of art; through the eternal Word, God freely creates creatures that are not eternal. William rejects the Peripatetic view that the Creator necessarily produced the first intelligence, from which there necessarily arose subsequent intelligences, with the agent intellect—the cause of the material world—coming tenth in order. Against this view, William maintains that God is the only cause of being. He gives a lengthy account of the creation of the universe that presents a curious combination of the Genesis account with Aristotelian cosmology. He draws this part to a close with a discussion of the locations of paradise, purgatory, and hell.

The second part of the first principal part investigates whether the universe is eternal or had a beginning. William distinguishes eternity from perpetuity and time: eternity is a simple duration that is all at once; both time and perpetuity have past, present, and future, but perpetuity has a beginning and no end while time has a beginning and an end. William argues against the positions of Aristotle and Avicenna that the world is eternal and offers proof that it had a beginning. He also argues against the Platonic claim that souls have no beginning, against the Pythagorean doctrine of the transmigration of souls, against the belief in the cyclic return of everything with the end of the Great Year (thirty-six thousand or forty thousand years), and against Origen's view that bodies will ultimately be annihilated. In the rest of this part William focuses on the resurrection of human bodies, the state of glory of the blessed, and the punishment of the damned. He steers a middle path between the Muslim paradise of sensual pleasures and a heaven of purely spiritual joys that would render bodily resurrection pointless and raises questions about how the life of glory approximates the timeless eternity of God.

The third part of the first principal part deals with God's care and governance of the universe, especially with regard to human affairs. He argues that the Creator has provident care for each and every thing and illustrates the workings of providence in the natural world. Then he turns to the question of why bad things happen to the good, while the evil thrive. He gives lengthy arguments against fate and the Fates and defends contingency in things and human freedom in the face of divine providence and foreknowledge.

The second principal part of *De Universo* deals with the spiritual universe. Knowledge of it surpasses the knowledge of the corporeal universe as a spiritual nature surpasses every bodily nature. William reminds his reader that one honors God "by loving and seeking the knowledges which illumine and direct our souls in order to magnify him and to know and contemplate his supereminence and glory." Previous philosophers have left behind almost nothing on the spiritual universe, save a few stories—perhaps because of the loftiness of the subject, the limitations of the human intellect, and the remoteness of spiritual substances from ordinary life. The ancients divided the spiritual universe into three parts: the separate intelligences utterly removed from matter, the good spirits that the Christians call angels, and the evil spirits that they refer to as bad angels or devils. The divisions of the second principal part correspond to these topics.

William first deals with the opinion of Aristotle on the separate intelligences—an opinion that was, he says, followed by many of the

Greeks and all of the Arabs. William's objection to Aristotle's position lies in his having removed from these intelligences "all will and love and other dispositions to act and virtues" so that they are mere intelligences. William argues that such beings must be perfect in virtue as well as in knowledge. He rejects the Aristotelian doctrine that the souls of the nine heavens love and seek the separate intelligences, since only the Creator should be loved and sought. He argues against al-Ghazali's view that the first principle produces only the first intelligence, against Aristotle's and al-Farabi's position that souls separated from bodies become numerically one, and against Aristotle on the location of the first intelligence. He rejects Aristotle's position on the agent intellect (as he knew it from the Arabs) and Plato's doctrine of an intelligible world largely because, as he understands them, they usurp the roles of the Creator and of the Word who is the archetype and exemplar of the universe. He also rejects the claim that one separate intelligence creates another. Returning to the Platonic archetypal world, he rejects it as the basis for ordinary knowledge; thus he provides a step toward a more naturalistic explanation of human knowing that restricts the role of divine illumination.

The second part of William's treatment of the spiritual universe argues that the angels are purely immaterial substances, thus rejecting the doctrine of spiritual matter. He maintains, however, contrary to the Averroist view, that the separate intelligences are each numerically one and that their separation from matter does not destroy their multiplicity. He deals with the number of the good angels, their differences, powers, knowledge, growth in knowledge, and the perfection of their will. He discusses their apparitions and whether they assumed real bodies. The sins of some of the angels occupy much of the remainder of this part, which contains 163 chapters.

The third part of the second principal part deals with the evil spirits. After discussing the natural and essential dispositions they share with the holy spirits, William turns to their acquired disposition, namely, malice, which is not the work of nature or of the Creator. He treats their differences and order, the trials and possessions with which they afflict humans, divination, works of magic, necromancy, incubi and succubi, their coupling, generation, and offspring.

In the prologue to *De Anima* William notes that the knowledge of the human soul with which he intends to deal is superior to natural philosophy that cannot treat the soul as image and likeness of God. A single science must deal with the image and its truth, and that science is *Magisterium Divinale et Sapientiale*. *De Anima* has seven chapters. Chapter 1 begins with Aristotle's definition of soul as "the perfection of an organic natural body having life potentially," but interprets "organic" in an Augustinian sense, such that the body is the organon, or instrument, that the soul uses; he rejects the idea that the body has life potentially. He criticizes those who deny the existence of the human soul, arguing that it is impossible to know that one is not, for in knowing that one is not, one would know that one is, and that which knows is the soul. The soul is a substance.

Chapter 2 sets out to explain the essence of the soul. William argues against the views that the soul is a number or a harmony; he shows that the soul is incorporeal, neither a heavenly body nor fire nor any body at all. The soul is without parts, for the act of knowing is instantaneous and indivisible. The soul is a spiritual substance that uses the body and its members for its operations, but the operations properly belong to the soul. Against Aristotle, William insists that it is the soul, not the person, who knows intellectually. Unlike the souls of other animals, the human soul is free. He likens the human soul to a well-ordered kingdom in which the will is king and emperor, the intellective power his counselor, and the lower powers his ministers.

Chapter 3 maintains the soul's simplicity and unity; the soul's powers are not parts or something added to the soul. Rather, as the Creator's power is God himself, so the powers of the soul are the soul itself. The intellective power is corrective of itself and of the senses, but the will which issues commands is the more noble power—something, William notes, that Aristotle and his Greek and Arab followers have all missed. Since all the powers of the soul are the one spiritual substance, the will is cognitive and the intellect is appetitive. The soul is not properly a part of an individual: from Avicenna's *Kitab al-Najat* one can see that "a man thinking of himself, without the use of any corporeal sense, finds that the body is not part of himself. Hence, he finds that his soul is his whole being or his whole essence." When one person says to another, "Think of this," he is speaking only to what can think, and that is the soul. The body is part of a person and falls within the definition of the human being in the same way that a horse falls within the definition of a horseman. That some claim that they do not know their souls is due to their long familiarity with the senses.

In chapter 4 William argues that an embryo has a soul as soon as it is completely formed, and that abortion is murder. Chapter 5 says that the soul is not produced by the parents but created and infused by God alone. William argues extensively against the materialist view of Alexander of Aphrodisias, who held that the soul was generated from the tempering of the elements and their qualities. The soul is not created outside the body prior to its infusion.

William is adamant that in the state of natural felicity the intellect could know singulars; if it could not, it could not know its Creator and would be deprived of the source of its happiness. Souls existing in that state had little care to know sensible things. Now, however, as the result of Original Sin, the human body has infected and corrupted the soul and cast it down from its noble state to the ignorance of brute animals. Yet merciful God has provided the remedies of baptism and grace by which humans can rise up and come to the perfect rest of glory.

The soul needs the body only for certain activities, as a guitar player needs a guitar only for guitar playing. The activities of the soul are never activities of the instrument; thus, the power of seeing belongs to the soul, not to the eye, and remains in the soul after death. The soul vivifies the body by an activity that is not voluntary but natural; death is the cessation of this influence due to the body's loss of the ability to receive it. The soul has the natural ability to exist and to increase in perfection forever.

Chapter 6 continues the discussion of the soul's immortality, arguing that infirmities and weaknesses do not occur in the soul, but in the body. Furthermore, bodily ills do not harm the soul but often strengthen it. The soul's natural desire for endless existence and happiness reveals its immortality, which is not an acquired disposition or one removed by vices.

William argues for immortality from "the roots" of divine goodness, providence, justice, magnificence, generosity, and glory. He adds the testimony of eyewitnesses and of Scripture and the experiences of ecstasy and rapture. The soul is wholly in each part of the body, though the body is better said to be present in the soul than the soul in the body.

Chapter 7 takes up the likenesses of the soul to the triune God. William defines the intellect as "the power that is able to apprehend spiritual and abstract, or stripped, and invisible things, whether they are singular or universal." Those who claim that the intellect knows only universals deprive it of the intellectual operation for which it was created: the clear and immediate vision of the Creator. Hence, they would deprive the intellect of its perfection and its beatitude. Moreover, if the nature of intellect were such that it could not know singulars, the divine intellect, too, would be unable to know individual things. William rejects the existence of the agent intellect, whether as a part of the soul or as a separate substance. He holds that "the human soul is naturally constituted and ordered as if at the horizon of two worlds. One of these worlds is the world of sensible things to which it is joined by its body; the other is the Creator himself . . . the eternal truth and the eternal exemplar of the clearest expression and the cleanest and purest mirror of universal revelation." In this mirror the soul reads off the first principles of truth, for the knowledge of which Aristotle mistakenly posited the agent intellect.

One of William's life long concerns was the problem of clergy holding a plurality of benefices. His *De Collatione et Singularitate Beneficiorum* (The Bestowal and Singleness of Benefices, circa 1228) was written about the time of his consecration to the episcopacy, and he continued his battle against this abuse as bishop. In 1235 he convoked the masters of the university to discuss the legality of the practice.

Around 1240 William wrote *Rhetorica Divina, sive Ars Oratoria Eloquentiae Divinae*, possibly the last part of his *Magisterium Divinale et Sapientiale*. Its pastoral and liturgical character indicates that it was aimed principally at the clergy of the diocese; it was the most popular of William's works and was still being copied two centuries later. Trading on the ambiguity of the Latin *oratio*, he examines the nature of prayer in comparison to classical oratory and then develops other, more symbolic and biblical comparisons.

In 1240 William presided over the condemnation and burning of the Talmud. In the following year he again convoked the masters to condemn a list of ten heretical propositions. Although as bishop he had the authority to make such a condemnation by himself, his habit of convoking the masters for such purposes may have contributed to the later custom whereby the masters exercised this function on their own. At least one of the condemned propositions censured a view that attenuated, apparently as a result of Avicenna's noetics, the doctrine of the immediate vision of God by the blessed. William himself had long championed an immediate vision of God as humanity's ultimate felicity.

William was a close friend and confidant of Blanche of Castille, the queen regent, and then of her son, Louis IX. Examples of his lively and at times biting wit have been recorded, along with examples of his frankness in dealing with the royal family. For example, William told Louis that he was out of his mind in planning a crusade in 1247, though he failed to dissuade the king from undertaking it. William remained bishop of Paris until his death on 30 March 1249. He was buried in the Abbey of St. Victor.

William's influence on subsequent philosophy and theology has perhaps been less than one might expect. Several factors may account for this lack of influence. First, William did not have the backing of a religious order that would adopt his philosophy and theology as its own and promote its study. Second, he was followed closely by the two giants of Scholasticism, Thomas Aquinas and Bonaventure, who have rightly dominated the scene. Third, he wrote in a difficult style that must have challenged his thirteenth-century readers as much as it challenges the reader of today. Fourth, he seems not to have chosen his audience wisely, for he did not write principally for the schools but for a wider learned readership; one might wonder whether, as a result, he was ignored in the schools.

It is known, however, that Aquinas read parts of the *Magisterium Divinale et Sapientiale*, and in many respects William's doctrine of being anticipated Aquinas's ideas on the role of being in the constitution of created beings. But perhaps William's principal legacy was not any particular doctrine but his leadership in taking seriously the philosophies of Aristotle and his Arab followers. William did not merely realize the value of these philosophies for the development of a Christian wisdom but also saw that the challenge of these non-Christian systems had to be met on their own level, that is, as philosophies. He was one of the first in the West to meet them on that level, and he did so with success.

References:

Baudoin C. Allard, "Note sur le 'De immortalitate animae' de Guillaume d'Auvergne," *Bulletin de philosophie médiévale*, 18 (1976): 68-72;

P. Anciaux, "Le sacrament de Pénitence chez Guillaume d'Auvergne," *Ephemerides Theologicae Lovanienses*, 24 (1948): 98-118;

Bernardo C. Bazán, "Pluralisme de formes ou dualisme de substances," *Revue philosophique de Louvain*, 67 (Fall 1969): 30-73;

Alan E. Bernstein, "Esoteric Theology: William of Auvergne on the Fires of Hell and Purgatory," *Speculum*, 57 (July 1982): 509-531;

Bernstein, "Theology between Heresy and Folklore: William of Auvergne on Punishment after Death," *Studies in Medieval and Renaissance History*, 5 (1982): 5-44;

Helmut Borok, *Der Tugendbegriff des Wilhelm von Auvergne (1180-1249): Eine moralhistorische Untersuchung zur ideengeschichtlichen Rezeption der aristotelischen Ethik* (Düsseldorf: Patmos, 1979);

P.-M. de Contenson, "La théologie de la vision de Dieu au début du xiiie siècle: Le 'De retributionibus sanctorum' de Guillaume d'Auvergne et la condamnation de 1241," *Revue des sciences philosophiques et théologiques*, 46 (1962): 409-444;

Guglielmo Corti, "La sette parte del *Magisterium divinale et sapientiale* di Guglielmo di Auvergne," in *Studi e Richerche di Scienze Religiose in Onore dei Santi Apostoli Petro et Paulo nel XIX Centenario del loro Martirio* (Romae: Facultas Theologica Pontificae Universitatis Lateranensis, 1968), pp. 289-307;

Leo Davis, "Creation according to William of Auvergne," in *Studies in Mediaevalia and Americana*, edited by Gerard G. Steckler and Leo Donald David (Spokane, Wash.: Gonzaga University Press, 1973), pp. 51-75;

Aimé Forest, "Guillaume d'Auvergne, critique d'Aristote," in *Etudes Médiévales offertes à Augustin Flictie* (Paris: Presses Universitaires de France, 1952), pp. 67-79;

René A. Gauthier, "Notes sur le début (1225-1240) du prémier 'averroisme,' " *Revue des sciences philosophiques et théologiques*, 66 (July 1982): 321-374;

Etienne Gilson, "La notion d'existence chez Guillaume d'Auvergne," *Archives d'histoire doctrinale et littéraire du moyen âge*, 21 (1946): 55-91;

Gilson, "Pourquoi saint Thomas a critiqué saint Augustin," *Archives d'histoire doctrinale et littéraire du moyen âge*, 1 (1926): 5-127;

Gilson, "Les sources gréco-arabes de l'augustinisme avicennisant," *Archives d'histoire doctrinale et littéraire du moyen âge*, 4 (1929): 5-149;

Palémon Glorieux, "Le tractatus de poenitentia de Guillaume d'Auvergne," in *Miscellanea Moralia*, Bibliotheca Ephemeriarum Theologicarum Lovaniensium, series 1, volume 3 (Louvain: Nauwelaerts, 1949), pp. 551-565;

Richard Heinzmann, "Zur Anthropologie des Wilhelm von Auvergne," *Münchener Theologische Zeitschrift*, 16 (1965): 27-36;

Gabriel Jüssen, "William of Auvergne und die Entwicklung der Philosophie in Übergang zur Hochscholastik," in *Thomas von Aquin im philosophischen Gespräch*, edited by Wolfgang Kluxen (Freiburg & Munich: Alber, 1975), pp. 185-203;

Josef Kramp, "Des Wilhelm von Auvergne 'Magisterium Divinale,'" *Gregorianum*, 1 (1920): 538-613; 2 (1921): 42-103, 174-195;

Artur Landgraf, "Der Traktat *De Errore Pelagii* des Wilhelm von Auvergne," *Speculum*, 5 (April 1930): 168-180;

Ephrem Longpré, "Guillaume d'Auvergne et Alexandre de Halès," *Archivum Franciscanum Historicum*, 16 (1923): 249-250;

Longpré, "Guillaume d'Auvergne et l'Ecole Franciscaine de Paris," *La France Franciscaine*, 5 (1922): 426-429;

Stephen P. Marrone, *William of Auvergne and Robert Grosseteste: New Ideas of Truth in the Early Thirteenth Century* (Princeton: Princeton University Press, 1983);

Amato Masnovo, *Da Guglielmo d'Auvergne a S. Tommaso d'Aquino*, 3 volumes, second edition (Milan: Vita et Pensiero, 1946);

Masnovo, "Guglielmo d'Auvergne e l'università di Parigi dal 1229 al 1231," in *Mélanges Mandonnet*, volume 2 (Paris: Vrin, 1930), pp. 191-232;

Ernest A. Moody, "William of Auvergne and his Treatise De Anima," in his *Studies in Medieval Philosophy, Science, and Logic: Collected Papers, 1933-1969* (Berkeley & Los Angeles: University of California Press, 1975), pp. 1-109;

J. Reginald O'Donnell, "The Notion of Being in William of Auvergne," *Proceedings of the American Catholic Philosophical Association*, 21 (1946): 156-165;

O'Donnell, "The Rhetorica Divina of William of Auvergne: A Study in Applied Rhetoric," in *Images of Man in Ancient and Medieval Thought* (Louvain: Louvain University Press, 1976), pp. 323-333;

Albrecht Quentin, *Naturkenntnisse und Naturanschauungen bei Wilhelm von Auvergne* (Hildesheim: Gerstenberg, 1976);

Jan Rohls, *Wilhelm von Auvergne und der mittelalterliche Aristotelismus* (Munich: Kaiser, 1980);

Stephan Schindele, *Beiträge zur Metaphysik des Wilhelm von Auvergne* (Munich: Kastner & Lossen, 1900);

Beryl Smalley, "William of Auvergne, John of La Rochelle and Saint Thomas on the Old Law," in *St. Thomas Aquinas 1274-1974: Commemorative Studies*, 2 volumes (Toronto: Pontifical Institute of Mediaeval Studies, 1974), II: 11-71;

Roland J. Teske, "The Identity of the 'Italici' in William of Auvergne's Discussion of the Eternity of the World," in *Proceedings of the Patristic, Medieval and Renaissance Conference* (Villanova, Pa.: Augustinian Historical Institute, 1990), pp. 189-201;

Teske, "William of Auvergne on the Eternity of the World," *Modern Schoolman*, 67 (March 1990): 187-205;

Teske, "William of Auvergne's Rejection of the Agent Intelligence," in *Supportive Confrontation: Greek and Medieval Studies in Honor of Leo Sweeney, S. J.*, edited by William J. Carroll (New York: Lang, forthcoming);

Noël Valois, *Guillaume d'Auvergne, évêque de Paris (1228-1249): Sa vie et ses ouvrages* (Paris: Picard, 1880);

Roland de Vaux, *Notes et textes sur l'avicennisme latin aux confins des xiie-xiiie siècles* (Paris: Vrin, 1934).

Manuscripts:

A list of the known extant manuscripts of William of Auvergne's writings can be compiled from Palémon Glorieux's list in his *Répertoire des Maîtres en Théologie de Paris au XIIIe Siècle* (Paris: Vrin, 1933), pp. 315-320, along with the articles by Baudoin Allard listing additions to Glorieux's list in the *Bulletin de la société internationale pour l'étude de philosophie médiévale*, 5 (1963): 147-148 and *Bulletin de philosophie médiévale*, 10-12 (1968-1970): 212-224. The only major philosophical work of William's in a modern critical edition is the *De Trinitate*, edited by Bruno Switalski, who lists the known extant manuscripts as Vatican City, Biblioteca Apostolica Vaticana, Borghese 351; Douai, Bibliothèque Municipale, MS 454; Cambrai, Bibliothèque de la Ville, MS 483; Tours, Bibliothèque Publique, MS 421; Chartres, MS 475 (destroyed in World War II); Paris,

Bibliothèque Mazarine 3477; Oxford, Bodleian Library, Laudianus Miscellaneus 146; Vatican City, Biblioteca Apostolica Vaticana, Vaticanus Latinus 6741. Of these he ranks Borghese 351 as the best. Glorieux lists seventeen manuscripts for the *De Universo*; they are in Brussels, Cambrai, Chartres, Erfurt, Klosterneuburg, Munich, Oxford, Paris, Rome, and Venice. Ballard has added fifteen more to that list; they are in Cambridge, Munich, Nuremberg, Oxford, Paris, and Rome. Glorieux lists four manuscripts for the *De Anima*: one in Chartres, two in Paris, and one in Rome; Ballard has added two more manuscripts in Rome. Ballard has also discovered six manuscripts of the *De Immortalitate Animi*, all of which bear William's name. In doing so, he has provided strong evidence that William is the author of all versions of the work, some of which had been attributed to Dominicus Gundissalinus.

William of Conches

(circa 1090 - circa 1154)

John H. Newell, Jr.
College of Charleston

PRINCIPAL WORKS: *Glosae super Boetium* (Glosses on Boethius [*De Consolatione Philosophiae*], written circa 1120-1125);
Glosae super Macrobium (Glosses on Macrobius [*De Somnio Scipionis*], written circa 1125);
Philosophia Mundi (Philosophy of the World, written circa 1125-1130);
Glosae in Iuvenalem (Glosses on Juvenal, written circa 1130; attribution uncertain);
Glosae super Priscianum (Glosses on Priscian, written circa 1130; revised circa 1150);
Glosae super Platonem (Glosses on Plato [*Timaeus*], written circa 1135-1144);
Moralium Dogma Philosophorum (The Doctrines of Moral Philosophers, written circa 1145-1150; attribution uncertain);
Dragmaticon (Dialogue about Physical Substances, written circa 1147-1149).

EDITIONS: *Dialogus de Substantiis Physicis [Dragmaticon Philosophiae]*, edited by Guilielmus Gratarolus (Strasbourg: Iosias Rihelius, 1567; reprinted, Frankfurt am Main: Minerva, 1967);
"Glosae super Platonem," in *Ouvrages inédits d'Abélard pour servir a l'histoire de la philosophie scholastique en France*, edited by Victor Cousin (Paris: Imprimerie Royale, 1836), pp. 646-657;
"Glosae super Boetium," excerpts edited by C. Jourdain, in *Notices et extraits des manuscrits de la Bibliothèque Imperiale et autres bibliothèques*, volume 20, part 2 (Paris: Imprimerie Impériale, 1862), pp. 40-82;
Moralium Dogma Philosophorum, edited by John Holmberg (Uppsala: Almqvist & Wiksell, 1929);
"Glosae super Boetium" and "Glosae super Platonem," excerpts edited by J. M. Parent, in his *La Doctrine de la création dans l'école de Chartres* (Paris: Vrin, 1938), pp. 122-177;
"Ein Timaioskommentar in Sigtuna," edited by Toni Schmid, *Classica et Mediaevalia*, 10 (1949): 220-266;
"Deux redactions des gloses de Guillaume de Conches sur Priscien," edited by Edouard Jeauneau, *Recherches de théologie ancienne et médiévale*, 27 (1960): 212-247;
Glosae super Platonem, edited by Jeauneau (Paris: Vrin, 1965);
"Glosses on Macrobius's *De Somnio Scipionis*," excerpts edited by Helen E. Rodnite, in her "The Doctrine of the Trinity in Guillaume de Conches' Glosses on Macrobius: Texts and Studies," Ph.D. dissertation, Columbia University, 1973;

Philosophia mundi: Ausgabe des 1. Buchs von Wilhelm von Conches' Philosophia, mit Anhang, edited by Gregor Maurach (Pretoria: University of South Africa, 1974);

Philosophia, edited by Maurach (Pretoria: University of South Africa, 1980);

Glosae in Iuvenalem, edited by Bradford Wilson (Paris: Vrin, 1980).

Despite his enormous productivity, his renown among his contemporaries, and his considerable influence on his successors (from students and contemporaries such as John of Salisbury and Bernard Silvestris to such fourteenth-century humanists as Geoffrey Chaucer, Giovanni Boccaccio, and Lino Salutati), William of Conches has not received the kind of attention that has been lavished on some of his better-known contemporaries, such as Peter Abelard, Bernard of Clairvaux, and John of Salisbury. As of 1992 none of William's works had been translated into English, and few had been made available in modern critical editions, although the Pontifical Institute of Mediaeval Studies was planning critical editions of all his works. There still exist no detailed studies of William's theological thought, no published examination of his moral philosophy, and no book-length study in English of his thought. This situation is especially regrettable because an examination of William's writings reveals an important aspect of twelfth-century thought.

Little is known about William's life, and what is known has been called into question with the controversy initiated by R. W. Southern over the existence and importance of the School of Chartres. Whether or not William taught at Chartres, he certainly studied there under Bernard of Chartres. And he is appropriately called a Chartrian because of the influence Bernard had on him, an influence he shared with Thierry of Chartres, Gilbert de La Porrée, John of Salisbury, and Bernard Silvestris.

William was born in the small Norman town of Conches sometime in the late eleventh century, probably around 1090 but perhaps as early as 1080. He was a student of Bernard of Chartres probably in the second decade of the twelfth century; by about 1120 he had himself become a master—probably at the cathedral of Chartres, and if not there, then at Paris. He was renowned as a grammarian and a natural philosopher, and he composed works in both fields.

Thoroughly imbued with the classics and with the Neoplatonic tradition, William viewed the works of antiquity in a way quite different from that of most of his predecessors and contemporaries. He saw the pagan writings not as Egyptians to be despoiled (as had Augustine, Peter Damian, and Bernard of Clairvaux) but as giants to be used as a basis of support for his own inquiries. In his *Glosae super Priscianum* (Glosses on Priscian, circa 1130, revised circa 1150), William writes: "He says well that moderns are more perceptive than ancients but not wiser. The ancients had no writings except what they composed. We, however, have all our writings and in addition all which have been composed from the beginnings until our time.... Whence we are as a dwarf placed on the shoulders of a giant. That dwarf sees farther, not from his own size, but from the size of what is placed under him." William is the earliest source for this well-known simile, which, according to William's student John of Salisbury, originated with William's teacher, Bernard of Chartres.

William composed glosses on the major sources of twelfth-century Neoplatonism—Plato, Boethius, and Macrobius. He also wrote glosses, or at least lectured, on Martianus Capella, Priscian, and Juvenal. In his *Glosae super Platonem* (Glosses on Plato [*Timaeus*], circa 1135-1144) William explains that he calls his works glosses because they not only provide the general argument of the text, as would a commentary, but also define words and explain the author's arguments and their context.

In all of his glosses William's main method of explicating the text is through such verbal and contextual explanations. Each gloss is, thus, a constant explanation of the meaning of a word or the intention of the author. For example, in his *Glosae super Platonem* William argues that Plato did not advocate giving all women in marriage by lot. He explains that Plato divided the people into classes, and only when two men from the same class sought a woman from that class was the use of lots prescribed. "This we are able to prove by reason and to conjecture from the author's words." He interprets Plato and the other ancients in such a way as to go beyond the apparent literal meaning to a more subtle reading which he finds more acceptable; by minutely examining each word for every possible meaning, he adroitly finds confirmation for his interpretation.

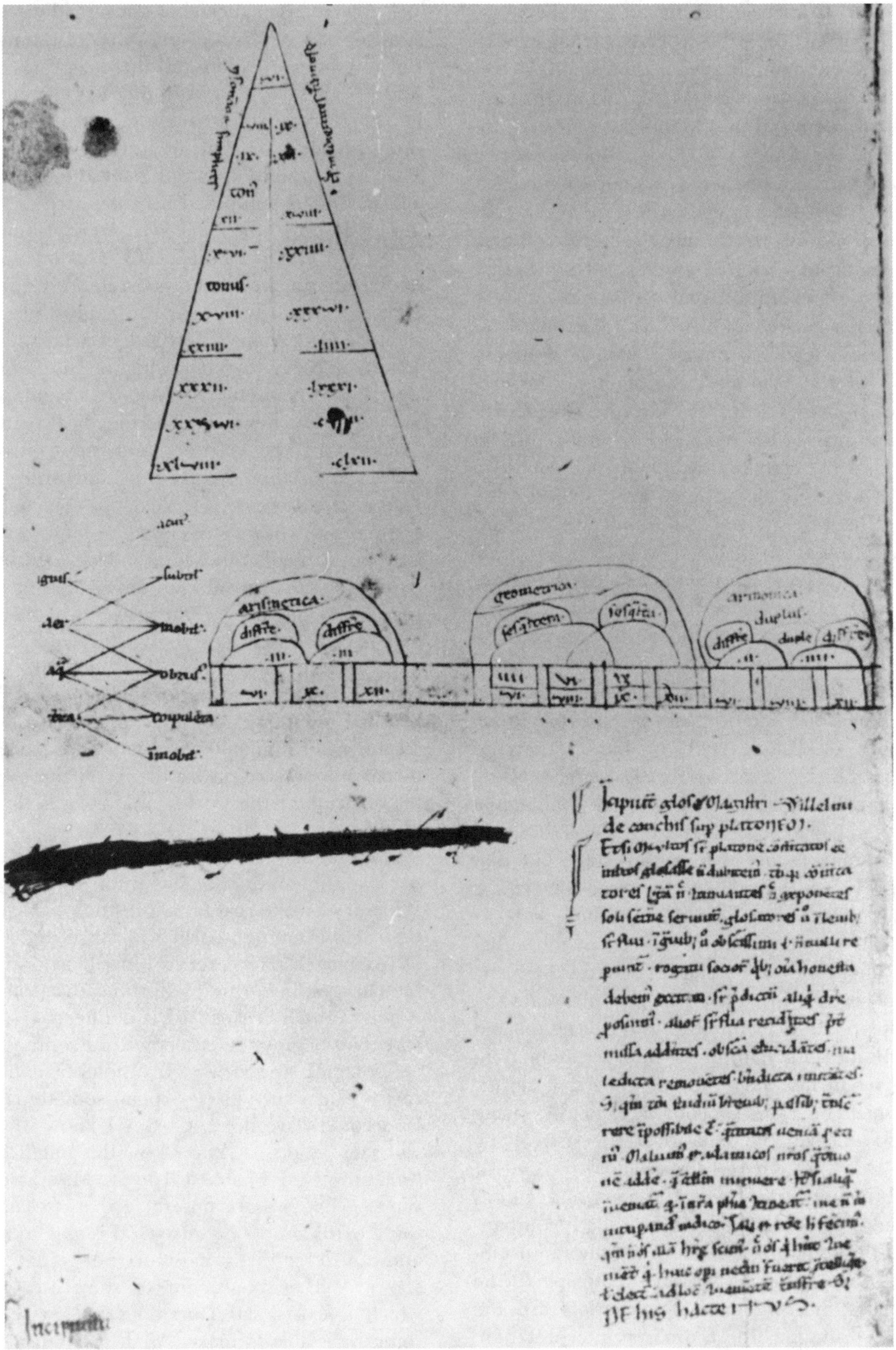

Page from a manuscript for William of Conches's Glosae super Platonem *(Biblioteca Nazionale, Florence, ms. Conv. Sopp. E.8.1398, f°1v)*

But when such verbal and contextual explication will not suffice, William reads the pagan writers in an unhesitatingly allegorical fashion. He repeatedly refers to Plato as "speaking through myth [*integumentum*] as was his custom." He insists that the works of Plato, Boethius, and Macrobius contain neither errors nor anything superfluous. In *Glosae super Platonem* he argues, "If anyone would know not only the words but also the meaning of Plato, he would find not heresy but the most profound philosophy hidden by a covering [*integumentum*] of words." A good example of this allegorical interpretation is William's analysis of the Platonic description of the creation of human souls. Plato says the Creator divided the primordial mixture into souls equal in number to the stars and assigned each soul to a star. Having thus placed them as in a chariot, he showed them the nature of the universe. William considers this myth in detail in both *Glosae super Platonem* and *Glosae super Boetium* (Glosses on Boethius [*De Consolatione Philosophiae*], circa 1120-1125). He criticizes those who, reading the passage literally, accuse Plato of heresy; he insists that Plato nowhere says that all souls are created at the same time. He proposes two possible interpretations of Plato's myth of the creation of human souls. In *Glosae super Platonem* he explains that when Plato said that God chose souls equal to the number of stars he did not mean that God made as many souls as there are stars, but that God provided that the stars would determine how long each soul would be united with its body. The stars are called "vehicles of the souls" not because they carried the souls across the heavens but because by the influence of the stars the body is prepared so that the soul can be created in it. Besides this naturalistic interpretation, William gives in his *Glosae super Boetium* a moralistic one, which he views as equally valid. By saying that God placed the souls over the stars, Plato meant that through reason, which is the gift of God, humanity transcends the stars and attains knowledge of God. The stars are called "companions of the souls" because both are always in motion and are rationally moved. According to the naturalistic interpretation, the chariots are the stars; according to the moralistic interpretation, the chariots are reason and understanding, by which the soul is led above the stars (the natural world) to God (the supernatural). For William one interpretation does not exclude the other.

By means of such allegorical readings of classical sources, William offers some of the most insightful interpretations of these writings in the Middle Ages. While continuing to revere authority, he places reason as a judge to decipher the often cryptic sayings of his authorities.

In the midst of writing these glosses in the 1120s William composed his first work of systematic philosophy, the *Philosophia Mundi* (Philosophy of the World, circa 1125-1130). This investigation of the natural world shows an interest quite foreign to those of such near contemporaries as Anselm of Canterbury, Bernard of Clairvaux, and Hugh of St. Victor. Drawing on the works on which he wrote his detailed commentaries, as well as on the newly available medical writings of Constantine the African and others, William strives to present a consistent and ordered picture of the universe. He develops the concept of the natural world as a closed system created by God but subsequently acting independently in accordance with natural laws discernible to human reason. He begins with the creation of the world; examines the nature and structure of the sublunary and supralunary worlds, including discussions of the cause of natural phenomena such as heat and lightning; and concludes with a detailed treatment of humanity. Scholars have placed particular importance on his theory of the elements, his doctrine of the world soul, and his theory of knowledge.

What is perhaps most striking about this work is the confidence in reason that it reveals. William seems to realize that his rational examination of the natural world will make him the object of attack. He defends himself against possible charges of heresy by arguing that something is heretical not because it has not been written before but because it is against the faith. He directly attacks the view of his monastic contemporaries that it suffices to explain something to say God could have done it: "But I know what they will say, We do not know how this might be, but we know God is able to do it. Miserable creatures! What is more miserable than to say something exists simply because God is able to make it and not to see that it exists so, nor to have a reason why it exists so, nor to show any use for which it exists. For God does not make everything he is able to make. As the peasant is accustomed to say, 'God can make a calf from a tree trunk. Has he ever done it?' Let them either show a reason or use for which it exists, or let them cease declaring it exists in such a fashion."

Blind acceptance of the natural world is not enough; one must use one's God-given reason to seek out the true nature of things.

A good example of William's use of reason to explain the origin and nature of things is his discussion of the creation of the human body. He says that following the creation of the other animals by the forces of nature, Adam's body similarly arose from a certain part of the earth where there was an equality of the four elements. For William, the account in Genesis does not literally mean that God created Adam's body but that the forces of nature, which God had created, produced his body from the mud. Having his body created by natural causes strengthens man's ties to nature; he is not distinct from the natural world but a part of it.

William also endeavors to apply a naturalistic interpretation to Eve's creation: "But since what is nearest to equality is, even if less, nevertheless somewhat temperate, it is likely that the body of woman was created from the nearby mud. And, therefore, woman is neither the same as man nor is she entirely different from man. Nor is she so temperate as man because the hottest woman is colder that the coldest man. And this is what the divine page says, 'God made woman from the side of Man.' For it ought not to be believed literally that God tore a rib from the first man." William thus insists on the comprehensibility of the world and emphasizes that man and woman are part of nature.

As William seems to have foreseen, he did come under attack for some of his ideas, at about the same time that Peter Abelard was being condemned at the Council of Sens in 1140. William was attacked in general for undue reliance on human reason and pagan sources and for meddling in the hidden secrets of God; in particular, he was attacked by William of Saint-Thierry for his doctrine of the world soul and his interpretation of the creation of Eve. Perhaps partly in response to these criticisms, in the early 1140s William withdrew from teaching in the schools to the court of Geoffrey of Anjou, where he continued to write and also tutored Geoffrey's sons, including Henry Plantagenet, the future king of England. At Geoffrey's court he rewrote his *Philosophia Mundi* in the form of a dialogue between a philosopher and a duke, the *Dragmaticon* (Dialogue about Physical Substances, circa 1147-1149). In this work he does not repeat his doctrine of the world soul, and he retracts his interpretation of the creation of Eve; but this retraction seems to be a withdrawal from a minor point rather than a real change in his thinking. Indeed, in the *Dragmaticon* William pursues his argument for the autonomy of the forces of nature and even brings in new sources to support his views. He also laments the current state of the church, in which the care of souls is committed to children and fools ignorant of what a soul is. In these passages William clearly attacks those monastic writers who condemned his writings without having adequately studied natural philosophy.

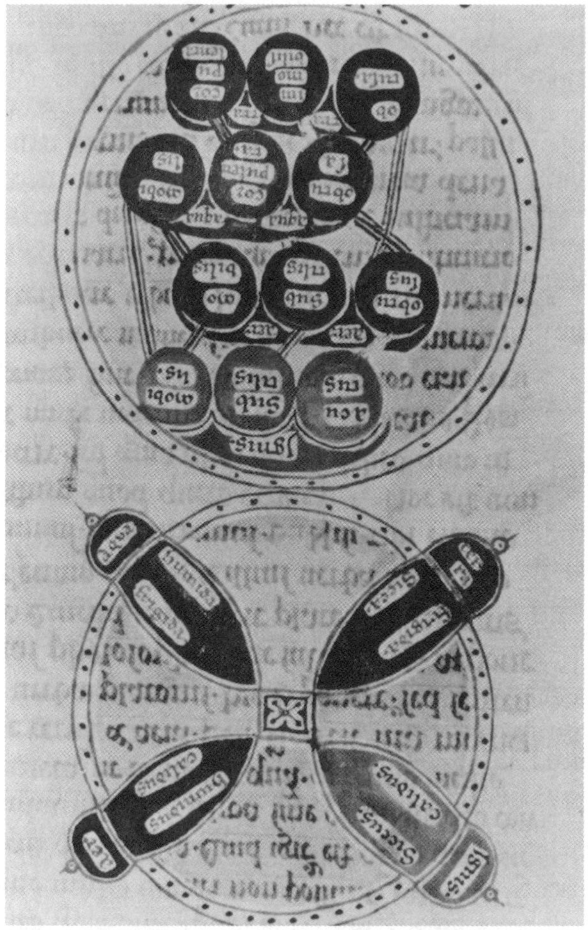

Illumination from a manuscript for William's Dragmaticon, *showing the interrelationships of the four elements (Paris, Bibliothèque Nationale, Ms lat.6415, f.6rb)*

At about the same time he was composing the *Dragmaticon* William was compiling the *Moralium Dogma Philosophorum* (The Doctrines of Moral Philosophers, circa 1145-1150), a guide to princely behavior drawn from Cicero and Seneca perhaps intended as an aid to his young charges at Geoffrey's court. The work develops a theme that appears repeatedly in William's writings, that life affords the opportunity for self-perfection. In contrast to the traditional emphasis on the debilitating effects of the Fall and on God's predestination, William insists that it is not grace or fate or fortune that makes a person what he or she is. Like Pico della Mirandola three centuries later, William argues that each person's destiny lies in that person's own hands. By striving for knowledge and virtue, a person can improve intellectually and morally; each individual possesses the capability of rising to the level of a god or descending to the level of a beast.

William of Conches is a prime example of a medieval humanist in the first half of the twelfth century. He viewed the ancient pagan writings not only as models of eloquence but also as sources of wisdom. Against criticism by his monastic contemporaries that he was deserting his faith for philosophy, he insisted that the ancient writings complemented rather than contradicted Christian revelation. William pushed this reliance on the classics to the limit and followed his arguments to their logical conclusion. Pressures from the more conservative monastic writers and the need to absorb the newly available Aristotelian works made it impossible to maintain this synthesis intact through the twelfth century. William's writings, nevertheless, influenced Latin and vernacular writers for more than two hundred years and were among the medieval writings retained in the libraries of the Renaissance humanists in fourteenth-century Italy.

References:

Marie-Dominique Chenu, *La théologie au douzième siècle*, second edition, Etudes de philosophie médiévale, 45 (Paris: Vrin, 1957); translated by Jerome Taylor as *Man, Nature, and Society in the Twelfth Century* (Chicago: University of Chicago Press, 1967);

Jules Alexandre Clerval, *Les écoles de Chartres au moyen âge du Ve siècle au XVIe siècle*, Memoires de la Societe archeologique d'Eure-et Loir, 11 (Paris: Picard, 1895), pp. 144-272;

Pierre Courcelle, "Etude critique sur les commentaires de la Consolation de Boèce (IXe-XVe siècles)," *Archives d'histoire doctrinale et littéraire du moyen âge*, 12 (1939): 5-140;

Philippe Delhaye, "Une adaptation du *De Officiis* au XIIe siècle: Le *Moralium dogma philosophorum*," *Recherches de théologie ancienne et médiévale*, 16 (1949): 227-258; 17 (1950): 5-28;

Delhaye, " 'Grammatica' et 'Ethica' au XIIe siècle," *Recherches de théologie ancienne et médiévale*, 25 (1958): 59-110;

Peter Dronke, *Fabula: Explorations into the Uses of Myth in Medieval Platonism*, Mittellateinische Studien und Texte, 9 (Leiden: Brill, 1974);

Dronke, "New Approaches to the School of Chartres," *Annuario de estudios medievales*, 6 (1969): 117-140;

Pierre Duhem, *Le système du monde* (Paris: Hermann, 1915);

Heinrich Flatten, *Die Philosophie des Wilhelm von Conches* (Coblenz: Gorres, 1929);

Karin Margareta Fredborg, "The Dependence of Petrus Helias' *Summa super Priscianum* on William of Conches' *Glosae super Priscianum*," *Université de Copenhague: Cahiers de l'Institut du moyen âge grec et latin*, 11 (1973): 1-57;

Eugenio Garin, *Studi sul platonismo medievale* (Florence: Monnier, 1958);

R. A. Gauthier, "Les deux recensions du *Moralium dogma philosophorum*," *Recherches de théologie ancienne et médiévale*, 21 (1953): 171-260; 22 (1955): 51-58;

Palémon Glorieux, "Le Moralium dogma philosophorum et son auteur," *Recherches de théologie ancienne et médiévale*, 16 (1949): 360-366;

Martin Grabmann, *Handschriftliche Forschungen und Mitteilungen zum Schrifttum des Wilhelm von Conches und zu Bearbeitungen seiner naturwissenschaftlichen Werke*, Sitzungsberichte der Bayerischen Akademie der Wissenschaften, 10 (Munich: Verlag der Bayerischen Akademie der Wissenschaften, 1935);

Tullio Gregory, *Anima Mundi: La filosofia di Guglielmo di Conches e la scuola di Chartres* (Florence: Samson, 1955);

Nikolaus M. Häring, "Chartres and Paris Revisted," in *Essays in Honor of Anton Charles Pegis*, edited by J. Reginald O'Donnell (Toronto: Pontifical Institute of Mediaeval Studies, 1974), pp. 268-329;

Charles Homer Haskins, *The Renaissance of the Twelfth Century* (Cambridge, Mass: Harvard University Press, 1927);

Edouard Jeauneau, *"Lectio philosophorum": Recherches sur l'Ecole de Chartres* (Amsterdam: Hakkert, 1973);

Helen Rodnite Lemay, "Science and Theology at Chartres: The Case of the Supracelestial Waters," *British Journal for the History of Science*, 10 (November 1977): 226-236;

Richard P. McKeon, "Medicine and Philosophy in the Eleventh and Twelfth Centuries: The Problem of the Elements," *Thomist*, 24 (April, July, October 1961): 211-256;

John H. Newell, Jr., "Rationalism at the School of Chartres," *Vivarium*, 21 (November 1983): 108-126;

Newell, "Twelfth-Century Theories of Knowledge: New Directions at the School of Chartres," *The Proceedings of the PMR Conference*, volume 6 (Villanova, Pa.: Augustinian Historical Institute, Villanova University, 1985), pp. 161-173;

Ynez V. O'Neill, "William of Conches and the Cerebral Membranes," *Clio Medica*, 2 (1967): 13-21;

O'Neill, "William of Conches' Description of the Brain," *Clio Medica*, 3 (1968): 202-223;

J. M. Parent, *La doctrine de la création dans l'école de Chartres* (Paris: Institut d'Etudes médiévales, 1938);

Reginald Lane Poole, *Illustrations of the History of Medieval Thought and Learning*, second revised edition (London: Macmillan, 1920);

Theodore Silverstein, "*Elementatum*: Its Appearance among the Twelfth-Century Cosmogonists," *Mediaeval Studies*, 16 (1954): 156-162;

R. W. Southern, *Medieval Humanism and Other Studies* (Oxford: Blackwell, 1970);

Southern, *Platonism, Scholastic Method, and the School of Chartres* (Reading, U.K.: Reading University Press, 1979);

Winthrop Wetherbee, *Platonism and Poetry in the Twelfth Century* (Princeton: Princeton University Press, 1972);

John R. Williams, "The Quest for the Author of the *Moralium Dogma Philosophorum*, 1931-1956," *Speculum*, 32 (October 1957): 736-747.

Manuscripts:

Most of William of Conches's writings remain unedited in manuscript copies widely distributed throughout the world, from Baltimore to Heiligenkreuz and from Copenhagen to Rome. Probably the largest and most important holdings are the Bibliothèque Nationale in Paris and the Bayerische Staatsbibliothek in Munich.

William of Sherwood

(1200/1205 - 1266/1271)

John Longeway
University of Wisconsin—Parkside

PRINCIPAL WORKS: *Introductiones in Logicam* (Introduction to Logic, written circa 1250?);

Syncategoremata (Treatise on Syncategorematic Words, date of composition unknown);

Insolubilia (Insolubles, date of composition unknown; attribution doubtful);

Obligationes (Obligations, date of composition unknown; attribution doubtful—probably written by Walter Burley);

De Petitionibus Contrariorum (On Contrary Assumptions, date of composition unknown; attribution doubtful).

EDITIONS: *Die Introductiones in Logicam des Wilhelm von Shyreswood,* edited by Martin Grabmann, Sitzungsberichte der Bayerischen Akademie des Wissenschaften, Philosophisch-historische Abteilung, Jahrgang 1937, Heft 10 (Munich: Verlag der Bayerishche Akademie der Wissenschaften in Komission bei der C. H. Beck'schen Verlagsbuchhandlung, 1937);

"The Syncategoremata of William of Sherwood," edited by R. O'Donnell, *Mediaeval Studies,* 3 (1941): 46-93;

"The logical treatises *De obligationibus*: An introduction with critical texts of William of Sherwood (?) and Walter Burley," edited by Romuald Green, Ph.D. dissertation, Louvain University, 1963;

"Insolubilia Guillelmi Shyreswood (?)," edited by M. L. Roure, in his "La problematique des propositions insolubles au XIIe siècle et au debut du XIVe, suivie de l'édition des traités de W. Shyreswood, W. Burleigh et Th. Bradwardine," *Archives d'histoire doctrinale et littéraire du moyen âge,* 37 (1970): 248-261;

"Some Thirteenth-Century Tracts on the Game of Obligation III: The Tract De petitionibus contrariorum, usually attributed to William Sherwood," edited by L. M. De Rijk, *Vivarium,* 14 (May 1976): 26-49.

CRITICAL EDITION: "William of Sherwood, 'Introductiones in Logicam': Critical Text," edited by Charles H. Lohr, Peter Kunze, and Bernhard Mussler, *Traditio,* 39 (1983): 219-299.

EDITIONS IN ENGLISH: *William of Sherwood's Introduction to Logic,* translated by Norman Kretzmann (Minneapolis: University of Minnesota Press, 1966; London: Oxford University Press, 1966);

Treatise on Syncategorematic Words, translated by Kretzmann (Minneapolis: University of Minnesota Press, 1968).

William of Sherwood was an English logician of the thirteenth century. His works are representative of the consolidation in medieval thought of supposition theory and the treatment of syncategorematic terms with the exposition or analysis of propositions whose logical form is not evident on their face. If the *Insolubilia* (Insolubles), *Obligationes* (Obligations), or *De Petitionibus Contrariorum* (On Contrary Assumptions) are correctly attributed to William, he also provides one of the earliest discussions of semantic and pragmatic self-referential paradoxes in the Middle Ages.

William was probably born in Nottinghamshire between 1200 and 1205. He studied at Oxford, and was a master there by 1252. Norman Kretzmann and Martin Grabmann claim that he taught at Paris between 1240 and 1248; but L. M. De Rijk argues convincingly that there is no reason to suppose he was ever at Paris, and the chief manuscript for his works is in an English hand. Although later generations took little note of William, Roger Bacon praises him as a logician above Albert the Great in his *Opus Tertium* (Third Work, 1266-1272). William became treasurer of Lincoln between 1254 and 1258 and was granted a special dispensation to hold a benefice with cure of souls in 1258. He died, from the evidence of references in Bacon's writings, between 1266 and 1271.

All of William's surviving works are logical, though lost works on the *Libri Quatuor Sen-*

tentiarum (Four Books of Sentences, 1157-1158) of Peter Lombard, on which he would have lectured in gaining his doctorate in theology, and a set of *Distinctiones Theologicae* (Distinctions Relevant to Theology) are reported. The *Introductiones in Logicam* (Introduction to Logic, circa 1250?) consists of six chapters. The first corresponds, broadly speaking, to Aristotle's *On Interpretation*; the second to the *Isagoge* (Introduction) of Porphyry; the third, dealing with syllogism, to Aristotle's *Prior Analytics*; the fourth to Aristotle's *Topics*; and the sixth to Aristotle's *Sophistical Refutations*. As in Peter of Spain's *Tractatus* (Treatise, circa 1230), another important introduction to logic from about the same time, however, Boethius is in fact the proximate source for much of what is in these chapters. The third tract includes one of the earliest occurrences of the mnemonic rhyme, "*Barbara celarent*," used by medieval students to memorize the figures and moods of the syllogism.

The most interesting material in the *Introductiones in Logicam* occurs in the fifth tract, the discussion of the "properties of terms"—*significatio* (signification), *suppositio* (supposition), *copulatio* (copulation), and *appellatio* (appellation). Signification is the "presentation of the form of something to the understanding" by a term. A term is said by William to "supposit" a form if it signifies that form "as subsisting and capable of being ordered under something else"—that is, if it signifies the form as an actually existing thing and so as capable of being "ordered under" a predicate (being made a subject of predication). A term is said to "supposit for" (*pro*, in the place of) another term when, in a given context, it is to be interpreted so that the other term is the logical subject of the predicate under consideration whereas supposition is the meaning the term has in the context of a sentence. Copulation is like supposition, except that it belongs to adjectival terms that describe, rather than substantive terms that refer. Appellation is the "present correct application" of the term, that is, the collection of those things of which the term can correctly be predicated using the present-tense verb *is*. The most important of these concepts is supposition, which provided medieval logicians with a tool to do the work that modern logicians do with quantifier theory. (There were important differences in the medieval approach, though. Supposition occurs within a natural language; there was no attempt to construct an artificial language for the uses of logic. The result was that a plethora of rules governing the different types of supposition had to be introduced to handle all sorts of special contexts in Scholastic Latin.)

As William of Sherwood defined supposition, the supposition of a term (or of the thought or concept associated with it) is specified by indicating the other terms that it stands in for. Thus, the meaning of a term in context is specifiable syntactically (that is, purely in consideration of the relation of the linguistic elements to each other), without reference to semantics (that is, the relation of terms to the extralinguistic realities they stand for). This view is a precursor of the nominalism of William of Ockham and the "terminist" tradition of logic after him, for it avoids reference to any universal other than terms (words, thoughts, or concepts) that a common term such as *man* might be said to signify, while still allowing the universal meaning of the term to be displayed and analyzed. (One should compare William's approach to supposition with that of Peter of Spain; the latter is rooted in a moderate realism—a belief in the actual existence of universals—rather than in an incipient nominalism. Supposition is divided by William into material supposition, which occurs when the word supposits for itself, as in "*man* is a monosyllable" or "*man* is a name," and formal supposition, which occurs when the word supposits for what it signifies. One type of formal supposition is simple supposition, when the word supposits for the form it signifies, as in "man is a species." The other type of formal supposition is personal supposition, which occurs when the word supposits for the individuals that fall under the form it signifies, as in "a man is running." Personal supposition is divided into determinate and confused. The first occurs when the word supposits for some single (undetermined) thing, as in "a man is running." (The single "thing" will be a term, like *Socrates*, or the concept of Socrates.) The second occurs when a word supposits for more than one thing. Confused personal supposition is either mobile or immobile—mobile if one can move from the general case to the specific, as with *man* in "every man is running," and immobile if one cannot, as with *animal* in "every man is an animal" (one cannot infer that every man is *this* animal). Rules concerning the type of supposition to be found in each term in a categorical statement, and allowable inferences from one sort of supposition to another, follow. For instance, an affirmative distributive sign, such as *every*, placed before the subject term, renders the term "merely" confused, while a negative distributive sign, such as *no*, placed before the subject, confuses the predicate distributively. One can argue from a statement containing a distributively confused term to a statement that has a similar structure, except that the term is reassigned a determinate supposition; thus, one can infer from "no man is any horse" that "some horse is no man." But one cannot argue from merely confused to determinate supposition; thus, one cannot move from "every man is an animal" to "some animal is every man."

The *Syncategoremata* (Treatise on Syncategorematic Words, date of composition unknown) extends supposition theory to sentences containing syncategorematic words—words that have no signification on their own but alter the signification of terms within the sentence in which they occur. Often, a syncategorematic word will alter the supposition of terms associated with it by the introduction of a negation or a sign of universality. Such words include *whole, all, every, but, only*, and others of this sort, but also, according to William, such terms as *begins* and *ceases*. The analysis of sentences containing *begins* breaks an apparent single categorical proposition into a logical combination of categorical propositions, one of which turns out to contain a negation. Thus, "Socrates begins to be white" might be exposited as "Socrates was not white before now, and is now white," or as "Socrates is not now white, but immediately after this he will be white."

The treatise *Insolubilia* (Insolubles, date of composition unknown) deals with semantic paradoxes of self-reference, such as the liar paradox in which one utters, "I am now saying a falsehood." The sentence cannot, it seems, be true, for from its truth it follows that it is false; nor can it be false, for from its falsehood it follows that it is true. The treatise mentions several approaches to the paradox. One approach, taken in the earliest known treatment of insolubles but rejected by *Insolubilia* and by the whole later tradition before the seventeenth century, takes it that one who utters the offending statement "says nothing." The treatise ascribed to William objects that the insoluble statement is perfectly meaningful, since it obeys the rules of grammar, so that one indeed says something when one says it. A second approach claims that the statement must mean "I am saying some falsehood other than this statement I am now making" and advances the rule that a term cannot supposit for the whole of which it is a part, so that self-reference is outlawed; thus, the term *falsehood* must be taken to supposit for a second sentence. The treatise objects that this approach rules out perfectly harmless cases, such as "every name signifies some substance with a quality," in which *name* should be taken to supposit for itself. But though William rejects the rule, he argues that in the sentence "I am saying a falsehood" the term *falsehood* must supposit for some sentence other than the one of which it is a part. The principle of charity, according to which a sentence is to be construed so that it does not mean something absurd and at least *could* be true, is to be invoked here. So the sentence really means "I am saying, at this moment, some falsehood other than the one I am uttering in saying this." The sentence is indeed false, since it is false that I am saying anything else false at this moment, for I am saying nothing else at all. But from this falsehood it does not follow that it is false that I am saying something false, but only that it is false that I am saying something else (other than what I am saying) that is false. And so one cannot argue that I am saying something true.

The treatise *Obligationes* (Obligations, date of composition unknown) is probably not by William of Sherwood; it is similar to a longer and more fully developed treatise known to be by Walter Burley, down to the examples advanced. In any case, it deals with paradoxes that arise in the context of a dialectical game forming part of the training in the medieval curriculum of logic. In this game, a person would be asked either to defend a given proposition advanced under certain hypothetical conditions, or to deny it under those conditions, and to reply to the questions of his opponent without becoming entangled in contradiction. Consistency, not plausibility, was aimed at, and the propositions were generally highly artificial. In the course of the game a paradox might arise because the proposition made some reference to the "obligations" of the person defending or denying it. "Obligations" are rules of the dialectical game that allow or outlaw certain inferences that can arise in the course of the game. So if the proposition under discussion refers to some rule which bears on the evaluation of the proposition, the proposition might have to be evaluated as true just in case it is false and vice verse. The treatise, then, deals with "pragmatic" paradoxes, that is, paradoxes that arise not because of the semantic content of propositions alone but because of that content together with the circumstances in which they are uttered. In practice, many of the examples in such treatises turn out to be equivalent to *insolubilia*.

References:

H. A. G. Braakhuis, "The Views of William of Sherwood on Some Semantical Topics and Their Relation to Those of Roger Bacon," *Vivarium*, 15 (November 1977): 111-142;

Jorge E. Gracia, "Propositions as Premisses of Syllogisms in Medieval Logic," *Notre Dame Journal of Formal Logic*, 16 (October 1975): 545-547;

Roland Houde, "Ńote sur une correction erronée," *Dialogue*, 6 (1967-1968): 583-584;

Raúl Iriarte and Néstor Otero, "Guillermo de Shyreswood y algunos antecedentes medievales de la filosofía del lenguaje," *Cuadernos del Sur*, no. 10 (1968-1969): 124-131;

Klaus Jacobi, "Drei Theorien über die Funktion aussagen verknupfender Zeichen: Die Diskussion des Junktors 'si' bei Wilhelm von Shyreswood," in *Sprache und Erkenntnis im Mittelalter: Akten des VI. Internationalen Kongresses für Mittelalterliche Philosophie der Societé internationale pour l'étude de la philosophie Mediévale* (Berlin: De Gruyter, 1977), pp. 385-397;

Jacobi, "Die Modalbegriffe in den logischen Schriften des Wilhelm von Shyreswood und in anderen Kompendien des 12. und 13. Jahrhunderts: Funktionsbestimmung und Gebrauch in der logischen Analyse," *Studien und Texte zur Geistesgeschichte des Mittelalters*, 13 (1980): 41-48, 328-331;

Jacobi, "Wilhelm von Shyreswode and die Dialectica Monacensis," in *English Logic and Semantics from the End of the Twelfth Century to the Time of Ockham and Burleigh: Acts of the Fourth European Symposium on Medieval Logic and Semantics, Leiden-Nijmegen, 23-27 April 1979*, edited by H. A. G. Braakhuis, C. H. Kneepkens, and L. M. De Rijk (Nijmegen: Ingenium, 1981), pp. 99-130;

Charles F. Kielkopf, "The Specific Reading of A-Propositions in a Defense of William Sherwood," *Notre Dame Journal of Formal Logic*, 20 (October 1979): 735-740;

Alain de Libera, "The Oxford and Paris Traditions in Logic," in *The Cambridge History of Later Medieval Philosophy*, edited by Norman Kretzmann, Anthony Kenny, and Jan Pinborg (Cambridge: Cambridge University Press, 1982), pp. 174-187;

Gerald W. Lilje, "Signification and Supposition in the Logic of William of Sherwood," M.A. thesis, University of Illinois, 1964;

Alfonso Maierù, *Terminologia logica della tarda scolastica*, Lessico intelletuale Europeo, 8 (Rome: Edizioni dell'Ateneo, 1972);

John Malcolm, "On Grabmann's Text of William of Sherwood," *Vivarium*, 9 (November 1971): 108-118;

Jan Pinborg and Sten Ebbesen, eds., "Thirteenth Century Notes on William of Sherwood's Treatise on Properties of Terms. An Edition of Anonymii Dubitationes et notabilia circa Guilelmi de Shyreswode introductionum logicalium Tractatum V from ms Worcester Cath. Q.13," *Cahiers de l'Institut du Moyen-Âge grec et latin*, no. 47 (1984): 103-141;

L. M. De Rijk, "Some Thirteenth-Century Tracts on the Game of Obligation," *Vivarium*, 14 (May 1976): 26-49;

M. L. Roure, "La problématique des propositions insolubles au XIIe siècle et au début du XIVe, suivie de l'édition des traités de W. Shyreswood, W. Burleigh et Th. Bradwardine," *Archives d'histoire doctrinale et littéraire du moyen âge*, 37 (1970): 205-326;

Mary J. Sirridge, "William of Sherwood on Propositions and Their Parts," *Notre Dame Journal of Formal Logic*, 15 (July 1974): 462-464;

Paul Vincent Spade, "Insolubilia," in *The Cambridge History of Later Medieval Philosophy*, edited by Kretzmann, Kenny, and Pinborg (Cambridge: Cambridge University Press, 1982), pp. 246-253;

Eleonore Stump, "Obligations: A. From the Beginning to the Early Fourteenth Century," in *The Cambridge History of Later Medieval Philosophy*, edited by Kretzmann, Kenny, and Pinborg (Cambridge: Cambridge University Press, 1982), pp. 315-334;

Stump, "William of Sherwood's Treatise on Obligations," *Historiographica Linguistica*, 7 (1980): 249-261.

Manuscripts:

All extant works by William of Sherwood are in a manuscript in the Bibliothèque Nationale, Paris (Ms. Lat. 16617). A second copy of the *Synacategoremata* is in the Bodleian Library, Oxford University (Ms. Digby 55).

Appendix

Translators of the Twelfth Century: Literary Issues Raised and Impact Created

Translators of the Twelfth Century: Literary Issues Raised and Impact Created

Richard Lemay
City University of New York, Emeritus

A sure sign of a qualitative step forward in the growth of a young civilization toward literary maturity is the outburst of a wave or waves of translations from the accumulated treasures of an older civilization. After a period of incubation the younger, fresher offshoot in humanity's collective striving for fuller self-realization reaches a certain level of consciousness of, adaptability to, and appetite for higher intellectual values—particularly of a literary or scientific kind—harbored by a neighboring, more experienced civilization with which it happens to have been put into living contact. History records many such situations; indeed, once favorable conditions have prevailed for a sufficiently long time, almost deterministically there emerges this phenomenon of a transfer of ideas and experiences from the more sophisticated to the younger culture made receptive by prolonged contact and familiarity.

The process may take place in successive stages that aim at satisfying a seemingly irrepressible and growing appetite; but it can just as well burst out as an unforeseen explosion imparting to a culture an irreversible direction of development that would have been quite different without that fateful contact and acculturation. As an instance of the first type one may recall the translations from Greek to Arabic which have been stressed in the research of Richard Walzer, S. M. Stern, Franz Rosenthal, and Abd al-Rahman Badawi. Of the second type are the late Byzantine translations from the Latin in philosophy and science in the wake of the contact with Latin culture produced by the conquest of the empire during the Fourth Crusade in 1204. This article will concentrate on the extraordinarily significant and as yet inadequately treated phenomenon of the twelfth-century Latin translations from Arabic works of science and philosophy that supplied fodder for Scholastic speculation and intellectual exploration for nearly four centuries afterward. In this strictly defined perspective we shall first examine the achievements of the principal European translators of the twelfth century with a view to ascertaining the stimulants, goals, and the literary background and preparation which attended the emergence of the movement. We will also examine the translation methods which were followed, either those inherited from earlier translators (such as Boethius) or those forged under necessity. From the resulting style of the products and their diffusion, we shall try to assess the influence exerted by this remarkable movement on the literary conceptions and ideals of medieval and Renaissance Europe. Our aim is to bring to light the enormously stimulating and, in the main, lasting impact of the work of twelfth-century translators on the future direction of European creativity in literature and thought.

The vogue of Arabic scientific material took hold among European scholars as early as the beginning of the twelfth century. It is safe to reckon as of near insignificance the dabbling with Arab science in the eleventh century by Gerbert and his school (principally Hermann Contractus or Hermann the Lame, author of a treatise on the astrolabe), on the one hand, and the Catalan monastic world of Montserrat and Ripoll, on the other. These naive scholars grasped practically none of the significance of what they were casually borrowing, they never brought it to any level of original development, and they distorted the few genuine elements of mathematics they borrowed from the flourishing Arab culture of their time. Their minds were simply too crude and unprepared for any fruitful absorption of the sophisticated astronomy and mathematics of the Arab world, a world of which they perceived but a glimpse.

With the opening of the twelfth century a deliberate and systematic movement of committing to the Latin language the scientific treasures of contemporary Arab science (essentially mathematics and astronomy) began to manifest itself. Whether this Latin demand represented a new awareness engendered by protracted contacts with higher levels of Muslim society during the Crusades, both Eastern and Iberian, it is not possible to determine. It first shines through the production of John of Seville, the first translator of importance and perhaps the source of inspiration of the whole movement. John is quite visibly answering a newly arisen demand among Latin scholars. He often alludes to "our Latin intellectual habits" as contrasted to Arab ones; sometimes he practically excludes himself from this tradition by referring to "the Latins" as if they were an external group.

During most of his career he worked in an area of the Iberian Peninsula that was then a sort of no-man's-land recently recovered for the Christian groups—in the north of what was to become the Kingdom of Portugal around 1140. He seems to have been of Jewish descent, if Ibn Daud (or Avendeuth) is part of his name, which is likely in spite of the arguments against it by M. T. d'Alverny and Manuel Alonso. He was in some way related to the well-known "vizier Sisnando Davidiz" (the equivalent of "son of David" or "Ibn Daud"), a Jewish native of Tentugal who was captured as a child, trained in Muslim Seville, and eventually became a refugee to his native region of north Portugal, which he helped Ferdinand of Galicia to reconquer and of which he was made lifetime vizier (he died in 1091). Sisnando Davidiz could be considered the real founder of Portugal, since the one usually recognized as such—Alfonso I, the son of Countess Teresa and Count Henry of Burgundy—simply inherited from his mother a territory that she had received in appanage shortly after 1091 but which had been consolidated and made self-administering by Sisnando Davidiz during the thirty years of his viziership.

John Avendauth Hispalensis, or John of Seville, produced most of his translations in the region of "Limia" or "Lima," the area created and administered by Sisnando. Although he bears the name, John probably never was in Seville; he maintained the cognomen, obviously, on account of the reputation achieved when his relative Sisnando was the vizier of al-Mu'tamid of Seville before escaping to the Christian side. Almost inescapably John of Seville has to be linked with this family, in some sufficiently close connection to be able to make use of the name.

In fact, he was probably the son of Sisnando Davidiz. As such, he would have had an inclination toward Jewish culture, which he exemplifies in translating practically the whole of the astrological works of the Jewish astrologer Ma'sha'llah of Baghdad and a good part of the works of another Jewish astrologer from Baghdad, Sahl ben Bisr, a disciple of Ma'sha'llah. He was a prominent figure among the upper crust of Christian society of the area: he dedicated a translation of a medical portion of the *Secret of Secrets* of Pseudo-Aristotle to the Countess Teresa, who followed Sisnando Davidiz in the administration of the region around Lima. The terms used to address the queen show John to be in close and friendly relation with her. John was on equally familiar terms with the French monk Maurice Bourdin, who was the first bishop of Braga, then archbishop of Coimbra, and finally "Pope" Gregory VIII (1118-1121; antipope in the official list). John "Avendauth of Seville" obviously belonged to the highest levels of lay, ecclesiastical, and scholarly circles of nascent Portugal culture.

John of Seville's enormous production as a translator reflects a substantial demand for such works from Latin circles. The most reliable lists of his works are those drawn up in the nineteenth century by F. Wüstenfeld and M. Steinschneider. Their authority has not been seriously affected by the controversy that raged for some thirty years of the twentieth century around the identity and works of John of Seville. The last unchallenged work of John of Seville was announced in 1936 by José Maria Millás Vallicrosa, who had recently discovered a previously unknown work by John Avendauth dedicated to two English friends. But after 1940, in a series of articles in *Al-Andalus*, Alonso sought to dismantle the personality and production of John of Seville, in which effort he was at first partially followed by d'Alverny. L. Thorndike nearly abandoned his earlier trust in the historical role of John of Seville as a translator from the Arabic and a mover of twelfth-century intellectual "renaissance." The earliest manuscripts of John's translations unmistakably identify the translator by name and clearly locate his activity in the region of Limia. The later confusion stems from the ineptitude of scribes, whose blunders are taken as evidence by modern scholars who feel ill at ease with some aspects of the intellectual production of medieval scholars. Traits of John's personality transpire clearly through his long efforts. An imposing number of stylistic and psychological characteristics render identification of his production nearly infallible, contrary to the objections of Alonso and d'Alverny.

The translations produced by John of Seville, exclusively from the Arabic, display a high level of understanding of the subject matter—usually mathematics, astronomy, or meteorology, some medicine, little of philosophy proper. At the same time, due both to John's apparently weak command of the Latin language, on the one hand, and to the undeveloped scientific vocabulary of Latin, on the other, his translations smack of their oriental origin. They produced, as a result, a new form of expression in Latin which was likely to appear repulsive to the taste of their intended users. In one passage John confesses that in translating scientific works the text must be rendered word for word, if possible, for fear of letting some "scientific" finery be lost in the transfer.

The method is so systematically adhered to that the present writer, in preparing a critical edition of an Arabic text, has often relied on John's Latin rendering to supply the answer to crucial doubts about the Arabic manuscript. Being of Semitic background, John apparently felt no inhibition in producing twisted sentences that were nearly unintelligible to a Latin reader. Grammatically idiomatic turns of phrase of the Arabic were transposed directly into the Latin idiom, where they did not fit and were likely to take the reader aback. This practice may be considered a distinctive trait of John's manner as a translator and can be used as a criterion for identifying his work. No other translator of the period worked this way, not even those who have traditionally been considered partisans of the word-for-word translation method.

Either John was ignorant of the proper Latin terms for particular technical expressions or, more likely, the Latin scientific vocabulary was not sufficiently developed at that time for him to have had at hand a standard guide. Most ancient Greek works of science—Ptolemy's *Almagest*, for instance—had never been translated into Latin in classical times. Much of the Greek technical vocabulary, therefore, had never found an apt equivalent in classical Latin. Hence, John is often impelled to coin his own Latin barbarisms replicating the Arabic idiom (for example, *elementari, elementantur, elementati sunt, elementans* for different uses of the Arabic root *taba'a*), at times merely transliterating into Latin consonants the skeleton of the Arabic word. The ultimate significance of John's trailblazing effort is that it probably engendered a lively controversy among twelfth-century Latin intellectuals as to the respective roles and limits of *sapientia* (science) as opposed to *eloquentia* (rhetoric or ornateness of expression) in the new learning that was dawning among them under the impact of the neighboring and thriving Arab culture.

A contemporary of John of Seville was the Jewish physician Moshe Sefardi; he became known as Petrus Anfulsus after his conversion in 1106, taking his new name from his godfather, King Alfonso I of Aragon. Petrus Anfulsus (or Pedro Alfonso) became important among translators from the moment he moved from his native Spain to London, where he had been called as a physician to King Henry I (Beauclerc) around 1110.

In England Petrus seems to have been shocked by the lack of scientific interest and training he found among supposedly learned men of the Latin world, and for a while he tried to act as a catalyst for their education by inviting them to absorb from the real source of learning at that time: that expressed in the Arabic language, a world of which he himself was an outstanding product. For their benefit he produced his best-known Latin work, *De Disciplina Clericalis*, an ethical treatise aimed at informing them about the lore of practical wisdom embodied in Arabian literature. He expanded this solicitude in an address to all Europeans in his celebrated *Letter to the Peripateticians of Francia* (that is, to the philosophers or would-be philosophers of Europe). In more scientific pursuits he is credited with a translation of one form of the astronomical *Canons* and *Tables* of al-Hwarizmi. Petrus Anfulsus's endeavors on behalf of the uplifting of Latin science can be dated between 1110 and 1115. It can thus be related, in time and in intention, to John of Seville's parallel effort, with the difference that Petrus's work was carried out directly in the midst of European society. Petrus may have been the direct inspiration for the career of Adelard of Bath, one of the earliest European translators of science from the Arabic in the twelfth century, and may have engendered a specifically English drive to acquire Arab science that was soon to be represented by Robert of Chester, Daniel of Morley, Roger of Hereford, Alfred of Sareshel, Michael Scot, and Robert Grosseteste.

Petrus Anfulsus's production should be given great credit for awakening the European consciousness from its slumber and for disclosing the high-minded cultural values expressed in the literary monuments of the contemporary Arab civilization. Another strain in Petrus's influence can be seen in the evolution of language in his time. As a Spaniard and a Jew he was familiar with the two major linguistic tools flourishing at that time in the literate world of the Iberian Peninsula, both Semitic: Hebrew and Arabic. He can be presumed also to have been familiar with the rapidly maturing romance of Spain, which produced at approximately his time the great poem *El mio Cid*. The Latin of his *Letter* is shot through with Romance and Arabic idioms; the definite article, unknown to classical Latin, pops up everywhere in his style in the guise of useless, even obtrusive demonstrative or personal pronouns which render the reading cumbersome for a classicist. Medieval, especially Scholastic, Latin would be radically and irreversibly affected by these stylistic and grammatical traits. The monuments of medieval European culture acquired their main differences from the classical ones, at least in the field of literature, precisely from these new strains already observable in the literary and scientific production of Petrus Anfulsus and John of Seville at the beginning of the twelfth century.

Adelard of Bath's adventure in the field of translation from the Arabic began around 1110, about the time of the presence of Petrus Anfulsus at the English court. In addition to the probable influence of Petrus, Adelard was likely inspired by the English savant Prior Walcher of Malvern, a self-proclaimed listener and imitator of Petrus Anfulsus. Adelard's career fits into the earliest phase, from about 1110 to 1130, of the movement of translations from the Arabic. He produced some of the earliest scientific translations from the Arabic, probably anticipated only by John of Seville and Petrus Anfulsus. Adelard was apparently the earliest "native" European to dabble in this new field, and his production has all the imperfections attributable to such novelties. His choice of "scientific" texts to be translated is awful: they are works dealing with the technique of astrology rather than with its assumed scientific foundations.

His method of translation betrays a woeful incompetence. In his translation of Abu Ma'sar's *Muhtasar* as *Ysagoge Minor Japharis*, apparently because of his inability to grasp the meanings of operations or concepts involved, he spatters his copy with a host of untranslated technical terms which confer on his text an esoteric note. In addition, he frequently mistranslates basic scientific notions. Midway through the translation of an astrological vade mecum, the *Centiloquium* of Pseudo-Ptolemy, he gives up the effort; he must have felt unequal to the still relatively simple task. This conclusion follows from the very inadequate level of performance achieved in the limited portion completed. The translation in both surviving independent copies (London, BL Sloane 2030 and Lyons, Bibl. Munic. 328) ends with the thirty-ninth proposition out of one hundred, and it does so throughout the many copies of a later conflated text into which Adelard's thirty-nine propositions were absorbed. Adelard did not even attempt a translation of the commentary, a much too sophisticated piece of epistemological and scientific contents.

The learned public of the time must have included scholars like Adelard himself, but the great majority was made up of classicists, dialecticians, or divines. They seem to have rated his products rather unfavorably, since even Adelard's later and "major" translations were either systematically improved by others or were taken up again from scratch in fresh versions superseding his own. The *Centiloquium* saw four other translations in the same century, and the *Ysagoge Minor Japharis* practically disappeared after the translations of Abu Ma'sar's *Introductorium Maius*. In short, although he was an enthusiastic adventurer into fields of intellectual endeavor which were new and bold for his times, Adelard's precocious awakening hardly went beyond a mere dabbling into a superior neighboring culture.

With regard to their style, Adelard's writings inevitably fall into the trap of barbaric Latin striving to parade in the trappings of Arab science. It would be hard to find in early-twelfth-century Latin expression a sentence as awkwardly clumsy as this one from Adelard's translation of the *Centiloquium*, first proposition: "Erit itaque sumenda forma iudicii in hoc opere et currentibus hunc cursum ex anima et inquisitione, scilicet in eo quod superat supra ipsum revelatio naturarum et servientis effectus vel vestigium." John of Seville's translations constantly indulged in the same kind of subservience to the sentence structure of his Arabic originals, but John's Latin sentences made at least minimal sense.

Mention of the special category of translators apparently working in tandem is indispensable in a survey of the work of translators of the twelfth century for several reasons, all compelling. One is the need to rid historical research of the prevailing assumption that actors in this novel field regularly worked in tandem or even in troika, one member each a specialist in one of the languages involved: Arabic, Romance, Latin, or Hebrew. Such specialization did take place, as in the project of the translation of the Koran set up by Peter the Venerable, or in the celebrated case of John of Seville and Domingo Gundisalvo working on the translation of the *De Anima* of Avicenna for Archbishop Raymond of Toledo. But this arrangement was rather exceptional. The bulk of the production of each translator was normally effected singly and consequently is ascribable to each translator individually. What appeared to be a team of translators, such as Hermann of Carinthia and Robert of Chester in the Rioja, or Abraham Savasorda and Plato of Tivoli in Barcelona, was usually a partnership or companionship (even a homosexual one, as in the case of Hermann and Robert) of congenial individuals working in the same field and coming together for the sake of providing mutual comfort and support, but each worker keeping to his own program and accomplishing his translations alone. The association may sometimes have inspired a definite direction in the program of translation, as in the case of Robert of Chester's abandoning some project to answer Hermann of Carinthia's demand that Robert translate al-Kindi's *Judicia* for him. Despite their close association, the translation of the *Judicia* was done by Robert alone and was never claimed by Hermann.

Second, it is imperative to clear away the hypothesis of the existence of a "College of Translators" supposedly established in Toledo by Archbishop Raymond. Collaboration under the patronage of the archbishop in the 1140s is attested for one translation alone, that of the *De Anima* of Avicenna, translated by John of Seville and Gundisalvo. Each member of this short-lived team had an extensive, independent career on his own as a translator or author, and few of their individual works can be connected with the patronage of Archbishop Raymond.

The temporary association set up by the archbishop seems only to have been a flicker of reaction to the "canonical" visit of Peter the Venerable, the abbot of Cluny in Spain, in 1142 (Archbishop Raymond was a French Cluniac monk, hence to some degree subject to Peter's jurisdiction). During his sojourn in Spain, undertaken primarily to settle the problem of unpaid subsidies Spanish monarchs had promised Cluny for its help in the Reconquista, Peter discovered Christian scholars (presumably all clerics) translating Arabic works of science. Apparently disturbed by this reverse of an apologetic duty to be expected from good Christians, Peter succeeded in engaging—for a time only—two of these translators, Robert of Chester and Hermann of Carinthia, (with much prayer and emolument, it is asserted by Peter) in the translation of religious literature of the Muslims, including a translation of the Koran, to provide an arsenal of arguments for an "intellectual crusade" envisaged against Islam. For a while Peter hoped to convince his friend Bernard of Clairvaux to undertake this crusade, or at least to give it his blessing. He was soon disappointed, for Bernard's attitude toward Islam was quite alien to the idea of an intellectual approach. Instead of agreeing to Peter the Venerable's suggestion, Bernard preached the Second Crusade at Vézelay (1144). The translation effort sponsored by Peter was not totally lost, however, for Peter wrote his own apologetic treatise against Islam, which can be dated about 1148.

For Hermann and Robert, hitherto so closely associated, the unexpected encounter with the abbot of Cluny signaled an irreparable breach—on ethical grounds raised by Peter the Venerable, it can be assumed. Within a year or so after their collaboration on Peter's project, Robert of Chester was working alone in translating the *Alchemy* of Morienus, taking great pains in his prologue to expurgate his name from some stain. He never mentions here, or at any time during a career spanning several more decades, his former "inseparable" companion.

Soon after the breach in 1143 Hermann was at Salerno, presumably working on translations of medical works until he learned of the arrival in Sicily of a Greek codex of Ptolemy's *Almagest.* Since his partnership with Robert in Spain had been for the purpose of translating the *Almagest*—a project which their separation cut short—Hermann rushed to Sicily in search of the "wandering" Henricus Aristippus, who held the precious codex. Henricus raised difficulties about lending it to Hermann; but, with the support of Admiral Eugenius of Sicily, Hermann finally laid his hands on the *Almagest.* He translated it in Palermo around 1150, according to the marginal note inserted by the scribe for the illuminator in the Florence manuscript, which seems to be a contemporary, unfinished copy of the translation.

Hermann seems to have died before seeing his cherished project to its final completion.

Robert of Chester may be the English scholar and translator Robertus Fortunae, who visited Sicily in 1156, apparently to inquire about translations. Henricus Aristippus tried to lure him into staying in Sicily by describing the opportunities at hand, further dedicating to him his translations of the Platonic dialogues *Phaedo* and *Meno*. Robertus brought the translations back to England, and they survive in a transcription in an Oxford manuscript (Corpus Christi College 243) made—probably directly from this Sicilian copy brought back by Robertus—by the Flemish scholar Frederick Nagel around 1450.

The few cases of actual joint translation include the translation of the astrological work *Elections* in Barcelona around 1134, claimed in its colophon to have been done by Plato of Tivoli and Abraham Savasorda (or Bar Hiyya or An-Nasi). It is a word-for-word rendering, with a minimum of Latin correction. Another case of joint translation is that of the *De Anima* of Avicenna, translated for Archbishop Raymond of Toledo by John of Seville and Domingo Gundisalvo. John says that he rendered (probably orally) each Arabic vocable into Romance (Spanish), which Gundisalvo turned into Latin. Therefore, the Latin style of this translation is exclusively Gundisalvo's, the correctness of the understanding of both technical and linguistic features of the original being credited to John of Seville.

Yet another well-known instance of collaboration is the case of Gerard of Cremona translating the *Almagest*, "with the help of the Mozarab Galippus." (Professor Paul Kunitzsch of Munich is investigating this translation with the intention of preparing a critical edition.) This translation is the only one for which it is attested (by Daniel of Morley) that Gerard used a collaborator. A statement by Gerard's *socii* (associates) in a eulogy after his death in 1187 has been used to assume a regular collaboration arrangement between them and Gerard, but the *socii* make no claim of direct collaboration in translation. The enterprise of Gerard was so extensive, so prolonged, and so obviously well organized that he may eventually have set up a team of coworkers who would do all the parallel jobs, such as procuring good manuscripts, transcribing or supervising the work of copyists, and so on. No further collaboration in translation after that with Galippus is asserted by anyone.

An assumed collaboration of Hermann of Carinthia's translation of the *Almagest* from the Greek must be rejected. It has been said, on the basis of a misinterpretation of the preface of this work, that Hermann acknowledged the help of Admiral Eugenius in the translation. Correct reading of Hermann's admittedly intricate Latin periods shows that the help he acknowledges having received from Eugenius merely extended to using his prestige and political influence to pressure Henricus Aristippus to surrender the Greek codex for Hermann to translate—a task which Aristippus had probably hoped to reserve for himself.

Conflict among the early generations of translators as to the proper or best methods of translation appears to have been rife for a time, although the evidence is surprisingly meager. Its ultimate solution profoundly affected the evolution of European expression during the Latin Middle Ages.

Up to the beginning of the twelfth century, European letters was in the doldrums. Scientific interest had long been deadened by the exclusive use of late Roman compendia, which contained stale rhetorical recitals of frozen axioms. Latin letters did not fare much better after the early triumph of Germanic invaders and settlers. A brief spurt of energy burst out in Carolingian times, only to quiet down again for another three centuries.

In the late eleventh and early twelfth centuries a renewed interest in Classical letters expressed itself in scattered schools where the Latin classics held sway again. The most important were Chartres and Orléans, but the schools of northern France frequented by Adelard of Bath, Peter Abelard, and Daniel of Morley sponsored and encouraged learning and thought, involving attention to literary expression. This stirring of Latin minds in favor of education has been loosely labeled a renaissance. Chartres, in particular, is now known—essentially on the testimony of John of Salisbury, who later became its bishop—to have been a nursery of good, even excellent Latin study in the tradition of Cicero. The ideal of classical Latin which was fostered for some generations at the School of Chartres was mastery of *eloquentia*. A riper ideal of learning, including a core of philosophical speculation, found expression at Chartres in the coupling of *eloquentia* with *sapientia*. It appears probable that the inspiration was Boethius's *Consolation of Philosophy*. At any rate, the full scope of this recently installed program was stamped with the celebrated distich made so familiar by the experience of Chartres: "Sapientia sine eloquentia parum prodest. Eloquentia sine Sapientia nihil prodest, multum obest."

But the historical achievement of Chartres' school manifested itself principally in the dominance of *eloquentia*, while stale compendia of the science of a dead past filled the part of sapientia. Hence a universal trait shared by men of learning of the Latin twelfth century was an overwhelming preoccupation with *eloquentia* at the expense of *sapientia*. What little science there was inevitably sank under the weight of eloquentia, or style in expression.

It is here that the vicissitudes affecting the early translations, especially rival translation methods, had a major impact. Two principal camps can be registered in the conflict: one wondered how much of eloquentia must be maintained as the mark of a civilized culture when transferring the intellectual goods from another culture; the other side wondered how far the borrowed elements can strive at identity with the original foreign ideals, at the cost of enormous insults to the rules of polished eloquentia.

Modern students of medieval translations have often observed that some of them follow a path of ad verbum (word-for-word), thereby producing Latin works whose style and general quality owe more to the original language than to Latin rhetoric or taste. This phenomenon is observed in translations from the Greek as well as in those from the Arabic. From the modern aspersions on the unpalatable literalness, eventually qualified as "slavishness," of the medieval translations, it is perhaps time to go back to ascertainable factors in the medieval outlook which may offer a more accurate picture of the efforts and merits of these translators.

Twelfth-century translators openly expressed an earnest preference for, or defense of, a literal method of translation. This preference is most clearly stated by John of Seville, who appears to have set the pattern for later generations of translators. In a prologue to his translation of a brief medical portion from the Pseudo-Aristotelian *Secret of Secrets*, John confesses to Countess Teresa of Lima that his previous translations did not familiarize him with medical subjects but that he had agreed to do this one at the instance of the queen. He then justifies his preference for a word-for-word translation. John declares that he did not totally espouse the wording of his original; this, he thinks, is not done by any interpreter. But as much as it is in his power, he will at times render the sense, and at times the very wording as well. No one should wonder at this apparent deficiency of his, since practically all translators had acted similarly. He states in no uncertain terms his determination to follow the original word for word, for a paramount reason: the need for accuracy of truth. If this solution should appear clumsy to some, let them blame it on his own shortcomings alone.

The rather general character of this defense indicates that John wishes to protect the whole of his earlier production. Hence, one suspects that his method had already raised some kind of criticism. He is no doubt anticipating that a divergence in attitude will soon develop among translators not strictly confined to the literary standards of the Iberian Peninsula. Adelard of Bath, for instance, had translated a book on amulets by Thabit ben Qurra, which is called *Tilasmat* in Arabic and which Adelard titled in Latin *Liber Prestigiorum*. When translating the same work later, John of Seville alludes to this "foolish" Latin translator who had attempted the work before him.

Much later, apparently, in his work of astronomy dedicated to two English friends, Gauco and William, John comes again to the topic of the right method of translation. This time he lays particular emphasis on the need to be explicit—overlong if necessary—in a scientific work ("Nunc vero ne lectorem cupientem aliquid quo animus eius delectetur citius invenire videamur verbis superfluis onerare, ac pro modico labore plurima verba iactando proferre, decrevimus ut dixi ad presens de his omnibus silere, et ad ea que promisimus quibuscumque verbis quiverimus tendere"). John then turns into an axiomatic statement his view of the proper literary standing of a work of science: in a short work, he writes, verbosity exposes the work to contemptibility, it engenders tedium in readers and numbs keenness of the mind "Verba enim multa in exiguo opere et opus contemptibile reddunt, et legentibus fastidium generant atque ingenii acuitatem pervertunt." In a magnum opus, on the contrary, abundance of words tempts the reader; it enhances the work by making it appear desirable and sharpening the wit ("In magno vero opere legentem sollicitant, opus commendant et ad eius dilectionem invitant atque ingenium acuunt").

In the prologue written in 1140, to his translation of *Liber Introductorius in Astrologiam*

Abuma'xar Albalachi (the *Kitab al-Mudhal al-Kabir* of Abu Ma'sar), the rival translator Hermann of Carinthia stages a discussion between himself and his "inseparable companion" Robert of Chester on the subject of the proper method of translation. Hermann and Robert seem to have issued from the School of Chartres; at the very least, they were imbued with the "classicist" ideal of Latin letters set up by Cicero and maintained, particularly in the matter of translations, by Boethius, the ideal Christian scholar for the Chartrians. Such men, fresh from a Latin school of such excellence, were likely to be the staunchest critics of John of Seville's method of "literal" translation which had produced such monstrous Latin monuments as John of Seville's translation of the same work of Abu Ma'sar: *Liber in quo est Maior Introductorius Abumasar astrologi ad scientiam iudiciorum astrorum et tractatus eius super eadem iudicia cum disputatione rationali et auctentica et figure signorum atque nature*. The discussion between Hermann and Robert represents a statement of method most sharply opposed to John's proclamation. Hermann and Robert propose to keep closer to the steps indicated by Boethius in matters of translations into Latin. Hermann first states his pronounced discomfort facing the "prolixity" of the Arabic language and authors, with which he contrasts the assumed "sobriety" of Latin scholars and authors. Hermann had at first been of a mind to eliminate all "useless verbiage" in his Arab source, until Robert reminded him of the "Boethian" rule which no interpreter—not even Hermann himself in the past—was wont to break. The rule, set forth in the prologue of Boethius's translation of the *Arithmetica* of Nicomachus, states that in transferring an alien source into one's own language a translator may be allowed to follow his own path expatiating where the source has been too concise in omitting some indispensable background, or cutting down on useless prolixity. Yet, hearing of Hermann's intention to skip passages from his source, especially toward the beginning, Robert reminds his companion of the "limits" of the Boethian rule: in following a different path from that of your source, see that you do not run too far away from it. For if you omit any portion, especially at the beginning, anyone in a position to check the source will ascribe omissions not to cleverness (*industria*) but to ignorance; and thereby the merits of your work will be diminished, and we ourselves (Robert takes seriously Hermann's fiction of a joint authorship) shall become the objects of blame for distortion. This rule was, therefore, the charter of Latin translators from the Arabic in the twelfth century who were still profoundly attached to the Boethian and Ciceronian ideal of pure latinity. Here and in his other translations or original works (*Astronomia*, Ptolemy's *Planispherium*, Euclid's *Elements*, his translation of the *Almagest* from the Greek) constant effort tended toward upholding a "classical" ideal in literary excellence and a novel respect for science from the Arabs.

The eulogy written by Gerard of Cremona's associates at the time of his death indicates that Gerard had come to Toledo around 1144, right after completing his studies in Western schools. Gerard was drawn to Spain by the lure of the *Almagest*, absent from the scope of any European school in his time but known to be accessible in some form in Spain. He remained in Toledo for the last forty-three years of his life. Gerard mastered Arabic in Toledo and trained himself in the trade of translating works of science by remaking already existing translations. The bulk of these "remakes" consists of works translated by John of Seville, although some translations by Gundisalvo, such as al-Farabi's *De Ortu Scientiarum*, were also involved. John's method of word-for-word translation was definitely preferred by Gerard in all his later translations from the Arabic over the more literary approach of Hermann of Carinthia and Robert of Chester. Furthermore, since the association of Hermann and Robert was abruptly interrupted by Peter the Venerable, it did not have enough time to hold its own in the controversy. The final result was that an improved method of "literal" translation imitated from John of Seville and given an acceptable literary finish by Gerard of Cremona won the day by the end of the twelfth century.

Translations from Arabic continued to be produced in the same vein in the early thirteenth century, especially by Michael Scot and Hermannus Alemanus. There was some stiff and prolonged resistance on the part of an "orthodox" section of the clergy at the incipient University of Paris, culminating, in the period from 1210 to 1215, in a sweeping condemnation of books of natural science of Arabic origin. The prohibitions were still in force during the crisis of 1229 to 1231 at the young university, and they were endorsed and reiterated at this time by the papacy. As late as the First Council of Lyon (1245) the prohibitions of 1210 still held sway, only to disappear mysteriously shortly afterwards; by 1253 the

English Nation at the university was introducing into its curriculum some of the prohibited *libri naturales* of Aristotle.

Two capital events in the mid thirteenth century seem to have coalesced to decide the fate of previous translations from the Arabic, some of which were by then in their second century of existence. Perhaps the most effective of these, although in an indirect way, was the part played by Emperor Frederick II in promoting the reading and teaching of the natural and metaphysical works of Aristotle and of his Arab expounders. In a letter addressed to scholars of his realm Frederick exalts the natural sciences, together with the books that propound them, as a model for the core of a true liberal education and as the new ideal of Latin thought. Many of these works fell under the Parisian prohibitions of 1210 to 1215; Frederick deliberately promoted them in open defiance of the papacy and the councils. One senses in the emperor's words a consciousness of the reliability of these foreign texts, translated according to the "literal" method from the Arabic. John of Seville's word-for-word method, perfected by Gerard of Cremona, thus obtains pride of place. One can see the inescapable threat to good style and to orthodox thought which loomed thereby. No doubt Frederick's encouragement and implied protection conferred on the flood of translations since the twelfth century an aura of desirability that could have proved irresistible of itself alone; but the second capital event that was to irreversibly alter the fate of the translations from the Arabic was the publication of the *Speculum Astronomiae* by Albert the Great about 1250.

After approximately 1250, therefore, owing to Frederick II's propaganda in their favor and to the publication of the *Speculum Astronomiae*, a quasi-canonical work that removed the forty-year-old church prohibitions against them, the bulk of the translations from the Arabic enjoyed an immense popularity. These translations, done in a style slavishly dependent on that of their Arabic originals, had an enormous impact on the evolution of Scholastic language, thought, and literary expression.

A prominent contemporary testimony concerning the literary or semantic quality of translations from the Arabic in the twelfth and early thirteenth centuries is that of Roger Bacon. On its face, this testimony should carry much weight on account of the privileged position of its utterer: Bacon was a student in Paris at the time of the prohibitions against the *libri naturales*, of the papal renewals of sanctions against their use, and of Frederick II's propaganda in their favor. Bacon's aspersions on these translations, suffer, however, from a measure of factual inaccuracy. According to Bacon, the first translations came to be known at Paris around 1230 when Michael Scot arrived there from Toledo with his own translations, in particular of the Aristotelian *On the Heavens* and *History of Animals* in Avicenna's version. Bacon must, however, have known about the condemnations of 1210 to 1215. He may have pretended ignorance to avoid aggravating his case with the authorities of his Franciscan order, who already had several scores against him. Whatever the case, Bacon's declarations on the age and quality of previous translations from the Arabic carry little weight, if any.

By the second half of the thirteenth century the work of the Dutch scholar William of Moerbeke reoriented schoolmen's interest from the Arabic to the Greek sources, bringing to dominance a trend observable earlier in Robert Grosseteste and Barthelemy of Bruges. It can be concluded from the condemnations of 219 propositions in Paris in 1277 that Emperor Frederick's crusade in favor of secular learning was definitely put to an end. Henceforward the Ockhamist theology of God's absolute power, totally divested from any accountable role in the physical universe, was to prevail as the rule of orthodox thinking. But the damage to European literary expression caused by the unchecked use of translations from Arabic would persist.

Anti-Arabism can be seen in the early manifestations of Italian humanism, starting with Dante at the turn of the trecento. The attitude of Dante toward translations of science from the Arabic is evident in the words of Nemrod in canto 31 of the *Inferno*, verse 67: they are not pure gibberish but Arabic words entirely justified in accordance with the medieval translators' rules of transliteration of Arabic consonants. Not a single consonant in the six-word line violates these rules, and the result is a dreadful sentence which aims to point out the harmful effect of dependence on science to understand the structure of the cosmos.

Dante had acquired the conviction that the science of nature, which depends on perception by the fallible senses, can only offer a false lure, of which Nemrod is here shown as a signal victim—the first in merit and in chronology. Dante read in the medieval *Liber Nembrot* wild claims about the unlimited powers of science to improve the human condition, claims that sounded to him pretty close to the propaganda directed by Frederick II at his scholars. In addition to a worship of science, the *Liber Nembrot* proposed a theory—acquired through use of "computus"—describing the structure of the universe in which the principal cosmic force was situated at the center of the earth. It is now given to Dante, through poetry and revelation, to discover Nemrod's error and the general uncertainty of science as regards universal truth. Although it might be broadly apprehended by the poetical faculty, reality is fully knowable only through revelation and not through obtuse human science. Nemrod's error in claiming truth for science of the merely rational type led him to the "abyss of stupidity" where he now lies, precisely at that spot in the cosmos where the *Liber Nembrot* had taught the cosmic source of life and intelligence to reside. In reality the center of the earth, according to revelation—confirmed by Dante's poetical vision under the guidance of Virgil—is the point farthest away from the seat of Intelligence, which, according to Aristotelian tradition, lies at the periphery of the universe. At the center is the "abyss of stupidity," and its denizen Nemrod, fixed there for eternity, has also been reduced to utter stupidity. Arabic line 67, "Rafel mai amech za bi almi," says in effect: "This abyss is devoted to stupidity, with me on account of science." But why should the biblical Nemrod use the Arabic language? Obviously because the Arabic culture was the dominant channel by which this danger from science had been permeating European culture for too long a time for Dante's taste, representing a continued threat of error and stupidity for Christian minds and souls privileged with the "true" revelation. In the *Divine Comedy* Nemrod is selected as the type of the confirmed "scientist"—the originator, moreover, of such an order of minds—and his exemplary punishment is meant to warn away his would-be imitators. Any orientation toward pure science inevitably involved dependence on the translations from the Arabic. The Arabic tongue is viewed by Dante as the appropriate language for Hell, just as Hebrew, the language of Adam, is the appropriate language for Heaven. Did not the fierce Cerberus, guardian of the "gates of Hell," shout his warning in Arabic: "bab as-saitan, bab as-saitan" (Pape Satan, Pape Satan)?

Dante's historic plea to Christian minds to rid themselves of their unhealthy, unholy reliance on Arab science inaugurated a trend that soon became manifest among the first recognized Italian humanists: Petrarch in particular, whose abhorrence of anything smacking of Arab culture—not merely Averroism in the university—is evident. Witness his poem *Africa,* the inspiration of which is to reclaim for Europe old Roman rule of Africa from Islamic domination. There was here a kind of national aspiration—perhaps already sensed in Roger of Sicily's capture of al-Mahdia in the twelfth century.

While Dante's warning against translations from the Arabic focused on the mental aberration they might cause, anti-Arabism among the later humanists had as its principal constituent a rejection of the barbaric Latin of medieval Scholasticism. Hence, the oft-praised "affection" for classical forms of Latin so prominent among Italian humanists was not merely a spontaneous revival of love for the ancient classics as such, but was more like a sequel to the rejection of the Arabic fashions in thought and expression introduced on a massive scale two centuries earlier through translations. Those enthusiastic devotees of *humaniores litterae* did not realize that by cleaning the tainted medieval pool they were throwing the baby away with the soiled waters. For the advance in the field of science stimulated by the Arabian imports had been genuine, if only by making all ancient hypotheses available for serious and thorough reconsideration. From Ockham to Copernicus, the prestige of ancient scientific and philosophic authorities, now looked at directly, unashamedly dwindled away to leave an open field for minds such as those of Galileo and Sir Isaac Newton.

This hitherto little noticed, certainly deemphasized anti-Arabism in the literary ideals of the early Renaissance was likely the principal force behind the humanists' efforts to procure new translations directly from the Greek. Since there is really nothing new under the sun, the new fashion in translation had to confront problems of method and style similar to those encountered and solved by the twelfth-century translators. Again, the literality of translations would come under attack.

An apt specimen of the humanists' low opinion of medieval translations, coupled with an outline of a different ideal of translation, may be found in a letter of Leonardo Bruni defending his translation of the *Nicomachean Ethics* of Aristotle. Bruni knew of two translations of the *Ethics* that preceded his: one from the Arabic (the author of which he does not mention; it was probably Barthelemy of Bruges, whose translation of the *Ethics* is met with in many medieval manuscripts) and a second from the Greek by a member of the Order of Friars. The latter is evidently Robert Grosseteste, bishop of Lincoln and an early teacher of the Franciscan order at Oxford. Bruni's criticism, spelled out through specific examples, is principally directed at the latter translation, although his aspersions on medieval translations as "distortions" of Aristotle's thought clearly embrace both. So inept are these translations, Bruni says, that if Aristotle were alive he would repudiate them. Boethius was a man of good taste (*viro eleganti*) and well versed in both Greek and Latin. His translations are vastly different from these: they are undefaced by awkward terms such as *eutrapeliam*, *architectonicam*, *bomolchos*, and *agricos*, for which there existed perfectly adequate Latin equivalents. Boethius would not mistake *tristitia* for *dolor*, *honestum* for *bonum*, or use *eligere* instead of *expetere*. These more recent versions, on the contrary, are "unlatin" (*non verba*), they exhibit no ornamentation of discourse (*non dicendi figura*), and they lack any literary style (*non eruditio litterarum*). Bruni's aspersions are all concerned with correction of speech and quality of style; a "literary" treatment is paramount, even indispensable, according to his conception of an ideal translation. Earlier in the same letter he claims as his own an approach to Plato's works which he considered to be in sharp contrast to that of his predecessors. While Hermann of Carinthia, one of the most genuinely humanist translators (if a rather inaccurate one) in the first half of the twelfth century, was aiming to make his translations conform as closely as possible to the "rhetorical" ideal (*eloquentia*) of the Latin scholars, Leonardo Bruni, the fifteenth-century Italian humanist, sets for himself, as an ideal for his translations, an arbitrarily "latinized" Plato whose assumed good taste will be his exclusive guide. In closing his letter Bruni confesses that when he was made to realize that medieval translators acted as if they were throwing feces (*tanta traductionis faece coinquinari videam*) at Aristotle's books, works in no way less precious than the most beautiful paintings, he could not but react in the same way as if someone was throwing feces at a painting by Giotto (*Equidem si in pictura Jotti quis faecem projiceret, pati non possem*).

From this letter, therefore, as well as from equally disparaging comments on medieval translators in the preface to his translation of the *Nicomachaean Ethics*, one may conclude that among the Italian humanists—for whom Leonardo Bruni may be judged an acceptable mouthpiece—a new ideal of translation manifested itself in a two-faceted form. It was most critical of medieval accomplishments, on grounds above all of their uncouth language and style, and it was instinctively anti-Arab in feeling. The second facet of the humanist translation ideal was a goal of rendering foreign models with utmost literary taste, which implied a relative lack of concern for the thought content of the works to be translated.

A most unpalatable aspect of the latter tendency was the humanists' amazing craving for the Hermetic books, which were perceived as the expression of a purer "pristina theologia." Twelfth-century translators such as John of Seville, Hermann of Carinthia, and Gerard of Cremona were attracted by the contemporary, actually flourishing, and immediately verifiable state of Arab science and learning. Italian humanists with their exclusively "rhetorical" bent fostered by their revulsion against a medieval expression marred (to their taste) by Arab culture, aimed at somersaulting backward two thousand years. In the process they were, in fact, belittling centuries of steady advance along the paths created by the ancient Greeks themselves and furthered by Persian, Indian, and Arab contributions. In the *Inferno* episode contrived around Nemrod, Dante appears to have inaugurated that fateful trend of a preference for a prophetic/Christian ideal versus science, hence for a literary, rhetorical ideal over thought content, in his followers among the humanists.

This humanistic orientation, by deliberately rating literature (*eloquentia*) above thought content (*sapientia*), somewhat paralleled twelfth-century thought previous to the impact of translations from the Arabic. This orientation seemingly delayed for some two hundred years the emergence of bold thinkers willing to discard a hallowed past whose sole merit was that it was "their own." After the Parisian condemnations of 1277, circumstances had apparently become ripe for a wholly novel orientation in science and thought. Yet the antimedieval, anti-Arab bent of the early humanists went the other way, nostalgically entertaining an antiquated ideal of rhetoric as against a scientific one based on recent international achievement and oriented toward the future.

BIBLIOGRAPHY

Printed Works of Translators

The present author has edited John of Seville's 1133 translation of Abu Ma'sar's *Kitab al-Mudhal al-Kabir ila 'Ilm Ahkam an-Nujum* together with the original Arabic text of 848 and Hermann of Carinthia's translation of the same work in 1140. Publication of all these texts in one collection is planned by the Istituto Universitario Orientale of the University of Naples. The multifold comparison thus made possible should help illustrate the translators' conflicting attitudes with respect to style.

John of Seville's style in his translations dons a wholly Semitic garb; on the other hand, in his "original" works (needless to say, inspired mainly from his earlier translations), John's Latin style becomes at least tolerably readable. As for "original" works by John that could illustrate his "normal" Latin expression, one has a choice of at least two separate printed works. The most recent one is *De Cursu Planetarum,* an astronomical work edited by José Maria Millás Vallicrosa (*Osiris,* 1 [1936]: 451-475). Astrology is never far from John's special interests: this work attempts to give directions on how to adjust astrological predictions to the movement of the eighth sphere described by Thabit ben Qurra. Another "original" work of John's, available in an early printed edition (Nuremberg, 1548), is his *Epitome Totius Astrologie*. This work is purely astrological and preserves many Arabic terms.

The literary performances of Hermann of Carinthia can also be assessed from good specimens in print. His major "naturalistic" work, the *De Essentiis,* was lifted from obscurity when Manuel Alonso published it in 1946. In the immediate postwar period Alonso was unable to verify that what is probably the only authentic copy of the *De Essentiis,* the Naples manuscript, was still preserved; thus he fell back on two unsatisfactory copies in English libraries. In 1982 C. S. F. Burnett produced a critical edition of the *De Essentiis,* taking the Naples manuscript into account; this edition has some serious faults, however, and should be used with caution.

Another significant piece of Hermann's original expression is to be found in the dedicatory letter to his teacher Thierry of Chartres (June 1143) in his translation of the *Planispherium* of Ptolemy from the Arabic of Maslama al-Majriti. The letter has been reproduced in print many times, most reliably by Johan Ludvig Heiberg in *Ptolemaei: Opera Astronomica Minora* (1907).

As a scholar thoroughly trained in the classical tradition of Bernard of Chartres, Hermann displays an astonishing mastery of the Ciceronian period to express the most varied forms of thought. His translation of Abu Ma'sar's *Introductorium Maius* was printed in Augsburg in 1489 by E. Ratdolt and in Venice in 1506 from the worst manuscript sources and is additionally marred by innumerable misprints. The critical collection mentioned above should help in assessing Hermann's distressing tendency to abbreviate, condense, and force into a Ciceronian straitjacket an unwieldy Arabic original.

The present writer has recently identified in a unique manuscript the "lost" *Astronomia* of Hermann and has prepared it for publication. The startling character of this fortunate retrieval, accompanied by a further identification of canons written by Hermann to accompany astronomical tables (not present in the manuscript) borrowed in large part from al-Battani, is increased through the additional discovery that the work reproduces, in its own inimitable Latin style, the entire *De Forma Mundi* (*Hai'at al-Alam*) of the Arab scientist ibn al-Haitam. Every sentence of ibn al-Haitam's work is there in Hermann's Latin but interlaced with extensive comments, additions, and criticisms by Hermann of the low state of astronomical knowledge among his contemporaries and a reminder that true knowledge is to be found among the Arabs. Hence exists the need for translations.

As to the humanistic Renaissance translators and their new methods or intentions, essential points may be garnered from Leonardo Bruni's preface to his translation of the *Nicomachean Ethics* of Aristotle, or in the works of Hieronymus Bagolinus, the translator of Alexander of Aphrodisias in the sixteenth century. The present writer has reproduced some of Bagolinus's remarks on his aims in the 1957 edition of the *De Fato* of Pietro Pomponazzi.

Manuscripts

Translation endeavors in the early twelfth century were not likely to cater to refined literary taste or even to exhibit minimal originality. "Substantific marrow"—as François Rabelais would label it—was the principal, nearly exclusive aim sought after. On the other hand, the "literary" aspect of the Chartrian philosophical tradition, represented by Bernard and Thierry, together with some of their disciples, such as John of Salisbury and Peter of Blois, might be expected to exhibit decent Latin expression.

Such an ideal was entertained above all by Hermann of Carinthia, who produced a stream of Latin texts derived from the Arabic but with a remarkable mastery of Ciceronian taste. He seems to have been imitated in this endeavor by his contemporary and probably rival translator Hugh of Sanctalla, who was working for Bishop Michael of Tarrazona. Hugh's style, however, is overly pompous and recherché, a far cry from the lucidity and easy flow achieved by Hermann. In both cases the achievement was made at the expense of fidelity to the original Arabic. Since virtually all these endeavors dealt with works of science, the extremely prosaic, at times even barbaric form of word-for-word method prevailed early in the first wave of translation from the Arabic. John of Seville's method, adopted and applied systematically for some four decades by Gerard of Cremona, secured the triumph of *sapientia* over *eloquentia* in medieval translations until the Italian Renaissance. The evidence for this historical development remains hidden in manuscript form and is virtually unknown to modern scholarship. Two notable instances of conflict and conciliation of methods of expression may be cited: Abu Ma'sar's *Introductorium Maius in Astronomiam* and the *Centiloquium* of Ahmad ibn Yusef (Pseudo-Ptolemy).

The overly literal translation of the *Introductorium Maius in Astronomiam* by John of Seville, in its original form of 1133, rests today in the valuable manuscript O. 8. 34 in the Trinity College Library at Cambridge; it may be an "original edition" of the finished production of John. This translation seems to have been so unpalatable to a scholar of the Chartrian mold such as Hermann of Carinthia that the latter undertook in 1140 another translation of the same text, surely from an Arabic original and not as a "remake" of John's version. Hermann's version espoused the canons of Ciceronian Latin and Boethian translation rules, producing the much altered and interlarded text found today in two early and good manuscript copies: Naples, Biblioteca Nazionale, ms. VIII. C. 50, and Oxford, Corpus Christi College, ms. 95. Contemporary readers seem to have held it in discredit rather early, and the manuscript transmission did not proliferate as did John of Seville's version. Hermann's text is the only one that has seen the light of printing, in an incunabulum edition of 1489 at Augsburg by Erhard Ratdolt, but this edition obnubilates the true fate of this version during the Middle Ages.

The discrediting of Hermann's version was completed by Gerard of Cremona, who, arriving in Toledo circa 1144 to begin a long career as translator, chose to practice John's word-for-word method but with the elimination of John's idiosyncratic Arabic style. Gerard remade John's version to support the public lectures on astrology he gave in Toledo. It would appear that the working copy of this revision has survived in the British Library ms. Harley 3631, ff. 1-57, and a spruced-up original edition may be in the Vatican ms. lat. 5713 (II) ff. 104-135.

The *Centiloquium (Liber Fructus)*, a forgery written by the Egyptian physician/mathematician/astrologer Ahmad ibn Yusuf circa 922, early attracted the attention of twelfth-century Latin scholars. Five translations may be dated from the twelfth century. The first is by Adelard of Bath, beginning with the words "*Doctrina stellarum.*" It translates only the first thirty-nine Verba, without the commentary which is the essence of the work. Adelard seems to have given up his effort before reaching the middle of the work either because of incompetence or rivalry from other translations (the former is probably the reason). Two independent manuscript copies of this translation survive: London, British Library, Sloane 2030, f. 87 r-v, and Lyon, Bibliothèque Municipale, ms. 328. Sometime during the thirteenth century Adelard's partial translation was incorporated into the tradition of the translation by Plato of Tivoli, together with another, probably incomplete version by Hermann of Carinthia or someone from his circle, beginning "Mundanorum mutatio." This triple conflated text survives in several excellent manuscript copies. Plato of Tivoli's version was done in Barcelona in 1136 and begins "Iam scripsi tibi, Iesure." The majority of surviving manuscripts of the *Centiloquium* carry this version, but surviving manuscripts of the version beginning "*Mundanorum mutatio*" are nearly as plentiful as those by Plato of Tivoli.

A fourth version is by Hugh of Sanctalla. Hugh's link with the late portion of the rule of Bishop Michael of Tarrazona and his much more scrupulous rendering of the Arabic indicate that this version is later than the others. It survives in only two known manuscripts: Madrid, Biblioteca Nacional, ms. 10009, and Naples, Biblioteca Nazionale, ms. VIII. D. 4, ff. 3r-30v.

Finally, an anonymous version beginning "Iam premisi libros" stands apart as the only one that knows the true name of the commentator, which it gives in the form of Abugafarus (sometimes distorted as Bugafarus). Since this version left only eight copies, including St. Petersburg (Russia) Academ. cod. F. 8. N. ff. 142-152 and Basel, University Library ms. F. III. 33, ff. 1-8, and since its correct identification of the author remained unknown throughout the medieval tradition, one may conclude that it did not spread at all. Because of its coarse Latin, resembling closely the translations by John of Seville, it is likely that this somewhat inchoate translation is by him.

In all, more than 150 complete or partial manuscript copies survive of this text in its various translations. The literary problems engendered by the movement of translations from the Arabic in the twelfth century would be illustrated with an astonishing degree of precision by a systematic study of this manuscript literature. Plato's version was printed at least twice in the incunabula period: in Venice in 1484 by Erhard Ratdolt (before he moved his presses to Augsburg circa 1488) and in Venice again in 1493 by the Brothers Locatelli, who may have used the plates of Ratdolt, only slightly modified. Since the *Centiloquium* continued to attract attention in the late Middle Ages, four other versions were produced: one by William of Aragon, probably in the fourteenth century (apparently but a paraphrase of existing translations); a second by Conrad Heingarter, the Swiss astrologer in the service of the Bourbon court at Moulins during the second half of the fifteenth century; a third by George of Trebizond in Italy, circa 1450; and a fourth by Gioviano Pontano, circa 1495. William of Aragon's and Heingarter's translations remained in manuscripts, but either George of Trebizond's or Pontano's versions fill all the printed editions after 1500. Thus, direct access to this tremendously important medieval text is available nearly exclusively through manuscript copies; only two incunabula editions give a glimpse of it, and a very confused one at that.

Checklist of Further Readings

Adler, Cyrus, Isidore Singer, and others, eds. *The Jewish Encyclopedia*, 12 volumes. New York & London: Funk & Wagnalls, 1901-1906.

Altmann, Alexander. "Jewish Philosophy," in *History of Philosophy, Eastern and Western*, volume 2, edited by Sarvepalli Radhakrishnan. London: Allen & Unwin, 1953, pp. 76-92. Reprinted in *Philosophy A to Z*, edited by James Gutmann. New York: Grosset & Dunlap, 1963, pp. 89-104.

Altmann. *Studies in Religious Philosophy and Mysticism*. Ithaca, N.Y.: Cornell University Press, 1969.

Anawati, Georges. *Etudes de philosophie musulmane*. Paris: Vrin, 1974.

Anawati. "Le Neoplatonism dans la pensée musulmane: Etat actuel des recherches," in *Plotino e il Neoplatismo in Oriente e in Occidente*. Rome: Accademia Nazionale dei Lincei, 1974, pp. 339-405.

Arberry, Arthur. *An Introduction to the History of Sufism*. London & New York: Longmans, Green, 1943.

Arberry. *Revelation and Reason in Islam*. London: Allen & Unwin, 1957.

Arberry. *Sufism: An Account of the Mystics of Islam*. London: Allen & Unwin, 1950.

Armstrong, Arthur H., ed. *The Cambridge History of Later Greek and Early Medieval Philosophy*. Cambridge: Cambridge University Press, 1967.

Ashworth, E. J. *The Tradition of Mediaeval Logic and Speculative Grammar from Anselm to the End of the Seventeenth Century: A Bibliography from 1836 Onwards*. Toronto: Pontifical Institute of Mediaeval Studies, 1978.

Badawi, Abd al-Rahman. *Histoire de la philosophie en Islam*, 2 volumes. Paris: Vrin, 1972.

Baudrillart, Alfred, ed. *Dictionnaire d'histoire et de géographie ecclesiastiques*, 22 volumes. Paris: Letouzey & Ané, 1912-1988.

Benson, Robert, and Giles Constable, eds. *Renaissance and Renewal in the Twelfth Century*. Cambridge, Mass.: Harvard University Press, 1982.

Berman, Lawrence V. "Medieval Jewish Religious Philosophy," in *Bibliographical Essays in Medieval Jewish Studies: The Study of Judaism*, volume 2, by Berman and others. New York: Published for the Anti-Defamation League of B'nai B'rith by Ktav, 1976.

Bochenski, Joseph M. *A History of Formal Logic*, translated by Ivo Thomas. Notre Dame, Ind.: University of Notre Dame Press, 1961.

Boehner, Philotheus. *Medieval Logic*. Chicago: University of Chicago Press, 1952.

Brehier, Emile. *The History of Philosophy: The Middle Ages and the Renaissance*, translated by Wade Baskin. Chicago: University of Chicago Press, 1965.

Bullough, Vern L. *The Development of Medicine as a Profession: The Contribution of the Medieval University to Modern Medicine*. Basel & New York: Karger, 1966.

Carra de Vaux, Bernard. *Les penseurs de l'Islam*, 5 volumes. Paris: Geuthner, 1921-1926.

Carré, Meyrick. *Realists and Nominalists*. London & New York: Oxford University Press, 1946.

Chenu, Marie-Dominique, O.P. *Nature, Man, and Society in the Twelfth Century*, translated by Jerome Taylor and Lester K. Little. Chicago: University of Chicago Press, 1968.

Chenu. *La théologie au XIIe siècle*. Paris: Vrin, 1957.

Clagett, Marshall. *Nicole Oresme and the Medieval Geometry of Qualities and Motions*. Madison: University of Wisconsin Publications in Medieval Science, 1968.

Clagett. *Studies in Medieval Physics and Mathematics*. London: Variorum Reprints, 1979.

Cobban, Alan. *The Medieval Universities: Their Development and Organization*. London: Methuen, 1975.

Copleston, Frederick. *A History of Philosophy*, volume 2: *From Augustine to Scotus*; volume 3: *From Ockham to Suarez*. London: Burns & Oates, 1950-1953.

Craig, William. *The Kalam Cosmological Argument*. New York: Lane, 1979.

Crombie, Alistair C. *Augustine to Galileo*. London: Falcon, 1952. Revised as *Medieval and Early Modern Science*, 2 volumes. Garden City, N.Y.: Doubleday, 1959.

De Ghellinck, Joseph. *Le mouvement théologique de XIIe siècle*, second edition. Bruges: Editions "De Tempel," 1948.

D'Entrèves, Alessandro. *The Medieval Contribution to Political Thought*. London: Oxford University Press, 1939.

De Wulf, Maurice. *Philosophy and Civilization in the Middle Ages*. Princeton: Princeton University Press, 1922.

Dijksterhuis, Eduard Jan. *The Mechanization of the World Picture*, translated by C. Dikshoorn. Oxford: Clarendon Press, 1961.

Edwards, Paul, ed. *The Encyclopedia of Philosophy*, 8 volumes. New York: Macmillan, 1967.

Efros, Israel. *The Problem of Space in Mediaeval Jewish Philosophy*. New York: Columbia University Press, 1974.

Efros. *Studies in Medieval Jewish Philosophy*. New York & London: Columbia University Press, 1974.

The Encyclopaedia of Islam, 10 volumes projected. Leiden: Brill, 1954-

Encyclopedia Judaica, 10 volumes ("Aach" to "Lycra"). Berlin: Eschkol, 1928-1934.

Encyclopedia Judaica, 16 volumes. Jerusalem & New York: Macmillan, 1972.

Fakhry, Majid. *A History of Islamic Philosophy*. New York & London: Columbia University Press, 1970.

Fakhry. *Islamic Occasionalism*. London: Allen & Unwin, 1958.

Forest, A., Fernand Van Steenberghen, and M. de Gandillac. *Le mouvement doctrinal du XIe au XIVe siècle*, volume 13 of *Histoire de l'église*. Paris: Bloud & Gay, 1951.

Fortin, Ernest. *Dissidence et philosophie au moyen âge: Dante et ses antécédents*, Cahiers d'Etudes Médiévales, volume 6. Paris: Bellarmin, 1981.

Gardet, Louis, and M. M. Anawati. *Introduction à la théologie musulmane*. Etudes de philosophie médiévale, volume 37. Paris: Vrin, 1948.

Gilson, Etienne. *History of Christian Philosophy in the Middle Ages*. New York: Random House, 1955.

Gilson. *Reason and Revelation in the Middle Ages*. New York: Scribners, 1955.

Gilson. *The Spirit of Medieval Philosophy*. New York: Scribners, 1936; London: Sheed & Ward, 1950.

Glorieux, Palémon. *La littérature quodlibétique*, 2 volumes. Volume 1, Le Saulchoir, Kain, Belgium: Revue des sciences philosophiques et theologiques, 1925; volume 2, Paris: Vrin, 1935.

Grabmann, Martin. *Die Geschichte der Scholastischen Methode*, 2 volumes. Freiburg & Saint Louis, 1909-1911.

Grabmann. *Mittelalterliches Geistesleben: Abhandlungen zur Geschichte der Scholastik und Mystik*, 3 volumes. Munich: Hueber, 1926-1956.

Grant, Edward. *Much Ado about Nothing: Theories of Space and Vacuum from the Middle Ages to the Scientific Revolution*. Cambridge & New York: Cambridge University Press, 1981.

Grant. *Physical Science in the Middle Ages*. New York: Wiley, 1971.

Grant, ed. *A Source Book in Medieval Science*. Cambridge, Mass.: Harvard University Press, 1974.

Guttmann, Jacob. *Die Scholastik des 13. Jahrhunderts in ihren Beziehungen zum Judenthum und zur jüdischen Literatur*. Breslau: Marcus, 1902.

Guttmann. *Das Verhältnis des Thomas von Aquino zum Judenthum und zur jüdischen Literatur*. Göttingen: Vandenhoeck & Ruprecht, 1891.

Guttmann, Julius. *Philosophies of Judaism*, translated by David W. Silverman. Philadelphia: Jewish Publication Society of America, 1964.

Harnack, Adolf von. *History of Dogma*, 7 volumes, translated by Neil Buchanan, James Millar, Ebenezer Brown Speirs, William M'Gilchrist, edited by Alexander B. Bruce. London: Williams & Norgate, 1896-1899; Boston: Little, Brown, 1899-1903.

Haskins, Charles. *The Renaissance of the Twelfth Century*. Cambridge, Mass.: Harvard University Press, 1939.

Haskins. *The Rise of Universities*. New York: Holt, 1923.

Haskins. *Studies in Medieval Culture*. Oxford: Clarendon Press, 1929.

Hastings, James, John A. Selbie, and others. *Encyclopaedia of Religion and Ethics*, 13 volumes. Edinburgh: Clark, 1908-1926; New York: Scribners, 1908-1926.

Heer, Friedrich. *The Medieval World*, translated by Janet Sondheimer. New York: New American Library, 1963.

Henry, Desmond Paul. *Medieval Logic and Metaphysics: A Modern Introduction*. London: Hutchinson, 1972.

Hourani, George F. *Islamic Rationalism: The Ethics of Abd al-Jabbar*. Oxford: Clarendon Press, 1971.

Hourani, ed. *Essays on Islamic Philosophy and Science*. Albany: State University of New York Press, 1975.

Hyman, Arthur, ed. *Essays in Medieval Jewish and Islamic Philosophy*. New York: Ktav, 1977.

Ijsewijn, Jozef, and Jacques Paquet, eds. *The Universities in the Late Middle Ages*. Louvain: Louvain University Press, 1978.

Joel, Issachar. *Index of Articles on Jewish Studies*. Jerusalem: Magnes Press, Hebrew University, 1969- .

Kantorowicz, Ernst Hartwig. *The King's Two Bodies*. Princeton: Princeton University Press, 1957.

Katz, Steven. *Jewish Philosophers*. Jerusalem: Keter, 1975.

Kenny, Anthony, Norman Kretzmann, and Jan Pinborg, eds. *The Cambridge History of Later Medieval Philosophy*. Cambridge & New York: Cambridge University Press, 1982.

Klibansky, Raymond. *The Continuity of the Platonic Tradition*. London: Warburg Institute, 1939.

Kneale, William Calvert, and Martha Kneale. *The Development of Logic*. Oxford: Clarendon Press, 1962.

Knowles, David. *The Evolution of Medieval Thought*. Cambridge & New York: Cambridge University Press, 1962.

Knuutila, Simo, ed. *Reforging the Great Chain of Being: Ancient and Medieval Modality*. Dordrecht & Boston: Reidel, 1980.

Kretzmann, Norman, ed. *Infinity and Continuity in Ancient and Medieval Thought.* Ithaca, N.Y.: Cornell University Press, 1982.

Kretzmann, ed. *Medieval Philosophy in the Philosophy Curriculum.* San Francisco: Council for Philosophical Studies, 1981.

Leff, Gordon. *The Dissolution of the Medieval Outlook.* New York: New York University Press, 1976.

Leff. *Heresy in the Later Middle Ages: The Relation of Heterodoxy to Dissent, c. 1250-1450*, 2 volumes. Manchester, U.K. & New York: Barnes & Noble, 1967.

Leff. *Medieval Thought.* Harmondsworth, U.K.: Penguin, 1958.

Leff. *Paris and Oxford Universities in the Thirteenth and Fourteenth Centuries: An Institutional and Intellectual History.* New York & London: Wiley, 1968.

Lindberg, David C. *Theories of Vision from al-Kindi to Kepler.* Chicago: University of Chicago Press, 1976.

Lindberg, ed. *Science in the Middle Ages.* Chicago & London: University of Chicago Press, 1978.

Lottin, Odon. *Psychologie et morale au XIIe et XIIIe siècles*, 6 volumes. Volumes 1-4, Louvain: Abbaye du Mont Cesar, 1942-1954; volumes 5-6, Gembloux, Belgium: Duculot, 1959-1960.

Madkour, Ibrahim. *L'Organon d'Aristote dans le monde Arabe*, second edition. Paris: Vrin, 1969.

Maier, Anneliese. *An der Grenze von Scholastik und Naturwissenschaft*, second edition. Rome: Edizione di storia e letteratura, 1952.

Maier. *Metaphysische Hintergründe der spätscholastischen Naturphilosophie.* Rome: Edizione di storia e letteratura, 1955.

Maier. *Die Vorläufer Galileis im 14. Jahrhundert.* Rome: Edizione di storia e letteratura, 1949.

Maier. *Zwei Grundprobleme der scholastischen Naturphilosophie*, second edition. Rome: Edizione di storia e letteratura, 1951.

Marenbon, John. *From the Circle of Alcuin to the School of Auxerre.* Cambridge & New York: Cambridge University Press, 1981.

Maurer, Armand A. *Mediaeval Philosophy: St. Augustine to Ockham*, second edition. Toronto: Pontifical Institute of Mediaeval Studies, 1982.

McIlwain, Charles Howard. *The Growth of Political Thought in the West.* New York: Macmillan, 1932.

McInerny, Ralph M. *A History of Western Philosophy*, volume 2: *Philosophy from St. Augustine to Ockham.* Notre Dame, Ind.: University of Notre Dame Press, 1970.

McMullan, Ernan, ed. *The Concept of Matter in Greek and Medieval Philosophy.* Notre Dame, Ind.: University of Notre Dame Press, 1963.

Moody, Ernest. *Studies in Medieval Philosophy, Science, and Logic*. Berkeley, Los Angeles & London: University of California Press, 1975.

Moody. *Truth and Consequence in Mediaeval Logic*. Amsterdam: North-Holland Publishing Co., 1953.

Morewedge, Parviz, ed. *Islamic Philosophical Theology*. Albany: State University of New York Press, 1979.

Morewedge, ed. *Studies in Islamic Philosophy and Science*. Albany: State University of New York Press, 1974.

Morrall, John. *Political Thought in Medieval Times*. London: Hutchinson, 1958.

Mundy, John. *Europe in the High Middle Ages*. New York & London: Longman, 1973.

Murdoch, John E., and Edith D. Sylla, eds. *The Cultural Context of Medieval Learning: Proceedings of the First International Colloquium on Philosophy, Science, and Theology in the Middle Ages—September 1973*. Dordrecht & Boston: Reidel, 1975.

Murray, Alexander. *Reason and Society in the Middle Ages*. Oxford: Oxford University Press, 1978.

Nasr, Seyyed Hossein. *An Introduction to Islamic Cosmological Doctrines*, revised edition. London: Thames & Hudson, 1978.

Nasr. *Science and Civilization in Islam*. Cambridge, Mass.: Harvard University Press, 1968.

The New Catholic Encyclopedia, 17 volumes. New York: McGraw-Hill, 1967.

Oberman, Heiko. *The Harvest of Medieval Theology*. Cambridge, Mass.: Harvard University Press, 1963.

Paré, Gerard, Adrien Brunet, and Pierre Tremblay. *La renaissance du XIIe siècle: Les écoles et l'enseignement*. Paris: Vrin, 1933.

Pearson, James Douglas. *Index Islamicus*. Cambridge: Heffner, 1958- .

Peters, Francis E. *Aristotle and the Arabs: The Aristotelian Tradition in Islam*. New York: New York University Press, 1968.

Potts, Timothy C. *Conscience in Medieval Philosophy*. Cambridge: Cambridge University Press, 1980.

Rand, Edward. *The Founders of the Middle Ages*. Cambridge: Cambridge University Press, 1928.

Rashdall, Hastings. *The Universities of Europe in the Middle Ages*, 3 volumes, edited by Frederick Maurice Powicke and Alfred Brotherston Emden. Oxford: Clarendon Press, 1936.

Rescher, Nicholas. *The Development of Arabic Logic*. Pittsburgh: University of Pittsburgh Press, 1964.

Rescher. *Studies in Arabic Philosophy*. Pittsburgh: University of Pittsburgh Press, 1967.

Rescher. *Studies in the History of Arabic Logic*. Pittsburgh: University of Pittsburgh Press, 1963.

Rosenthal, Erwin. *Political Thought in Medieval Islam.* Cambridge: Cambridge University Press, 1958.

Rosenthal, Franz. *Knowledge Triumphant: The Concept of Knowledge in Medieval Islam.* Leiden: Brill, 1970.

Ross, James F., ed. *Inquiries into Medieval Philosophy.* Westport, Conn.: Greenwood, 1971.

Sarton, George. *Introduction to the History of Science,* 3 volumes. Baltimore: Williams & Wilkins, 1927-1948.

Scholem, Gershom Gerhard. *Major Trends in Jewish Mysticism,* second edition. New York: Schocken, 1946.

Sharif, Mohammed, ed. *A History of Muslim Philosophy,* 2 volumes. Wiesbaden: Harrassowitz, 1963-1966.

Smalley, Beryl. *The Study of the Bible in the Middle Ages,* second edition. New York: Philosophical Library, 1952.

Southern, Richard. *The Making of the Middle Ages.* New Haven: Yale University Press, 1953.

Southern. *Medieval Humanism and Other Studies.* Oxford: Blackwell, 1970.

Spade, Paul Vincent. *The Mediaeval Liar: A Catalogue of Insolubilia-Literature.* Toronto: Pontifical Institute of Mediaeval Studies, 1975.

Steinschneider, Moritz. *Die Arabischen Übersetzungen aus dem Griechischen.* Leipzig: Harrassowitz, 1897; reprinted, Graz: Akademische Druck-und Verlagsanstalt, 1960.

Strauss, Leo. *Persecution and the Art of Writing.* Chicago: Free Press, 1952.

Synan, Edward A. "Latin Philosophies of the Middle Ages," in *Medieval Studies,* edited by James M. Powell. Syracuse, N.Y.: Syracuse University Press, 1976, pp. 277-311.

Thorndike, Lynn. *A History of Magic and Experimental Science,* 8 volumes. New York: Macmillan, 1923-1958.

Ullmann, Walter. *The Individual and Society in the Middle Ages.* Baltimore: Johns Hopkins University Press, 1966.

Ullmann. *Law and Politics in the Middle Ages.* Ithaca, N.Y.: Cornell University Press, 1975.

Ullmann. *Medieval Political Thought.* Harmondsworth, U.K. & Baltimore: Penguin, 1975.

Vacant, A., E. Mangenot, and E. Amann, eds. *Dictionnaire de théologie catholique,* 18 volumes. Paris: Letouzey & Ané, 1903-1972.

Vajda, Georges. *L'Amour de Dieu dans la théologie juive du Moyen Age.* Etudes de philosophie médiévale, 46. Paris: Vrin, 1957.

Vajda. "Les études de philosophie juive du Moyen Age depuis le synthèse de Julius Guttmann," *Hebrew Union College Annual,* 43 (1972): 125-147; 45 (1974): 205-242.

Vajda. "Les études de philosophie juive du Moyen Age 1950-1960," in *Die Metaphysik im Mittelalter*, edited by Paul Wilpert. Berlin: De Gruyter, 1963, pp. 126-135.

Vajda. *Introduction à la pensée juive du Moyen Age*. Paris: Vrin, 1947.

Vajda. *Jüdische Philosophie*. Volume 19 of *Bibliographische Einführungen in das Studium der Philosophie*. Bern: Francke, 1950.

Vajda. *Recherches sur la philosophie et la kabbale dans la pensée juive du Moyen Age*. Paris: Mouten, 1962.

Van Steenberghen, Fernand. *La bibliothèque du philosophie médiéviste*. Louvain: Publications Universitaires, 1974.

Van Steenberghen. *Philosophie des Mittelalters*. Bibliographische Einführungen in das Studium der Philosophie, 17. Bern: Francke, 1950.

Vignaux, Paul. *Philosophy in the Middle Ages: An Introduction*, translated by E. C. Hall. New York: Meridian, 1959.

Vinogradoff, Paul. *Roman Law in Medieval Europe*, second edition. Oxford: Clarendon Press, 1929.

Von Grunebaum, Gustave. *Medieval Islam*, second edition. Chicago: University of Chicago Press, 1953.

Von Grunebaum, ed. *Logic in Classical Islamic Culture*. Wiesbaden, 1970.

Wallace, William A. *Causality and Scientific Explanation*, volume 1: *Medieval and Early Classical Science*. Ann Arbor: University of Michigan Press, 1972.

Walzer, Richard. *Greek into Arabic: Essays on Islamic Philosophy*. Oxford: Cassirer, 1962.

Watt, William Montgomery. *Islamic Philosophy and Theology*. Edinburgh: Edinburgh University Press, 1962.

Watt. *Islamic Political Thought: The Basic Concepts*. Edinburgh: Edinburgh University Press, 1968.

Weinberg, Julius Rudolf. *A Short History of Medieval Philosophy*. Princeton: Princeton University Press, 1964.

Weisheipl, James A., O.P. "Curriculum of the Faculty of Arts at Oxford in the Early Fourteenth Century," *Mediaeval Studies*, 26 (1964): 143-185.

Weisheipl. *The Development of Physical Theory in the Middle Ages*. New York: Sheed & Ward, 1960.

Wolfson, Harry Austryn. "The Amphibolous Terms in Aristotle, Arabic Philosophy and Maimonides," *Harvard Theological Review*, 31 (1938): 151-173.

Wolfson. "The Classification of Sciences in Medieval Jewish Philosophy," in *Hebrew Union College Jubilee Volume*, edited by David Philipson and others. Cincinnati: Hebrew Union College, 1925, pp. 263-315.

Wolfson. "The Classification of Sciences in Medieval Jewish Philosophy: Additional Notes," *Hebrew Union College Annual,* 3 (1926): 371-375.

Wolfson. "The Double Faith Theory in Clement, Saadia, Averroës and St. Thomas," *Jewish Quarterly Review,* new series 33 (1942): 213-264.

Wolfson. "The Internal Senses in Latin, Arabic and Hebrew Philosophical Texts," *Harvard Theological Review,* 29 (1935): 69-133.

Wolfson. *Philo: Foundations of Religious Philosophy in Judaism, Christianity and Islam,* 2 volumes. Cambridge, Mass.: Harvard University Press, 1948.

Wolfson. *The Philosophy of the Church Fathers.* Cambridge, Mass.: Harvard University Press, 1956.

Wolfson. *The Philosophy of the Kalam.* Cambridge, Mass.: Harvard University Press, 1976.

Wolfson. *Repercussions of the Kalam in Jewish Philosophy.* Cambridge, Mass.: Harvard University Press, 1979.

Wolfson. *Studies in the History of Philosophy and Religion,* volumes 1 and 2, edited by Isadore Twersky and George Williams. Cambridge, Mass.: Harvard University Press, 1973-1977.

Zimmermann, Albert, ed. *Die Auseinandersetzungen an der Pariser Universität im XIII. Jahrhundert.* Berlin & New York: De Gruyter, 1976.

Contributors

Deborah L. Black .... *Pontifical Institute of Mediaeval Studies, Toronto*
Jerome V. Brown .... *University of Windsor, Canada*
Anthony J. Celano .... *Stonehill College*
Bernard Cullen .... *Queen's University of Belfast*
Idit Dobbs-Weinstein .... *Vanderbilt University*
Thérèse-Anne Druart .... *Catholic University of America*
Donald F. Duclow .... *Gwynedd-Mercy College*
Paul Edward Dutton .... *Simon Fraser University*
André Goddu .... *Stonehill College*
Jeremiah Hackett .... *University of South Carolina*
Peter King .... *Ohio State University*
Richard Lemay .... *City University of New York, Emeritus*
P. Osmund Lewry, O.P. ....*Blackfriars, Oxford, and Pontifical Institute of Mediaeval Studies, Toronto*
R. James Long .... *Fairfield University*
John Longeway .... *University of Wisconsin—Parkside*
Thomas A. Losconcy .... *Villanova University*
Charles H. Manekin .... *University of Maryland*
J. C. Marler .... *Saint Louis University*
Michael E. Marmura .... *University of Toronto*
Bernard McGinn .... *University of Chicago*
Ralph McInerny .... *University of Notre Dame*
Anthony Murphy .... *Saint Bonaventure University*
John H. Newell, Jr .... *College of Charleston*
B. B. Price .... *York University*
T. M. Rudavsky .... *Ohio State University*
James South .... *Duke University*
Edward A. Synan .... *Pontifical Institute of Mediaeval Studies, Toronto*
Roland J. Teske, S.J. .... *Marquette University*
Frederick Van Fleteren .... *LaSalle University*

Cumulative Index

Dictionary of Literary Biography, Volumes 1-115
Dictionary of Literary Biography Yearbook, 1980-1990
Dictionary of Literary Biography Documentary Series, Volumes 1-9

Cumulative Index

DLB before number: *Dictionary of Literary Biography,* Volumes 1-115
Y before number: *Dictionary of Literary Biography Yearbook,* 1980-1990
DS before number: *Dictionary of Literary Biography Documentary Series,* Volumes 1-9

A

C

D

E

F

G

H

I

K

L

M

Cumulative Index

Modern Novelists–Great and Small (1855), by Margaret Oliphant DLB-21
"Modern Style" (1857), by Cockburn Thomson [excerpt] DLB-57
The Modernists (1932), by Joseph Warren Beach DLB-36
Modiano, Patrick 1945- DLB-83
Moffat, Yard and Company DLB-46
Monkhouse, Allan 1858-1936 ....DLB-10
Monro, Harold 1879-1932 ....DLB-19
Monroe, Harriet 1860-1936 ....DLB-54, 91
Monsarrat, Nicholas 1910-1979 ....DLB-15
Montale, Eugenio 1896-1981 ....DLB-114
Montagu, Lady Mary Wortley 1689-1762 ....DLB-95, 101
Montague, John 1929- DLB-40
Montgomery, James 1771-1854 ....DLB-93
Montgomery, John 1919- DLB-16
Montgomery, Lucy Maud 1874-1942 ....DLB-92
Montgomery, Marion 1925- DLB-6
Montgomery, Robert Bruce (see Crispin, Edmund)
Montherlant, Henry de 1896-1972 ....DLB-72
The Monthly Review 1749-1844 ....DLB-110
Montigny, Louvigny de 1876-1955 ....DLB-92
Moodie, John Wedderburn Dunbar 1797-1869 ....DLB-99
Moodie, Susanna 1803-1885 ....DLB-99
Moody, Joshua circa 1633-1697 ....DLB-24
Moody, William Vaughn 1869-1910 ....DLB-7, 54
Moorcock, Michael 1939- DLB-14
Moore, Catherine L. 1911- DLB-8
Moore, Clement Clarke 1779-1863 ....DLB-42
Moore, Dora Mavor 1888-1979 ....DLB-92
Moore, George 1852-1933 ....DLB-10, 18, 57
Moore, Marianne 1887-1972 ....DLB-45; DS-7
Moore, Mavor 1919- DLB-88
Moore, Richard 1927- DLB-105
Moore, Richard, The No Self, the Little Self, and the Poets DLB-105
Moore, T. Sturge 1870-1944 ....DLB-19
Moore, Thomas 1779-1852 ....DLB-96
Moore, Ward 1903-1978 ....DLB-8
Moore, Wilstach, Keys and Company DLB-49
The Moorland-Spingarn Research Center DLB-76
Moraga, Cherríe 1952- DLB-82
Morales, Alejandro 1944- DLB-82
Morales, Rafael 1919- DLB-108
More, Hannah 1745-1833 ....DLB-107, 109
Morency, Pierre 1942- DLB-60
Moretti, Marino 1885-1979 ....DLB-114
Morgan, Berry 1919- DLB-6
Morgan, Charles 1894-1958 ....DLB-34, 100
Morgan, Edmund S. 1916- DLB-17
Morgan, Edwin 1920- DLB-27
Morgner, Irmtraud 1933- DLB-75
Morin, Paul 1889-1963 ....DLB-92
Morison, Samuel Eliot 1887-1976 ....DLB-17
Moritz, Karl Philipp 1756-1793 ....DLB-94
Morley, Christopher 1890-1957 ....DLB-9
Morley, John 1838-1923 ....DLB-57
Morris, George Pope 1802-1864 ....DLB-73
Morris, Lewis 1833-1907 ....DLB-35
Morris, Richard B. 1904-1989 ....DLB-17
Morris, William 1834-1896 ....DLB-18, 35, 57
Morris, Willie 1934- Y-80
Morris, Wright 1910- DLB-2; Y-81
Morrison, Arthur 1863-1945 ....DLB-70
Morrison, Charles Clayton 1874-1966 ....DLB-91
Morrison, Toni 1931- DLB-6, 33; Y-81
Morrow, William, and Company DLB-46
Morse, James Herbert 1841-1923 ....DLB-71
Morse, Jedidiah 1761-1826 ....DLB-37
Morse, John T., Jr. 1840-1937 ....DLB-47
Mortimer, John 1923- DLB-13
Morton, John P., and Company DLB-49
Morton, Nathaniel 1613-1685 ....DLB-24
Morton, Sarah Wentworth 1759-1846 ....DLB-37
Morton, Thomas circa 1579-circa 1647 ....DLB-24
Möser, Justus 1720-1794 ....DLB-97
Mosley, Nicholas 1923- DLB-14
Moss, Arthur 1889-1969 ....DLB-4
Moss, Howard 1922- DLB-5
The Most Powerful Book Review in America [*New York Times Book Review*] Y-82
Motion, Andrew 1952- DLB-40
Motley, John Lothrop 1814-1877 ....DLB-1, 30, 59
Motley, Willard 1909-1965 ....DLB-76
Motteux, Peter Anthony 1663-1718 ....DLB-80

N

O

P

Q

R

S

T

U

V

W

Y

Z

ISBN 0-8103-7592-3
90000
9 780810 375925

80: *Restoration and Eighteenth-Century Dramatists,* First Series, edited by Paula R. Backscheider (1989)

81: *Austrian Fiction Writers, 1875-1913,* edited by James Hardin and Donald G. Daviau (1989)

82: *Chicano Writers,* First Series, edited by Francisco A. Lomelí and Carl R. Shirley (1989)

83: *French Novelists Since 1960,* edited by Catharine Savage Brosman (1989)

84: *Restoration and Eighteenth-Century Dramatists,* Second Series, edited by Paula R. Backscheider (1989)

85: *Austrian Fiction Writers After 1914,* edited by James Hardin and Donald G. Daviau (1989)

86: *American Short-Story Writers, 1910-1945,* First Series, edited by Bobby Ellen Kimbel (1989)

87: *British Mystery and Thriller Writers Since 1940,* First Series, edited by Bernard Benstock and Thomas F. Staley (1989)

88: *Canadian Writers, 1920-1959,* Second Series, edited by W. H. New (1989)

89: *Restoration and Eighteenth-Century Dramatists,* Third Series, edited by Paula R. Backscheider (1989)

90: *German Writers in the Age of Goethe, 1789-1832,* edited by James Hardin and Christoph E. Schweitzer (1989)

91: *American Magazine Journalists, 1900-1960,* First Series, edited by Sam G. Riley (1990)

92: *Canadian Writers, 1890-1920,* edited by W. H. New (1990)

93: *British Romantic Poets, 1789-1832,* First Series, edited by John R. Greenfield (1990)

94: *German Writers in the Age of Goethe: Sturm und Drang to Classicism,* edited by James Hardin and Christoph E. Schweitzer (1990)

95: *Eighteenth-Century British Poets,* First Series, edited by John Sitter (1990)

96: *British Romantic Poets, 1789-1832,* Second Series, edited by John R. Greenfield (1990)

97: *German Writers from the Enlightenment to Sturm und Drang, 1720-1764,* edited by James Hardin and Christoph E. Schweitzer (1990)

98: *Modern British Essayists,* First Series, edited by Robert Beum (1990)

99: *Canadian Writers Before 1890,* edited by W. H. New (1990)

100: *Modern British Essayists,* Second Series, edited by Robert Beum (1990)

101: *British Prose Writers, 1660-1800,* First Series, edited by Donald T. Siebert (1991)

102: *American Short-Story Writers, 1910-1945,* Second Series, edited by Bobby Ellen Kimbel (1991)

103: *American Literary Biographers,* First Series, edited by Steven Serafin (1991)

104: *British Prose Writers, 1660-1800,* Second Series, edited by Donald T. Siebert (1991)

105: *American Poets Since World War II,* Second Series, edited by R. S. Gwynn (1991)

106: *British Literary Publishing Houses, 1820-1880,* edited by Patricia J. Anderson and Jonathan Rose (1991)

107: *British Romantic Prose Writers, 1789-1832,* First Series, edited by John R. Greenfield (1991)

108: *Twentieth-Century Spanish Poets,* First Series, edited by Michael L. Perna (1991)

109: *Eighteenth-Century British Poets,* Second Series, edited by John Sitter (1991)

110: *British Romantic Prose Writers, 1789-1832,* Second Series, edited by John R. Greenfield (1991)

111: *American Literary Biographers,* Second Series, edited by Steven Serafin (1991)

112: *British Literary Publishing Houses, 1881-1965,* edited by Jonathan Rose and Patricia J. Anderson (1991)

113: *Modern Latin-American Fiction Writers,* First Series, edited by William Luis (1992)

114: *Twentieth-Century Italian Poets,* First Series, edited by Giovanna Wedel De Stasio, Glauco Cambon, and Antonio Illiano (1992)

115: *Medieval Philosophers,* edited by Jeremiah Hackett (1992)

Documentary Series

1: *Sherwood Anderson, Willa Cather, John Dos Passos, Theodore Dreiser, F. Scott Fitzgerald, Ernest Heming-*

(Continued from front endsheets)